Writer's Guide to Places

WRITER'S GUIDE ▶▶▶▶ to PLACES

Don Prues and Jack Heffron

WRITER'S DIGEST BOOKS
CINCINNATI, OHIO
www.writersdigestbooks.com

Visit our Web site at www.writersdigest.com for information on more resources for writers.

To receive a free weekly e-mail newsletter delivering tips and updates about writing and about Writer's Digest products, register directly at our Web site at http://newsletters.fwpublications .com.

07   06   05   04   03   5   4   3   2   1

Library of Congress Cataloging-in-Publication Data

Prues, Don
  The writer's guide to places: a one-of-a-kind reference for making the locales in your writing more authentic, colorful and real / Don Prues, Jack Heffron.
    p.   cm.
  Includes index.
  ISBN 1-58297-169-2
    1. United States—Description and travel. 2. Canada—Description and travel. 3. United States—History, Local. 4. Canada—History, Local. 5. Fiction—Authorship—Handbooks, manuals, etc. 6. Setting (Literature)—Guidebooks. 7. Characters and characteristics in litera-ture—Handbooks, manuals, etc. I. Heffron, Jack. II. Title.

E169.04 P78   2002
917.3—dc21

2002027433
CIP

Edited by Donya Dickerson and Meg Leder
Designed by Sandy Kent
Cover by Lisa Buchanan
Production coordinated by Michelle Ruberg

Jack Heffron is the author of *The Writer's Idea Book*. His nonfiction has appeared in a variety of publications, including *Oxford American*, *Utne Reader*, *Bookstreet USA*, *Pages*, and *The AKC Gazette*. His piece "Fake Bullets in Louisiana" was listed in *Best American Travel Writing 2000*. His fiction has appeared in a number of literary journals, including *TriQuarterly*, *North American Review*, and *The Journal*. Two of his stories have been nominated for the Pushcart Prize and another was anthologized in *Ohio Short Fiction*. He was a founding editor of *Story* magazine and series editor for *Best Writing on Writing*. He is a freelance writer and editorial consultant in Cincinnati, Ohio.

Don Prues writes and edits. Before he started freelancing, Don was the editor of *Guide to Literary Agents*, assistant editor of *Writer's Market*, and managing editor of critics.com, kids-in-mind.com, and mediascreen.com. His recent projects include editing *An Expression of The Community: Cincinnati Public Schools' Legacy of Art and Architecture* (by photographer Robert A. Flischel), writing *Formatting and Submitting Your Manuscript* (with Jack Neff), and taking a six-month backpacking trip overseas (with his wife, Jennifer Lile).

Putting together a book of this magnitude is no easy task, and therefore it's probably no surprise that many people have been involved in this project. Before listing them all, we would like to thank one person who deserves special mention: George Schuhmann. He demonstrated not only that he's a darn good writer and researcher but also that he's a trusted, reliable friend who comes through when you need him. He contributed much to this book, helping with places from as far north as Vancouver to as far south as Miami. Thank you, G.

Also, our editors at Writer's Digest did a wonderful job of assisting us along the way. We are most grateful for their patience and guidance, especially Meg Leder and Donya Dickerson—you guys kept us on the ball, and the book in order, even in the midst of a company move. Your edits and suggestions were quite helpful. The same can be said of Amanda Prenger, who had the Herculean task of copyediting this book. We know it wasn't easy, and we thank you for your diligence.

We obviously had to conduct a number of interviews with a plethora of folks from all over the continent to get their "insider's take" on the city, state, or province at hand. Many of these interviews took place over the phone, but just as many were e-mail exchanges, in which respondents would answer a list of questions about their locale. Everybody who helped did a great job. In fact, many of our contacts were so helpful and had such familiarity with and enthusiasm for their "place" that they pretty much wrote the entire section at hand themselves.

Indeed, we are indebted to a great many people, especially the following folks who freely contributed to this project and gave us their time, knowledge, and insight about what Faulkner called their "little postage stamp of native soil." For without them, this book could not have been written. So, without further ado, we sincerely thank:

Jared Adams
Susan Amalong
Kurt Angermeier
June and Roger Apel
Paul Asher
Sue Bauer
Sheila Bender
Adam Blake
Anne Bowling
Kristy and Steve Broers
Jeff and Chalice Bruce
Christi Bruce
Deb Bruce
Pat Brug
Beth Burwinkel
Mike Cafferky
Sharon DeBartolo
  Carmack
Allyson and Tom Cermak
Ken and Susan Cheney

Julie Christensen
Kathy and Al Ciabattoni
Jamie and Kelly Clymer
Kristen Clymer
Donna Collingwood
Terra Colvin
Carrie Conlon
Brad Crawford
Katie DeNicola
Mike DeNicola
Katie DeRossitt
Alex Davis
Marco Pasquale
  DePompa III
Donya Dickerson
Frankie Dietz
Kathleen and Brent
  Duncan
John Elliott
Molly Fairbanks

Molly Fanning
Robert Fathman
Barry Field
Meg Files
Tom and Kathy Foegle
John Garvey
Mark and Deb Garvey
Steve Goedde
Lisa Gonzales
Kelly Milner Halls
Jane and Gus Hamre
Jan and Al Hauser
Steve Hawkins
Sharon Hordes
Mark Huffman
Jerry Jackson Jr.
Heather Dakota Jansen
Steve Jenike
Nicole Johnson
Rick Johnston

Susan Johnston
Diane Jones
Wendy Knerr
Cindy Laufenberg
Jennifer Lile
Roger and Marcia Lile
Kirk and Laurie Little
Andrew Lucyszyn
Delores McCarthy
Donnette McCommas
Jennifer McGrath
Errol Miller
Pat Miller
Candy Moulton
Mark Novak
Jenny O'Rourke
Mike and Rene Peeden
Steve Peters
Jim Pope
Alice Pope
Denise Prues
Erin Prues
Margie Prues
Marlene Prues
David Radabaugh
Amy Ratto
Neil and Lanna Ray
Nicky Robertshaw
Harry Rosengrants
I.J. Schechter
Betty Shafer
Graham Shelby
France Griggs Sloat
Meg and Rob Spicer
Todd Stump
Steve Sullivan
Chris Theim
David Tompkins
Erica Velasco
Nancy Wall
Bill Wallace
David Warner
Mike Willins
Amy Wolgemuth
Monica Wood
Susan Zierinberg

Table of Contents

U.S. States and Cities

Canadian Provinces and Cities

One of the most common adages for the fiction writer is "write what you know." You hear this time and time again at writers conferences, in writing workshops, and, yes, even in several Writer's Digest publications. The rationale behind such a thought makes sense, of course, because what you know comes fastest and easiest to you. Naturally, this is why so many fiction writers—and often the best of them—invariably inject autobiographical elements into their works. However, writing what comes fast and easy doesn't ensure that you're writing what's best. In fact, writing only about what you know can be out-and-out restraining.

This book is for the writer who wants to stretch himself, who doesn't necessarily care to write about only what he knows. Think about it: Imagination often requires us to take a trip beyond what we know—after all, that is what imagination is all about, isn't it? Most of the best writers are imaginative; they are not simply recorders and regurgitators.

Our aim in this book is to offer you a sense of many places you might not be familiar with but might be interested in writing about, from seedy cities and spread-out states to street corners and small town squares. Of course, this is a reference book and therefore lacks the storytelling sense of place that many of your favorite novelists provide. Our goal, however, is not to tell a story; it's to provide you with information you can use to create your own stories in various settings other than your hometown.

What Does This Book Offer You?

- Facts and peculiarities about the places covered. This lets you know the basics that your character would know and might even take for granted.
- A brief history and some significant events in the state, city, or province you choose, so you can understand what your character has thought about or been influenced by, or what your character's forebears actually went through.
- Insight into your character, from her rivalries to what she's proud and ashamed of to local slang your character is likely to hear or utter. This will help you create a *type* of character from the area you're studying.
- Local food your character is likely to eat. This will help you get to know your character's appetite, and

you can specifically inject what he ingests into your story, if you care to.
- This book provides you with an overall sense of the locale. We hope it will be a catalyst for you to pass that same (or even better) sense of locale on to your readers, in your own story.

How to Use This Book

- Use it as a time-saving research tool. There's lots of good information here, and we've already scoured the Web sites and interviewed the locals to get their take on their locale, so you don't have to. But you can always delve deeper . . .
- Use it as an idea generator. You might find in here things about a place you're already writing about—but you haven't thought about some of the aspects of the area that we point out. Or, you might not yet know where you want to send a character—you know he has to leave home and come back, a typical motif in the hero's journey, but you don't know where to send him. Flip through these pages and uncover a place you think would be suitable for your character in the context of your story.
- Use it to create a setting. Since we offer information on such subjects as people, neighborhoods, and religion, you should have no problem setting a scene in the places we've outlined in this book.
- Use it to add subplots to your story. Here's an example: Take Neil Simon's play *Lost in Yonkers,* which was also made into a movie in 1993. The story takes place in an apartment above a candy shop, but some of the subplots revolve around the father traveling and writing letters home to the kids, providing bits and pieces about the different people in the different locales. He travels throughout the South and writes from Georgia, Alabama, Louisiana, and Texas, telling his boys strange tidbits of information about the place he's writing from. Neil Simon might not have known any of those states well, but in the context of his story, he didn't need to do extensive research in order to write a little about them. You might run into a similar situation in one of your stories or novels.
- Use it for its serendipitous factor. Just page through and you'll be surprised at how one interesting nugget of information can trigger something in your mind.

Before you know it, a new story—your new story—will have already begun.

- Finally, use it however you want. The book is divided into two major sections: the United States and Canada. In the first section of the book, each U.S. state is followed by the selected city(s) within that state, and all are arranged alphabetically. In the second section of the book, the major Canadian provinces and their selected cities are arranged in the same way. It's easy to follow.

So Where Do You Go From Here?

Well, that's where our **For Further Research** sidebars come into play. Each chapter has several nonfiction books and Web sites for you to consult; each of these will add depth to your knowledge of the place at hand. In the **Still Curious? Why Not Check Out** section, we list various novels, movies, memoirs, television shows, plays, and other publications and media related to the area in that chapter. Either they're set in the area, filmed in the area, or just give a sense of the area and its people.

You can also do what we've done:

- **Consult the guidebooks.** There's a whole host of them out there that we've consulted; we are grateful for all of the following: *Access, CitySmart, Compass American, Eyewitness Travel Guides, Fodor's, Frommer's, Insiders' Guides, Lonely Planet, Mobil Travel Guides, Moon Publications,* and *The Rough Guides.* While each series differs from the others, all offer lots of good information. The only drawbacks are that the books cost money, the information can be dated, they're all geared toward tourists and not writers, and most of the information is available—free and easy—if you find the right Web sites.

- **Call convention and visitors bureaus and chambers of commerce.** This can be helpful to get local touristy information, but most likely you'll be offered a free information packet. In general, unless you have a specific question to ask, calling these places is often not that helpful and can even be frustrating. They all want to just send you a packet, most of which consist of glossy tourist brochures boostering the place at hand and its proprietors. In essence, you get a big book of coupons and attractions. Along these "helpfulness lines," we have found some geographical curiosities. Southern visitors bureaus tend to be friendly and

helpful. Maybe we've been lucky, but many often had an older native on the line who's lived in the area for fifty years and worked at the bureau for nearly as long. Such folks were always polite, patient, and knowledgeable, especially in the smaller Southern cities. In the North, especially the Northeast, we were met with impatient replies: "What do you need to know? Sir, all the information you'll need is in our visitor's packet. Now would you like to give me your address?" We were also shocked by all the young, unknowledgeable voices on the other end, asking how they could help but then not being able to our question, which always led to the inevitable, "But I'll be glad to send you an information packet, sir." This was true from Texas to Toronto.

- **Scour Web sites.** What we've found works best is to start with a few general sites about the area, like the official state or city site. While these sites often only tout what's great and overlook the shortcomings of the area, they give a good sense of what the area is proud of, what it thinks of itself, or how it would like to be perceived. Then you can move on to more targeted searches, like historical eras, specific street names, neighborhoods, or even restaurant and club names. To get a broad, objective view of the area, go to sites, such as http://historychannel.com, www.50states.com, http://infoseek.go.com, and http://encarta.msn.com. They contain good, informative facts and manageable essays about many places, with good links to other sites as well.

- **Call libraries.** Librarians are great for leading you in the right direction. If they can't find the answer for you, they'll put you in touch with someone who will. Next to interviewing locals themselves, we've found librarians in all cities and states indispensable and most helpful. The only problems are that you have to wait on hold often (which can be expensive when it's long distance), they usually don't e-mail information to you (they prefer to mail it to you), and if you want information faxed to you and you're out of state, it can be quite expensive—up to ten dollars for just one page!

- **Interview the locals.** This is by far the best way to get an honest take on a city, including the dirt on and quirks of an area; this is how we got lots of our information. Guidebooks and visitors bureaus won't tell you that locals in Dallas call the Cowboys the "Cryboys," that those in Atlanta have unkindly acronyms for their rapid transit system, and that Toronto feels at once envied and despised by its fellow Canadians.

- **Go to some of these places.** Take a vacation to one of the areas that tickles your fancy and seems appealing for setting a story. Go and talk to the locals, tell them you're writing a book, ask about their pasts and the town's past—before you know it, you might have three novel ideas in hand with just one trip. Moreover, there's nothing like being there to get a true sense of the place and the people. If you do decide to travel to one of the places in this book, the previously mentioned guidebooks can be invaluable for finding places to stay and eat, and for seeing the best sights in an orderly fashion.

A Few Caveats

- This is certainly not the last word on any of these places, for entire books have been written about each of them. The few pages of information we provide for each area are mere starting points for you, windows into these places but not open doors—the door-opening part is up to you.
- This book is not encyclopedic in scope or content. We will invariably upset some readers by what we have *not* included. We do have at least one section for each state, but we've mostly focused on the major metropolitan areas for the cities, and not all of these have their own chapter, of course.
- We don't guarantee to list every significant historical event or famous person that has to do with an area, nor do we catalog every fact or tell about every neighborhood. These sections are mere samplings to give you a taste of the locale at hand; they're not entrées unto themselves. We hope to whet your writing appetite and then let you decide what you want to devour.

- Please keep in mind that the Average Daily Temperature for a city is the mean average temperature (a combination of average night and day highs and lows). It is not an average daytime temperature. Hence, most of the temperatures will seem rather low—some places hit 100° during the day in July but at night go down to 70°. Thus the average daily temperature is 83° for July. Go to www.weather.com for specifics.
- We've included the ethnic makeup for most of the states and cities included here. However, since we've included them in percentages, you'll find that the numbers don't always add up to 100 percent. This occurs due to rounding. For more information on this subject, check the Web site of the U.S. Census Bureau at www.census.gov.
- Finally, we cannot guarantee all the information in this book will be entirely accurate when you read it. We have done our best, but with so many facts and figures, it's inevitable that errors might occur—to proclaim ourselves infallible would be just silly.

The importance of setting to a story cannot be over-emphasized. Take Stephen King's novels and what they evoke about the small towns of Maine; or Rebecca Harding Davis's *Life in the Iron-Mills* about West Virginia coal mines; or William Faulkner's Yoknapatawpha County based on Oxford, Mississippi; or Holden Caulfield's experience of New York City in J.D. Salinger's *Catcher in the Rye;* or Tony Hillerman's New Mexican novels and what they tell us about the Southwest. Like these writers, you can do a great job providing readers with a good sense of where the story takes place, of the setting that is so crucial to the story at hand.

With that, we will let you step inside the book, wherever it is you want to go.

UNITED STATES

▶▶▶▶▶ *States and Cities*

Alabama

Alabama Basics That Shape Your Character

![Map of Alabama showing cities including Huntsville, Birmingham, Tuscaloosa, Montgomery, and Mobile, bordered by Tennessee, Mississippi, Georgia, Florida, and the Gulf of Mexico]

Motto: We Dare Defend Our Rights

Population: 4.4 million

Prevalent Religions: Christianity, particularly Southern Baptist, Methodist, Pentecostal, and Roman Catholic

Major Industries: Steel, iron, piping, poultry, eggs, cattle, nursery stock, peanuts, cotton, vegetables, milk, soybeans, lumber, paper, mining, rubber and plastic products, transportation equipment, apparel

Ethnic Makeup (in percent): Caucasian 71.1%, African-American 26%, Hispanic 1.7%, Asian 0.7%, Native American 0.5%, Other 0.7%

Famous Alabamians: Hank Aaron, Nat King Cole, Zelda Fitzgerald, Lionel Hampton, W.C. Handy, Emmylou Harris, Helen Keller, Coretta Scott King, Harper Lee, Carl Lewis, Joe Louis, Willie Mays, Jim Nabors, Jesse Owens, Rosa Parks, George Wallace, Hank Williams Sr.

Significant Events Your Character Has Probably Thought About

- Alabama seceded from the Union on January 11, 1861 (the fourth state to do so).
- The designing of the Confederate Battle Flag. "The Southern Cross" was created, designed, and first flown in Alabama; the year was 1861.
- The Battle of Mobile Bay on August 5, 1864, when Admiral David Farragut issued his famous command, "Damn the torpedoes, full speed ahead."
- From 1910 to 1915, the boll weevil destroyed most of the state's cotton crop. Although this was an initial blow for farmers, the devastation forced them to diversify their farming, which has paid off.
- The formation of the Dixiecrats. A splinter group of Southern Democrats in the 1948 elections who rejected President Harry Truman's civil rights platform.
- The 1948 presidential election. Incumbent President Harry Truman's name did not even appear on the 1948 presidential ballot in Alabama. (The Dixiecrats had Strom Thurman as their candidate.)
- The 1955–56 Montgomery Bus Boycott. This major event was initiated by Rosa Parks, who refused to surrender her seat to a white male passenger in December 1955.
- The 1956 establishment of the Army Ballistic Missile Agency. Formed in Huntsville's Redstone Arsenal, this agency has played a major role in bomb making, rocket launching, and space exploration.
- George Wallace's 1962 inaugural speech. The proud governor uttered his famous line, "Segregation now, segregation tomorrow, segregation forever."
- The University of Alabama on June 11, 1963. Governor George Wallace physically tried to prevent two black students from entering school doors.
- The bombing of the Sixteenth Street Baptist Church on September 15, 1963. Four young girls were killed and twenty-one adults injured on this Sunday morning, spawning a series of race-related violence in Alabama.
- "Bloody Sunday" on Edmund Pettus Bridge in Selma. On March 7, 1965, black protest marchers were attacked by local police and state troopers armed with

tear gas, billy clubs, and even dogs. This was the beginning of the 1965 Selma-to-Montgomery Voting Rights March, led by Martin Luther King Jr.

- The 1970 election, in which two black men were elected to the state legislature (first time in Alabama history).
- The 1982 gubernatorial election. Twenty years after his "segregation forever" speech, George Wallace changed his segregationist stance and unexpectedly won the majority of the black vote as well as the general election.
- In 1986, Guy Hunt became the first elected Republican governor of Alabama since Reconstruction.

Alabama Facts and Peculiarities Your Character Might Know

- Mobile held its first Mardi Gras in 1830, which makes it the oldest Mardi Gras festival in North America.
- Montgomery was the capital of the Confederate States of America.
- Montgomery introduced the electric trolley system to the world, back in 1886.
- Founded in 1881, Tuskegee Institute was the first university in the world dedicated to educating black students.
- No other state in the nation contains all the major natural resources needed to make iron and steel.
- The town of Enterprise might be the only place in the world to erect a monument in honor of an insect: the Boll Weevil Monument.
- The Auburn campus is one of the most historic and beautiful in the South; its chapel is on the National Register of Historic Places.
- Fort Payne is proud to host a museum in honor of the state's favorite musical group, Alabama (now there's a surprise!).
- Fort McClellan is home to the United States Army Chemical Corps Museum, which houses thousands of chemical warfare relics.
- Throughout the twentieth century, Alabama was the largest supplier of cast-iron and steel pipe products in the states.
- For the past half century, Alabama has been at the forefront of space technology. The Huntsville crew built the rocket that put Neil Armstrong on the moon.
- Governor George Wallace served four terms in office.
- Alabama has the lowest property taxes in the country.

Your Character's Food and Drink

Barbecue pork, beef, and—more recently—chicken. Hot dogs and corn dogs. Grapico soft drink, Buffalo Rock ginger ale, Golden Eagle table syrup, redeye gravy, thickening gravy, ham, hash browns, and biscuits 'n' gravy. Main courses are fried chicken, hickory smoked ribs, deep-fried catfish, country fried steak, and chitlins. Veggies include okra, collard greens, black-eyed peas, green beans, and corn on the cob. Breakfast food favorites tend to be bacon, sausage patties, ham, hash browns, flaky biscuits, biscuits 'n' gravy, and grits. Side and dessert dishes are corn bread, pecan pie, pudding, and peach cobbler.

Myths and Misperceptions About Alabama

- **Race relations haven't changed since the horrible events in the early 1960s.** Many Alabamians are in fact quite proud of how they've "owned up" to their racist past. In fact, instead of simply burying history, they've elected to expose and deal with it, as is evident in The Birmingham Civil Rights Institute and other memorials throughout the state.
- **It's still at the back end of everything and the forefront of nothing.** Alabama is actually a leader in space technology (Alabamians' elbow grease worked the nuts and bolts to put the first man on the moon) and computer information systems (Huntsville is known as the Silicon Valley of the South).
- **Nobody from outside wants to relocate to Alabama.** This isn't true. Many people think they don't want to go to Alabama but once they get there, they don't

The Civil Rights District in Birmingham

For Further Research

Books

Alabama Bound: Contemporary Stories of a State, edited by James Colquitt

Alabama: The History of a Deep South State, by William Warren Rogers

The Art of Fiction in the Heart of Dixie: An Anthology of Alabama Writers, edited by Philip D. Beidler

Bad Blood Tuskegee Syphilis Experiment, by James Howard Jones

A Blockaded Family: Life in Southern Alabama During the Civil War, by Parthenia Antoinette Hague

Daybreak of Freedom: The Montgomery Bus Boycott, edited by Stewart Burns

Essays on Alabama Literature, edited by William T. Going

Fighting Words: Words on Writing From 21 of the Heart of Dixie's Best Contemporary Authors, edited by Bill Caton

Many Voices, Many Rooms: A New Anthology of Alabama Writers, edited by Philip D. Beidler

Pickett's History of Alabama: And Incidentally of Georgia and Mississippi From the Earliest Period, by Albert James Pickett

The Schoolhouse Door: Segregation's Last Stand at the University of Alabama, by E. Culpepper Clark

Seeing Historic Alabama, by Virginia Van der Veer Hamilton and Jacqueline A. Matte

The Walking City: The Montgomery Bus Boycott, 1955–1956, edited by David J. Garrow

A War in Dixie: Alabama V. Auburn, by Ivan Maisel, et al

Web Sites

www.dir.state.al.us (Alabama Department of Industrial Relations)

www.archives.state.al.us./aho.html (state history)

http://quickfacts.census.gov/cgi-bin/state_QuickLinks ?01000 (U.S. Census info)

http://Alabama.citysearch.com/ (state information and links)

Still Curious? Why Not Check Out

All Over but the Shoutin', by Rick Bragg

The Bad Seed, by William March

B-Four, by Sam Hodges

A Christmas Memory, by Truman Capote

Cottonmouth, by Julian Lee Rayford

"The Cracker Man," by Helen Norris

Crazy in Alabama, by Mark Childress

A Cry of Absence, by Madison Jones

Jealous-Hearted Me and Other Stories, by Nancy Huddleston Packer

To Kill a Mockingbird, by Harper Lee

The Last of the Whitfields, by Elise Sanguinetti

The Long Night, by Andrew Lytle

Marbles, by Oxford Stroud

Mother of Pearl, by Melinda Haynes

Norma Rae

The Story of My Life, by Helen Keller

Sweet Mystery, by Judith Hillman Paterson

Tongues of Flame, by Mary Ward Brown

The Untidy Pilgrim, by Eugene Walter

The Weight of the Cross, by Robert Bowen

---

want to leave. So Alabama's the place where nobody wants to go but everybody wants to stay.

- **Manufacturing is driving the state.** Not any more. The famed steel and iron mills that held Alabama afloat in the twentieth century are dying. Taking their place are the health and retail industries, which are leading the way for Alabama in the twenty-first century.

Interesting Places to Set a Scene

- **Auburn.** This quaint college town is steeped in Confederate history. Auburn University has twenty-one thousand students, which is the largest on-campus enrollment in the state. There's also a big football rivalry between Auburn and the University of Alabama.
- **Birmingham.** (See page 10 for an extensive look at Birmingham.)
- **Huntsville.** The first English-speaking settlement in Alabama, Huntsville is deemed the space and rocket capital of the world. In the 1950s, Dr. Wernher Von Braun and company developed military rockets for the U.S. Army at Redstone Arsenal, and then NASA began using the facilities to build and test space rocket launchers. Huntsville is also known as the Silicon Valley of the South; its high-tech workforce is the third largest in the country.
- **Mobile.** This is Alabama's major harbor town and old-

est city, and it is also the third oldest Latin town east of Mexico. Mobile was once the capital of the Louisiana area until 1720. It was also a major seaport for the Confederacy during the Civil War. For ten days in February, Mobile celebrates its long-standing Mardi Gras. Despite modernization, Mobile retains much of its old French and Spanish heritage.

- **Monroeville.** In 1997, the Alabama state legislature officially deemed this historic little town "The Literary Capital of Alabama." There's good reason, as it's the childhood home of famous writers Harper Lee, Truman Capote, and, more recently, Mark Childress, author of the best-selling *Crazy in Alabama*. Monroeville holds the Alabama Writers Symposium each May.

- **Montgomery.** This socially historic city was chosen in 1846 to be the state capital. Then, in 1861, Jefferson Davis was sworn in as the president of the Confederacy in Montgomery—and Montgomery became the capital of the Confederate States of America. This is also the place where Rosa Parks helped usher in a time of great social change by refusing to move to the back of the bus. And in 1965, Martin Luther King Jr. finished his Selma-to-Montgomery march on the state capital steps (and gave a most memorable speech).

- **Selma.** This river town will forever remain in the history books as a cradle for the Civil Rights movement. In fact, there's an entire Martin Luther King Jr. Street and several historical sites. Perhaps Selma's most memorable event is "Bloody Sunday" (March 7, 1965), which occurred on the Edmund Pettus Bridge. Marchers heading for Montgomery were thwarted by state troopers armed with billy clubs, tear gas, and even dogs. This event led to the Voting Rights Act of 1965.

- **Tuscaloosa.** This "black warrior" town is one of the state's major industrial centers (tires, chemicals, wiring, steel) and home to the University of Alabama's nineteen thousand students. If there's one thing this city loves, it's the Crimson Tide and Paul "Bear" Bryant (who led the team to twelve national titles). The corridor from Birmingham to Tuscaloosa was ranked the third best metro area in the nation for starting and growing a business (according to a 1997 study by MIT's Cognetics, Inc.). Tuscaloosa is also home to several art museums and historic homes.

- **Tuskegee.** This college town has something special about it—and it's not a football team. It's Tuskegee University. Originally Tuskegee Institute, the university was founded on July 4, 1881, by Booker T. Washington, and it was the first in the world dedicated to educating black students. At first the university was nothing but a dilapidated church and shanty, but now the campus boasts 161 buildings, spans 165 acres, and has over 5,000 students.

Birmingham

Birmingham Basics That Shape Your Character

Birmingham's skyline

Courtesy of Birmingham Convention and Visitors Bureau

Population: 265,968 in the city; 921,106 in the Greater Metro area

Prevalent Religions: Southern Baptist, Protestant, Roman Catholic (mostly in the north, where many Italians reside), Buddhist, and nondenominational (in the university area, near University of Alabama at Birmingham)

Top Employers: University of Alabama at Birmingham (UAB), U.S. Government, BellSouth, State of Alabama, Baptist Health System, Bruno's Grocery Stores, Jefferson County Board of Education, Birmingham Public Schools, City of Birmingham, Jefferson County Government, Wal-Mart, AmSouth Bank, SouthTrust Bank, Alabama Power Company, Regions Financial Corporation, Drummond Company, Blue Cross and Blue Shield, Carraway Methodist Medical Center, Children's Health System, USX Corporation, Compass Bank, American Cast Iron Pipe Company, Brookwood Medical Center, Tyson Foods

Per Capita Income: $27,896

Average Daily Temperature: January, 42° F; July, 80° F

Ethnic Makeup (in percent): Caucasian 58.1%, African-American 39.4%, Hispanic 1.6%, Asian 0.9%, Native American 0.2%, Other 0.6%

Newspapers: *Birmingham Post-Herald* (morning daily) and *Birmingham News* (afternoon and Sunday)

Other Publications: The weekly *Birmingham World* has served the black community since 1930. *Black & White* is the best source for cultural and entertainment happenings. *Birmingham* is a slick, glossy monthly magazine. And the *Birmingham Business Journal* is the weekly business paper.

Birmingham Facts and Peculiarities Your Character Might Know

- Cast from Birmingham iron ore in 1904, the 55-foot Vulcan statue overlooking the city is the largest steel sculpture in the world and the second largest statue in the United States, behind the Statue of Liberty.
- Alabama's first KKK klavern was organized here in 1916.
- Local Erskine Hawkins composed the famous jazz standard "Tuxedo Junction," which included the sound of an old streetcar on the move in Birmingham.
- The Barber Vintage Motor Sports Museum (boasting over six hundred vintage motorcycles) is deemed one of the top three motor sports museums in the world.
- The horrible year of 1963, which changed Alabama forever (see the following points).
- On April 16, 1963, Martin Luther King Jr. penned his famous "Letter From Birmingham Jail."
- In the summer of 1963, Police Commissioner Eugene "Bull" Connor ordered fire hoses and attack dogs on student civil rights marchers.
- The September 15, 1963 bombing of the Sixteenth Street Baptist Church. This horrific act claimed the lives of four young black girls attending Bible study that Sunday morning.
- It's home to *Southern Living* magazine. What started out in 1966 as a regional magazine with a couple thousand regional subscribers now has over twelve million subscribers worldwide.
- Former Mayor Richard Arrington was Birmingham's first black mayor; he was elected in 1979 and served a whopping five terms (until 1999).
- The Birmingham Civil Rights Institute opened its doors in 1992.
- In May of 2001, a Birmingham jury convicted Thomas Blanton Jr. on four counts of first-degree murder in the attack on the Sixteenth Street Baptist Church in 1963.
- City nicknames include "The Magic City," "Steel City," "Pittsburgh of the South," and—during its racial past—"Bad Birmingham," "Bombingham," and "Tragic City." Locals prefer "The Magic City."

If Your Character . . .

If Your Character Is Alternative and Grungy, she lives in Five Points South. Right near the heart of UAB, Five Points South is swarming with Bohemians, restaurants, bookstores, coffeehouses, clubs, poetry readings, and other campus activity.

If Your Character Smells of Money, he lives in Mountain Brook. This is the opulent area of Birmingham. With plenty of traces of old money, Mountain Brook houses extremely large Victorian homes and a few mansions.

If Your Character Is All About Business, she lives in one of the bedroom communities along Highway 280. These middle- to upper-middle-class residential areas are home to many Birmingham business men and women. So are Mountain Brook and Over the Mountain.

If Your Character Is a Rich Computer Geek, she lives in Over the Mountain. Out and above the mixed neighborhoods in Birmingham, Over the Mountain is a community up on a hill that overlooks the valley of the city.

If Your Character Is a Family Man, he lives in Hooper. Hooper is just your average middle-class community for someone who puts family before business.

If Your Character Wears a Blue Collar at Work, he lives in Irondale. This residential blue-collar town is now rather famous. The Irondale Cafe, also known as "The Original Whistle Stop Cafe," was the inspiration for Fannie Flagg's novel (also turned into a movie) *Fried Green Tomatoes at the Whistle Stop Cafe.* It still feeds hungry bellies seven days a week. Tarrant, Fairfield, and Millville are also old mill towns.

Local Grub Your Character Might Love

Hot dogs and barbecue rule. Barbecue pork and beef restaurants are pretty much all over the place, as are hot dog stands. The Golden Rule is the primary local barbecue chain. Small hot dog stands (with sauerkraut on the dogs) were popular in the 1950s and 1960s, but most mom-and-pop stands fell to the wayside. Sneaky Pete's Hot Dogs is the primary hot dog chain; it has been around since 1915. Bottega, Café Bottega, and Highlands Bar & Grill (Chef Frank Stitt is considered the "best chef in Alabama") are for those characters with deep pockets and exquisite tastes. There's also a strong Italian community in north Birmingham, with genuine Italian restaurants and grocery stores. Other local favorites include Grapico soft drink, Buffalo Rock ginger ale, Golden Eagle table syrup, redeye gravy, thickening gravy, salt-cured ham, hash browns, and biscuits 'n' gravy.

Interesting and Peculiar Places to Set a Scene

- **Twentieth Street South at Eleventh Avenue South.** This corner in Five Points South is surrounded by tree-shaded streets and is graced by a Frank Fleming sculpture and a fountain called *The Storyteller.* A perfect area for a romantic encounter.
- **Arlington Antebellum Home and Gardens.** This Greek Revival home was built in 1845, and the gardens have been growing since. There are lots of period antiques in this old house at 331 Cotton Avenue SW.
- **On top of Red Mountain in Vulcan Park.** The huge statue of the mythical god of fire and metalworking (Vulcan) oversees Birmingham from Vulcan Park, a most romantic area in the late evening (especially atop the 124-foot observation tower, when the lighted city looks so beautiful). Or, the park can be a deadly place in the middle of the night. The Vulcan's torch changes colors depending on whether everything is safe and sound in the city (green light = no accidents; red light = an accident has occurred).
- **Sixteenth Street Baptist Church at 1530 Sixth Avenue North.** A landmark for Birmingham and the world, the Sixteenth Street Baptist Church is where four little girls were killed while attending Sunday services.
- **The Alabama Theatre.** The 1920s can still be encountered in this downtown theatre that features films from today and yesterday. The Wurlitzer organ and Art Deco architecture make "The Alabama" a special place to locals and to those who wish they'd lived in the Jazz Age.
- **The Birmingham Civil Rights Institute.** Across the street from the Sixteenth Street Baptist Church, this museum and popular tourist spot was built "to remember revolution and reconciliation."
- **The Fourth Avenue District.** This is the historic black business area of Birmingham. Although the district has become more integrated over the years, it is still predominantly a self-sufficient African-American neighborhood.

For Further Research

Books

Bearing the Cross: Martin Luther King Jr. and the Southern Christian Leadership Conference, by David J. Garrow

Blessed Are the Peacemakers: Martin Luther King Jr., Eight White Religious Leaders, and the Carry Me Home: Birmingham, Alabama, the Climactic Battle of the Civil Rights Revolution, by Diane McWhorter

An Easy Burden: The Civil Rights Movement and the Transformation of America, by Andrew Young

The Eyes on the Prize: Civil Rights Reader: Documents, Speeches, and Firsthand Accounts From the Black Freedom Struggle, 1954–1990, by Clayborne Carson

Letter From Birmingham Jail, by S. Jonathan Bass

Parting the Waters and *Pillar of Fire*, by Taylor Branch

Race and Place in Birmingham: The Civil Rights and Neighborhood Movements, by Bobby M. Wilson

Reweaving the Fabric: How Congregations and Communities Can Come Together to Build Their Neighborhoods, by Ronald E. Nored

Walking With the Wind: A Memoir of the Movement, by John Lewis

Web Sites

www.ci.bham.al.us/ (official city site)

www.bcvb.org/ (Greater Birmingham Convention and Visitors Bureau)

http://birmingham.bcentral.com/birmingham/ (*Birmingham Business Journal*)

www.birminghamchamber.com/ (Birmingham Area Chamber of Commerce)

www.bhammag.com/ (*Birmingham* magazine)

www.ci.bham.al.us/library/default.jsp (city library network)

www.birminghamemployment.com/ (Birmingham employment)

Still Curious? Why Not Check Out

Eyes on the Prize

Four Little Girls

Fried Green Tomatoes at the Whistle Stop Cafe, by Fannie Flagg

The Journal of Biddy Owens: The Negro Leagues, by Walter Dean Myers

Soul of the Game

Thanh Ho Delivers: A Novel, by Fred Bonnie

The Watsons Go to Birmingham: 1963, by Christopher Paul Curtis

---

- **The Riverchase Galleria.** This is a shopping city in its own right that rests under the Western Hemisphere's longest skylight. It has a huge parking lot and over two hundred specialty shops and department stores.
- **The Twenty-Second Street Jazz Cafe.** This is the most authentic jazz club in Birmingham (it's actually more like a New York jazz club). A small, dark, low-lighted place with all the intimacy and jazz ambience your character can take. There's great live music, too.
- **Rickwood Field.** This is the oldest professional baseball park in the United States. Completed in 1910, it was originally the home of the Birmingham Coal Barons. Although the field remains intact, games are no longer played there, as it's being turned into the Museum of Southern Baseball History.

Exceptionally Grand Things Your Character Is Proud Of

- With its six Fortune 500 companies, Birmingham has more Fortune 500 companies per capita than any other city in Fortune's top 10 ranking, and it has the second highest concentration of the nation's largest companies in the Southeast (Atlanta has the highest).
- Downtown's restoration and revitalization.
- Birmingham is the cultural center of Alabama (museums, a ballet, an orchestra, etc.).
- Confronting and honoring up to its civil rights past.
- The Sandy Bottom community. Once a rundown area of hopelessness and neglect, this area is now being revitalized by those who live there—a testament to what community involvement can accomplish.
- Pets and vets. In 2002 a group of forty-three Birmingham veterinarians—over half of the city's animal doctors—teamed up to open the city's first twenty-four-hour emergency clinic.

Pathetically Sad Things Your Character Is Ashamed Of

- Birmingham's civil rights past.
- Former Police Commissioner Eugene "Bull" Connor.

- Steel and iron mill pollution.
- The city's record on education. According to the 2000 census, 28 percent of those over age sixteen are high school dropouts and thus have no diploma or GED.
- That nearly 40 percent of births in Birmingham are to single mothers.

Your Character Loves

- Football.
- Its iron and steel industries; they built Birmingham.
- The Redmont Hotel.
- Royal Cup Coffee and Red Diamond coffees.
- Birmingham Botanical Gardens.

- The UAB Medical Center.
- Stock car racing.

Your Character Hates

- Pretentious, self-righteous Yankees.
- Being stereotyped as a backward southerner.
- That people won't let go of Birmingham's civil rights history.
- The loss of mill and manufacturing jobs in and around Birmingham.
- The U.S. Justice Department's twenty-year, allegedly unwarranted pursuit of former Mayor Richard Arrington. (The feds thought he was involved in some shady business deals, which turned out to be unfounded.)

Alaska

Alaska Basics That Shape Your Character

Motto: North to the Future

Population: 626,932

Prevalent Religions: Christianity, particularly Baptist and Episcopalian, Roman Catholic, Methodist, Lutheran, Presbyterian, and nondenominational, also Buddhism and Bahá'í

Major Industries: Petroleum and natural gas, gold and other mining, food processing, lumber and wood products, tourism, seafood, nursery stock, dairy products, vegetables, livestock

Ethnic Makeup (in percent): Caucasian 69.3%, African-American 3.5 %, Hispanic 4.1%, Asian 4.0%, Native Alaskan 15.6 %, Other 1.6%

Famous Alaskans: Clarence L. Andrews, Aleksandr Baranov, Margaret Elizabeth Bell, Benny Benson, Vitus Bering, Susan Butcher, William A. Egan, Carl Ben Eielson, Henry E. Gruennig, B. Frank Heintzleman, Walter J. Hickel, Sheldon Jackson, Joe Juneau, Sydney Lawrence, Ray Mala, Tommy Moe, Virgil F. Partch

Significant Events Your Character Has Probably Thought About

- The first discovery of gold on Gastineau. Auk Tlingit Chief Kowee led Joe Juneau and Richard Harris to the veins of gold in 1880.
- Plans began in 1914 for the Alaska Railroad, and Anchorage became a construction campsite.
- Alaska became a state in 1958.
- A 1964 earthquake devastated much of the state.
- The Alaskan Pipeline, extending from Prudhoe Bay to Valdez, was completed in 1977.
- The 1980s put Alaska in a deep recession; several banks and businesses went bankrupt, and many folks lost their jobs and left the state.
- The Exxon Valdez accident in 1989 put eleven million gallons of crude oil into Prince William Sound.
- In 1991 Congress voted to close the Arctic National Wildlife Refuge to oil development.
- Still suffering from the recession, the *Anchorage Times,* once Alaska's largest newspaper, closed its doors in 1992.
- In 1993 a federal verdict slapped Exxon with a five-billion-dollar fine for the 1989 spill.
- A Japanese refrigerator ship went aground near Unalaska in 1997, spilling about thirty-nine thousand gallons of fuel.
- In 1998 Alaska's economy was on the rebound, as the unemployment rate hit a record low of 5.8 percent.
- An Alaska Airlines jet crashed near Los Angeles in 2000, killing eighty-eight people, including Interior Alaska Native leader Morris Thompson.
- Lots of state and national debates in 2002 over drilling in the Arctic National Wildlife Refuge.

Alaska Facts and Peculiarities Your Character Might Know

- Walking on the mud flats on Alaska's beaches is dangerous: Every year people get stuck, start sinking, and unfortunately die.
- Residents are huge on "buy Alaska"; everyone encourages buying products made in their home state.
- The famous Klondike gold rush took place from 1897–1900.
- Hockey player Scott Gomez, a Mexican American from Anchorage, brought home the 2002 Stanley Cup.
- Possessing almost 3.2 million acres of land and water, Alaska's state park system is America's largest.

- The state is commonly called "The Last Frontier" or "Land of the Midnight Sun."
- What those in the lower forty-eight call a snowmobile, Alaskans refer to as a snow machine.
- A rich Russian past is still visible in some parts of the state, like in Sitka, Kodiak, and Ninilchik, where onion-domed churches still grace the skyline.

Your Character's Food and Drink

Alaskans love their Pacific Rim dishes, including King and Dungeness crab, Pacific prawns, tenderloin beef medallions, Sitka foods, salmon, halibut, red snapper, shrimp, and various other shellfish. Meaty favorites are popular, especially beef, pork, moose steaks, and buffalo burgers. Those in Anchorage boast of Moose's Tooth Pizza and Micro Brewery (the best pizza and beer in the state, they say), and The Bear Tooth Theatre Pub and Grill. Also in Anchorage is Simon and Seaforts, which is one of the few restaurants that serves wild game *and* fresh seafood.

Things Your Character Likes to Remember

- An estimated four thousand people marched in Anchorage to show solidarity and to bring attention to native rights issues.
- Big Game Alaska Wildlife Park. A rescue shelter for wild animals, from eagles and owls to bears and moose.
- Edgar Nollner, the last surviving musher from the 1925 diphtheria serum run from Anchorage to Nome.
- Joe Redington Sr., founder of the Iditarod Dogsled Race.
- The beauty and the cleanliness of the state.
- The Miners and Trappers Ball—one huge costume party in a warehouse.
- Olympic gold medal-winner Tommy Moe.

Things Your Character Would Like to Forget

- Even though Alaska has plenty of oil, gas prices are still much higher than in most states.
- Alaskan Independence Party Chairman Joe Vogler mysteriously disappeared in 1993, and his body was later found near Fairbanks.
- Many cities and villages in the state are only accessible by plane or boat.
- Tourists in their RVs stopping in the middle of the highway to photograph wildlife.
- The high cost of living.

- How time-consuming and expensive it is to travel anywhere outside of the state.
- The problems with racism—especially against Natives.

Myths and Misperceptions About Alaska

- **Alaskans live in igloos.** They live in houses and apartments like the rest of us.
- **It's always cold.** Only in the winter, but summer months are quite tolerable and even pleasant.
- **It's always dark.** Only in the winter.
- **It's always sunny.** Only in the summer.
- **It's always raining.** Only in Juneau, which does in fact get a lot rain. But the rest of Alaska remains fairly dry.
- **Alaska was part of the Louisiana Purchase.** Nope. The United States purchased Alaska from Russia in 1867.

Interesting Places to Set a Scene

- **Anchorage.** Alaska's largest city accounts for nearly 40 percent of the state's population. The discovery of huge petroleum and natural gas reserves in the Prudhoe Bay region in 1968 sparked interest in the area—the population has more than quadrupled since (although it still hasn't reached 300,000). These days Anchorage is Alaska's cosmopolitan city, with malls and several national clothing shops and restaurants; it's also an international transportation hub and one of the nation's primary defense centers.
- **Arctic Man.** About ten thousand people and one thousand RVs congregate in this isolated part of the state

Anchorage amidst snow-capped peaks

For Further Research

Books

Alaska, by Dow Scoggins

The Alaska Almanac: Facts About Alaska: With the Wacky Wisdom of Mr. Whitekeys, edited by Roseanne Pagano

Coming Into the Country, by John McPhee

Discovering Denali: A Complete Reference Guide to Denali National Park and Mount McKinley, Alaska, by Dow Scoggins

Gold Rush Women, by Claire Rudolf Murphy and Jane G. Haigh

Good Time Girls of the Alaska-Yukon Gold Rush, by Lael Morgan

Highliners, by William McCloskey

How Heavy Is the Mountain, by Tim Rundquist

The Klondike Fever, by Pierre Berton

The Reader's Companion to Alaska, edited by Alan Ryan

Web Sites

www.state.ak.us/ (official state site)

www.dced.state.ak.us/tourism/ (visitor info)

http://sled.alaska.edu/ (vast electronic library)

www.juneau.org/akla/ (Alaskan authors site)

www.usgennet.org/usa/ak/state1/ (state history)

Still Curious? Why Not Check Out

Alaska, by James Michener

Bird Girl and the Man Who Followed the Sun: An Athabaskan Indian Legend From Alaska, by Velma Wallis

The Call of the Wild, by Jack London

Into the Wild, by Jon Krakauer

Looking for Alaska, by Peter Jenkins

Mystery, Alaska

Northern Exposure

Outside Passage: A Memoir of an Alaskan Childhood, by Julia Scully

The Seal Wife, by Kathryn Harrison

(Summit Lake near Paxson) every April for Alaska's biggest tailgate party. It's billed as hosting the world's toughest downhill ski races, mostly because it pairs skiers against snow machines for a wild ride down a mountain. Your character can ski and snow machine for several days if he's up for it, or he can do what most folks do—drink, drink, and drink.

- **Beluga Point.** A scenic stop along Turnagain Arm offers your character a good chance of seeing either a Dall sheep on a hillside or a beluga whale in the deep blue sea.

- **The Bush Company.** This is a tongue-in-cheek monikered and quite popular Anchorage strip club. If your desperate character needs to hang around some bright warm bodies on a cold, dark winter night . . . this could be his place.

- **Denali National Park.** This is mountain country at its finest. The park contains the massive Mount McKinley (20,320 feet), North America's highest point, and many other snow-capped peaks. It's also home to glaciers, tundra, and an abundance of wildlife, including moose, grizzly bears, mountain sheep, and wolves. Since the only road through the park is closed to the public, your character must take a crowded bus over an old gravel road for hours just to get to the park. But there's no place like it in the world, an awesome setting for an adventure story. . . .

- **Fairbanks.** The urban center of Alaska's interior, Fairbanks had a gold boom at the turn of the twentieth century and then faded. But mining, lumbering, tourism (dogsled races are a big deal here), and the oil industry keep the city afloat today. It has art galleries, theaters, a symphony, museums, and other cultural offerings. Fort Wainwright and Eielson Air Force Base are big employers, as is the University of Alaska.

- **Fur Rondy.** A two-week-long party in the middle of winter, Fur Rondy was established as a bartering station for trappers to sell their furs and pelts and for gold miners to sell their gold. Now, it survives as an excuse for a party.

- **Gwennies Old Alaska Restaurant in Spenard.** A legendary restaurant that locals have been frequenting for years, known for having just about the best sourdough pancakes anywhere—some folks even get beer with breakfast (but it has to be after 10:00 A.M.).

- **Juneau.** Alaska's capital rests at the base of two awesome peaks, Mount Juneau and Mount Roberts. Although it was once a gold miner's town, Juneau survives today as the Panhandle's main trade center, thanks to its ice-free harbor, seaplane base, and airport. As with Fairbanks, government is a major employer, but fishing, lumber, and tourism are also important to the economy.

- **Sheep Creek Lodge.** About two hours north of Anchorage near Talkeetna, this very lively bar is a getaway destination for city dwellers and a comfy pit stop for weary road warriors. Have your character spend the night in one of the cabins available for highway travelers.

- **Talkeetna.** This funky, little old mining town has only two paved streets, a two-block "downtown" area, a railroad depot, two lodges, rustic log cabins, and clapboard buildings.
- **The Iditarod Dogsled Race.** The one-thousand-mile, one-month mushfest stretches from Anchorage to Nome and is known the world over. What isn't so well known is that the race commemorates a medical mission that took place during a 1925 diphtheria epidemic.

Arizona

Arizona Basics That Shape Your Character

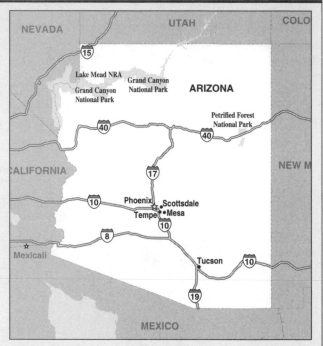

Motto: *Ditat Deus* (God enriches)

Population: 5 million

Prevalent Religions: Roman Catholic, Baptist, Methodist, and Church of Jesus Christ of Latter-day Saints

Major Industries: Manufacturing (electronic and aerospace machinery, electrical and transportation equipment), mining (predominately copper), tourism, agriculture (cotton, citrus fruits, vegetables), cattle ranching

Ethnic Makeup (in percent): Caucasian 75.5%, African-American 3.1%, Hispanic 25.3%, Asian 1.8%, Native American 5.0%, Other 11.6%

Famous Arizonans: Linda Carter, César Chávez, Cochise, Alice Cooper, Barbara Eden, Geronimo, Barry Goldwater, Charlie Mingus, Stevie Nicks, Linda Ronstadt, Kerri Strug, Mare Winningham

Significant Events Your Character Has Probably Thought About

- A thriving Native American culture existed in this land for more than a thousand years before Spanish explorers found it in the 1500s during their search for gold in the Seven Cities of Cibola. The Hohokam and the Anasazi were the principle people of the area until the 1400s.
- Spanish missions were built in the area in the seventeenth century, but Native American tribes—including the Hopi, Apache, Pueblo, and Pima—remained the dominant societies. They killed missionaries and destroyed settlements to retain their land.
- Arizona land north of the Gila River was annexed by the United States as part of the New Mexico Territory in 1848, after the Mexican War. The remainder of the state was annexed as part of the Gadsden Purchase in 1853.
- During the Civil War, the Arizona/New Mexico Territory sympathized with the Confederacy, though not officially. No resources or men were committed to either side. After the war, the territory was a popular area for settlement by disenfranchised Southern soldiers.
- In 1869 geologist John Wesley Powell and a small group of aides completed the first successful passage of the Grand Canyon.
- Wars with Apache Native Americans kept whites from settling in large numbers. By the late 1870s, the Apache threat had been minimized. Geronimo surrendered in 1886. Access to the East and to California through new railroads brought more settlers to the area.
- The Wild West was pretty wild in the Arizona Territory. Fights with Apaches and the frenzied boom-and-bust towns led to murder and mayhem, best remembered by the Gunfight at the O.K. Corral in Tombstone in 1881. Wyatt Earp, the best-known combatant in the fight, had come to the territory seeking wealth in the mining business.
- The opening of the Roosevelt Dam in 1911 brought a steady source of water to the area, creating greater opportunities for agriculture and settlement.
- Arizona achieved statehood on February 14, 1912, becoming the forty-eighth state.
- In the 1920s, work began on a highway system to ease travel throughout the state.
- The population of the state nearly tripled between 1960 and 1990 as Rust Belt industries moved to the

Sun Belt. The economy boomed, but the influx of residents taxed the water supply. In the 1980s the Central Arizona Project diverted larger supplies of water from the Colorado River to Tucson and the Phoenix area.

Arizona Facts and Peculiarities Your Character Might Know

- The name *Arizona* derives from the Pima Native American word *arizonac*, which means "little spring place."
- Arizona stays on Mountain Standard Time throughout the year. Friends in the East often forget this fact.
- Arizona is the sixth largest state in land area. It ranks twentieth in population.
- Arizona is home to more saguaro cacti than is any other state, and it has adopted the cactus as an unofficial symbol. The flower of the cactus, which is the official state flower, blooms in May and June. The age of a cactus is determined by its height and its number of arms. The saguaro is the largest American cactus.
- Arizona contains more Native American reservation land—38 percent—than does any other state. Oraibi, founded by the Hopi, is the oldest Native American settlement in the United States. Only California and Oklahoma have larger Native American populations than Arizona.
- Arizona produces more copper than any other state.
- Grand Canyon National Park is located mostly within the borders of Arizona.
- Kitts Peak National Observatory, located in the town of Sells, contains the world's largest solar telescope.
- The state did not have a major-league baseball team until 1998, when the Arizona Diamondbacks were created. However, in February and March since 1947 the state has hosted spring training, called the Cactus League. The Arizona Fall League in October and November attracts top players from throughout the minor leagues.

Your Character's Food and Drink

Arizonans make their food with plenty of hot spices. Chiles can be an ingredient in most any dish, and locals pride themselves on liking things "the hotter the better."

Mexican and Southwestern cuisine is dominant throughout the state. In the past decade or two, these dishes have become much more common throughout the country, but as recently as the 1970s and 1980s, favorites such as chorizo and queso were considered exotic in other regions.

Though salsa is a common food everywhere now, Arizonans pride themselves on their unusual exotic recipes, which include a variety of chiles, beans, and other fresh vegetables.

Arizonans tend to enjoy a healthy lifestyle. Healthy foods, therefore, are popular throughout the state.

Southern Arizona is a leading producer of citrus fruits, primarily oranges, grapefruits, lemons, and tangerines. The availability of fresh fruit makes it a favorite, especially as a cool treat in the hot months.

Things Your Character Likes to Remember

- The Diamondbacks (known locally as the "D'backs") beating the Damn Yankees to win the World Series in 2001.
- The weather. That's why many of them moved here.
- The Grand Canyon. They don't call Arizona "The Grand Canyon State" for nothing. Folks here are proud of this national treasure.

Rock formations in Monument Valley

© PhotoDisc/Getty Images

For Further Research

Books

Arizona: A Cavalcade of History, by Marshall Trimble

Arizona: A History, by Thomas E. Sheridan

Arizona Myths, Fallacies, and Misconceptions, by John D. Neuner

Arizona Place Names, by Will Croft Barnes

And Die in the West: The Story of the O.K. Corral Gunfight, by Paula Mitchell Marks

The Great Arizona Orphan Abduction, by Linda Gordon

The Hohokam: Ancient People of the Desert, by David Grant Noble

A Natural History of the Sonoran Desert, edited by Steven J. Phillips and Patricia Wentworth Comus

Over the Edge: Death in Grand Canyon, edited by Thomas M. Meyers and Michael P. Ghiglieri

Vacant Eden: Roadside Treasures of the Sonoran Desert, by Abigail Gumbiner

Web Sites

www.arizonaguide.com (state tour site)

www.azinfo.com/ (tour and info site)

www.arizonacenter.net/ (state info and links directory)

www.pr.state.az.us/parklist.html (state parks guide)

www.azcentral.com/ (news and info site)

Still Curious? Why Not Check Out

A number of Westerns have been set in or shot in Arizona, a list too long to include here.

Animal Dreams, by Barbara Kingsolver

A Boy Called Hate

Capirotada: A Nogales Memoir, by Alberto Alvaro Ríos

Fire in the Sky

Grand Canyon Celebration: A Father-Son Journey of Discovery, by Michael Quinn

Patton

Jerome

Joanna Brady series by J.A. Jance (These novels are set in Bisbee and Cochise Counties.)

Lazy B: Growing Up on a Cattle Ranch in the American Southwest, by Sandra Day O'Conner

Murphy's Romance

Raising Arizona

Starman

We're So Famous, by Jaime Clark

Things Your Character Would Like to Forget

- Electing J. Fife Symington III as governor. Twice. He resigned in disgrace in 1997 after being convicted on seven felony charges for illegal business practices. Elected in 1990, Symington had a reputation as a great businessman, and despite pending criminal charges of fraud and extortion, voters reelected him in 1994.

- The Native American and Hispanic populations exert a strong influence on the culture of the state, but many still live below the poverty line.

Myths and Misperceptions About Arizona

- It's a dry heat. True, but when the temperature is over a hundred, it still feels really hot.

- It's full of rich retirees. Places like Sun City and Paradise Valley drew retirees from the north by the thousands for many years, and, yes, they still come. But Arizona is one of the fastest-growing states in the country, based largely on economic opportunity for young professionals.

Interesting Places to Set a Scene

- **Bisbee.** Founded as a copper-mining town, Bisbee is located near the Mexican border. Surrounded by desert, it is strongly influenced by its Mexican neighbor. The one-hundred-year-old Copper Queen Hotel offers plenty of Old West details for setting a scene.

- **Chandler.** In 1912 Dr. Alexander Chandler founded this first planned community in the state, and his legacy lives on in Dr. A.J. Chandler Park. Chandler lies twenty minutes south of Phoenix and has been absorbed into the sprawl of that city.

- **Four Corners.** There's not much here other than a photo opportunity. Located in the northwesternmost corner of the state, this is the only place in the country where four states meet. People sprawl in various contortions to have a foot or hand in each of the states, and the area buzzes with tourists and vendors.

- **Dry riverbeds.** Many of the state's rivers don't flow in the heat of summer. The dry riverbeds, even in the middle of busy towns and cities, offer great places for scenes.

- **Flagstaff**. One of the highest U.S. cities at seven thousand feet, Flagstaff is also one of the coolest spots in the state and is a magnet for folks from Phoenix and Tucson seeking respite from the long hot summer. The San Francisco mountains attract tourists, as does the city's proximity to the Grand Canyon, but the growing sector of high-tech industries attracts new residents, too.
- **Grand Canyon**. Occupying the northwest corner of the state, this wonder of the world is tough to beat as a setting. Forged by the Colorado River, which runs through it, the Canyon is one of the most recognized places in the country. Your only problem as a writer is finding something fresh to say about it.
- **Prescott**. Prescott is a city in transition. It calls itself "Everybody's Hometown" and prides itself on a small-town atmosphere and good fishing on Watson and Granite Basin Lakes, as well as at the Willow Springs reservoir. But more recently it has become a popular getaway for the Hollywood glitterati in search of a more authentic place to live.
- **Sedona**. Known as a hotbed of New Agers and psychics, Sedona has commercialized its reputation in recent years, sort of Eccentrics 'r' Us. Beautiful red-rock mountains surround the town, and it features plenty of places for buying stones and receiving tarot readings.
- **Tombstone**. Called "the town that wouldn't die," Tombstone almost went the way of other desert boomtowns, but it has turned itself into a tourist attraction by relying on its roots in the Old West. Your characters can watch a reenactment of the Gunfight at the O.K. Corral every day.
- **Winslow**. A small town made famous in "Take It Easy" by The Eagles in the line "Standing on a corner in Winslow, Arizona," the town features a banner marking "the corner." Across the street is Standing on the Corner Park, complete with a bronze statue of a guitar-playing Eagle. If your character is a girl in a flatbed Ford, she may want to slow down here.
- **Yuma**. Snuggled in the southwestern corner of the state near both the California and the Mexican borders, Yuma used to be a small, rugged western city, one closely identified with Mexico and the Colorado River. Since 1990, however, it's been the third fastest-growing city in the country.

Phoenix

Facts and Peculiarities Your Character Might Know

- The Hohokam Native Americans flourished in the Salt River Valley that is now Phoenix for nearly a thousand years, until the 1400s. They built a system of irrigation canals to water their crops, a system that white settlers used while developing the city in the 1800s.
- White settlers founded the city in 1867. Because the new city was built on the land of an ancient and departed civilization, it was named Phoenix, after the mythical bird that rises from its own ashes.
- Phoenix was made the capital of Arizona Territory in 1889 and remained the capital when Arizona achieved statehood in 1912.
- Nearly two-thirds of the state's population lives in the Phoenix metro area. More than 1.3 million people live in the city itself, making it the sixth-largest city in the United States.
- The Phoenix metro area is one of the fastest-growing spots in the country.
- Before the economic boom began in the 1960s, Phoenix was known mostly as a great place to retire. Sun City and Leisure World were big attractions for retirees from the cold North.
- For many years, the city had only one major-league sports team, the National Basketball Association Phoenix Suns. They now have a team in every major sport: Arizona Cardinals (football), Arizona Diamondbacks (baseball), Phoenix Coyotes (hockey), and the Phoenix Mercury (women's basketball).
- All the money, clean air, and sunshine wouldn't seem to be a recipe for great rock and roll, but the area has launched more than its share of music stars, including Alice Cooper, the Gin Blossoms, the Meat Puppets, and The Refreshments.

If Your Character . . .

If Your Character Is Alternative and Grungy, he lives in Tempe, near Arizona State University, or in the neighborhoods within the Phoenix city limits.

If Your Character Smells of Old or Big Money, she lives in Scottsdale, Fountain Hills, or the Biltmore area. The

Phoenix Basics That Shape Your Character

A sculpture at Frank Lloyd Wright's Taliesan.

Population: 1.3 million in the city; 3.25 million in the Greater Metro area

Prevalent Religions: Roman Catholic, Baptist, and Methodist

Top Employers: Honeywell, Intel, Microchip Technology, Boeing, Southwest Airlines, Arizona State University, Wells Fargo

Per Capita Income: $27,617

Average Daily Temperature: January, 54°; July, 94°

Ethnic Makeup (in percent): Caucasian 71.1%, African-American 5.1%, Hispanic 34.1%, Asian 2.0%, Native American 2.0%, Other 16.4%

Newspaper: *The Arizona Republic*

Free Weekly Alternative Paper: *Phoenix New Times*

northeastern area is known for its upscale communities.

If Your Character Is All About Business, she works in downtown, though other business and commercial centers are spread throughout the city. Tempe and the East Valley are home to a lot of new high-tech industries.

If Your Character Is a Rich High-Tech Geek, he lives in the East Valley in areas such as Ahwatukee, Gilbert, or Apache Junction.

If Your Character Is Raising a Family, he lives in Chandler, Mesa, or the southeastern area. The western suburbs and bedroom communities such as El Mirage, Glendale, and Litchfield Park, are growing, too.

If Your Character Wears a Blue Collar at Work, she lives in Tempe, Mesa, Gilbert or the neighborhoods within the Phoenix city limits.

Local Grub Your Character Might Love

A city this size offers any and all types of ethnic cuisine to its residents. Many restaurants, however, favor a southwestern approach.

Mole. No two people make it exactly the same way. Generally, it's a thick sauce made of chiles, vegetables, nuts, and southwestern spices, along with enough chocolate to make it sweet and creamy. Authentic Mexican is common. Locals pride themselves on spotting imposters.

Interesting and Peculiar Places to Set a Scene

- **Arizona Biltmore.** Located at the foot of Squaw Peak, this luxurious old hotel recalls the city's early resort days. It was designed by Albert Chase McArthur, a student of Frank Lloyd Wright, and drew attention from the Hollywood glitterati looking for a weekend escape. Near the hotel is the William Wrigley Jr. mansion, a palatial estate built by the king of chewing gum.
- **Chandler.** Located twenty miles south of Phoenix, Chandler has been consumed into the metro area by urban sprawl. Sun Belt mania has turned it from a quaint farming community into a fast-growing city with sophisticated citizens working in high-tech industries. The annual Ostrich Festival, a bow to Chandler's history of ostrich ranching, draws visitors from throughout the Phoenix metro area.
- **Fountain Hills.** This is a wealthy area filled with retirees as well as successful professionals. It's best known for the fountain in the center of the city, which shoots water 560 feet in the air and is listed by the Guinness folks as the highest fountain in the world.
- **Glendale.** The state's fourth-largest city, Glendale also is one of the fastest-growing cities. Located in the West Valley, Glendale is a fun-in-the-sun spot for tourists and retirees. New residents also are drawn to the area by the high-tech industries in the cities to the east. It's best known for its myriad antique shops.
- **Mesa.** Located in the booming East Valley, Mesa is one of the fastest-growing cities in the United States, a hotbed of high-tech industries. Largely known for its military base before the tech companies moved in, Mesa retains a bit of old desert charm but mostly is a dense urban center.
- **Scottsdale.** Developed as a high-class retirement city, along with nearby Paradise Valley, Scottsdale remains one of the wealthiest areas in metro Phoenix. The McDowell Mountains and Sonoran Desert give it natural beauty, and the fine homes, many featuring classic southwestern architecture, make it one of the more beautiful spots in the state. For golf, tennis, spas, and fine dining, this is the place to be.
- **South Mountain Park.** Located within the Phoenix city limits, it's the largest municipal park in the world, boasting more than fifty-eight miles of trails. Locals looking for a morning jog before work or for a quick getaway from the baking concrete of the city come here.
- **Sun City.** Though just one of several retirement meccas in Greater Phoenix, Sun City is synonymous with old folks from the North. It's located in the northern section of the West Valley, and though it looks dated amid the newness of other areas, it does offer the Sundome Center, a concert venue that's the largest single-level facility in the country.
- **Tempe.** Best known nationally as the home of Arizona State University, the National Football League's Arizona Cardinals, and the annual Fiesta Bowl, Tempe also is home to many high-tech industries. It is a place of rich cultural diversity as residents of various races from all over the world come here to work and study. It's the westernmost city in the thriving East Valley area.

Exceptionally Grand Things Your Character Is Proud Of

- The Diamondbacks. Sure, they just bought up the best players from other teams, like the Yankees always do. But in the 2001 World Series, they beat the Yankees.
- The scenery, mountains, and beauty of the state.
- The thriving economy. People from across the coun-

For Further Research

Books

Camelback: Sacred Mountain of Phoenix, by Gary Driggs

Greater Phoenix: The Desert in Bloom, by Hugh Downs

Historic Scottsdale: A Life From the Land, by Joan Fudala

The Old U.S. 80 Highway Traveler's Guide (Phoenix-San Diego), by Eric J. Finley

Phoenix: The History of a Southwestern Metropolis, by Bradford Luckingham

Phoenix in the Twentieth Century: Essays in Community History, edited by G. Wesley Johnson Jr.

Phoenix and the Valley of the Sun: A Photographic Portrait, by editors of Twin Light Publishers

Web Sites

www.ci.phoenix.az.us/ (Phoenix city government site)

www.phoenixcvb.com/ (Greater Phoenix Convention and Visitors Bureau)

www.phoenixonline.com/ (info and chat about Phoenix)

www.allaboutphoenix.com/ (visitor and travel info)

Still Curious? Why Not Check Out

Arizona Highways magazine and the line of Arizona Highways books

Concrete Desert, by Jon Talton

Flamingos, by Marc Savage

Jerry Maguire

La Maravilla, by Alfredo Vea Jr.

Let Their Spirits Dance, by Stella Pope Duarte

My Life as a Girl, by Elizabeth Mosier

The Night Bird Cantata, by Donald Rawley

The Trunk Murderess: Winnie Ruth Judd, by Jana Bommersbach

Until Your Heart Stops, by T.M. McNally

Waiting to Exhale

What Planet Are You From?

---

try relocate here every day. The city must be doing something right.

- The cultural diversity.

Pathetically Sad Things Your Character Is Ashamed Of

- Maricopa County Sheriff Joe Arpaio. A strutting, self-promoting bully who calls himself "America's Toughest Sheriff," Arpaio spends much more time blowing his own horn than he does catching criminals. The mere mention of his name to locals sparks laughter or rage, eye-rolling or blushing.
- In 2001 Scottsdale resident Robert Fisher blew up his house, killing his wife and two children. Despite extensive effort by law enforcement and coverage on *America's Most Wanted*, he has not been caught.
- The Cardinals. Since they arrived here, they've never been any good.
- The homeless. The city's warm weather attracts them, as does the growing population.

Your Character Loves

- The weather. In summer, one-hundred-degree temperatures are not unusual, but folks here adjust their schedules to get outside in the cool hours in the morning. And in the winter the days are sunny and warm.
- John McCain. In these cynical times, politicians don't get much love, but many folks from Phoenix love this outspoken senator.
- Bank One Ballpark. The state-of-the-art ballpark with retractable dome is a favorite spot for fans, most of whom call it "BOB."
- Golf. Locals love it, the snowbirds and retirees love it, and the tourists love it, too. In the hot months, tee times are usually early or late in the day.
- The proximity to a number of wonderful places, such as the Grand Canyon, the desert, Mexico—even California and the ocean are not far.

Your Character Hates

- Traffic on I-10. There's a price to pay for all the growth and prosperity. Phoenixians pay it in traffic jams and road rage.
- The pollution. It hangs over the valley like a brown cloud. As more cars get on the highways, the situation will get worse.
- The heat. From May to mid-October, it can be brutal.

Tucson Facts and Peculiarities Your Character Might Know

- Evidence exists that hunter-gatherers lived in the Tucson Valley as early as 10,000 B.C. The Hohokam Native Americans thrived there for over a thousand years, until the middle of the fifteenth century. They developed into the Pima and Tohono O'odham tribes, who were the primary occupants when Spanish explorers arrived in the 1500s.
- Father Eusebio Francisco Kino founded Mission San Xavier del Bac in 1699, the northernmost mission in the Spanish empire in the New World.
- The first Spanish settlement in the area was the Presidio de San Augustin de Tucson, which was built in 1775 to house soldiers. Tucson considers this year its birth date. In the 1990s, archaeologists began to unearth the presidio walls, which are buried beneath the city next to the Pima County Courthouse.
- Tucson became part of the United States in 1854 in the Gadsden Purchase and was the capital of the Arizona Territory from 1867 to 1877. The city began to grow in the late 1870s, when the Southern Pacific Railroad arrived and gold and silver deposits were discovered in the Pima County area.
- *Tucson* is derived from the Pima Native American word *stjukshon*, meaning "spring at the foot of the black hill."
- Actress Barbara Eden and pop singer Linda Ronstadt are from Tucson. Author Barbara Kingsolver has lived here for many years.
- Despite the stifling heat, Tucsonans love the outdoors. Hiking the surrounding mountains is a popular pastime, as is bicycling. *Bicycling Magazine* named Tucson one of the three best cycling cities in the country.
- Bird-watching is a popular pastime in the city, especially among retired folk. Southern Arizona attracts hundreds of species, and groups of binocular-wearing older gentlemen climbing around in the cool hours after dawn are a common sight.
- Within very short drives of Tucson, your characters will find vast Native American reservations. To the west lies the Tohono O'odham reservation. The San

Tucson Basics That Shape Your Character

A typical road in Arizona

Population: 750,000

Prevalent Religions: Roman Catholic, Baptist, and Methodist

Top Employers: University of Arizona, Raytheon Missile Systems, Davis-Monthan Air Force, Phelps Dodge Mining Company

Per Capita Income: $25,445

Average Daily Temperatures: January, 51°; July, 87°

Ethnic Makeup (in percent): Caucasian 62.7%, African-American 3.1%, Hispanic 29.6%, Asian 2.1%, Native American 2.5%, Other 0.1%

Newspapers: *Arizona Daily Star* (morning), *Tucson Citizen* (evening)

Free Weekly Alternative Paper: *Tucson Weekly*

Xavier and the Pasqua Yaqui reservations lie to the south of the city.

If Your Character . . .

If Your Character Is Alternative and Grungy, he lives in the warehouse district downtown, the barrio district downtown, or Los Lomas on the far west side.

If Your Character Smells of Old Money, he lives in the Catalina Foothills, Sabino Canyon, El Encanto, or Colonia Solana. There's a lot of new money here, too.

If Your Character Has New Money, she lives in the Catalina Foothills, Sabino Canyon, or one of the many new high-priced homes being built on a daily basis throughout the outer rim of the city.

If Your Character Is All About Business, he works in downtown, though business centers are spread throughout the city. For a city of this size, the downtown area is small. East Broadway has a number of business parks.

If Your Character Is a Rich Snowbird, he lives in Star Pass, Catalina Foothills, or Rancho Distoso.

If Your Characters Are Raising a Family, they live in Sam Hughes, though, again, new suburbs are springing up everywhere, primarily on the far east side for this type of character.

If Your Character Wears a Blue Collar at Work, he lives in South Tucson, anywhere on the south side, or in the Flowing Wells area to the north of downtown.

Local Grub Your Character Might Love

Tucsonans like their food hot and spicy. Mexican restaurants serving authentic dishes loaded with chiles abound. Locals pride themselves on enjoying food hotter than their visitors can stand it.

Southwestern cuisine is impossible to avoid, and steak is a favorite throughout the state.

Any kind of ethnic food is available.

Mexican beer—Pacifico, Dos Equis, Bohemia, Carta Blanca, Modello Negro—is popular. If your character prefers margaritas, the drink is very easy to find. Many of the Mexican and southwestern restaurants pride themselves on their margaritas.

Interesting and Peculiar Places to Set a Scene

- **Mission San Xavier del Bac.** This old mission attracts tourists as well as locals. The beautiful, white Spanish-style church and courtyard are located just outside the city. Near the mission, Native Americans in makeshift booths vend fry bread.
- **Biosphere 2.** This three-acre laboratory is the world's largest controlled environment for the study of plant growth and other Earth systems. Run by scientists from Columbia University, Biosphere 2 is a source of pride for Tucsonans, who can take a guided tour through part of the facility. In case you're wondering, Biosphere 1 is the Earth.
- **Congress Hotel.** One of the oldest hotels in the city, Congress Hotel was built during the railroad days. It's been restored and has a quaint cafe that attracts locals. In the ballroom on Fridays and Saturdays, dances attract the college crowd.
- **Fourth Avenue.** This eclectic shopping district near the University of Arizona draws a mix of people, from students to artists to wealthy locals to the down-and-out. Caruso's Italian restaurant and Antigone bookstore are two popular haunts.
- **Electric Park.** In February and March, Electric Park is the spring training home to the Arizona Diamondbacks and the Chicago White Sox. The cozy stadium is part of the Kino Veterans Memorial Community Center and Sports Complex, which contains twelve fields. When the teams head north in April, the park is home to the minor-league Tucson Sidewinders.
- **Old Tucson.** Sure it's fake, but it's definitely scene fodder. Columbia Studios built this Old West town in 1939 to shoot *Arizona*. Throughout the heyday of Western movies and TV shows, it was used regularly by Hollywood studios. Now it's mostly a tourist attraction. Actors dressed in Old West garb entertain visitors.
- **Saguaro National Park.** A forest of the giant saguaro cacti, Saguaro National Park draws more than a million visitors per year. It's also a popular getaway for Tucsonans who live close by. Tucsonans love the big cactus and know the general facts about it. The cactus can grow as tall as fifty feet and can live up to two hundred years. It begins to grow arms after the first seventy-five years. You can approximate its age by the number of arms.
- **Sabino Canyon.** Another nearby and popular getaway for locals, Sabino Canyon is loaded with weekend hikers. It's nestled in the Catalina Mountains south of town and does not allow motorized vehicles other than park shuttles. For less physically ambitious visitors, the shuttles offer guided tours.
- **South Tucson.** A mile-square area in the southern section of the city, South Tucson is populated predominately by Mexican Americans with low incomes. It's a high-crime area in need of greater economic oppor-

For Further Research

Books

The Book of Tucson Firsts, by Larry Cox

El Charro Café: Tastes and Traditions of Tucson, by Carlotta Flores

Fighting Sprawl and City Hall: Resistance to Urban Growth in the Southwest, by Michael F. Logan

Los Tucsonenses: The Mexican Community in Tucson 1854–1941, by Thomas E. Sheridan

Tucson: The Life and Times of an American City, by Charles Sonnichsen

Tucson: The Old Pueblo, by Lisa Schnebly Heidinger

Web Sites

www.ci.tucson.az.us (city government site)

http://iwtucson.com/ (city guide)

www.insidetucson.com/ (city events and entertainment site)

www.dotucson.com/ (city entertainment guide)

www.hereintucson.com/ (city Internet directory)

www.pima.com/ (Pima County main site)

www.desertusa.com/ (desert information and attractions)

www.aztucson.com/ (visitor information and site directory)

Still Curious? Why Not Check Out

The Bean Trees, by Barbara Kingsolver

Cold Blooded: The Saga of Charles Schmid, the Notorious "Pied Piper of Tucson", by John Gilmore

Kiss of the Bees, by J.A. Jance

Naked Pueblo: Stories and *Goats: A Novel*, by Mark Jude Piorier

Nothing but the Truth, by Richard Parrish

Shelter, by Bobby Burns

Tales From the Geronimo, by Scott Frank

The Twenty-Seven Ingredient Chili Con Carne Murders, by Nancy Pickard and Virginia Rich

---

tunities. Though known for its authentic Mexican restaurants, the crime keeps tourists away at night.

Exceptionally Grand Things Your Character Is Proud Of

- The desert and desert life. Locals are quick to show off the mountains that ring the city, as well as the desert and the grand saguaros.
- The tradition of cooperation between Caucasians, Native Americans, and Hispanics. Locals relish the richness and diversity of their culture. Celebrations by Native Americans who live on the nearby reservations draw huge local crowds.
- The Primavera Foundation. A local organization dedicated to helping the homeless.

Your Character Loves

- Mount Lemmon. It's a favorite place for local hikers.
- Lute Olson. The Wildcat coach is beloved.
- The desert in spring.
- Sentinel Peak Park, which is called "A" Mountain because of the large whitewashed "A" that sits near the top of the eastern slope facing the city. It's a particular favorite for University of Arizona students.

- Poetry. The Tucson Poetry Festival takes place in early spring. Tucson is one of the leading cities in poets per capita.

Your Character Hates

- The "snowbirds." Though the economy depends upon winter tourists from the North, especially those who invade the town in search of sun and golf, locals (those not working in the tourist industry) sometimes view the tourists as nuisances. Snowbirds tend to drive slowly and hold up traffic.
- Developers who are razing the desert, destroying natural habitats for plant and animal life.
- The city's uncontrolled growth. People who have lived here for many years feel the loss of political power to snowbirds and retirees. The latter have elected strongly pro-business local governments who have not been as sensitive to social services and the environment.
- The taste of CAP water. The Central Arizona Project diverted water from the Colorado River to supply Tucson and the Phoenix metro area. The stuff tastes terrible.

Arkansas

Arkansas Basics That Shape Your Character

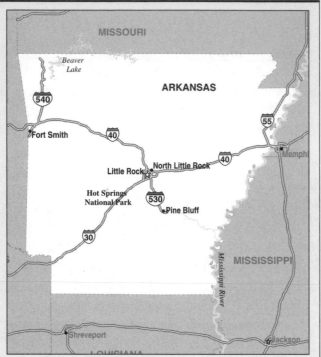

Motto: The People Rule

Population: 2.67 million

Prevalent Religions: Christianity, particularly Southern Baptist and Pentecostal

Major Industries: Food processing, poultry and eggs, soybeans, sorghum, cattle, cotton, rice, hogs, milk, electric equipment, fabricated metal products, machinery, paper products

Ethnic Makeup (in percent): Caucasian 80.0%, African-American 15.7%, Hispanic 3.2%, Asian 0.8%, Native American 0.7%, Other 1.5%

Famous Arkansasans: Maya Angelou, Helen Gurley Brown, Glen Campbell, Johnny Cash, Eldridge Cleaver, Dizzy Dean, John Gould Fletcher, Al Green, John H. Johnson, Scott Joplin, Alan Ladd, Douglas MacArthur, Mary Steenburgen, CK Williams, Miller Williams

Significant Events Your Character Has Probably Thought About

- Arkansas seceded from the Union in 1861 to join the Confederacy.

- The election of Hattie Caraway in 1932. "Silent Hattie" became the first woman elected to the U.S. Senate, only twelve years after women were given the right to vote. And she served three terms.
- The 1955 election of Governor Orval Eugene Faubus. The mountain man (and six-term governor!) from the town of Greasy Creek achieved national prominence by defying the Supreme Court's *Brown v. Board of Education* ruling against segregation.
- The 1957 Little Rock Central High integration crisis. Nine African-American teenagers set the stage for the Civil Rights movement as they stood bravely at the doors of the school and demanded nonsegregated education, with no help from Governor Faubus.
- Sam Walton opened his first Wal-Mart store in Bentonville in 1962.
- In 1966 Winthrop Rockefeller became the first elected Republican governor in ninety-two years.
- Bill Clinton won his first of several gubernatorial elections in 1979.
- In 1992 homeboy Bill Clinton was elected president of the United States, and Jim Guy Tucker became governor of Arkansas.
- James and Susan McDougal, the Clintons' partners in their failed Whitewater real estate investment, were sent to jail on fraud charges in 1996.
- Jim Guy Tucker resigned as governor, also in 1996, after a federal jury convicted him a felon for shady business deals associated with the Clintons and the McDougals.
- The shooting at Westside Middle School in Jonesboro in March of 1998. Two boys, ages eleven and thirteen, gunned down four female students and one teacher.

Arkansas Facts and Peculiarities Your Character Might Know

- Arkansas was the twenty-fifth state to join the Union.
- The southwestern region of the state is known for its logging and paper industries, as well as its spartan towns.
- The southeast delta area is poor with lots of low-income farming and cotton communities.
- Arkansas has quite varied elevations, spanning from

only 54 feet above sea level in the far southeast corner to 2,753 feet at Mount Magazine in the northwest Ozark Mountains.

- Arkansas is the only place in North America where diamonds have been found.
- Stuttgart has gained notoriety throughout the world for its duck-calling contest.
- Hot Springs Mountain is literally a fountain of steaming water, with forty-seven hot springs (averaging 143° temperatures) flowing from its southwestern slope.
- Mountain View is home to one of the largest producers of handmade dulcimers in the world.
- They've tried to rename Arkansas "The Natural State" a number of times; as of yet, it's still just plain old "Arkansas."

Your Character's Food and Drink

Standard Arkansas fare includes barbecue, beef cuts, fried chicken, prime rib, quail, shrimp, fried catfish sandwiches, watermelon, rack of lamb, corn bread, coleslaw, okra, and traditional veggies. Barbecue restaurants and down-home diners and buffets are popular in Arkansas, as are steak houses and "all you can eat" cafeterias. McClard's Bar-B-Q in Hot Springs is perhaps the most famous restaurant in the state (President Clinton has boasted of filling up there on more than several occasions). The specialty is a big rib platter piled over with fries and a side of coleslaw. Nu-grape is a favorite state soft drink.

Things Your Character Likes to Remember

- The Bath Houses in Hot Springs.
- Arkansas's natural diversity and resources, especially its hot springs and rolling mountains.
- The Arkansas Razorbacks (the "Hogs").
- Sam Walton.
- Bill Clinton.

Things Your Character Would Like to Forget

- Governor Faubus and the 1957 Little Rock Central High integration crisis.
- The Jonesboro shootings.
- Bill Clinton.

Myths and Misperceptions About Arkansas

- **The residents are uneducated.** While pockets of the state are still a bit backward, Arkansas has invested a lot of money in education over the years. It is one of the better-paying southern states for teachers.
- **Bill Clinton is the state's most cherished son.** Guess again. Sam Walton and General Douglas MacArthur are held in much higher esteem than the state's only president.
- **They don't like to gamble.** Wrong! The residents of Arkansas do in fact love to gamble, but everybody goes to Memphis and Mississippi to do it.

Interesting Places to Set a Scene

- **Eureka Springs.** Set in a precipitous gorge in the Ozarks, this charming mountain town is called "Little Switzerland" by many. It's been a refuge to hosts of artists, writers, and eccentrics, thanks to its Old Victorian homes, gingerbread houses, medicinal springs, and zigzag streets that wind around old brick buildings on sloped mountain sides.
- **Fayetteville.** This agricultural experiment station and trade center (canneries and food processors) is the state's big college town, as it's home to the University of Arkansas. Urban sprawl has become a problem in recent years.
- **Hot Springs.** Surrounded by lakes and mountains, Hot Springs is by far the most memorable big city in Arkansas. An old cosmopolitan city that as of late is also a teeming art center, it is also the boyhood home of Bill Clinton (although he lived his first several years in Hope). The city boasts the Arlington and Majestic Hotels, the Magic Springs theme park, and Hot Springs National Park (a long block of old bath

The Old State House in Little Rock

Courtesy of Little Rock Convention & Visitors Bureau

For Further Research

Books

The Best of Times: America in the Clinton Years, by Haynes Johnson

Down From the Hills, by Orval Eugene Faubus

Faubus: The Life and Times of an American Prodigal, by Roy Reed

Let Us Build Us a City: Eleven Lost Towns, by Donald Harington

A Living History of the Ozarks, by Phyllis Rossiter

Roadside History of Arkansas, by Alan Paulson

Web Sites

www.state.ar.us/ (official state site)

www.arkansas.com/ (visitor info)

www.arktimes.com/ (state news)

www.asl.lib.ar.us/arloc.htm (state library site)

www.ark-ives.com/ (state history commission)

www.hsu.edu/dept/alf/links.html (state literary forum)

Still Curious? Why Not Check Out

Maggody and the Moonbeams: An Arly Hanks Mystery, by Joan Hess

A Painted House, by John Grisham

Paradise Lost: The Child Murders at Robin Hood Hills

Queen of October, by Shelley Fraser Mickle

Shiloh Autumn: A Novel, by Bodie and Brock Thoene

Sugar, by Bernice L. McFadden

houses on the main strip that has soaked the likes of FDR, Babe Ruth, and Al Capone). As your character walks along the brick promenade, he's also likely to encounter the seedy side of the city, coming face-to-face with drug dealers and prostitutes. During prohibition there was plenty to drink in Hot Springs as well (which could explain Al Capone's preference for the place).

- **Little Rock.** Although this Arkansas River city of 175,000 is the state's capital and largest city, there's not an abundance of things in Little Rock to make it an interesting place in which to set a scene. As one native described it, Little Rock is "A nonplace big place. I'll take Hot Springs any day." What does, however, make Little Rock unique is its importance to the state; it's the administrative, commercial, and transportation center of Arkansas. The city received some negative world press in 1957 when federal troops had to be sent in to enforce a Supreme Court ruling against segregation in public schools. Of course, the governor's mansion is a treat (as everyone saw from the outside during President Clinton's victory speech in 1992), as are the art and natural history museums and the IMAX theater.

- **Mountain View.** The self-proclaimed "Folk Capital of America," this little mountain town does its best to preserve the pioneer way of life by trying to keep everything the way it used to be, albeit in a quasi-touristy kind of way.

- **Pine Bluff.** Have your character visit the only museum in the country devoted to band instruments and the history of the band movement in America. Pine Bluff is also world renowned for producing archery bows.

Significant Events Your Character Has Probably Thought About

- In 1848, James Marshall discovered gold, sparking the California gold rush.
- The Compromise of 1850 permitted California to enter the Union as a free state.
- The Chinese Exclusion Act of 1882 pushed the Chinese out of the labor force; many locals had been losing jobs to Chinese immigrants, who were cheaper labor.
- In 1913, the California Alien Land Act declared that those ineligible for U.S. citizenship could not own land in the state.
- The influx during the 1930s of displaced farm workers caused profound dislocation in the state's economy. Read John Steinbeck's *The Grapes of Wrath* for a sense of what life was like during this period.
- Industry in California expanded rapidly during World War II; the production of ships and aircraft attracted many workers who later settled in the state.
- Many African-Americans came to the state during World War II to work in the war industries. By the 1960s, they constituted a sizable minority in the state, and racial tensions began to rise.
- Also in the 1960s, migrant farm workers in California formed a union to obtain better pay and working conditions.
- In the late 1970s, Californians staged a "tax revolt," passing legislation to cut property taxes.
- California grew rapidly during the 1970s and 1980s, especially the state's interior, which experienced a large influx of immigrants from Mexico, China, the Philippines, and Asia.
- The 1989 earthquake killed about sixty people and injured thousands in Santa Cruz and the San Francisco Bay area.
- Another earthquake rocked the Northridge area and killed sixty people in 1993.
- California voters approved Proposition 187 in 1994, which prohibited the state from providing welfare, education, and nonemergency medical services to illegal immigrants.

California Basics That Shape Your Character

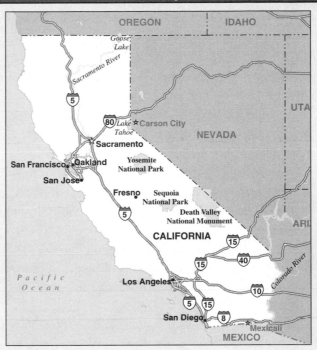

Motto: Eureka!

Population: 33.9 million

Prevalent Religions: They're all here, of course, but Roman Catholics have the greatest numbers, followed by Lutherans and Baptists.

Major Industries: Electronic components and equipment, aerospace, film production, food processing, petroleum, computers and computer software, tourism, vegetables, fruits and nuts, dairy products, cattle, nursery stock, grapes, wine

Ethnic Makeup (in percent): Caucasian 59.5%, African-American 6.7%, Hispanic 32.4%, Asian 10.9%, Native American 1.0%, Other 16.8%

Famous Californians: Julia Child, Leonardo DiCaprio, Joe DiMaggio, Isadora Duncan, John Charles Frémont, Jerry Garcia, William Randolph Hearst, Sidney Howard, Jack London, George Lucas, Richard Nixon, Isamu Noguchi, George Patton, Robert Redford, Sally Ride, John Steinbeck, Shirley Temple, Earl Warren, Tiger Woods

California Facts and Peculiarities Your Character Might Know

- It has the largest population and the largest economy of any state in the country.
- Both the highest and the lowest points in the lower forty-eight states are in California and are within one hundred miles of one another: Mount Whitney is 14,495 feet high; Bad Water in Death Valley is 282 feet below sea level.
- Hillside Cemetery in Culver City is thought to be home to the greatest number of dead celebrities in the United States.
- The state motto, "Eureka!" (a Greek word meaning "I've found it!"), was coined in 1849 during the California gold rush.
- The redwood is the official state tree. Some of the giant redwoods in Sequoia National Park are more than two thousand years old.
- San Jose was the state's first capital in 1805. Within four years, Monterey, Vallejo, and Benicia all became capitals before Sacramento was settled upon as the capital in 1854.
- About 500,000 seismic tremors are detected in California annually.
- Both of California's senators are Jewish women—Barbara Boxer and Dianne Feinstein. Now where else has this happened? Only here!
- Noted public figures from California include Ronald Reagan, Adlai Stevenson, Richard Nixon, and Earl Warren.
- The state produces about seventeen million gallons of wine each year.
- Most folks don't think of California when they think of rodeos, but the nation's largest three-day rodeo is held in Red Bluff.
- Jerry Brown was perhaps the most eccentric governor in state history and definitely its greatest New Ager. He was nicknamed "Governor Moonbeam."

Your Character's Food and Drink

The state offers everything, of course, because it's a melting pot of cultures. California is credited with creating "fusion cuisine," which blends different types of food. Some dishes are a mix of Mexican, Spanish, Italian, Asian, and other international tastes. Then, of course, there's "California cuisine," which embodies a light approach to cooking, with lots of fresh, locally grown veggies like tomatoes, avocados, peppers, herbs, and lettuces as well as grains, citrus fruits, and fresh seafood. The emphasis in "California cuisine" is on the ingredients (healthiness and flavor) and not so much on the cooking of the presentation. There are lots of vinaigrette dressings, cheeses, and breads to go with all those fresh fruits and vegetables. To drink, Californians love water with lemon, and many love to sip homegrown wines from the state's many famous vineyards.

Things Your Character Likes to Remember

- The USS *Potomac*. Hundreds of volunteers devoted over twelve years to restoring FDR's "Floating White House."
- Traveling along the Southern California coast, either by car or on one of the rails.
- Going to Calistoga to enjoy one of its pleasant mud baths.
- Taking a hot air balloon ride over Napa Valley.
- The Jerry Brown years—when he was reelected to a second term in 1978, it was by the largest vote margin in California's history.
- California has some of the best golf courses in the world.
- That California is really the trendsetter and pack leader for the rest of the country—things happen here way before they do elsewhere.
- No matter where you are in California, you're not too far away from the ocean or the mountains.

Things Your Character Would Like to Forget

- Earthquakes.
- The electric power mess that has frustrated the state in recent years.
- Proposition 14. A 1964 initiative measure allowing racial discrimination in the sale or rental of housing in the state (later declared unconstitutional by the U.S. Supreme Court).
- Japanese-American internment camps.
- The high cost of living.
- The constant influx of newcomers.
- The Pacific Gas and Electric cover-up regarding toxic water, as portrayed in *Erin Brockovich*.

Myths and Misperceptions About California

- **There's gang violence every day everywhere.** The unfortunate streaks of gang-related violence in Los

Angeles and other big cities have given the state a bad rap.

- **It's all big cities.** Not at all. The natural wonders and expanses of land and small towns make up most of the state.
- **They're all just a bunch of crazy liberals.** Actually, Californians often vote Republican. The GOP has played a more dominant role than the Dems in California politics, especially during the last half of the twentieth century—from the end of World War II through the mid-1990s, five of the seven governors were Republicans.

Interesting Places to Set a Scene

- **The Alabama Hills.** These rocks and hills and eroded granite look like another planet. The result is a picture-perfect movie set, which it has been for such films as *King of the Khyber Rifles*, *Tremors*, and *Star Trek V: The Final Frontier*.
- **Avenue of the Giants.** More than fifty thousand acres of giant redwood trees surround this corridor in Northern California.
- **Berkeley.** Home to Alice Waters, "the queen of California cuisine"; several divinity schools; and, of course, University of California, Berkeley (the main campus of the University of California), which has a worldwide reputation for its academics and was a harbinger for student protests and the counterculture of the 1960s and 1970s. The spirit of the famous 1964 "Free Speech" movement still lingers in Berkeley, as does the variety of life and people. Perhaps your character might think of what Clark Kerr, former chancellor of Berkeley, said back in the 1950s: "If you are bored with Berkeley, you are bored with life."
- **Big Sur.** This ninety-mile stretch of coastline is nothing but breathtaking (and a good place to toss a body or escape for a romantic getaway).
- **Bodega Bay.** Bodega Bay became known around the world as the setting for Alfred Hitchcock's *The Birds*. They (the birds) are still flying about in the marshes. This is also a good spot for your character to sip some local wine or watch the hundreds of fishing boats come and go, dropping off their catches at Tides Wharf.
- **Cambria.** This tiny artist's colony has only a few eateries, inns, bed-and-breakfasts, and shops. The area hasn't been encroached upon by major land developments—yet. There's an ongoing debate as locals are upset with a developer who recently purchased quite a bit of land near the town. Gray whales, which pass through the area in winter, and elephant seals can be seen from the shores.

- **Coachella Valley.** Have your character take off on one of the tram cars 8,500 feet above the desert floor. Who says deserts are entirely boring?
- **Death Valley.** It's the heat that's the problem.
- **Gold Country.** With its Sutter's Fort, historic Old Sacramento, and restored 1927 riverboat-turned-hotel-turned-locomotive museum, this area has history and knows how to flaunt it. It does, of course, celebrate its history during the gold rush. These days, your character can bike along the river's waterfront or take a balloon ride above it. Then, if he's ready for a drink, he can end his day with a stop at Murphy's for some local wine.
- **Lake Tahoe.** It's a major vacation and recreation spot from winter (skiers) to summer (mountain bikers, boaters, swimmers), and it has gambling resorts along the Nevada state line.
- **Los Angeles.** (See page 36 for more specifics on Los Angeles.)
- **Manzanar War Relocation Center.** This eight-hundred-acre national historic site is a living history lesson, the spot where more than ten thousand Japanese Americans were corralled and detained during World War II.
- **Mendocino.** Filled with tiny art galleries, small wooden houses, and old-time general stores, this Northern California artist's colony (started in the 1950s) might make your character think she's in New

A typical California surfer

© PhotoDisc/Getty Images

England, thanks to the homes and the architecture. The port town used to be fairly active, but these days only about a thousand people reside here. Mendocino used to be the backdrop for that Sunday night murder mystery show, *Murder, She Wrote*.

- **Monterey.** Your family man character could easily find himself here with the kids, as Monterey is often called "Disneyland by the Sea" thanks to all the family-friendly activities like the aquarium and Fisherman's Wharf. Monterey is also known for its Cannery Row, where they used to pack sardines en masse (about twenty-five tons a night at its peak in the early 1900s). Check out John Steinbeck's *Cannery Row*.

- **Napa Valley.** Both the Napa Valley and neighboring Sonoma Valley make up California's premier wine country, which has an international reputation for producing some of the best wines in the world. The small town of Copia is a mix of museums, gardens, and The American Center for Wine, Food & the Arts—a museum where your character can learn an epicurean's secrets and see kitchenware from Julia Child's home!

- **Oakland.** This football—and baseball—loving city is San Francisco's working-class neighbor. Although it lacks the culture and chic of San Francisco, Oakland has survived, thanks to its shipping port, railroad yards, shipyards, chemical plants, pharmaceutical companies, computer manufacturers, glassmakers and other blue-collar businesses. For many, what is most notable about Oakland is that it was home to Jack London (and Heinold's First and Last Chance Saloon won't let your character forget it!).

- **Ocean Beach.** The beach is notorious for its rip currents, but things seem worse than ever these days. In 2002 the beach was deemed by Francis Smith of University of California, Berkeley as "the most hazardous and dangerous piece of shoreline associated with an urban environment in the whole United States."

- **Ojai.** The rather private Ojai Valley contains eucalyptus groves and small ranches that rest amidst lush green hills; it has been a mecca for artists and writers for years. To give you an idea of how remote, beautiful, and imaginary this place is, Frank Capra chose to shoot the 1937 utopian film *Lost Horizon* here.

- **Palm Springs Resorts.** World-famous for its golf resorts, swimming, sunbathing, and tennis courts, Palm Springs used to be associated with retirees swinging their irons and college students getting silly on spring break. This is changing, as young Hollywooders and a plethora of gays and lesbians are frequenting "the Springs." It's deemed the best European-style vacation spot on the West coast.

- **Sacramento.** (See page 41 for more specifics on Sacramento.)

- **San Diego.** (See page 45 for more specifics on San Diego.)

- **San Francisco.** (See page 49 for more specifics on San Francisco.)

- **San Jose.** San Jose was the state capital from 1849 to 1851. This brother of San Francisco is well known for its fruit-growing, computers, electronics, mineral springs, Japanese gardens, wineries, food-processing industries, and aircraft and motor-part manufacturing. San Jose's population has grown rapidly—some say by 70 percent—in the past twenty-five years. Both the city's Tech Museum of Innovation and its repertory theater have recently found new homes in cool buildings.

- **Santa Cruz.** Surrounded by hills and redwoods, this seaside city sports a replica of a mission established here in 1791 and the notoriously partying school, the University of California at Santa Cruz.

- **Santa Barbara.** This is an expensive, relaxed community of fashionable boutiques, chic cafes, antiques stores, healthy eateries, white sands, umbrellas, beaches, students, volleyball, and Spanish architecture (especially evident are all the red tile roofs). The city's main street, State Street, is beautiful as well, as many local artists sell their works under the palm trees on the green median. The Santa Barbara Mission, called "Queen of the Missions," is also here, overlooking the city and the sea.

- **Sequoia National Park.** If the forty-foot-wide base of the world's largest living tree isn't enough to put your character in jaw-dropping awe, perhaps the site of one of the black bears that curls up under a fallen log to sleep would. A tree-hugger's dream . . . too bad he can't get his arms around most of these giant natural wonders.

- **Yosemite.** Although a major flood wiped out a lot of the man-made elements (campgrounds, cottages, bridges, etc.) in the Yosemite Valley to the disappointment of many visitors and park employees, the flood made one thing clear: You deal with Yosemite on Yo-

For Further Research

Books

American Exodus: The Dust Bowl Migration and Okie Culture in California, by James N. Gregory

Ansel Adams' California, edited by Andrea Stillman

Assembling California, by John McPhee

Atlas of California, by Michael W. Donley

California: The Geography of Diversity, by Crane S. Miller and Richard S. Hyslop

California: A History, by Andrew F. Rolle

California: An Illustrated History, by T.H. Watkins

California: Land of Contrast, by David W. Lantis

A Companion to California, by James D. Hart

The Fourth Wave: California's Newest Immigrants, by Thomas Muller

The Golden State: California History and Government, by Andrew F. Rolle

Paradise Lost, by Peter Schrag

Rush for Riches: Gold Fever and the Making of California, by J.S. Holliday

The Seven States of California: A Natural and Human History, by Philip L. Fradkin

Web Sites

www.ca.gov/state/portal/myca_homepage.jsp (state site)

www.californiahistory.net/ (state history)

www.travelcalifornia.com/ (visitor's info and tourism)

www.californiahistoricalsociety.org/ (historical society)

www.calwriters.com/ (writers' site)

www.writersmonthly.com/ (Southern California writers' site)

http://gocalif.ca.gov/ (tourism)

Still Curious? Why Not Check Out

American Son: A Novel, by Brian Ascalon Roley

Billy Straight, by Jonathan Kellerman

California Rush: A Novel, by Sherwood Kiraly

California's Daughter: Gertrude Atherton and Her Times, by Emily Wortis Leider

Cannery Row, by John Steinbeck

Collecting Sins: A Novel, by Steven Sobel

Education of a Felon: A Memoir, by Edward Bunker

Erin Brockovich

The Harry Bosch Novels: The Black Echo, The Black Ice, The Concrete Blonde, by Michael Connelly

Highwire Moon: A Novel, by Susan Straight

Hoyt Street: An Autobiography, by Mary Helen Ponce

The Lights of Earth: A Novel, by Gina Berriault

Lost Horizon

Sister Noon, by Karen Joy Fowler

Snow Mountain Passage: A Novel, by James D. Houston

semite's terms, not yours. This is one thing your character needs to remember. The park is a wondrous work of nature; it contains the world's largest slab of granite (El Capitan), North America's highest waterfall (Yosemite Falls), one of the world's biggest trees (Grizzly Giant), and a most breathtaking mountain (Half Dome). It's a natural playground—the perfect setting for an adventure story.

Los Angeles

Los Angeles Basics That Shape Your Character

The City of Angels is now a sprawling metropolis

Population: 3.8 million in the city; 9.9 million in Greater Metro Area

Prevalent Religions: They're all here, but it's mostly Catholic, Pentecostal, nondenominational, Judaism, Muslim, and Buddhist

Top Employers: County of Los Angeles, State of California, Los Angeles Unified School District, U.S. Government, City of Los Angeles, Boeing, Kaiser Permanente, Ralphs Grocery Company, Walt Disney Company, Kelly Services, Bank of America, Target, Pacific Bell, ABM Industries, University of Southern California

Per Capita Income: $27,606

Average Daily Temperature: January, 60° F; July, 82° F

Ethnic Makeup (in percent): Caucasian 46.9%, African-American 11.2%, Hispanic 46.5%, Asian 10.0%, Native American 0.8%, Other 25.7%

Newspapers and Magazines: *Los Angeles Times, Los Angeles Daily News, La Opinión, Los Angeles Magazine, Irvine Spectrum News, Los Angeles Business Journal, Southern California Business Trends, Los Angeles Family, L.A. Parent*

Free Weekly Alternative Papers: *Los Angeles Downtown News, Los Angeles Independent, L.A. Weekly, New Times L.A.*

Los Angeles Facts and Peculiarities Your Character Might Know

- A joke among Southern Californians is that San Diego is where California began, but Los Angeles has always been where it is headed.
- Los Angeles is a city of excess, with more everything than almost any other place: It's more varied, more cosmopolitan, more gracious, more grotesque, more strange.
- This is a city of handshakes. People are always auditioning in Los Angeles, and they want to present their best selves first, hoping the person they're being introduced to is connected to someone (who's connected to someone).
- Everything's for sale in Los Angeles: In busy areas, you'll find merchants selling things from blankets, trinkets, boas, and artwork to chair massages and photo-ops in front of Los Angeles landmarks.
- The number of languages spoken in Los Angeles is amazing and varied.
- When you are in a store, the people behind the counter are as ethnically diverse as those waiting in line.
- There are lot of first-generation Americans, with many of these folks sharing homes and apartments.
- Los Angeles is very industrious, with people always on the move, doing or looking at something.
- When they went up in 1923, the big white letters that spell "Hollywood" read "Hollywoodland" to promote the area's real estate. The city bought the letters in 1949 and simplified the name.
- There's more than just palm trees here, including lots of banana trees, birds of paradise, pine trees, citrus trees, kumquat trees, and others.
- Balconies in Los Angeles seem to have become extensions of homes, not just sitting areas. For example, you'll often see bicycles, couches, toys, plants, old televisions, and storage boxes. Read Janet Fitch's *White Oleander.*
- Los Angeles is also a city of renters, not landowners.
- Everything turns into entertainment in Los Angeles, as there always seems to be breaking news stories, car chases, holdups, and so on. Since so many people

have video cameras, much of it gets caught on tape as well.

- Although the days of Valley talk seem long ago, it's not uncommon to hear phrases like, "What's up?" "Hey, girlfriend!" and "What's goin' on?"
- The city in some ways has no city center. Because it's so sprawled out and there is so much activity in so many places, it's been called "forty-nine suburbs in search of a city."

If Your Character . . .

If Your Character Is Alternative and Grungy, he lives in West Hollywood. A variety of "alternative" lifestyles are represented here, from the residents to the stores. The place is wrought with lots of tattoos, body piercings, gays, motorcyclists, punk types, and struggling actors. Similar areas are Venice Beach and Melrose Avenue.

If Your Character Smells of Old Money, he lives in Pasadena. Old, attractive, refined homes and gardens, as well as upscale restaurants, make up this historic area. Especially interesting is "Old Pasadena," where the city's oldest homes are preserved. Similar places are Palos Verdes, Malibu, the Wilshire District, and Beverly Hills.

If Your Character Smells of New Money, she lives in Brentwood. This nice upper-class community became famous because a certain ex-pro-football player "allegedly" stabbed his wife to death here.

If Your Character Is a Young Movie Star, she lives in Hollywood Hills. It's here, not in Hollywood or Beverly Hills, where the young stars live these days. The houses are cool, have pools and gardens, and are far too big for most of these single folks.

If Your Character Is an Old Movie Star, he lives in Beverly Hills. The area was once nothing but a ranch with a farmhouse. Now, however, it's a five-mile spectacle of million-dollar homes, servants, gardeners, and security systems.

If Your Character Is Down-and-Out, she lives in San Pedro. This is one of the poorest areas in the city and seems very third worldly.

If Your Character Is Having an Affair, he's going to the other side of town. That's what people do here. A lot of them have affairs, and they just go to the other side of town for an evening or for an entire weekend in a hotel room. Since Los Angeles is so big, there's little risk of having that chance encounter with the spouse.

Local Grub Your Character Might Love

Seafood. Get this fact: Los Angeles consumes the most seafood in the United States—eating $1.5 billion worth of fish annually! That tops even Boston, New York, San Francisco, Miami, and Chicago. There's lots of Mexican food here, too, of course. Ethnic restaurants are on almost every corner: Chinese, Italian, Caribbean, Iranian, Thai, Brazilian, Japanese, French, and anything American. Los Angeles folks with less money tend to get lots of fast food, like McDonalds, Burger King, and Taco Bell. Some favorite local restaurants and eateries include The Hollywood Hills Coffee Shop, Grill 53, Musso and Frank Grill, Ocean Avenue Seafood, Wolfgang Puck Café, Valentino, Prego, Buffalo Club, Schatzi on Main, Morton's, Cobalt Cantina, La Scala, Emporio Armani Express Café and Restaurant, The Grill, and Balducci's Trattoria.

Interesting and Peculiar Places to Set a Scene

- **Boardwalk in Venice Beach.** Your character is going to run into pamphleteers, poets, musicians, street performers, and others. And the sunset is always lovely. . . .
- **Broadway.** Nowhere in town does the Los Angeles Latino community do more shopping than here. It's very crowded with the sights and sounds (and smells!) of Latin America.
- **Downtown.** Your character won't have to travel far to run into one of the city's many homeless, who tend to gather here as well as at the beaches.
- **Grand Central Public Market.** This huge indoor marketplace bustles with shoppers of every age and race. Booths of all sorts sell almost anything that grows under the sun, swims in water, or crawls or walks on land.
- **Hollywood Boulevard.** The freaks apparently do come out at night in this area of town, where sidewalks are filled with some of the city's strangest-dressed characters. It's also home to male and female hookers, drug

addicts, and runaway teens trying to make it on the streets.

- **In a car.** A lot seems to happen in cars in Los Angeles. There's a joke that drivers have a latte in one hand, a sandwich in the other, a cell phone to their ear, and steer with their knees. They only put the latte in the cup holder to put on makeup, shave, brush their hair and teeth, or change clothes.

- **Little Tokyo.** Just as you imagine, it's filled with Japanese citizens, Japanese clothing shops, and delicious Japanese food. Have your character grab her chopsticks and enjoy a meal here, but not until she checks out the nearby Japanese American National Museum, which catalogs one of the darkest moments in U.S. history—the Japanese-American internment camps during World War II.

- **Mulholland Drive.** Your character can't get better vistas of both valley and city than when traveling on this escalating windy road.

- **Outside the Capitol Records building.** Your character might walk by this landmark, look up, and wonder, "Is this supposed to be a stack of pancakes or a stack or records?" The answer, of course, is the latter. A lot of good songs have come from within those walls.

- **Pacific Park.** This mini-amusement park pays homage to the amusement parks of the past that once dotted the Pacific Coast. Aside from the dozen or so amusement rides is the hand-carved merry-go-round featured in *The Sting*.

- **Pasadena's Doo Dah Parade.** While this area of town is known for its Rose Bowl and Tournament of Roses Parade, this alternative parade might make for a better story. Although it lacks floats, themes, prizes, judges, and organization, it has crazy marchers (some in amazingly strange getups) handling everything from lawn mowers and baby buggies to shopping carts and big wheels. Authorities had to ban tortillas from the parade because so many people were throwing them at each other.

- **Pershing Square.** If your character wants to be surrounded by a bunch of suits all day, this is where he needs to be. Once the working day is over, however, the area becomes fairly deserted.

- **The Santa Monica Pier.** People gather here for everything from concerts and strolling to munching on cotton candy and popcorn. The area is particularly beautiful at night when white lights swing along the edge of the pier.

- **South Central.** This mostly African-American community received national attention during the Los Angeles Riots in 1992 after the Rodney King verdict. While many of the burned and busted buildings are back in business, this is still a rough part of the city with its share of shootings and gangs.

- **The bar at The Beverly Hills Hotel.** Your character should have no problem catching a few celebrities here—they like bars, they like Beverly Hills. Maybe your character can figure out a way to get them to like him, too. The drink prices are high, but since we're living in a fictional universe, money's irrelevant.

- **The Hollywood Bowl.** Not only is this the world's largest outdoor amphitheater, it is also one of the best places in the world to catch a concert—and definitely one of the most relaxing places in all of Los Angeles. Have your character take her blanket and picnic lunch for a wonderful evening of music under the stars.

- **The Plaza Downtown.** This is the heart of the city and home to Cinco de Mayo and other Mexican festivals. You won't find Steven Spielberg and Tom Cruise here (but maybe at a Dodgers game), but Los Angeles's business and Hispanic communities love the area.

- **The Theater District.** While it's not Broadway, this strip of theaters runs for blocks and includes such legendary venues as the Million Dollar Theater, the Los Angeles United Artists, and The Los Angeles Theater. The district is on the National Register of Historic Places.

- **Venice.** While patterned after Venice, Italy, with lots of canals and singing boatmen, some of the canals have been filled in and concreted (good place for a detective character to uncover a body?). It was a resort area in the 1920s and 1930s, but now it bustles with the young, the hip, the cutting edge, and the duck feeders.

- **Wilshire Boulevard between Sycamore and Fairfax Avenues.** This stretch of road is nicknamed "Miracle Mile" because it's a six-lane street with offstreet parking and numerous Art Deco buildings. It's one of the best drives—and walks, if your character plans to foot it—in the city.

For Further Research

Books

Geography of Rage: Remembering the Los Angeles Riots of 1992, by Jervey Tervalon

Ecology of Fear: Los Angeles and the Imagination of Disaster, by Mike Davis

The Fragmented Metropolis: Los Angeles, 1850–1930, by Robert M. Fogelson

Looking for Los Angeles: Architecture, Film, Photography, and the Urban Landscape, edited by Charles G. Salas and Michael S. Roth

Los Angeles: The Architecture of Four Ecologies, by Reyner Banham

Los Angeles and the Automobile: The Making of the Modern City, by Scott L. Bottles

Los Angeles: The Centrifugal City, by Rodney Steiner

The Los Metropolis, by Howard J. Nelson

The Los Angeles River, by Blake Gumprecht

Translating LA: A Tour of the Rainbow City, by Peter Theroux

Vanity Fair's Hollywood, by Christopher Hitchens

We Got the Neutron Bomb: The Untold Story of L.A. Punk, by Marc Spitz and Brendan Mullen

William Mulholland and the Rise of Los Angeles, by Catherine Mulholland

Web Sites

www.latimes.com/ (*Los Angeles Times*)

www.ci.la.ca.us/ (official city site)

www.co.la.ca.us/ (Los Angeles County site)

www.lapl.org/ (public library)

www.usc.edu/isd/archives/la/ (history)

www.losangelesalmanac.com (city almanac)

www.hollywood.com (movies)

Still Curious? Why Not Check Out

Blade Runner

Boyz N the Hood

Charlie's Angels

Clueless

Coldheart Canyon: A Hollywood Ghost Story, by Clive Barker

Flesh and Blood, by Jonathan Kellerman

L.A. Story

L.A. Confidential

Old Los Angeles

Scenes From a Mall

Short Cuts

Slouching Toward Bethlehem, by Joan Didion

The Black Dahlia, by James Ellroy

The Black Echo, by Michael Connelly

The Player The Sting

Thieves' Paradise, by Eric Jerome Dickey

Valley Girl

White Oleander, by Janet Fitch

Exceptionally Grand Things Your Character Is Proud Of

- Beaches and clubs.
- Rodondo Beach.
- West Hollywood.
- The Getty Center.
- Hosting the 1984 Summer Olympics.
- The Dodgers and the Lakers.
- Thomas Bradley. He was the city's first black mayor, elected in 1973.
- Specialty bookstores like The Cook's Bookstore and The Traveler's Bookcase.
- Loyola Marymount University; University of California, Los Angeles; and University of Southern California—all great schools.
- You can get anything you want in Los Angeles from drugs to phony IDs to the best meals, shops, theater, and jazz.
- You can go from the sunny beach to the snowy mountains to the dry desert in less than two hours.
- Diversity—it's everywhere.

Pathetically Sad Things Your Character Is Ashamed Of

- The Los Angeles Police Department—the Rodney King incident.
- Smog.
- Rudeness on the freeways.
- The O.J. Simpson trial.
- Crime.

- Gang violence.
- Homelessness.
- The lack of public transportation.
- The city's dependence on cars. Nearly everyone has a car, or they can't get around.
- Sprawl.

Your Character Loves
- Driving on Mulholland Drive on a clear day.
- Sneaking into the back-lot tours at Warner Brothers and Paramount Studios.
- Mother's Beach.
- Movies.
- The up close look at Hollywood.
- Billboards.
- Gossip.
- Discount stores—they're everywhere and are well stocked, especially those dollar stores.
- Limousines.
- Movie shoots.
- Movie stars.

- Getting tickets to a TV talk show.
- Mexican food.
- Seafood.
- Farmer's markets.
- Gold's Gym. It's where celebs and your average fitness folks work out side by side.
- Surfing, roller-blading, bicycling, skiing.

Your Character Hates
- Woody Allen's quips in *Annie Hall*: that the only cultural advantage to living in Los Angeles is being able to turn right on a red light, and that they don't throw away their garbage in Los Angeles but turn it into TV shows.
- Northern California and Orange County.
- Breathing in the smog.
- Traffic jams.
- Waiting. Los Angeles folks tend to want everything a minute ago.
- Being in the mountains at night—cell phones don't usually work there.

Sacramento

Sacramento Facts and Peculiarities Your Character Might Know

- Spanish explorer Gabriel Moraga came here in the 1800s and gave the area its name.
- Europeans wiped out many local Native American tribes in the 1800s, and the discovery of gold in 1848 turned the city into a bustling boomtown.
- In addition to being the state capital, Sacramento is one of California's primary educational and cultural centers.
- Sacramento is one of the fastest-growing areas in the state and in the country.
- Sacramento's downtown underwent a much-needed revitalization in the 1960s and 1970s.
- Patty Hearst and company came to Sacramento in 1974 to rob a few banks—but they also killed an innocent bystander.
- The city is a shipping, processing, and canning center for such agricultural products as fruit, vegetables, rice, wheat, and dairy goods, most of which are produced in Central Valley.
- President Gerald Ford was almost assassinated here in 1975.
- Several military bases near the city closed during the 1990s, which rocked the area economically.
- In the latter half of the 1990s, most of the military facilities were converted into high-tech industries.
- Several of the previously mentioned high-tech industries originated in Silicon Valley and then opted to set up shop here.
- ARCO Arena is home of both the Sacramento Kings (National Basketball Association) and the Sacramento Monarchs (Women's National Basketball Association).
- The American River Parkway right outside of town offers ample opportunities for fishing and rafting as well as pleasant riverside trails for walking, jogging, and bicycling.
- *Newsweek* magazine recently named Sacramento one of the ten best cities in the United States.

If Your Character . . .

If Your Character Is Trendy, she shops in Central City. This area has lots of coffeehouses and boutique stores,

Sacramento Basics That Shape Your Character

A pond and roses set against the state capital building

Population: 407,000 in the city; 1.9 million in the Greater Metro area

Prevalent Religions: Christianity (Baptist, Roman Catholic, Lutheran, nondenominational, United Methodist, Presbyterian), Judaism, Reform Judaism, Muslim, and Buddhism

Top Employers: Intel, McClellan Air Force Base, University of California, Davis Medical Center, Hewlett-Packard, City of Sacramento, ASI Children's Center, Sacramento County, New United Motor Manufacturing, U.S. Army Corps of Engineers, Siemens Transportation Systems, California Department of Transportation, California Water Resources Control Board, Franchise Tax Board

Per Capita Income: $26,000

Average Daily Temperature: January, 45° F; July, 76° F

Ethnic Makeup (in percent): Caucasian 48.3%, African-American 15.5%, Hispanic 21.6%, Asian 16.6%, Native American 1.3%, Other 17.4%

Newspapers and Magazines: *The Sacramento Bee, Sacramento Magazine, Sacramento Business Journal*

Free Weekly Alternative Papers: *Sacramento Gazette, Sacramento News and Review, The Sacramento Observer*

from independent, expensive local shops to national chain stores. It's in a cool part of town. Even if your character doesn't buy anything, this is The Place to Be Seen Shopping in Sacramento.

If Your Character Is a Middle-Class Family Man, he lives in Citrus. This is typical suburbia, with strip malls all around and houses in little bunches. The area is home to many middle-income families.

If Your Character Loves Nature, she's spending time in one of the city's 120 parks. The most popular is probably William Land Park, site of the Sacramento Zoo.

If Your Character Wears a Blue Collar at Work, he lives in Freeport. The bait shops far outnumber the grocery stores here. This, in essence, is a fishing area.

If Your Character Needs to Recapture the Pioneer Spirit of California, he's at Sutter's Fort State Historic Park. The famous John Sutter established this outpost in 1839. The park board has restored the fort to its 1850ish rustic grandeur, with such exhibits as a blacksmith's forge, a cooperage, a bakery, and a jail.

If Your Character Smells of Money, he resides in The Fabulous 40s. Yes, Fortieth Street and up are where the rich folks live, including the California governor, who has a little mansion up there. There are lots of big homes in the Fabulous Forties, with even bigger lots and plenty of old money. Land Park is a similar area.

Local Grub Your Character Might Love

Your character will love California cuisine, of course, but Sacramento offers lots of eating options. Barbecuing is big with families during the summer. For the best on local eateries, check out these local favorites: Oasis (Syrian-owned lunch spot that combines the cuisines of Northern Africa with more Americanized Italian cooking); Willie's Burgers on Sixteenth Street (chili burgers); Bread Shed Café (cheap Chinese); Fulton Avenue's Thai Cottage (great Thai food). Other favorites are Aïoli Bodega Española, Il Fornaio Flower, Kirby's Creekside Restaurant, Paragary's Bar and Oven, and Cliff House (great views above the American River).

Interesting and Peculiar Places to Set a Scene

- **Downtown near the University of California, Davis.** What used to be a town where cow-tipping was the big event is now a hopping university area, all educated, artsy, and bustling, with hip stores, spas, and salons up and down the stretch. Have your character

hop into some cool used clothes at Lulu's Fashion Lounge or grab some natural fiber at Samira's. Then she can slip into some sandals at Birkenstock Plus and head out to many more specialty stores, bookstores, and art galleries. This is definitely the coolest, most active area of town.

- **The Fifty-Seventh Street Antiques Row in East Sacramento.** This area is legendary for the quality and variety of its merchandise, offered by more than one hundred dealers in eight stores.

- **The Graduate.** This favorite pizza- and sandwich-type restaurant goes over well with the college kids; it could be the outdoor patio and the pool tables, but it's more likely the fifty-six-tap bar that spits out nearly every lager, pilsner, and ale your character could dream of drinking.

- **Oak Park.** The streets are tough here, as this once-quaint residential area has in a way been taken over by gangs. The community is a strange mix of young gang members out of work and old retirees who've been living in their homes for years.

- **Happy hour at the Paragon.** When you need to have your character in a blue-collar setting with a bunch of Busch- and Bud-drinking maintenance men, mechanics, electricians, and carpenters, this is the place. The Paragon is Sacramento's working-man's bar, a place where they're munching on a burger and fries while watching the Kings beat the Lakers, happily waiting for Shaq to miss another free throw.

- **On a bike.** Sacramento is a casual biker's paradise— the city's as flat as a pancake. With no major hills to thwart your almost-in-shape character, she should have no problem exploring the town on two wheels, especially as she cruises through Old Sacramento and peddles along the American River Parkway.

- **On a steam locomotive ride along the Sacramento River.** Have your character set off on a six-mile noisy train ride just like they used to after the gold rush. Sacramento boasts one of the finest locomotive museums anywhere, evident in its 105 locomotives and rail cars—all works of art and tributes to those who knew there had to be a better transportation option besides horses. Your character can also learn the fascinating story of the transcontinental railroad.

- **Outside the California State Capitol.** If your character wants to prove he's tired of being around the locals, he can always come here—because no locals do! The

For Further Research

Books

History of the Sacramento Valley, by J.W. Wooldridge

Sacramento, Heart of the Golden State, by Joseph McGowan

History of Sacramento County, by George F. Wright (editor)

Sacramento: An Illustrated History (1839–1874), by Thor Severson

Web Sites

www.sacbee.com/ (*The Sacramento Bee*)

www.sacramento.com/ (city site)

www.tourvision.com/explore/history.html (tourism and history)

www.oldsacramento.com/historical (history of Old Sacramento)

www.lib.csus.edu/guides/sturmt/sactohistory.htm (city history)

www.sacramento.org/film/ (city film festival)

www.sacpublishers.org/ (Sacramento Publishers and Authors)

Still Curious? Why Not Check Out

Ali: A Girl of Sacramento Streets, by Richard Epstein

An Angry World, by Kendall Person

Blaize of Glory, by Louise Crawford

Do No Harm, by Bruce Bob

False Accusations, by Alan Jacobson

Katapult, by Karen Kijewski

The Last Swan in Sacramento, by Stephen Bly

Lucky Numbers

Frankie and Johny

Another 48 Hrs.

American Beauty

The General's Daughter

What's Love Got to Do With It

River's Edge

---

building, by the way, is a big granite model of the U.S. Capitol and is definitely Sacramento's most distinctive landmark.

- **Rafting down a river.** Since Sacramento rests at the confluence of the American and Sacramento Rivers, rafting is a popular way to spend a nice day, especially on the American River. Have your character don a life jacket and set off for summer's day full of splashing and smashing fun.

- **Sutter Street.** This is the primary street in the preserved railroad town, which these days is dotted with specialty stores, antique shops, little galleries, and classic saloons.

Exceptionally Grand Things Your Character Is Proud Of

- Mather. This town just east of Sacramento does a great job finding housing, job training, and employment programs for previously homeless adults and families.

- Sacramento's first Sephora cosmetics store. It opened in 2002, and, yes, it is the number one beauty retailer in France, and Europe's largest. That means all the cosmetics, fragrances, and skin-care products ought to go over well here.

- Its art museums and galleries. Over one hundred galleries are in the area, and the most impressive (to many) is the Crocker Art Museum, which boasts an exceptional collection of nineteenth-century California paintings.

- Its performing arts. Yes, Sacramento has it all: the Sacramento Symphony, the Sacramento Theater Company, the Sacramento Ballet, the Camellia Symphony, and the Sacramento Opera.

Pathetically Sad Things Your Character Is Ashamed Of

- Its reputation (or lack thereof). Sacramento still isn't deemed a "big" noteworthy city by most of the country.

- Lynette "Squeaky" Fromme fired upon President Ford in an assassination attempt right here in Sacramento, back in 1975.

- Hagin Oaks. This struggling area of town really needs help, as revitalization of this poor and neglected neighborhood hasn't happened yet.

Your Character Loves

- The Sacramento Kings.
- Parks—all 120 of them!
- Theater.
- River activities.
- Antique shopping. It's becoming really popular here these days, especially with places like Le Jardin, the trendy French antiques shop in town.
- Museums.
- Wine.
- Fresh veggies—they're all over.

Your Character Hates

- That the Lakers won the seventh game of the play-offs in 2002.

- The loss of the military bases.
- The year 1850. In January a flood swept houses and livestock downstream. Doctors couldn't bury the city's dead so they sewed them into blankets and sunk them in the floodwaters. Then in the summer Sacramento was hit by a cholera epidemic that killed over six hundred people—including seventeen physicians—in less than a month. And then there were the Squatter Riots—bloody gun battles over land claims that wreaked economic havoc on the city.
- Patty Hearst and the Symbionese Liberation Army (SLA). They came to Sacramento in 1974 and robbed two banks (Guild Savings and Loan Association, and the Crocker National Bank in Carmichael) and gunned down Myrna Lee Opsahl in the process.

San Diego

San Diego Facts and Peculiarities Your Character Might Know

- Juan Rodriguez Cabrillo first landed at Point Loma in 1542.
- It's the second-largest city in California and the seventh-largest city in the country, following New York, Los Angeles, Chicago, Houston, Philadelphia, and Phoenix.
- It doesn't really have much in common with its northern neighbors, Los Angeles and San Francisco. It has no great mythological past or historical legacy—no gold rush, no free-love revolution, no heydey of Hollywood, no Haight-Ashbury, no City Lights Bookstore.
- The city is known for its restaurants, music, movies, performing arts, museums, outdoor recreation, beaches, and sports.
- Tijuana, Mexico, is only eighteen miles south of the city.
- Thoroughbred racing at Del Mar is big here.
- Legend has it a ghost resides in one of the rooms at the Hotel Del Coronado (where Bing Crosby was a regular patron).
- Tourists flocked here like crazy after *Top Gun* became such a hit—many scenes were shot both at the U.S. Naval Air Station and in the city.
- Charles Lindbergh's Spirit of St. Louis was built in San Diego.
- The city is a major commercial center, it is one of the country's chief military ports, and it has a major tuna-fishing harbor.
- San Diego is also known for its biomedical industry, which accounts for as much as two-thirds of the city's employment. As of late, however, the fastest-growing industry in town is telecommunications.
- Before the San Diego–Coronado Bridge was built, cars were transported by five ferries (the San Diego, the Coronado, the Crown City, the North Island, and the Silver Strand).
- The city's convention center has an ocean-themed roof, complete with sails.
- When people say "The Murph" they're referring to Jack Murphy Stadium, which has recently been re-

San Diego Basics That Shape Your Character

An aerial view of San Diego's waterfront

Population: 1.2 million in the city; 2.8 million in the Greater Metro area

Prevalent Religions: Roman Catholic, Protestant, Buddhist, Muslim, Jewish, and Hindu

Top Employers: Sony Technology Center, Hewlett-Packard, AT&T Global Business Communications Systems, Kaiser Permanente, Science Applications International Corporation, Alaris Medical Systems, Children's Hospital and Health Center, City of San Diego, GDE Systems Inc., U.S. Military

Per Capita Income: $26,067

Average Daily Temperature: January, 57° F; July, 71° F

Ethnic Makeup (in percent): Caucasian 60.2%, African-American 7.9%, Hispanic 25.4%, Asian 13.6%, Native American 0.6%, Other 17.2%

Newspapers and Magazines: *San Diego Union-Tribune, San Diego Magazine*

Free Weekly Alternative Paper: *San Diego Reader*

named Qualcomn Stadium. Now people call it "The Q" (but some still refer to it as "The Murph").

If Your Character . . .

If Your Character Is Alternative and Grungy, he lives in Mission Beach. This area and neighboring Ocean Beach and Pacific Beach are where young, single San

For Further Research

Books

La Jolla: A Celebration of Its Past, edited by Patricia Daly-Lipe and Barbara Dawson

Landmarks: Sculpture Commissions for the Stuart Collection at the University of California, San Diego, by Mary Livingstone Beebe

Rise and Fall of San Diego: 150 Million Years of History Recorded in Sedimentary Rocks, by Patrick L. Abbott

San Diego: Air Capital of the West, by Mary L. Scott

San Diego: An Introduction to the Region, by Philip R. Pryde

San Diego: Where Tomorrow Begins, by Dan Berger, Peter Jensen, and Margaret C. Berg

A Short History of San Diego, by Michael McKeever

Stranger Than Fiction: Vignettes of San Diego History, by Richard W. Crawford

Successful San Diegans, by Lee T. Silber

Web Sites

www.sandiego.org (San Diego Convention and Visitors Bureau)

www.sandiego-online.com (*San Diego Magazine*)

www.signonsandiego.com (city info)

www.gaslamp.org (Gaslamp Quarter history)

www.digitalcity.com/sandiego (lifestyle guide)

www.sandiegoinsider.com (San Diego Insider)

www.sdreader.com (*San Diego Reader*—clubs and events)

Still Curious? Why Not Check Out

Blue, by Abigail Padgett

Double, by Marcia Muller and Bill Pronzini

Finnegan's Week, by Joseph Wambaugh

Generation X: Tales for an Accelerated Culture, by Douglas Coupland

The Hotel Detective, by Alan Russell

La Jolla Spindrift, by Jack Trolley

Playback, by Raymond Chandler

Renegade

Silk Stalkings

Simon and Simon

Some Like It Hot

Top Gun

Traffic

Wirecutter, by John Brizzolara

Diegans make their homes. The areas have busy nightlife scenes, lots of beaches, and plenty of casual, inexpensive places to eat.

If Your Character Smells of Old Money, he lives in Mission Hills. This mansion-filled community comes from very old money, and these people are exceedingly rich, owning homes that are just big for big's sake. This is excess at its finest. The Alvarado Estate is also home of the rich and famous, as is Delmar.

If Your Character Needs to Shop, she's spending time at Mission Valley. This area near San Diego's Old Town is loaded with suburban sprawl and more shopping centers than any sensible shopper could wish for.

If Your Character Smells of Money, she lives in La Jolla. This is like Los Angeles's Rodeo Drive but with a smaller feel. Right on the sea, the area is home to those wealthy folks who could live anywhere in town but choose here—La Jolla has fancy restaurants, upscale

shops, and an attractive beach. The University of California, San Diego is here as well.

If Your Character Flies Jets for the Navy, he's spending time in Coronado. This rather resort-looking area of the city is accessible only by ferry or bridge, so many folks think it's an island. Not so—it's a peninsula. The northern part of it houses the outrageously huge U.S. Naval Air Station—home to lots of retired admirals. *Top Gun,* anyone?

Local Grub Your Character Might Love

Three types of food rule here: Mexican, seafood, and Californian. There's also a California-French cuisine. Your character can choose from a mix of clever salads, top-quality seafood, juicy meats, prime steaks, seasonal veggies, garnishes, eggplant salads, and lots of vinaigrettes. Clam chowder in an edible bread bowl is big, as is Sunday brunch that might feature an apple-sausage-omelet breakfast ripe with fresh fruit. A good wine often goes with the evening meal. Local favorite eateries include The Old Town Mexican Café, Roberto's, Foggy Burger's, Potato Shack in Encinitas, Seau's, Rubio's Fish and Lobster Tacos, Sports City Café and Brewery, and the San Diego Brewing Co.

Interesting and Peculiar Places to Set a Scene

- **Balboa Park.** When your character needs to get away from the busyness of life, send him here for some serenity. Have him stroll along the many walkways and gaze upon the pretty pavilion, the lush gardens, the gushing fountain, and the spectacular Spanish-Moorish buildings that line El Prado. The park is also home to the world's largest outdoor organ, an Omnimax theater, a nationally acclaimed theater, some restaurants, the world-famous San Diego Zoo, the Museum of Art, the Museum of Photographic Arts, and the Reuben H. Fleet Science Center. Enough here for a series of books. . . .
- **Coves Black's Beach.** For some fun in the sun with only the breeze and a few grains of sand for a coverup, have your character come to Coves Black's Beach. That's right, it's a nudist beach, so he'll be able to rest more than just his bare feet in the sand . . . not sure why he'd want to, but the option is there.
- **Dog Beach.** San Diego started a trend that others cities have followed—having a place where Rusty can roam free with lots of other canine companions. This place is unique because there aren't many beach towels and picnic baskets—just lots of wet dogs shaking the water of their backs.
- **Gaslamp Quarter.** This once rather rough and depressing area is now one of the hippest spots in town. The streets are lined with restaurants, cafes, nightclubs, galleries, theaters, and trendy shopping areas, and the Horton Plaza is here.
- **Hillcrest.** Although this area was in sad shape in the 1960s and 1970s, it's now San Diego's answer to New York's SoHo or Los Angeles's West Hollywood. It's jammed with cool restaurants, galleries, and avant-garde boutiques. Much of the city's gay community now lives here.
- **Little Italy.** This tiny community on the northern edge of downtown looks and smells like most other Italian pockets in major cities. It's the best place your character will want to go for pasta, pizza, gelato, espresso, and interesting Italian characters.
- **Mission Bay and the beaches.** If you plan on sending your character to San Diego for a vacation and need her to send a postcard home, it should be of this area. Mission Bay is not just beautiful, but it's also a great recreation area that's ideal for sailing, windsurfing, swimming, and waterskiing.
- **Old Town.** If you need to set a scene in a museum or in old-time San Diego, this is your place. The area houses three major parks—Old Town State Historic Park, Presidio Park, and Heritage Park—and numerous museums, most of which revisit life in the city during its formative years. Your character will have no problem seeing her share of tourists here either.
- **On the boardwalk.** This area of Mission Beach is a pleasant mix of lovers watching sunsets; fitness freaks running, bike-riding, or in-line skating; and families with kids.
- **Orange Avenue.** Your character will find lots of cute shops and boutiques along this stretch, as well as fancy resorts and hotels, such as the legendary Hotel Del Coronado. Orange Avenue is part of Coronado, which is known for its popular sand-duned beaches, fine restaurants, and a downtown area that's reminiscent of a small Midwestern town.

Exceptionally Grand Things Your Character Is Proud Of

- San Diego hasn't lost its small-town ambiance.
- That it's not Los Angeles or San Francisco—no Hollywood, no earthquakes, no hype.
- Torrey Pines Golf Course.
- The San Diego Zoo, home to almost five thousand animals and insects.
- The ocean.
- The weather (it's always sunny!).
- The Tidal Caves in La Jolla.
- Fiesta Island during the OTL (over the line) contest, in which 1,150 softball teams (of three persons each) compete for two weekends. Fifty thousand people attend.
- Hotel Del Coronado.
- Ramona's Marriage House in Old Town.
- The Children's Pool in La Jolla.
- The Del Mar Racetrack and Fairgrounds.
- The Del Mar Fair. This two-week fair draws large crowds who enjoy the entertainment, livestock, and rides.

- The University of California, San Diego.
- Some of the world's best medical facilities.

Pathetically Sad Things Your Character Is Ashamed Of

- McDonald's Massacre at San Ysidro.
- The Brenda Spencer shooting.
- The poor and homeless Hispanic population.

Your Character Loves

- Hiking up Cowles Mountain at sunrise and sunset on clear days.
- The Coronado Islands.
- Surfing.
- Roller-blading around Mission Bay.
- The San Diego Padres—they were National League Champs in 1998.
- Dan Fouts.
- The Old Point Loma Lighthouse, built in 1854.

San Francisco

San Francisco Facts and Peculiarities Your Character Might Know

- The city covers only forty-nine square miles.
- It is the second most crowded city in the country, next to Manhattan.
- It was settled by the Spanish, who established a mission (which still exists) and a fort (Presidio), which is now a national park.
- There are no cemeteries within the city limits. They were all moved to make room for more living people. Colma got all the bodies, making it a city in which the dead outnumber the living.
- Alcatraz is only a half mile away in the middle of the Bay.
- While most San Franciscans aren't gay, gays and lesbians do make up a significant percentage of the city's population and are a strong political force.
- San Francisco Bay is the largest land-locked harbor in the world.
- It is one of the most politically liberal cities in the country, and conservatives here tend to be more middle-of-the-road than right wing.
- The Golden Gate Bridge is the only mile of road in the United States where you can get a ticket for running out of gas.
- The term *sandlot* was coined in San Francisco (boys literally played ball on sand lots in San Francisco), and the poem "Casey at the Bat" was written by *The San Francisco Examiner*'s Ernest Thayer in 1888.
- In 1995 Willie Brown Jr. became San Francisco's first African-American mayor.
- San Francisco is ethnically diverse, with one of the largest percentages of Asians in the United States (30 percent and growing).
- It grew up almost overnight as a result of the California gold rush of 1849.
- Small businesses play a big role in the economy; more than 80 percent of the city's nearly thirty-four thousand businesses have fewer than fifteen employees.
- Residents are big travelers and love to take short trips to Sonoma or Napa Wine Country, Mendocino, or Big Sur. Many go to Lake Tahoe for summer or winter

San Francisco Basics That Shape Your Character

The houses of San Francisco

Population: 776,733

Prevalent Religions: Not known as a religious city but has a diverse range of denominations and churches (540 in all), including Protestant, Roman Catholic, Jewish, Greek and Russian Orthodox, Bahá'í, Buddhist, and Hindu.

Top Employers: City and County of San Francisco, University of California, San Francisco, San Francisco Unified School District, Wells Fargo, U.S. Postal Service, AT&T (communication), Pacific Gas and Electric; Pacific Bell, Cal Pacific Medical Center, ABM Industries (national janitorial company), Gap Inc.; Macy's; Bechtel Engineering, Levi Strauss and Company, Charles Schwab and Company, Chevron, United Airlines

Per Capita Income: $49,695

Average Daily Temperature: January, 48.5° F; July, 62.2° F

Ethnic Makeup (in percent): Caucasian 49.7%, African-American 7.8%, Hispanic 14.1%, Asian 30.8%, Native American 0.4%, Other 0.5%

Newspapers and Magazines: *San Francisco Chronicle, The San Francisco Examiner, San Francisco Magazine, San Francisco Business Times, Napa Valley Business Times*

Free Weekly Alternative Papers: *The San Francisco Bay Guardian, SF Weekly, San Francisco Times*

getaways. Europe and the Far East are popular long-trip destinations.

- *Bridge and tunnel* means you're commuting to and from the East Bay.
- *Hella* is a corruption of *hell of* and means "extremely." For example, if you were really drunk you would say, "I'm hella wasted."
- *Nickle and dime* refers to the 510 area code in the East Bay. One could say he or she lives over in the "nickle and dime."

If Your Character . . .

If Your Character Is Trendy, she shops on Union Street. Union Street is the bustling hub of San Francisco, with dozens of hotels and department stores and numerous trendy shops, galleries, and boutiques. Stores like bebe and Betsey Johnson are here.

If Your Character Is a Middle-Class Family Man, he lives in Richmond (Russian or other Caucasian) or Sunset (Asian or Caucasian) or Fillmore (if African-American). These are San Francisco's most populated residential areas. While not exactly the suburbs, they are large areas with lots of small but costly houses mixed in with local shops and eateries.

If Your Character Loves Nature, she's spending time in Marin Headlands, Mount Tamalpais, or Golden Gate Park. Or, among the Redwoods just north of the city, or down along the Big Sur coast.

If Your Character Is a Rich Computer Geek, he lives in SOMA. This is where the now-defunct dot-com revolution took place. The businesses may have evaporated, but the dot-comers are still around.

If Your Character Wears a Blue Collar at Work, he lives in Bay View (African-American), Excelsior (mixed), or the Mission (Hispanic and others). Working-class and union members tend to be in the southern tier of the city. Here you find row after row of modest, two-story split-level houses, very plain; some better maintained than others.

If Your Character Must Rid Himself of the Body He Just Killed, he's taking the corpse down Highway 101 to toss it off one of those steep cliffs that drops straight into the Pacific.

If Your Character Smells of Money, she resides in a house on one of the hills looking down on the city. Some of the most spectacular views in the Bay Area can be seen from the mansions up here: Nob Hill, Pacific Heights, Seacliff (Robin Williams lives here), Twin Peaks.

Local Grub Your Character Might Love

San Franciscans eat out more than folks in other U.S. cities, and one of the biggest games in town is finding the newest, trendiest restaurant. San Francisco is one of the premier restaurant cities in the country and has well-respected cooking schools (San Francisco Culinary Academy, for instance). Alice Waters, across the Bay in Berkeley, is generally credited with developing and promoting what has come to be called "California" cuisine. See the California chapter for more on California cuisine. The diversity of cultures in town also encourages great interest in various foods: Chinese, Japanese, Italian, French, Thai, and Vietnamese all contribute to the mix.

Local old-time favorites include Hangtown Fry and Joe's Special (egg dishes). For a classic San Francisco meal, there is nothing better than Pacific Coast cracked crab with the area's famous and unique sourdough bread, all washed down with a chilled bottle of fine California white wine. The martini, which is alleged to have been created in San Francisco, is popular, as are gin and vodka ("Vitamin V") and very dark-roasted, strongly brewed coffee. Also big are fancy vegetarian or vegan restaurants like Herbivore, Millenium, and Greens (a high-end, pricey, all-vegetarian restaurant). Sushi and dim sum (little plates of different Chinese foods, kind of like Spanish tapas) are popular. The huge burritos at the Mexican restaurants in the Mission are very inexpensive. Other favorites are Capps Corner (an old Italian bar and family-style restaurant.), Café Trieste, Moose's (society people, movers and shakers, and politicians), Fifth Floor Restaurant (very trendy), Lulu's (busy, noisy, and trendy), Ella's, Slanted Door Vietnamese restaurant (trendy in the Mission), Foreign Cinema (also in the Mission where you sit in a kind of patio watching old foreign films while having dinner), and Chez Panisse (the mother church of California cuisine, just across the Bay in Berkeley and home to Alice Waters).

Interesting and Peculiar Places to Set a Scene

- **Sixth Street.** This is San Francisco's most notorious skid row, with lots of down-and-out young people of every persuasion, struggling immigrants, sad derelicts, bums, and some working-class folk trying to make it.

- **Barbary Coast.** Named after the pirate coast of North Africa, this legendary waterfront area has been hopping since the 1849 gold rush. Gamblers, gangsters, brothels, saloons, and disreputable boardinghouses have given the area a notorious reputation throughout the world. The entertainment strip is still pretty raunchy and caters to adolescent males, Japanese tourists, and tired and lonely businessmen.

- **Beach Blanket Babylon.** This wild and wacky cabaret show has been running nonstop for over twenty-five years at the Club Fugazi. Gay, campy "musical review humor" dominates, with song parodies, impersonations, and outrageous costumes.

- **Castro and Eighteenth Streets.** The focal point of this intersection is the old Castro Theater, a relic from the glory days of movie palaces. The Castro area is one of the most prominent centers for gay and lesbian life in America; hopping gay and lesbian bars line the streets.

- **Chinatown.** It is really a world unto itself. Most San Franciscans who aren't Chinese have little to do with it, mostly because it is a tourist mecca (and a legitimate one at that). However, thousands of Asians do live in this crowded, busy, colorful, unique quarter of town. Amy Tan or Maxine Hong Kingston novels give a good feel for Chinatown.

- **City Lights Bookstore.** Kerouac Alley's famed bookstore, City Lights was founded by poet Lawrence Ferlinghetti in 1953 and became the cradle of the Beat movement. A literary landmark, gathering place, and pilgrimage destination for many writers and fringe intellectuals, City Lights also has published cutting-edge social and political books since the 1950s, the most famous of which is Allen Ginsberg's *Howl and Other Poems.*

- **Crissy Field.** A brand-new addition to the city that is carved out of the Presidio, this is where joggers, au pairs, business folk, and tourists gather to enjoy the breathtaking views of the Golden Gate Bridge and Marin County.

- **Financial District.** Belden Place is an alley full of outdoor restaurants where people of all types meet for lunch. Also nearby is Sam's Grill, a classic businessman's restaurant and very "Old San Francisco."

- **Golden Gate Bridge.** More people allegedly take their lives from this hanging expanse than from anywhere else in the world. Another interesting place for a scene is the old fort right below the bridge, called Fort Point.

- **Golden Gate Park's Japanese Tea Garden.** If your character needs to get away from the hustle and bustle of the city, have her go here, especially on Sundays when they close the park to cars.

- **The intersection of Fifth and Market.** With its cable car turnaround, Nordstroms, tourists, bums, chess players, street-corner preachers, bongo players, and locals going about their shopping, this is as close to being the heartbeat of the city as any place in town.

- **Irish bars along Geary Boulevard.** Although many have disappeared, there are still some good old Irish bars here (O'Shea's is a legendary one) and scattered around downtown. Harrington, in the Financial District, is where Saint Patrick's Day crowds go crazy, requiring the police to close the street for the day.

- **John's Grill.** This downtown restaurant is the closest thing to a literary landmark outside of City Lights, since this is where Dashiell Hammett ate while writing *The Maltese Falcon.* There's even a replica of the Falcon on the premises.

- **The Marina Green along the Bay front.** Most days people of all ages are flying beautiful kites here in the ever-present breeze.

- **North Beach.** North Beach is the old Italian section of town; it's very crowded, but people love living here. Jane Jacobs, the great social critic, called it one of the truly great urban places in the country back in the 1960s—and not much has changed since. The narrow streets, sidewalk cafes, and active nightlife give it a European look. North Beach was home to the Beat Generation, and it still has a strong bohemian feel.

- **Redwood Park.** This is right near the Transamerica Pyramid. It's easy to catch workers out here having lunch, especially on Friday afternoons in the summer when there's always live music.

- **SOMA.** This area South of Market Street is a ware-

For Further Research

Books

The Contested City, by John H. Mollenkopf

Eat This, San Francisco: A Narrated Roadmap to Dives, Joints, All-Night Cafes, Noodle Houses, Buffets, and Other Cheap Places to Eat in the Bay Area, by Dan Leone

The Great San Francisco Trivia and Fact Book, by Janet Bailey

Historic San Francisco: A Concise History and Guide, by Rand Richards

The Mayor of Castro Street: The Life and Times of Harvey Milk, by Randy Shilts

Once Upon a City, by Mark Gordon

San Francisco As You Like It: Twenty Tailor-Made Tours for Culture Vultures, Shopaholics, Neo-Bohemians, Fitness Freaks, Savvy Natives, and Everyone Else, by Bonnie Wach

San Francisco Almanac, by Gladys Hansen

The San Francisco Bay Area, by Mel Scott

A Short History of San Francisco, by Tom Cole

Web Sites

www.sfgate.com/chronicle (*San Francisco Chronicle*)

www.examiner.com (*The San Francisco Examiner*)

www.indybay.org/ (news)

www.zpub.com/sf50/sf/ (history)

www.enclave.org/write/ (San Francisco writers site)

www.sfbg.com (*The San Francisco Bay Guardian*; gay lesbian news and events)

Still Curious? Why Not Check Out

2nd Chance, by James Patterson (with Andrew Gross)

The Bachelor

Basic Instinct

Bullitt

Dead Midnight, by Marcia Muller

Dirty Harry

McTeague: A Story of San Francisco, by Frank Norris

Mrs. Doubtfire

The Oath, by John T. Lescroart

Pale Truth: The California Chronicles, by Daniel Alef

The Rock

San Francisco Stories: Great Writers on the City, edited by John Miller

Tales of the City, by Armistead Maupin

The Towering Inferno

Vertigo

---

house/loft kind of neighborhood, with lots of computer and art types. SOMA is the new trendy neighborhood, and condos, live/work lofts, and apartments are replacing some of the old industrial warehouses. Dance clubs and fancy new restaurants abound, and the focal point is the Pac Bell baseball park along the restored waterfront.

Exceptionally Grand Things Your Character Is Proud Of

- Bridges, hills, phenomenal views (from almost anywhere in the city), the skyline.
- Its reputation for culture (museums, opera, theater, the Beat movement) and sophistication (exceptional food and wine).
- The 49ers (they were once a dynasty).
- Legendary nightclubs like The Hungry I, Purple Onion, Jazz Workshop, El Matador (all nationally famous but all gone now). Many top entertainers (The Kingston Trio, Phyllis Diller, Bob Newhart, Woody Allen, Barbra Striesand) began their careers here.
- Harvey Milk. The city's first elected openly gay politician was assassinated along with Mayor George Moscone in 1978. Milk is now a legend; operas and films have been written about him.
- Lefty O'Doul. He played and coached in the 1930s and 1940s, and now a bridge and, more appropriately, a bar/restaurant are named in his honor.
- Barry Bonds. He hit a record-breaking seventy-three home runs in 2001.
- Carol Doda. The former file clerk and cocktail waitress bared her breasts at The Condor in the 1960s, thus introducing the concept of the topless nightclub to America.
- The Gay, Lesbian, Bisexual, Transgender Parade. It's held in late June and is one of the biggest events of the year in San Francisco. Everyone attends, including families.

- Its universities (Cal-Tech; Stanford; University of San Francisco; University of California, San Francisco; University of California, Berkeley).
- North Beach's Telegraph Hill. Coit Tour, a monument to firemen in the Russian Hill area, and Washington Square, with the lovely St. Peter and Paul Church, are the two main focal points in North Beach.

Your Character Loves

- Herb Caen. Called "Mr. San Francisco," Caen died several years ago, but you'd never know it. The city celebrates Herb Caen Days, and the *San Francisco Chronicle* reprints his old columns. Caen chronicled living in San Francisco and created an image of the city that was both real and mythical (part of the image he helped create was the city as a hard-drinking town).
- The weather in the fall—a nice Indian summer in early September.
- Bloody Marys at Club Deluxe on Sunday afternoons.
- Anchor Steam beer. A revived local brew that the early San Franciscan immigrants used to make.
- Sunday brunch at the Ramp down by the Bay.
- Music concerts at the Warfield or the Fillmore.

Your Character Hates

- Earthquakes. The two biggies were in 1906 and 1989 (during the World Series).
- That much of the Financial District and most of the Marina sit on a landfill highly susceptible to earthquakes.
- Traffic, double-parked cars and trucks, inconsiderate drivers.
- Southern California/Los Angeles.
- People who call it "Frisco."
- Tourist hangouts like Pier 39, Fisherman's Wharf, and Powell Cable Cars.
- That outsiders assume everyone in town is gay.
- To see tourists in shorts turning blue and shivering because they don't know any better—due to the topography of the Bay and the ocean, it is actually quite cold and foggy, even during the summer months.

Colorado

Significant Events Your Character Has Probably Thought About

- Lieutenant Zebulon Pike discovered the peak that bears his name. He was unable to reach the summit, ironic in that today a person can drive to the top.
- In 1858 gold was discovered near Cherry Creek, sparking the first of many gold and silver rushes to the state and ushering in a mining industry that dominated Colorado for more than a hundred years.
- The gold rushes displaced a number of Native American tribes, including the peaceful Southern Cheyenne led by Black Kettle. In 1864 an army led by Colonel John Chivington massacred more than two hundred Native Americans on the Sand Creek reservation, sexually mutilating the corpses and later presenting their trophies to cheering crowds in Denver.
- The first juvenile court system in the country was instituted in Colorado in 1869.
- Colorado achieved statehood on August 1, 1876.
- The repeal of the Sherman Silver Purchase Act in 1893 devalued silver and sent the already staggering Colorado economy into chaos.
- Hot Sulphur Springs, the state's first sports skiing area, opened in 1911, beginning the ski resort industry that would boom by the 1960s.
- In 1947 the ski area at Aspen Mountain opened, ushering in the first wave of ski bums and bunnies. Aspen's success as a ski resort inspired many other towns in the state to market themselves in this way.
- The Air Force Academy was completed near Colorado Springs in 1958.
- In 1973 the Eisenhower Tunnel on Interstate 70 opened, creating easier access from Denver to the Rocky Mountain resorts.
- In the summer of 2002, wild fires spread throughout the state. A number of towns were evacuated and millions of dollars worth of property was destroyed.

Colorado Facts and Peculiarities Your Character Might Know

- The word *Colorado* means "colored red" in Spanish and was first applied to the Colorado River.
- Colorado is called "The Centennial State" because it achieved statehood in 1876, when the United States turned one hundred years old.
- Katherine Lee Bates was inspired by the view from Pike's Peak to compose "America the Beautiful."
- It has the highest mean elevation of the fifty states, boasting fifty-four peaks above fourteen thousand feet. Climbers call such peaks "fourteeners."
- Though Pike's Peak is much more famous, Mount Elbert is the highest peak in the state and the second highest in the continental United States.
- The road leading to Mount Evans is the highest paved road in North America.

- Doc Holliday's grave is located in Glenwood Springs at the top of a steep hill. Unfortunately, Doc's body isn't there. Locals believe he lies in one of the yards in the neighborhood at the bottom of the hill.
- There are more microbreweries per capita in Colorado than in any other state in the country.
- The vast majority of Coloradoans live east of the Front Range. It's tough to get lost, therefore, going from one city to the next, because when the mountains are on your left you know you're headed north; when the mountains are on your right, you're going south.

Your Character's Food and Drink

In Denver and the ski resorts, your characters can find any kind of exotic and ethnic cuisine. In the less cosmopolitan towns, the fare is much more basic.

Cowboy traditions live on in the state, making beef a favorite food. In many places, your characters can find rattlesnake, elk, and bison on the menu or the dinner table. All of the local microbreweries make Colorado a great state for beer. Despite the beef and beer, Coloradoans tend to be health conscious. Organic fruits and vegetables are popular, as are the growing number of health-food stores and groceries.

Things Your Character Likes to Remember

- Colorado was the second state in the country to give women the right to vote.
- Colorado was the second state in the country to ratify the amendment outlawing child labor.
- Colorado has the highest mean elevation of any state.
- The Denver Broncos have won two Super Bowls and have played in six. They are one of the most successful franchises in the game. Beloved quarterback John Elway was famous for leading numerous comebacks during the 1980s and 1990s. Coloradoans bleed Bronco orange.
- In 1972 the state turned down the 1976 Olympics, fearing that too much attention would attract more people to the area and ruin its unique charms.
- Colorado is world famous for its skiing.

Things Your Character Would Like to Forget

- The state made national headlines in 1992 when it passed the controversial Amendment 2, which stated that gays and lesbians could not file discrimination cases based on gender preference.

- During World War II, the town of Amache hosted a Japanese-American internment camp.
- The Broncos lost four Super Bowls before winning their first one in 1999.
- In the nineteenth century, relations with Native American tribes were noteworthy mostly for broken treaties and betrayals, such as the infamous Sand Creek massacre of 1864.
- The murder of eighteen students by fellow students at Columbine High School in Littleton in 1999.
- The tabloids have kept the murder of five-year-old JonBenet Ramsey of Boulder a topic of discussion for years.

Myths and Misperceptions About Colorado

- **Colorado is full of cowboys, and meals are primarily beef.** The bigger cities are diversified in economy and cuisine. Although the state is proud of its cowboy heritage, it is a multifaceted place that has moved beyond its past.
- **Colorado is a tourist mecca for rich folk seeking a Rocky Mountain high.** The ski towns attract the wealthy vacationer, but Colorado is much more diversified than the average state because of its climate and topography variety. For every yuppie, there is a hippie; for every wealthy skier, there is a blue-collar worker.
- **Colorado has little crime.** The boom in population since 1960 has brought with it a fairly high crime rate.
- **The skies are big and clear.** Denver suffers from one of the worst smog problems in the country.

A skier on the Colorado slopes

© PhotoDisc/Getty Images

For Further Research

Books

American Indians in Colorado, by J. Donald Hughes

Buildings of Colorado, by Thomas J. Noel

The Colorado Book, edited by Eleanor M. Gehres, Sandra Dallas, Maxine Benson, and Stanley Cuba

The Colorado Guide, by Bruce Caughey and Dean Winstanley

Colorado: A History of the Centennial State, by Carl Abbott, Stephen J. Leonard, and David McComb

The Contested Plains: Indians, Goldseekers, and the Rush to Colorado, by Elliott West

Historical Atlas of Colorado, by Thomas J. Noel, Paul F. Mahoney, and Richard E. Stevens

A History of Skiing in Colorado, by Abbott Fay

Web Sites

www.colorado.com/ (state travel and visitor information)

www.colorado.gov (The state's official Web site)

http://coloradobyways.org (guide to scenic roads in the state)

www.archives.state.co.us/info.html (state history and facts)

www.state.co.us/business_dir/chambers.html (index of and links to chambers of commerce throughout the state)

Still Curious? Why Not Check Out

Angle of Repose, by Wallace Stegner

Centennial, by James A. Michener

Dumb and Dumber

Plainsong, by Kent Haruf

Remember Me: A Novel, by Laura Hendrie

The Shining

Interesting Places to Set a Scene

- **Aurora.** Though it developed with its own identity, Aurora is now considered part of the Denver metro area. It grew as a result of two military bases—Lowry and Fitzsimmons—both of which have been closed in recent years. Far less touristy than most cities in the state, Aurora thrives as a place of strong businesses and sprawling suburbs.

- **Boulder.** Boulder is an eclectic place where aging hippies and young wanderers mix with well-heeled tourists and locals. At the Naropa Institute, classes are countercultural and draw students from across the country. Your characters can stroll down the Pearl Street Mall, a street full of shops, galleries, and restaurants, where the mix of scruffy street musicians and tourists makes for exceptional people-watching.

- **Colorado Springs.** Your characters can drive Pike's Peak Highway or take the Cog Railway up to the top to see the purple mountain's majesty. Also consider The Garden of the Gods, a park filled with unusual formations of red sandstone. The exhibits at the Ghost Town Museum are so homely, they have a charm of their own. At the swanky Broadmoor Hotel, a suite can cost up to $2,100 per night. "The Springs" is considered the glamour spot of the Front Range, but it isn't as posh as the ski resort towns.

- **Fort Collins.** Home to Colorado State University, Fort Collins is not picturesque, but it's located within an hour's drive of Rocky Mountain National Park and Wyoming. If your characters want to stay within the city limits, try the Old Town shopping area. Or, send them to The Gym of the Rockies, well known locally for its forty-foot climbing wall and freestanding climbing boulder.

- **Glenwood Springs.** Called "Deadwood Springs" by the climbers, rafters, and snowboarders who flock to the area, Glenwood Springs lacks the panache of the snazzier mountain towns. However, it boasts the world's largest hot springs pool, an unglamorous spot that nonetheless offers warm waters and spectacular views of the surrounding mountains.

- **Pueblo.** In a state that's more than 80 percent white, Pueblo prides itself on its ethnic diversity. Forty percent of the population is Hispanic, and the culture of the town draws much of its flavor from that percentage. The heart of Pueblo can be found along Union Avenue, where the street life is varied and colorful.

Interesting Places to Set a Scene—The Ski Resort Towns

- **Aspen.** Trendy resorts rise and fall in popularity, but Aspen remains the crown jewel. It attracts the rich, famous, and beautiful to its slopes throughout the winter. Many old buildings remain from the town's mining days, but these have been renovated and turned into pricey restaurants and shops. Nearby Snowmass, always in the shadow of Aspen, is gaining a reputation of its own.

- **Steamboat Springs.** Known locally as Ski Town U.S.A., Steamboat was one of the first resorts in the state. Nestled in the Yampa River valley, Steamboat lays much farther north than the well-known resorts along I-70 and offers less glitz and glamour. Still, it draws wealthy vacationers by the thousands. Nearby hot springs are open throughout the year.
- **Summit County.** This is the fastest-growing resort area in the state. Skiers need not drive all the way to Vail or Aspen on I-70 from Denver now that posh new resorts have opened in Breckinridge, Dillon, Frisco, and Silverthorne. The Arapahoe Basin, another popular ski resort, is also located in Summit County.
- **Telluride.** Your characters will find an odd mix of people here: rich and famous skiers, artists, Bohemians, well-heeled family vacationers, rugged and enterprising locals. Located at the foot of the San Juan Mountains, Telluride became a trendy spot in the 1970s and hasn't succumbed to the glitter of other resorts. A quick hike out of town leads to Bridal Veil Falls, Colorado's largest waterfall.
- **Vail.** A very "cool" spot in the 1970s and 1980s, Vail has great slopes and a trendy crowd, glamorous restaurants and nightclubs, and swanky condos where skiers party and play. But there's a phony, manufactured quality about the town, somewhat like an amusement park.

Denver

Denver Basics That Shape Your Character

Aerial view of the "Mile High" city

Population: 2.4 million

Prevalent Religions: Southern Baptist, Protestant, Buddhist, and Roman Catholic

Top Employers: United Airlines, Coors, Lockheed Martin, Sun Microsystems, Merrill Lynch, AT&T

Per Capita Income: $36,058

Average Daily Temperature: January, 30° F; July, 74° F

Ethnic Makeup (in percent): Caucasian 55.3%, African-American 15%, Hispanic 27.8%, Asian 3.3%, Native American 1.4%

Newspapers: *Denver Post* (Thursday-Sunday), *Rocky Mountain News* (Monday-Wednesday)

Free Weekly Alternative Papers: *The Onion*, *Westword*

Denver Facts and Peculiarities Your Character Might Know

- Denver was named for James Denver, who was the governor of Kansas Territory, which at the time included eastern Colorado. The city was little more than a mining camp, and hopes were high that the governor would bless it with political favors. Unfortunately, he resigned before the name became official and proved to be of no use at all.
- The motley group of founding fathers built the town to be close to the gold strikes in Cherry Creek and the South Platte River, despite warnings from Native American residents that the area was susceptible to floods. The fathers ignored the advice, and the town had to be rebuilt a few years later after it was destroyed by a flood. It also was destroyed by a fire.
- The "Mile-High City" is exactly that. The fifteenth step of the Colorado State Capitol Building is exactly 5,280 feet above sea level. If your character goes to a Rockies baseball game and sits in the purple seats, she'll be a mile high.
- Famous gunfighter and lawman Bat Masterson worked for a while as a bouncer in a saloon and whorehouse located across the street from the elegant Brown Palace Hotel. Distinguished businessmen and politicians used a tunnel built under the street to visit the "ladies" without being seen entering such a den of iniquity.
- Denver lays claim to inventing the cheeseburger, citing the Humpty Dumpty Drive-In restaurant as its birthplace in 1935. The restaurant is long gone, but most histories of the city maintain that it's the home of the cheeseburger.
- Denver's thriving economy and booming population have created urban sprawl, with new suburbs carving into the nearby mountains on a regular basis. The eastern suburb of Aurora is now the third-largest city in the state, while suburban Lakewood on the west side is the fourth-largest city.
- Starting as a boomtown during the gold and silver strikes in the 1850s, Denver has been a boom-and-bust town ever since. As recently as the 1980s, the city built its three tallest buildings within a two-year span only to have its economy collapse, leaving many floors of empty office space—the highest vacancy rate in the country.
- Denver has the largest park system of any city in the country, with 205 parks within the city limits and more than 20,000 acres of parkland in the surrounding area.
- Denver is known to some as the "Baby Boomer City," because it lists more boomers among its residents than does any other city in the country.

If Your Character . . .

If Your Character Is Alternative and Grungy, she lives on Colfax Street. A bizarre collection of neighborhoods collide on the longest continuous street in North America, including high-crime areas riddled with drugs and prostitutes. This also is where the grunge crowd clusters, where it's hip to be poor.

If Your Character Is Alternative but Afraid of Colfax Street, he lives in Boulder or Fort Collins. These nearby cities are close enough for a commute to Denver and hip enough—both are college towns—to attract the alt crowd.

If Your Character Smells of Old Money, he lives in Cherry Creek. Just the mention of this area of town to Denverites evokes the smell of old money.

If Your Character Is All About Business, he works in downtown. Denver is a city of suburbs, but the business of business still takes place in the middle of town.

If Your Character Is Young and Rich, she lives in The Lofts of LoDo. This is the trendiest part of town, in the heart of the social and business whirl. Your character can walk to work and walk home from the chic bistros.

If Your Character Is All About Raising a Family, she lives in Arapaho County, Boulder County, Jefferson County, or Longmont. The city is ringed by a number of sprawling suburbs within a short commute to the city, though as the city continues to expand, traffic is becoming more of a problem.

If Your Character Wears a Blue Collar at Work, he lives in Aurora, Longmont, or Loveland. These working-class suburbs bloomed after World War II.

Local Grub Your Character Might Love

Beef—any way you want it. Denver is the birthplace of the cheeseburger and the Denver omelet. Both are still popular. Western fare is also popular, such as rattlesnake, buffalo, and Rocky Mountain oysters.

Denver is becoming more and more of a cosmopolitan city, and it offers plenty of exotic fare from Asia, Africa, Europe, and the Middle East. For drinks, Denver hosts more microbreweries than does any other city

in the country. Nearby Golden is home to the Coors Brewery, which was considered a rare pleasure to Easterners before improvements in shipping technology made the beer much easier to buy in the 1980s. Despite all the great food and beer, Denver prides itself on being America's slimmest major city, citing a 1996 U.S. government report as proof.

Interesting and Peculiar Places to Set a Scene

- **LoDo.** The Lower Downtown area is full of shops, restaurants, cafes, and plenty of street activity. The Sixteenth Street mall—a walking promenade—is the heart of LoDo. Your characters can go broke fast in the trendy stories, or they simply can sit on a bench and people-watch.
- **Molly Brown House.** She didn't go down with the Titanic, earning her the sobriquet "unsinkable." Her house, located on Capitol Hill, is now a museum and brings old Denver to life.
- **Denver International Airport.** Sprawled across fifty-six square miles, the airport's unique architectural design and expanse of surrounding countryside offers plenty of opportunity for description. As one comedian said, it's "conveniently located in western Nebraska," which isn't exactly true, but your characters will have a long drive into town, mostly through flat, barren country broken only by an occasional chain hotel or restaurant.
- **Red Rock Amphitheater.** This natural outdoor area is set in red sandstone cliffs and is the setting for many concerts. Many big-name national acts have played here.
- **Colfax Street.** A weird confluence of the grunge scene, prostitution and drugs, and other types of street life, this is the place to set the midnight meeting rife with potential violence and oozing with urban texture.
- **The Buckhorn Exchange restaurant.** Denver's oldest saloon and restaurant features more than five hundred stuffed animal heads in the dining area.
- **Larimer Square.** Deep in the heart of downtown, between Fourteenth and Fifteenth Streets, your characters can shop, eat, drink, or, if they're feeling particularly romantic (and a little corny), they can take a horse-drawn carriage ride.
- **The U.S. Mint.** This facility is the second-largest storehouse of gold bullion in the country, next to Fort Knox. If your characters are tourists, they can take a

For Further Research

Books

Denver: The City Beautiful and Its Architects, 1893–1941, by Barbara S. Norgren and Thomas J. Noel

Denver International Airport: Lessons Learned, by Paul Stephen Dempsey, Andrew R. Goetz, and Joseph S. Szyliowicz

Denver: From Mining Camp to Metropolis, by Stephen J. Leonard and Thomas J. Noel

Denver in Slices, by Louisa Ward Arps

Molly Brown: Unraveling the Myth, by Kirsten Iversen

The Seamy Side of Denver, by Phil Goodstein

Web Sites

www.denver.org/ (travel guide for state)

www.denvergov.org/ (Denver Metro Convention and Visitors Bureau)

http://denver.citysearch.com/(calendar of events and listings of restaurants and stores)

www.denverchamber.org/ (Denver Metro Chamber of Commerce)

http://www.denver.com/ (city guide)

http://www.allabout-denver.com/ (travel and visitors guide)

http://coloradowebsites.com/dr-colorado/ (tourism web site)

Still Curious? Why Not Check Out

Denver, by John Dunning

Primary Suspect

Things to Do in Denver When You're Dead

The Unsinkable Molly Brown

Waiting to Exhale, by Terry McMillan

---

tour (which is strictly forbidden at Fort Knox). If your characters are ambitious thieves, they can try to take some of the bullion home with them.

Exceptionally Grand Things Your Character Is Proud Of

- Denver is one of the fastest-growing large cities in the country.
- Denver has approximately three hundred sunny days per year. Despite its reputation for snow, it actually enjoys a dry, arid climate, receiving just eight to fifteen inches of precipitation each year.
- The "best snow in the world."
- Back-to-back Super Bowl championships.
- Being physically fit. According to a recent survey, it's the fittest large city in the country.
- It's also the best-educated city in the country, with the highest percentage of college graduates.
- Molly Brown. The home of the "unsinkable" one remains a popular tourist attraction, and her fiery, resilient, western spirit epitomizes how the city likes to see itself.

Pathetically Sad Things Your Character Is Ashamed Of

- The shooting spree at Columbine High School in suburban Littleton.
- Appearing too rowdy and western.
- Appearing too right wing.
- Appearing too left wing.

Your Character Loves

- Trucks and SUVs.
- The Broncos, the Rockies, and the Avalanche.
- Hiking, climbing, skiing, and many other outdoor sports and recreations.
- Getting into the mountains on the weekends.
- Ties to the state's Old West roots.

Your Character Hates

- Californians. In the 1980s and 1990s, Californians came to the state en masse. Coloradoans wish they'd go home.
- Pollution.
- Being seen as too cowboy.

Connecticut

Significant Events Your Character Has Probably Thought About

- English settlers arrived here in 1636.
- The Pequot War of 1637 was a major battle in which colonists annihilated many of the Pequot Native Americans.
- *The Hartford Courant* began publishing in 1764 and hasn't stopped, making it the oldest U.S. newspaper still being published.
- Local Benedict Arnold switched allegiance in 1780 by surrendering a fort to the enemy in return for a royal commission in the British army and a sum of money.
- Thomas Jefferson becoming president in 1800 didn't fare so well with Connecticut, as it was a Federalist stronghold.
- Immigrants from eastern and western Europe flocked here at the end of the nineteenth and beginning of the twentieth centuries.
- Connecticut thrived financially from the 1950s through the 1980s, as major industries from General Electric to Union Carbide made their headquarters here.
- The Cold War made Connecticut a major producer of nuclear-powered submarines and military helicopters.
- Several race riots occurred in big cities in the state during the late 1960s.
- The late 1980s and early 1990s were tough times for the state: Defense spending was cut, manufacturing jobs were lost, the young sought jobs elsewhere, and retirees moved to places with sunnier skies and lower taxes.
- The state's first gambling casino opened on the Mashantucket Pequot reservation in 1992, vastly improving economic conditions and leading to many improvements on the reservation.
- Senator Joe Lieberman was Al Gore's running mate during the highly contested and controversial 2000 presidential election.

Connecticut Facts and Peculiarities Your Character Might Know

- Connecticut allegedly came up with the first written "constitution" (known as the Fundamental Orders) and thus is known as "The Constitution State."

Connecticut Basics That Shape Your Character

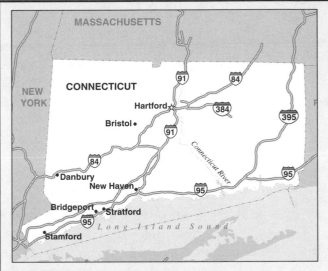

Motto: He Who Transplanted Still Sustains

Population: 3.4 million

Prevalent Religions: Christianity, particularly Roman Catholic, as well as some Baptist, Methodist, Lutheran, Episcopalian, and Church of Jesus Christ of Latter-day Saints; also Judaism and Muslim

Major Industries: Transportation equipment, machinery, electric equipment, fabricated metal products, chemical products, scientific endeavors, eggs, dairy products, cattle instruments

Ethnic Makeup (in percent): Caucasian 81.6%, African-American 9.1%, Hispanic 3.4%, Asian 2.4%, Native American 0.3%, Other 4.3%

Famous Nutmeggers: Ethan Allen, Benedict Arnold, P.T. Barnum, Henry Ward Beecher, John Brown, Samuel Colt, Oliver Ellsworth, Nathan Hale, Robert N. Hall, Katharine Hepburn, Collis Potter Huntington, Charles E. Ives, Edwin H. Land, Annie Leibovitz, John Pierpont Morgan, Frederick Law Olmsted, Kenneth H. Olsen, Rosa Ponselle, Adam Clayton Powell Jr., Benjamin Spock, Harriet Beecher Stowe, Noah Webster

- Although Connecticut is one of the nation's wealthiest states, its three largest cities—Bridgeport, Hartford, and New Haven—are among the nation's poorest.
- It's the nation's third smallest state—only ninety

miles wide and fifty-five miles long. Rhode Island and Delaware are smaller.

- Among the economic disasters of the early 1990s: 125,000 manufacturing jobs were lost, and the Colt Firearms Company filed for bankruptcy.
- The state didn't impose an earned income tax until 1991.
- Connecticut is divided into five sections: the eastern highland and the western highland, which are separated by the Connecticut Valley lowland, the Taconic area (highest point in the state), and the coastal lowlands.
- The television show *Judging Amy* takes place in Hartford.
- Mr. American Dictionary himself, Noah Webster, published his first dictionary here in 1807.
- It was said that over half of George Washington's army in 1776 was from Connecticut.
- Connecticut claims to be home to many "firsts," from the first typewriter to the first Polaroid camera to the first helicopter and the first color television set.
- It's the fourth most congested state in the nation.
- Connecticut lacks a major geographic wonder; aside from its shores and rivers, it's comparatively dull topographically.
- New Haven haircutters actually placed cut pumpkin shells on their customers' heads to ensure a uniformly round hairstyle. All who got their locks cut this way were rightfully nicknamed "pumpkin heads."
- President George W. Bush was born here—not in Texas—in 1946.
- About fifty insurance companies are headquartered in Hartford, giving it the moniker of "Insurance City."

A replica of the Amistad at Mystic

Your Character's Food and Drink

Your Connecticut character loves clams, lobster, and mussels fresh from Long Island Sound. She also likes typical Northeastern cuisine, which includes seafood, of course, that's often cooked into chowders or served boiled or steamed. Traditional accompaniments are baked beans and corn, and dinner at family gatherings might end with berry or nut pies and cobblers.

Things Your Character Likes to Remember

- Many movie stars and notable people make their homes here: Paul Newman and Joanne Woodward, Tom Cruise, Gwyneth Paltrow, Marlo Thomas and Phil Donahue, Brooke Shields, Martha Stewart, Jack Welsh.
- Connecticut has been home to some great writers: Harold Bloom, Robert M. Coates, Charlotte Perkins Gilman, Harry Harrison, Eugene O'Neill, Wallace Stevens, Harriet Beecher Stowe, and Mark Twain.
- In 1974 Ella Grasso became the state's first elected female governor.
- The Civil War. It was good for the state's economy, as the demand for weapons, munitions, and textiles stimulated the state's industrial output.
- Its numbers of classic colonial small villages.
- Going to the beach or sailing.
- Cross-country skiing.
- Dining and dancing in South Norwalk.
- Fishing off the beaches or piers.
- To read—Connecticut publishes about 144 newspapers.
- The town of Groton. It offers tours of the world's first nuclear submarine.
- Going to "The City" (New York City) at Christmastime.
- That she's away from the crime and other problems in New York.
- There's no shortage of water—the state boasts several rivers, plus the entire southern end of the state has the Long Island Sound.
- Yale. The university has educated the likes of Gerald Ford, William Howard Taft, Noah Webster, Eli Whitney, Bill Clinton, and others.
- The New York Yankees or Mets.
- The Boston Red Sox.

Things Your Character Would Like to Forget

- Traffic on I-95 any time of the day.
- Bridgeport politics. Mayor Joseph Ganim was in-

dicted by a federal grand jury for racketeering charges.

- Bridgeport. Although it's located in wealthy Fairfield County, Bridgeport is an economically depressed city that flirted with filing for bankruptcy toward the end of the twentieth century.
- The World Wrestling Federation (WWF)—it's headquartered in Stamford.
- The New York Yankees or Mets.
- The Boston Red Sox.

Myths and Misperceptions About Connecticut

- **Everyone in Connecticut is snobby.** While many do make a decent amount of money, the majority of people are very open-minded and do a great deal of charitable work.
- **Connecticut gets an overabundance of snowfall.** No, it doesn't. Connecticut is not stereotypical of New England, which does get a lot of snow. Being the southernmost state and along the water, the temperatures tend to stay a bit more moderate, keeping the snowfall accumulations down.
- **Insurance has kept the state financially sound.** Guess again—industry has. Thanks to railroads, canals, and cheap immigrant labor, Connecticut has been one of the industrial wonders of the country, having produced everything from Colt and Winchester firearms and Stanley tools to International silverware and Seth Thomas clocks to Hitchcock chairs and Royal typewriters.

Interesting Places to Set a Scene

- **Essex.** This is a dream of a New England town. Residents feel so safe that they swear they leave their doors unlocked. Most residents are college educated, and the income levels are as high as the big trees that border the streets and hover over the shops. The town's main street is postcard-perfect, as residents bustle about going to and from the many shops and squares.
- **Greenwich.** This area is loaded with multimillion-dollar homes boasting plenty of acreage at premium dollar. Typical Connecticut wealth is on display here, and, of course, Greenwich is safe and far away from the dirty tentacles of the big city.
- **Hartford.** Connecticut's capital and second largest city has been undergoing hard times, including a sinking reputation that it just can't shake. The reason: The city is filled with miles of dilapidated housing projects, unkempt lawns, vacant lots filled with knee-high weeds, and seemingly empty old factory buildings. The insurance business Hartford is so well known for has been in the doldrums for years. Aside from the impressive Old State House, Wadsworth Atheneum, and Mark Twain Home, there's little in Hartford these days that's interesting or inspiring.
- **Main Street, Westport.** Chic shops, quaint storefronts, cobblestone streets, historic buildings, angled parking spaces, SUVs, pleasant walkways, beautiful leaves in the fall, and good-looking, confident, upper-class New Englanders make up this Norman Rockwell postage stamp of America. There has to be a surprisingly dysfunctional story amidst all the perfection. . . .
- **New Haven.** Home to one of the world's best universities (Yale), this city isn't much without the university and the New Haven Green, a big expanse of greenery that was once set aside for citizens to graze their livestock, bury their dead, and spend leisure hours strolling its paths. Now it's filled with college students leaving campus to party in the park, nature lovers birdwatching, illicit lovers having a tryst, and homeless folks looking for a shady summer home.
- **Norwalk's Calf Pasture Beach.** This thirty-three-acre beach and park offers a panoramic view of Long Island Sound and the Norwalk Islands—a great place for your character to enjoy a summer's day.
- **Ridgefield.** Its main street is one hundred feet wide, with ancient, towering elms, maples, and oaks draping over it. If your character likes that, he'll really be swept away by the massive nineteenth-century houses set back from the street with their plush green lawns. This is a most romantic place to fall in love, no matter what time of year.
- **Sherwood Island.** A popular spot for inland residents who crave sand, sunshine, and saltwater but don't have a friend with a home on the Sound. Since access to most of the beachfront on Long Island Sound is limited, Sherwood's mile and a half of beach is especially attractive. The area also has marine trails through tidal marshland. It's one of the more popular birding locations as well, with frequent sightings that make the Rare Bird Alert.
- **Stamford.** The state's largest city has been growing, as new, flashy mid-rise office buildings have been

For Further Research

Books

The Captain From Connecticut, by C.S. Forester

The Colt Legacy: The Colt Armory in Hartford, 1855–1980, by Ellsworth S. Grant

Connecticut, by William Hubbell

Connecticut: A Geography, by Thomas R. Lewis and John E. Harmon

Connecticut in Transition: 1775–1818, by Richard Joseph Purcell

New Haven: A Guide to Architecture and Urban Design, by Elizabeth Mills Brown

The New Haven Railroad Along the Shore Line: The Thoroughfare From New York City to Boston, by Martin J. McGuirk

From Puritan to Yankee, by Richard L. Bushman

Web Sites

www.state.ct.us/ (official state site)

www.lib.uconn.edu/CTWriters/ (state writer's site)

www.cthistoryonline.org/ (state history online)

www.cthum.org/redirect.htm (state culture)

www.connpost.com/ (state news)

www.fairfieldct.org/ (the town of Fairfield)

www.hartfordadvocate.com/ (Hartford news and events)

Still Curious? Why Not Check Out

The Baby-Sitter's Club

Christmas in Connecticut

A Connecticut Yankee in King Arthur's Court, by Mark Twain

The Ice Storm

Judging Amy

The Mantis Murder

The Palm at the End of the Mind, by Wallace Stevens

The Paragon, by John Knowles

Revolutionary Road, by Richard Yates

Stillmeadow Daybook, by Gladys Bagg Taber

Young at Heart

---

erected to headquarter at least a dozen Fortune 500 companies. Stamford's lively downtown—with theaters, shops, tree-lined streets, plazas, stylish restaurants, and people spending money—makes capital Hartford look like "the Connecticut city that was."

- **The North End of Bridgeport.** This area is predominately populated by people of Italian heritage, Pacino or DeNiro style. You may think you're in Naples as you smell the sauce cooking from the sidewalks and see clothes hanging from lines out the windows.

- **The Trout Brook Valley.** Over one thousand acres are open to the public in the Trout Brook Valley area which is somewhat larger than Central Park in New York City. Recreational activities include hiking, cross-country skiing, horseback riding, dog walking, off-road bicycle riding, picnicking, seasonal fishing, and restricted seasonal hunting. This is where an outdoorsy character is likely to spend her time.

- **The Yale campus.** What student wouldn't die to go to school here? One of the most prestigious universities in the world also hosts a beautiful campus. Yale's University Center is the city's oldest building, and its Natural History Museum can't be matched. As you can imagine, the campus teems with black-turtle-necked English majors deriding Derrida, plaid-coated historians espousing the New Historicists, and young, angst-ridden Nietzscheans extolling the death of God. Then, of course, there are the countless students wandering from hall to hall in a haze, certain of their immediate destination (the next class) but of little else.

Significant Events Your Character Has Probably Thought About

- The first European explorers came to Delaware from the Netherlands, but the first settlement flew the flag of Sweden. A group led by Peter Minuit from the Dutch West India Company created the first settlement in 1638 on a site that is now the city of Wilmington. Minuit bargained with Indian residents to expand the settlement, which he called New Sweden.

- In 1655 fighting between New Sweden and a territory called New Netherland, commanded by Peter Stuyvesant, ended Swedish rule in the colonies. In turn, the Dutch were thrown out by the English in 1667.

- The next combatants for the land were colonies: Pennsylvania and Maryland. Pennsylvania won, controlling the "Three Counties" until 1704, when they were made a self-governing colony.

- During the Revolutionary War, the British captured New Castle, Delaware's capital city. Colonists quickly moved the capital to Dover, where it has remained since 1777.

- In 1829 the Chesapeake and Delaware Canal was completed. It remains a popular landmark in the state.

- Though Delaware was loyal to the Union during the Civil War, more than two thousand blacks remained slaves until 1863. Delaware voted against Abraham Lincoln in the 1860 and 1864 elections.

- In the second half of the nineteenth century, Delaware often associated itself with the restored southern states.

- The du Pont family grew to be one of the most powerful forces in the state during the twentieth century, controlling politics and giving huge donations to improve the educational and park systems.

Delaware Facts and Peculiarities Your Character Might Know

- Delaware was the first state to ratify the U.S. Constitution and therefore calls itself "The First State."

- Delaware sometimes is called the "Blue Hen State." The blue hen is the official state bird and is known as a fierce fighter. During the Revolutionary War, soldiers from the state used them in cockfights.

Delaware Basics That Shape Your Character

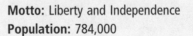

Motto: Liberty and Independence

Population: 784,000

Prevalent Religions: Methodist, Roman Catholic, and Jewish

Major Industries: Chemicals products, rubber, plastic and synthetic products, fishing (mostly crabs, clams, and oysters), agriculture (predominantly broiler chickens and eggs)

Ethnic Makeup (in percent): Caucasian 74.6%, African-American 19.2%, Hispanic 4.8%, Asian 2.1%, Native American 0.3%, Other 2.0%

Famous Delawareans: Valerie Bertinelli, the du Pont family, Henry Heimlich, George Thorogood

- Delaware also is known as "The Diamond State," "The Peach State," and "Small Wonder." Thomas Jefferson, who thought it was a little jewel of a state, gave it the first name. The second name refers to the state's production of peaches until a blight in the late 1800s. Publicists recently created the last name to attract tourists.
- Rhode Island is smaller in land area than Delaware, which is only ninety-six miles long and, at its narrowest point, only nine miles wide. Only five states have fewer residents.
- Explorer Samuel Argall was blown off course and into Delaware Bay, which he named for the first governor of Virginia, Thomas West, Lord De La Warr. The name soon was applied to the bay, the nearby river, and the land in the vicinity.
- Delaware is the only state without a national park system.
- The DuPont chemical company began in 1802, when E.I. du Pont opened his gunpowder mill near Wilmington.
- Locals speak of Delaware as two states in one: The north is primarily urban and industrial, while the south is rural and focuses primarily on farming and fishing. The Chesapeake and Delaware Canal is usually considered the dividing line. Delawareans speak of living "above [or "north"] of the canal" or "below [or "south"] of the canal."
- The state has only three counties: New Castle, Kent, and Sussex. Nearly 70 percent of the population lives in New Castle, the northernmost county. Dover, the capital, is located in Kent County, in the middle of the state.

"The Greens" in Dover

- Delaware's corporate taxes are very low, leading a number of businesses to incorporate in the state even though they are based elsewhere.
- In 1974 school children sent petitions to the state general assembly, asking that the ladybug be made the state's official insect. Their request was approved.

Your Character's Food and Drink

Steamed crabs are a favorite food in Delaware. Delaware fishermen bring in plenty of crabs, oysters, and clams, and you'll find some restaurants that serve them raw. A great local meal features raw bluepoint crab, raw oysters, and steamed clams spread across a newspaper-covered table where they're cracked and eaten. A pitcher of cold beer completes the repast. Grotto's Pizza, begun in Rehoboth Beach, is a popular chain in the state. Chicken and turkey farming are big here, especially in the southern counties, and so fowl dinners are common. Capriotti's in Wilmington is famous for its turkey subs. In Wilmington and, to a lesser extent, in Dover, locals can find most ethnic foods.

Things Your Character Likes to Remember

- It's "The First State." And, as the state tourism buttons proclaim, "It's good to be first."
- The smallness of the state creates a sense of community and identification.
- The proximity of the ocean and Chesapeake Bay. Shore activities are the most popular pastime.
- The minor league Wilmington Blue Rocks attracts a lot of local interest from baseball fans, especially in New Castle County. Delawareans, particularly in the north, follow the fortunes of the Philadelphia sports teams.

Myths and Misperceptions About Delaware

- **It's named after the Delaware Native Americans.** While a number of states were named for a Native American term or phrase, in Delaware, the opposite is true. The Europeans called the local people "the Delaware." They called themselves *Lenni Lenape,* or "the original people."
- **Nothing happens in Delaware.** The beaches in the south are crowded in summer, drawing tourists from throughout the region, especially from Washington DC. The northern area around Wilmington buzzes with industry and people.

For Further Research

Books

Cruising the Chesapeake, by William H. Shellenberger
The Delaware Indians, by Clinton A. Weslager
Delaware Trivia, by Phil Milford
The National Waterway: A History of the Chesapeake and Delaware Canal, 1769–1965, by Ralph D. Gray
Shipwrecks, Sea Stories, and Legends of the Delaware Coast, by David J. Seibold and Charles J. Adams III

Web Sites

www.visitdover.com/ (Kent County Convention and Visitors Bureau)
www.cityofdover.com/ (City of Dover's official Web site)
http://delaware.gov/ (state government information)

www.hsd.org/ (state historical society)
www.visitsoutherndelaware.com/ (tourism for southern Delaware
www.visitwilmingtonde.com/ (Greater Wilmington Convention and Visitors Bureau)
www.delaware.com/ (area resources and information)
www.visitdelaware.net/ (tourism for Delaware)

Still Curious? Why Not Check Out

Fatal Embrace, by Cris Barrish and Peter Meyer
A Gentleman's Game: A Novel, by Tom Coyne
The Judas Pool, by George Owens
And Never Let Her Go: Thomas Capano, the Deadly Seducer, by Ann Rule

Interesting Places to Set a Scene

- **Betheny Beach.** This beach resort popular with Delawareans is located in the southern part of the state. Chief Little Owl, a twenty-six-foot sculpture honoring the Native Americans, greets visitors to the beach. The sculpture features a long face with an eagle on top of it. Far less glamorous than many Atlantic resorts, Betheny—the town and the beach—offers quiet relaxation. A recent survey chose the beaches of southern Delaware as the cleanest in the country.
- **Dover.** Dover is the capital and the second largest city in the state. The wide green parks and red-brick colonial buildings create a genteel atmosphere. That atmosphere is balanced nearby with the large Dover Air Force Base and Dover Downs, a 140,000-seat sports facility that features a NASCAR track (the "Monster Mile") and a harness-racing track. Casino gambling is legal on the property, which also features a luxury hotel.
- **New Castle.** The original capital of Delaware, New Castle once bustled with activity and commerce. It's now mostly a quaint spot for tourists. Located on the Delaware River across from New Jersey, it attracts frequent visitors from Philadelphia.
- **Rehoboth Beach.** This largest and best known of Delaware's beaches draws visitors from several nearby states. Its most popular landmark is the mile-long boardwalk. On the boardwalk, your characters can find a bandstand, where summer concerts (mostly local entertainers) draw a crowd. Mango Mike's, a Caribbean restaurant, is a popular hangout.
- **Wilmington.** The largest city in the state and the only one of significant size and population, Wilmington is located in northern Delaware in the Brandywine Valley. It's the economic, political, and cultural center of the state. Unlike the rest of the state, Wilmington has a northern atmosphere and energy, based on industry, finance, and entertainment. Many people in Wilmington commute to nearby Philadelphia. The du Pont name has been supreme in this city for more than a hundred years.

Florida

Florida Basics That Shape Your Character

Motto: In God We Trust

Population: 15.9 million

Prevalent Religions: Christianity, including Southern Baptist, Roman Catholic, Santería (Cuban Catholicism), Pentecostal, Episcopalian, also Judaism

Major Industries: Tourism and related services, agriculture (citrus, sugarcane, fishing and fisheries), small-scale manufacturing, paper and pulp, aerospace, real estate, international banking

Ethnic Makeup (in percent): Caucasian 65.4%, African-American 14.6%, Hispanic 16.8%, Asian 1.7%, Native American 0.3%, Other 3.0%

Famous Floridians: Julian "Cannonball" Adderley, Dave Barry, Faye Dunaway, Zora Neale Hurston, James Weldon Johnson, Butterfly McQueen, Jim Morrison, Tom Petty, Sidney Poitier, Janet Reno, Ben Vereen

Significant Events Your Character Has Probably Thought About

- Florida seceded from the Union in 1861; approximately thirty-nine thousand of the eighty-six thousand people living in Florida at the time were African-American slaves.

- In the 1880s, railroad magnates began building train lines from the Northeast to Miami and from Richmond, Virginia, to Tampa.

- Revolution in Cuba sparked the Spanish-American War in 1898. Tampa was the army command post from which Teddy Roosevelt and his Rough Riders set out for San Juan Hill.

- A Florida real estate boom that followed the Spanish-American War was halted in the late 1920s by cold winters, hurricanes, and the Wall Street crash.

- Florida's population doubled to almost 2 million between 1920 and 1940, and approximately 2.5 million tourists were visiting the state annually by the beginning of World War II.

- The War Department began testing missiles at Cape Canaveral in the 1940s, leading to its development later as the base of operations for the National Aeronautics and Space Administration (NASA) and the Kennedy Space Center.

- In 1959 Fidel Castro's revolution started a wave of immigration from Cuba. Significant numbers of refugees have also come to Florida from Nicaragua (75,000 people in the 1980s) and Haiti (125,000 people, many on homemade wooden boats).

- Walt Disney World opened in 1971, leading to the development of numerous other theme parks that, along with the beaches, attract over forty-three million visitors annually to Florida. More than a third of Florida's tourists come from overseas.

- A boom in business development in the 1980s led many companies to relocate their headquarters to Florida. Banking, insurance, pharmaceutical, and real estate development companies found a home here, as did somewhat less-desirable smugglers and traders of illegal drugs.

Florida Facts and Peculiarities Your Character Might Know

- Florida has the fourth largest state population in the country.

- The population is growing by more than seven hundred people a day, with about half coming from other parts of the United States (the other two-quarters are immigrants and new births).

- Most of Florida is flat, flat, flat. Its highest point, Britton Hill on the Alabama border, is the lowest of any state (345 feet).
- Florida is the lightning capital of the country, with Clearwater being the most-struck city.
- St. Augustine is the oldest continuously inhabited European settlement in North America.
- Greater Miami is the only metropolitan area in the United States bordered by two national parks: Everglades National Park to the west and Biscayne National Park to the east.
- The country's first scheduled domestic jet flights began in 1959 with a short trip between St. Petersburg and Tampa.
- Florida is the wettest state in the country, with most of the rain coming from June to September. The winter is usually quite dry.

Your Character's Food and Drink

Chain restaurants dominate the sprawling suburban culture of much of the state, but Florida's influx of immigrants from Jamaica, Cuba, South America, Haiti, and the Northeast add delicious variety—jerk chicken, roast pork, fried plantains, *cafe Cubano* (strong and sweet Cuban coffee), kosher delicatessens—to the increasingly common shopping mall fare. Seafood is in season much of the year, and favorites include broiled stone crabs, turtle soup, baked kingfish, conch fritters, shrimp, and big game fish such as marlin, tarpon, and dolphinfish. Inland lakes provide catfish and bass to go with such traditional southern fare as turnip greens, grits, and sweet potato pie. In addition to traditional citrus fruits, roadside stands offer mangos, papayas, coconuts, and avocados.

Things Your Character Likes to Remember

- It's never cold. While temperatures may dip into the forties in northern parts of the state during the winter, highs stay in the eighties throughout most of the year in the south.
- Large waterfowl and other migrating birds often soar against fantastic pink sunsets.
- A huge, slow-moving river, two hundred miles long and up to seventy miles wide, originates in the state's midsection and flows slowly southward through countless acres of saw grass, culminating in the Everglades National Park.
- Florida's vegetation is lush and varied: High temperatures and humid sea air keep the land green all year long. Even strip malls have palm trees lining their parking lots.
- Florida has served as a base of operations for American military training and supply operations for over a century.
- The TV series *Miami Vice* changed the city's image from that of a stodgy retirees' haven to a hip, pastel-colored metropolis of fashionable chaos.
- Up north they're shoveling snow, and I'm lying out by the pool . . . .

Things Your Character Would Like to Forget

- Florida's reluctance to grant women the right to vote. It was the last state in the country to do so, waiting until 1969.
- The race riots in Miami in 1980 and 1982.
- A wave a violent attacks against foreign tourists in the early 1990s.
- Hurricane Andrew, which in 1992 devastated many parts of South Florida, killing twenty-three people, destroying sixty thousand homes, and causing twenty billion dollars of damage.

One of the state's Alligator Crossing road signs

For Further Research

Books

200 Quick Looks at Florida History, by James C. Clark

African-Americans in Florida, by Maxine D. Jones

Al Burt's Florida: Snowbirds, Sand Castles and Self-Rising Crackers (Florida History and Culture Series), by Al Burt Jr.

Black Society in Spanish Florida, by Jane Landers and Peter H. Wood

The Book Lover's Guide to Florida: Authors, Books, and Literary Sites, by Kevin M. McCarthy

Crime Fiction and Film in the Sunshine State: Florida Noir, edited by Steve Glassman and Maurice O'Sullivan

Cuban Miami, by Robert M. Levine and Moisés Asís

Dave Barry Is Not Making This Up, by Dave Barry

The Idea of Florida in the American Literary Imagination, by Anne E. Rowe

Maximum Insight: Selected Columns of Bill Maxwell, by Bill Maxwell

Southern Discomfort: Women's Activism in Tampa, Florida 1880s–1920s, by Nancy A. Hewitt

Zora in Florida, edited by Steve Glassman and Kathryn Lee Seidel

Web Sites

www.cityoforlando.net (Orlando)

www.tampagov.net (Tampa)

http://fcit.usf.edu/florida (educational resources about Florida)

www.ci.miami.fl.us (Miami)

www.ci.jax.fl.us (Jacksonville)

www.pac-info.com/list.php?nid=21 (public records)

www.tallynews.com (Tallahassee alternative weekly)

www.floridamagazine.com (*Florida Monthly* magazine)

www.miami.com/mld/miamiherald (*The Miami Herald*)

Still Curious? Why Not Check Out

100% Pure Florida Fiction, edited by Susan Hubbard and Robley Wilson

Florida in Poetry: A History of the Imagination, edited by Jane Anderson Jones and Maurice J. O'Sullivan

Ghosts of St. Augustine, by Dave Lapham

The Key West Reader: The Best of the Key West's Writers 1830–1990, edited by George Murphy

A Land Remembered, by Patrick D. Smith

Little Havana Blues: A Cuban-American Literature Anthology, edited by Delia Poey and Virgil Suarez

More Florida Stories, edited by Kevin M. McCarthy

Naked Came the Manatee: A Novel, by Dave Barry et al.

Tellable Cracker Tales, by Annette J. Bruce

Their Eyes Were Watching God, by Zora Neale Hurston

- The city of Miami's bankruptcy, declared in 1996.
- Elian Gonzales, a six-year-old Cuban refugee whose fate (should he be allowed stay in the United States with his Miami relatives or be sent back to Cuba to his father?) brought national attention and a raid by armed national guards in the spring of 2000.
- The presidential election of 2000, wherein the state's antiquated voting machines fueled a painful, protracted national debate about dimpled, pregnant, and hanging chads.

Myths and Misperceptions About Florida

- **Florida's population growth is due to an influx of retirees.** Actually, although almost 18 percent of Florida's population is over the age of sixty-five, it's families with children, both from the North as well as from the Caribbean and Latin America, who account for much of the new growth.
- **Florida is all beaches, condos, and Mickey Mouse.** The state's interior and panhandle, not to mention the Everglades, present many landscapes unique to Florida. And its diversity of population and cultures rivals that of any other state.
- **It's a nice place for an evening walk.** Of the ten most dangerous U.S. cities for pedestrians, five are in Florida, with Tampa holding the number one spot. Better to stay on the beach.
- **Florida is just for old people.** (Someone once referred to Miami as "God's waiting room.") In fact, many children of retirees visit their parents only to find that they, too, would like to live in Florida, hence the influx of young families from the Northeast and Midwest.

Interesting Places to Set a Scene

- **Daytona Beach.** This is the current major spring break destination and site of the Daytona International Speedway.
- **The Everglades.** The Everglades consists of two and a half million acres of water and saw grass, punctuated by small islands ("hammocks") that support hardwood tropical trees. Herons, spoonbills, egrets, alligators, and countless other species make this an unforgettable landscape. In some parks on the fringes of the Everglades, boardwalks lead you over the marshy surface.
- **Fort Lauderdale.** Locals got fed up with the antics of spring break revelers and took back their town; the beaches are now more family friendly. The city itself is one of the most tightly segregated in the country, with whites living on the east side and minorities (mostly African-Americans) living on the west side.
- **Gainesville.** This college town, home to the University of Florida, has lots of student-oriented restaurants and bars.
- **Key West.** Hemingway lived here for almost ten years before moving to Cuba. Tennessee Williams spent thirty-four years here. The sunset itself is a major party event, and divers come here from all over the world to swim among the exotic fish and miles of coral.
- **Jupiter Island.** This is home to many of the wealthy for whom Palm Beach isn't exclusive enough. Outsiders are looked at with suspicion.
- **Miami.** What doesn't go on here? Famous for its nightlife (Will Smith's "second home"), Miami is a busy, sprawling city with no real center. Traffic is a free-for-all, with rusty station wagons vying for lanes with sleek Jaguars. Over 90 percent of the residents of Hialeah, on the west side, count Spanish as their native language. Huge festivals celebrating the diverse cultures of the city take place at least once a month. And at night, the party never stops!
- **Miami Beach.** Most of the architecture in Florida is merely serviceable, but the Art Deco buildings of South Beach (the southern tip of Miami Beach) create a fantastic backdrop for moneyed leisure and nightlife.
- **Palm Beach.** Home to the rich and famous, Palm Beach is notable for its lack of strip malls and neon. Petite Marmite is a restaurant favored by celebrities. Polo is a favorite pastime.
- **Pensacola.** This city in the western panhandle is noted for its charming ante- and post-bellum architecture. It's also near a huge naval air base that is home to the Blue Angels precision flight squad.
- **Suwannee.** This small town is near where the river of song (officially called "Old Folks at Home" but known to most as "The Suwannee River," for its opening line: "Way down upon the Sewanee River, far, far away") empties out into the Gulf after its journey down from Georgia. Popular for canoeing, camping, diving, and lazily floating down the river on an inner tube. Note: It's spelled "Suwannee," not "Sewanee" as the song spells it; composer Stephen Foster never even saw the river.
- **Tallahassee.** The state capital is situated halfway between St. Augustine and Pensacola. Although it's the seat of state government and the skyline is dominated by the twenty-two-story capitol building, Tallahassee has managed to maintain its small-town southern charm.
- **West Palm Beach.** Originally the "servants' town" for the other Palm Beach, West Palm Beach has plenty of strip malls, along with the noteworthy Norton Museum of Art. Much of the area between here and the huge Lake Okeechobee is given over to sugarcane cultivation.

Jacksonville

Jacksonville Basics That Shape Your Character

Amelia Island Plantation

Population: 778,900

Prevalent Religions: Various denominations of Christianity, especially Baptist, Presbyterian, and Episcopalian

Top Employers: Winn-Dixie Stores, Blue Cross and Blue Shield of Florida, Bank of America, Baptist Health System, United Parcel Service, Convergys, Citibank, CSX Transportation

Per Capita Income: $26,868

Average Daily Temperature: January, 52° F; July, 82° F

Ethnic Makeup (in percent): Caucasian 65.8%, African-American 29.6%, Hispanic 4.2%, Asian 2.8%, Native American .1%, Other 1.4%

Newspapers and Magazines: *The Florida Times-Union, Jacksonville Business Journal, Jacksonville Daily Record, Florida Trend, Black Family Today*

Free Weekly Alternative Paper: *Folio Weekly*

Jacksonville Facts and Peculiarities Your Character Might Know

- The city is named after Andrew Jackson, who was the provisional governor of Florida before becoming president.
- Jacksonville describes itself as being in the "First Coast" area because it was the first area settled by Europeans in North America.
- The St. Johns River, like the Nile, is one of the few rivers in the Northern Hemisphere that flows northward.
- Jacksonville, unlike much of Florida, actually has mild (read: perceptible) seasons. Winter freezes occur occasionally, and summertime highs reach the nineties.
- James Weldon Johnson, a famous Jacksonville lawyer, wrote the popular song "Lift Every Voice and Sing." He was the first African-American admitted to the Florida Bar.
- A fire burned down most of the city in 1901.
- Limp Bizkit got its start in Jacksonville.
- Harriet Beecher Stowe settled down to write in Mandarin, in south Jacksonville.
- If there's one thing Jacksonville just can't get enough of, it's not the sun or the surf but classic southern rock. Rumor has it you've got a better chance of running into a snowflake than into someone who doesn't love Lynyrd Skynyrd.
- Geographically, Jacksonville is the largest city in the United States. It is also the largest city in Florida, with a population almost twice that of Miami proper.

If Your Character . . .

If Your Character Smells of Money, he lives in Dr.'s Lake or San Marco. These are some of the country's wealthiest neighborhoods. Both provide easy access to the yacht piers.

If Your Character Is All About Business, she lives in Ponte Vedra, Riverside, or Avondale. These neighborhoods on the western side of the St. Johns River are a short commute from downtown.

If Your Character Is a Family Man, he lives in Orange Park or Windsor Park. The kids can even walk to school in this leafy east-side suburb.

If Your Character Wears a Blue Collar at Work, she lives in North Jacksonville or Middleburg. North of Twentieth Street, there are lots of new apartment complexes as well as trailer homes here. This area is away from the beach.

For Further Research

Books

Jacksonville, edited by the Jacksonville Historical Society

Jacksonville: Crown of the First Coast, introduction by J. Wayne Weaver and Delores Barr Weaver

Jacksonville Diary: Behind the Microphone, by Ed Bell

Jacksonville: Reflections of Excellence, by Deborah Gianoulis et al.

Keeping the Faith: Race, Politics, and Social Development in Jacksonville, Florida, 1940–1970, by Abel A. Bartley

A River Runs Backward, by the Junior League of Jacksonville

Web Sites

www.jaxweb.com (general info)

www.coj.net/ (city of Jacksonville)

www.myjaxchamber.com (chamber of commerce)

www.jacksonville.com (*The Florida Times-Union*)

www.folioweekly.com (*Folio Weekly*)

http://64.176.211.78/EverythingJacksonville/media.html (extensive local links)

Still Curious? Why Not Check Out

The Flamingo Rising, by Larry Baker

A House on Hubbard Street, by Louise Stanton Warren

Palmetto Leaves, by Harriet Beecher Stowe

Plenty Good Room, by Teresa McClain-Watson

Scar Lover, by Harry Crews

Short Stories: The Story of a Refugee, by Rea-Silvia Costin

G.I. Jane

If Your Character Likes to Hunt, he lives in Westside. Wooded areas characterize this vast area between Jacksonville proper and Florida's interior.

If Your Character Is Hip and Trendy, he lives in Atlantic Beach or Neptune Beach. This is the good beach life for most folks.

Local Grub Your Character Might Love

In Florida, you have to go north to go south. Fried chicken, black-eyed peas, buttermilk biscuits, and other southern staples are much more common here than in other parts of Florida. Besides the burgers, pizza, and hot dogs that compose the primary diet of most north Floridians, catfish and gator tail may make an appearance on the dinner plate. Firehouse Subs is a favorite local chain.

Interesting and Peculiar Places to Set a Scene

- **The Riverwalk.** This mile-long boardwalk along the St. Johns is good for pier fishing or a sunset stroll.
- **The Crazy Horse Saloon.** The young and ungroomed enjoy this country-and-western joint on Jacksonville's Southside.
- **Five Points.** Five Points is an area in the middle of the Riverside neighborhood. Street performers add to the general zaniness of the freaks and freak-wanna-bes who hang out by the Marquee Theater and in the local coffee shops.
- **Tree Hill Nature Center.** With its walk-through butterfly house, this is one of the few truly green spaces left in the city.
- **Pete's Bar.** This is a folksy, down-home kind of place in Neptune Beach where the waitresses still call you "honey."
- **The Broken Spoke in Arlington.** On University Boulevard right off Arlington Speedway, this is a popular and crazy nightspot, but it's in an area with lots of crime.
- **Amelia Island.** Just north of Jacksonville, this is the site of the historical Fort Clinch. The fine white beaches are covered with tiny fragments of quartz that have washed down from the Appalachians.
- **St. Augustine.** To the north, this very old city (the oldest in North America) is supposedly riddled with ghosts.
- **Sunday at Conch House.** This resort on Anastasia Island is home to a marina, a restaurant, an inn, a bar, and the hoppin' "Reggae Sunday," a dock party that's become a local legend, complete with bands, beers, boats, and drunken folks.
- **Caps.** Only known to beach people, your character can pull up to the dock of this local bar in his boat and listen to live music.

- **An old gas station at the beach that is now Angie's Subs.** You'll find some of the best subs in the state at this "gas-station-turned-sub shop." And only the most local of the locals know this place exists. It's right on the beach and a lovely place for a romantic encounter.

Exceptionally Grand Things Your Character Is Proud Of

- Jacksonville was the busiest military port in the country during the 1991 Gulf War.
- The Jacksonville Jaguars.
- Player's Championship.
- The Jacksonville Fair for two weeks in downtown.

Pathetically Sad Things Your Character Is Ashamed Of

- The Duval County School Bus Debacle of 2001. Political infighting and lawsuits led to lots of stranded kids and angry parents as the school buses stayed put.

- The Ditch. A famous saying among the more privileged is "Don't go over the ditch," meaning into the inner coastal waterway. It's a rough part of town.

Your Character Loves

- Weekend getaways to the beach.
- Fishing, deep sea or pier.
- Golf.
- Shopping.
- Boat races.
- Dog races.
- Speedways.

Your Character Hates

- Georgia. The Georgia-Florida football rivalry is unsurpassed, with hotel room always booked during the weekend of game day.
- The Better Jacksonville Plan—a redevelopment plan that's had residents up in arms and complaining daily on the evening news.

Miami

Miami Facts and Peculiarities Your Character Might Know

- Miami is world-renowned for its beaches and night-life: twenty miles of white sandy beaches, and more clubs and bars than any reasonable person could hope to patronize in a lifetime.
- Miami is an international financial center and handles the bulk of all U.S. trade with Latin America.
- It is the world's largest cruise ship port.
- It is also one of the most transient places in the United States. Just over half of Miami-Dade residents are foreign-born, and only 60 percent of the remainder were born in Florida.
- Sixty-eight percent of residents speak a language other than English at home.
- Much of the city is made up of "planned communities," although the planners might not have anticipated the swell of year-round population that followed the invention of air-conditioning.
- The Coconut Grove neighborhood is one of the oldest planned communities in the country, and at one time was home to Robert Frost, Harriet Beecher Stowe, Alexander Graham Bell, and Tennessee Williams.
- "It's not the heat. . . ." Summertime humidity usually hovers between 90 percent and 100 percent, so even with a high of "only" ninety degrees, you're shirt's going to be soaked by the time you get to the other side of the parking lot.
- Hurricane season lasts from June to November. Ever since Andrew in 1992, people take the watches and warnings seriously.
- Tight clothes are popular with just about everyone, even those whose bellies bulge from underneath their baby-tees.

If Your Character . . .

If Your Character Wears a Blue Collar at Work, he lives in North Miami, Glenwood Heights, or Pinewood Park. Buildings seem to age faster in the sea air, and wealthier residents tend to fan outward to the suburbs. Lake Lucerne is near both the Pro Player Stadium (Dolphins, Marlins) and the expressways, so the commute's not as bad.

Miami Basics That Shape Your Character

The Miami Strip

Population: 2,253,362 in Miami-Dade County. Miami itself (population 350,000) is one city among twenty-nine municipalities in the county, including Miami Beach and Coral Gables. Let's just worry about Miami-Dade County for now, because that's what people usually mean when they refer to "Miami."

Prevalent Religions: Roman Catholicism, Santería (Cuban Catholicism), various denominations of Protestantism, Judaism, and representatives of just about any other religion in the world.

Top Employers: American Airlines, Precision Response Corporation, University of Miami, Baptist Health Systems, BellSouth, Florida Power and Light, Publix Supermarkets, Royal Caribbean International, Celebrity Cruises, United Airlines

Per Capita Income: $24,733

Average Daily Temperature: January, 67° F; July, 83° F

Ethnic Makeup (in percent): Caucasian 69.7%, African-American 20.3%, Hispanic 57.3%, Asian 1.4%; Native American .2%, Other 4.6%

Newspapers and Magazines: *The Miami Herald, Daily Business Review, El Nuevo Herald, Sun-Sentinel* (Broward County), *Miami Metro, South Beach Magazine, Ocean Drive, Wire, South Florida Business Journal, South Florida Parenting*

Free Weekly Alternative Newspapers: *Miami New Times, Miami City Link*

If Your Character Is African-American and Smells of Money, he lives in Coconut Grove. Coconut Grove is extremely diverse in its ethnic makeup and range of houses, but there is a large community made up of the descendents of settlers from the Bahamas.

If Your Character Is Caucasian and Smells of Money, she probably lives in Broward or Palm Beach County, not Miami. She commutes to the downtown office on I-95. If she really lives in Miami (and plenty of rich Caucasians do), she's in Coral Gables, with its lush foliage, waterways, overhanging trees, and golf courses.

If Your Character Is Down-and-Out, he lives in Liberty City, Overtown, or Little Haiti. The area between the airport and downtown is, to put it mildly, economically depressed. It's home to many people who are fleeing even worse conditions elsewhere in the world. This was the site of the race riots in the early 1980s.

If Your Character Is a Hispanic Family Man, he lives in Hialeah. NW Forty-Ninth Street is the main commercial strip through this second largest Dade County city. About 90 percent of residents speak Spanish as their native language.

If Your Character Is Excited About Shopping Malls, she lives in Aventura. From many of the new high-rises, you can make out the Aventura Mall, which is packed every day of the week with professionals shopping for shirts, retirees sifting through bargain bins, and surly teenage "rebels" who sneer at it all.

Local Grub Your Character Might Love

Just about everything is available in Miami at any time of the year. The restaurants and grocery stores overflow with treats from all over the world, but you're especially likely to find Cuban, Haitian, Jamaican, and South American foods. From Cuba alone, you've got *boniato* (somewhat like a sweet potato), *mojo* (a sauce or marinade made from oil, herbs, and lime juice), *ropa vieja* ("old clothes"; shredded beef cooked in tomato sauce), *cafe Cubano* (strong, sweet coffee), and crispy Cuban bread. Stone crabs are in season all winter, and they are best broiled and served with a tart mayonnaise or fresh lemon juice. Big ocean fish (swordfish, marlin, dolphin-fish, tarpon) are always popular. Roadside vendors sell coconut, citrus fruits, bananas, pineapples, mangos, papayas, avocados, and guavas. And don't forget all those kosher delis!

Interesting and Peculiar Places to Set a Scene

- **The basketball court at Flamingo Park.** A noisy, derisive, and at times appreciative crowd ogles the fierce competition between eager teenagers, smooth-talking hustlers, and wiry old hands.
- **Brickell Avenue.** This street is lined with gleaming skyscrapers that look out over the aquamarine Biscayne Bay.
- **A capoeira training academy.** This Afro-Brazilian martial art is quite popular in Miami, and its lithe practitioners stretch, twirl, kick, and flip over the mats to the sound of *berimbaus* (West African string instruments).
- **Miami Beach.** This was built on a sandbar in Biscayne Bay. Tops are optional along the stretch from Sixty-Fifth to Seventy-Eighth Streets. Why be modest when you're gorgeous?
- **Carnaval Miami.** This nine-day festival in March has parades, a beauty contest, lots of concerts, cooking contests, and even a Latin drag queen show. The Calle Ocho festival follows, and Little Havana is up all night cooking and making music.
- **The Miami Book Fair in November.** This book fair is popular with writers and readers from all over the country.
- **South Beach.** In the daytime, the sun gleams off the pink and turquoise Art Deco buildings all along the shimmering white strand. At night, this is quite possibly the party center of the United States. Haven for the hip, young, and beautiful, South Beach is what Will Smith was referring to when he sang about Miami as his second home.
- **The Caribbean Marketplace in Little Haiti.** This is the Miami version of the one in Port-au-Prince, with lots of colorful crafts, paintings, and food. Goat head, anyone?
- **The Fairchild Tropical Gardens.** The thing is, with all of Miami's sunshine and rain, you can't stop anything green from growing, so you may as well enjoy it. Palm trees dot the city (even the parking lots of auto dealers), but people come here to enjoy everything green and tropical.

For Further Research

Books

Black Miami in the Twentieth Century, by Marvin Dunn
Building Marvelous Miami, by Nicholas M. Patricios
City on the Edge: The Transformation of Miami, by Alejandro Portes and Alex Stepick
Going to Miami: Exiles, Tourists, and Refugees in the New America, by David Rieff
Knights of the Fourth Estate: The Story of The Miami Herald, by Nixon Smiley
The Life and Times of Miami Beach, by Ann Armbruster
Miami Now! Immigration, Ethnicity, and Social Change, edited by Guillermo J. Grenier and Alex Stepick
Miami: In Our Own Words, edited by *The Miami Herald*

Web Sites

www.miaminewtimes.com (*Miami New Times* alternative weekly)
www.m-dcc.org (chamber of commerce)
www.beaconcouncil.com/links2/gov.asp (government links)
www.miami.com/mld/miamiherald (*The Miami Herald*)
www.oceandrive.com (*Ocean Drive* fashion and style magazine)

Curious? Why Not Check Out

The Aguero Sisters, by Cristina Garcia
The Birdcage: A Novel, by Robert Rodi et al.
Bitter Sugar, by Carolina Garcia-Aguilera
In Cuba I Was a German Shepherd, by Ana Menendez
In the Fast Lane: The True Story of Murder in Miami, by Carol Soret Cope
Going Under: A Novel, by Virgil Suarez
Miami, by Joan Didion
Moon People: A Novel, by Sondra Shulman
Suitable for Framing, by Edna Buchanan
Welcome to Miami, by Michael Largo

Exceptionally Grand Things Your Character Is Proud Of

- Everyone dreams of coming for a visit, 'cause nobody parties like Miami!
- The Beethoven by the Beach Festival.
- Robert Beatty—the man has a great record as a constructive and heroic reformer. He's been called "the conscience of the town."

Pathetically Sad Things Your Character Is Ashamed Of

- Race riots.
- Municipal bankruptcy.
- Reckless drivers.
- Attacks against tourists.
- Environmental degradation.
- The Elian Gonzales controversy.
- The 2000 presidential election disaster.

Your Character Loves

- Merengue, samba, salsa, Cuban jazz.
- Betting on jai alai, horses, dogs, whatever.
- Free shots offered by liquor promoters on Saturday night.
- The Marlins (baseball).
- The Dolphins (football).
- The Heat (basketball).
- The Panthers (hockey).
- The University of Miami (Hurri)'Canes.
- Thongs.
- Mah-jongg.

Your Character Hates

- *Miami Vice*. People think the city is really like the portrayal on the television show. It has changed a lot since then.
- Those idiot drivers who exceed the speed limit.
- Those idiot drivers who don't exceed the speed limit.

Orlando

Orlando Basics That Shape Your Character

A typical downtown Orlando street

© Corrie Decker

Population: 190,000 in the city; 900,000 in the Greater Metro Area

Prevalent Religions: Representatives of just about anything, but mostly Protestantism, with a bit of an evangelical streak (Benny Hinn set up his television-ministry shop here, and The Gideons International is centered in nearby Ocala).

Top Employers: Walt Disney World, Universal Studios Florida, Orlando Regional Healthcare System, Florida Hospital, Lockheed Martin, Central Florida International Investments, University of Central Florida, Darden Restaurants, SunTrust, AT&T Wireless

Per Capita Income: $24,120

Average Daily Temperature: January, 60° F; July, 82° F

Ethnic Makeup (in percent): Caucasian 72.9%, African-American 13.8%, Hispanic 10.5%, Asian 2.5%, Native American 1%, Other 2.8%

Newspapers and Magazines: *Orlando Sentinel*, *Orlando Times* (African-American community), *Orlando Business Journal*, *Orlando Magazine*

Free Weekly Alternative Newspapers: *Orlando Weekly*, *Watermark* (gay and lesbian news)

Orlando Facts and Peculiarities Your Character Might Know

- Orlando's theme parks make it not only the number one tourist destination in the country, its annual forty-three million visitors make it the number one tourist destination in the world.
- Here are some of the area theme parks and attractions: Sea World, Universal Studios, Gatorland, Alligatorland Safari Zoo, Circus World, Splendid China, Medieval Times, King Henry's Feast, Wet 'n Wild, Fun 'n' Wheels, Ripley's Believe It or Not!, Cypress Gardens, and a little place off Route 4 called Walt Disney World.
- The area is dotted with hundreds of lakes, from humble Clear Lake to huge Lake Apopka.
- Although average temperatures range from the low fifties at night in the winter to the mid-nineties during the day in summer, inland summers are very humid, without the ocean breezes that "cool" many other parts of Florida into the low nineties.
- The boy bands O-Town, Backstreet Boys and 'N Sync all got their starts here.
- Other celebrities from Orlando include Tiger Woods, Wesley Snipes, Mandy Moore, and Shamu, the killer whale.
- This is the center of the citrus belt in Florida. From the car window, you can see rows and rows of rounded trees shoot off into the horizon.
- Cattle are also an important agricultural product. There are hundreds of small ranches in this part of the state. Many are located, not coincidentally, near dinner theaters.
- Orlando has a strong concentration and commitment to aerospace and electronics industries. A lot of the economy is dependent on them.
- Forty-three percent of the population works in tourist-related jobs (for hotels, restaurants, theme parks, the airport, the Dumbo ride, and so on).

If Your Character . . .

If Your Character Is a Trendsetter, she lives in Thornton Park. Lots of newly renovated houses, fashionable shops, and fun restaurants make this one of the hippest and most sought-after areas in Orlando.

If Your Character Is Crazy About Theme Parks, he lives in Bay Hill. Just minutes from Universal Studios, Sea World, Wet 'n Wild, and Ripley's Believe it or Not, there's never a dull (or quiet) moment—except, of course, on the golf course.

If Your Character Is a Culture Maven, she lives in Winter Park. Lots of trees, nice old houses, parks, theaters, and museums characterize this old suburb of Orlando. (That is, old for Orlando; it was founded in 1887.)

If Your Character Is a Family Man, he lives in Altamonte Springs. Just north of the Orlando city limits, it makes for an easy commute. Altamonte Springs is notable for its parks and schools and total suburbanization.

If Your Character Is Down-and-Out, he lives in Pine Hills, west of downtown. It's really the area between Pine Hills and downtown Orlando that's the poorest. Many Caribbean immigrants have taken up residence here, and some have been able to establish small businesses, but in general this is Orlando's down-and-out section.

If Your Character Works in the Citrus Industry, she lives in Winter Garden (not to be confused with Winter Park). Hundreds of people involved in the packing and juicing sectors live and work here.

If Your Character Is a Recent Immigrant From Elsewhere in the World, he lives on Oak Ridge Road, west of Orange Blossom Trail. This long street is lined with the businesses and homes of people from Asia, Africa, and the Middle East.

Local Grub Your Character Might Love

Did somebody say Applebees? Chain restaurants are the norm here, as in most of Florida, but the enormous influx of international visitors has left its mark on the restaurant scene. Orlando residents have easy access to the seafood (big sea fish, shrimp, crabs) that most Floridians enjoy, in addition to the catfish, bass, perch, and scampi that splash through the surrounding lakes. The steaks produced from local cattle ranches also are widely lauded.

This is the heart of citrus country, and oranges and grapefruit are plentiful. Some of the best oranges are actually green; most of these are dyed before shipping, but locals eat them in all their verdant splendor.

Interesting and Peculiar Places to Set a Scene

- **The Beacham Theater.** This movie house on Orange Street was built in the 1920s. It later hosted musical acts and is currently the Tabu nightclub. And one more thing: It's HAUNTED!!
- **The Walk of Fame on the campus of Rollins College in Winter Park.** The five hundred stones that border the Mills Lawn are inscribed with the names of famous people from various fields of endeavor. The college itself is located at the end of Park Avenue, the sedate and fashionable main thoroughfare of Winter Park.
- **Orange Avenue.** This is the main street downtown, site of flashy new skyscrapers, Egyptian revival buildings, and, because it's Florida, plenty of Art Deco facades.
- **Orange Blossom Trail.** With plenty of nice and not-so-nice hotels in the area, this is by far Orlando's red-light district (although nobody in town will admit it!).
- **A boat in Lake Harris in the Mount Dora neighborhood.** Here's a real Florida pastime for a lazy evening: The sun sets slowly on the egrets and the alligators and you. Finally, it's cooling off out here . . .
- **A rodeo.** These are popular in the area around Kissimmee (accent on the second syllable), and the locals south of Orlando love a good bull session.
- **Walt Disney World.** The resort is divided into several sections: The Magic Kingdom (Main Street USA, Adventureland ["Pirates of the Caribbean"], Frontierland ["Country Bear Jamboree"], Fantasyland ["It's a Small World"], Tomorrowland ["Space Mountain", MGM Studios), EPCOT Center (comprising the somewhat-educational Future World and World Showcase), and the largest of the theme parks, Disney's Animal Kingdom, which features real African wildlife as well as genuine fabricated unicorns and dinosaurs.
- **A hot air balloon ride over the theme parks.** Have your character go vertical and then look down on the really small people in the world. Great for a broad view of the parks.

Exceptionally Grand Things Your Character Is Proud Of

- More people come to Orlando to vacation every year than to any other place in the world.
- Magic Coach Doc Rivers.

For Further Research

Books

Married to the Mouse: Walt Disney World and Orlando,
   by Richard E. Foglesong
The Other Orlando, by Kelly Monaghan
Orlando: The City Beautiful, by Glenda E. Hood et al.
Orlando: Sunshine Sonata, edited by Mike Thomas et al.

Web Sites

www.cityoforlando.net (local government)
www.downtownorlando.com (downtown in the city of
   Orlando)

www.orlandoonline.com (flashy city site)
www.orlandosentinel.com (main newspaper)
www.orlando-times.com (African-American newspaper)
www.orlandoweekly.com (alternative weekly)

Still Curious? Why Not Check Out

Bellemere, by Walter G. Allen Jr.
Cross-Check, by Janice Law
Lassus, by Jerome Roche
A Matter of Perspective, by Kevin Robinson
Street Level, by Bob Truluck

A Pathetically Sad Thing Your Character Is Ashamed Of

• This is where the whole boy-band thing unleashed itself on an unwary America.

Your Character Loves

• Fun, fun, fun!
• Golf, golf, golf!

• Citrus and sunshine.
• Weekend getaways to diverse amusements.
• The Orlando Magic (basketball).
• Fishing.
• Low-humidity days.

Your Character Hates

• Tourist drivers—they stink.
• That Orlando is deemed a tourist town and little else.

Tampa

Tampa Facts and Peculiarities Your Character Might Know

- Tampa is Florida's third largest city, after Jacksonville and Miami. It's located in Hillsborough County, across Tampa Bay from St. Petersburg.
- Tampa has the seventh largest port in the United States.
- Much of the architecture reflects the Art Deco style popular throughout Florida. Most houses are no more than one story.
- In the 1880s, railroad mogul Henry B. Plant completed a train route to Tampa from Richmond, Virginia.
- Plant also built the Tampa Bay Hotel to lure tourists. It's still around, although it's now part of the University of Tampa campus. Its silver minarets create an unusual outline in the cityscape.
- Tampa has a long history as a military outpost. It was a base of operations during the Spanish-American War (1898), with thousands of soldiers setting up camp here, including Teddy Roosevelt and his Rough Riders. Clara Barton, founder of the American Red Cross, established a hospital. Winston Churchill, a journalist at the time, reported on the war while staying at the Tampa Bay Hotel.
- There is a U.S. Operations Command headquartered at the nearby MacDill Air Force Base.
- Radio evangelism got its start here in the 1930s.
- Busch Gardens began as a minor attraction for people who'd just finished a tour of Busch Brewery.
- Hillsborough County is famous for its strawberries, and nearby Plant City is the site of a huge annual strawberry festival.

Tampa Basics That Shape Your Character

Tampa's skyline

Population: 303,000

Prevalent Religions: Various denominations of Christianity

Top Employers: Verizon Florida, Bank of America, St. Joseph's Hospital, TECO Energy, Citigroup, Caspers Company, Busch Gardens, University of South Florida, Walter Industries Inc., University of Tampa

Per Capita Income: $27,304

Average Daily Temperature: January, 60° F; July, 82° F

Ethnic Makeup (in percent): Caucasians 79.4%, African-American 10%, Hispanic 8.6%, Asian 1.6%, Native American .3%, Other 2.3%

Newspapers: *Tampa Tribune, Tampa Bay Business Journal, St. Petersburg Times*

If Your Character . . .

If Your Character Smells of Money, he lives in Culbreath Isles. This area is filled with massive homes overlooking the Bay and plenty of yacht owners. Or Golfview: For the country club set, huge houses set among leafy suburban landscapes. Or Bayshore. Home prices range from one to six million dollars. No loitering, please.

If Your Character Is All About Business, she lives on Davis Island. This artificial island was built in the 1920s. Its nice houses are next to the downtown business district.

If Your Character Is a Family Man, he lives in Westchase. This well-off community is allegedly more environmentally friendly than most neighborhoods.

If Your Character Wears a Blue Collar at Work, she lives in the Downtown Area. No need to transfer buses on the way to the cigar factory or the dock.

If Your Character Is Retired, he lives in St. Petersburg. This is across the Bay.

For Further Research

Books

The Immigrant World of Ybor City: Italians and Their Latin Neighbors in Tampa, 1885–1985, by George E. Pozzetta and Gary R. Mormino

Politics and Growth in Twentieth-Century Tampa, by Robert J. Kerstein et al.

Tampa: A Pictorial History, by Hampton Dunn

Things Remembered: An Album of African-Americans in Tampa, compiled by Rowena Ferrell Brady

Web Sites

www.eflorida.com/all_facts.html (info about each county)

www.tampagov.net (city of Tampa government)

www.tampachamber.com (chamber of commerce)

www.tampatrib.com (*Tampa Tribune*)

www.pewcenter.org/doingcj/research/r_ST2000tampa1.html (an extensive survey of Tampa residents in which they express their opinions on everything from education to crime to the moral state of the nation)

Still Curious? Why Not Check Out

Bodies in the Bay, by Mason L. Ramsey

Tampa Review, literary journal of the University of Tampa

Local Grub Your Character Might Love

Seafood, especially shrimp. Mullet and grouper are traditionally fried, but options now include grilling, poaching, or smoking. Crabs are in season from mid-October to mid-May. Fried alligator isn't too hard to find. Steak houses are ubiquitous.

Interesting and Peculiar Places to Set a Scene

- **Bern's Steak House.** A local eatery noted for its funeral parlor decor and extensive wine list.
- **Tampa Port Authority.** Tanker pilots from all over the world pass through town while dropping off bananas or picking up the shrimp catch.
- **Busch Gardens.** Lions and tigers and gators! Busch Gardens is divided into: Serengeti (free-roaming animals), Nairobi (petting zoo), Timbuktu (rides, plus a somewhat incongruous German beer hall called the Festhaus), and Congo (more roller coasters).
- **Nick Bollettieri Tennis Academy (in Bradenton, to the south).** This has served as a training ground for such tennis greats as Andre Agassi, Monica Seles, Jim Courier, and Anna Kournikova.
- **The Florida State Fair.** It's held here in February. Check out the size of that pig!
- **The Gasparilla Invasion.** This is also held in February. Locals dress up as puffy-sleeved pirates as they steer the *Jose Gasparilla*, decked out in colorful flags and blasting its cannons, to the mouth of the Hillsborough River. Pirates lead the parade through downtown.
- **Ybor City.** Over 500 million cigars are rolled here each year.

Exceptionally Grand Things Your Character Is Proud Of

- MacDill Air Force Base played a major role as a military post in the Gulf War.
- The business district has been revitalized in the past twenty years.
- The Tampa Aquarium.

Pathetically Sad Things Your Character Is Ashamed Of

- International freighter traffic has polluted the bay and beaches of Tampa; neighboring St. Petersburg, Pinellas County, and Sarasota have the nice beaches.
- Seddon Island development.
- Transiency—too many people come and go without staying.
- Tampa's crime rate. Over two hundred people are murdered annually.

Your Character Loves

- Canoeing in Hillsborough River State Park.
- Gorgeous sunsets.
- Golf.
- Tampa Bay Buccaneers (football).
- Tampa Bay Devil Rays (baseball).
- Tampa Bay Lightning (hockey).
- Tampa Bay Mutiny (soccer).

Your Character Hates

- The encroaching sprawl.
- That the beach downtown is no good anymore.

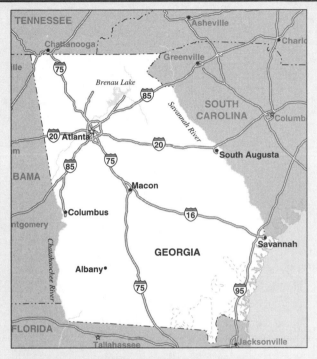

Significant Events Your Character Has Probably Thought About

- The Battle of Bloody Marsh in 1742. Although he declared Georgia a settlement in 1733, General James Oglethorpe had to defeat the Spanish in 1742 for permanent control over the area.
- The Trail of Tears. Thousands of Cherokees were forced from their homes and imprisoned in camps, until they were ultimately sent on a thousand-mile march westward. Four thousand of them died.
- Georgia became the fourth state to join the Confederacy (1861).
- The burning of Atlanta by General William Tecumseh Sherman in 1864. Sherman and his Union troops torched Atlanta and then moved on to capture Savannah in his famous March to the Sea.
- Jefferson Franklin Long's two-year term in the House of Representatives. Although his time in Congress was short (from 1869 to 1871), Franklin was the first African-American to serve in the House.
- On April 20, 1868, Atlanta became Georgia's capital.
- In 1886, Dr. John Pemberton of Atlanta invented Coca-Cola.
- On February 25, 1948, nineteen-year-old Martin Luther King Jr. was ordained associate minister at Ebenezer Baptist Church in Atlanta.
- The 1974 murder of Alberta Williams King. Martin Luther King Jr.'s mother was gunned down during services at the same Ebenezer Baptist Church in which her son had been ordained.
- Jimmy Carter's election as president in 1976.
- The December 2001 shooting of DeKalb County sheriff-elect Derwin Brown, who was slain in his driveway shortly after telling thirty-eight county workers that their jobs were in jeopardy.

Georgia Facts and Peculiarities Your Character Might Know

- The sweet and famous Vidalia onion has been successfully grown only in the fields around Vidalia and Glennville.
- Georgia was the last of the first thirteen original colonies.

Georgia Basics That Shape Your Character

Motto: Wisdom, Justice, and Moderation

Population: 8.18 million

Prevalent Religions: Christianity, particularly Southern Baptist, Lutheran, Pentecostal, and Roman Catholic

Major Industries: Paper products, chemical products, electric equipment, tourism, poultry and eggs, peanuts, cattle, hogs, dairy products, vegetables, textiles and apparel, transportation equipment, food processing

Ethnic Makeup (in percent): Caucasian 65.1%, African-American 28.7%, Hispanic 5.3%, Asian 2.1%, Native American 0.3%, Other 2.4%

Famous Georgians: B-52s, Black Crowes, Jim Brown, Erskine Caldwell, Jimmy Carter, Ray Charles, Ty Cobb, Charles Coburn, James Dickey, Lawrence Fishburne, Newt Gingrich, Amy Grant, Joel Chandler Harris, Larry Holmes, Holly Hunter, Indigo Girls, Little Richard, Martin Luther King Jr., Carson McCullers, Johnny Mercer, Margaret Mitchell, Flannery O'Connor, Otis Redding, Burt Reynolds, REM, Julia Roberts, Jackie Robinson, RuPaul, Dean Rusk, Janelle Taylor, Clarence Thomas, Travis Tritt, Alice Walker, Trisha Yearwood

- Cordele knows a good melon when it sees one—it's deemed the "Watermelon Capital of the World."
- Georgia is known as "The Peach State," "The Cracker State," and "The Empire State of the South."
- President Franklin D. Roosevelt chose "The Little White House" in Warm Springs as his second home so he could soak in its healing, hot-spring waters. He died here in 1945.
- The city of Rome can brag about Marshall Forest, the only natural forest within city limits in the country.
- Georgia has flown six flags in its history: England, Spain, Liberty, Georgia, the Confederate States of America, and the United States. Hence the amusement park, Six Flags Over Georgia.
- Plains is the hometown of Jimmy Carter.
- Georgia is the largest state east of the Mississippi River.
- Springer Mountain is the southern terminus on the Appalachian Trail.
- Georgians have a variety of accents, from the nasally twang of the mountain folk to the southern drawl of the farmers to the polite and soft-spoken lilt of inhabitants from the older, wealthier areas along the coast.

Your Character's Food and Drink

Barbecue stands and restaurants still cook the whole pig. The meat is pulled off the bone for sandwiches, and the ribs are deliciously tender; both meat and ribs are bathed in a mouth-watering tangy sauce. Brunswick stew is a typical side dish.

Things Your Character Likes to Remember

- Taking the family to Six Flags Over Georgia.
- The Etowah Mounds Historic Site in Cartersville.

Atlanta's skyline at sunset

© PhotoDisc/Getty Images

- The Chieftains. They have their own museum in Rome (Georgia, not Italy).
- Macon's Wesleyan College was the first college in the states to offer degrees to women (1836).
- Stone Mountain boasts the largest sculpture in the world, honoring Confederate heroes Jefferson Davis, Stonewall Jackson, and Robert E. Lee.
- Georgia produces more peanuts, pecans, and peaches than does any other state.
- Georgia has a varied landscape, with the Appalachian foothills in the north, beautiful coastal areas in the east, swamps in the south, and soil-rich fields in the center.
- Eli Whitney's creation of the cotton gin. Although from Connecticut, Whitney was in Savannah tutoring at a nearby plantation when he came up with his great invention, which led to Savannah becoming a major cotton producer.
- The Hawkinsville Civitan Club's Annual Shoot the Bull Barbecue Championship. With their mouth-watering barbecue recipes in hand, southerners from all over converge on this Georgia town to partake in a big 'n' beefy cook-off. What's best is that the funds raised go toward finding a cure for Down's syndrome.

Things Your Character Would Like to Forget

- Slavery.
- The Trail of Tears.
- Sherman's March to the Sea, during which he ravaged much of the state.
- Andersonville Prison. This infamous Civil War prison existed for only fourteen months but confined more than forty-five thousand Union solders, of which nearly thirteen thousand died (from disease, malnutrition, or exposure to the elements).
- The bomb set off during the 1988 Summer Olympics in Atlanta.
- Ray Brent Marsh, the owner of the Tri-State Crematory crematorium in Noble. It's hard to forget this guy; he's the one who in 2002 was arrested for dumping hundreds of corpses into a lake instead of doing his job and cremating them.

Myths and Misperceptions About Georgia

- **Peanuts and peaches are the only foods that come out of Georgia.** Wrong. Each year Georgia hosts the Inter-

For Further Research

Books

Beyond Atlanta: The Struggle for Racial Equality in Georgia, 1940–1980, by Stephen G. N. Tuck

The Condemnation of Little B, by Elaine Brown

A Dream of a Tattered Man: Stories From Georgia's Death Row, by Randolph Loney and Will D. Campbell

An Education in Georgia: Charlayne Hunter, Hamilton Holmes, and the Integration of the University of Georgia, by Calvin Trillin

Georgia Ghosts, by Nancy Roberts

Growing Up Cuban in Decatur, Georgia, by Carmen Agra Deedy

Highbrows, Hillbillies, and Hellfire: Public Entertainment in Atlanta 1880–1930, by Steve Goodson

Negrophobia: A Race Riot in Atlanta, 1906, by Mark Bauerlein

One Family, by Vaughn Sills

Recasting: Gone With the Wind in American Culture, edited by Darden Asbury Pyron

Time to Reconcile: The Odyssey of a Southern Baptist, by Grace Bryan Holmes

Whisper to the Black Candle: Voodoo, Murder, and the Case of Anjette Lyles, by Jaclyn Weldon White

Web Sites

www.state.ga.us/ (official state site)

www.georgia.org/ (Georgia tourism)

www.savannahnow.com/ (Savannah news)

www.tybeemsc.com/ (coastal marine info)

www.cviog.uga.edu/Projects/gainfo/gahist.htm (state history)

www.georgiawriters.org/ (writer's organization)

Still Curious? Why Not Check Out

Athens, GA—Inside/Out

Blindsighted, by Karin Slaughter

Delirium of the Brave, by William C. Harris Jr.

Glory

The Legend of Bagger Vance

Literary Savannah, edited by Patrick Allen

Midnight in the Garden of Good and Evil

Midnight in the Garden of Good and Evil, by John Berendt

Monster's Ball

Roots, by Alex Haley

---

national Poultry Trade Show, the largest poultry convention in the world.

- **Farming products like cotton are what make Georgia a leading agricultural state.** Actually, Georgia leads the nation in the production of paper and board, tufted textile products, and, of course, processed chicken.

- **Georgia produces more peaches than any other state.** Not so. Both California and South Carolina out-produce "The Peach State."

Interesting Places to Set a Scene

- **Athens.** This nineteenth-century college town is home to the University of Georgia and several splendid architectural gems. It's also known for its botanical garden, its art museum, and its musicians, including the likes of REM, the B-52s and the Indigo Girls.

- **Atlanta.** (See page 87.)

- **Augusta.** The state's third oldest city (and capital from 1785 to 1795), Augusta is most famous today for hosting the Masters Golf Tournament each April. Augusta's riverwalk makes for a most romantic saunter, and its Olde Town is a classy neighborhood punctuated with several antebellum and Victorian homes.

- **Clayton.** A small mountain community that can boast of being the gateway to the "Grand Canyon of the East," Tallulah Gorge (a yawning canyon only second in depth to the Grand Canyon in Arizona). Loaded with flea markets, boutiques, folk art, art and antique shops, artists and nature lovers, Clayton is a bohemian character's gem of a hometown.

- **Donhelson.** Site of the nation's first gold rush in 1828, this is a typical example of a small Georgia town, with a central cobblestoned square and an old-time county courthouse.

- **Macon.** What make Macon visually unique are the 100,000 flowering Japanese cherry trees rubbing elbows with the homes of the antebellum South. This city was home to poet Sidney Lanier, who had a bridge named in his honor in 1956. The city also boasts of its music heritage. It has the Georgia Music Hall of Fame and is home to Otis Redding, The Allman Brothers Band, Little Richard, and others. It's home to the Harriet Tubman African-American Museum as well.

- **Madison.** Known as "the town Sherman refused to burn" and once called "the most cultured and aristocratic town on the stagecoach route from Charleston to New Orleans," Madison is a blast from the past. It has stately mansions, colonial homes, wide lawns, and enormous oak trees draped in Spanish moss. The brick-sidewalked town square is as it's been for years, making it an ideal place for a walk down memory lane.

- **The Okefenokee Swamplands.** With its cypress trees, canals, bogs, gators, and singing birds, the 400,000-acre Okefenokee Wildlife Refuge is a natural wonder and a sanctuary for numerous flora and fauna, many of which are endangered.

- **Savannah.** You're probably not going to outdo the popularity of what locals simply call "The Book" (John Berendt's *Midnight in the Garden of Good and Evil*), but Savannah still can be a treasure trove as the setting for your story. Founded in 1733, Savannah is Georgia's oldest city and, not coincidentally, has the country's largest historic district (two and a half square miles), with over twenty cobblestone squares, huge southern mansions, plentiful gardens, quaint boutiques, and city parks with oaks draped in Spanish moss. A great walking city with a wonderful waterfront to boot.

- **The one-hundred-mile Eastern Coast.** Georgia's entire Atlantic coast, from the Savannah River in the north to the St. Mary's River in the south, is a series of golden-nugget beaches and islands. The seaside and island communities offer a great combination of Piedmont southern belles and hard-core, weathered fisherman. The homes and grounds are just awesome. Much of *The Legend of Bagger Vance*, for example, was filmed on Jekyll Island and in Savannah.

Atlanta Facts and Peculiarities Your Character Might Know

- Atlanta today is a fairly clean city thanks to the beautification that took place for the 1996 Summer Olympics.
- Homelessness is pervasive and visible here, especially along Peachtree Avenue.
- The city is socioeconomically segregated: The north is primarily Caucasian and upper income, while poorer African-American communities live in the south. There doesn't seem to be much of a middle class.
- Interstate ramp numbers are strange here—they don't correspond to mile markers but are numbered sequentially (one ramp may be labeled Exit 5 and another labeled Exit 6, but twenty miles might be between them).
- Although it's a big city, Atlanta seems small because of its friendly, down-home feel. Strangers will greet others on the street and exchange pleasantries at grocery stores, the bank, the barber, and so on.
- When someone says "MARTA," they're referring to the public transit system: Metropolitan Atlanta Rapid Transit Authority.
- MARTA is a poor public transit system—it's not reliable, and it doesn't encompass much of the expansive city.
- Almost everyone owns a car here, especially in the suburbs, because there's no mass transit system allowing people to get downtown.
- Much of Atlanta's population is transient—people come and stay for a short while and then they go elsewhere.
- Atlanta's downtown area is fairly dead after business hours.
- It's definitely the melting pot of the South, with many Asians and Hispanics, so people of different ethnicities naturally interact with each other.
- That said, you'll still hear good ol' southernisms like "hun," "y'all," and "fixin'."
- Atlanta is one of the few major cities that doesn't rest near a major body of water.
- On and around the Georgia Tech campus, it's quite common to hear people say, "To Hell With Georgia."

Atlanta Basics That Shape Your Character

Heading into the city

Population: 416,474

Prevalent Religions: Christianity, particularly Southern Baptist, Lutheran, Pentecostal, and Roman Catholic, also Buddhist

Top Employers: Delta Airlines, BellSouth, U.S. Postal Service, Wal-Mart, AT&T, Lucent Technologies, Hewlett-Packard, Scientific Atlanta, Equifax, Electronic Data Systems, Emory University, CNN, Worldspan, McKesson HBOC Inc., NCR Corporation, NOVA Corporation, ALLTEL Corporation, Compaq

Per Capita Income: $45,473

Average Daily Temperature: January, 41, F; July, 79, F

Ethnic Makeup (in percent): Caucasian 33.2%, African-American 61.4%, Hispanic 4.5%, Asian 1.9%, Native American 0.2%, Other 3.2%

Newspapers and Magazines: *The Atlanta Journal-Constitution, Atlanta Magazine, Atlanta Jewish Times, Atlanta Daily World, Southern Voice, Atlanta Business Chronicle, Atlanta Catalyst, Atlanta Tribune, Atlanta Parent, Our Kids Atlanta*

Free Weekly Alternative Paper: *Creative Loafing*

Don't worry, they're not bad-mouthing their state; they're talking about their greatest rival, the University of Georgia.

If Your Character . . .

If Your Character Is Alternative or Grungy, he's hanging out in Little Five Points. This is the hip section of town for the young, alternative crowd—it's eclectic, with small-scale concert venues, bars, ethnic foods, local markets (not grocery stores!), and small shops of all sorts.

If Your Character Is Trendy, she's shopping in Buckhead. This area is home to high-end boutiques, upscale salons (offering massages, herbal wraps, and all-day spas), upper-middle-class Caucasians, beautiful homes, and old money.

If Your Character Smells of Old Money, he lives in Jones-borough or Newnan. These areas south of the city have big plantation homes with deep southern roots and wealth. *Gone With The Wind* was filmed here, and, yes, Margaret Mitchell herself even lived in one of the areas.

If Your Character Is a Rich Computer Geek, he lives in Virginia Highlands. This is one chic area, with bars, restaurants, residential apartments and lofts, and those on the cutting edges of technology. He might also live in Midtown, depending on his taste.

If Your Character's Got a Thing for Sweet Soda, she's hanging out at World of Coca-Cola. Atlanta is the birth-place—in 1892—of this world-famous beverage. At the museum today, your caffeinated character can try Coke products from around the world and explore all the old classic bottles, signs, billboards, bottle openers, and commercials.

If Your Character Is a Middle-Class Family Man, he lives in Marietta. This large suburb is more upper to middle class. It's north of the city, and if your character lives here he probably has one or two SUVs or minivans in his driveway and a swing set in his backyard.

If Your Character Wears a Blue Collar at Work, she lives in College Park or Eastpoint. Actually, anywhere in the south end of the city is blue collar, with lots of row houses and small yards.

Local Grub Your Character Might Love

Atlantans love typical southern food, of course, but these days Atlanta offers your character just about any-thing he wants to dig his teeth into. People here brag like crazy about Mellow Mushroom, which they say has pizza better than the best in Chicago. Fellini's Pizza is a chain with about half a dozen locations in the city (open late). The Kudzu Café allegedly has the best smoked pork chops in town. The Aurora Coffeehouse is a meager but favorite local hangout. Both the Sun Dial Restaurant and Bar in the Westin Hotel and the Polaris at the Hyatt Regency are revolving, overpriced restaurants with great views of the city. The Casbah is a favorite local Moroccan Restaurant, if your character likes belly dancers and tarot card readings with his meal. The Buckhead Diner is not only the place to eat but also the place to be seen in Atlanta. The Horseradish Grill is known for its meaty contemporary southern cuisine. Finally, The Varsity offers some of the best dogs, burgers, onion rings, grease, and atmosphere in the city—a greasy spoon if there ever was one.

Interesting and Peculiar Places to Set a Scene

- **A Cappella Books.** When your character feels like flipping through lots of old dust jackets or finding an out-of-print book, she should be here. There's even a special section of the store devoted to the Beat Generation.
- **Buckhead.** Locals call it the Beverly Hills of Atlanta (both Elton John and the governor have mansions here), and this is where your underprivileged character might go to fantasize about what it's like to have lots of money.
- **CNN Studios.** Sure, it's touristy and a major plug for Ted Turner and company, but this place is impressive. Have your character take a guided tour of the studios, as he watches behind-the-scenes filming of this global news network that broadcasts to millions of viewers daily. He can also have lunch at the food court and catch some of the anchors ingesting a meal in between shifts.
- **Criminal Records.** With a name like this it's no surprise Criminals has more than CDs. The store specializes in small-label CDs, magazines, and comics, and it even has books!
- **Cyclorama.** Before moving pictures captured scenes, people used to paint them. This impressive wide-angle view is a series of paintings—or one big painting, depending on how you look at it—of the Battle of Atlanta. Atlanta is a living phoenix, having risen

For Further Research

Books

Atlanta and Environs, by Harold H. Martin

Atlanta Architecture: Art Deco to Modern Classic, 1929–1959, by Richard M. Craig

Atlanta History: A Journal of Georgia and the South, edited by Andy Ambrose

Atlanta Walks: A Comprehensive Guide to Walking, Running, and Bicycling the Area's Scenic and Historic Locales, by Ren and Helen Davis

Atlanta, 1847–1890: City Building in the Old South and the New, by James M. Russell

Henry Grady's New South: Atlanta, a Brave and Beautiful City, by Harold E Davis

Race and the Shaping of Twentieth-Century Atlanta, by Ronald H. Bayor

Regime Politics: Governing Atlanta, 1946–1988, by Clarence N. Stone

Requiem for a Lost City: A Memoir of Civil War Atlanta and the Old South, by Sarah Conley Clayton and Robert Scott Davis Jr.

Web Sites

www.accessatlanta.com/ajc/ (*The Atlanta Journal-Constitution*)

www.atlanta.com/ (local guide)

http://atlanta.indymedia.org/ (Atlanta's independent media site)

www.ci.atlanta.ga.us/ (official city site)

www.atlhist.org/ (Atlanta History Center)

www.atlhist.org/WhatsNew/html/atlantahistory.htm (history)

Still Curious? Why Not Check Out

Atlanta, by Sara Orwig

Atlanta Graves, by Ruth Birmingham

Atlanta Heat, by Robert Coram

Benjamin Smoke

Dawn's Early Light: Ralph McGill and the Segregated South

Deliverance

Imagineering Atlanta, by Charles Rutheiser

A Man in Full, by Tom Wolfe

The Players Club

Ralph McGill: A Biography, by Barbara Barksdale Clause

The Visitor, by Sheri S. Tepper

---

from the ashes into something quite splendid. General William Tecumseh Sherman could be rolling in his grave.

- **Fadó.** An upper-income Irish character will inevitably be caught here, as this Buckhead Irish Pub rings of clanking pints of Guinness, loud drunken Irishmen, and old Irish songs.
- **Olympic Park.** As your character strolls through this twenty-one-acre park, her memories will be jolted back to the 1996 Summer Olympics, when several great moments occurred but also when the bomb went off. It's in the heart of downtown.
- **The Atlanta Botanical Gardens.** These southerners love their gardens, and this place is no exception—if anything, it is exceptional. And it even has big birds and colorful butterflies.
- **The Fox Theater.** No other theater in Atlanta is as legendary as The Fox. Originally built in the 1920s as the Yaarab Temple Shrine Mosque (headquarters of the Shriners organization), this historic theater is a city landmark.
- **The Masquerade.** This huge, multilevel club has various dance floors, pool tables, and bars. It's perfect for a younger character who likes hanging around other Goths and folks with tattoos and piercings who listen to alternative rock and dance all night.
- **Underground Atlanta.** Lots of shops, boutiques, cobblestone, locals, tourists, and folks of all ethnicities can be found here—and it's all underground (hence the name). Your character could spend hours shopping and dining here, and candy shops offer the best samples of tasty southern treats.
- **Little Five Points.** Part business community and part neighborhood, this is by far the coolest, hippest spot in Atlanta, some say in the entire South. Bohemians and grungers hang out with those involved in the arts and theater. A very eclectic crowd in a very interesting area (bars, cafés, galleries, etc.).

Exceptionally Grand Things Your Character Is Proud Of

- Its southern heritage.
- The 1996 Summer Olympics.
- Sports greats like Hank Aaron, Dale Murphy, Greg Maddux, and Dominique Wilkins.
- Education—Georgia Tech is deemed one of best schools in the South, and Spelman, Morehouse, and Clark-Atlanta are some of the premier African-American institutions in the country.
- It's still a very friendly city.
- It's had both a black female police chief (Beverly J. Harvard) and mayor (Shirley Franklin)—Martin Luther King Jr. would be proud.

Pathetically Sad Things Your Character Is Ashamed Of

- MARTA is a filthy public transit system.
- Traffic is jammed and rotten.
- Segregation.
- Atlanta is one of the most dangerous cities in the country thanks to the economic and racial tensions Atlanta has 2,729 violent crimes per year, and the U.S. city average is only 446.

Your Character Loves

- Zoo Atlanta.
- Martin Luther King Jr.—he went to college in Atlanta.
- Jimmy Carter—his library and museum are here.
- Georgia Tech football—John Heisman (people still brag about how his team, and the most treasured trophy in college football is named in his honor).
- The Underground, the city's favorite mall.
- The Coca-Cola Museum
- Ted Turner.
- Waffle House restaurants—they're all over the city.
- The University of Georgia or Georgia Tech—but definitely not both.

Your Character Hates

- General Sherman. He only torched the entire city. . . .
- The bombing during the 1996 Summer Olympics.
- Criticism. Atlantans are known for not handling verbal attacks on the city very well—residents get upset when someone from outside the city makes a negative comment about it.
- Traffic jams and all the associative honking.
- The University of Georgia or Georgia Tech—but definitely not both.

Hawaii

Significant Events Your Character Has Probably Thought About

- In 1778, James Cook discovered the Hawaiian Islands.
- Franklin Roosevelt was the first president to visit Hawaii, in 1934.
- The bombing of Pearl Harbor on December 7, 1941.
- Hawaii became the fiftieth state in 1959.
- Jack Lord and the *Hawaii Five-O* series was first shot here in 1969.
- The Kilauea volcano erupted in 1983 on The Big Island.
- John Waihee became the first U.S. governor of Hawaiian descent when he was elected in 1987.
- In 1992, Hurricane Iniki wreaked serious damaged to Kauai and parts of Oahu.
- President Bill Clinton apologized to Hawaiians for the 1893 overthrow of their kingdom.
- By winning the 1994 gubernatorial race, Ben Cayetano became the first governor of Philippine descent.
- Hawaii's last sugar plantation closed in 1995.
- In 1999, voters (well, only 8.7 percent, or nine thousand of them) elected to form the Hawaiian Convention, an "anti U.S. occupation" group that would establish state sovereignty.

Hawaii Facts and Peculiarities Your Character Might Know

- Hawaii has its own time zone (Hawaiian Standard Time).
- It is made up of eight different islands (Niihau, Kauai, Oahu, Molokai, Lanai, Kahoolawe, Maui, and Hawaii.)
- It is the "Aloha State."
- The wind blows east to west in Hawaii (unlike on the continent where it blows west to east).
- The state fish is—try saying this—the Humuumunukunukuapuaa (whomoo whomoo newkoo newkoo ah pu ah ah).
- Hawaii is really isolated from the rest of the world: It's 2,390 miles from California; 3,850 miles from Japan; 4,900 miles from China; and 5,280 miles from the Philippines.
- Hawaii is the only state in the nation that grows coffee.

Hawaii Basics That Shape Your Character

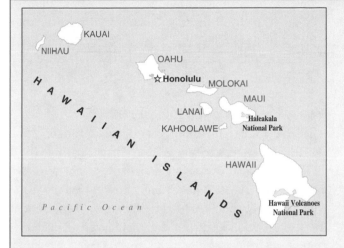

Motto: The Life of the the Land Is Perpetuated in Righteousness

Population: 1.2 million

Prevalent Religions: Christianity, mostly Roman Catholicism and Congregationalism, also Buddhism, Shinto, Hinduism, Taoism, Judaism, and Muslim

Major Industries: Sugarcane, pineapples, nursery stock, livestock, macadamia nuts, tourism, food processing, apparel, fabricated metal products, stone, clay, and glass products

Ethnic Makeup (in percent): Caucasian 24.3%, African-American 1.8%, Hispanic 7.2%, Asian 41.6%, Native American 0.3%, Other 1.3%

Famous Hawaiians: Tia Carrere, Steve Case, Don Ho, Bette Midler, Ellison Onizuka, Harold Sakata, James Shigeta, Don Stroud

- People greet each other with the *shaka,* a hand gesture in which the three middle fingers are folded into the palm while the thumb and pinky are extended. Then they give the hand a little wiggle.
- Hawaii supplies over one-third of the world's commercial supply of pineapples.
- Most of the world's macadamia nuts are grown in Hawaii.
- Most folks speak English, as that's the unifying language, but it's usually mixed with some form of Ha-

waiian (and there are several forms of Hawaiian).

- Some Hawaiian words and meanings: *Howzit?* ("come try"), *Ohana* ("family"), *Kine Grindz* ("local food"), *Brah* ("brother" or "buddy").
- Others include *Pau Hana* (pow-hahna), which means "work is finished"; *Mahalo* (many people think it means "trash" because it's on all the "rubbish" cans, but it means "thank-you"); *Kama'aina* ("local"), and this is also the discount that vendors and stores give to locals.

Your Character's Food and Drink

There are hundreds of different dishes throughout the islands. At home, sticky rice (rice that clumps together) is a main staple in the meals. Many Asian foods are mainstays here, such as various types of Japanese, Chinese, Korean, and Thai foods. Of course, Pacific Rim or Hawaiian regional cuisine is big and consists of combinations of grilled shrimp with taro chips, yellowfin tuna, and Peking duck in a gingery sauce (called *ginger-lilikoi*, meaning "passion fruit"). Sushi (called *poke*) is very popular. The luau, a traditional Hawaiian feast, is held on special occasions like baby christenings; most of the food served at luaus is not eaten at home, like poi (a paste from cooked taro corms, or roots), pig, and even pineapple. Local fruits and veggies such as mangos, papayas, coconuts, bananas, breadfruit, oranges, strawberry guavas, thimbleberries, mountain apples, Methley plums, and avocados are everywhere. As for local eateries, Zippy's is practically on every corner in Honolulu, and Sam Choy's has a great reputation but is a little pricey. Hawaiian-made fruit juices are the drinks. Favorite drinks with alcohol include fruity wine and beer and, of course, tropical drinks like piña colada, mai tai, and blue Hawaii.

Things Your Character Likes to Remember

- The islands themselves. Anywhere on any island, around almost every corner, is an excellent view. If you go hiking into the mountains, you get the rain forest feel without all the strange animals.
- The Aloha spirit. By law Hawaiians are required to make a conscious effort to adhere to the aloha spirit, which is the "coordination of mind and heart" and "each person must think and emote good feelings to others."
- Almost everyone here drives with aloha (consider-

ation and respect for fellow motorist). More often than not people casually drive below the speed limit, and you can always count on someone letting you over. Stick a *shaka* sign out the window, and the person in the other lane will slam on his brakes to let you over. Just remember to give a little *Mahalo* wave to thank him afterward.

- The beauty of the oceans and beaches. Compared to California beaches, Hawaii beaches are clean and beautiful.
- The University of Hawaii—it's the only major college in the state.
- Not working, and just hanging out at the beach, surfing, fishing, and eating instead.
- First birthdays. First-birthday parties are an all-out celebration—lots of food, games, prizes, more food, cake, and so on.

Things Your Character Would Like to Forget

- Corruption in the government. Hawaiian government officials are constantly being investigated for wrongdoing.
- Non-locals, unless they are tourists spending money.
- Speeders.
- The congested traffic.

Myths or Misperceptions About Hawaii

- **That the aloha spirit is everywhere.** It's only where the tourists are spending the money. The more money, the more aloha.
- **Waikiki Beach is the best beach on Oahu.** The prettier beaches actually are on the west side of the island, but locals like to keep them for themselves. Waikiki is one of the calmest beaches, but there are so many tourists that the beach tends to get dirtier than the others.
- **Hawaii only has beaches, not mountains.** Guess again. If it weren't for the volcanoes that created the extremely large mountains, there'd be no beautiful beaches because there'd be no Hawaiian Islands.

Interesting and Peculiar Places to Set a Scene

- **Ala Moana Mall.** This open-air mall has plenty of trendy shops, like Gucci and Neiman Marcus. There are also plenty of Hawaiian specialty shops pushing Hawaiian heritage jewelry and local knickknacks and mementos. Several surf shops are here as well.

What's interesting is that the parking lot is huge, due to the fact that most people drive. The lot is always filled with big buses transporting loads of tourists to and from Honolulu's largest mall.

- **Chinatown.** When your character steps foot in Honolulu's Chinatown, he'll think he's in, well, China (actually the area is filled with Asians of all sorts—Vietnamese, Thai, Filipino, Chinese, and so on). Few places in the states have such a concentrated array of temples and shrines, dragons and moon cakes, art galleries and antique shops, noodle factories and cheap peep shows.

- **Hawaii Kai.** Your wealthy character resides here in Honolulu's upscale neighborhood. Windy streets, relatively spacious yards (space is at a premium), and large houses make up this area. Most homes have brass gates in the front yard, lots of windows—and no cinder blocks! Asians are often seen as hired hands taking care of the grounds.

- **Honolulu.** Flashy office skyscrapers, Victorian homes, churches of all sorts, a New England missionary, and a grand royal palace all rub shoulders in this capital city. Outside of the busy streets, it's not uncommon to see canoers and kayakers hugging the coastline, drifting past suited businesspeople taking a lunch break on a pier as motorboats cruise in and out of the harbor. You could easily set a scene here or in one of the four green gardens around the city that make up the Honolulu Botanical Gardens. Then there's the Arizona Memorial, which commemorates the 1,100 who died during the bombing of Pearl Harbor. There's also the ever-popular, high-rise-hotel-filled, touristy Waikiki area.

- **Maui.** Home to Haleakala (Ha-lay-ah-ja-lah) Crater, the world's largest dormant volcano, Maui is where your character will go if she's a tourist and has an interest in the island's many famous attractions, from the Haleakala Crater to the old whaling town of Lahaina to the lovely road to Hana. Maui's Kaanapali Beach can't be matched for people-watching, especially international tourists with cash to spend on drinks and lazy fun in the sun.

- **Molokai.** The most "natural" Hawaiian Isle, Molokai, especially its east end, is a tropical rain forest (parts of the island get 240 inches of rainfall annually!). If your character really wants to get away from it all and experience natural Hawaii at is finest, it's here he should go. Have him make his home in one of the island's tent cabins and take to the Molokai Ranch Wildlife Park, which is a haven for many rare African and Indian animals.

- **Niihau.** This privately owned island is loaded with livestock. Nobody goes here, unless they make a helicopter landing. Only about 250 people populate this sixty-nine-square-mile isle.

- **The North Shore of Oahu.** This is surfer country. More surfers live and hang out here than line any beach in California. If your character is a beach bum or a surfer, he lives here in a small surfer shack or apartment. Nobody ever dresses up here; they all walk around in trunks, shorts, and sandals (or barefoot). Your character will be hard-pressed to find a man wearing a buttoned-up shirt. Surfers really do own this area of Honolulu, as evidenced by the big yellow "Surfer X-ing" signs (with a surfer guy icon) that dot the area.

- **The Wainea side (the west) of Oahu.** This entire west side of the island is very dry and not tropical. Most homes are small and made with corrugated tin roofs, and they are occupied by lots of native Hawaiians. There are no zoning laws here, so a nice, big home

Pu'uhonua o Honaunau Historical Park

For Further Research

Books

Fragments of Hawaiian History, as Recorded by John Pap Ii, edited by Dorothy B. Barrère

Hawaiian Dictionary, by Mary Kawena Pukui and Samuel H. Elbert

The Hawaiian Kingdom, by Ralph S. Kuykendall

Hawaiian Mythology, by Martha Warren Beckwith

Keneti: South Sea Adventures of Kenneth Emory, by Bob Krauss

Legacy of the Landscape, by Patrick Vinton Kirch

The Legends and Myths of Hawaii, by King David Kalakaua

Shoal of Time, by Gavan Daws

Surfer's Guide to Hawaii: Hawaii Gets All the Breaks, by Greg Ambrose

Web Sites

www.honoluluadvertiser.com/ (Honolulu news)

www.planet-hawaii.com (tourist info)

www.state.hi.us/ (official state site)

www.ascehawaii.org/heritage.html (history and heritage)

www.outinhawaii.com/ho.html (outdoor info)

www.ohananet.com/weblinks/art.htm (art and architecture)

http://starbulletin.com/ (news)

www.HawaiianKingdom.org (state sovereignty info)

Still Curious? Why Not Check Out

Baywatch Hawaii

Blue Hawaii

From Here to Eternity

Hawaii, by James A. Michener

A Hawaiian Reader, edited by A. Grove Day and Carl Stroven

Hawaii Five-0

Jurassic Park

Magnum P.I.

Pearl Harbor

Picture Bride

Raiders of the Lost Ark The Return of Lono, by O.A. Bushnell

Song of the Islands

Stories of Hawaii, by Jack London

Talking to the Dead and Other Stories, by Sylvia Watanabe

Tora! Tora! Tora!

Waterworld

can rest right next to one (or several) of the shanties. Most homes are on the ocean and at the foot of the mountain, rather than up on the hill (as with Pearl City).

- **Pearl City.** This is a typical middle-class Hawaiian neighborhood. Most homes are close together with hardly any side yards. Most are on steep hills with no lawns—maybe a patch of grass at most—and are almost always single level and made out of cinder blocks or "board 'n' batten" panel. There are no decks and no front porches. But since all the houses are on a hill, no matter where you live you get wonderful views of Pearl Harbor.

Significant Events Your Character Has Probably Thought About

- The Jesuits came here and established the Cataldo mission in the early 1840s; it still stands as the oldest structure in the state.
- Gold mining in the 1860s jump-started Idaho's economy.
- Idaho had to build its first major prison in 1872, which held inmates until the building was placed on the National Register of Historic Places in 1974.
- In 1879 the weekly *Idaho Enterprise* was first published (and the presses still keep turning every week).
- Spanning over one million acres in southeast Idaho, the Caribou National Forest was established as a natural refuge in 1907 by Teddy Roosevelt's administration.
- Idaho became the first state in the nation to elect a Jewish governor when Moses Alexander took office in 1914.
- Shelley held its first annual Spud Day in 1927; it's been going on since.
- In 1982 Idaho became the first state in the nation to outlaw the insanity plea for defendants.
- Democratic challenger Richard Stallings defeated incumbent George Hansen in 1984 in the closest Idaho congressional race in history; he won by a mere 170 votes.
- The 1992 "incident" at Ruby Ridge. U.S. Marshals and FBI and BATF agents assailed the home of Randy and Vicki Weaver, killing Vicki, son Sammy, and the family dog. In 1993 Randy Weaver was found innocent of weapon and murder charges; he and the surviving Weavers won $3.1 million in civil damages.

Idaho Facts and Peculiarities Your Character Might Know

- Idaho is home to several ghost towns, including Silver City, Yankee Fork, Gold Dredge, and the Sierra Silver Mine.
- Rigby claims it's "the birthplace of television," since local Philo Farnsworth was a pioneer of TV technology.
- *Spendy* means "expensive," as in, "That looks like a spendy set of boots ya got there."

Idaho Basics That Shape Your Character

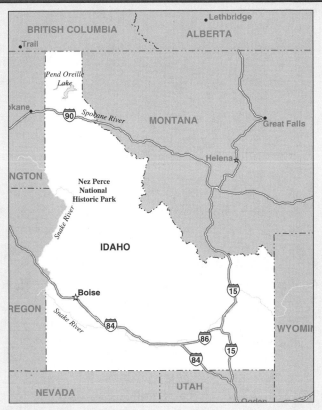

Motto: It Is Perpetual

Population: 1.29 million

Prevalent Religions: Christianity, especially Roman Catholic, Baptist, and Methodist, also a small portion of Lutheran, Presbyterian, and Church of Jesus Christ of Latter-day Saints, and even fewer Pentecostal and Episcopalian

Major Industries: Cattle, dairy goods, potatoes, hay, wheat, peas, beans, sugar beets, electronic and computer equipment, processed foods, lumber, chemical manufacturing, tourism

Ethnic Makeup (in percent): Caucasian 91.0%, African-American 0.4%, Hispanic 7.9%, Asian 0.9%, Native American 1.4%, Other 4.2%

Famous Idahoans: Gutzon Borglum, Carol Ryrie Brink, Frank F. Church, Fred Dubois, Vardis Fisher, Ezra Pound, Robert E. Smylie, Henry Spalding, Picabo Street, Lana Turner

- Idaho actually has a law that forbids one citizen to give another citizen a box of candy that weighs more than fifty pounds.
- Idaho is topographically diverse: Many mountains in Idaho reach elevations of around eight thousand feet, but then the terrain plummets to around fifteen hundred feet in Hells Canyon.
- The Lewis and Clark Highway (U.S. Highway 12) is the shortest route from the Midwest to the Pacific Coast and the longest highway within a national forest in the nation.
- With its 2.3 million acres and parts of six national forests, the Frank Church–River of No Return Wilderness Area is the largest wilderness area in the lower forty-eight states.
- People in Boise are active. These outdoorsy types show their physical fitness daily, particularly in the north end of Boise, where people of all ages get where they're going by peddling bikes instead of driving.
- It is typical for residents to own guns.
- Sun Valley has become a favorite home for Hollywooders, with the likes of Bruce Willis, Demi Moore, Jamie Lee Curtis, Tom Hanks, and Arnold Schwarzenegger taking up residences here.

Your Character's Food and Drink

People in Idaho like their meat and, you guessed it, potatoes. Beef is a staple, with beef jerky being a popular snack. Buffalo burgers are also consumed more here. Goldy's eggs Benedict has quite a reputation (Goldy's is a hip Boise breakfast place where there is always a line to get in), as does the prime rib at the Stage Coach Inn.

Things Your Character Likes to Remember

- Liberty and freedom. Idaho's laws rarely infringe on individual or property rights.
- Idaho's beautiful scenery and recreational opportunities (world-class skiing, kayaking, hiking, backpacking, fishing, whitewater rafting, snowmobiling, snowshoeing, and snowboarding).
- Randy Weaver and family. The Idaho public in general feels that the Weavers were heroic for exercising their individual rights and standing up to the feds.
- Family and religious values, particularly those set forth by the Church of Jesus Christ of Latter-day Saints (healthy lifestyle, personal achievement, friendship, service, and family).

- Boise is deemed a great place to raise kids; it has a multitude of city parks, Zoo Boise, and a low crime rate.
- When Evil Knievel tried (and failed) to jump the Snake River Canyon near Twin Falls.
- Only one highway (a two-laner at that) connects northern and southern Idaho.
- Ernest Hemingway wrote parts of *For Whom the Bell Tolls* in Sun Valley.
- The Sawtooth Mountains.
- Mountain biking, running, or hiking in the Boise Foothills.
- Cross-country skiing in the moonlight on Bogus Basin's Nordic trails.
- Snowshoeing from yurt to yurt with a handful of friends.
- Soaking naked in natural hot springs.
- The Boulder, White Cloud, or Pioneer Mountains.
- Whitewater rafting the Middle Fork of the Salmon River.
- Trucks. Idahoans refer to their large pickup trucks as their "rigs."
- Camping. It's surprising how universal it is for Idaho families to be interested in camping; many camp every weekend in the summer.
- Seven Devils' Peaks, one of the highest mountain ranges in Idaho. It includes Heaven's Gate Lookout, where sightseers can look into four states.
- Women skiers: Natives Christin Cooper and Picabo Street won Olympic medals. Cooper won in 1984, and Street won in 1994 and 1998.

Things Your Character Would Like to Forget

- Ernest Hemingway committed suicide here (near Ketchum) in 1961.
- Claude Dallas. In 1982, he murdered two Idaho Fish and Game Wardens and in 1986 escaped from the Idaho State Penitentiary. He was caught in 1987.
- The Idaho Legislature.
- Idaho's reputation as a haven for white supremacists.
- Its poor education system.
- Californians.
- Incomers.
- Liberals.
- Bill Clinton.
- Abortion doctors.
- Automobile traffic and shopping malls.

- The federal government telling him what he can and can't do, particularly with property.

Myths and Misperceptions About Idaho

- **Idaho harbors large numbers of white supremacists and hate groups.** Actually, there are only tiny groups concentrated in northern Idaho. To put it in perspective, when the Aryan Nations had its national gathering recently, fewer than fifty people attended. And by some estimates, Idaho's human rights organizations outnumber its extremist organizations by ten to one.
- **The only things worth remembering about Idaho are its potatoes.** While the spuds are good and profitable, there's a lot more going on here, like students going to great schools, white water rafting, and outdoor activities of all sorts.

Interesting Places to Set a Scene

- **The lunch counter at the Boise Coop.** The unwashed hippy crowd hangs out and eats the fresh and untainted gourmet foods at this nontraditional, all-organic grocery store/cafe.
- **Boise.** There is a surprising disconnect between many young people in Boise and the state's general populous. Those in Boise are fantastically healthy and athletic-looking folk with expensive sunglasses on their heads and fancy footwear on their feet (Gore-Tex boots in the winter and fashionable river sandals in the summer). Many drive new Subaru wagons and eat sushi. The mild weather and proximity to the Boise Foothills makes Boise somewhat of an outdoor mecca (skiing, mountain biking, kayaking). It draws a crowd that you might find just as easily living in San Francisco or Portland, Oregon.
- **Silver City.** This bizarre ghost town on the Oregon Border offers a glimpse into the Wild West of the mid- to late-1800s. During its heyday, Silver City had a brewery, several ore mines and general stores, two hotels, a newspaper, and two lumberyards. In case you're wondering, it had its brothels as well, mostly along what was called "Virgin Alley."
- **The Kamiah Valley.** Rich in the heritage and legends of the Nez Perce, it was here among the ancestors of the present-day Nez Perce that the Appaloosa horse was first bred, primarily for use as a war animal.
- **The Cross on top of Table Rock.** Crowned by an illuminated forty-foot-high cross overlooking Boise, Table Rock is a popular make-out spot and teen hangout. But people of all ages drive or hike up at sunset to see the spectacular view of the Treasure Valley below.
- **The Anniversary Inn in Boise.** This themed hotel has a collection of different suites, all lavishly decorated a la Disney (Treasure Island, Ford's Theatre, and so on). Middle-aged Idahoan couples blow a wad of cash every year to stay here on their anniversary. The owners are Mormon, so to book a room your character must be married (or at least pretend to be).
- **Dinner at the Stage Coach Inn.** This dark, smoky, wagon-wheelesque, western-style steak-and-potatoes place has retained its early sixties feel (complete with refillable blue cheese and thousand island salad dressing trolleys). Waitresses still wear fringed uniforms/costumes reminiscent of Pocahontas. The Stage Coach is known for its strong cocktails and consumer-driven staff. FYI: Those who take the orders and deliver the meals are not called "servers"; they're "waitresses."
- **McCall.** Many wealthy Boiseans have understated but well-equipped "cabins" in this old and picturesque town that's built around a seven-mile alpine lake. *Holiday Inn* was filmed here.
- **The annual God and Country Rally in Nampa.** Every year for over three decades on the Wednesday preceding Independence Day, the people of the Treasure Valley celebrate their religious and patriotic freedoms. This good old-fashioned rally attracts thousands who are proud of their god, flag, and country.
- **The Marsing sprint boat races.** People in jet boats (yes,

Idaho's Snake River

For Further Research

Books

Beyond Burlap: Idaho's Famous Potato Recipes, by Junior League of Boise

Idaho for the Curious: A Guide, by Cort Conley

It's Fun to Remember, by Warren H. Brown

Lay the Mountains Low: The Flight of the Nez Perce From Idaho and the Battle of the Big Hole, August 9–10, 1877, by Terry C. Johnston

River of No Return, by Johnny Carrey and Cort Conley

River Tales of Idaho, by Darcy Williamson

Standing Up to the Rock, by T. Louise Freeman-Toole

Sun Valley: An Extraordinary History, by Wendolyn Spence Holland

Where the Morning Light's Still Blue: Personal Essays About Idaho, edited by William Studebaker and Rick Ardinger

Web Sites

www.accessidaho.org/ (official state site)

www.uidaho.edu/ (university site)

www.visitid.org/ (visitor's info)

www.idahogeology.org/ (state geology site)

www.idahopotato.com/ (Idaho potato site)

www.ci.boise.id.us/public_works/news/ (Boise news)

www.logcablit.org/ (writer's resource site)

www.idahostatesman.com/news/history/ (state history)

Still Curious? Why Not Check Out

Across Open Ground, by Heather Parkinson

Angle of Repose, by Wallace Stegner

The Complete Short Stories of Ernest Hemingway, by Ernest Hemingway

In His Arms, by Robin Lee Hatcher

Holiday Inn

The Idaho Review

Pale Rider Pure Gold, by Warren Wassom

The River Wild

boats, not skis) speed around at warp speeds on a curvy, shallow water track. It's normal for drivers to flip out onto the bank and tumble. The festival draws an interesting crowd, as Marsing is a small Snake River town that's a mix of farmers, ranchers, wine connoisseurs (there's a Tuscan-style winery), and espresso addicts.

Significant Events Your Character Has Probably Thought About

- Illinois become the twenty-first state in 1818.
- In 1846, Brigham Young and fellow Mormons left Nauvoo for the Great Salt Lake in Utah.
- The 1908 Springfield race riots spawned the 1909 formation of the National Association for the Advancement of Colored People (NAACP).
- In 1925, Evanston native Charles Dawes became Calvin Coolidge's vice president and received the Nobel Peace Prize for his "Dawes Plan," which helped restore the German economy after World War I.
- In 1949, Gwendolyn Brooks became the first African-American to win a Pulitzer Prize with her book of poetry, *Annie Allen*; she was later named Illinois poet laureate in 1968.
- During the 1950s, Illinois auditor Orville Hodge was convicted of stealing $1.5 million from the state. Governor Otto Kerner had a similar fate in 1973 when he was convicted of receiving ample funds for partaking in the sale of a racetrack while in office.
- The 1993 floods became the worst in the state's history, covering over 500,000 acres of land and causing $1.5 billion of crop and property damage.
- Governor Jim Edgar won the largest reelection margin in the twentieth century in 1994 with 64 percent of the vote. For the first time in thirty-eight years, a single party (Republicans) controlled all statewide offices and both chambers of the general assembly.
- Illinois declared a moratorium on the death penalty in 2000.

Illinois Facts and Peculiarities Your Character Might Know

- Edgar Lee Masters published his famed *Spoon River Anthology* in 1915.
- Using the steel from a broken saw blade, John Deere designed the first self-scouring steel plow in Detour in 1837.
- The first railroad bridge across the Mississippi River spanned from Rock Island, Illinois, to Davenport, Iowa (1856).
- Abraham Lincoln (Republican) and Stephen A. Doug-

Illinois Basics That Shape Your Character

Motto: State Sovereignty, National Union

Population: 12.4 million

Prevalent Religions: Christianity, particularly Roman Catholic, Church of Jesus Christ of Latter-day Saints, Baptist, Methodist, Lutheran, and Pentecostal, also Judaism

Major Industries: Corn, soybeans, hogs, cattle, dairy products, wheat, machinery, food processing, electric equipment, chemical products, printing and publishing, fabricated metal products, transportation equipment, petroleum, coal

Ethnic Makeup (in percent): Caucasian 73.5%, African-American 15.1%, Hispanic 12.3%, Asian 3.4%, Native American 0.2%, Other 5.8%

Famous Illinoisans: Jane Addams, John Bardeen, Bonnie Blair, Gwendolyn Brooks, Dick Butkus, Al Capone, John Chancellor, Hillary Clinton, Richard Daley, Roger Ebert, Benny Goodman, Gene Hackman, Hugh Hefner, Charlton Heston, David Mamet, Carl Sandburg, James Tobin, Dick and Jerry Van Dyke, Charles Rudolph Walgreen, Frank Lloyd Wright

las (Democrat) had seven debates in their 1858 run for the Senate, and Douglas won the election. Two years later, however, Lincoln won the presidency.

- Democrats nominated Salem native William Jennings Bryan (of the 1925 Scopes Trial fame in Tennessee) as their presidential candidate three times. He lost every election.
- The worst tornado in U.S. history wreaked havoc on Illinois, Missouri, and Indiana, killing 695 people.
- Governor Adlai Stevenson was the 1956 Democratic nominee for president but lost to Dwight D. Eisenhower.
- HAL, the computer in *2001: A Space Odyssey*, was "born" in Urbana on January 12, 1997.

Your Character's Food and Drink

Chain restaurants dominate much of the state. Chicago, of course, loves its pizza, as does the northern part of the state, and the Mormons have their Jell-O, baked ham, and funeral potatoes. The rest of the state, however, mostly eats meat-and-potato fare.

Things Your Character Likes to Remember

- Hometown boy Abraham Lincoln was elected president in 1860.

Cityscape of downtown Chicago

© PhotoDisc/Getty Images

- The Jim Thompson years. This popular governor was elected in 1976 to his first of four terms, making him the longest-serving governor in Illinois history.
- Ray Kroc opened the country's first McDonald's in Des Plaines in 1954.
- Two out of the three major candidates in the 1980 presidential election were born in Illinois: Ronald Reagan (in Tampico, 1911) and John Anderson (in Rockford, 1922).
- Literacy. In 2001 Illinois was the first state to receive the Five-Star Policy Program Award for literacy from the International Reading Association.
- The tallest man in documented medical history was Robert Pershing Wadlow from Alton. He was 8 feet, 11.1 inches tall. The poor guy died at age twenty-two.

Things Your Character Would Like to Forget

- The 1844 assassinations of Mormon leaders.
- Known as the "Salt King of Southern Illinois," John Crenshaw was involved in illegally kidnapping free blacks and selling them back into slavery.
- In 1979 an American Airlines plane crashed at O'Hare International Airport, killing 275 people.
- Pipe bombs in mailboxes. Many were found in eastern Illinois and several other states in 2002.

Myths and Misperceptions About Illinois

- **Everyone's from Chicago.** There's a whole state outside of the big city by the big lake.
- **Other than Chicago, they're all farmers.** Many in the state are educators, businesspeople, computer specialists, and industrial workers.
- **It's pronounced "Illinoiz."** That's wrong. The correct pronunciation is "noi" not "noiz."
- **John Wilkes Booth shot Abraham Lincoln in Illinois.** Lincoln was actually shot in Ford's Theatre in downtown Washington, DC, but his body was moved to Springfield. So he is, in fact, buried in Illinois but was killed in DC.

Interesting Places to Set a Scene

- **Bloomington/Normal.** The *Utne Reader* recently named Bloomington the "most enlightened" community in Illinois. The economy is based on agriculture and farming; electronic equipment is also manufactured here. In 1856 the state Republican Party was organized in Bloomington, at which time Lincoln de-

For Further Research

Books

Abraham Lincoln: Speeches and Writings 1832–1858, by Abraham Lincoln

A. Lincoln, Esquire: A Shrewd, Sophisticated Lawyer in His Time, by Allen D. Spiegel

Awesome Almanac: Illinois, by Jean F. Blashfield

The Black Civil War Soldiers of Illinois: The Story of the Twenty-Ninth U.S. Colored Infantry, by Edward A. Miller Jr.

Journal of the Abraham Lincoln Association, edited by Thomas F. Schwartz

Lake Effect, by Rich Cohen

Sugar Creek: Life on the Illinois Prairie, by John Mack Faragher

The Transformation of Rural Life: Southern Illinois, 1890–1990, by Jane Adams

Web Sites

http://alexia.lis.uiuc.edu/~sorensen/hist.html (state history site)

www.100.state.il.us/ (official state site)

www.state.il.us/hpa/ (historic preservation agency)

www.commerce.state.il.us/ (commerce and community affairs)

www.digitalcity.com/peoriaarea/news/ (central Illinois news)

Still Curious? Why Not Check Out

Abe Lincoln in Illinois

Far From Home: Life and Loss in Two American Towns, by Ron Powers

Poor White Trash

A Supposedly Fun Thing I'll Never Do Again, by David Foster Wallace

Time Will Darken It, by William Maxwell

---

livered his famous "lost speech" (no copy of it is known to exist). Illinois State University is in adjacent Normal (formerly North Bloomington).

- **Champaign Urbana.** The twenty-six thousand students at the University of Illinois at Urbana-Champaign are a big part of this small city of forty thousand. When your character walks the streets, she'll notice an odd mix of frat boys, sorority girls, local drop-out grungers, pamphleteers, and U.S. fighter pilots who visit on the weekends from nearby Chanute Air Force Base.

- **Chicago.** (See page 103 for more detailed information on the Windy City.)

- **East St. Louis.** Forty-ounce bottles of malt liquor and yellowed Zig-Zag rolling papers sit side by side in the uncut grass, as prostitutes and poor, fatherless teenage boys pass drugs and commit crime on the street. Rickety run-down homes and smoke-filled corner bars make up this sad, dirty, and unsafe area—a good place for a murder or a drive-by shooting (of which there are many).

- **Naperville.** It's not the shops and restaurants along the tree-lined streets in downtown that make this city interesting—it's the concerned parents and smart kids. Naperville boasts two nationally recognized school districts, a reputable college, and a library that was selected first in the country for two consecutive years. Not surprisingly, Naperville also was recently voted the number one city in the country to raise children.

- **Nauvoo.** Joseph Smith and his Church of Jesus Christ of Latter-day Saints followers built a bustling little town here in 1939. With its twelve thousand citizens, it was one of the largest towns in the state at the time, until a militia jailed Smith and forced many of his fellow Mormons to join Brigham Young on his trip to Utah. *Nauvoo* means "beautiful place," and you can see why—this peaceful small town on a bend in the Mississippi River is sleepy and historic, with little red-brick stores, a big white-framed mansion, an old hotel, Smith's log cabin, and in 2002 the brand-new Nauvoo Illinois Temple.

- **Our Lady of the Snows Shrine in Belleville.** Your character won't find a better place for surrounding herself with such a plethora of virgin-birth devotees. This odd place, which is owned and operated by the Missionary Oblates of Mary Immaculate, is one of the largest outdoor shrines in North America. The unique architecture and creative landscaping lend a touch of serenity to the grounds.

- **Peoria.** This old lake and river city is not just one of the state's oldest settlements, but a trade and transportation hub as well. Have your character work in one of the plants where grain, livestock, and coal are processed. Or, he could be a taster at one of the large distilleries or breweries. Or, he even could be the "star guy" at the local planetarium in Lakeview Park, which also has a community theater and an arts and sciences center. Peoria is a city that's busy without being big, industrial without being ugly, and historic without being gimmicky.

• **Springfield.** Let the ghost of Abraham Lincoln (whose remains are nearby) creep into your story about this Illinois capital (which became the capital thanks in no small part to Lincoln himself). Our sixteenth president lived and practiced law here from 1837 to 1861, and his home is a preserved national historic site. Lincoln gave his "House Divided" speech at the old capitol building and his farewell address at the Depot Museum. Poet Vachel Lindsay was born here as well.

• **The DuQuoin State Fair.** This Midwestern landmark brings in more than 400,000 fair-goers who enjoy harness racing, auto racing, music, and women in cutoffs and halter tops carrying big balls of blue cotton candy. DuQuoin boasts of being the first fair in the nation to hold stage shows at night. Read David Foster Wallace's essay "Getting Away From Already Pretty Much Being Away From It All" (about the Illinois State Fair) for a little inspiration.

Chicago Facts and Peculiarities Your Character Might Know

- The correct pronunciation of *Chicago* is actually "shi-CAWG-o," but most Chicagoans and Midwesterners say "shi-COG-o."
- Remember the "superfans" on *Saturday Night Live* and how much they loved Polish sausage, ribs, and Mike Ditka? Their mannerisms and speech patterns were *not* exaggerated. Male genitalia is often referred to as "the package" and pronounced "pake- ij"; that is, "Ay, nice package" would sound like "Ay, nishe pake-ij." Something that is "over there" is actually "ooo-ver by 'der'."
- In addition, *sausage* is pronounced "sass-ij," and when addressing a group, a Chicagoan might refer to them as "you's guys." In traffic, you might hear the term "f—in' jagoff."
- *Chicago Tribune* sports editor Arch Ward (1896–1955) organized the first baseball All-Star Game, which was played at Comiskey Park and won by the American League.
- The Stevenson Expressway (I-55) is referred to as the "Double Nickel."
- Charles Lindbergh flew daily mail delivery flights between Chicago and St. Louis.
- The 1958 fire at Our Lady of Angels Elementary School killed ninety-two children and three nuns.
- Chicago got dumped with twenty-three inches of snow in 1963.
- The 1968 Democratic National Convention got out of hand, with 650 arrests.
- Chicago has more private boat ships than anywhere in the world. Hard to believe, but true.
- The Sears Tower was finished in 1942.
- In 1978 the *Chicago Daily News,* the city's last afternoon newspaper, ceased publication.

If Your Character . . .

If Your Character Is Alternative and Grungy, he lives in Wicker Park and Bucktown. These two communities on the northwest side of town are the oldest, most eclectic neighborhoods in the city. The area is known to have one of the largest populations of working artists and musicians in the country. This artsy population, plus the cultural and ethnic diversity of the area, make it popular for trendy residents and retailers, unique boutiques, cutting-edge art galleries and theaters, and hip restaurants and bars.

Chicago Basics That Shape Your Character

The famous Buckingham Fountain

Population: 2.9 million in the city; over 9.1 million in the Greater Metro area

Prevalent Religions: Christianity, primarily Roman Catholicism, dominates, but Chicago is home to almost all religions.

Top Employers: U.S. Government, Archdiocese of Chicago, Dominick's Finer Foods, Target, United Airlines, Abbott Laboratories, Motorola Inc., American Airlines, Northwestern University, University of Chicago, Advocate Health Care, Cook County/City of Chicago, Jewel-Osco, Bank One, Exelon Corporation, Chicago Public Schools

Per Capita Income: $34,612

Average Daily Temperature: January, 21° F; July, 73° F

Ethnic Makeup (in percent): Caucasian 42%, African-American 36.8%, Hispanic 26%, Asian 4.3%, Native American 0.4%, Other 16.5%

Newspapers and Magazines: *Chicago Tribune, Chicago Sun-Times, Daily Herald, Chicago Magazine*

Free Weekly Alternative Papers: *Chicago Reader, The Chicago Reporter, Newcity Chicago*

If Your Character Smells of Money, she lives on the North Shore. Huge homes on big lots make up this secluded neighborhood. People who live here can sit back on their extensive decks and feel the breeze come in from Lake Michigan, all while sipping martinis before dinner.

If Your Character Is All About Business, she works in the Financial District. This is downtown's business central, with skyscrapers that house expansive office suites with windowed views of Lake Michigan below.

If Your Character Is a Family Man, he lives in Evanston. Home to Northwestern University, many professors live in the nice suburban homes here. The winding streets are shady and pleasant and away from the hubbub of the city.

If Your Character Is Down-and-Out, he lives in the South Side of Chicago. The city's poor were once centralized in high-rise buildings just south of the city, but they are a bit more spread out than they used to be.

Local Grub Your Character Might Love

Stuffed pizza is a Chicago favorite. If you've never had one, just imagine a regular pizza with about a solid inch of cheese (after it's been cooked) and an extra layer of pizza dough on top. The pizza is covered with sauce, and the "toppings" are stuffed inside. Chicagoans also enjoy the ever-popular Italian beef sandwich, which comes with the options of cheese (mozzarella), sweet peppers (usually sautéed green peppers) or hot peppers, and hot giardinera (a mix of hot peppers, celery, onions, and carrots in oil). Add a big chunk of Italian sausage to the Italian beef sandwich, and you have the "beef combo"—essentially a heart attack on a bun. The combo is ordered either "red" (with tomato sauce) or "dipped" (dipped in au jus). Oh, and don't forget cheese fries. The Chicago hot dog is somewhat unique—it's a kosher dog with no ketchup (ever!), served on a poppy-seed bun. It comes with half slices of tomato, a pickle spear, sport peppers, sweet piccalilli (the fluorescent green variety), and the coup de grace, celery salt. The "Polish" version is a grilled kielbasa on a hot dog bun, served with optional kraut and peppers.

Some favorite local eateries are Giordano's, Gino's East, Uno's, Lou Malnati's (pizza), Gene and George-tti's, Morton's, Smith Wollensky (steak), Reza's (Mediterranean), Rosebud on Rush or Mia Francesca (Italian), and of course, any of the many Vienna Beef stands.

Interesting and Peculiar Places to Set a Scene

- **The Courtyard of the Fifth Presbyterian Church on Michigan Avenue.** Your character must know that this could easily be one of the most romantic areas in the city. The courtyard is just so green and quiet and beautiful and secluded—it's that "special place" for many Chicagoans. Other romantic areas are Olive Park and the Japanese garden at the Botanical Gardens in Glencoe.

- **Grant Park.** This park on the Lake Michigan shore is an art lover's paradise. Amidst the pleasant, winding walkways and breezy off-the-lake winds is not only the Chicago Art Institute but some one hundred outdoor sculptures by some of the world's most noted artists, such as Marc Chagall, Joan Miró, Henry Moore, Claes Oldenburg, and Pablo Picasso. The latter's unnamed sculpture is the city's favorite (and certainly the most photographed by visitors). During warm weather there is always some performance or exhibition as part of the city's long-running "Under the Picasso" multicultural program.

- **North Avenue Beach.** Walk along the beaches and your character will see sunbathers in bikinis, lovers kissing on a blanket, kids building sand castles near the water, mountain bikers riding along the walkways, twenty-somethings swing dancing on the plaza, and people enjoying cold drinks or ice-cream cones from the snack shop. This is Chicago's own Hilton Head, and residents love it.

- **Lincoln Park's Clark Street.** This is Chicago's international avenue. As your character strolls up Clark, she'll encounter people and restaurants from around the world, from mom-and-pop Greek walk-ups to all-in-the-family-owned Ethiopian sit-downs to Indian buffets to small coffee-and-pancake shops. The streets bustle, especially at night.

- **Lincoln Park Zoo.** This place is great not only because it's free but also because it's beautiful. Where else can you hang out with lions, tigers, and bears while gazing out upon the wide expanse of shuffling white tips on Lake Michigan?

- **Michigan Avenue.** Along Michigan Avenue lies the "Magnificent Mile," Chicago's famous shopping district. Your character will see shopping bag after shopping bag as fashionable folks walk the streets of the strip filled with stores like Crate and Barrel, Bloomingdale's, Nieman Marcus, Pottery Barn, and Tiffany & Co. During the holiday season, the streets and storefronts are aglow with lights, bright boxes, bows, and garlands—a beautiful place for two characters in love to do some last-minute shopping.

- **North Avenue.** This is where your character could find a drug dealer or solicit a prostitute. Recently the Chicago Police Department has been cracking down on the area.
- **Oak Park.** Shady streets and pleasant, well-kept Victorian and Tudor homes mark this Chicago suburb. Ernest Hemingway was born here; even Frank Lloyd Wright built a few homes in the area.
- **O'Hare's underground walkways.** The corridors that take passengers from the parking garage to the terminals are one heck of a spot to set a scene. Lots of street musicians congregate here because of the streams of passersby and also for the great natural reverb. Even in the winter a street musician can make a quite a few bucks here. Have your character toss a few bucks into a musician's open guitar case or onto his spread-out bandana.
- **Pacific Gardens Mission on South Michigan Avenue.** This is where Chicago's homeless congregate, for no other place will take them. It's not uncommon to see several sad-looking folks in tattered clothing standing out on the street smoking cigarettes and occasionally begging for handouts.
- **The Cal-Sag Canal.** Does one of your characters need a great place to dump a corpse? Here's the perfect spot.
- **The South Side.** This mostly African-American neighborhood full of projects is still poor, but the projects are being razed with the hopes of building more respectable housing that residents will care for and appreciate.
- **The Steppenwolf Theatre.** In 1998, Steppenwolf was the only arts organization awarded a National Medal of Arts—presented by Bill and Hillary Clinton in a White House ceremony—and for good reason. The place is legendary, as it was started in the 1970s by the likes of John Malkovich and Gary Sinise, who are still involved with the theatre today. The old, unpretentious building on a nonglitzy street is surrounded by small, independent eateries.

Exceptionally Grand Things Your Character Is Proud Of
- Wrigley Field.
- The city's architecture (Louis Sullivan, Mies van der Rohe, Frank Lloyd Wright, Dankmar Adler).
- Literary tradition (Upton Sinclair, Saul Bellow, Theodore Dreiser, Richard Wright).
- Social reformers (Jane Addams, Upton Sinclair, Women's Christian Temperance Union).
- Music. The Chicago Blues Festival is the largest free-admission Blues Festival in the world, and Chicago jazz is legendary, thanks to all the jazz clubs, the Chicago Jazz Festival (oldest in the city), and the Jazz Institute of Chicago.
- Higher education. The University of Chicago and Northwestern University are both here, and both are exemplary schools.
- The Chicago Bears. They won the professional football championship in 1933, 1940, 1941, 1943, 1946, 1963, and 1986.
- Chicago theater-chain owner John Balaban established WBKB, the first television station in Illinois.

Pathetically Sad Things Your Character Is Ashamed Of
- The Cubs.
- Political corruption.
- Graft, de facto segregation of neighborhoods.
- Gangsterism.
- The 1919 Chicago White Sox. The players were accused of gambling on the World Series, which they lost to the Cincinnati Red Legs.
- The seventeen Chicago attorneys, police officers, and judges who were indicted in 1987 for "Operation Greylord" on charges of improperly influencing court cases.
- After the death of Secretary of State Paul Powell in 1970, $800,000 was found in shoe boxes in his Springfield hotel room.
- The "Chicago Seven" defendants were convicted on charges relating to violence at the 1968 Democratic National Convention; the decision was overturned in 1972.
- Dan Rostenkowski, from 1959–1995 he served in Congress until he was indicted on corruption charges and sentenced to seventeen months in federal prison after pleading guilty to two counts of misuse of public funds.

For Further Research

Books

Capone: The Life and World of Al Capone, by John Kobler

Chicago: Growth of a Metropolis, by Harold M. Mayer and Richard C. Wade

Chicago: Metropolis of the Mid-Continent, by Irving Cutler

The Chicago School of Architecture, by Carl W. Condit

Chicago: Transformations of an Urban System, by Brian J.L. Berry et al.

City of the Century: The Epic of Chicago and the Making of America, by Donald L. Miller

Creating Chicago's North Shore, by Michael H. Ebner

The Great Chicago Fire, by Robert Cromie

Nature's Metropolis: Chicago and the Great West, by William Cronon

Web Sites

www.chicagotribune.com/ (*Chicago Tribune*)

www.ci.chi.il.us/ (city's official site)

www.suntimes.com/index/ (*Chicago Sun-Times*)

www.chicagohs.org/ (Chicago Historical Society)

www.lib.ohio-state.edu/guides/chicagogd.html (Chicago Manual of Style)

www.choosechicago.com (visitor's bureau)

Still Curious? Why Not Check Out

About Last Night . . .

The Adventures of Augie March, by Saul Bellow

The Big Silence, by Stuart Kaminsky

Blink

Brian's Song

Conspiracy: The Trial of the Chicago 8

High Fidelity

The Jungle, by Upton Sinclair

Meet the Parents

Memoirs of an American Citizen, by Robert Herrick

Message in a Bottle

Native Son, by Richard Wright

Never Been Kissed

The Precipice, by Elia W. Peattie

Queen Bee, by Eugene Kennedy

Return to Me

Sister Carrie, by Theodore Dreiser

Twenty Years at Hull House, by Jane Addams

While You Were Sleeping

Your Character Loves

- Hanging out at the Lincoln Park Zoo (it's free!).
- Bare-handed 16″ softball. An only-in-Chicago game similar to softball but without gloves. There's even a "Chicago 16″ Softball Hall of Fame."
- The bars are open until 4:00 A.M.
- The lakefront and how well it is preserved (with parks and beaches).
- Jane Addams.
- Richard J. Daley.
- Clarence Page, the first African-American columnist to receive the Pulitzer Prize.
- Saul Bellow. He won the Nobel Prize in Literature.
- Studs Terkel—Chicago's greatest journalist.

Your Character Hates

- The Asian longhorn beetle that destroyed hundreds of trees in the city.
- New Yorkers.
- Green Bay Packers.
- The weather.
- The St. Louis Cardinals.
- The Mets.

Significant Events Your Character Has Probably Thought About

- Indiana became a state in 1816.
- Although born in Kentucky, Abraham Lincoln spent his childhood in Spencer County.
- The American Federation of Labor (AFL) was organized in Terre Haute in 1881.
- In 1911 the Indianapolis Motor Speedway held the nation's first long-distance auto race. The winner averaged 75 miles an hour and won a whopping $14,000; today Indy 500 speeds average 170 miles an hour, and the prize is $1.2 million.
- South Bend's Studebaker Company was the nation's largest producer of horse-drawn wagons and later became a major carmaker.
- From 1900 to 1920, Indiana was a major auto manufacturer, producing more than two hundred different makes of cars.
- In 1934 Chicago gangster John Dillinger escaped from Crown Point Jail without a shot being fired. Whether he carved a wooden "pistol" doesn't much matter—he embarrassed state law enforcement enough by driving off in Sheriff Lillian Holley's car.
- During World War II, Republic Aviation in Evansville supplied Allied forces with the P-47 fighter plane.
- During the 1972 Summer Olympics, Indiana University's Mark Spitz won a record-breaking seven gold medals.
- In 1989 Dan Quayle became the forty-fourth vice president.
- Bobby Knight, the general of Indiana basketball, was fired in 2000 after twenty-five years as the Hoosiers' head coach.

Indiana Facts and Peculiarities Your Character Might Know

- Indiana has a town called Santa Claus, which, not surprisingly, receives thousands of wish lists during the weeks before Christmas.
- While driving around the state in the late fall, your character must be careful of hitting deer during the "rut" season.
- Southern Indiana's limestone is deemed the best in

Indiana Basics That Shape Your Character

Motto: The Crossroads of America

Population: 6.1 million

Prevalent Religions: Christianity, particularly Roman Catholic, and also Baptist, Methodist, Lutheran, Presbyterian, Pentecostal, Jewish, Mennonite, and Amish

Major Industries: Corn, soybeans, hogs, cattle, dairy products, eggs, steel, electric equipment, transportation equipment, chemical products, petroleum and coal products, machinery

Ethnic Makeup (in percent): Caucasian 87.5%, African-American 8.4%, Hispanic 3.5%, Native American 0.3%, Asian 1.0%, Other 1.6%

Famous Hoosiers: Larry Bird, Hoagy Carmichael, James Dean, Eugene Debs, Theodore Dreiser, Jimmy Hoffa, The Jacksons, David Letterman, Eli Lilly, Shelley Long, John Mellencamp, Joaquin Miller, Jim Nabors, Cole Porter, Ernie Pyle, Dan Quayle, Red Skelton, Rex Stout, Booth Tarkington, Kurt Vonnegut Jr.

the world—just ask the Empire State Building, the Pentagon, the Treasury, and several other government buildings.

- *Rebel Without a Cause* star James Dean is from the small town of Marion.
- With its thirty-two covered bridges, Parke County deems itself the "Covered Bridge Capital of the World."
- Indiana is nicknamed the "Cross Roads of America" for good reason: More major highways intersect in Indiana than in any other state.
- The original Coca-Cola bottle was designed and blown in Terre Haute.
- The Hoosier State has had its share of major prize winners: Albert Beveridge won the Pulitzer Prize for *The Life of John Marshall*; Harold Urey won the Nobel Prize in Chemistry for his discovery of deuterium; Ernie Pyle won the Pulitzer Prize in Foreign Correspondence; Paul Samuelson won the Nobel Prize in Economics.
- Sarah Walker (she called herself "Madame J.C. Walker") became one of the first female millionaires by creating her hair-straightening treatment.
- There's a big rivalry between Indiana University in Bloomington and Purdue University in West Lafayette (they pretty much hate each other).
- Many Hoosiers talk with a "drawl" and pronounce their short "i" as a long "e": *fish* is "feesh" and *dish* is "deesh" (mostly in the southern part of the state).

Your Character's Food and Drink

Meat and potato foods are mainstays here. Brain sandwiches (pork brains mixed with a batter of flour, baking soda, salt and pepper, and eggs, and then mixed into a dough and dropped into a pan and fried) are big (and were allegedly created) in Evansville. Country fried biscuits and apple butter are popular in the south. Most residents prefer beer over wine and Coke or Pepsi over orange juice and water. There's a big disconnect among the college towns and the rest of the state. For example, vegan, vegetarian, and international foods (Greek, Thai, Mediterranean, Vietnamese) are popular near the college campuses, as in Bloomington, Muncie, and South Bend.

Things Your Character Likes to Remember

- More than one hundred species of trees are native to Indiana.
- Wayne County's Fountain City was called the "Grand Central Station of the Underground Railroad." It's estimated that Levi and Katie Coffin provided overnight lodging for more than two thousand runaway slaves.
- Muncie's Ball State University was built mostly from funds contributed by the founders of the Ball Corporation, a company than made glass canning jars.
- High school football.
- Deer hunting and showcasing his new gun rack.
- Riding motorcycles or snowmobiles on the farm.
- Covered bridges.
- Riverboat casinos.
- John Mellencamp.
- The Bobby Knight era.
- The Jackson 5.

Things Your Character Would Like to Forget

- The Great Depression. The unemployment rate in southern Indiana reached 50 percent.
- Nearly 80 percent of Indiana was covered with forest before the pioneers arrived. Now only 17 percent of the state is forested land.
- George O'Leary. In 2001 he had to resign as Notre Dame's football coach within a week after being hired because he lied about playing football in college.
- All the KKK and NRA activity in the state.
- Pulling off hundreds of ticks at Brookville Lake.
- Bobby Knight's unbridled antics.
- Michael Jackson after he got weird.

Myths and Misperceptions About Indiana

- **That it's all rural and backward.** While Indiana does have a number of rural and farming communities, it

© PhotoDisc/Getty Images

The Sim Smith Bridge in Parke County

For Further Research

Books

Grand Dragon: D.C. Stephenson and the Ku Klux Klan in Indiana, by M. William Lutholtz

Hoosier Faiths: A History of Indiana's Churches and Religious Groups, by L.C. Rudolph

Indiana History: A Book of Readings, by Ralph D. Gray

The Indiana Way: A State History, by James H. Madison

Jokelore: Humorous Folktales From Indiana, by Ronald L. Baker

In Lincoln's Footsteps: A Historical Guide to the Lincoln Sites in Illinois, Indiana, and Kentucky, by Don Davenport

A Lynching in the Heartland: Race and Memory in America, by James H. Madison

Web Sites

http://my.evansville.net/my-bin/index.cgi (Evansville news)

www.terrehaute.com/ (Terre Haute visitor's info)

www.ipfw.edu/ipfwhist/indihist.htm (state history)

http://siw.00author.com/anthologies/ (Southern Indiana writers group)

www.thetimesonline.com/ (state news)

www.thestarpress.com/ (Muncie news)

www.post-trib.com/cgi-bin/pto-today/news/z1 (Gary news)

Still Curious? Why Not Check Out

Alice of Old Vincennes, by Maurice Thompson

Blue Chips

From Dawn to Daylight, by Eunice Beecher

The Hoosier Schoolmaster, by Edward Eggleston

A League of Their Own

Reckless Driver, by Lisa Vice

Sister Carrie, by Theodore Dreiser

When Knighthood Was in Flower, by Charles Major

---

also has Indianapolis, with its 800,000 mostly sophisticated residents.

- **That residents actually know what a Hoosier is.** Residents don't have a clue. There are many crazy theories about the origin of the word. The one certainty is that Hoosiers bear their nickname proudly.

Interesting Places to Set a Scene

- **Bern.** Many Mennonite and Amish people live on this farmland in northwestern Indiana. Because these folks are forbidden to drive cars, use electricity, or go to public places for entertainment, your character will find more than her share of horse-drawn carriage roads, big-barned farms, little bonnets, long beards, dark nights, and quality leather and woodworking craftsmanship—all trademarks of the Amish.

- **Bloomington.** The state's most popular college town is home to the exceptionally beautiful Indiana University. The wooded campus is a park unto itself, containing everything from a small stone chapel and a cemetery to a sculpture of Adam and Eve to the world's largest student union building to the legendary Assembly Hall, where the Hoosiers have won many nail-biting games (and Bobby Knight has thrown many temper tantrums and chairs). See *Breaking Away* to get a real sense of the campus, although Memorial Stadium, where the Little 500 bicycle races were once held, has been replaced by a five-hundred-tree arboretum. Bloomington is also John Mellencamp country and home to several eclectic shops and restaurants.

- **Brown County.** This place is known as Indiana's art community. When people say they're going to Nashville, they're coming here (to Brown County's Nashville). Have your character take a carriage ride, browse through an art gallery, watch an artist at work, or sip some of the local wines in this quiet, peaceful refuge. This is a favorite weekend getaway for those in other parts of the state.

- **Columbus.** Architectural wonder-buildings (by the likes of I.M. Pei and Eliel Saarinen) and a lively downtown (with nineteenth-century storefronts) make this a cool place to set a scene. At 37,000 residents, Columbus is small, but few cities can match its innovation and architectural design. It's been called "a living lab for architecture," because it welcomes new styles, embraces old styles, and cares about aesthetics. Locals even call Fifth Street the "Avenue of the Architects."

- **Evansville.** Called "Plastics Valley," this Ohio River town has been the rail and river shipping hub for southwestern Indiana, northwestern Kentucky, and southeastern Illinois. Although it's still pretty much an industrial town (refrigeration/air-conditioning equipment, aluminum, pharmaceuticals, excavating machinery, and plastics), the University of Evansville and a few technical colleges have made Evansville the educational and cultural heart of southern Indiana. The city can boast of having an aviary, a museum of arts and sciences, a zoo, and even its own symphony orchestra (San Diego can't beat that!). It's also known as the home of "brain sandwiches."

- **Fort Wayne.** Indiana's second largest city rests at the confluence of the Maumee and the St. Mary's and St. Joseph Rivers. After the Battle of Fallen Timbers (1794), General "Mad Anthony" Wayne built Fort Wayne on the site of a Miami Indian village. It grew into a city that has shaped Shelley Long, Dave Thomas, Bill Blass, and TV inventor Philo Farnsworth.

- **Indiana Dunes.** On the southern edge of Lake Michigan, this stark landscape is a unique spot in Indiana. The uncrowded beaches and barren lands make a marked contrast to the corn-covered green fields and warm, welcoming towns that dot the rest of the state.

- **Indianapolis.** (See page 111 for an extensive look at Indianapolis.)

- **Parke County's Covered Bridge Festival.** So it's not Robert James Waller's Madison County, but your character will find more covered bridges (thirty-two) here than any where else in the country (and allegedly the world). Deemed the best festival in the state—thanks to those covered bridges, several arts and crafts booths, antiques and flea market dealers, and the smoke-filled, mouth-watering air from the barbecued food—all set in the midst of October's colorful fall foliage.

- **Saint Mary-of-the-Woods College.** Just outside of Terre Haute, this sixty-seven-acre wooded campus with fitness trails, swimming pools, lakes, and horse stables has been home to thousands of Catholic schoolgirls who eventually become nuns.

- **Wyandotte Cave.** One of the largest caves in the nation can be found in southern Indiana's Crawford County. Have your character go spelunking for a little adventure.

Indianapolis

Indianapolis Facts and Peculiarities Your Character Might Know

- Indy has a strong auto-racing heritage, featuring the three largest single-day sporting events in the world: the Indianapolis 500, the Brickyard 400, and the SAP United States Grand Prix.
- The military loves local Richard Gatling, who invented the rapid-fire machine gun back in 1862.
- It's one of largest cities in the country not built on a major waterway.
- This capital is largely Republican, as is the entire state.
- Indy has hosted several National Collegiate Athletic Association (NCAA) Final Four Championships.
- It's home to the NCAA Headquarters.
- The Raggedy Ann doll was the brainchild of local Marcella Gruelle in 1914.
- Local grocer Gilbert Van Camp used an old family recipe of pork and beans in tomato sauce, opened up a canning company, and now Van Camp's pork and beans is an American favorite.
- The *Saturday Evening Post* is published in Indianapolis.
- Indianapolis hosted the Pan American Games in the summer of 1987.
- It considers itself—and rightfully so—the "Amateur Sports Capital of the World."
- It's the nation's twelfth largest city, and it prides itself as a place rich in the arts, culture, history, and time-honored traditions.

If Your Character . . .

If Your Character Is a Generation X-er, he hangs out in Broad Ripple. There he may be going to concerts at the Vogue or watching the local skateboarders show off near Starbucks and quaint little outdoor diners.

If Your Character Is a Shopaholic, she's spending all her time in The Fashion Mall, Castleton Square Mall, or Circle Center Mall. Well, they're all malls—one pretty much looks like the next.

If Your Character Is a Middle-Class Family Man, he lives in Brownsburg or Greenwood. These average middle-class communities of modest homes and nice green

Indianapolis Basics That Shape Your Character

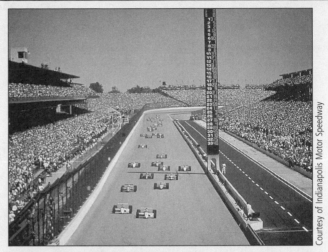

Courtesy of Indianapolis Motor Speedway

Another day at the Indianapolis Motor Speedway

Population: 818,014

Prevalent Religions: Christianity, particularly Roman Catholic, and also Baptist, Methodist, Lutheran, Presbyterian, Pentecostal, and Jewish

Top Employers: Eli Lilly and Company, Marsh Supermarkets/Village Pantry, St. Vincent Hospitals, Methodist Hospitals, Kroger, Community Hospitals, Delphi Interior and Lighting Systems, Allison Transmissions/GMC, Allison Engine Company, Delphi Energy and Engine Management Systems

Per Capita Income: $30,523

Average Daily Temperature: January, 26° F; July, 75° F

Ethnic Makeup (in percent): Caucasian 70.5%, African-American 24.2%, Hispanic 2.67%, Asian 3.9%, Native American 0.3%, Other 2.0%

Newspapers and Magazines: *The Indianapolis Star, Indianapolis Business Journal, Indianapolis Monthly, Indy's Child*

Free Weekly Alternative Paper: *Nuvo News Weekly*

lawns are for those who work hard but still put family before business.

If Your Character Wears a Blue Collar at Work, he lives in the Thirty-Eighth Street Corridor. This entire stretch is one blue-collar block after the next, with rows of red-brick houses nearly stacked on top of each other. Other blue-collar communities are Beech Grove, Avon, Plainfield, and Speedway.

If Your Character Smells of Money, she resides in the Geist Area. Big, sprawling homes with a few acres unto themselves make the Geist Area an exceptionally grand part of the city. Carmel, Zionsville, and certain areas of Eagle Creek are also home to Indy's upper crust.

Local Grub Your Character Might Love

Meat and potato foods are mainstays here. Ruth's Chris Steak House, Shulas, and St. Elmos are your character's favorites for a succulent steak, as is Kona Jack's Fish Market for seafood. For a departure from steak and fish, your character might go to P.F. Chang's China Bistro, Carabbas, the Rathskellar, the Claddagh Irish Pub, Don Pablos, or Schlotzky's deli. It's big here for folks to gather for dinner while watching a basketball or football game on TV at a place like Champps or Champions. Downtown's Old Spaghetti Factory is a favorite for cheap and sloppy meals for the family, as are Arni's and Puccinis for pizza. A big-deal burger joint is Googies Burgers. And don't forget the Van Camp's pork and beans.

Interesting and Peculiar Places to Set a Scene

- **Broad Ripple.** A village unto its own with interesting little boutiques, fashionable clothing shops, brew pubs, cozy restaurants, and show-off adolescent skateboarders, this area of town is about as hip and cool as Indy gets.
- **Conner Prairie.** Your character can catch contemporary outdoor summer concerts at this Fishers, Indiana open-air living history museum. Or, she can take a trip back in time at one of the five historic areas, including a frontier village that plays the part of nineteenth-century settlers in the Old Northwest Territory. Conner Prairie was deemed the most authentic and entertaining museum by *U.S. News & World Report* in 1989.
- **Conseco Fieldhouse.** This retro-themed home of the Indiana Pacers and the Indiana Fever can't be overlooked, for it is all about basketball, which is, after all, one of the three major things those in Indianapolis care about (the other two: auto racing and kids).
- **Fountain Square historic district.** If antiques are what

your character is looking for, this area southeast of downtown boasts more than two hundred antique dealers, specialty stores, and art galleries.
- **IMS (Indianapolis Motor Speedway).** Fast cars, beer-drinking men, halter-topped women—it's Middle America at its finest.
- **Indianapolis City Market.** Here your character will find an international mixture of eclectic merchants who sell everything from Greek, Indian, Latino, and German delicacies to pigs feet and Turkish tapestries. He'll also be able get his shoes shined or his back massaged if he's in the mood. The market house itself is on the National Register of Historic Places.
- **Monument Circle.** This city's centerpiece is the site of water cascading into collecting pools, spring and summer festivals, lunchtime concerts, and several monuments, including "Miss Indiana," a 130-foot bronze statue named *Victory* that sits atop the 284-foot spire on the Soldiers' and Sailors' Monument. Your character can take a Space Needle-ish elevator ride 230 feet up to a glass-enclosed observation area—a good place for an Indy kiss, a Hoosier murder, or just a pleasant panoramic view of the city.
- **The Basement of the Indianapolis City Market.** The unique basement of the market is from the original 1886 Tomlinson Hall structure, which eventually went up in flames in 1958. Locals refer to the area simply as the "catacombs" and warn, "If you ever get a chance to see it, you'll understand why."
- **The Indianapolis Zoo.** If your character has kids, they will love this place. It's the only zoo in the nation that's an accredited zoological park, botanical garden, and aquarium all in one. Most noteworthy are the impressive dolphin pavilion (world's second largest) and aquarium, and the "biomes," where thousands of animals rest and roam in an open air, quasi-cageless setting.
- **The NCAA Hall of Champions.** No other place in the world celebrates intercollegiate athletes like this one, which is big on interactive exhibits showcasing cool multimedia presentations of college greats before they moved on to better-paying ventures.
- **White River State Park.** If your character has an interest in Native American culture and art, this is where she needs to be. Amidst the lovely trees and flowers, the Eiteljorg Museum is the main instructional showplace for all things Native American.

For Further Research

Books

City Smart: Indianapolis, by Helen Wernle O'Guinn and Betsy Sheldon

The Encyclopedia of Indianapolis, edited by David J. Bodenhamer and Robert G. Barrows

Indiana Blacks in the Twentieth Century, by Emma Lou Thornbrough, Lana Ruegamer

Indiana Legends: Famous Hoosiers from Johnny Appleseed to David Letterman, by Nelson Price

The Indianapolis ABCs: History of a Premier Team in the Negro Leagues, by Paul Debono

Indianapolis: Crossroads of the American Dream, by Richard G. Lugar

Indy: Seventy-Five Years of Racing's Greatest Spectacle, by Rich Taylor

Kidding Around Indianapolis, by Layne Scott Cameron

A Season On the Brink: A Year With Bobby Knight and the Indiana Hoosiers, by John Feinstein

Web Sites

www.indygov.org/ (official city site)

www.indychamber.com (chamber of commerce)

www.indystar.com/community/ (news)

http://indianapolis.about.com/ (current events, tourism information)

www.indianapolis.com/history/ (local history)

Still Curious? Why Not Check Out

Breaking Away

Hard Rain

Hoosiers

The Indy Man, by Janet Dailey

Justly Proud: A German American Family in Indiana, by Beverly Raffensperger Fauvre

The Magnificent Ambersons, by Booth Tarkington

Pride and Protest: The Novel in Indiana, by Jeanette Vanausdall

Exceptionally Grand Things Your Character Is Proud Of

- The Colts, Pacers, and Hoosiers.
- Revitalization of downtown and some of its neighborhoods.
- The character of the people—they're generally helpful and full of hospitality.
- Children's Museum of Indianapolis, ranked by *Child* magazine as the "best children's museum" in the country.
- Its arts and theater, especially for a town this size. This includes Cloewes Hall (Bulter University) and Hilbert Theatre on the Circle.
- Conseco Fieldhouse and Murat Theatre.
- The Monon Trail.

Your Character Loves

- Memorials. Considered second only to Washington, DC, in number.
- Basketball.
- Taking the kids to the Children's Museum.
- Jane Pauley, David Letterman, Kurt Vonnegut Jr.—they're all from here.

Your Character Hates

- Being stereotyped as a pot-growing redneck by outsiders.
- Seeing pathetic hicks consistently interviewed on the evening news.
- Either Indiana University or Purdue—but not the both.
- The humidity.
- People always saying, "It's not the heat, it's the humidity."
- There are few hills for sledding in the winter.
- Monster truck shows (well . . . some residents do like them).

Iowa

Iowa Basics That Shape Your Character

Motto: Our Liberties We Prize and Our Rights We Will Maintain

Population: 2.92 million

Prevalent Religions: Christianity, particularly Roman Catholic, Methodist, and Lutheran, some Presbyterian, Pentecostal, and Baptist

Major Industries: Hogs, corn, soybeans, oats, cattle, dairy products, food processing, machinery, electric equipment, chemical products, printing and publishing, primary metal

Ethnic Makeup (in percent): Caucasian 93.9%, African-American 2.1%, Hispanic 2.2%, Asian 1.3%, Native American 0.3%, Other 1.3%

Famous Iowans: Tom Arnold, Buffalo Bill (William F. Cody), Johnny Carson, Mamie Eisenhower, George H. Gallup, Susan Glaspell, Herbert Hoover, Ann Landers, Glenn Miller, Harriet Nelson, Radar O'Riley, David Rabe, Harry Reasoner, Slipknot, Wallace Stegner, James A. Van Allen, Abigail Van Buren, John Wayne, Andy Williams

Significant Events Your Character Has Probably Thought About

- Iowa became a state in 1846, with Iowa City as its capital (which was changed to Des Moines in 1857).
- Many Iowans were opposed to the United States entering World War I because they had strong ties to Germany and Ireland and didn't want their country siding with Britain.
- In 1917, then-governor William Harding banned the speaking of any foreign language in public.
- During World War II, several farm-machine factories in the state switched to producing military equipment.
- In the 1950s, Iowa's farmers began moving to the cities; by 1960 the urban population of Iowa was for the first time higher than its rural population.
- The state's population suffered serious decline in the latter half of the twentieth century, as it lost three seats (it went from eight to five) in the House of Representatives from 1960 to 1990.
- In the 1970s, Governor Robert Ray invited many Asian refugees from the Vietnam War into the state, which diversified its population.
- During the late 1970s and early- to mid-1980s, about sixteen thousand farms in Iowa shut down.
- In 1985, Governor Terry Branstad had to declare a state of emergency because economic times were so bad.
- In 1991, the state legalized riverboat gambling.
- Davenport and other central Iowa river towns were awash during the 1993 floods.

Iowa Facts and Peculiarities Your Character Might Know

- Imes Bridge is the oldest of Madison County's legendary six covered bridges.
- Elk Horn in the largest Danish settlement in the United States.
- Kalona is the largest Amish community west of the Mississippi River.
- Quaker Oats, in Cedar Rapids, is the largest cereal company in the world.
- Cornell College is the only school in the nation to have its entire campus listed on the National Register of Historic Places.
- Local Herbert Hoover became the thirty-first president of the United States.
- John Wayne, whose birth name was Marion Robert Morrison, grew up in Winterset.
- Nearly everyone has a set of rugged Carhartts coveralls, especially farmers and construction workers. On college campuses you can tell which kids come from

farms because they wear Carhartts, but it's not anything to be ashamed of (it's cool).

- Some Mormons, disillusioned with the leadership of Brigham Young and opposed to polygamy, the practice of having more than one wife, remained in the Midwest. They founded the Reorganized Church of Jesus Christ of Latter-day Saints, which had its headquarters in Lamoni, Iowa, for thirty-nine years.
- Several German Pietist groups found their way to Iowa. The Community of True Inspiration bought thousands of acres in eastern Iowa and established seven villages known as the Amana Colonies.
- The Amish, followers of a conservative Mennonite faith, also established farms in Iowa and practiced their traditional lifestyle.
- There seems to be a sheltered naïveté about Iowans; they tend to come across as provincially optimistic.
- This is one friendly state. There's a small-town cordiality even in big places like Des Moines. Everyone says "Hi" on the street.

Your Character's Food and Drink

German food is big here, including smoked hams and sausages, fresh pastries, and homemade wines. The "Iowa chop" is a huge, boneless pork chop. Your character will find lots of pork and barbecue places in Iowa. Corn on the cob is huge, but overall fruits and vegetables aren't a major part of an Iowan's diet, except in the cities.

Things Your Character Likes to Remember

- The University of Iowa Writers' Workshop. It has an unsurpassed international reputation for fostering great writers, including the likes of Ray Bradbury, Flannery O'Connor, and Kurt Vonnegut Jr.
- George Washington Carver went to Iowa State.
- The education system in the state is well above the national average.
- The way everybody comes together to help during the floods, and during difficult times in general—everybody is your neighbor and you take care of them.
- It's wrong to judge another person. Iowans are very accepting of differences.

Things Your Character Would Like to Forget

- How he's perceived by the rest of the country (this is a big concern here).

- The Iowa paradox: Residents at once seem so proud of Iowa but also so ashamed of it. They complain about Iowa but don't leave.

Myths and Misperceptions About Iowa

- **The farmers are all hicks and hillbillies.** Most are nice, articulate, literate, congenial—many even have college degrees.
- **It's flat.** Iowa rolls like bedcovers and pillows. Beautiful, green rolling space.
- **It's always dry and brown.** It snows a lot, especially above I-80. Snowmobiles can be found all over the northern part of the state, especially in the country. All houses have snowblowers, not just shovels.
- **Iowa isn't near any water.** Iowa is actually the only state whose east and west borders are 100 percent water.

Interesting Places to Set a Scene

- **Des Moines.** Although there's no major university here (other than Drake University, a Jesuit school), Des Moines is Iowa's major city for two reasons: insurance and publishing. Next to Hartford, Connecticut, Des Moines is the largest insurance city in the states. In addition, media giant Meredith Corporation is located here, publisher of such national magazines as *Better Home and Gardens* and *Ladies Home Journal* are published here.
- **Cedar Rapids.** This industrial powerhouse of a city actually does rest near the rapids of the Cedar River. Industries here include the production of farm hard-

An aerial view of Iowa's farmland

© PhotoDisc/Getty Images

For Further Research

Books

A Brit Among the Hawkeyes, by Lord Acton Richard
Growing Up in Iowa: Reminiscences of Fourteen Iowa Authors, edited by Clarence A. Andrews
Iowa: A Bicentennial History, by Joseph Frazier Wall
Iowa History and Culture, by Patricia Dawson and David Hudson
Iowa: The Middle Land, by Dorothy Schwieder
Iowa Off the Beaten Path, by Lori Erickson and Tracy Stuhr
Iowa and Some Iowans, by Betty Jo Buckingham and Eleanor Blanks
Take This Exit and *Take the Next Exit: New Views of the Iowa Landscape*, edited by Robert F. Sayre

Web Sites

www.mtmercy.edu/iafiction/iowafor.htm (Iowa writers)
www.state.ia.us/ (official state site)
www.heartofiowa.com/history/ (state history)
www.iowahistory.org/ (state historical society)
www.uiowa.edu/~iww/ (University of Iowa Writers' Workshop)

Still Curious? Why Not Check Out

Boy Life on the Prairie, by Hamlin Garland
The Bridges of Madison County, by Robert James Waller
Code Sixty-One: A Novel, by Donald Harstad
Field of Dreams
The Hawkeye Trilogy, by Herbert Quick
A Jury of Her Peers, by Susan Glaspell
The Music Man
New Hope, by Ruth Suckow
The Straight Story
A Thousand Acres, by Jane Smiley
What's Eating Gilbert Grape

---

ware, electronics, cereal, corn products, and milk-processing machinery.

- **The Amana Colonies.** These seven quaint villages were established in the mid-1800s by a German religious group. Don't confuse the Amana with the Amish—your character will find no horse-drawn buggies here. Technology also is not a problem, as the Amana have become relatively well known for their appliances, especially refrigerators and air conditioners. The houses and barns are filled with homemade wineries, smoked meats, fresh pastries, quaint shops, restaurants, handcrafted furniture, quilts, and lots of brooms and looms.

- **Davenport.** This river city is part of what's known as the Quad Cities metropolitan area. Aside from getting flooded and impressing the world with its community coming together during tough times, Davenport is the chiropractic capital of the states, thanks to the Palmer College of Chiropractic. If your character wants to help flooded neighbors, needs to have his back cracked, or has to toss a body off the historic Government Bridge, this is his city.

- **Madison County.** You know what this place looks like if you've seen the movie or read the book *The Bridges of Madison County*. The six covered bridges are a sight to behold, especially the big red Roseman Bridge.

- **Sioux City.** This is another river city, but this time it's the Missouri. Sioux City benefits greatly from being on the Missouri's banks, as it is now a recreational area near the water. Your character can come here and dance on the pavilion, stroll the lovely riverside park, or try to win a few bucks at the riverboat casino.

- **Fort Madison.** Fort Madison's days as a steamboat, logging, and railroad center are for the most part gone. Today three things put this city on the map: paints, pens, and a penitentiary. It makes the paints and pens and then ships them out of town, but the city's not so lucky with the penitentiary—it and its inhabitants are here to stay. It's the state's only maximum-security prison, so inmates come and rarely leave.

- **Council Bluffs.** What makes Council Bluff stand out is not that it was settled by Mormons in the mid-1800s, nor that Lewis and Clark made their first "council bluff" with the Native Americans here—it's the fifty-six-foot golden spike at the corner of Twenty-First Street and Ninth Avenue. But this is not where the Union Pacific and Central Pacific railroads met to form the Union Pacific; the big spike must be a hoax of some sort.

- **Dubuque.** This river town was the state's first European settlement. Although once a mining and banking area, it is now one of the state's major industrial centers and is home to several publishing, printing, and software companies. The riverboat casinos are hopping on the weekends, as is "Music on the March," a drum and bugle competition that takes place each July.
- **Iowa City.** One of the Midwest's favorite college towns, this is the intellectual and cultural center of the state. The downtown pedestrian plaza hops with shoppers and students, the latter of which can be found hanging out at the street-side cafes and restaurants, listening to local bands at the outdoor stage, or playing chess on the life-size chessboard. Or, if your character is like many writers in Iowa City, she's locked in a room behind her PC trying to pen some dazzling bit of fiction for the writers workshop.
- **Ames.** It's a college town in which students make up about half the city's population. A lot of residents, however, are not affiliated with Iowa State—but they don't want to live in Des Moines! They want the college culture of Ames. The Vishas festival at the end of the school year is huge and can get out of hand.

Kansas

Kansas Basics That Shape Your Character

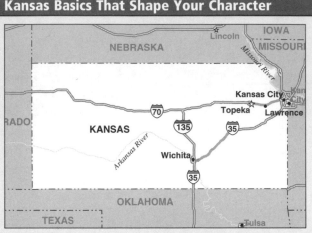

Motto: To the Stars Through Difficulties

Population: 2.68 million

Prevalent Religions: Roman Catholic, Baptist, Methodist, some Lutheran and Presbyterian, and fewer Pentecostal and Episcopalian, also Church of Jesus Christ of Latter-day Saints and Jewish

Major Industries: Cattle, transportation equipment, food processing, printing and publishing, chemical products, machinery, apparel, wheat, sorghum, soybeans, hogs, corn, petroleum, mining

Ethnic Makeup (in percent): Caucasian 86.1%, African-American 5.7%, Hispanic 7.0%, Asian 1.7%, Native American 0.9%, Other 3.4%

Famous Kansans: Walter P. Chrysler, Bob Dole, Amelia Earhart, Dwight D. Eisenhower, Dennis Hopper, William Inge, Buster Keaton, Harold Lloyd, Edgar Lee Masters, Gordon Parks, Charles "Buddy" Rogers, Damon Runyon, Barry Sanders, W. Eugene Smith, William E. Stafford, William Allen White

Significant Events Your Character Has Probably Thought About

- Kansas was a crucial battleground in the fight over slavery between 1858 and 1859. It was finally admitted as a free state in 1861, just before the Civil War.
- Argonia elected Susanna Madora Salter as the nation's first female mayor in 1887.
- In 1919, Wichita built the state's first airplane factory.

Wichita went on to become one of the nation's top plane manufacturing cities.

- In 1939, Wichita's Hattie McDaniel became the first African-American woman to win an Academy Award, for her supporting role in *Gone With the Wind*.
- Dan and Frank Carney opened the first Pizza Hut in Wichita in 1958. Now it's the largest pizza restaurant chain in the world, with over 300,000 employees in ninety countries.
- In 1969, Bob Dole won his first of many senatorial elections; he left the Senate in 1996 for a failed run for the presidency.
- In 1990 and 1997, Kansas wheat farmers produced way too much wheat, enough to make thirty-three to thirty-five billion loaves of bread, or enough to provide everyone on Earth with more than six loaves each. Needless to say, a lot of it had to go to waste.
- In August of 1999, a majority of the Kansas Board of Education voted to pass a new statewide science curriculum that promoted creationism, wiping out virtually all mention of evolution and related concepts in K-12 schools.

Kansas Facts and Peculiarities Your Character Might Know

- The graham cracker was named after the Reverend Sylvester Graham, an alleged whole-wheat flour fanatic.
- Most cartographers will tell you that Lebanon is the geographic center of the United States.
- Kansas City is divided into Kansas City, Kansas, and Kansas City, Missouri (called KCK and KCMO). Most people think that Kansas City is just in Kansas, but the majority of it is on the Missouri side.
- Kansas State (K-State) always has a great football team and a pathetic basketball team. The University of Kansas (KU) always has a great basketball team and a pathetic football team. Thus, peace is always maintained and the universe keeps its balance.
- The town of Tonganoxie was well known in the state because the dyslexic person who made the road sign pointed people to "Tognanoxie" (he reversed the first *n* and the *g* in the sign, either by mistake or so only

he could read it!). The sign stayed that way for almost three decades before it was fixed.

- Forget Chicago—Dodge City is one of the windiest cities in the nation.
- When a tornado destroys a town, victims take particular care *not* to remove debris from roads and begin repairing damaged public properties. That way, when Federal Emergency Management Agency (FEMA) representatives arrive, the damage looks, well, like a tornado hit, and the city gets more disaster relief funds.
- If you're from Leavenworth County, you probably tell people you're "doing time in Leavenworth," one of the most notorious state prisons in the country.
- Students from the University of Kansas refer to Kansas State (K-State) as "Gay State."
- Students from K-State refer to the University of Kansas (KU) as "Gay U."

Your Character's Food and Drink

Kansans like their cattle. Of course, Kansas City barbecue rules, as does grilling pork, chicken, and hot dogs; baby back ribs; grilled pork chops; fried chicken; hickory smoked ribs; meatloaf; chili; catfish; and fried steak. Veggies include okra, collard greens, black-eyed peas, green beans, and corn on the cob. Breakfast food favorites tend to be bacon, sausage links, ham, hash browns, and biscuits.

Things Your Character Likes to Remember

- He has a home where the buffalo roam. (Yes, "Home on the Range" is the official state song).
- Having survived the Dust Bowl of the 1930s.
- Wheat. The state produces more of it than any other place in the world.
- Grain elevators. Hutchinson has one that's a half-mile long, consists of one thousand bins, and holds forty-six million bushels.
- Horses. The Kansas State University College of Veterinary Medicine lets the big mammals rest on waterbeds when they're in surgery.

Things Your Character Would Like to Forget

- Tornadoes.
- The Reverend Fred Phelps of the Westboro Baptist Church in Topeka. He showed up at Matthew Shepard's funeral in Wyoming with signs carrying mes-

sages such as "God Hates Fags" and "Matt's in Hell." Phelps and the Westboro Baptists are nationally known as one of the worst anti-gay hate groups in America.

Myths and Misperceptions About Kansas

- **Everyone in Kansas loves *The Wizard of Oz.*** Almost everyone in Kansas hates *The Wizard of Oz.* Some businesspeople have tried to start a Wizard of Oz theme park in Kansas for the last two decades, but Kansans keep finding ways to stop it.
- **The Kansas City Royals, Kansas City Chiefs, and Kansas City Wizards play in Kansas.** Sorry—they all play in Missouri.

Interesting Places to Set a Scene

- **The Missouri River.** Stretching from northeastern Kansas (Leavenworth County) down past Kansas City, this body of water has many branches that extend into many towns in northeastern Kansas. Most towns in northeastern Kansas therefore have a spot where people frequently go to "watch the river." The Missouri River is also used frequently by murderers to dump bodies—now there's an idea.
- **Frontier Army Museum in Fort Leavenworth.** One of the finest collections of nineteenth-century horse-drawn vehicles is the highlight of this museum. General George Custer's horse sleigh, a carriage that carried Abraham Lincoln during his visit to Leavenworth, and a 1917 Jenny biplane used to track Pancho Villa are among the many items on exhibit. It's also home to the Buffalo Soldier memorial.
- **Council Grove.** One of the state's most historic towns; in fact, the entire settlement has been designated a

A wagon train near Topeka

For Further Research

Books

Charles W. Quantrell: A True History of His Guerilla Warfare on the Missouri and Kansas Border During the Civil War of 1861 to 1865, by John P. Burch

The Great Kansas Bond Scandal, by Robert Smith Bader

I Love Kansas, by Richard Taylor

Outlaws on Horseback: The History of the Organized Bands of Bank and Train Robbers Who Terrorized the Prairie Towns of Missouri, Kansas, Indian Territory, and Oklahoma for Half a Century, by Harry Sinclair Drago

Pioneer Women: Voices from the Kansas Frontier, by Joanna L. Stratton and Arthur Meier Jr.

The Repeal of the Missouri Compromise, by P. Ormal Ray

West of Wichita: Settling the High Plains of Kansas, 1865–1890, by Craig Miner

What Kansas Means to Me: Twentieth-Century Writers on the Sunflower State, edited by Thomas Fox Averill

Web Sites

www.accesskansas.org/ (news and events)
www.ku.edu/ (university site)
http://skyways.lib.ks.us/history/ (Kansas history)
www.washburn.edu/reference/bridge24/Kansas.html (contemporary Kansas writers)

Still Curious? Why Not Check Out

A Boy and His Dog, by Harlan Ellison

Daltons! The Raid on Coffeyville, Kansas, by Robert Barr Smith

Kansas

The Kid From Kansas

The Life and Legend of Wyatt Earp

The Persian Pickle Club, by Sandra Dallas

Smallville

To Watch the River, by Thomas Wade Oliver

The Will: A Novel, by Reed Arvin

National Historic Landmark. Council Grove was the last provision stop on the Old Santa Fe Trail between the Missouri River and Santa Fe, and the town is filled with landmarks of the frontier West, including the Last Chance Store and the Hays House Restaurant, both of which have been in business since 1857. The latter is the oldest continuously operating restaurant west of the Mississippi.

- **Lawrence.** Two cools things about Lawrence are its Fire Station No. 4, which was a station site on the Underground Railroad, and the fact that William S. Burroughs lived here for the last years of his life. In fact, Burroughs helped start a small coffeehouse/bar in town. After his death, the city issued a William S. Burroughs three-dollar bill that was used as legal tender in some city stores.

- **Riverboat casinos.** It may not be what Ike and Tina had in mind, but "rollin' on the river" aboard one could be an experience sure to float a character's boat. The Missouri River just north of downtown Kansas City has become the site of some of the area's hottest entertainment spots. With four riverboats, Kansas City offers a number of opportunities to court Lady Luck.

- **Historic Fort Hays Day in Hays.** Two full days of living history, including demonstrations of butter churning, tatting, rope making, rug weaving, whittling, stone-post cutting, and more.

- **Liberal's International Pancake Race.** Have your female character partake in this wacky battle. Kansas women compete against women in Olney, England, running a 415-yard, S-shaped course with a pancake in a skillet, flipping it en route.

- **Topeka.** If your character needs a shrink, have him head to Topeka, the state capital and home to the world-recognized Menninger Foundation psychiatric clinic.

Significant Events Your Character Has Probably Thought About

- Daniel Boone exploring the area and blazing the Wilderness Trail in 1767.
- The birth of Abraham Lincoln in a log cabin on Sinking Spring Farm in 1809.
- The Hatfield-McCoy feud. This vendetta started in 1863 and lasted until the 1890s, causing much bloodshed and anguish between two families and two states (Kentucky and West Virginia).
- In 1904 the Kentucky Legislature passed Day Law, which prohibited the co-education of African-American and Caucasian students.
- The Black Patch War in 1907. Hired hands lawlessly (but effectively) boycotted against the monopolistic practices of the tobacco industry. The state militia finally forced a truce in 1908.
- Colonel Harlan Sanders began cooking his famous Kentucky Fried Chicken in 1930 at a gas station in Corbin.
- In the 1930s, the United Mine Workers of America (UMW) in Harlan County staged a violent strike, drawing national attention to "bloody" Harlan.
- The son of a poor Graves County tobacco farmer, seventy-one-year-old Alben W. Barkley became the oldest U.S. vice president when he entered the office in 1949.
- The energy crisis of the 1970s was good for Kentucky, because the state's large coal supply was in high demand.
- A political scandal that started as a small horse-racing investigation in 1992 spread like wildfire and brought convictions to fifteen state legislators.
- In 1997, two years before Columbine, a Paducah fourteen-year-old entered Heath High School and opened fire on a prayer group, killing three girls and wounding five other students.

Kentucky Facts and Peculiarities Your Character Might Know

- Curiously, both Abraham Lincoln (president of the Union) and Jefferson Davis (president of the Confed-

Kentucky Basics That Shape Your Character

Motto: United We Stand, Divided We Fall

Population: 4.1 million

Prevalent Religions: Christianity, particularly Southern Baptist, Pentecostal, Lutheran, and Roman Catholic

Major Industries: Horses, tobacco, cattle, dairy products, hogs, soybeans, corn, transportation equipment, car manufacturing, petroleum, natural gas, electric equipment, machinery, food processing, aluminum, coal, tourism

Ethnic Makeup (in percent): Caucasian 90.1%, African-American 7.3%, Hispanic 1.5%, Asian 0.7%, Native American 0.2 %, Other 0.6%

Famous Kentuckians: Muhammad Ali, Wendell Berry, Kit Carson, the Clooneys (Rosemary, George, and Nick), Johnny Depp, Crystal Gayle, Sue Grafton, David W. Griffith, bell hooks, the Judds, Barbara Kingsolver, Abraham Lincoln, Loretta Lynn, Thomas Merton, Bill Monroe, Patricia Neal, Diane Sawyer, Adlai Stevenson, Allen Tate, Hunter S. Thompson, Robert Penn Warren

eracy) were born in Kentucky, within one year and one hundred miles of each other.
- Pike County can boast of being the world's largest producer of coal.
- A Henderson teacher named Mary Wilson came up with the idea of Mother's Day in 1887. Now, of course, it's a national holiday.
- Kentucky can be partitioned into four basic quadrants: the coal country in the eastern mountains, the cave country in the south and central areas, the horse-laden

bluegrass farms surrounding Lexington's northern plains, and the lakes and rolling farmlands in the west.

- The largest amount of gold in the world—more than six billion dollars worth—is stashed in the vaults at Fort Knox.
- In 1983 Martha Layne Collins became the first woman elected governor of Kentucky.
- Many Kentucky towns are named after European cities, including Athens, London, Paris, Frankfort, and Versailles. But here it's not "Ath-ens" but "Ay-thens" (long *a*), and it's not "Ver-SIGH" but "Ver-SALES."
- Some things about Kentucky are just downright ironic: State Treasurer James W. "Honest Dick" Tate embezzled $247,000 and fled the state. Frederick Moore Vinson of Louisa was born in a jail but became Chief Justice of the U.S. Supreme Court. You can buy and sell alcohol in Christian County, but in Bourbon County you can't. And Barren County is alleged to have the most fertile ground in the entire state. Finally, legendary horse Man o' War won every race in his career except one, in which he lost to a horse appropriately named Upset.

Your Character's Food and Drink

Kentuckians love typical southern cuisine, such as southern fried chicken, bean soup, country ham, hog jowl bacon or meat with beans, pork chops, mustard greens, corn, green beans, Kentucky wonder beans, catfish, collard greens, spinach, and corn bread. Breakfast favorites are bacon, sausage links, country ham, hash browns, biscuits 'n' gravy, and grits. Dessert dishes are pecan pie, pudding, and cobbler. Popular drinks include mint julep and the legendary Kentucky bourbons and whiskeys, from moonshine and Wild Turkey to Jim Beam and Maker's Mark (all of which have distilleries here).

Things Your Character Likes to Remember

- The Kentucky Derby.
- Bluegrass music.
- University of Kentucky basketball—residents say they "bleed blue."
- Farming. There were still ninety thousand farms in Kentucky in 2000.
- Cars. Kentucky is the nation's fourth leading producer of motor vehicles.
- Tobacco. About 450 million pounds of it are grown annually.
- Kentucky bourbon. Nearly all of the world's bourbon comes from Kentucky.
- Post-it notes. Everybody in the world uses them, but they're manufactured exclusively in Cynthiana (and the exact number produced is a secret).
- Senator John Sherman Cooper. A champion of civil rights, he represented Kentucky for twenty-one years.

Things Your Character Would Like to Forget

- That Kentucky never chose sides in the Civil War.
- The filth and the squalor of eastern Kentucky.
- Much of the land is scarred and ravaged from strip mining.
- Winchester was recently on the *National Geographic* list of the one hundred worst cities in America.
- In 1970, it was the last of all the states in the number of school years its adults had completed: an average of 9.9 years compared with a national average of 12.1.

Myths and Misperceptions About Kentucky

- **Bluegrass is really blue.** It's called "bluegrass," but it's actually green. In the spring, however, "bluegrass" does produce bluish purple buds.
- **They're proud of their mountain roots.** Not in the big cities. Although about one-third of people from Lexington can trace their roots to small towns in the Appalachian Mountains, many don't admit it.
- **Kentucky was a Confederate state during the Civil War.** With thirty thousand residents fighting for the Confederacy and sixty thousand for the Union, Kentucky

One of Kentucky's many country roads

For Further Research

Books

Ante-Bellum Kentucky: A Social History, 1800–1860, by F. Garvin Davenport

Days of Darkness: The Feuds of Eastern Kentucky, by John Ed Pearce

A Geography of Kentucky: A Topical-Regional Overview, by Wilford A. Bladen

How the West Was Lost: The Transformation of Kentucky From Daniel Boone to Henry Clay, by Stephen Aron

Kentucky: A Bicentennial History, by Stephen A. Channing

The Kentucky Encyclopedia, edited by John E. Kleber et al.

Kentucky Government and Politics, edited by Joel Goldstein

A New History of Kentucky, by Lowell H. Harrison and James C. Klotter

Our Kentucky: A Study of the Bluegrass State, edited by James C. Klotter

Pioneer Ghosts of Kentucky, by Wilma Winton

Violence in the Black Patch of Kentucky and Tennessee, by Suzanne Marshall

Web Sites

www.kentucky.com/mld/kentucky/ (current events)

www.kydirect.net/ (official state site)

www.rootsweb.com/~kypoc/ (African-American state history)

www.tourky.com/tourky/html (tourism)

www.kdla.state.ky.us/ (libraries and archives)

http://kentuckywriters.org/ (writer's site)

Still Curious? Why Not Check Out

In Country, by Bobbie Ann Mason

The Kentuckians, by Janice Holt Giles

Kentucky Authors: A History of Kentucky Literature, by Mary Carmel Browning

A Literary History of Kentucky, by William S. Ward

One of the Children Is Crying, by Coleman Dowell

River of Earth, by James Still

Taps for Private Tussie, by Jesse Stuart

---

actually had its own Civil War going on. Although a slave-holding state, it also had a large abolitionist population.

Interesting Places to Set a Scene

- **Ashland.** This is Appalachian coal and mining country. Aside from coal and oil, the two things important to Ashlanders are the Paramount Theatre (on the National Register of Historic Places) and musicians who've come from the area, including Billy Ray Cyrus, the Judds, Ricky Skaggs, Loretta Lynn, Crystal Gayle, Dwight Yoakam, and Patty Loveless. They've even named U.S. 23 the Country Music Highway, because it's spawned so many successes in Nashville.

- **Berea.** Berea College stands for everything that's right about education. It was integrated in the early 1900s, before other schools welcomed diversity. All students receive full-tuition scholarships, but they also must spend twenty hours a week working on a mountain craft or doing community service. The campus, which sits amidst the rolling hills of the Appala-

chian Mountains, is the most beautiful in the state.

- **Land Between the Lakes.** This is the largest inland peninsula in the country. In 1963 President John F. Kennedy designated it a national recreation area to show that it could be turned into a profitable asset. The plan worked, as the area brings in millions of visitors and millions of dollars. People come to camp, hike, boat, and fish; other highlights are a nature center, a living history farm, a planetarium and an observatory, horse stables, and a huge elk and bison prairie.

- **Lexington.** (See page 125 for an extensive look at Lexington.)

- **Louisville.** (See page 128 for an extensive look at Louisville.)

- **Mammoth Cave.** It's what its name implies: the world's longest cave. It was first promoted in 1816, making it the second oldest tourist attraction in the states. Today it receives loads of visitors, who come to see stalagmites, stalactites, underwater lakes, and aboveground deer. This area was important for providing gunpowder.

- **Northern Kentucky.** Newport and Covington are the two primary cities here, and in many ways, they are extensions of Cincinnati. Newport had been known for its strip joints and sad cafes, but as of late it has a world-class aquarium and an entertainment plaza. Covington is known for its waterfront, historic neighborhoods, restaurants, and the Cathedral Basilica of the Assumption, which is modeled after Notre Dame and reputedly has the largest stained-glass church window in the world.

- **Red River Gorge.** Part of Kentucky's extensive Daniel Boone National Forest, this geological gem is called "Land of the Arches," because it's home to the world's largest array of natural arches (over one hundred). If your character is a backpacker, mountain climber, rapeller, or canoer, she's spending a lot of time here.

- **Shaker Village.** From 1805 until 1859 they shared common property, practiced equality between the sexes, believed in pacifism, practiced celibacy, and shook and trembled to rid themselves of evil. Though they are gone (the celibacy thing caught up with them), the Shakers cannot be forgotten, as their village of horse paths, unique brick-and-stone architecture, and simplified furniture is testament to them. Shaker Village will send your character on a trip back in time and will teach him a lesson in self-sufficiency.

- **Sinking Spring Farm.** This is where Honest Abe was born. What makes the area unique is not the log cabin (which most historians agree isn't the cabin of Lincoln's birth), but the monument around it. It's an impressive granite-and-marble structure with fifty-six steps (one for each year of Lincoln's life) and massive double front doors—all sticking out like a sore thumb smack in the wooded hills of Kentucky.

Lexington Facts and Peculiarities Your Character Might Know

- Lexington was settled in 1775 and was so cosmopolitan that at one point it was nicknamed the "Athens of the West."
- Some of the most beautiful country in the world surrounds Lexington in the bluegrass region of Kentucky.
- Legendary Wildcat basketball coach Adolph Rupp got his job in 1930 when he walked into the search committee meeting and said that he was the best coach in America. Rupp coached at the University of Kentucky (UK) for forty-two years and won 876 games and four NCAA championships.
- The city bills itself, understandably, as the horse capital of the world.
- Lexington has high schools named after Henry Clay, "The Great Compromiser," and poet Paul Laurence Dunbar, both of whom have roots to the area.
- William Shatner raises horses just outside of town.
- Rupp Arena. At the time of its inception, critics railed against it as folly, saying you would never get that many people to watch a basketball game in Lexington—these days about twenty-four thousand fans pack Rupp Arena for every Wildcats game.
- George Blanda, the oldest man to score a point in the National Football League (NFL), graduated from UK in 1948 and played twenty-six seasons in the NFL, leaving the game when he was forty-nine.
- Twin brothers Morgan and Marvin Smith, who photographed many of the stars of the Harlem Renaissance, had ties to Lexington.
- WUKY in Lexington (which began as WBKY) is the oldest university-licensed FM station in the country.

If Your Character . . .

If Your Character Is Alternative and Grungy, he lives in a gutted old house near UK on Maxwell Street or Rose Street. This area of town is college and adolescent central.

If Your Character Smells of Old Horse Money, she lives on Versailles Road on a horsefarm, or out past Old Paris

Lexington Basics That Shape Your Character

A new barn at Calumet Farms

Population: 260,512 in the city; 424,778 in the Greater Metro area

Prevalent Religions: Christianity, particularly Southern Baptist, Pentecostal, Lutheran, and Roman Catholic

Top Employers: Ashland Inc., Clark Material Handling Company, General Electric, GTE Products Corporation, Johnson Controls, Lexmark International, Link-Belt Construction Equipment Company, Long John Silver's, Square D Company, Toyota Motor Manufacturing, Tokico (USA) Inc., Trane Company, The Valvoline Company, United Parcel Service, University of Kentucky (UK)

Per Capita Income: $29,000

Average Daily Temperature: January, 31° F; July, 76° F

Ethnic Makeup (in percent): Caucasian 81%, African-American 13.5%, Hispanic 3.3%, Asian 2.5%, Native American .2%, Other 1.2%

Newspapers and Magazines: *Lexington Herald-Leader, The Lane Report, Thoroughbred Times*

Free Weekly Alternative Papers: *ACE Weekly, Community Voice, Kentucky Kernel*

Pike. People who come from old horse money also live on Russell Cave Road.

If Your Character Smells of Non-Horse Money, she lives downtown, near Transylvania in an expensive townhouse or high-rise. If she's in the Gratz Park subdivision, she'll be overlooking another fine place called Greenbrier, off Winchester Road.

If Your Character Smells of Basketball Money, he lives on The Island. A causeway on each side of the street leads up to The Island, which is not really a big island but a rich, guarded community on a small island. The homes are huge, ritzy, and very private. Eddie Sutton and Rick Patino lived here.

If Your Character Is a Family Man, he lives on Gainesway Drive or Beacon Hill Road. Single- and two-story family ranch houses on almost identical-sized plots of land make up these two middle-class areas of town. Red Cliff Road or Mary Todd Elementary are two other middle-class, integrated areas.

If Your Character Wears a Blue Collar at Work, she lives in Northside or Windburn Drive. A mix of Caucasians and African-Americans makes up these communities, which often have small, simple homes or poor apartment complexes. The convenience store in the area probably has steel bars across the windows.

Local Grub Your Character Might Love
Lexingtonians love typical southern fare (see Kentucky listing on page 121). Local favorite places for your character to grab a bite to eat, including Joe Bologna's, in what used to be an old synagogue, complete with stained glass windows (best pizza and breadsticks in town); Tolly Ho (greasy spoon by UK campus, open twenty-four hours); Deshay's on Main and Broadway across from Triangle Park. (One local professed: "The stuffed mushrooms kick ass!"); Jozo's Bayou Gumbo (Cajun food); The Louden Café (cheap and fattening); and The Atomic Café on Limestone Street (the carrot soup is a favorite).

Interesting and Peculiar Places to Set a Scene
- **Alfalfa's.** This vegetarian hangout across from UK's main entrance established itself in the 1960s as a conversation-filled gathering place; it has been serving the coffeehouse crowd ever since.
- **At a Wildcat game in Rupp Arena.** Not only will your character get a big taste of what it's like to bleed blue, she'll also be entertained by one darn good basketball game. Heck, she might even spot Ashley Judd, who has frequented many games.
- **Austin City Saloon.** Lexington's original country bar is where country music star John Michael Montgomery played for five years before he hit it big. Have your character grab his hat and boots and get scootin'.
- **Just west of Rupp.** This industrial, rough section of town is poor and scary. This is where old, junked cars and a big quarry meet the local drug dealers. Your character could cause or get into a lot of mischief here.
- **Keeneland.** This is often called the most beautiful and historic racecourse in the world. But if you set a scene here, make sure it's in the spring or fall, as Keeneland only holds races six weeks a year—three in April and three in October.
- **Lynagh's.** The O'Round burgers here are tops in the city and probably in the region (the menu says each is the size of a small hubcap).
- **The abandoned castle near Versailles.** With its battlements, outer walls, and conical towers, this looks like an old European castle built of aged stone, but it was actually erected in the 1960s and mostly consists of concrete blocks. On a hillside in the middle of beautiful horse country, the place has been abandoned for most of its existence. Telltale stories abound about those who've dared others to spend the night on the grounds.
- **The Bar.** A Lexington legend, this downtown nightclub (used to be Johnny Angel's) has been the city's main gay late-night spot for years. The industrial dance music keeps playing loudly, and female impersonators keep performing weekly.
- **The Festival of the Bluegrass.** The top bluegrass and gospel festival in the world is held at the Kentucky Horse Park Campgrounds. The likes of Alison Krauss and Union Station come here to perform for what's becoming quite an international audience.
- **The Kentucky Horse Park.** This is the only equestrian theme park in the world. Spanning over a thousand acres, it's a horse lover's paradise. Your character can explore it in many ways—by foot, on a shuttle, in a horse-drawn carriage, or even on a saddle.
- **The Kentucky Theatre.** This is where Lexingtonians go to see offbeat, foreign, and classic films. The theater also provides an intimate live concert venue for all types of music, from bluegrass to rock.
- **The Red Mile in May.** It's noted red soil is rumored to make this the fastest harness track in the world. It's

For Further Research

Books

Bossism and Reform in a Southern City: Lexington, Kentucky, 1880–1940, by James Duane Bolin

Call to Post: Winning Kentucky Recipes, edited by Beth H. Clifton

History of Fayette County, Kentucky, by William Henry Perrin

History of Lexington, Kentucky, by George Washington Ranck

Lexington in Good Taste, by Lani Basberg and Jeanne Jennings

Vestiges of the Venerable City: A Chronicle of Lexington, Kentucky, by Clay Lancaster

Web Sites

www.kentucky.com/mld/heraldleader/ (news)

www.uky.edu/AS/English/news/ (UK writers)

www.imh.org/ (Kentucky Horse Park)

www.visitlex.com/quick/facts.html (visitor's guide)

www.louisville.edu/library/ekstrom/govpubs/states/kentucky/kyplaces/lexington/lexhist.html (Lexington history)

Still Curious? Why Not Check Out

The Bean Trees, by Barbara Kingsolver

The Bluegrass Conspiracy: An Inside Story of Power, Greed, Drugs and Murder, by Sally Denton

Blue Grass of Kentucky

Bluegrass King, by Janet Dailey

In Country

A Kentucky Cardinal: A Story, by James Lane Allen

Kentucky Heat, by Fern Michaels

Kentucky Rich, by Fern Michaels

Lexington's oldest existing racecourse (built in 1875), and the Memorial Stakes Days (Memorial Day weekend) is the most celebrated chili fest in the state.

- **Triangle Park.** Cascading fountains and flowering pear trees make up this city park, where three streets meet. It's a pleasant and relaxing retreat for many who work in the office buildings nearby.

Exceptionally Grand Things Your Character Is Proud Of

- UK Basketball. The Wildcats are seven-time NCAA champions, have their own museum, and fans say they bleed blue.
- When the Wildcats won their first title in 1921. Kentucky won the game on a free throw. Fans celebrated in the streets for days, classes were cancelled, and the university president posted guards around the armory.
- Writer Wendell Berry taught at UK and now lives on a farm west of Lexington.
- Marvin Gaye's family comes from the area.
- Pulitzer Prize winners Angelo Henderson and Don Whitehead.
- Thomas Hunt Morgan (the father of modern genetics; he won the Nobel Prize in 1933).

- William N. Lipscomb won the Nobel Prize for Chemistry in 1976.

Pathetically Sad Things Your Character Is Ashamed Of

- The fire at the Wild Turkey distillery in May of 2000. Nearly twenty thousand barrels of flaming bourbon spilled into the Kentucky River, killing and intoxicating thousands of fish.
- Eddie Sutton. Although he won Coach of the Year in 1986, the 1988 recruiting scandal angered and embarrassed—and still haunts—many fans.

Your Character Loves

- An Adolph Rupp story. A favorite he used to tell was about a woman who normally sat behind the bench with her husband and sons. One day Rupp came out before the game and saw she was sitting alone, so he asked where her husband was. She said he had died the week before. Rupp said, "Oh, I'm sorry. And where are your sons?" Her response: "They're at the funeral."
- Ashley Judd, Sam Shepard, Johnny Depp, George Wolfe, George Clooney, Harry Dean Stanton, Jim Varney, John Michael Montgomery.
- Bobbie Ann Mason and Barbara Kingsolver.

Louisville

Louisville Basics That Shape Your Character

Louisville skyline at night with Ohio River in the foreground

Population: 256,231 in the city; 1,025,598 in the Greater Metro area

Prevalent Religions: Mostly Christian (Southern Baptists and Presbyterians both have theological seminaries here) with a sizable Roman Catholic population, also a small but visible Jewish community and some Buddhist and Muslim immigrants

Top Employers: United Parcel Service, Jefferson County Public Schools, Ford Motor Company, GE Appliances, Norton Healthcare, Kentucky State Government, Jewish Hospital, University of Louisville, Kroger, Humana Inc., Bank One Kentucky, LG&E Energy Corporation, CARITAS Health Services, Catholic Archdiocese of Louisville, Vencor Inc., Baptist Hospital East, Publishers Printing Company

Per Capita Income: $23,085

Average Daily Temperature: January, 32° F; July, 78° F

Ethnic Makeup (in percent): Caucasian 77.4%, African-American 18.9%, Hispanic 1.8%, Asian 1.4%, Native American 0.2%, Other 0.7%

Newspapers and Magazines: *The Courier-Journal, Business First, Louisville Magazine*

Free Weekly Alternative Papers: *LEO (Louisville Eccentric Observer), Louisville Music News*

Louisville Facts and Peculiarities Your Character Might Know

- Louisville was named after France's King Louis XVI for that country's assistance during the American Revolution. The mayor of Montpellier later gave Louisville a statue of Louis XVI, which now stands in front of City Hall. (Locals suspect, however, that this donation may have stemmed in part from that king's immense unpopularity in France: Who wants a statue of an effete aristocrat who sparked a violent revolution?)
- Despite the provenance of the name, it's pronounced "Loo-uh-vul" or "Loo-vul."
- Louisville is located on the Falls of the Ohio River and is sometimes called "Falls City."
- The Kentucky Derby, run the first Saturday in May at Churchill Downs, is the preeminent horse-racing event in the world.
- Thunder Over Louisville, the kickoff for Derby Month, is the largest annual fireworks event in the country. It also features an air show over the river, with military jets streaking above the city throughout the third weekend in April.
- The governments of the city of Louisville and Jefferson County merged recently to form "Greater Louisville."
- Frederick Law Olmsted designed many of the city's parks, neighborhoods, and parkways.
- The first restaurant cheeseburger is widely believed to have been served at Kaelin's on Newburg Road, which is still in operation. Kaelin's was also one of the first outlets for Colonel Harlan Sanders's new fried chicken recipe.
- "You all" is heard more often than "y'all," but Louisvillians do "warsh" their clothes.
- No matter how much education you have, it's where you went to high school that often determines your social life here.
- As a city, Louisville is not quite southern and not quite midwestern. Less charitable visitors might describe it as a town of "southern efficiency and northern charm," but residents know the opposite is true.
- Some famous Louisvillians: Muhammad Ali, Diane Sawyer, Tom Cruise, Foster Brooks, Bob Edwards,

Zachary Taylor, Pee Wee Reese, Colonel Harlan Sanders, Louis Brandeis, Hunter S. Thompson.

If Your Character . . .

If Your Character Is an African-American Family Man, he lives in Portland. Portland was originally its own city and is still important to river traffic. Most of the homes here are small, shotgun-style houses, with many larger townhouses and clapboard houses mixed in. There are lots of churches, too. In local parlance, the "West End" of Louisville is generally considered the African-American side of town, with the "East End" populated by rich Caucasians, and the "South End" populated by poor Caucasians. These "End" terms are too broad to be meaningful and are in fact used less often these days (in favor of actual neighborhood names); nevertheless, they are still in use and are not wholly inaccurate.

If Your Character Is a Caucasian Family Man, he lives in Butchertown. Historically associated with soap-makers, brewers, and—you guessed it—butchers, the close, shotgun houses here are overshadowed by the twin spires of St. Joseph's Church, the old Oertel's Brewery building, and the Hadley Pottery Company, which is famous for its stoneware.

If Your Character Is an Aspiring Young Musician, she lives in The Highlands. This area roughly surrounds Bardstown Road, near Cherokee Park and Cherokee Triangle, with a lot of older homes and apartments. It's not far to walk for her gig at Twice Told Café.

If Your Character Is a Small Business Owner, she sets up shop in St. Matthews. Despite the presence of the popular St. Matthews Mall, this area is characterized by non-chain hardware stores, dry cleaners, clothing stores, and the like.

If Your Character Is a Wealthy Businessperson Who Commutes, he lives in Anchorage. This neighborhood of big houses provides easy access to the freeways. You'll find lots of wide driveways for all the Land Cruisers and Expeditions "needed" for the commute into downtown.

If Your Character Wears a Blue Collar to Work, he lives in Fern Creek or Pleasure Ridge Park (PRP). These southeastern communities are home to thousands of people who know the Gene Snyder Expressway all too well. PRP isn't too far from Fort Knox.

If Your Character Is a Well-Off Artistic Type, she lives in St. James Court. Designed in imitation of popular British styles of the mid-nineteenth-century, the grand houses of this neighborhood are arranged around a central strip of grass and trees. Statues and iron street lamps lend a cultivated air to the broad streets. The annual St. James Art Fair in October is wildly popular with all sorts of Louisvillians.

If Your Character Is a Professional Who Spurns Those Faceless New Suburban Developments Way Out Where There Used to Be Farms, he lives in Cherokee Triangle. There are a *lot* of big, old Queen Anne and Victorian houses here, many with wide porches, turrets, scrolling, or gingerbread shingles—or all of these—arrayed on tree-lined streets with genuinely useful sidewalks. This is another Frederick Law Olmsted neighborhood.

Local Grub Your Character Might Love

Some southern favorites like pork chops, fried fish, and sweet tea are common, but others, such as grits and sweet potato pie, are less so. Benedictine spread was popularized by a local restaurant a century ago and is still a favorite; it's a puree of cucumber, cream cheese, onion, salt, and mayonnaise (sometimes with a little green food coloring), and it's used as a vegetable dip and a sandwich spread. The "Hot Brown," first served at the fancy Brown Hotel downtown, is a baked, open-face sandwich made with bacon, tomato, mushrooms, and turkey (or country ham), topped with onions sautéed in butter, milk, and cheddar and parmesan cheeses. Bearno's and Impellezeri's serve the best local pizza, although the national chain Papa John's got its start here and is still popular. Chess pie is a buttermilk dessert that can be flavored with lemon, coconut, or chocolate. But the chocolate-and-walnut Derby pie is a springtime favorite, as is the mint julep, a potent (and often off-putting) mixture of bourbon, mint, lemon, and sugar that is best enjoyed from a silver cup at the Downs.

Interesting and Peculiar Places to Set a Scene

- **Bardstown Road.** This commercial and residential corridor is the heart of popular/youth culture in Louis-

For Further Research

Books

African-American Life in Louisville, by Bruce M. Tyler

The Binghams of Louisville: The Dark History Behind One of America's Great Fortunes, by David Leon Chandler and Mary Voelz Chandler

Crack of the Bat: The Louisville Slugger Story, by Bob Hill

Derby Magic, by Jim Bolus

The Encyclopedia of Louisville, edited by John E. Kleber et al.

Louisville: The Greatest City, by Muhammad Ali (Introduction)

The Wall Between, by Anne Braden

Web Sites

www.louky.org/default.htm (general and government info)

http://planetlouisville.com/explore.htm (regional info)

www.gotolouisville.com (Greater Louisville Convention and Visitors Bureau)

www.louisville.com/loumag (*Louisville Magazine*)

www.courier-journal.com (*The Courier-Journal*)

Still Curious? Why Not Check Out

Absence of Reason, by Linda Y. Atkins

Aindreas: The Messenger, by Gerald McDaniel

The Great Gatsby, by F. Scott Fitzgerald (Daisy was from Louisville, remember?)

More Ten-Minute Plays From Actors Theatre of Louisville, edited by Michael Bigelow Dixon

Passion and Prejudice: A Family Memoir, by Sallie Bingham

The Proud Highway: Saga of a Desperate Southern Gentleman, 1955–1967, by Hunter S. Thompson

Society of Salty Saints, by Micheal Elliott

The Stonemason: A Play in Five Acts, by Cormac McCarthy

Win, Place, or Die, by Carolyn Keene

---

ville. Hip restaurants, music stores (Ear X-tacy is the favorite), galleries, bars, clothing shops, bookstores, and musical venues line Bardstown road from I-264 to the intersection at Broadway and Baxter. Your character might want to take a walk here on a weekend evening to see and be seen.

- **Frankfort Avenue.** With an increasing number of cafes, shops, and restaurants, this area is "the new Bardstown Road." Mom's Music is a haven for local musicians, who record, teach, learn, and perform here.

- **A bar with a band.** Louisville has an active independent music scene, from small clubs like Stevie Ray's Blues Club, Maier's St. Matthews Tavern, Twice Told Café, and The Rudyard Kipling, to larger, multistage venues, like old stalwarts the Butchertown Pub and the Phoenix Hill Tavern, and the newer, enormous O'Malley's Corner at Second and Liberty.

- **Churchill Downs.** Ladies in stylish pastel sun hats. Men in suits, from fancy and fashionable to rumpled and stained. Ostentatious horse owners chomping on cohibas. Nervous jockeys speaking diverse forms of Spanish. Drunken revelers at The Infield in various stages of undress. It must be springtime. . . .

- **Rames Food Mart.** Located right across the street from Churchill Downs, this little Arabic store can provide you with pistachio halvah in between bets on the ponies.

- **Crescent Hill Reservoir.** The walkways around the still waters of the reservoir are popular with joggers and dog walkers.

- **Iroquois Park at Sunset.** The dying light casts a russet glow on the marshes and meadows. . . .

- **An alley.** The city is filled with interesting back alleys, which are not necessarily dangerous places; in fact, they often present charming ways of navigating the city.

- **Riverfront Park.** This newly developed park complements the older Belvedere as a place to play on a jungle gym, have a picnic, listen to an outdoor concert, or just watch the steamboats and barges on the Ohio.

- **Old Louisville along Third or Fourth Street.** The Victorian and Italianate mansions here are a great social backdrop, both those that still house the wealthy and those that have been divided into apartments for the city's less-affluent young people.

Exceptionally Grand Things Your Character Is Proud Of

- The Derby.
- Artificial heart research.

- The Louisville Slugger baseball bat (and its new museum downtown).
- Muhammad Ali, the Louisville Lip.
- Actors Theatre of Louisville's annual New Play Series.

Your Character Loves

- The Cards (University of Louisville Cardinals basketball team).
- The Cats (University of Kentucky Wildcats basketball team).
- The Cards-Cats game, when the Cards then hate the Cats.

- Derby Month.
- The State Fair in August.
- Bourbon.
- High school sports.

Your Character Hates

- Spaghetti Junction (where I-64, I-65, and I-71 converge).
- The traffic jams after Thunder Over Louisville.
- Using a turn signal.
- That clunky newscaster word *Kentuckiana*.

Louisiana

Louisiana Basics That Shape Your Character

Motto: Union, Justice, and Confidence

Population: 4.68 million

Prevalent Religions: French Catholic in the south, Protestant, Pentecostal, and nondenominational in the north, Buddhism, Voodooism, and other fringe religions in and around New Orleans

Major Industries: Tourism, chemical products, petroleum and coal products, food processing, transportation equipment, paper products, seafood, cotton, soybeans, cattle, sugarcane, poultry and eggs, dairy products, rice

Ethnic Makeup (in percent): Caucasian 63.9%, African-American 32.5%, Hispanic 2.4%, Asian 1.2%, Native American 0.6%, Other 0.7%

Famous Louisianians: Louis Armstrong, Truman Capote, Van Cliburn, Fats Domino, Louis Moreau Gottschalk, Bryant Gumbel, Lillian Hellman, Dorothy Lamour, Jerry Lee Lewis, the Marsalis brothers, Jelly Roll Morton, Huey Newton, Cokie Roberts, Kordell Stewart

Significant Events Your Character Has Probably Thought About

- The settling of Lafayette Parish by French-speaking Acadians in the mid-1700s. The Acadians were soon joined by Creoles (those of African, West Indian, and European descent). Louisiana was under Spanish rule at the time.
- The Louisiana Purchase in 1803. Thomas Jefferson paid France fifteen million dollars for the Louisiana Territory, which consisted of 828,000 square miles of land west of the Mississippi River.
- In 1812, Louisiana became a state.
- Louisiana joined the Confederate States of America in 1861.
- In 1862, Port Hudson's Corps d'Afrique became the first American army to enlist African-American officers.
- In 1901, the first oil well was tapped in Louisiana. It led to a century's worth of economic prosperity for those in the oil industry.
- The election of the notoriously corrupt Governor Huey Long in 1928.
- The assassination of Huey Long in 1935 in the Baton Rouge state capitol building.
- The 1943 election of country singer and Baptist member Jimmie Davis, the only U.S. governor elected to the Country Music Hall of Fame, the Nashville Songwriter's Hall of Fame, and the Gospel Music Hall of Fame.
- The 1959 election of "The Earl of Louisiana," Earl Long (Huey's equally corrupt, good ol' boy brother).
- The 1983 Special Olympics International Summer Games, which were held in Baton Rouge.
- In 1988 televangelist Jimmy Swaggart was caught consorting with a prostitute at the "No-Tell Motel" in New Orleans. Ouch!
- The 1988 election of David Duke to the U.S. House of Representatives.
- In 1991, Duke ran for governor and nearly beat incumbent Edwin Edwards, who before the election joked, "The only way I won't get reelected is if I get caught in bed with a live boy or a dead woman." Edwards won by only 2 percent of the vote.

Louisiana Facts and Peculiarities Your Character Might Know

- Louisiana is known as "The Mardi Gras State," "Cajun Country," "Sportsman's Paradise," "The Bayou State," and "The Pelican State."

- Louisiana was named in honor of King Louis XIV.
- Louisiana is the only state with a large population of Cajuns, French descendants driven out of Nova Scotia and New Brunswick in the 1700s for refusing to pledge allegiance to England.
- English, Irish, and Scottish Protestants from the East Coast settled northern Louisiana in the early nineteenth century.
- Musically, northerners prefer country and western, while jazz, zydeco and Cajun music rule in south Louisiana.
- Religiously, the south is French Catholic; the north is Protestant; the middle is a mix of both.
- Northern Louisiana has more in common politically, culturally, and philosophically with Mississippi and Alabama than it does with southern Louisiana.
- Geographically, the terrain in the southwest is flat and grassy, in the northeast it's a delta, in the northwest it's forested, and in the middle it's rolling hills. Spanish moss and cypress swamps can be found in the southeastern part of the state.
- The Ouachita River is the dividing line between the delta in the east and the forested rolling hills to the west.
- A *pirogue* is a small, flat-bottom boat poled through a bayou.
- Louisiana's 450-foot-high capitol building is the tallest capitol building in the United States.
- Louisiana is the only state in which political subdivisions are called "parishes," not "counties."
- Bonnie and Clyde were ambushed and killed in Gibsland; their car (with their bludgeoned bodies still in it) then was towed to Arcadia, some thirty miles away.

Your Character's Food and Drink

See the New Orleans chapter for a list of Cajun favorites. Beef, catfish, barbecued pork, and crawfish are the four most popular foods in the state outside of Acadiana. Pralines are the state's favorite sweets. Avita spring water and Dixie beer are local liquid favorites. Daiquiri shops, in which you drive up in your car and order a daiquiri (alcohol included), are found throughout the state.

Things Your Character Likes to Remember

- That there's more natural variety in Louisiana than in most southern states: timber forests, oceanfronts, large fishing ponds, several rivers for fishing and boating, lush vegetation for growing crops, and good swampland for alligators.
- The Cajuns and Catholics in the south of the state are exceptionally proud of their heritage.
- The Courir de Mardi Gras, in which costumed, masked characters on horseback run wild through the countryside north of Lafayette.
- The *joie de vivre* ("joy of living").
- The song "You Are My Sunshine." This unofficial state anthem was written and recorded by none other than Governor Jimmie Davis.
- The historic antebellum homes that dot the state.
- The short and pleasant winters.

Things Your Character Would Like to Forget

- The hot and humid summers.
- The pollution caused by many factories, especially in the Baton Rouge area.
- Louisiana is forty-ninth in the nation in teacher's pay.
- Louisiana consistently ranks as one of the nation's poorest states.
- High auto and health insurance rates. Thanks to poor road conditions and lots of drunk driving, auto insurance is more expensive here than in the rest of the South. Health insurance is high, too, thanks to pollution, smoking, drinking, and a poor diet that consists of fried food high in fat and cholesterol.
- A "Long" list of corrupt politicians, from the Long boys to Edwin Edwards.

Myths and Misperceptions About Louisiana

- **All Louisianans are Cajuns.** They are not. Only a small section of the state (Acadiana) contains Cajuns. You'll

The swampy Atchafalaya Basin in Cajun Country

For Further Research

Books

A Black Patriot and a White Priest: André Cailloux and Claude Paschal Maistre in Civil War New Orleans, by Stephen J. Ochs

Celebrations on the Bayou: Invitations to Dine in Cotton Country Style, by Junior League of Monroe

The Earl of Louisiana, by A.J. Liebling

History of Louisiana Volume I: The French Domination, by Charles Gayarré

Landscape Guide: The South-Central States, by Tom Clote Jr.

Lee's Tigers: The Louisiana Infantry in the Army of Northern Virginia, by Terry L. Jones

Louisiana Buildings, 1720–1940: The Historic American Buildings Survey, edited by Jessie Poesch

Louisiana Houses of A. Hays Town, by Cyril E. Vetter

Web Sites

www.state.la.us/ (official state site)

www.louisianatravel.com/ (tourist information)

www.wlf.state.la.us/apps/netgear/page1.asp (wildlife and fisheries site)

www.crt.state.la.us/crt/profiles/history.htm (state history)

www.ibiblio.org/laslave/ (Afro-Louisiana history and genealogy)

http://centrallouisiana.net/almanac/ (state almanac)

www.shreve.net/~nola/ (Louisiana romance writers)

www.cajungrocer.com (Cajun food and photos)

Still Curious? Why Not Check Out

All The King's Men, by Robert Penn Warren

A Cajun Dream, by Cherie Claire

Gotta Get Next to You, by Lynn Emery

A Lesson Before Dying, by Ernest J. Gaines

Louisiana Blue, by David Poyer

Louisiana Power & Light, by John Dufresne

My Louisiana Sky

The Passions of Princes, by Eloise Genest

She Flew the Coop: A Novel Concerning Life, Death, Sex, and Recipes in Limoges, Louisiana, by Michael Lee West

Through My Eyes, by Ruby Bridges

be hard-pressed to find a Cajun or a Creole in northern Louisiana.

- **Everybody in Louisiana speaks French.** Not at all. In fact, few northerners in Louisiana speak French.

- **Louisiana is the cultural capital of the South.** Sure, New Orleans offers its share of art museums, playhouses, clubs, and upper-crust restaurants. But New Orleans is only one small part of the state.

Interesting Places to Set a Scene

- **Metairie.** This river town is home to the longest bridge over water in the world. At twenty-four miles, the Lake Pontchartrain Causeway connects Metairie with St. Tammany Parish.

- **New Orleans.** (See page 135 for more information on New Orleans.)

- **Alexandria.** Alexandria is wedged between the rolling hills and piney woods in the north and the mossy swamplands in the south.

- **West Monroe.** If your character can't wait to buy what some call junk and others call treasures, she'll want to step into West Monroe. It's an antique collector's heaven.

- **Gueydan.** A French name for "slow-moving river," Gueydan is known worldwide as the "Duck Capital of America" in recognition of its abundance of waterfowl. A beautiful place that's both a bird watcher's and a duck hunter's dream—come true.

- **Great River Road.** Also known as "Plantation Country," this corridor parallels the Mississippi River, stretching from Baton Rouge to New Orleans, and passes by numerous stately antebellum mansions and plantations.

- **Covington.** Unlike most of Louisiana, which is, quite frankly, steeped in pollution, Covington is an environmentalist's safe haven. The town lies in a region referred to as the "Ozone Belt," and it has long been known for its clean air and water.

- **Lafayette.** With a population of 100,000, Lafayette stakes its claim as the capital of southern (French) Louisiana, also called Acadiana. It's also a hip and wild college town, thanks to the University of Louisiana at Lafayette's nearly twenty thousand ragin' Cajuns.

New Orleans

New Orleans Facts and Peculiarities Your Character Might Know

- It hosted the 1984 World's Fair.
- It's divided into "parishes," not "neighborhoods," "suburbs," or "counties" (but parishes are similar with what other states call counties).
- It's the most festive city in the world, home to the biggest party on Earth (that's Mardi Gras) and many others: The New Orleans Jazz and Heritage Festival, The Tennessee Williams Literary Festival, The French Quarter Festival, The Greek Festival, The Reggae Riddums Festival, White Linen Night, Washington Parish Free Fair, Essence Afro-American Music Festival, and Christmas, New Orleans Style!
- Forget restricted liquor-selling hours; you can buy a drink all day, any day, any time—just no glass in the streets!
- Jackson Square, memorializing Andrew Jackson and the Battle of New Orleans, is one of the most recognized memorials in the world.
- It's very Catholic, especially compared to the rest of the state. Acadiana is full of French, Spanish, and Italian people who brought old-style Catholicism with them when they arrived. It's also loaded with Irish Catholics.
- Over six million people gather to view the annual Mardi Gras parade.
- Residents don't care if you're straight, gay, male, female, androgynous, or a pleasant mix of all.
- That said, New Orleans actually has quite a few racial tensions between African-Americans and Caucasians, but tourists rarely see this side of things.
- Refugee Santo Dominican slaves brought Voodooism to New Orleans toward the end of the eighteenth century.
- Its "unofficial slogan" is "Let the good times roll!" ("Laissez les bons temps rouler!").
- "The Big Easy," which stems from the earliest days of jazz, is the city's unofficial nickname, according to locals. It's also called "The Paris of the Americas," "America's International City," "The Gateway to the Americas," "The City That Care Forgot," and "The Crescent City."

New Orleans Basics That Shape Your Character

Ah, the French Quarter's architecture. . .

Population: 484,674 in Orleans Parish; 1.2 million in the Greater Metro area

Prevalent Religions: Roman Catholicism abounds, but just about anything goes here, from New Age to Protestantism to Voodooism.

Top Employers: Avondale Industries, Tulane University, Hibernia Corporation, Ochsner Clinic Foundation, JCC Holding Company (Harrah's Casino), BellSouth, Lockheed Martin, Entergy Corporation, Al Copeland Investments, Whitney Holding Corporation, Oreck Corporation, *The Times-Picayune*, Boh Bros. Construction Company, Hilton New Orleans, Acme Truck Line Inc.

Per Capita Income: $25,960

Average Daily Temperature: January, 53° F; July, 83° F

Ethnic Makeup (in percent): Caucasian 28.1%, African-American 67.3%, Asian 2.3%, Hispanic 3.1%, Native American 0.2%, Other 0.9%

Newspapers and Magazines: *The Times-Picayune, New Orleans Magazine, Louisiana Life, New Orleans CityBusiness, Louisiana Technology Journal, Ambush Magazine* and *Impact Gulf South Gay News* (both gay publications), *The New Orleans Tribune* (African-American community), *Aqui New Orleans* (Spanish community), *Jewish Civic Press* (Jewish monthly)

Free Weekly Alternative Paper: *Gambit Weekly*.

- Ernest Morial was elected in 1979 as the first African-American mayor of New Orleans, and he's served a whopping five terms in office!
- New Orleans has hosted more Super Bowl games than any other city.

If Your Character . . .

If Your Character Is a Struggling Artist, he lives in The Lower Garden District. Your creator will have lots of company in this run-down area that's home to numerous starving artists, suffering writers, and low-income musicians. Also popular with struggling artists are The Warehouse District and The French Quarter. An up-and-coming place for Bohemians is the Faubourg Marigny, a district adjacent to the Quarter on the other side of Esplanade Avenue.

If Your Character Is All About Business, he works in The Central Business District. Dominated by The Superdome, high-rise hotels, and office buildings, this "American" area of New Orleans also sports upscale malls, the Convention Center, and Spanish Plaza. Your character could also live in Metairie, the major suburban part of town, in Jefferson Parish (as opposed to Orleans Parish).

If Your Character Is a Tourist, he's hanging out in The French Quarter. A grid of narrow streets with bars, street vendors, hurricane drinkers, and small homes with wrought iron gates, balconies, and French doors, The Quarter is by far the most touristy part of New Orleans, particularly Bourbon Street and Jackson Square.

If Your Character Is All About Fine Cuisine, he dines at Emeril's, Bayona, or Mike's on the Avenue. Call this the triumvirate of fine of dining in New Orleans. All three restaurants serve top-notch cuisine from internationally renowned chefs (yes, Emeril's chef is none other than the Food Network's Emeril Lagasse). Following coat-and-tie dress codes is a must.

If Your Character Is a Family Man, he lives in Algiers. Tucked in a bend in the Mississippi River, Algiers is flat-out suburbia. Its claim to fame is its Mardi Gras museum, which is deemed one of the best in the world.

If Your Character Is Hip, he lives in The French Quarter, The Warehouse District, or Faubourg Marigny. All three of these neighborhoods are abuzz with funky bars, street vendors, curbside musicians, bookstores, and restaurants. The cost of living in the touristy Quarter is, of course, much higher than in Warehouse or Faubourg.

If Your Character Smells of Money, he lives on St. Charles Street or Audubon Place. Can you say "deep pockets in a big house"?

If Your Character Wears a Blue Collar at Work, he lives in Kenner. This longtime residential area has small brick houses and rows of neighborhood blocks.

Local Grub Your Character Might Love

The muffuletta (gobs of olive salad and stacks of meat on a big sesame bun) and the po'boy (a submarine-ish, French bread sandwich) are the two most popular sandwiches in New Orleans. If your character wants a po'boy "dressed," she's saying she wants mayonnaise, lettuce, and tomato on it. Other favorite dishes include andouille, bananas foster, barbecue shrimp, beignets, boudin, bouillabaisse, cafe au lait, crawfish, debris, étouffée, filé, gumbo, jambalaya, mirliton, pain perdu, plantain, soul Creole, and tasso (smoked pork). The city's signature drinks include the hurricane (rum and fruit juices) and the Sazerac (rye and bitters in an artificially glazed absinthe glass). A few old-school dining places: Galatoire's, Antoine's and Arnaud's. A few new-school dining places: Emeril's, Dick & Jenny's, and Jacques Imo's, Casamento's.

Interesting and Peculiar Places to Set a Scene

- **Lafitte's Blacksmith Shop.** With its blend of straights and gays and lesbians, Lafitte's is the sing-along piano bar in New Orleans. The atmosphere is impressively Old New Orleans—it's entirely lit by candles.
- **Esplanade Avenue.** World renowned for its grand Italianate mansions in serious neglect, this vein of a street is also the dividing line between The French Quarter and Faubourg Marigny. The Marigny used to be rather inexpensive but is no longer that cheap. One little note: Edgar Degas, in his lone visit to the United States, stayed in his relative's home on Esplanade; he even painted a bit here.
- **Preservation Hall.** Known simply as "The Hall" to locals, this classic jazz joint is a touristy, but uniquely New Orleans, venue. The Hall is basically a dirty room with a few benches and plenty of floor room for

sitting in awe at the musicians' feet (big, soft, and dirty cushions are provided).

- **Tremé.** Big and little brass bands and Louis Armstrong Park (with the famous Congo Square at its center) mark this historic and deep-rooted African-American neighborhood, which was once a red-light district. Current trumpeter Kermit Ruffins hails from the Tremé.
- **Faulkner House Books on Pirate's Alley.** This is where William Faulkner lived when he wrote his first novel, *Soldier's Pay*, before he moved to Oxford, Mississippi. Now it's a quaint bookshop that specializes in first editions of the former tenant's work (and other rare books).
- **The Mint.** The funniest, craziest club for catching male and female revues. A favorite hangout for straights and gays set on seeing some skin.
- **Tipitina's.** What started out as "the place to be" for New Orleans funk, Cajun, reggae, and rhythm and blues, Tipitina's received stiff competition once the House of Blues opened during 1994's Mardi Gras. But Tipitina's fought back and established three clubs in the city, all of which are now hoppin' local favorites; tourist are much more likely to head to House of Blues.
- **Pirate's Alley near St. Louis Cathedral.** With its long, shady streets, this walkway is one of the most romantic in New Orleans, as is Pere Antoine's Alley, which is on the other side of the cathedral. Faulkner's bookshop is on this alley.
- **Rawhide.** A wacky-and-wild, country-and-western dance club is popular with local gays and lesbians.
- **Victorian Lounge.** Velvet-covered chairs, a pressed-tin ceiling, and a wood-burning fireplace make this a most romantic setting for a character needing to fall in love or planning to pop the question.
- **Michaul's Live Cajun Music Restaurant.** Have your character take a free dance lesson (the "two-step" is popular) at this one-of-a-kind, good-time club.
- **Praline Connection Gospel and Blues Hall.** This Warehouse District hall is renowned for its exceptional soul food, but your character won't be bored by the blues music, either.
- **Howlin' Wolf.** For college students and younger adult characters into cutting-edge music, the Howlin' Wolf is it. Other popular spots swarming with students are Vic's Kangaroo Café (blues music), the House of Blues, Pat O'Brien's, and Carrolton Station.
- **Café DuMonde.** This legendary café opened as a coffee stand back in 1862 in the French market. It is still serving up coffee, Beignets (square French doughnuts in powdered sugar), and other treats twenty-four hours a day, seven days a week.
- **T.T.'s Club.** Owned and entertained by the female impersonator T.T. Thompson, this drag club (impromptu shows pop up whenever someone's in the mood) is the perfect place for your cross-dresser.
- **The Esplanade Lounge in the Royal Orleans Hotel.** If you're looking for someplace cozy where your character can have an affair, Esplanade Lounge is it—a mellow piano player, dim lights, tasty desserts, and a room upstairs.
- **Café Havana.** In the name of Cuba, this cigar bar is all about smoke. If it's related to tobacco, your character can find it here.
- **New Orleans Historic Voodoo Museum.** Does your character need to brush up on or purchase ju ju bags, exotic potions, transformative powders, healthy spirits, and voodoo charms (*gris gris*)? Look no further than this dark and danky museum, devoted to the twenty thousand or so voodoo practitioners in the city.
- **Royal Street** and **Magazine Street.** Art galleries, antique shops, boutiques, and other independent retailers make these hip strips many a window shopper's dream.

Exceptionally Grand Things Your Character Is Proud Of

- The recent crime rate, which is at a twenty-seven-year low.
- "Ladies in Red" streetcars. The city owns and runs seven vintage streetcars painted red with gold trim—a historical reference to the old French Market.
- Anything Creole or Cajun.
- New Orleans or "Dixieland" jazz.
- The 2002 Super Bowl, in which the underdog New England Patriots scored a winning field goal with no time remaining to upset the highly favored St. Louis Rams.
- The Port of New Orleans.
- Shibboleths. Examples for New Orleans include weird street pronunciations: Burgundy (Bur-*gun*-dy), Calliope (*Kal*-ee-ope), Carondelet (Ka-*ron*-da-let), Chartes (*Char*-ters), Conti (*Con*-tie), Fontainebleau (*Foun*-ten-blow), Milan (*My*-lan), and Tchoupitoulas (Chop-a-*too*-lus).
- A long list of corrupt politicians (yes, some are proud of this).

For Further Research

Books

Frenchmen, Desire, Good Children and Other Streets of New Orleans, by John Churchill Chase

Gumbo Shop: A New Orleans Restaurant Cookbook, by Richard Stewart

The Last Madam: A Life in the New Orleans Underworld, Christine Wiltz

Legends of New Orleans, by Pableaux Johnson

Literary New Orleans, edited by Judy Long

New Orleans: Elegance and Decadence, by Richard Sexton and Randolph Delehanty

New Orleans Stories: Great Writers on the City, edited by John Miller and Genevieve Anderson

Obituary Cocktail: The Great Saloons of New Orleans (2nd Edition, Expanded) and *The Majesty of the French Quarter*, by Kerri McCaffety

Portraits From Memory: New Orleans in the Sixties, by Darlene Fife

Zombification: Stories From National Public Radio, by Andrei Codrescu

Web Sites

www.insideneworleans.com/ (things to do in the city)

www.neworleansonline.com/ (city events and tourism information)

www.neworleanscvb.com/new_site/general.cfm (New Orleans Metropolitan Convention and Visitors Bureau)

www.marigny.homestead.com/ (local's guide to New Orleans)

www.nolalive.com/ (city news)

www.neworleansshowcase.com/books.html (great regional and local book site)

www.neworleans247.org/ (geared toward those who are relocating)

www.frenchquarter.com/ (French Quarter site)

www.neworleansmagazine.com/ (local magazine)

www.tennesseewilliams.net/ (Tennessee Williams literary festival site)

www.louisianamusic.org/ (music site)

Still Curious? Why Not Check Out

Angel Heart

Blaze

Cat People

A Confederacy of Dunces, by John Kennedy Toole (This is a big book down here; the main character, Ignatius Reilly, has a statue on Canal Street.)

A Conversation With David Halberstam, interviewed by Randy Fertel (video)

Dinner at Antoine's, by Frances Parkinson Keyes

Easy Rider

Feast of All Saints, by Anne Rice

Interview With The Vampire

JFK

Lives of the Saints, by Nancy Lemann

Midnight Bayou, by Nora Roberts

The Moviegoer, by Walker Percy

The Pelican Brief

Pretty Baby

A Streetcar Named Desire

Suddenly, Last Summer

Wild at Heart

Pathetically Sad Things Your Character Is Ashamed Of

- The condition of some of the old homes on Esplanade Avenue.
- Racial tensions.
- A long list of corrupt politicians (yes, some are ashamed of this).

Your Character Loves

- Lucky Dogs—these famous hot dogs still fill a hungry tummy like they have for years.
- The Saints.
- Historic homes.
- Pluralism.
- Mardi Gras beads (but only during Mardi Gras!).
- A good party.

Your Character Hates

- Bad food.
- Disrespectful tourists.
- Narrow minds.
- A dull party.

Significant Events Your Character Has Probably Thought About

- Scandinavian Leif Ericson landed in Newfoundland and may have ventured as far south as Maine in A.D. 1000. John Cabot, sailing for England, may have arrived in 1497. The first confirmed arrival, however, occurred in 1524, when Giovanni da Verranzano, sailing for France, reached Maine shores.

- The French established the first European settlement in Maine in 1604 at the mouth of the St. Croix River, but after enduring a harsh winter, the settlement moved to Nova Scotia. The English established a colony in 1607, but it did not last through the first winter.

- In 1652 Maine was annexed by Massachusetts as a territory. The French, the British, and the Native Americans fought over Maine until the French surrendered their claims in the colonies in 1763. French culture remains part of the state's legacy and identity.

- After the Revolutionary War, Mainers began to object to control by Massachusetts. The feud continued until Maine achieved statehood on March 15, 1820, as part of the Missouri Compromise.

- Hannibal Hamlin was the first Mainer to serve in the executive office, serving as vice president under Abraham Lincoln from 1860 to 1864.

- Maine soldiers distinguished themselves at the Battle of Gettysburg in 1863, repelling a Confederate counterattack. The victory was considered a turning point in the Civil War. Joshua Lawrence Chamberlain, who still ranks as one of the state's great heroes, led the troops.

- In 1884, James G. "Blaine From Maine" ran for president against Grover Cleveland and lost by a slim margin. Serving in various offices—including Speaker of the House and secretary of state—Blaine was one of the most powerful political figures of his day.

- In the twentieth century, the state's natural resources and manufacturing power declined. Population dropped as Mainers sought jobs elsewhere. After World War II, the state began to rely more on tourism, which conflicted with the interests of wood-based industries.

- After 1970, population began to rise again as Maine

Maine Basics That Shape Your Character

Motto: *Dirigo* (I lead)

Population: 1.3 million

Prevalent Religions: Roman Catholic, Baptist, and Methodist

Major Industries: Wood-product manufacturing, fishing and fishing-related industries, tourism, agriculture (primarily fruit, vegetables, and dairy)

Ethnic Makeup (in percent): Caucasian 96.9%, African-American 0.5%, Hispanic 0.7%, Asian 0.7%, Native American 0.6%, Other 0.6%

Famous Mainers: "L.L." Bean, Dorothea Dix, John Ford, Sarah Orne Jewett, Stephen King, Henry Wadsworth Longfellow, Edna St. Vincent Millay, Judd Nelson, Edward Arlington Robinson, Joan Benoit Samuelson

marketed itself as a pristine place of natural beauty and simple lifestyles.

Maine Facts and Peculiarities Your Character Might Know

- Maine supplies 90 percent of the country's lobsters.
- Maine is the country's leading supplier of blueberries,

producing nearly 99 percent of the nation's annual crop.

- The name "Maine" may have derived from English explorers who called the area "mainland," or it may come from the region of Maine in northwestern France.
- Eastport is the easternmost city in the country. It's also the only U.S. city to be ruled by a foreign government. Great Britain ruled it from 1814 to 1818.
- Acadia is the second most visited national park in the country.
- Although Paul Bunyan usually is associated with the upper Midwest, Mainers claim he was born in Bangor, where a thirty-one-foot statue stands in Bass Park. Bangor resident Stephen King brought the statue to life in his novel *It*.
- Margaret Chase Smith, a resident of Skowhegan, won a seat in the Senate in 1948. She was the first woman to be elected to that congressional house and the first woman to serve in both houses.
- Cataloger "L.L." Bean began his mail-order company in 1912, selling waterproof boots. He opened a store in Freeport in 1917 and gradually added outdoor wear to his line. The company is now world famous for quality products and 100 percent customer satisfaction.
- In the 1980s, Portland's Judd Nelson found fame in Hollywood as part of the Brat Pack, starring in such movies as *The Breakfast Club* and *St. Elmo's Fire*. Freeport's Joan Benoit Samuelson won the first gold medal in the women's marathon at the 1984 Summer Olympics.
- In 1988 George H.W. Bush ran for president as a native son of several states, including Maine. Born in Massachusetts, raised in Connecticut, and based fi-

nancially and politically in Texas, Bush spent much time at his oceanfront home in Kennebunkport, which became a familiar name to the country during his administration. Mainers tend to be clannish, and so unless you were born and raised in the state, you'll never be a true native.

- Mainers who live in the northern part of the state, mostly in rural locales or in small blue-collar towns, see southern Mainers as affected yuppies who lack the hardy spirit associated with the state. Southern Mainers see the north part of the state as less sophisticated.

Your Character's Food and Drink

The lack of ethnic diversity in Maine, outside of Portland, leads to a menu of mostly American cuisine. It's a Saturday-night tradition in much of the state to serve hot dogs and beans for dinner. Another Maine tradition is the Saturday-night church supper, where the fare is largely American. These suppers are popular even in the cosmopolitan centers.

In Portland your character will find a variety of ethnic restaurants. Its location near the coast also makes Portland, and most of the other coastal cities, a great place for seafood. Native Mainers love Moxie, a brown soft drink not unlike root beer but with a sharp, medicinal taste. Originally marketed as a nerve medicine, Moxie was one of the first soda pops in the country. Now it's mostly a Maine drink. Visitors will be encouraged to try it and will be told, after grimacing through the first gulp, "It's an acquired taste."

A hoagie or a sub sandwich in Maine is called an "Italian." If your characters are looking for a cheap drunk straight from the bottle, they'll forego bourbon for a bottle of Allen's Coffee Brandy. Whoopee pie, a type of sandwich with two cakey, chocolate-chip cookies on either side of a white, creamy filling, is a popular dessert.

Things Your Character Likes to Remember

- Mainers aren't, by nature, braggarts, and you won't hear them crow about the state's accomplishments. They do like to exaggerate about the weather, however. They note with pride the worst storms, the heaviest snowfalls, and the coldest freezes.
- The great years of the Boston Celtics. Mainers tend to dislike people from Massachusetts, but they love

© PhotoDisc/Getty Images

Old lobster buoys in eastern Maine

the Boston sports teams. The parade in Portland following the New England Patriots Super Bowl win in 2002 was the most attended event in the history of the city.

- The natural beauty. Mainers take pride in their natural wonders—the ocean, the mountains, the forests. The state welcome sign includes the logo "The way life should be."

Things Your Character Would Like to Forget

- People from out of state buying up oceanfront property. Hollywood has found Maine, as have the well heeled in much of the country. The new money is driving out shore people who have lived their whole lives in the towns. Class rage abounds.
- The ringleaders of the 9/11 tragedy stayed in Portland on the tenth and got their Boston flight through a Portland connection.
- The ice storm of 1998, when some people were without power for weeks. (Of course, they also like to remember this storm. See "Things Your Character Likes to Remember.")
- The fact that the Boston Red Sox haven't won the World Championship since Babe Ruth left.

Myths and Misperceptions About Maine

- **The Greens are in constant battle with the huge logging companies.** While Mainers protect the natural splendor, they also want to keep the wood-product corporations in the state.
- **The accent.** Once upon a time the Maine accent was strong, with broad *a* sounds and dropped *r*'s. They spoke of "Bah Hahbah" ("Bar Harbor") and "pahking the cah" ("parking the car"). But with each generation it recedes. TV-crazed teens in the current generation seem to have lost the accent completely.
- **Mainers are tight-lipped Yankees.** Mainers are sometimes seen as somber, stoic, and hardheaded. Visitors, therefore, are often surprised to find them friendly and gregarious.

Interesting Places to Set a Scene

- **Aroostook County.** Known by Mainers simply as "The County," Aroostook County, the largest in Maine, occupies the northernmost part of the state. The sparsely populated area attracts vacationers seeking to get away from it all. Lakes, rivers, and pine forests

abound, along with miles of coastline. Particularly popular are Presque Isle and Aroostook State Park.

- **Augusta.** The capital city, Augusta boasts the capitol building itself and Blaine House, the beautiful governor's mansion named after James G. Blaine. Other than these attractions, Augusta is a bit drab. Southern Mainers call it "Disgusta."
- **Bangor.** This central city seems to stay above the bickering between north and south Maine. How a person says the name of the town is a litmus test for his or her Mainer-ness. Mainers call it "Bang-gore," while outsiders call it "Bang-ger." Your characters will find a number of historic buildings as well as a thriving, if small, downtown area.
- **Bar Harbor.** Once a port town focused mostly on fishing, Bar Harbor now relies on tourist dollars. Located on the Atlantic, it offers breathtaking views and various tourist activities. Readers of a certain age might remember a TV commercial for a cold remedy that featured interviews with the hardy folk of Bar Harbor, whose sniffles during the long Maine winters were put to rest by the medicine.
- **Bethel.** This town is quaint with a capital *Q*. It has rows of craft and antique shops, a grassy common in the center of town, and restored Victorian homes with gingerbread to spare. The nearby Sunday River Bridge has been photographed and painted so often locals call it "The Artist's Bridge." Bethel also enjoys a growing reputation as a ski resort.
- **Cape Elizabeth.** Even the name evokes wealth and beauty. Located in the Greater Portland area, Cape Elizabeth features gorgeous homes and natural splendor. If your Maine character has a lot of money, she probably lives here.
- **Mount Katahdin.** A terminus for the Appalachian Trail, Mount Katahdin is one of the most famous mountains in the East. It's located in Baxter State Park, which was created on land donated by Percival Baxter, a successful businessman and politician intent on preserving the natural beauty of the state.
- **Portland.** The largest city in the state, Portland also is the most cosmopolitan. More than a quarter of the state's population lives in Greater Portland, which includes South Portland, Cape Elizabeth, and other thriving bedroom communities. Portland is the artistic, cultural, economic, and social center. It has an extensive park system, known locally as "The Emer-

For Further Research

Books

A Year in the Maine Woods, by Bernd Heinrich

Maine Jeopardy: Answers and Questions About Our State, by Carole Marsh (Carole Marsh Maine Books is a series of books that features the state.)

Maine: The Seasons, by Terrell S. Lester

Northern Farm: A Glorious Year on a Small Maine Farm, by Henry Beston

Web Sites

www.visitmaine.com/home.php (state tourism site)

www.state.me.us/ (state government site)

www.maineguide.com/ (visitor information site)

www.mainetoday.com (state information site)

Still Curious? Why Not Check Out

Most of the books by **Stephen King** and some of the movies based on his books

Belfast, Maine (documentary)

The Cider House Rules, by John Irving

Empire Falls, by Richard Russo

Ernie's Ark, by Monica Wood

In the Bedroom

My Only Story: A Novel, by Monica Wood

The Beans of Egypt, Maine, by Carolyn Chute

The Best Maine Stories, edited by Sanford Phippen et al.

The Man Without a Face

The Many Faces of Paper (documentary)

The Wooden Nickel, by William Carpenter

A mystery series set in Eastport, by Sara Graves

ald Necklace." The city is located on a peninsula jutting into Casco Bay, and it offers plenty of spectacular views of the water.

- **Waterville.** This is a town of contrasts. Colby College, an elite private school, sits in the middle of a dying blue-collar town where textile mills once bloomed. Conflicts between the well-heeled students and down-on-their luck town folk are not unusual. For settings with similar culture clashes, check out Lewiston, home to Bates College, and Brunswick, home to Bowdoin College.

Significant Events Your Character Has Probably Thought About

- In 1634 the English ships The Ark and The Dove sailed into the Potomac, bringing 140 colonists to the area.
- Just after the Revolutionary War ended, Annapolis became the nation's capital for nine months (1783–1784) and was the site for the signing of the Treaty of Paris in 1784.
- Maryland opted in 1791 to give up some land for the creation of what is now the District of Columbia.
- The U.S. Naval Academy was founded at Annapolis in 1845.
- What's deemed "The First Blood of the Civil War" was shed in Baltimore in 1861, shortly after Abraham Lincoln passed through Baltimore's President Street Station on the way to his inauguration.
- On September 17, 1862, twenty-three thousand soldiers either died or were seriously wounded in the Battle of Antietam; this turned out to be the bloodiest single-day battle of the war.
- Ocean City opened in 1875 and has been one of the state's major beach resorts since.
- Johns Hopkins University was founded in Baltimore in 1876.
- The 1925 construction of the twelve-mile-long Deep Creek Lake put Garrett County on the map as a recreation area.
- In 1952 the Eastern Shore was finally opened to drivers when the Bay Bridge, stretching from Annapolis to Kent Island, was completed.
- Baltimore's Harborplace opened in 1980, spawning even more development on the area's waterfront.
- Maryland's Queen Anne's County was the site of the 1998 Wye River Summit—Middle East peace talks between Israel and Palestine.

Maryland Facts and Peculiarities Your Character Might Know

- A trip through southern Maryland seems like a journey through the Deep South.
- Upstate, or in the western peninsula of Maryland, is more like Appalachia than one would imagine.
- The eastern shore has either a kind of white trashi-

Maryland Basics That Shape Your Character

Motto: Strong Deeds, Gentle Words

Population: 5.3 million

Prevalent Religions: Roman Catholic, Baptist, and Methodist, smaller portions of Lutheran, Presbyterian, Pentecostal, Episcopalian, Judaism, Muslim, and Church of Jesus Christ of Latter-day Saints

Major Industries: Seafood, poultry and eggs, dairy products, nursery stock, cattle, soybeans, corn, electric equipment, food processing, chemical products, printing and publishing, transportation equipment, machinery, primary metals, coal, tourism

Ethnic Makeup (in percent): Caucasian 64.0%, African-American 27.9%, Hispanic 4.3%, Asian 4.0%, Native American 0.3%, Other 1.8%

Famous Marylanders: Spiro T. Agnew, John Barth, Eubie Blake, John Wilkes Booth, James M. Cain, Samuel Chase, Frederick Douglass, Philip Glass, Billie Holliday, Johns Hopkins, Francis Scott Key, Thurgood Marshall, H.L. Mencken, Babe Ruth, Harriet Tubman, Leon Uris, Frank Zappa

ness (to put it negatively) or an antiquated charm (to put it in a more positive light).

- Marylanders (outside of the DC area) are known for being laid-back.
- Aside from being a naval center, Annapolis is known as one of the world's great sailing capitals.
- Trees cover 43 percent of Maryland's land.
- The DC-Baltimore corridor is all about movement

(fast cars, impatient drivers), unlike the rest of the state.

- Maryland is a national leader in the production of blue crabs and soft-shell clams; it also produces lots of other seafood.
- Sixteen of Maryland's twenty-three counties border tidewater.
- Maryland is varied geologically: The highest point in is 3,360 feet above sea level (Backbone Mountain), and the lowest point is 174 feet below sea level (Bloody Point Hole).
- Early in its history, the area became known for its religious tolerance.

Your Character's Food and Drink

The most obvious local food in Maryland is the seafood from the Chesapeake Bay. Crab cakes of all sorts are all over. Hard- and soft-shell crabs are usually seasoned with Old Bay Spice, which is a sort of cayenne spice. Food, like a lot of things, is influenced by the state's position on the coast. This accounts for your character's love of decadent seafood, but also her insistence to sweeten the iced tea.

Things Your Character Likes to Remember

- Clara Barton. She founded the American Red Cross, using her home in Glen Echo headquarters.
- Elizabeth Ann Bayley Seton. This Emmitsburg saint—literally!—was canonized in 1975. She formed the Sisters of Charity.
- Its workers. Maryland was first state to enact workers' compensation laws (1902).
- The Methodist Church. It was formally organized in the United States in 1784 at Perry Hall.

Coastal Maryland at its finest

© PhotoDisc/Getty Images

- Fooling the British. In the wee hours on a night in 1813, Saint Michaels residents had been warned a British attack was coming, so they put lanterns on the masts of ships and in the tops of the trees. This smart move caused the cannons to overshoot the town. Only one house was damaged; it's called the "Cannonball House."
- The Orioles and Ravens when they win.
- Jousting. Yep, it's the state sport.

Things Your Character Would Like to Forget

- The Orioles and Ravens when they lose.
- That its neighbors consider it a somewhat backward state.
- That Maryland was on the losing side of the Civil War—there are still many Confederate flags flying here.
- That it's deemed a blue-collar state. Professionals don't really aim to move here (unless it's near DC).

Myths and Misperceptions About Maryland

- **They're all good ol' boys.** Maryland gets a bad rap because it's so close to DC.
- **All Marylanders are alike.** Not true. In fact, the ways of life of mountainous Marylanders are incomprehensible to the state's water folk, and vice versa. And Maryland has grown in diversity, thanks to the development and housing of many research institutes and campuses.
- **Race relations and attitudes haven't changed in decades.** Many Marylanders have lost that racist edge, even if some of the larger cities are still rather segregated.
- **One Maryland mystery.** Who was the first person to pick up a live Atlantic blue crab, hold it without being attacked or injured by the gigantic pincer claws, and then think, "I'm going to eat you"? There's probably some myth about this person . . .

Interesting Places to Set a Scene

- **Annapolis.** This capital city is an interesting mix of government workers, tourists, naval officers, and sailboats. Many argue that Annapolis is culturally and economically more akin to neighboring DC than it is to cities and town in its own state.
- **Assateague Island.** Wild beaches and wild ponies, of course. This thirty-seven-mile, windswept barrier is-

For Further Research

Books

A Guide to Civil War Sites in Maryland: Blue and Gray in a Border State, by Susan Cooke Soderberg

The Antietam and Fredericksburg, by Francis Winthrop Palfrey

Maryland Lost and Found . . . Again, by Eugene L. Meyer

Maryland: A Middle Temperament, 1634–1980, by Robert J. Brugger et al.

Maryland: A New Guide to the Old Line State, by Earl Arnett et al.

Maryland's Geology, by Martin F. Schmidt Jr.

Slavery and Freedom on the Middle Ground: Maryland During the Nineteenth Century, by Barbara Jeanne Fields

Web Sites

www.state.md.us/ (state site)

www.marylandwriters.org/ (Maryland Writers' Association)

www.mdhs.org/ (state historical society)

http://trainweb.com/mvmra/wmrhs/ (Maryland railroad history)

http://home.att.net/~secondmdus/sites.html (Maryland's Civil War history)

Still Curious? Why Not Check Out

The Accidental Tourist, by Anne Tyler

The Bloody Ground, by Bernard Cornwell

Chesapeake, by James A. Michener

Death in September: The Antietam Campaign, by Perry D. Jamieson

Divine Evil, by Nora Roberts

Landscape Turned Red: The Battle of Antietam, by Stephen W. Sears

Mason and Dixon, by Thomas Pynchon

Not Guilty, by Patricia MacDonald

The Sugar House, by Laura Lippman

---

land is the perfect spot for a nature-loving character, who can engage in swimming, canoeing, crabbing, clamming, hunting, surf fishing, bird-watching, and, yes, off-road vehicle riding.

- **Chesapeake City.** This quaint city is dotted with several inns, restaurants, tiny shops, and nineteenth-century structures. Chesapeake and Delaware Canal runs right through the middle of town. As your character sits along the canal enjoying his day, he might be greeted by a tall ocean freighter as it passes under the city's high-arching bridge.

- **Chestertown.** This town can boast that it possesses Washington College, the only college to which George Washington himself lent his name. The town is full of tall, old trees that make the streets shady and pleasant. There are also several well-preserved mansions in the area.

- **Crownsville during the Maryland Renaissance Festival.** If your character is into lancing and jousting and all things sixteenth century, this is her slice of heaven. That the festival runs for three months ought to tell you what a big deal it is. In addition to reenactments, galloping horses, armor, and jousting, there's plenty of food, crafts, and fun bits of entertainment.

- **Frederick.** If your character is into history, he might like to visit this home to both the Revolutionary and Civil War history. The city is still well preserved, with many eighteenth- and nineteenth-century structures. Since Antietam Battlefield, site of the bloodiest day of the Civil War, is nearby, your character shouldn't be surprised to learn that twenty-nine of the town's buildings were turned into hospitals during the war.

- **Labor Day in Crisfield.** Where else but in Maryland can your character attend the National Hard Crab Derby and Fair? Crisfield is a tiny seafood town that has made its living thanks to the mighty crab. Have your character partake in festivities, which include fireworks, music, rides, a hard crab race, and, of course, the crab-picking contest.

- **Ocean City.** High-rise hotels, motels, condos, crowded beaches . . . you get the picture.

- **Rocky Gap Country/Bluegrass Music Festival.** Country music fans flock to Cumberland for this major summer outdoor concert. Have your character step into this scene to experience Marylanders partying at their finest, as they jam to the likes of Willie Nelson, Travis Tritt, Hank Williams Jr., and others.

- **Talbot County.** While fishing and crabbing are important here, nothing has affected the area like the shipbuilding industry. Talbot County these days has a lot of hotels, inns, and restaurants. Its two villages, Easton and St. Michaels, are quite historic and touristy; they boast nineteenth- and twentieth-century works of art, colonial and Victorian homes, inns and restaurants along tiny streets and wooden walkways, piers that reach out to the water, and the cool, Art Deco Avalon Theater that was built in 1921.

- **The Southern Shore.** The counties that make up this area are home to the old-time crabbing and fishing industries. Because the land is so flat and the elevation is so low, wetlands cover much of the shore. Migrating waterfowl love it here, too, but outsiders don't visit all that often.

- **Upper Chesapeake Bay.** Perfectly preserved mansions, pretty waterfront towns, and a strong maritime tradition make up this summery area. For your character to get a breathtaking view of it all, see if she can finagle her way to the top of Concord Point Lighthouse, one of the of oldest operating lighthouses in the East.

Baltimore

Baltimore

Baltimore Facts and Peculiarities Your Character Might Know

- The Cleveland Browns football team moved to Baltimore in 1996 and was renamed the Ravens.
- Francis Scott Key wrote "The Star-Spangled Banner" here in 1818 (apparently while watching Fort Mc-Henry get bombarded).
- Baltimore celebrated its two-hundredth anniversary in 1997 with the opening of a new $150 million harbor.
- Baltimore can boast of having one of the world's largest natural harbors.
- Much of Baltimore's economy these days focuses on research and development, especially in the areas of aquaculture, pharmaceuticals, medical research, and medical services.
- Oriole Park at Camden Yards opened in 1992.
- The city has loads of private laboratories but is also home to over sixty federal research labs.
- Convention Center at the Inner Harbor is the place to go for convention-type events.
- Many middle- to upper-class folks still have personal cooks and nannies (often of a different ilk).
- When people greet each other, they're matter-of-fact about it (except for some of Baltimore's artsy folks, who do the hugging-and-kissing bit).
- All adults say "hon" to women and young men, but guys wouldn't say that to each other.
- The town is very segregated, racially and economically.
- That said, ethnicity in Baltimore is quite varied, making it the most diverse area in the state.

If Your Character . . .

If Your Character Is Trendy, she shops in Towson. This shopping area just outside of Baltimore is pretty much its own city, with a huge mall and lots of other smaller stores lining the streets. Towson University is here as well.

If Your Character Is a Middle-Class Family Man, he lives in Federal Hill. This area's beautiful row homes are owned by your average family-yuppie folks. Other areas include Dundalk, Towson, or one of the bedroom communities off the I-95 corridor.

Baltimore Basics That Shape Your Character

© PhotoDisc/Getty Images

Baltimore's skyline

Population: 651,154 in the city; 2.5 million in the Greater Metro area

Prevalent Religions: Christianity, mostly Roman Catholic, Baptist, Methodist, and fewer Pentecostal, Lutheran, and Presbyterian, also Judaism, Muslim, and Church of Jesus Christ of Latter-day Saints

Top Employers: Johns Hopkins University, LifeBridge Health, University of Maryland Medical System, Baltimore Gas and Electric Company, Bank of America, General Motors Truck Group, St. Agnes Health Care, Allfirst Bank, St. Paul Companies, Verizon Communications, Baltimore Sun Company, Union Memorial Hospital, Bon Secours Health Care, Zurich Commercial

Per Capita Income: $34,237

Average Daily Temperature: January, 35° F; July, 80° F

Ethnic Makeup (in percent): Caucasian 31.6%, African-American 64.3%, Hispanic 1.7%, Asian 1.5%, Native American 0.3%, Other 2.1%

Newspapers and Magazines: *The Baltimore Sun, Baltimore Times, Baltimore Magazine, Baltimore Business Journal, The Daily Record, Baltimore's Child*

Free Weekly Alternative Papers: *The Baltimore Guide, Baltimore Chronicle, Baltimore City Paper*

If Your Character Loves Nature, she's spending time in Robert E. Lee Park. It's a pleasant city park named after the Confederate general. People come here to walk their dogs, picnic, and toss Frisbees. Patapsco River State Park, Lock Raven Reservoir, and Sandy Point State Park (close to Annapolis) are also favorite spots for nature lovers.

If Your Character Wears a Blue Collar at Work, he lives in Essex. Right on the water, this is where someone's father's father worked on the boats. Locals sit around and have crab feasts, and many of the small homes are covered in "Formstone"—siding that looks like fake stone.

If Your Character Smells of Old Money, she resides in Roland Park. Rich equestrians just love this area, which boasts lots of old money and grand estates, many with horses and lots of land. Sparks and Cockeyesville are similar.

If Your Character Smells of New Money, he resides in White Marsh. To the northeast of town on the I-95 corridor, this used to be a marsh but they filled it in. Now its covered with nice, new homes and a classy mall.

Local Grub Your Character Might Love

What makes Baltimore stand out from other cities is that people go nuts over blue crabs. They buy them in big bushels—like a box of fifty—take them home, cover the table with newspaper, dump the crabs on the table, and hammer away at ripping apart the sea creatures. It's a tradition to spend hours of family time doing this. Residents also love Pit Beef (barbecue) with vinegar and salt; horseradish is a popular topping as well. Onions and peppers are big on hot dogs and sandwiches. As with most big cities, street vendors and hot dog carts can be found about town. Baltimore also has many ethnic restaurants, from those classic Italian spots in its Little Italy to the Indian, Moroccan, and Caribbean eateries that pop up near the universities and research centers.

Interesting and Peculiar Places to Set a Scene

- **Artfest.** Affiliated with Maryland Art Institute, this is the big-deal art festival of the season. Have your character grab a glass of her favorite wine and mingle with the city's art lovers about the relevance of all things beautiful.

- **Camden Yards.** It's baseball time here, old-park style. Your character might just want to engage in some dog eating and beer drinking, but he can forget singing all about buying peanuts and Cracker Jacks—the seventh-inning stretch song here isn't the legendary "Take Me Out to the Ballgame" but "Thank God I'm a Country Boy."

- **Druid Hill Park.** This was the first planned park in the country, as explained on a plaque in the park. Inside the park is the Baltimore Zoo and nearby is the racetrack. Unfortunately, the area of town surrounding the park has become rough, with drug pushers making deals in the park and homeless people sleeping on its benches.

- **Dundalk.** This industrial area is on the water, which means it's a very good place to dump a body . . .

- **East Baltimore and SW Baltimore.** These are two of the city's seedy, unsafe neighborhoods. Your character will have no problem finding lots of drugs, drug addicts, bums, and people who are generally down on their luck.

- **Falls Creek.** What were once thriving mills along the river are now shops with artists hard at work on their craft or on a sale. The historical area is only three or four blocks and there's no parking, but your character can always hop on the light rail system, which runs by here.

- **Federal Hill.** This historic market area bustles with shoppers of all persuasions and ethnicities. Although it's an indoor market, it stretches for a few blocks, with vendors selling anything a palate could want.

- **Fells Point.** This old maritime area is a mix of yuppietypes and fortunate college kids. The area is touristy, with lots of bars, parties, clubs, and chic restaurants, but no parking spaces.

- **Mount Washington.** This hip part of town is filled with cool boutiques, lots of vegetarian restaurants, offbeat shops, interesting people, and pamphleteers.

- **Pikesville.** Near Liberty Heights, this area is historically Jewish, with lots of older Jewish East Coast women shopping, shopping, and shopping.

- **SoWeBe.** This Southwest Baltimore festival is a combination of a hippie love fest, an artsy gathering, and a rock concert. Have your character partake in the festivities—hey, good grunge, bitchin' bands, awesome arts, buckets of beer. . . . You could have fun just imagining you're there.

For Further Research

Books

Baltimore Iconoclast, by William Hughes

Baltimore: A Not Too Serious History, by Letitia Stockett

Baltimore Then and Now, by Alexander D Mitchell IV

Baltimore Transitions: Views of an American City in Flux, by Mark B. Miller

Black Social Capital: The Politics of School Reform in Baltimore, 1986–1998, by Marion Orr

The Flag, the Poet and the Song: The Story of the Star-Spangled Banner, by Irvin Molotsky

Greetings From Baltimore: Postcard Views of the City, by Bert Smith

Journeys to the Heart of Baltimore, by Michael Olesker

The Price of Freedom: Slavery and Manumission in Baltimore and Early National Maryland, by T. Stephen Whitman

Web Sites

www.ci.baltimore.md.us/ (official city site)

www.baltimore.org/ (Baltimore Area Convention and Visitors Association)

www.sunspot.net/ (news)

http://baltimorecountymd.com/history.htm (city history)

Still Curious? Why Not Check Out

Back When We Were Grownups: A Novel, by Anne Tyler

Company Man: A Novel, by Brent Wade

The Crawlspace Conspiracy: A Novel, by Thomas Keech

Dead Luck, by Gregory Yawman

Hairspray

The Hearse Case Scenario, by Tim Cockey

In a Strange City, by Laura Lippman

Liberty Heights

Miss Susie Slagle's, by Augusta Tucker

My Baltimore Landsmen, by Herman Taube

Pecker

Sum of All Fears

Temples, by Vincent Williams

- **The Block.** Sailors used to cruise up here to get some loving from the brothels. Well, things haven't changed much. The area's "businesses," many of which are strip clubs and houses of prostitution, seem to be doing well. The place is busy and alive, especially once the sun goes down. There's even a police station near the area, but the officers pretty much let business carry on as usual.

- **The Preakness.** You might think the city's biggest event of the year is just a horse race, but it's not—it's a weekend-long event that riles up the whole city. Locals hold parades, have a 5K run, play polo, and even sponsor Preakness golf tournaments. Even if your character doesn't make it to the race, there's lots of interesting happenings throughout the week that'll be sure to spark a story idea.

Exceptionally Grand Things Your Character Is Proud Of

- The Orioles.
- The Ravens.
- "The Star-Spangled Banner" and Francis Scott Key.

- The city's aquarium.
- The reputation of its horse-racing industry.
- The bay.
- Memorial Stadium. When it was recently torn down, many people bought the seats and mementoes from the place so they could keep a part of the stadium.
- Edgar Allen Poe. This is where he lived and wrote many stories and poems.

Your Character Loves

- Helping others—even if it's trying to understand and cope with a heroin addict on the street.
- Private schools.
- Duckpin bowling—kind of like regular bowling but a little more challenging. It started here in 1900, and it's never spread beyond the city.
- Crabbing, fishing, boating.

Your Character Hates

- New Yorkers.
- The Yankees.
- The poor shape of the public schools.

Massachusetts

Massachusetts Basics That Shape Your Character

Motto: By the Sword We Seek Peace, But Peace Only Under Liberty

Population: 6.4 million

Prevalent Religions: Roman Catholicism rules the state, but small pockets of other Christians are here as well.

Major Industries: Seafood, scientific instruments, printing and publishing, nursery stock, dairy products, cranberries, vegetables, machinery, electric equipment, tourism

Ethnic Makeup (in percent): Caucasian 84.5%, African-American 5.4%, Hispanic 6.8%, Asian 3.8%, Native American 0.2%, Other 3.7%

Famous Bay Staters: Henry Adams, John Adams, Samuel Adams, Louisa May Alcott, Horatio Alger, Susan B. Anthony, F. Lee Bailey, Clara Barton, Alexander Graham Bell, William Cullen Bryant, e.e. cummings, Emily Dickinson, Ralph Waldo Emerson, Benjamin Franklin, Margaret Fuller, Erle Stanley Gardner, Robert H. Goddard, John Hancock, Nathaniel Hawthorne, Oliver Wendell Holmes, Jack Kerouac, Amy Lowell, James Russell Lowell, Robert Lowell, Samuel Morse, Sylvia Plath, Paul Revere, Norman Rockwell, Dr. Seuss (Theodor Geisel), Anne Sexton, Lesley Stahl, Paul Theroux, Henry David Thoreau, Mike Wallace, Barbara Walters, John Greenleaf Whittier, James Whistler, Eli Whitney.

Significant Events Your Character Has Probably Thought About

- Plymouth Colony started in 1620.
- In 1630, John Winthrop led the first large Puritan migration.
- King Philip's War took place in 1675–1676.
- The Minute Men got the American Revolution going by battling British troops at Lexington and Concord in 1775.
- Shays' Rebellion in 1786. Many areas were economically depressed after the American Revolution; Berkshire farmers rebelled.
- In the 1830s and 1840s, the state became the center of movements like Unitarianism and Transcendentalism.
- Massachusetts soldiers were apparently the first to die for the Union when fired upon by a secessionist mob in Baltimore in 1861.
- In the 1840s, waves of Irish immigrants began arriving here. Before century's end French Canadians, Portuguese, Italians, Russian Jews, Poles, Slavs, and Scandinavians all came as well.
- The creation of the Quabbin Reservoir in the late 1930s changed the shape of Massachusetts, wiping out four towns and pushing 2,500 residents to find new homes elsewhere.
- Local Senator John F. Kennedy became the thirty-fifth president in 1960.
- In 1988, former two-time governor Michael Dukakis ran for president and lost to George H.W. Bush.
- The 1990s were good for the state, thanks to its many high-tech companies.
- In the summer of 1999, John F. Kennedy Jr.'s plane crashed into the Atlantic Ocean just off Martha's Vineyard.

Massachusetts Facts and Peculiarities Your Character Might Know

- Northampton was the hometown of Calvin Coolidge.
- These folks love their museums—no other state has so many historical museums, museum villages, witch museums, rural museums, maritime museums, and, yes, even famous art museums.
- The state's cranberry crop is the nation's largest.
- Massachusetts was a major pioneer in the manufacturing of textiles and shoes.
- It's called the "Bay State" and hosts more than two dozen lighthouses.
- During the nineteenth century, the state was famous

for its intellectual activity, especially its writers and educators.

- The first successful liquid fuel rocket was launched by Dr. Robert H. Goddard in Auburn in 1926.
- Plymouth Plantation will keep your character stuck in about 1630, where this reconstructed settlement is swarming with pilgrims.
- The oldest music festival in the state is the long-running Worcester County Music Association Festival, which has been busting out tunes since 1858.
- The Nonotuck Mountain Range is one of the few east-west ranges in the world.
- The state's first official scenic road—the thirty-eight-mile stretch of Route 2 between Greenfield and Williamstown—was built in 1914. Now it's called The Mohawk Trail Highway and is sixty-three miles long.
- In 1944 Howard Aiken of Harvard developed the first automatic digital computer.
- Paul Revere and William Dawes never made it to Concord (they were arrested), but Samuel Prescott completed the journey and delivered the message.
- Massachusetts is the only one of the original thirteen states still governed by its original constitution (1780), which was, however, amended from 1917 to 1919.
- At 3,491 feet, Mount Greylock is the state's highest mountain.
- The state can brag about having nine Speakers of the House and four presidents
- The Americans and Minutemen lost the first battle of the Revolution; eighteen died and not a single redcoat suffered a death or an injury.

Your Character's Food and Drink

If your character's in the eastern part of the state, she's eating cod, lobster, fish and chips, fried clams, fried clam bellies, oysters, and any kind of seafood. Folks in the middle and western part of the state like seafood as well, but they tend to have meatier diets; the exception is near the university towns and medical centers, where tofu, soy milk, vegetarian restaurants, and ethnic foods rule (and so do smoothies).

Things Your Character Likes to Remember
- The Patriots.
- Its many universities.
- Its tradition in science and technology, from all those award winners at Massachusetts Institute of Technol-

ogy (MIT) to Lynn Margulis, the preeminent evolutionary biologist at the University of Massachusetts (UMass).

- Its literary greats: Ralph Waldo Emerson, Henry David Thoreau, Herman Melville, Nathaniel Hawthorne, Louisa May Alcott, Margaret Fuller, Charles Bulfinch, Emily Dickinson, Oliver Wendell Holmes, Henry Wadsworth Longfellow, James Russell Lowell, John Greenleaf Whittier; James Tate, John Edgar Wideman, Jack Kerouac.
- The National Yiddish Book Center at Hampshire College. It's the world's largest collection of Jewish literature from the last one thousand years.
- Pink flamingo lawn ornaments. They were first produced in Worcester in the 1950s by Union Products.
- Dick "The Derby" Smith of WORC. He was the first American deejay to air the Beatles. They were so grateful they gave Smith the gold record for their hit "She Loves You."
- The monkey wrench, the smiley face, white chocolate—all came from here.
- Emily Dickinson. She pretty much lived her whole reclusive life in Amherst.
- Robert Frost lived in Amherst as well, from 1931 to 1938, and also taught at Amherst College (after he left town).
- Edith Wharton lived at The Mount, a twentieth-century replica of a seventeenth-century mansion.
- Herman Melville lived at Arrowhead, his eighteenth-century farmhouse in Pittsfield.
- Jack Kerouac was born in Lowell and spent his last years there as well.

Things Your Character Would Like to Forget
- The cost of the Big Dig (the I-93 construction project that is taking too much time to complete and sucking up too much money) and its affect on potholes (due to lack of highway funds) for western Massachusetts.
- Bricks falling from the graduate library at UMass.
- Chappaquiddick. You know, the 1969 incident in which Ted Kennedy left the scene of the accident after he drove his Oldsmobile off a wooden bridge, drowning his passenger.

Myths and Misperceptions About Massachusetts
- **It's a liberal state.** Many in the state are quite stuck in their ways.

- **People aren't friendly.** They are friendly to family and friends, just not so much to strangers.
- **The only happening things take place in Boston.** There's a whole world in Massachusetts that has nothing to do with its big city.
- **Witch-hunts are still a brewing.** They stopped centuries ago.

Interesting Places to Set a Scene

- **The Berkshires.** Shakers and artisans have made Berkshire County their home, and it still hangs on to such legacies (though the Shakers, of course, are all dead). Making maple sugar is still a thriving business here today, primarily in the hill towns, an area with more sugarhouses than the rest of the state put together. March is sugar season, and people come to watch producers "boil off" the sap, which reduces it to liquid. Berkshire County also has been home to such literary residents as Herman Melville, William Cullen Bryant, Oliver Wendell Holmes, Nathaniel Hawthorne, Edith Wharton, and W.E.B. DuBois.
- **Cape Cod.** Named after the fish that filled the waters, the Cape is still a major fishing area, but it's also known for its homes (the Cape Cod design), its boatbuilding, its cranberry farms and bogs, and yes, its tourists. The Chatham Lighthouse is one of the most photographed sites on the island.
- **Deerfield.** It seems nothing post-nineteenth century has found its way into Deerfield. In fact, this town could be the best-preserved colonial village in New England, with dozens of houses dating to the seventeenth and eighteenth centuries.
- **Edgartown on Martha's Vineyard.** Edgartown is the gem town of Martha's Vineyard. White picket fences are covered in red roses, the homes of sea captains are preceded by pretty green lawns, and the Whaling Church bell rings to tell everyone it's time for dinner. The place gets packed, though, during the Fourth of July, when multitudes gather on Main Street to watch an old-fashioned parade.
- **Gloucester.** Nobody heard of this sleepy, little fishing town until Sebastian Junger's *The Perfect Storm* hit the best-seller lists. Since then the town has been swamped with tourists (but there's really not much to see other than the docks and the now-famous but tiny, low-ceilinged Crow's Nest Bar).
- **Lenox.** Aside from the Tanglewood Music Festival (see page 154), this city is known for its Shakespeare and Company. From late May to Labor Day, plays from The Bard and others take place at two outdoor amphitheaters and two indoor stages on the grounds of Edith Wharton's estate. Hundreds of summer "cottages" (yes, they're mansions) are here as well—Andrew Carnegie died here while spending time at his "cottage."
- **Lexington and Concord.** Henry David Thoreau, Ralph Waldo Emerson, The North Bridge, The Shot Heard Around the World, Walden Pond, the Transcendentalist Movement—it's all here in these two historically important towns outside of Boston.
- **Lowell.** This Merrimack Valley textile town, the country's first planned manufacturing city, boasts more than five miles of canals and several old brick mills on the water's edge. If your character doesn't like that unusual setting, she can wander around the many places Jack Kerouac spent some time—heck, she can even go to the Boott Mill Boarding House Museum and see Kerouac's backpack, his typewriter, and the original manuscript of *On the Road*. There is also The Jack Kerouac Commemorative in Eastern Canal Park.
- **Marblehead.** Yachts and yachts and more good yachts—that's what your character will find here in the self-proclaimed "Yachting Capital of America." The scene of all the various boats in the harbor is awesome, but so are the town's tiny flower-filled streets.
- **Martha's Vineyard.** Have your character hang out with the likes of James Taylor and company on this beautiful island. This was once a major whaling area, but that stopped years ago. There arc rows upon rows of little painted cottages on Oak Bluffs. Your character

© PhotoDisc/Getty Images

The famed House of Seven Gables

For Further Research

Books

A Guide to the History of Massachusetts, edited by Martin Kaufman et al.

Historical Atlas of Massachusetts, edited by Richard W. Wilkie and Jack Tager

A Little Commonwealth: Family Life in Plymouth Colony, by John Demos

Massachusetts: A Concise History, by Richard D. Brown and Jack Tager

Massachusetts: Portrait of the Land and Its People, by Georgia Orcutt

The Minutemen and Their World, by Robert A. Gross

Paul Revere's Ride, by David Hackett Fischer

Witchcraft at Salem, by Chadwick Hansen

Web Sites

www.mass-vacation.com/ (tourism)

www.mass.gov/portal/index.jsp (state government site)

www.doe.mass.edu/ (Massachusetts Department of Education)

www.memorablequotations.com/Dingle5.htm (quotes from state writers)

www.massculturalcouncil.org/grants/for_artists/ (Massachusetts Cultural Council)

www.concordma.com/arts.html (Concord literary history)

www.noho.com/artists.html (Northampton artists and writers)

Still Curious? Why Not Check Out

The Crucible, by Arthur Miller

The Dumb Shall Sing, by Stephen Lewis

Ethan Frome, by Edith Wharton

Home Town, by Tracy Kidder

The Key, by Peter Mars

The Ladies' Man: A Novel, by Elinor Lipman

Moby Dick, by Herman Melville

MotherKind: A Novel, by Jayne Anne Phillips

On the Road, by Jack Kerouac

Ralph Waldo Emerson: Essays and Lectures, by Ralph Waldo Emerson

The Scarlet Letter, by Nathaniel Hawthorne

Walden, by Henry David Thoreau

ought to know that alcohol (at least the selling of it) is prohibited on much of the island. Gay Head is home to Wampanoag Native Americans, who still dominate the area and spend their days making pottery from the area's rich clay.

- **Nantucket.** This narrow slice of an island (it's only about fourteen miles at its widest) was a major whaling hub for most of the nineteenth century, but then it, well, floundered. Now the island is mostly used for relaxation and vacation purposes, thanks to its historic houses, charming inns, cobblestone streets, museums, shops, and overall weathered New England coastal feel. Siasconst (pronounced "Sconset"), a village at the eastern corner of the island, was a haven for artists at the end of the nineteenth century. Why not have your character go to the top of the Sankaty Lighthouse and gasp at the views of the ocean and those amazing cranberry bogs?
- **Northampton.** This is often called a small-town version of San Francisco, thanks to its restaurants, cafes, theaters, clubs, crafts stores, galleries, fine jewelry,

artists, writers, activists, academics, and professionals. Smith College (1875), one of the first schools for women and a cradle for the feminist movement, is here, too. Betty Friedan, Sylvia Plath, Gloria Steinem, and Nancy Reagan, among others, went here.

- **Provincetown.** This little land's end tip of the cape is definitely the most colorful part of the island, and we're not talking the color of the changing leaves in autumn. In winter months, only about four thousand residents live here, but in the summer it rocks with at least seventy-five thousand, most of whom are Bohemians, artists, gays, transvestites, and others who feel free, act even freer, and party it up rather well.
- **Salem.** Witch-hunts anyone? Although Salem only has forty thousand residents, its history is one of the most fascinating and notorious in U.S. history. Your character can still find all sorts of witches here today, from wax witches to "real witches" (who just like the legacy—or are just plain weird) to witch houses. There are several witch museums, too. Today, Salem's busiest season is—surprise, surprise—Halloween, which

lasts for three weeks. Salem also has a maritime history museum and the House of Seven Gables, which inspired Hawthorne's novel of the same name.

- **Sandwich.** This picturesque town is Cape Cod's oldest (1637) and is legendary for its glassmaking. They still have glassblowing studios today, but what might interest your character more is the Heritage Plantation, with its antique-car collection and old-time carousel.
- **Stockbridge.** This town has *Saturday Evening Post* written (or painted) all over it. What's historically been a mix of modest farm homes and opulent mansions is today just plain quaint. Norman Rockwell lived here and painted several scenes from the area, the most famous of which is of the town's picturesque Main Street with the Berkshires in the background. And there's the famous Red Lion Inn, one of the few remaining American inns in continuous use since the 1700s, also immortalized in Rockwell's painting. Ah . . . those were the days.
- **Tanglewood Music Festival.** This is New England's big summer cultural affair. Have your character join in the fun and fugues at this music festival that takes place on a grand Berkshires estate. Of course, the Boston Symphony Orchestra is the house band, so to speak, and it always has plenty of guest musicians, from Itzhak Perlman to James Taylor.
- **The Berkshire Theatre Festival.** Great actors come here to perform in plays of all sorts. The big draw is the setting—the festivities are held in an 1887 casino and a converted barn.
- **Worcester.** With a population of 170,000, this is the state's (and New England's) second largest city. It has eight colleges and universities, and the twenty acres or so in the center of the town is deemed Medical City. Worcester also hosts an art museum, a theater company, a symphony, and one of the country's oldest music festivals. Worcester's civic symbol is the heart, representing its location in the heart of the state (and New England). It's no surprise, then, that Valentine's cards were first mass-produced here as well, thanks to the New England Valentine Company (1874).

Boston Facts and Peculiarities Your Character Might Know

- John Winthrop founded Boston in 1630 as the main settlement of the Massachusetts Bay Company.
- The Irish began to arrive in Boston in the 1840s when the potato famine devastated their home country. Bostonians weren't too welcoming: "No Irish Need Apply" signs went up everywhere.
- Boston was an early center of American Puritanism, with a fire-and-brimstone moral life but a dynamic intellectual life.
- The Battle of Bunker Hill was one of the first battles of the American Revolution.
- Many now deem City Hall an architectural eyesore and embarrassment, especially considering that most of the buildings in Boston are quite beautiful.
- Boston is a leading city in health care, with over twenty-five hospitals and many more community health centers.
- Boston has one of the largest student populations in the country.
- Many of Boston's old waterfront warehouses have been converted into luxurious condos.
- Many residents were upset when a whole community in the West End was wiped out to build City Hall, a couple of hospitals, and ugly, towering apartment buildings.
- Much of Boston was originally a marsh; the founding fathers filled it in and built on it.
- Bostonians have a habit of throwing "ie" on the ends of words: "statie" is state policeman, "Southie" is South Boston, "packie" is the package store, and "wallies" is Wallaston Beach.
- Boston locals do drop their *r*'s and add *l*'s. Some things your character might overhear in a Boston "bah": "He's gotta pach da cabbie"; "She's a wicked pissah"; "One more beeah"; "Yaa dood" and "Naa dood"; "That's bunk. I'm totally bullshit"; "Dat Allie, he's a good kid."
- Only a few folks talk like the Kennedy clan.
- Brahmins are all about propriety, social convictions, old wealth (tracing their lineage back to colonial

Boston Basics That Shape Your Character

A waterfront view of Boston's skyline

Population: 589,141 in the city; 1.2 million "day" population (those coming in to the city daily)

Prevalent Religions: Very Roman Catholic, various denominations of Protestantism, Judaism, and representatives of just about any other religion.

Top Employers: Eaton Vance Corporation, Analog Devices, RSA Security Inc., Employee Management Consultants Inc., Brooktrout Technology Inc., Biogen Inc., Staples Inc., Affiliated Managers Group, Millipore Corporation, State Street Corporation, Waters Corporation, Teradyne Inc., Candela Corporation, BJ's Wholesale Club Inc., Saucony Inc.

Per Capita Income: $36,285

Average Daily Temperature: January, 29° F; July, 73° F

Ethnic Makeup (in percent): Caucasian 54.5%, African-American 25.3%, Hispanic 14.4%, Asian 7.5%, Native American 0.4%, Other 7.8%

Newspapers and Magazines: *The Boston Globe, Boston Herald, Boston Magazine, Banker and Tradesman, Boston Business Journal, Mass High Tech, New England Economic Review, Boston Parents' Paper, New England Journal of Medicine*

Free Weekly Alternative Paper: *The Boston Phoenix*

times), and social status; they often wield considerable political power.

If Your Character . . .

If Your Character Is Trendy, she shops on Newberry Street. This eight-block stretch of cafes, restaurants, record stores, trendy restaurants, hair salons, spas, and clothing shops of all sorts has been compared to New York City's Fifth Avenue.

If Your Character Wears a Blue Collar at Work, he lives in Charlestown. With its row upon row of triple-decked apartment buildings (called "Irish Battleships"), Charlestown is a working-class American Irish neighborhood, poor in general but with some middle-class homes. People in Boston frequent here only to eat at a famous restaurant called Olives.

If Your Character Is a Struggling Irishman, he lives in South Boston. South Boston has a reputation as being one of the city's rough communities, with many housing projects in the area, many murals and graffiti painted on walls about the troubles in Ireland, and many washed-up old and poor Irish folk. Recently, however, the area has gone through a bit of gentrification due to its proximity to the financial district and Back Bay.

If Your Character Smells of Money, she resides in Back Bay. Epitomizing wealth and propriety, this is posh East Coast living at its finest. The Victorian houses are beautiful, the neighborhood is sanitized, and the streets are reminiscent of old Parisian boulevards. Of course, there's a splendid public garden for walking if your character tires of strolling the area's tree-lined, cobblestoned streets.

If Your Character is Gay and Wealthy, he lives in South End. This used to be a poor, mostly African-American neighborhood until the gay and lesbian community moved in and gentrified it—now it's an expensive place to call home. Columbus and Tremont Streets are home to many restaurants and shops that cater to gays and straights alike.

If Your Character Is Really Down-and-Out, she's hanging out in Roxbury. Boston's poverty-stricken, African-American ghetto, Roxbury is a dense urban area that's sad and sometimes scary. There's lots of crime, drugs, and litter here, but nearby is a breath of fresh air at Harvard's Arnold Arboretum.

Local Grub Your Character Might Love

Bostonians do love their seafood (lobster, cod, fish and chips, fried clams, fried clam bellies, oysters) and their ethnic foods. Huge Dim sum houses are in Chinatown, and numerous Italian offerings are in the North End. There also are lots of Irish pubs for Irish beer and food. Boston cream pie and Parker House rolls were invented in town as well. Here's a short list of some of your character's restaurant offerings: Locke-Ober Café, Grill 23 & Bar, Jake's Boss BBQ, Red Bones BBQ, Tim's Tavern, Sunset Grill, Mike's Pastry, Modern Pastry, Victoria Café, Ginza, Union Oyster House, Durgan Park, Santarpios, Dali, and On the Waterfront.

Interesting and Peculiar Places to Set a Scene

- **"A" Street.** Hundreds of artists have descended here on what once was a stretch of abandoned warehouses next to a post office. Now it's full of high-class lofts and galleries.
- **Boston Garden.** Manicured lawns and gardens make this a comfy green space for your park-loving character, as she sits and watches dogs chasing Frisbees, college students sitting on the grass for lunch, or lovers stealing a kiss on a bench under a tree.
- **Boston's Subway.** Busy with people coming and going, it's also a classic spot for musicians trying to make a few bucks—James Taylor, Janis Ian, Tracy Chapman, and others played these subways.
- **Charles River Esplanade.** This meandering park along the Charles River has a sailboat rental, a jogging path, and a hatch shell where free concerts and movies are held. Grungers and alternative types on skateboards frequent here for the music or just to hang out.
- **Faneuil Hall.** A series of old markets and a meetinghouse have been converted into a shopping mall with bars, restaurants, and general consumer garbage. Street performers, pamphleteers, noisy preachers, beggars, and pigeons are daily sites here.
- **Government Center.** Boston's old "shopping district" fell on hard times in the last part of the twentieth century but is now on the upswing. The New England Patriots's Super Bowl victory parade ended here at City Hall (which was built in the seventies and is horribly ugly). The City Hall Plaza hosts many shows and events in the summer.
- **Harvard Square/Harvard Yard.** Streets musicians, slackers, students, professors, and people of all ethnicities crowd this busy triangular square that's boarded by Harvard on one side and banks, restaurants, and boutiques on the other two sides. The legendary Out-of-

For Further Research

Books

The Art of Scandal: The Life and Times of Isabella Stewart Gardner, by Douglass Shand-Tucci

Bibles, Brahmins, and Bosses: A Short History of Boston, by Thomas H. O'Connor

Boston: A Brief History, by Charles F. Durang

The Boston Massacre, by Hiller B. Zobel

Cityscapes of Boston: An American City Through Time, by Robert Campbell

Emerson Among the Eccentrics: A Group Portrait, by Carlos Baker

The First Suburbs: Residential Communities on the Boston Periphery, 1815–1860, by Henry C. Binford

The Fitzgeralds and the Kennedys: An American Saga, by Doris Kearns Goodwin

Frederick Law Olmsted and the Boston Park System, by Cynthia Zaitzevsky

One Boy's Boston, 1887–1901, by Samuel Eliot Morison

Planning the City Upon a Hill: Boston Since 1630, by Lawrence W. Kennedy

Web Sites

www.bostonusa.com/ (Greater Boston Convention and Visitors Bureau)

www.boston.com/globe/ (*The Boston Globe*)

www.boston-online.com/ (current events)

www.historyproject.org/ (gay and lesbian history)

www.iboston.org/index2.php (history and architecture)

Still Curious? Why Not Check Out

Ally McBeal

Amistad

The Bell Jar, by Sylvia Plath

Blown Away

Boston Adventure, by Jean Stafford

The Bostonians, by Henry James

The City Below, by James Carroll

Couples, by John Updike

Faithful Are the Wounds, by May Sarton

Good Will Hunting

The Last Angry Man, by Gerald Green

The Last Hurrah, by Edwin O'Connor

The Last Puritan, by George Santayana

Next Stop Wonderland

One L, by Scott Turow

The Paper Chase

Superior Women, by Alice Adams

The Verdict

Town newsstand has been selling food for thought from the same kiosk since the 1920s.

- **Post Office Square.** This quaint little park in the heart of the financial district is a place where lots of suits lunch.
- **South Station.** This big, old granite train station is still the main Amtrak depot in Boston. The coffee bars, gift shops, and eateries make this quite a pleasant place for your character to sit and read the paper while waiting for his train to come in.
- **The Financial District.** As in most major cities, this area is dominated by tall buildings, lunch spots, and high-end department stores. The place is but a shell at night, as no one lives or hangs out here after business hours.
- **The Leather District.** This area of Boston is home to large, old manufacturing buildings, where all of New England's leather was processed. Now it's become Boston's Soho, with expensive converted lofts, a few art galleries, bars, and coffee shops. It's also home to South Station.
- **The North End.** This is Boston's Italian sector. It has lots of small storefronts, restaurants, espresso joints, food shops, and old Italian immigrants. This area used to be home to the Italian mob, but not so much anymore. Homemade ravioli and cured meats hang in many windows, and feasts and festivals abound throughout the summer.

Exceptionally Grand Things Your Character Is Proud Of

- Herself—Bostonians are known for having exaggerated senses of self-importance.
- Its place in national history. The Bunker Hill Memorial, for example, is a treasure that can be seen from all over the city. This is where Paul Revere apparently was for the whole "one if by land, two if by sea" thing.

- Education. Boston and the surrounding areas have a long intellectual history and today are home to over sixty universities, colleges, and research facilities.
- Boston Common. What a park.

Pathetically Sad Things Your Character Is Ashamed Of

- Enforced busing and the race riots of the early 1970s.
- Trading Babe Ruth to the Yankees (superstition says the Red Sox can never win a World Series because of a curse).
- The banning of gays in South Boston during the St. Patrick's Day Parade.
- Hard-drinking celebrities, from Kitty Dukakis to Ted Kennedy.
- James "Whitey" Bulger, the Irish mobster who murdered nineteen people.

Your Character Loves

- To argue. Bostonians love having heated discussions.
- The Celtics and the Red Sox.
- The New England Patriots, 2002 Super Bowl winners.
- His family. Bostonians are generally family-oriented.
- His Irish heritage.
- His Italian heritage.
- Running the Boston Marathon.
- Sports and politics.

Your Character Hates

- Yankees, New Yorkers, and sometimes it seems like everyone in general.
- The Big Dig. They've been burying I-93 and turning it into a tunnel with a park on top for years. It's taking forever to build, running way over budget, and causing major traffic issues.

Significant Events Your Character Has Probably Thought About

- The state was occupied for centuries by three dominant Native American groups: the Potawatomi, the Ojibwa, and the Ottawa. French fur trade brought the first Europeans to the area in the 1600s. Father Jacques Marquette founded the first settlement at Sault Ste. Marie in 1668.

- In the 1700s, England began moving into the area in search of furs. Their presence sparked fighting with the French. Both sides enlisted Native Americans' support, but the tribes tended to favor the French.

- After the French surrendered the land at the end of the French and Indian War in 1763, Ottawa Chief Pontiac led an alliance of Native American tribes against the British. Known as Pontiac's Rebellion, the war lasted three years and stretched as far east as Maryland.

- During the War of 1812, American forts in Michigan drew much fighting, as both sides sought control of the Great Lakes. The Battle of Raisin River and the Battle of Lake Erie remain well-known events in state history.

- Michigan achieved statehood on January 26, 1837.

- When the fur trade died in the 1830s, the state switched its economic focus to lumber and cut down its extensive pine forests. By the turn of the twentieth century, much of this natural resource had been depleted. Mining in the late nineteenth century also provided the area with a strong economy, and the presence of these metals led to the development of the auto industry.

- At the turn of the twentieth century, Detroit and nearby cities, such as Flint and Dearborn, became leaders in the new automobile industry.

- In 1903 Henry Ford founded the Ford Motor Company. By 1908 Model Ts were pouring off assembly lines, bringing affordable cars to the country.

- An invasion of lamprey eels nearly destroyed the Great Lakes fishing industry in the 1930s. A toxin was developed after World War II that destroyed the eels without harming other types of fish.

- The United Auto Workers union staged a series of strikes against the major car companies during the Great Depression. By 1941 all the companies had accepted the union.

- Racial conflicts plagued Michigan's industrial cities in the 1960s.

Michigan Basics That Shape Your Character

Motto: If You Seek a Pleasant Peninsula, Look About You

Population: 9.9 million

Prevalent Religions: Roman Catholic, Baptist, Methodist, and Lutheran

Major Industries: Automobile and other motor vehicles, motor vehicle parts, fabricated metal and chemical products, food processing, agriculture (primarily dairy products, fruits, and vegetables), tourism

Ethnic Makeup (in percent): Caucasian 80.2%, African-American 14.2%, Hispanic 3.3%, Asian 1.8%, Native American 0.6%, Other 1.3%

Famous Michiganders: Ellen Burstyn, Francis Ford Coppola, Thomas E. Dewey, Gerald Ford, Henry Ford, Julie Harris, Magic Johnson, Ring Lardner, Madonna, Terry McMillan, Ted Nugent, Iggy Pop, Gilda Radner, Della Reese, Martha Reeves, Diana Ross, Steven Seagal, Bob Seger, Tom Selleck, David Spade, Potter Stewart, Lily Tomlin, Danny Thomas, Jackie Wilson, Stevie Wonder

- The auto industry suffered its worst period during the 1970s and early 1980s, when gas prices skyrocketed and fuel-efficient cars from Japan dominated the market.

Michigan Facts and Peculiarities Your Character Might Know

- The name of the state is derived from the Ojibwa word *meicigama*, meaning "great water," which the Ojibwa used to name Lake Michigan.
- Since the middle of the nineteenth century, Michigan has been called "The Wolverine State." Michiganders like the evocation of aggressiveness and tenacity, but some historians believe it was an insult created by Ohioans or Native Americans, who found Michiganders rapacious and greedy. There are no actual wolverines in the state.
- The state is divided into two peninsulas: the upper (called the "U.P.") is sparsely populated and focused on tourism, especially camping and fishing; the lower (rarely called the "L.P.," sometimes called "the Mitten"), contains the major population and industrial centers, as well as extensive farmland.

A "superior" lakeshore view

© PhotoDisc/Getty Images

- Ask people from the lower peninsula where they're from in the state and odds are they'll show you the palm of their hand and point to the spot.
- Michigan borders four of the five Great Lakes. It has the longest freshwater shoreline of any state. Only Alaska has more total shoreline than Michigan.
- No matter where you are in the state, you're no more than eighty-five miles from the Great Lakes.
- The peninsulas have a bit of rivalry. Folks from the U.P. are called "you-pers" by those in the lower peninsula, who consider their northern neighbors less sophisticated. In the U.P., the other peninsula is seen as dirty and a bit full of itself.
- The five-mile-long Mackinac Bridge is one of the longest suspension bridges in the world. It connects the upper and lower peninsulas between Mackinaw City and St. Ignace. Before its completion in 1957, residents could travel between the peninsulas only by ferryboats. Michiganders call the bridge "the Mighty Mac."
- In 1817, the University of Michigan became the first state-established university.
- Michigan is the eleventh largest state in area, though thirty-eight thousand square miles of that area is the Great Lakes.
- Michigan leads all states in the production of cucumbers and is second in the production of dry beans.

Your Character's Food and Drink

Cherry everything. The state's production of cherries makes plentiful cherry desserts and wines, which your characters will find wherever they go. Tourists and Michiganders come for miles for the Mackinaw fudge. In fact, locals call tourists "fudgies." Detroit's brewing industry is mostly gone now, but the state has a number of popular microbrews. At the top of the list is the Great Lakes brand, which produces several types of beer. Wineries in the northwest part of the lower peninsula are growing, especially around Traverse City and Cadillac. The Chantal brand is popular throughout the state. In the larger areas, ethnic food of every variety is available, especially Middle Eastern, Hungarian, Greek, and Polish food.

Things Your Character Likes to Remember

- The Lions and Tigers and Pistons and Red Wings of Detroit have long histories in the state, and their championship seasons are remembered. The major universities—Michigan and Michigan State—also have proud traditions and have won national championships in a variety of sports.

- Native son Gerald Ford became president after Richard Nixon's resignation.
- Michigan was a leader in economic reform and development in the 1990s when it turned its sagging economy into one imitated by other states.
- The Motown Sound. The state has produced more than its share of music stars in pop, rock, and jazz.
- The festivals. Michiganders will travel far to attend festivals. The state fair is a source of pride, as is the Holland Tulip Festival, the National Cherry Festival, and the Toy Fair in Kalamazoo, among others.

Things Your Character Would Like to Forget

- The race riots of the 1960s. Detroit was the setting for much violence and destruction during this time. Race relations have been a source of conflict, as have relations between workers and bosses in the auto industry.
- The influx of foreign competitors in the auto industry, beginning in the 1970s. Though sound business decisions have reversed the industry's fortunes, its era of dominance in this market is over as the market is split by many competitors.
- Michiganders have a love-hate relationship with winter. The lake effect produces a lot of snow, and the Canadian winds produce a biting chill. Though skiing, cross-country skiing, and other winter sports are enjoyed, locals could do without so much snow.

Myths and Misperceptions About Michigan

- **It's one giant car plant.** It's still the "Motor Capital of the World," but first-time visitors will be surprised at the amount of farmland and unsettled shoreline in the lower peninsula and the rugged wilderness of the U.P.
- **The Michigan Militia.** The alliteration (and the nuttiness) of this organization has etched it into the national consciousness, but Michiganders tend not to be violent anti-government reactionaries.

Interesting Places to Set a Scene

- **Ann Arbor.** Home to the University of Michigan, there's a freethinking, sophisticated atmosphere in this city. Your characters will find a lot of coffee-houses, bookstores, and bohemian types here. It's the hometown of rock stars Iggy Pop and Bob Seger, and renowned author Charles Baxter teaches at the prestigious university writing program.
- **Battle Creek.** Known as "Cereal City," this is where kids have sent cereal box tops for the promotional prizes offered by the two major companies that built the town: Kellogg's and Post. From roadsides to the names of public centers, the influence of these companies on the city is everywhere. Also, the grave of Sojourner Truth is here.
- **Flint.** The city took a drubbing in the documentary *Roger and Me*, and the slumping auto industry has drubbed it even further. It's an industrial city, drab and smoky, and home to Fisher Body, Buick, and other factories. The factory workers, however, bring an ethnic richness to the city that give it character and interest.
- **Grand Rapids.** Hometown of President Gerald Ford, Grand Rapids is not grand so much as unassuming. In winter it draws skiers to the area, and in summer it is a pleasant rest stop for travelers headed farther north and west. The Grand River flows through town.
- **Isle Royale National Park.** The park includes Isle Royale, the largest island in Lake Superior, and approximately two hundred smaller islands. Cars are not permitted in the park, and there are no roads. The wilderness here preserves a habitat for plant life as well as for moose, wolves, and other animals. If your characters are serious about getting back to nature, they can do it here.
- **Kalamazoo.** Folks here catch grief about the odd name, though lyricists have had fun with it for decades. It's an industrial city, though winter skiing is popular with locals and tourists.
- **Lansing.** Located at the confluence of the Grand and Red Cedar Rivers, Lansing is the state capital. Like most cities in this part of the state, it relies heavily on industry, though state government offices also make a strong presence. To get away from all the business, send your characters to Cooley Gardens on Main Street, an interesting green space amidst the hustle and hassle.
- **Mackinac Island and Mackinaw City.** (Pronounced "mack-I-naw.") One of the oldest and most famous resorts in the state, this area attracts tourists from throughout the Midwest. No cars are allowed on the

For Further Research

Books

Buildings of Michigan, by Kathryn Bishop Eckert

Fishing the Great Lakes: An Environmental History, 1783–1933, by Margaret Beattie Bogue

Michigan: A History of the Wolverine State, by Willis F. Dunbar and George S. May

Michigan Place Names, by Walter Romig

A Most Unique Machine: The Michigan Origins of the Automobile Industry, by George S. May

Rites of Conquest: The History and Culture of Michigan's Native Americans, by Charles E. Cleland

Web Sites

www.michigan.org/ (state site for travel and business)

http://travel.michigan.org/ (state tourism site)

www.usgennet.org/usa/mi/state/ (American local history site)

www.michiganhistorymagazine.com/ (state history information)

Still Curious? Why Not Check Out

Almost Famous

Cumberland County, by John P. Schroeder

The Feast of Love, by Charles Baxter

Home Improvement

I Wish I Had a Red Dress, by Pearl Cleage

The Last Big Attraction

Master Hands

The Nick Adams Stories and *In Our Time*, by Ernest Hemingway

North of Nowhere, by Steve Hamilton

Roger and Me

Somewhere in Time

The Sporting Club, by Thomas McGuane

The Virgin Suicides, by Jeffrey Euginedes

Waiting for the Morning Train: An American Boyhood, by Bruce Catton

The Woman Lit By Fireflies, by Jim Harrison

island to preserve its natural beauty. Ferries run regularly from the city, which is considered a gateway to the U.P.

- **Sault Ste. Marie.** A small town in the eastern area of the U.P., Sault Ste. Marie (pronounced "soo-saint-marie" and known locally as "the soo") is a key tourist destination and a gateway to the rest of the peninsula and to Canada. In summer people come to fish and hunt. In winter they ski and ride snowmobiles. It's a place of natural beauty as well as racial harmony. More than 15 percent of the population is Native American.

- **Traverse City.** Best known for its production of cherries and cherry-related products, Traverse City also is home to Interlochen Academy, a world-renowned high school/boarding school for teens studying music, dance, drama, and art. Visitors flock here for the annual National Cherry Festival in July. The city is home to the World's Largest Cherry Pie.

Detroit

Detroit

Detroit Facts and Peculiarities Your Character Might Know

- Detroit was a trading center for Native Americans for hundreds of years before Europeans arrived.
- The city was founded in 1701 by Frenchman Antoine de la Mothe Cadillac, making it the oldest large city west of the Atlantic seaboard. In 2001, locals made much of their three hundredth birthday, staging a number of events and festivals to celebrate.
- The French named the city *Detroit* meaning "strait" or, more literally, "the narrow place," a name they had given the Detroit River, a slim channel that connects Lakes Erie and St. Claire. Detroit calls itself "The Motor City" or "Motown." Lately it's become cool (sort of) to call the city "the D."
- Detroit was the capital of the state until 1847.
- The city's population grew dramatically in the second half of the nineteenth century, as Polish and Eastern European immigrants came to find jobs in the shipping and shipbuilding industries. African-Americans from the South poured in during the early twentieth century for jobs in the auto industry.
- Since 1970, the population of Detroit has declined by more than 30 percent, the largest decrease of any major American city. The metro area, however, has continued to expand.
- In the early 1960s, Barry Gordy founded Motown Records, which produced African-American urban pop music that found a huge audience. Detroit singers such as Diana Ross, Smokey Robinson, and Stevie Wonder became national stars. The Motown Museum now stands at the place where "Hitsville USA" began.
- Famous for the Motown Sound, Detroit also is the hometown to other music stars, including Sonny Bono, Aretha Franklin, MC5, Mitch Ryder, Eminem, and Margaret Whiting.
- Detroit has the largest Arab community in the United States, with more than 300,000 residents.
- The Ambassador Bridge, which links Detroit with Windsor, Canada, is the world's longest international suspension bridge. If your characters prefer to drive under rather than over the water, they can take the tunnel, which is the first international connection tunnel in the world.
- James Vernor developed Vernor's ginger ale, the oldest soda pop in the country, in Detroit in 1865.

Detroit Basics That Shape Your Character

Inside the Detroit Historical Museum

Population: 951,270 in the city; 4 million in the Greater Metro area

Prevalent Religions: Catholic, Protestant, Muslim, Jewish

Top Employers: General Motors Corporation, Ford Motor Company, DaimlerChrysler Corporation, Volkswagen of America, Kmart, The Budd Company, Stroh's Brewing Company, American National Resources, Federal-Mogul Corporation

Per Capita Income: $31,472

Average Daily Temperature: January, 25° F; July, 74° F

Ethnic Makeup (in percent): Caucasian 12.3%, African-American 81.6%, Hispanic 5.0%, Asian 1.0%, Native American 0.3%, Other 2.5%

Newspapers: *Detroit Free Press, The Detroit News*

Free Weekly Alternative Paper: *Metro Times*

If Your Character . . .

If Your Character Is Alternative and Grungy, she lives near Wayne State University or in bohemian pockets of the Inner Ring suburbs. Ferndale is becoming a hot spot for this crowd.

If Your Character Smells of Old Money, he lives in Bloomfield Hills, Edison, Rochester, Birmingham, or St. Claire Shores where some old money families joined the "White Flight" to the farthest northern suburbs.

If Your Character Is All About Business, she works in Troy if she works in the newer businesses, such as banking. If she works in the auto industry, GM and Ford are downtown. Other new business, such as the growing health-care industry, is spread throughout the city but is concentrated in the expanding north.

If Your Character Is Newer Money, he lives in the northern suburbs, in Grosse Point, Romeo, West Bloomfield Hills, Rochester Hills, Auburn Hills, or Beverly Hills. The new money and new neighborhoods are located in the Outer Ring. The apartments and lofts in the revitalized riverfront area are becoming trendy homes for single professionals.

If Your Characters Are Raising a Family, they live in Dearborn, Royal Oak, Northville, or Troy. Most new homes are being built in the north where middle- to upper-middle class families live.

If Your Character Wears a Blue Collar at Work, he lives in Westland, Wayne, Livonia, Oak Park, and the suburbs on the west side. The Inner Ring suburbs are older and less advantaged.

Local Grub Your Character Might Love

Authentic Hungarian, Polish, Arab, Greek, and German ethnic foods are plentiful due to the city's strong ethnic groups. Arab restaurants are located mostly in Dearborn. Greektown is in the downtown area. As is most large cities, ethnic foods of nearly any type are available. Coney islands—chili-covered hot dogs in buns served with chopped onions and mustard—are popular. Sometimes called "coney dogs," these are Detroit's favorite sloppy food. Potato chips rule in Motown; the Better Made brand is an institution. Detroit was once a great brewing center, and though that star has faded in recent decades, the city is loaded, so to speak, with microbrews. Detroiters also find no end of ways to enjoy Michigan's annual crop of cherries and apples.

Interesting and Peculiar Places to Set a Scene

- **African World Festival.** Held annually in August, this festival draws more than a million people who come to celebrate their African heritage. It's a mix of live music, art, food, and cultural presentations.
- **Belle Isle.** Located in the Detroit River, this thousand-acre park is where the city comes to play, if only in a "family fun" way. It's best known for its aquarium and children's zoo and for its great views of the city. Locals gather here in great number to watch Fourth of July fireworks explode above the city skyline.
- **Detroit Zoo.** Located in Royal Oak, the Detroit Zoo was the first to create cageless habitats where the animals could roam in natural settings. Its best-known feature is the Arctic Ring of Life, a four-acre exhibit featuring polar bears and seals in any icy setting.
- **Fox Theater.** Once a crown jewel in the Fox chain, this magnificent building opened in 1928. By the 1970s, it was a relic, but Detroiters restored it rather than tearing it down. The refurbished building reopened in 1988 and is the setting for concerts as well as the city ballet.
- **Greenfield Village.** Henry Ford created this mythic village to preserve life as it was lived in the nineteenth century. The village is a collection of eighty houses and shops arranged to evoke a real American town. Actors dressed in period costume walk the streets.
- **Hart Plaza.** Located on the riverfront next to the Renaissance Center, Hart Plaza is Detroit Central. Its fountain is a local landmark and a gathering place for locals and visitors.
- **Henry Ford Museum.** Located in Dearborn next to Greenfield Village, the Ford Museum, founded by Henry himself, presents an eclectic mix of Americana treasures and junk, mostly gadgets and inventions. The theme here is American ingenuity. The city has a number of beautiful fine-art museums—such as the outstanding Institute of Arts—but if you're looking for a more unique setting, start here.
- **Pontiac.** A northern commuter city, Pontiac is where the young professional crowd lives and plays. Its suburbs are booming, and its restaurants and nightclubs are well loved by hip locals. Clutch Cargo's is known as a great place to dance and drink.
- **The Renaissance Center.** Completed in the 1980s as part of a push to revitalize downtown, the "Ren Cen" is a gargantuan, seven-tower complex of hotels,

For Further Research

Books

Before the Ghetto: Black Detroit in the Nineteenth Century, by David M. Katzman

Before Motown: A History of Jazz in Detroit, 1920–1960, by Lars Bjorn

Dancing in the Street: Motown and the Cultural Politics of Detroit, by Suzanne E. Smith

The Detroit Almanac: 300 Years of Life in the Motor City, edited by Peter Gavrilovich and Bill McGraw

Detroit Then and Now, by Cheri Y. Gay

Frontier Metropolis: Picturing Early Detroit, 1701–1838, by Brian Leigh Dunnigan

A Most Unique Machine: The Michigan Origins of the Auto Industry, by George S. May

The Origins of the Urban Crisis: Race and Inequality in Postwar Detroit, by Thomas J. Sugrue

The Purple Gang: Organized Crime in Detroit, 1910–1945, by Paul R. Kavieff

This Is Detroit: 1701–2001, by Arthur M. Woodford

The Tigers of '68: Baseball's Last Real Champions, by George Cantor

Whose Detroit, by Heather Ann Thompson

Web Sites

www.ci.detroit.mi.us/ (main city site)

www.detroitmusic.com (info and chat forums about the city music scene)

www.visitdetroit.com/ (tourism site)

www.freep.com/ (*Detroit Free Press*)

www.detroit.net/ (city info and links)

www.inmetrodetroit.com/ (entertainment and city info and links)

http://cityofdetroit.com/ (city info and links)

Still Curious? Why Not Check Out

The Amos Walker series of mystery novels, by Loren D. Estleman

Blue Collar

City Primeval: High Noon in Detroit, by Elmore Leonard

Detroit Rock City

Ernie Harwell: Stories of My Life in Baseball, by Ernie Harwell

The Final Season, by Tom Stanton

The Good Negress, by A.J. Verdelle

Grosse Point Blank

Last Year's Jesus: A Novella and Nine Stories, by Ellen Slezak

Mama, by Terry McMillan

Middlesex, by Jeffrey Eugenides

Mr. Mom

Paper Lion, by George Plimpton

Polish Wedding

Robocop

Them, by Joyce Carol Oates

---

shops, and offices located on the riverfront. Its crown jewel is the seventy-three-story hotel/convention center.

- **Wayne State University.** The campus features striking architecture, and the neighborhood surrounding it is home to artists, bohemians, and a thriving gay community. Trendy coffeehouses, shops, restaurants, and apartments fill the area.

Exceptionally Grand Things Your Character Is Proud Of

- The car industry. Though it's lost some of its former luster, the auto industry still is big business in Detroit. Experts had forecast the industry's demise, but in recent years it has made a comeback.
- Revitalized downtown. The movement of people and industries from the city to the surrounding suburbs has hurt the city's economy. Through great effort, the city has been able to lure new investors and residents back downtown.
- The music scene. From Motown to rock to jazz, music is a big deal in Detroit and has earned the city national recognition for decades.
- Comerica Park, the state-of-the-art home of baseball's lowly Tigers. Locals call it "CoPa" and by August rarely go to it.

Pathetically Sad Things Your Character Is Ashamed Of

- Race riots in the 1940s and 1960s. Racial strife and clashes between the working class and professional class have stained the history of the city. Today the core city and the Inner Ring suburbs are struggling, while the Outer Ring suburbs are middle to upper-middle class.

- In the latter part of the twentieth century, Detroit was known as "The Murder Capital of America."
- It's not a pretty city. Its reliance for so many years on heavy industry and its high unemployment as a result of the sagging American auto industry has made Detroit a less-than-attractive city in an otherwise beautiful state.
- In the late 1990s, the Lions and Tigers have been two of the worst teams in their leagues.

Your Character Loves

- Jazz. Though known as the home of the Motown Sound, Detroit is a hotbed for great jazz. The annual Montreux Jazz Festival draws fans from across the country, and locals rarely use its official new name: the Ford Detroit International Jazz Festival.
- Gordie Howe and the Red Wings. Hockey, in general, is a popular sport here.
- To gamble. For a number of years locals drove across the bridge to Canada for casino gambling. Now they stay in town and go to the MotorCity Casino or the MGM Grand Casino.
- The restored Fox Theater. Locals are proud of the beautiful building and will invariably include the Fox on the city tour for their out-of-town guests.

Minnesota

Significant Events Your Character Has Probably Thought About

- The early European explorers in the state were French trappers who hunted on land that was occupied mostly by Ojibwa and Dakota tribes. As early as the middle of the seventeenth century, councils were held with the native people, and several forts had been built by the end of the century.
- Treaties were signed in 1837 with the Dakota and Ojibwa, opening Minnesota to white settlement.
- On May 11, 1858, Minnesota became the thirty-second state in the union.
- Broken promises, bad treaties, and a new railroad sparked the Dakota War in 1862. Dakota warriors attacked a number of villages. Nearly four hundred warriors were arrested and convicted, though President Abraham Lincoln pardoned nearly all of them. Thirty-eight men were hanged in Mankato in December 1862.
- Charles Lindbergh of Little Falls piloted the first trans-Atlantic flight from New York to Paris, earning the status of national hero.
- Minnesotan Sinclair Lewis became the first American writer to win the Nobel Prize for Literature in 1930. A best-selling writer throughout the 1920s, Lewis's most famous novel was *Main Street*, an excoriating satire of small-town life that angered residents of his hometown, Sauk Center.
- As vice president to Lyndon Johnson in 1964, Hubert Humphrey became the first Minnesotan to be elected to national executive office. Four years later, he was the first Minnesotan to be nominated for president by a major political party. In 1984 fellow Minnesotan Walter Mondale was nominated for the post.
- The Mall of America, the country's largest indoor shopping complex, opened in 1992.
- In 1998, Reform Party candidate Jesse Ventura was elected governor, the first third-party candidate to win the job since 1936 and the first ever who had the nickname "The Body."

Minnesota Facts and Peculiarities Your Character Might Know

- The state is known as the "Land of 10,000 Lakes." In fact, there are 11,842 lakes that are each more than ten acres large.

Minnesota Basics That Shape Your Character

Motto: The Star of the North

Population: 5 million

Prevalent Religions: Roman Catholic, Lutheran, Baptist, and Methodist

Major Industries: Food processing, dairy products, agriculture (primarily corn, wheat, and soybeans), printing and publishing, mining (primarily iron ore), manufacturing of industrial machinery

Ethnic Makeup (in percent): Caucasian 89.4%, African-American 3.5%, Hispanic 2.9%, Asian 2.9%, Native American 1.1%, Other 0.2%

Famous Minnesotans: Loni Anderson, Warren Berger, Bob Dylan, F. Scott Fitzgerald, Judy Garland, J. Paul Getty, Garrison Keillor, Jessica Lange, Sinclair Lewis, John Madden, Kate Millett, Walter Mondale, Prince, Jane Russell, Winona Ryder, Charles Schultz, Dave Winfield

- Minnesota leads the nation in recreational boats per capita, with one in six people owning one.
- The name of the state is derived from the Dakota word for sky-tinted water or "water that looks like the sky." This word often was used to describe the many lakes.

- From the 1880s through the 1930s, Minnesota was known as the "Flour Capital of the World" because its mills processed grain for farmers throughout the region.
- Minnesota produces nearly 75 percent of the country's iron ore.
- The state reached a new low (temperature-wise) on February 2, 1996, when the thermometer dropped to sixty degrees below zero (Fahrenheit) in the town of Tower.
- Pop cultures icons Paul Bunyan (1914), Betty Crocker (1921), The Jolly Green Giant (1928), and The Pillsbury Doughboy (1965) were born here to pitch the products of Minnesota companies.
- The town of Darwin is home to the world's largest ball of twine. A thirty-year project for farmer Francis Johnson, the ball weighs nearly nine tons.

Your Character's Food and Drink

Freshwater fish are abundant. Walleye pike is served everywhere, from the dinner table to truck stops to four-star restaurants. Some restaurants regularly offer specials on "All the Walleye You Can Eat." Traditional Norwegian dishes are still served, though they are far less popular than in the past; they are staples of Lutheran church dinners. Any native of Minnesota has tried *lutefisk,* which is cod that has been soaked in lye and cooked. *Lefse,* a crepe eaten with butter and cinnamon, is another favorite. Both are served during the Christmas season. A "hot dish" is a casserole of varied ingredients that is brought to picnics and public dinners. The practice and the name are still quite common. Minnesota is the nation's leading producer of wild rice, and it is a popular food, especially in the northern part of the state.

Things Your Character Likes to Remember

- "The best state fair in the country." Minnesotans take pride in their annual fair, sometimes known locally as "The Great Minnesota Eat-In." Held in late summer on fairgrounds located between St. Paul and Minnesota, the fair attracts crowds from every part of the state.
- The Minnesota Twins have won several World Series. The Vikings have been to the Super Bowl four times and in the 1970s were well known for their defensive line, The Purple People Eaters.
- Minnesotans also take pride in being a hardy people who can endure the long, often harsh winters. When the winter is not robust, they're disappointed.
- Minnesota used to call itself "The Education State" because of its good education system and libraries.
- Mayo Clinic.
- Garrison Keillor and *A Prairie Home Companion*.

Things Your Character Would Like to Forget

- Electing Jesse Ventura. A former wrestler, Ventura won a narrow three-way race for governor. His election caught national attention, but most Minnesotans regret their choice. He had a big following among college students and other young voters, making his harsh cuts in the education budget ironic.
- The Vikings have been to the Super Bowl four times and lost them all, scoring thirty-four points in the four games combined. Any loss to the hated Green Bay Packers is worth forgetting.
- Mosquitoes. The lakes and swamps spawn these annoying bugs. Visitors often are surprised by the size and persistence of the mosquitoes, which appear at dawn and dusk from the end of May until early September. A popular T-shirt declares the mosquito "The State Bird."
- Potholes. The salt thrown on roads throughout the long winters eats up the pavement, creating many potholes. Minnesotans sometimes complain of having two seasons—winter and road construction. The salt also is tough on cars.
- Minnesota sits at the top of the Iowa-Kansas tornado belt, and southern Minnesota is sometimes hit hard.

© PhotoDisc/Getty Images

Bridges of the Twin Cities

For Further Research

Books

Cold Comfort: Life at the Top of the Map, by Barton Sutter

How to Talk Minnesotan, by Howard Mohr

The Minnesota Book of Days, by Tony Greiner

The Minnesota Guide, by Anne Gillespie Lewis

Minnesota Marvels: Roadside Attractions in the Land of Lakes, by Eric Dregni

Tastes of Minnesota: A Food Lover's Tour, by Donna Tabbert Long

Wild Rice Cooking: History, Harvesting, and Lore and Sugartime, by Susan Carol Hauser

Web Sites

www.mnhs.org/ (state historical site)

http://deckernet.com/minn/ (general state info and links)

www.state.mn.us/ (general information about the state; many links)

www.mnpro.com/ (state main site)

www.exploreminnesota.com/ (state tourism site)

Still Curious? Why Not Check Out

Fargo

Feeling Minnesota

The novels and stories of Garrison Keillor, best known for *Lake Wobegon Days*

Grumpy Old Men

The novels of Jon Hassler, including *A Green Journey, Grand Opening, North of Hope, Staggerford*

Look How the Fish Live and Wheat That Springeth Green, by J.F. Powers

Main Street, by Sinclair Lewis

Red Earth, White Earth, by Will Weaver

The Little House on the Prairie books, by Laura Ingalls Wilder (Wisconsin also claims Wilder's books.)

Myths and Misperceptions About Minnesota

- **The accent.** While you'll still hear the Scandinavian twang in the northern part of the state, the Minnesota accent has softened through the years. Minnesotans bristle when they hear themselves caricatured, as in the movie *Fargo*. One expression that does recall the Norwegian roots of many Minnesotans is "oof da," which is used in the state as an exclamation, along the lines of "goodness gracious."

- **The weather is always cold.** Every winter brings at least a few bad snowstorms, but summers are pleasant and warm—sometimes even hot.

Interesting Places to Set a Scene

- **Bemidji.** One of the creators of the TV series *Northern Exposure* is from Bemidji, and that sense of eccentricity and uniqueness are easy to find here. A strong bohemian community mixes with a blue-collar, conservative bunch. Lots of back-to-nature types. Bemidji has the "real" Paul Bunyan statue and claims to be his birthplace.

- **Brainard.** Joel and Ethan Coen set their film *Fargo* here. As in Bemidji, you'll find a Paul Bunyan statue; the towns carry on a joking rivalry about which one is the true home of the giant logger. There's also a car-racing track that has attracted some famous drivers, including movie star Paul Newman.

- **Boundary Waters Canoe Wilderness Area.** This area contains more than a thousand lakes and streams and lives up to the name "wilderness." Many of the lakes are paddle only, and serious campers can find truly primitive places. The town of Ely teems with outfitters and lodges, and the town of Grand Marais on Lake Superior offers great views and a less rigorous vacation. The crown jewel of the area is Lake Vermillion, which is dotted with small islands.

- **Duluth.** An international port city on Lake Superior, Duluth boasts the largest inland harbor in the country. It's an industrial city, but you also can take your characters for a romantic stroll along the three-mile walkway that rims the lake, or they can take the car along the North Shore Scenic Drive, a twenty-four-mile lakeshore trip on Old Highway 61. If things get really romantic, they can get married at Chapel on the Lake, a pristine white chapel located right on the shore.

- **The lakes.** You have more than twelve thousand to choose from for setting a scene. The biggest is Red Lake, which is more than twice the size of the second largest, Mille Lacs Lake. Other big lakes are Leech,

Winnebegoshish, and Vermilion. Fishing and boating are popular hobbies throughout the state.

- **New York Mills.** A small town located a hundred miles west of the Twin Cities, New York Mills enjoys a growing reputation as a cultural center. If your characters are seeking the artistic life, they'll find a home here.
- **Red Wing.** A small town nestled on the Mississippi River, an hour's drive south of the Twin Cities, Red Wing is quaint without being cute. Local boosters have christened it "The Desirable City," which would seem cloying if it weren't so true. Your characters will find a number of restored Victorian houses to tour. Train passengers still board and depart from the Old Milwaukee Depot, a stop along the Empire Builder's Chicago-to-Seattle run.
- **Rochester.** This town is home to the famous Mayo Clinic. If your character needs a world-class diagnosis for a health problem, send her here. If she's suffering from a bad haircut, send her to Rochester's other famous diagnostic clinic, Hair Gods, an upscale salon.
- **Split Rock Lighthouse.** You've seen photographs of this famous lighthouse, which sits on the edge of a cliff overlooking Lake Superior. Located less than an hour north of Duluth in the North Shore area, the lighthouse hasn't been in service since the mid-1960s, but it remains a popular destination for tourists and locals.

Minneapolis/St. Paul

Twin Cities Facts and Peculiarities Your Character Might Know

- Originally called "Pig's Eye," St. Paul was a center for French traders. Built on the east side of the Mississippi, it grew quickly, spreading to the west side of the river, which became Minneapolis.
- St. Paul was chosen as the capital of the newly created Minnesota Territory in 1849.
- As the cities grew, St. Paul became associated primarily with state government and with stockyards, becoming the region's primary meat-processing center. Minneapolis grew into the center for lumber and for grain mills.
- The 1890 national census showed, for the first time, that Minneapolis had surpassed St. Paul in population. By the end of the century, the younger city had become the stronger economic center.
- To generalize the differences between the cities, St. Paul is known as "the last city of the east," and Minneapolis is known as "the first city of the west."
- People who live in the state but outside the Greater Twin Cities area are said to live "out state."
- In 1961, the state boomed with major-league sports. The Minnesota Twins baseball team took the field for the first time, as did the Minnesota Vikings football team. The year before, the Minneapolis Lakers left to become the Los Angeles Lakers. Minnesotans waited until 1989 for a new NBA team, the Timberwolves.
- A throng of more than fifteen thousand shoppers waited for the doors to open for the first time at the Mall of America in August of 1992. The country's first enclosed mall, Southdale, opened in suburban Minneapolis in 1956.

If Your Character . . .

If Your Character Is Alternative and Grungy, he lives in Uptown or the Lake Harriet area, in Minneapolis. He also might live in the Riverside area. In St. Paul, your character lives in the Grand Avenue area, north of downtown.

If Your Character Is All About Business, he works in downtown in both cities, but more likely in downtown

Minneapolis/St. Paul Basics That Shape Your Character

Aerial view of downtown Minneapolis

Population: 3 million

Prevalent Religions: Catholic, Lutheran, Baptist, Methodist

Top Employers: General Mills, 3M Company, Northwest Airlines, the University of Minnesota, Archer Daniels Midland

Per Capita Income: $35,250

Average Daily Temperature: January, 12° F; July, 74° F

Ethnic Makeup (in percent): Minneapolis Caucasian 65.1%, African-American 18.0%, Hispanic 7.6%, Asian 6.1%, Native American 2.2%, Other 4.1% **St. Paul** Caucasian 67.0%, African-American 11.7%, Hispanic 7.9%, Asian 12.4%, Native American 1.7%, Other 1.0%

Newspapers: *Star Tribune* (called the "Strib" by some locals), *St. Paul Pioneer Press*

Free Weekly Alternative Papers: *Southwest Journal* (bi-weekly community paper of southwest Minneapolis), *City Pages*

Minneapolis. Eden Prairie, a Minneapolis suburb, also has a lot of industry and offices.

If Your Character Is a Moneyed, Young Professional, she lives in Prospect Park or Lake of the Isles in Minneapolis. In St. Paul, you'll find her in White Bear Lake.

If Your Character Has Big Bucks, he lives in Golden Valley or Minnetonka. Though lacking the genteel grace of Edina or Summit Avenue, these Minneapolis suburbs have big, new mansions and their residents enjoy a rich life.

If Your Character Is a Family Man, he lives in Bloomington, Apple Valley, Maple Grove, or White Bear Lake. These suburbs are part of what locals call the Outer Ring, in that they're new bedroom communities.

If Your Character Wears a Blue Collar at Work, he lives in Richfield or St. Louis Park in Minneapolis, and Hopkins in St. Paul. In the 1950s and 1960s, these suburbs housed the rising middle class. They're part of what's called the Inner Ring. In Minneapolis your character also might live in the Northside area.

Local Grub Your Character Might Love

The Twin Cities offer a variety of ethnic restaurants and have their share of great places for steak and seafood, but they're not known for any special regional dishes. The freshwater fish certainly is fresh, given the proximity of the lakes. Otherwise, your characters will find whatever is popular or trendy on the national scene. For particular Minnesota favorites, see "Minnesota" on page 167.

Interesting and Peculiar Places to Set a Scene

- **Bloomington.** Sure, it's just an overgrown suburb, but there's lots of stuff here. The Mall of America, for example. The Minneapolis-St. Paul airport is here, too. There are thirty-five hotels and lots of restaurants and entertainment facilities, many of them clustered around the airport and the mall. And there are lots of suburbs.
- **Farmer's Market.** Residents of both cities like to spend Saturday or Sunday mornings at the Farmer's Market on East Fifth Street in St. Paul. Fresh produce and fresh-cut flowers create an array of smells and sights amidst the overflowing stalls.
- **First Avenue and Seventh Street Eatery.** Hometown boy Prince played here in his film *Purple Rain.* The First Avenue section is a hip, slightly shabby nightclub with black-on-black decor. Patrons generally are cutting-edgers or wanna-bes. The Seventh Street Eatery attracts the same crowd hungry for a late-night repast. Your characters can enter either section through a separate door, though once inside, they can walk through a connecting door.
- **Foshay Tower.** A Minneapolis landmark, the thirty-two-story Foshay Tower was completed in 1929 and was the first skyscraper west of the Mississippi River. It was the tallest building in the city until late in the century, when new buildings were constructed in the downtown area. Its observation deck is still a favorite spot for locals and tourists, and it's a great place to set a scene.
- **Fort Snelling.** More a tourist or school field-trip destination than a hangout for locals, Fort Snelling is nonetheless a well-known landmark. It will bring interesting details and local history to any scene set here. The fort sits high on a hill overlooking the Mississippi and Minnesota Rivers and features actors dressed in period costume.
- **IDS Crystal Court.** Mary Tyler Moore tossed her tam in the air here during the credits of her 1970s sitcom. A small bronze statue on the corner of Seventh Street and Nicollet commemorates the moment. The matrix of the Nicollet Mall—a collection of offices, hotels, and shops connected by a skyway—the Crystal Court offers plenty of glass-enclosed space for your characters. Several suicides have occurred here in recent years, in case your character is thinking of ending it all.
- **Lowertown.** The artsy, bohemian part of St. Paul, this area includes the Farmer's Market and a wide assortment of galleries, studios, shops, and restaurants. Some in the bohemian set have objected to the renovation of this area and now find it too commercialized, but it remains a popular destination for the young and the hip.
- **Minneapolis City Hall.** If you want to add interesting juxtaposition to your scene, City Hall offers the look of the past amidst the modern, glass-and-steel downtown. More than a century old, the Minneapolis City Hall is made of red granite shaped in the architectural style of the late nineteenth century. It has a copper roof and a four-hundred-foot clock tower.

For Further Research

Books

City of Lakes: An Illustrated History of Minneapolis, by Joseph Stipanovich

The Falls of St. Anthony, by Lucile M. Kane

Minneapolis Then and Now, by Hanje Richards and Martin Howard

Minneapolis-St. Paul: People, Place, and Public Life, by John S. Adams

St. Paul: The First 150 Years, by Virginia Brainard Kunz

Twin Cities Then and Now, by Larry Millett

Web Sites

www.ci.minneapolis.mn.us/ (city government site)

www.minneapolis.org/ (Greater Minneapolis Convention and Visitors Association)

www.twincities.com/ (visitor and attractions information)

www.stpaulcvb.org/ (St. Paul Convention and Visitors Bureau)

www.ilovestpaul.com/ (city entertainment guide)

www.stpaul.gov/ (city government site)

Still Curious? Why Not Check Out

The Antelope Wife, by Louise Erdrich

A Definitive Guide to the Twin Cities in Poetry and Prose, edited by Chris Watercott

Dust to Dust, by Tami Hoag. Also, her earlier novel *Ashes to Ashes*

My Lesbian Husband, by Barrie Jean Borich

Untamed Heart

- **Minnehaha Park and Falls.** One of the most popular parks in the area, it includes a fifty-three-foot waterfall, a bronze mask of Dakota Chief Little Crow, a famous bronze statue of Hiawatha, and the Henry Wadsworth Longfellow House. Hiawatha was the hero of Longfellow's epic poem "The Song of Hiawatha," which was inspired by a trip he made to the area.
- **St. Paul Winter Carnival.** Heralded as the oldest and largest festival in the country, this ten-day event is held in late January. The tradition began in 1886 and includes ice sculptures and parades, a winter king and queen, and much eating, drinking, and revelry. The festival features an enormous castle, built from more than twenty-five thousand blocks of ice.
- **Summit Avenue.** A wide, elegant street in St. Paul, Summit Avenue is lined with magnificent old mansions and once was *the* place to live for the city's elite. Its most famous resident, F. Scott Fitzgerald, lived in one the more modest buildings, an eight-dwelling group of attached townhouses called Summit Terrace. The palatial estate of railroad robber baron James J. Hill also is on this street.

Exceptionally Grand Things Your Character Is Proud Of

- The Guthrie Theater. This theater and repertory company opened in 1963 and has gained an international reputation for artistic achievement.
- Artistic and cultural richness.
- The park system. The Twin Cities have more than two hundred parks and put them to use.
- The Twins, Vikings, and Timberwolves. Though league championships have eluded the Vikings and Timberwolves, the teams often finish with good records. The Twins, for a small-market team, have enjoyed surprising success.
- The educational system. The area has a number of colleges and universities, and the public education system at the grade and high school is also a source of pride.
- The lakes. In a state full of lakes, the Twin Cities take pride in those nearest them—Lake of the Isles, Lake Calhoun, and Lake Harriet. Together they form "the Chain of Lakes."
- WCCO. This fifty-thousand-watt, clear-channel station is a powerful institution in the Twin Cities.

Your Character Loves

- The Mall of America. Residents like to feign disinterest and even disdain for this giant shrine to chain retail, calling it "The MegaMall." But deep down they're proud of the attention it receives nationally. You won't need to twist an arm to get them to go.
- Sports stars, past and present. Special favorites: Kevin Garnett, Jim Kaat, Harmon Killebrew, Kevin McHale,

Kirby Puckett, Ron Yary and the Purple People Eaters.

- Going "north for the weekend." Even city-dwellers in Minnesota love the outdoors and usually spend their weekends boating, camping, and fishing. The cold weather rarely keeps them inside. Winter sports are among their favorite activities.
- The cold weather. You'll hear a note of pride in the voices of locals when they talk about the weather here. It's cold and snowfall is heavy, but people of the Twin Cities, especially natives of the state, love it.

Your Character Hates

- The cold weather. As much as they love it (see "Your Character Loves"), they complain about it, too. It makes life more difficult—driving, moving from place to place, dressing warmly for even the shortest forays outdoors. The downtown skyways help make movement in the city easier (and warmer), but commutes to and from downtown through snowstorms are tough.
- The mosquitoes. City workers spray for the annoying little bloodsuckers every summer, but the lakes and swamps throughout the state just make more.

Significant Events Your Character Has Probably Thought About

- On January 9, 1861, Mississippi seceded from the Union to join the Confederate States of America.
- The Siege of Vicksburg on July 4, 1863. This memorial battle (and defeat for the Confederacy) guaranteed Union control of the Mississippi River and signified the beginning of the end for Confederate forces.
- Mississippi's readmittance to the Union in 1870.
- The 1870 election, in which Mississippi's Hiram Revels became the nation's first African-American senator.
- In 1900, railroad engineer Casey Jones smashed his train near Vaughan, Mississippi, spurring a number of myths and songs about the tragic wreck.
- The 1927 Mississippi River Flood. This disaster wiped out almost three million acres of farmland, forcing thousands in the Delta to become homeless.
- In 1936 Governor Hugh White launched the state's "Balance Agriculture With Industry" program to promote both agricultural and industrial economic development.
- In 1962, James Meredith stepped foot in the University of Mississippi, establishing himself as the first African-American to attend one of Mississippi's segregated public colleges.
- The 1963 murder of civil rights activist Medgar Evers.
- Segregation officially ended in state public schools in 1969.
- In 1983, Lenore Prather became Mississippi's first woman Supreme Court justice.
- The 1991 gubernatorial election made Kirk Fordice, the self-proclaimed "Mississippi Miracle," the first Republican governor since Reconstruction. Then, in 1995, Fordice won a second term, becoming the first governor in over a century to be elected to two consecutive terms.

Mississippi Facts and Peculiarities Your Character Might Know

- William Grant Still composed the Afro-American Symphony.

Mississippi Basics That Shape Your Character

Motto: By Valor and Arms

Population: 2.85 million

Prevalent Religions: Christianity, particularly Southern Baptist, Pentecostal, Methodist, Lutheran, and Roman Catholic

Major Industries: Cotton, poultry, cattle, catfish, gaming, soybeans, dairy products, rice, gaming, clothing, furniture, lumber, food processing, electrical machinery

Ethnic Makeup (in percent): Caucasian 61%, African-American 36%, Hispanic 1.4%, Asian 0.4%, Native American 0.7%

Famous Mississippians: Bo Diddley, William Faulkner, Richard Ford, John Grisham, Jim Henson, Faith Hill, James Earl Jones, B.B. King, Elvis Presley, Eudora Welty, Tennessee Williams, Oprah Winfrey

- Burnita Shelton Mathews was the first female federal judge in the United States.
- The first nuclear submarine built in the South was produced in Mississippi.
- Liberty became the first town in the United States to erect a Confederate monument (1871).
- Friendship Cemetery in Columbus has been called "Where Flowers Healed a Nation." A year after the Civil War (April 25, 1866), the women of Columbus decorated both Confederate and Union soldiers' graves with bouquets and garlands of flowers. This gesture, which was repeated every year, was the impetus for what is now Memorial Day.
- The University of Mississippi Medical Center performed the world's first human-to-human lung transplant in 1963.
- In 1964 Dr. James D. Hardy performed the world's first heart transplant surgery (from chimp to a human, but the man only lived ninety minutes).
- Mamie Thomas was the first female mail carrier in the United States. She delivered mail by buggy to areas southeast of Vicksburg in 1914.
- Edward Adolf Barq Sr. invented root beer in Biloxi in 1898.
- The largest Bible-binding plant in the nation is Norris Bookbinding Company in Greenwood.

Your Character's Food and Drink

Main courses are fried chicken, hickory smoked ribs, deep-fried catfish, barbecued beef and chicken, seafood from the Gulf, country fried steak, and chitlins. Veggies run the gamut and include okra, collard greens, black-eyed peas, green beans, and corn on the cob. Breakfast food favorites tend to be bacon, sausage patties, ham, biscuits 'n' gravy, and grits. Side and dessert dishes include corn bread, pecan pie, pudding, flaky biscuits, and peach cobbler.

Things Your Character Likes to Remember

- Teddy Roosevelt's 1902 hunting expedition in Sharkey County. The president's refusal to shoot a captured bear cub spawned the creation of the stuffed teddy bear we all know and love.
- Mississippi has more churches per capita than does any other state.
- Memorial Day—it started in Columbus at Friendship Cemetery in 1866.
- Mississippi's state legislature was the first in the nation to incorporate a system of junior colleges.
- Its literary heritage: Richard Wright, William Faulkner, Eudora Welty, Barry Hannah, John Grisham.
- Juke joints.
- Delta Blues.

Things Your Character Would Like to Forget

- Mississippi suffered the largest percentage of people who died in the Civil War of any Confederate state. Seventy-eight thousand Mississippians entered the Confederate military. By the end of the war, fifty-nine thousand were either dead or wounded.
- The boll weevil. In 1907 this pesky creature destroyed most of the state's cotton crop, wreaking havoc on the economy as well as the land.
- That Martin Luther King Jr. tagged Mississippi "a desert state sweltering with the heat of injustice and oppression."
- Of the forty martyrs whose names are inscribed in the national Civil Rights Memorial in Montgomery, Alabama, nineteen were killed in Mississippi.
- Not until 1995 did Mississippi's state legislature finally ratify the Thirteenth Amendment outlawing slavery.

Myths and Misperceptions About the State

- **Citizens are "rednecks."** Although the word got its name from the sunburned red-collar line on plowboys out in the fields with their mules, the term refers to a white Southerner who conforms to the social behavior of his peers. Mississippians don't like that label. (They'd prefer being called "good ol' boys," which is a group of close friends you grew up with or have known for a long time. A cut above the rednecks.)

Courtesy Vicksburg Convention and Visitors Bureau

Monument in the Vicksburg National Military Park

For Further Research

Books

An American Insurrection, by William Doyle

Approaching the Magic Hour: Memories of Walter Anderson, by Agnes Grinstead Anderson

The Band Played Dixie: Race and the Liberal Conscience at Ole Miss, by Nadine Cohodas

Ghosts of Mississippi: The Murder of Medgar Evers, the Trials of Byron de la Beckwith, and the Haunting of the New South, by Maryanne Vollers

Let Us Now Praise Famous Men, by James Agee

Mississippi: An American Journey, by Anthony Walton

Mississippi: A History, by John Knox Bettersworth

My Mississippi, by Willie Morris

The Rising Tide: The Great Mississippi Flood of 1927 and How It Changed America, by John M. Barry

Walker Percy: A Southern Wayfarer, by William Rodney Allen

Web Sites

www.olemiss.edu/depts/english/ms-writers/ (Ole Miss's site)

www.mississippi.com (about the state)

www.mississippi.gov/ (official state site)

www.city.jackson.ms.us/ (Jackson site)

www.tupelo.net/ (Tupelo site)

www.greenville.ms.us/ (Greenville site)

www.vicksburg.org/ (Vicksburg site)

www.biloxi.ms.us/ (Biloxi site)

Still Curious? Why Not Check Out

As I Lay Dying, by William Faulkner

Church Folk, by Michele Andrea Bowen

Ghosts of Mississippi

High Lonesome, by Barry Hannah

Jordan County: A Landscape in Narrative, by Shelby Foote

Life on the Mississippi, by Mark Twain

Mississippi Burning

Native Son, by Richard Wright

The Oxford American: The Southern Magazine of Good Writing

Stories, Essays, and Memoirs, by Eudora Welty

A Time to Kill, by John Grisham

- **The cotton industry keeps the state financially sound.** Not so. Today industry, electronics, and digital technologies are on the rise, challenging cotton as the most profitable state product. Tourism and gaming also are becoming big boons to the state's economy.
- **All Mississippians are Bible-loving and God-fearing.** Many citizens say they don't care too much about organized religion these days. "Spiritual, not religious" is becoming the tag line, not "hell, fire, and brimstone." There's also more religious tolerance than there was in the past.
- **Caucasians still rule the state, even though segregation ended in 1962.** Not true. In fact, Mississippi now has the largest percentage of elected African-American officials in the United States.

Interesting Places to Set a Scene

- **Belzoni.** If your character is into fishing or eating catfish, Belzoni prides itself as "The Catfish Capital of the World." While pulling fish from the river has become a thing of the past (thank you, pollution), rumor has it there are more catfish farms in Belzoni than gambling boats in Biloxi.
- **Bay St. Louis.** A small-town-on-the-Gulf character's dream, Bay St. Louis boasts a quaint Old Town District with boardwalks, antique shops, art galleries, specialty boutiques, and intimate restaurants. The town also is home to several artists and writers, and others seeking inspiration from the beautiful coastal community.
- **Biloxi.** Vegas-type gaming and Gulf Coast waters make Biloxi a popular tourist spot. The oldest settlement on the Gulf Coast, historic Biloxi is a laid back, relaxing place—except during Mardi Gras, held on Fat Tuesday in February.
- **Canton.** If your character has flea market fever, send him to Canton. With over a thousand vending booths offering odds and ends of all sorts, this is the next best thing to heaven for barterers and traders. The interestingly architectural-preserved town square has a number of antique shops.
- **Clarksdale.** Sixty miles south of Memphis, Clarksdale

is the blue-noted heart of the Delta Blues (and has the state's best Delta Blues Museum).

- **Greenwood.** The town hosts Cotton Row, the nation's second largest cotton exchange. Greenwood is also on the National Register of Historic Places and is deemed "The Cotton Capital of the World."

- **Jackson.** The state capital, named after Andrew Jackson, was hometown to Eudora Welty. It also possesses the state's finest art, historical, and science museums. To many, Jackson epitomizes suburban sprawl.

- **Natchez.** It doesn't get more Old South than this. The oldest settlement on the Mississippi River and one of the wealthiest cities in the country during the antebellum years, Natchez sports over five hundred antebellum homes and buildings. This gateway to the West is a primary stop on the Natchez Trace (now parkway) that goes from Natchez to Nashville.

- **Oxford.** This is Faulknerland, his "little postage stamp of native soil." Not only did Faulkner live here, he also made Oxford the setting (it's the Jefferson of Yoknapatawpha County) for much of his fiction. Many writers since also have called Oxford home, as do the University of Mississippi (a.k.a. "Ole Miss"), the famous independent bookstore Square Books, and *The Oxford American: The Southern Magazine of Good Writing*. Oxford is no doubt the literary inkwell of Mississippi.

- **Tupelo.** This is Elvis's birthplace and childhood home, where the King roamed around in poverty until he was thirteen—and there's a museum to prove it. Another landmark and interesting place in Tupelo is Reed's independent bookstore, established in 1907.

- **Vicksburg.** The "Gibraltar of the Confederacy" fell to Union troops in 1863. Although this river town now relies on its casinos to keep the economy afloat, Vicksburg typifies the Old South, with its magnolia-covered streets, horse-drawn carriages, Victorian homes, and southern hospitality. The National Cemetery in the National Military Park is the second largest in the United States, next to Arlington National Cemetery in Washington, DC.

Significant Events Your Character Has Probably Thought About

- The "Missouri Compromise" of 1820 granted Missouri the right to enter the Union as a slave state.
- In 1865, Missouri became the first slave state to free slaves before the official U.S. adoption of the Thirteenth Amendment.
- The U.S. Supreme Court ignored Missouri's "separate but equal" laws and allowed Lloyd Gaines to be the first African-American man admitted to the University of Missouri law school in 1938.
- Franklin Roosevelt's death in 1945 pushed native Vice President Harry Truman into the presidency (he was elected to a second term in 1948).
- To alleviate the racial isolation of African-American students, in 1980 the state of Missouri was required to pay half the cost of school desegregation plans.
- The town of Times Beach had to be evacuated in 1982 after soil samples showed the grounds were contaminated with high levels of dioxin. Several lawsuits followed.
- A 1983 auto accident put Nancy Cruzan in a vegetative state, and the family fought for years to remove her from life support. *Cruzan v. Missouri* became the first right-to-die case heard by the U.S. Supreme Court.
- In 1992, Missouri voters approved riverboat gambling excursions on the Mississippi and Missouri Rivers.
- The Outstanding Schools Act—a $310 million measure to reform Missouri schools—passed in 1993, improving education in the state.

Missouri Facts and Peculiarities Your Character Might Know

- Missouri is the "Show Me State" and "The Birthplace of Jazz."
- Lake of the Ozarks is one of the largest artificial lakes in the world, with about fourteen hundred miles of shoreline.
- In 1838, Governor Lilburn Boggs issued an extermination order forcing all members of the Church of Jesus Christ of Latter-day Saints to leave the state.
- The first Capitol Building in Jefferson City burned in 1837, and the second structure—completed three

Missouri Basics That Shape Your Character

Motto: The Welfare of the People Shall be the Supreme Law

Population: 5.6 million

Prevalent Religions: Christianity, particularly Roman Catholic, Baptist, Methodist, Lutheran, Pentecostal, and non/inter-denominational, small segments of Judaism and Church of Jesus Christ of Latter-day Saints

Major Industries: Cattle, soybeans, hogs, dairy products, corn, poultry and eggs, transportation equipment, food processing, chemical products, electric equipment, fabricated metal products

Ethnic Makeup (in percent): Caucasian 84.9%, African-American 11.2%, Hispanic 2.1%, Asian 1.1%, Native American 0.4%, Other 0.8%

Famous Missourians: Robert Altman, Burt Bacharach, Thomas Hart Benton, Yogi Berra, Bill Bradley, Martha Jane Canary (Calamity Jane), Dale Carnegie, George Washington Carver, Walter Cronkite, T.S. Eliot, Eugene Field, Redd Foxx, James W. Fulbright, John Goodman, Betty Grable, Edwin Hubble, Langston Hughes, John Huston, Marianne Moore, Vincent Price, Ginger Rogers, Harry Truman, Mark Twain, Dick Van Dyke

years later—went up in flames when the dome was struck by lightning in 1911.

- St. Joseph, Missouri, is home to Aunt Jemima pan-

cake flour. Invented in 1889, it was the first self-rising flour for pancakes and the first ready-mix food available for commercial use.
- Outlaw Jesse James was killed by Bob Ford in St. Joseph in 1882.
- Many pronounce the state "Mazura."
- The McDonnell Douglas Aircraft Corporation got its start in 1967 when The McDonnell Aircraft Corporation merged with the Douglas Aircraft Company.

Your Character's Food and Drink

Favorites for Missourians include: catfish; thrown rolls from Lambert's Cafe in Sikeston; bread from the St. Louis Bread Company (which the rest of the country calls Panera); authentic mexican food (there are a lot of immigrants who work on farms); Tyson chicken; locally raised beef, corn, and wheat; and Kansas City barbecue. To drink, most folks love a cold Budweiser brewed in St. Louis.

Things Your Character Likes to Remember

- Mark Twain. Twain was born in Florida (Missouri, of course) in 1835.
- The University of Missouri-Columbia was founded in 1839 as the first public university west of the Mississippi River.
- The Missouri Woman's Suffrage Club. Formed in 1867, it was the first organization in the United States with a mission to promote the political enfranchisement of women.
- The Ellis Fischel State Cancer Center in Columbia. Opened in 1940, this was the first state-owned hospital west of the Mississippi devoted to the care of cancer patients.
- Walt Disney. He grew up in Marceline and modeled Disneyland's Mainstreet U.S.A. after his hometown.
- The "Missouri Waltz."
- Women in politics: Missouri's first female U.S. Representative was Leonor Sullivan (1952); Mary Gant became Missouri's first woman state senator (1972); Gwen B. Giles became Missouri's first African-American female senator (1977); Ann Covington became the first woman appointed to the Missouri Supreme Court (1987).

Things Your Character Would Like to Forget

- William Clarke Quantrill. Quite possibly the most dangerous and psychopathic man to fight in the Civil War (today he'd be called a terrorist). He led Confederates in a deadly border war between Southern sympathizers in Missouri and the Unionist Jayhawks of Kansas. He also spearheaded the 1863 massacre of nearly two hundred men and boys in Lawrence, Kansas.
- The 1925 Annapolis tornado. In three hours, it tore through the town and left a 980-foot-wide trail of demolished buildings, uprooted trees, and overturned cars. Almost 3,000 people were injured and 823 died.

Myths and Misperceptions About Missouri

- **St. Louis and Kansas City are right next to each other.** They're actually at opposite ends of the state.
- **It's flat.** It is actually quite hilly in some parts, and there is a mountain region, the Ozarks, in the south.
- **People in Missouri are uncultured.** The state thrives with culture—both large cities and small towns have museums, theaters, and other such high-brow places. The Nelson Museum in Kansas City is one of the best in the country. *The Missouri Review* is a very respected literary magazine.
- **Everyone is a farmer.** Not by a long shot. Of the 5.6 million residents, a mere 136,000 farm.

Interesting Places to Set a Scene

- **Bonne Terre.** This area, once the world's biggest lead-mining district, has the world's largest man-made caverns to prove it, as well as a billion-gallon underground lake. Scuba diving in the lake is popular, if your character's up (or should we say "down") for it.

Mark Twain's boyhood house in Hannibal

For Further Research

Books

Bald Knobbers: Vigilantes on the Ozarks Frontier, by Mary Hartman and Elmo Ingenthron

The Big Sea: An Autobiography, by Langston Hughes

The Devil Knows How to Ride: The True Story of William Clarke Quantrill and His Confederate Raiders, by Edward E. Leslie

The Essential Lewis and Clark, edited by Landon Y. Jones

A History of Missouri, by William E. Parrish

Inside War: The Guerrilla Conflict in Missouri During the American Civil War, by Michael Fellman

Jesse James: The Man and the Myth, by Marley Brant

Missouri: The Heart of the Nation, by William E. Parrish et al.

Missouri's Black Heritage, by Lorenzo Greene et al.

The Ozarks: An American Survival of Primitive Society, by Vance Randolph

Tom and Huck Don't Live Here Anymore: Childhood and Murder in the Heart of America, by Ron Powers

Web Sites

www.missouritourism.org (visitor info)

http://digmo.org/ (central Missouri news and current events)

www.showmenews.com/ (*Columbia Daily Tribune*)

www.coin.org/ (Mid-Missouri community information)

www.mohistory.org/ (Missouri Historical Society)

http://books.missouri.org/heritage/south.html (state literary info)

Still Curious? Why Not Check Out

The Disinherited, by Jack Conroy

King's Row, by Henry Bellamann

Living In Missouri

The Missouri Review

The Missouri Traveler

Old Fish Hawk, by Mitchell F. Jayne

The Shepherd of the Hills, by Harold Bell Wright

Show Me, by Janet Dailey

Unto These Hills: True Tales From the Ozarks, by Paul W. Johns

---

- **Columbia.** This home to the University of Missouri-Columbia is quickly becoming a veritable "restaurant town." The arts are big here as well, with many festivals throughout the year focusing on Missouri's heritage and its performing and visual arts. The Devil's Icebox cave at nearby Rock Bridge State Park is popular with spelunkers.
- **Fulton.** Winston Churchill gave his famous "Iron Curtain" speech here in 1946. The city boasts a reconstructed Sir Christopher Wren church, an impressive sculpture made from pieces of the Berlin Wall, and a Churchill Memorial. Local William Woods University is both a Christian school and a notorious party school. There also are a lot of drugs here that come from Kansas City and St. Louis.
- **Great River Road.** This long stretch of pavement follows the Mississippi from Canada to the Gulf of Mexico. In Missouri it offers lots of history, scenic vistas, small towns, and natural beauty. South of the Missouri-Iowa state line is a Civil War battlefield (Battle of Athens State Historic Site); the town of Louisiana, which has the most intact Victorian streetscape in Missouri; and the Clarksville area, which is well known for its large numbers of wintering bald eagles.
- **The Mark Twain Region.** Perhaps this is the most famous part of the Mississippi River because it was the boyhood home of Sam Clemens himself. River towns and villages make up most of the area, including Florida and the two-room cabin where Twain was born in 1835. The most significant area, of course, is Hannibal, the Mississippi River town that was the setting for all of Tom and Huck's adventures. The downtown historic district boasts Twain's house, restored to its exact mid-1800s appearance, and a Twain museum, filled with manuscripts and memorabilia. Nearby are the Becky Thatcher House and Judge Clemens's law office.
- **Hermann.** Founded by the Deutsche Ansiedlungs-Gesellschaft (German Settlement Society), Hermann is called "Little Germany" by many because of its German culture. But it's also known for its award-winning homegrown wines and authentic German food.
- **Jamesport.** This is Missouri's Amish country. With Amish foods, crafts, antiques, and tours, Jamesport knows how to offer outsiders glimpses into their Amish way of life. In nearby Gallatin is the squirrel cage

rotary jail that imprisoned the infamous James Gang.

- **Jefferson City.** Although it showcases the beautiful Renaissance-style Capitol Building and is home to Lincoln University (founded by Civil War vets in 1866), what really puts Jefferson City on the map are the sumptuous ice-cream treats at the legendary Central Dairy. People are often surprised that Jefferson City is the capital, not Columbia, St. Louis, or Kansas City.
- **Kansas City** (See page 183 for more information on Kansas City.)
- **The Osage Lakes Region.** The Truman, Stockton, and Pomme de Terre Lakes rule this area of west-central Missouri. Nearly half of the state's impounded waters are here, and together these lakes offer sixteen marinas and 1,369 miles of undeveloped shoreline. Your character will also find nuggets of history, scenic countryside, and quaint, friendly little towns. It's like taking a trip to Maine without leaving the Heartland.
- **Sedalia.** This is ragtime country. Scott Joplin, the official King of Ragtime, lived and played and composed here, putting ragtime on the national map. He's honored every June when fans flock here for the Scott Joplin Ragtime Festival. The Missouri State Fair is held here each August as well. Historic Bothwell Lodge could be a great setting for a story; it's a mighty stone castle that sits atop a 120-foot bluff.
- **Sikeston.** While the Jaycee Bootheel Rodeo is held here each August, what really puts Sikeston on the map is Lambert's Cafe, home of the famous, one-of-a-kind "throwed rolls." Lambert's is also known for its free "pass arounds"—servers walk around carrying big containers with a mixture of black-eyed peas, fried okra, fried potatoes, macaroni, tomatoes, sorghum, and honey. Lambert's is one of Missouri's most celebrated restaurants.
- **St. Joseph.** Walter Cronkite's hometown is where the Pony Express began and outlaw Jesse James was gunned down. The red-brick Pony Express Stables are now fully restored as a museum, as is the Patee House. Just down the street sits the house where James spent his last years before being shot to death by Bob Ford in 1882. This touristy but significant town hosts numerous museums, galleries, and historical sites. There's also the Stetson Hat Factory Outlet.
- **St. Louis** (See page 186 for more information on St. Louis.)
- **Ste. Genevieve.** Along Great River Road, this colonial village (established in 1735) sports the reputable Ste. Genevieve Winery, a museum dedicated to Native American and Civil War relics, and, most importantly, about fifty historic buildings built in the French Creole style. The town is dotted with several restored bed-and-breakfasts and old inns.

Kansas City

Kansas City Facts and Peculiarities Your Character Might Know

- Kansas City, not St. Louis, is the largest city in Missouri, although a good share of the metro area is in Kansas.
- It has more than ninety barbecue joints, from tiny, smoke-filled walk-ups to fancy, "please wait to be seated" restaurants.
- Kansas City's first barbecuer was Henry Perry, who worked out of a trolley barn, wrapped his ribs in newsprint, and sold them for just twenty-five cents a slab.
- Many of the world's most celebrated jazz players got their start in Kansas City.
- The city is a major wheat flour producer and auto and truck assembler.
- During the 1970s and 1980s, the suburbs grew so fast that the city itself started to suffer, as residents and businesses moved out.
- Ernest Hemingway once worked as a reporter for *The Kansas City Star*.
- Casino gambling has become a big deal here; locals call the stretch of the Missouri River just north of downtown "Little Las Vegas."
- Robert Altman, Calvin Trillin, Ed Asner, Burt Bacharach, and Tom Watson are just a few of the famous folks from the city.
- Kansas City was once a major stop along the California, Oregon, and Santa Fe Trails.
- Kay Barnes was elected as the first female mayor of Kansas City in 1999.

If Your Character . . .

If Your Character Is Trendy, she shops in The Plaza. The city's favorite open-air shopping bonanza is popular with crowds of all ages and persuasions. It's home to everything from gigantic department stores and trendy boutiques to small cafes and fancy restaurants.

If Your Character Smells of Money, he lives in Johnson County. This wealthy area of town is for those with deep pockets who are not ashamed to flaunt it. Grand homes, widespread yards, and BMWs make up this sanitized neighborhood.

Kansas City Basics That Shape Your Character

Kansas City's skyline

Population: 441,545 in the city; 1.7 million in the Greater Metro area

Prevalent Religions: Roman Catholics and Baptists rule the city, but there are also decent-sized groups of Methodists, Lutherans, and Pentecostals, Jewish and Mormon faiths also worship in the city.

Top Employers: A.G. Edwards & Sons Inc., Anheuser-Busch, AT&T, Bank of America, Barnes-Jewish Hospital, Boeing, City of Kansas City, Commerce Bank & Trust, DaimlerChrysler, Dierbergs Supermarkets, Dillard Department Stores Inc., Division of Adult Corrections, Division of Family Services, Edward D. Jones & Company

Per Capita Income: $30,225

Average Daily Temperature: January, 28° F; July, 80° F

Ethnic Makeup (in percent): Caucasian 60.7%, African-American 31.2%, Hispanic 6.9%, Asian 1.9%, Native American 0.5%, Other 3.2%

Newspapers and Magazines: *The Kansas City Star, Kansas City Kansan, Kansas City Magazine, Experience Kansas City, Kansas City Business Journal, The Daily Record*

Free Weekly Alternative Paper: *Pitch Weekly*

If Your Character Is All About Business, she works in Downtown. Like most cities, the central business district in Kansas City is its downtown, which has high-rise office buildings, restaurants, and lunch shops.

If Your Character Is a Family Man, he lives in Overland Park. This is middle-class America. Just have your character park his car on any street in the summer, and he'll see kids with beach towels going to the pool, sprinklers wetting the well-manicured lawns, and one SUV and one minivan in each driveway.

If Your Character Wears a Blue Collar at Work, she lives in Olathe. Residents in this area punch their time cards in the morning and clock out when the working day is done. Small, patterned homes with tiny yards are typical.

Local Grub Your Character Might Love

Barbecue. Period. The mother of all is Arthur Bryant's, which has a long, solid reputation as the best barbecue in town. Since there are over ninety barbecue joints in the city, your character's going to have to find a way to put on a bib and dine in at least one of them. In addition to barbecue, the city is known for its steak and hot wheat rolls. The Southwest Boulevard has a reputation for its variety of Mexican eateries, and Minsky's Pizza is a Kansas City legend. Locals also love their Natural Light Beer (commonly referred to as "Naty Light" or "beer-flavored water").

Interesting and Peculiar Places to Set a Scene

- **Eighteenth and Vine.** This was the hangout for Charlie Parker and other jazz greats. The area was in poor shape until a serious renovation project put the Jazz Hall of Fame and the Negro Leagues Baseball Museum here. Now this area bustles with tourists interested in the city's two favorite cultural offerings.
- **A Wedding at J.C. Nichols Memorial Fountain.** One of the city's landmarks, the Forty-Seventh and J.C. Nichols Parkway fountain seems to get flooded with more onlookers than water. It's actually a popular spot for newlyweds to get their photo taken on their wedding day. The four equestrian figures that make up the fountain each represent a famous river.
- **An Abandoned Warehouse North of the City by the River.** This is a safe place to do bad things. Does your character need to murder someone? Here's the place. Need to hide that body? Here's the place. Need to drop the weapon in the river to get rid of the evidence? Here's the place.
- **Country Club Plaza.** Since 1927 the plaza's streets have been bustling with shoppers. Now it's still the place to shop, but it's noted for its artwork, especially the many sculptures and fountains, portraying the likes of King Neptune, the Mermaid, and Bacchus.
- **Missie B's.** This is Kansas City's favorite gay bar, and it offers nightly drag shows. Your character will find it easy to strike up a conversation or relax with the welcoming crowd. The Chelsea also has its share of late-night drag queen shows.
- **Nichols.** This old, grungy restaurant is open twenty-four hours. It's full of adolescents and twenty-somethings sporting tattoos, odd piercings, strange hairdos, and clove or roll-your-own tobacco cigarettes.
- **Prospect Avenue.** Lots of people in this poor area are down on their luck and willing to do anything to improve their dire situations. It's not surprising that drugs, prostitution, and crime are the norm here.
- **Unity Village.** Started in 1951, it boasts 1,400 acres of fountains, a huge rose garden, two meditation gardens, woodlands, walking paths, ponds, a natural preserve, and a nature prairie. Amidst the serenity is a bell tower that chimes hourly and plays recitals several times daily. Unity Village is a popular site for outdoor weddings.
- **The City Market.** This is a small part of the larger area known as the River Market. It's one the city's most popular outdoor marketplaces. Your character can buy just about anything here.
- **Westport.** The nightclubs, fancy restaurants, and small boutiques make this historical area once of the city's key spots for entertainment, shopping, and dining. This is where your character could easily go for a night of drinking, dancing, and window-shopping.

Exceptionally Grand Things Your Character Is Proud Of

- The Negro League Baseball Museum.
- The Santa Fe and Oregon Trail.
- Its music heritage. Kansas City has long been noted for its music, particularly jazz and swing, which have been popular here since the 1930s.
- Its various jazz and blues festivals.
- The American Jazz Museum.
- The new Kansas City Zoo, especially its African exhibit.
- The Nelson-Atkins Museum of Art and the Kemper Museum of Contemporary Art and Design.
- The greeting-card publishing industry, which to many

For Further Research

Books

Celebrating Greater Kansas City, by Arthur S. Brisbane et al.

A City Divided: The Racial Landscape of Kansas City, 1900–1960, by Sherry Lamb Schirmer

From the Bottom Up: The Story of the Irish in Kansas City, by Pat O'Neill

The Grand Barbecue: A Celebration of the History, Places, Personalities, and Techniques of Kansas City Barbecue, by Doug Worgul

Kansas City Women of Independent Minds, by Jane Fifield Flynn

Missouri Pacific Northwest: A History of the Kansas City Northwestern Railroad, by I.E. Quastler

The Romantic Past of the Kansas City Region, 1540–1880, by William D. Grant

Short Tails and Treats From Three Dog Bakery, by Dan Dye and Mark Beckloff

Web Sites

www.experiencekc.com/main.html (city guide)

www.kansascityhistory.com/ (city history)

http://books.missouri.org/heritage/kc-area.html (literary site)

www.kcfountains.com/ (city fountains and statues)

www.zwire.com/site/news.cfm?brd=1425 (*The Kansas City Jewish Chronicle*)

Still Curious? Why Not Check Out

An Artist in America, by Thomas Hart Benton

Going to Kansas City

Kansas City

Kansas City Bomber Mrs. Bridge or *Mr. Bridge*, by Evan S. Connell

The Rise and Fall of Excellence, by Edward T. Matheny Jr.

---

has become as much a part of the city as barbecue and jazz.

- FOCUS Kansas City, the city's first city-wide planning process that was initiated in the early 1990s.
- George Brett, the city's favorite ballplayer.

Pathetically Sad Things Your Character Is Ashamed Of

- Most of the downtown area is in desperate need of revitalization.
- The city has one of the highest per capita crime rates in the nation; car theft is a big problem.

Your Character Loves

- Kansas City barbecue.
- Fountains (has the most outside of Rome).
- Jazz.

- The arts. The city really encourages and supports its artists.
- Livestock and grain—they've kept the city going.
- Steamboat landings.
- The Royals, the Chiefs, the Blades, the Wizards.
- The idea of a revitalized downtown.
- Tourists.
- Dogs—the Three Dog Bakery—a "for doggies only" bakery and store—has become a big hit. They even bake birthday cakes for man's best friend.

Your Character Hates

- St. Louis.
- Kansas City, Kansas.
- That people think Kansas City is in Kansas when most of it is in Missouri.
- Flooding, which happens often in the spring.

St. Louis

St. Louis Basics That Shape Your Character

The famous Gateway Arch

Population: 348,189 in the city; 1.1 million in St. Louis County; 2.6 million in the Greater Metro area

Prevalent Religions: Roman Catholics and Baptists are the most prevalent.

Top Employers: Emerson Electric Company; Monsanto Company; Ralston Purina; Edward D. Jones & Company; A.G. Edwards & Sons Inc.; Anheuser-Busch; Lambert-St. Louis International Airport; University of Missouri, St. Louis; Washington University

Per Capita Income: $30,382

Average Daily Temperature: January, 29° F; July, 80° F

Ethnic Makeup (in percent): Caucasian 43.8%, African-American 51.2%, Hispanic 2.0%, Asian 2.0%, Native American 0.3%, Other 0.8%

Newspapers and Magazines: *St. Louis Post-Dispatch, St. Louis Commerce Magazine, St. Louis Business Journal, St. Louis Small Business Monthly*

Free Weekly Alternative Paper: *Riverfront Times*

St. Louis Facts and Peculiarities Your Character Might Know

- St. Louis is considered "The Gateway to the West."
- The Lewis and Clark Expedition set out from St. Louis in 1804.
- Freed slaves during Reconstruction passed through here on their way to Chicago.
- St. Louis is northern, southern, eastern, and western all at once, and therefore hopelessly midwestern.
- After Central Park in New York, Forest Park is allegedly the second largest public park in the country.
- University St. Louis Loop's "Walk of Fame" pays tribute to the likes of Chuck Berry, Charles Lindbergh, Tina Turner, Vincent Price, Bob Costas, John Goodman, Kevin Kline, Phyllis Diller, Stan Musial, Ozzie Smith, Eugene Field, Jackie Joyner-Kersee, Senator John Danforth, and Scott Joplin.
- The ice-cream cone and iced tea were invented in St. Louis 1904.
- In 1927 Charles Lindbergh crossed the Atlantic in the *Spirit of St. Louis* (grandson Erik followed suit in 2002 and landed in Paris almost seventy-five years to the day).
- Sweeping areas of the city (especially north St. Louis) are all but abandoned. (The city's population has dropped drastically in the past decade.)
- Bill McClellan, a *St. Louis Post-Dispatch* columnist, once speculated that because St. Louis is a crossroads, people with real ambition and drive are always on their way somewhere else.
- Caucasian St. Louisans, particularly those from south St. Louis, tend to pronounce words the opposite of Bostonians ("pahk yah cah in Hahvahd yahd")—thus, words with *er* and *or* become *ar* (Highway 44 becomes "farty-far"). Just listen to Dick Gephardt, a south St. Louisan if ever there was one, who was parodied for his accent on *Saturday Night Live*.

If Your Character . . .

If Your Character Is a Bohemian or Grungy Generation X-er, she lives or hangs out in the U-St. Louis Loop, in the lofts on Washington Street, or on the north side of downtown. This area is home to lots of artists and creative types.

If Your Character Is Trendy, she shops in U-St. Louis, Central West End, The Galleria, and Union Station. All are great and fashionable shopping spots for any character wanting to window shop, browse, or purchase.

If Your Character Is a Middle-Class Family Man, he lives in South County. This county sports typical suburban homes and strip malls that don't necessarily have a community identity. Many areas are unincorporated and don't even have names. Other spots are Brentwood, Kirkwood, Webster Groves, Ballwin, and Ellisville.

If Your Character Loves Nature, she's spending time in one of these great St. Louis green spaces: Forest Park, Missouri Botanical Gardens, Shaw's Arboretum, Gray's Summit, Greensfelder County Park, Forest 44, West Tyson County Park, Castlewood County Park, Lone Elk Park, Babler State Park, Rockwoods Reservation. There's also a huge Boy Scout camp (Beaumont Scout Reservation) and a Kiwanis camp (Camp Wyman).

If Your Character Wears a Blue Collar at Work, he lives in Overland (African-American), Fenton or Oakville (Caucasian), South St. Louis, South County, St. Peters, or Wentzville.

If Your Character Smells of Money, he resides in Ladue, Clayton, Richmond, Heights, the Central West End, Chesterfield, or Wildwood. All very posh and gentrified neighborhoods with big homes, lots of property, and really expensive cars.

Local Grub Your Character Might Love

Since St. Louis folks stopped pulling anything to eat out of Old Man River years ago, today they rely on the following: St. Louis-style (thin crust) pizza, places like Ted Drewes' Frozen Custard (frozen custard is big here), toasted ravioli, Culpepper's chicken wings, and anything from "The Hill," the Italian neighborhood in St. Louis that offers many excellent restaurants.

Interesting and Peculiar Places to Set a Scene

- **The Admiral.** This massive, old boat once whisked away tourists and young, high school prom goers, but now it's been docked, relying more on casino cash flow than the undercurrent of the Mississippi.
- **The Amoco station at Clayton and McCausland.** This area marks the highest elevation in St. Louis with a huge Amoco sign.
- **Art Hill.** This big hill outside the art museum is where people come to sled when in snows.
- **The Carousel at Faust Park.** This indoor, original carousel is from the World's Fair.
- **Crown Candy Kitchen.** Ice cream, chili, and sandwiches are the specialties at this Old North St. Louis neighborhood eatery. The building dates to 1889, the old-fashioned soda fountain to the 1930s, and the antique jukebox and old Coca-Cola memorabilia all have their own histories as well.
- **Fitz's Root Beer Brewery in the U-St. Louis Loop.** Have your character grab a tasty sandwich as he hears the clanking glass bottles spin around on the bottling machines in front of him.
- **The Fox and the Hound.** This hotel bar in the Chesire Inn is small, dark, and cozy with couches and fireplaces and a well-known bartender.
- **The Jewel Box.** This small conservatory is in Forest Park.
- **Laclede's Landing.** Other than riverboat casinos, this is the main riverfront development in the city. It's a big entertainment district that's a popular place to go after sporting events, and it holds some of the few historic downtown buildings to be renovated. Banana Joe's, Morgan Street Brewery, The Old Spaghetti Factory, and many other bars/restaurants are here.
- **Riverfront North.** What was once a historic urban area bustling with German immigrants is now fairly abandoned with little bustling but litter in the wind. The city wants to do something with the big vacant lots but can't agree on what that something should be. This could be a great place for some clandestine activity down by the river.
- **Six Flags Over Mid-America.** Typical theme park fare, but well done and one of the biggest and most successful amusement parks in the Midwest (if you don't count Chicago).
- **Soulard Market.** This farmer's market is bustling on the weekends. All of the area farmers bring their produce, meat, live chickens, and whatever to sell for cheap. It draws a very mixed crowd.

For Further Research

Books

The 100 Greatest Moments in St. Louis Sports, by Bob Broeg and Bob Costas

After the Fall: Srebrenica Survivors in St. Louis, by Patrick McCarthy

Ain't but a Place: An Anthology of African-American Writings About St. Louis, edited by Gerald Early

Behind the Headlines: Stories About People and Events Which Shaped St. Louis, by G. Duncan Bauman and Mary Kimbrough

The Colored Aristocracy of St. Louis, by Cyprian Clamorgan

A Guide to the Architecture of St. Louis, by Frank Peters and George McCue

In Her Place: A Guide to St. Louis Women's History, by Katharine T. Corbett

Seeking St. Louis: Voices From a River City, 1670–2000, edited by Lee Ann Sandweiss

St. Louis: The Evolution of an American Urban Landscape, by Eric Sandweiss

Web Sites

www.stltoday.com/ (current events)

http://home.post-dispatch.com/ (news)

www.gaystlouis.com/ (gay and lesbian St. Louis)

www.nps.gov/jeff/history.htm (history)

http://stlouis.missouri.org/neighborhoods/history/ (history of city neighborhoods)

www.stlouiswritersworkshop.com/ (writer's site)

Still Curious? Why Not Check Out

The Great St. Louis Bank Robbery

Meet Me in St. Louis

The Obituary Writer, by Porter Shreve

The Pink Flamingo Murders, by Elaine Viets

Sweet St. Louis: A Novel, by Omar Tyree

- **The Tivoli.** This old restored movie theater is popular for seeing classic and art house films.
- **The Wineries.** This is a frequent day trip among yuppie types.

Exceptionally Grand Things Your Character Is Proud Of

- The St. Louis Arch.
- The St. Louis Zoo.
- The St. Louis sports teams: The Cardinals, The Rams, and The Blues.
- The renovated Union Station, a former railroad station that's now a huge mall, but in a good way.
- Missouri Botanical Gardens—a nationally known jewel in the city that holds thousands of plant species and attracts botanists from all over.
- The Tyson Research Center's World Bird Sanctuary. Walter Crawford's organization is known by ornithologists the world over for saving endangered bird species and reintroducing them into the wild.
- Local Susan Elizabeth Blow came up with the idea of a public kindergarten.
- The Tyson Research Center's Wolf Sanctuary. The program studies wolves and breeds them for reintroduction to the wild.

- Washington University. This nationally respected and ultra-expensive research school is known for its medical and research programs.
- The Pope's visit in 1999.
- St. Louis's golf opportunities. It has an impressive blend of private and public courses.
- KSHE 95, the stalwart rock station in St. Louis that helped build Sammy Hagar's career.

Pathetically Sad Things Your Character Is Ashamed Of

- Successful businessmen flock to the east side for an eyeful or a lap dance at the strip clubs.
- East St. Louis, which is right across the Mississippi River in Illinois, is a crime- and poverty-infested mess; it's also the city's landfill.
- That downtown has many individual bright spots, but overall government and business have done little to curb the exodus from the city; in the evenings and on weekends those streets are empty.
- Missouri's pro-slavery past.

Your Character Loves

- Mardi Gras in Soulard (allegedly the biggest Mardi Gras party outside New Orleans).

- The St. Patrick's Day Parade.
- Cardinal games with friends or family.
- Cycling on the Katy Trail.
- Saying things like "Show me!" and "What high school did you go to?"
- Soccer. With its private Catholic schools and mammoth youth soccer programs, St. Louis has traditionally produced pro soccer players at a rate far out of proportion to its size.

Your Character Hates

- The sprawl. St. Louis is one of the country's worst offenders, as everything is moving west, particularly northwest (St. Peters, St Charles) and west-central (Chesterfield, Ellisville, Wildwood).
- That Lambert-St. Louis International Airport is in St. Louis County—the county enjoys all those airport-related revenues, despite the fact that patrons use the airport to get to the city.
- The underlying dichotomy between city and county: The infrastructure and spirit of St. Louis lie in the city, but the population and the power are in the county.
- The heat and humidity in July and August.
- Mayors. As of this writing, the city's on its fourth mayor in nine years.
- The fact that to go to a nice restaurant on Saturday, you have to make reservations on Wednesday.
- Public transportation—it stinks (especially Metro-Link, the limited rail system).
- Out-of-date Lambert airport.

Montana

Montana Basics That Shape Your Character

Motto: Gold and Silver

Population: 902,195

Prevalent Religions: Christianity, with particularly large numbers of Roman Catholic and Lutheran, also Baptist, Methodist, Presbyterian, and Church of Jesus Christ of Latter-day Saints

Major Industries: Mining, lumber and wood products, food processing, tourism, cattle, wheat, barley, sugar beets, hay, hogs

Ethnic Makeup (in percent): Caucasian 90.6%, African-American 0.3%, Hispanic 2.0%, Asian 0.5%, Native American 6.2%, Other 0.6%

Famous Montanans: Dorothy Baker, Dana Carvey, Gary Cooper, Chet Huntley, Evel Knievel, Myrna Loy, David Lynch, George Montgomery, Martha Raye.

Significant Events Your Character Has Probably Thought About

- Nelson Story led a thousand longhorns from Texas to Montana in 1866, giving birth to Montana's cattle industry.
- The Battle of Little Bighorn (1876). Also known as Custer's Last Stand, because Sitting Bull, Crazy Horse, and company wiped out General George Custer's entire battalion.
- The Anaconda Copper Mining Company (1899). "The Company," as it was called, constructed railroads, built dams, controlled forests, oversaw banks, and even owned all the area newspapers.
- In 1910, Congress created Glacier National Park. Also

in 1910 the worst fire in state history burned millions of forested acres.
- Montana's booming economy during World War II. There was great demand for meat, grain, copper, and other metals.
- Oil being found in the Williston Basin in the 1950s boosted the state's petroleum industry.
- "Unabomber" Ted Kaczynski was arrested in 1996 at his remote cabin outside of Lincoln.
- The 1996 eighty-one-day standoff in Jordan. More than one hundred federal agents set up a perimeter around a farm inhabited by the anti-government group called the "Freemen."
- The horrible fires in the summer of 2000. The governor had to close off 21 percent of the state; thousands of residents were evacuated and hundreds of homes were destroyed.

Montana Facts and Peculiarities Your Character Might Know

- Montana is known as the "Headwaters State" because much of the water that flows to the rest of the nation comes from Montana mountains. It's also known as "Big Sky Country," "Land of Shining Mountains," "Mountain State," and "Bonanza State."
- Montana is a geological wonder, with mountains, canyons, rivers, valleys, forests, grassy plains, badlands, caverns, and even geysers. The eastern third of the state is plains, the central third is surrounded by "island" mountain ranges, and the western third showcases vast mountainous peaks, steep valleys, and crystal clear lakes.
- One of the first major gold fields was called Confederate Gulch, after Southerners—and there were many—who fled north after the Civil War and struck gold.
- The International Wildlife Film Festival is held here.
- Dogs are allowed in most stores and shops, especially in smaller towns.
- If someone's dog runs into a rancher's field, the rancher can legally shoot to kill the pooch.
- The legal age for marriage is a late-blooming sixteen.
- Cars always stop for bikers and walkers.

- Montana has more than its share of casinos, particularly on and near reservations.
- They say "rut" instead of "root" and "crick" instead of "creek."
- A lot of fly-fishing terms are thrown around like everyone knows what they mean.

Your Character's Food and Drink

The greater Montana population is all about red meat and beer. Bison burgers are becoming big, as are pickled eggs (at the dive bars) and bull testicles.

Things Your Character Likes to Remember

- Few outsiders come here, except in the summer to visit Glacier and Yellowstone.
- There's no restriction on open alcohol containers (even in cars).
- Paleontologist Jack Horner was the prototype for *Jurassic Park*'s Dr. Grant.
- Jeannette Rankin was the first woman to serve in Congress (elected in 1916) and the only member to vote against U.S. entry into World War II.

Things Your Character Would Like to Forget

- The 1917 mining disaster in Butte (168 men died).
- The ongoing war between environmentalists and the timber industry.
- Little Big Horn. Although the Sioux and Cheyenne were victors, this battle marked the beginning of the end for the Native Americans; they were soon forced to move to reservations.
- In 1999 Montana flunked the Center for Public Integrity's "Ethics Test." The state received a grade of 48 percent, which ranked each state on the disclosure and accuracy of public records.

Your Character Loves

- Skinny-dipping in natural hot springs.
- Floating down the Blackfoot River in an inner tube on a hot summer day, dodging fly fishermen.
- The timber industry.
- Environmental activism.
- Dive bars, many of which are housed in double-wide trailers and have cool names (the Buck's Club, the Elbow Room). The Blue Ribbon Bar in Red Lodge and The Dixon Bar in Dixon are legendary.
- Going to raucous fairs and festivals.

- Potlucks (there's a rumor that they happen every 2.3 seconds).

Your Character Hates

- Any infringement on what he perceives as his personal privacy.
- The many Hollywooders who buy houses here, and thus draw attention to the state.

Myths and Misperceptions About Montana

- **Ted Kaczinsky clones are everywhere.** Sorry, few residents actually live in secluded cabins, make bombs, and write manifestos.
- **They're all boot-scootin' cattle ranchers and chew-spittin' cowboys.** Get this: Nonprofit organizations, not ranches, are actually the leading employers in the state. Also, "cultural events" like theater and ballet are popular in urban areas.
- **Living here is a piece of cake.** Most people don't actually spend all day kicking back in the great out-

A waterfall at Clements Mountain in West Glacier

© PhotoDisc/Getty Images

For Further Research

Books

The Book of Yaak, by Rick Bass

A Bride Goes West, by Nannie T. Alderson and Helena Huntington Smith

Community and the Politics of Place, by Daniel Kemmis

Forty Years on the Frontier as Seen in the Journals and Reminiscences of Granville Stuart, edited by Paul C. Phillips

Great Plains, by Ian Frazier

The Last Best Place: A Montana Anthology, edited by William Kittredge and Annick Smith

The Song of the Dodo, by David Quammen

Tough Trip Through Paradise, 1878–1879, by Andrew Garcia

Web Sites

www.state.mt.us/css/default.asp (official state site)

www.mtbookco.com (state writers and literature)

www.montanawoman.com/mtwoman/index.html (*Montana Woman* magazine)

www.his.state.mt.us/ (historical society)

http://indiannations.visitmt.com/ (state Indian Nations site)

http://nature.org/wherewework/northamerica/states/montana/ (nature conservancy)

www.testyfesty.com (Testicle Festival Site, just for the fun of it!)

Still Curious? Why Not Check Out

Bitterroot, by James Lee Burke

The Horse Whisperer

Legends of the Fall One Sweet Quarrel: A Novel, by Deirdre McNamer

A River Runs Through It

A Stranger in This World: Stories, by Kevin Canty

Ten Tough Trips: Montana Writers and the West, by William W. Bevis

They Are Sleeping: Poems, by Joanna Klink

Wind From an Enemy Sky, by D'Arcy McNickle

Winter in the Blood, by James Welch

Winter Wheat, by Mildred Walker

Writing Montana: Literature Under the Big Sky, edited by Rick Newby and Suzanne Hunger

Young Men and Fire, by Norman McClain

doors—many must have at least two jobs because the state's economy is so bad.

Interesting Places to Set a Scene

- **A farmer's market.** These are all around the state and usually take place twice a week—on Tuesday nights and Saturday mornings—during the summer.

- **Butte.** Much of Montana's growth during the late nineteenth century stemmed from the mines in Butte (Butte Hill was called the "Richest Hill on Earth"), where Irish immigrants came and made themselves a home. Although the last mining pit shut down in the 1970s, the town is still loaded with drunken Irishmen, especially on St. Patrick's Day (when the whole place is one crazy beer fest).

- **Glacier National Park.** Known as the "crown jewel of the continent," Glacier is tied to Waterton Lakes National Park in Canada, forming the world's first International Peace Park. It has grizzly bears, wolves, elk, mountain goats, towering peaks, 250 lakes, waterfalls, and "Going to the Sun Road"—one of the most scenic drives in the world.

- **Hemp Fest.** Yes, it's a big pot festival. Held in Caras Park in late September, the fest features all sorts of hippies and hemp lovers. Your character will find quite an array of marijuana paraphernalia, including numerous hemp arts and crafts, and lots of information about the medical benefits of pot and hemp. There also are tasty treats with special ingredients.

- **Missoula.** Nestled in the Rocky Mountains, this scenic university town (University of Montana) is all about laid-back coffeehouses, historic bars, good parties, and cozy bookstores. It is also the cultural mecca of Montana, with several art galleries, museums, a ballet company, live theater, and even a symphony. If your character loves skiing, hiking, hunting, or fishing . . . they're all just minutes away.

- **Rock 'n' Roll Days.** People show off their old classic cars at this big festival during the day, but at night everyone drives on the main strip, where huge crowds scream and cheer for drivers to "burn rubber." Almost every driver does (even a police officer, who recently spun the cruiser's wheels to get the crowd going).

• **The Testicle Festival.** This fun-filled, three-day event takes place at the Branding Iron Bar and Grill in Charlo during the first weekend in June. "It is pretty much a big naked festival where people come from all over the country to eat fried bull testicles and participate in a variety of bizarre drunken games," says one local. Plenty of stories there.

• **Yellowstone.** This is home to Yellowstone Lake and the Upper and Lower Falls of the Yellowstone River, and the most famous geyser ever, Old Faithful. It's also known for its large herds of bison, elk, mule deer, and pronghorn antelope.

Nebraska

Nebraska Basics That Shape Your Character

Motto: Equality Before the Law

Population: 1.7 million

Prevalent Religions: Christianity, particularly Roman Catholic, also Lutheran, Methodist, Presbyterian, Pentecostal, Baptist, Episcopalian, and Church of Jesus Christ of Latter-day Saints

Major Industries: Cattle, corn, hogs, soybeans, wheat, sorghum, food processing, machinery, electric equipment, printing and publishing

Ethnic Makeup (in percent): Caucasian 89.6%, African-American 4.0%, Hispanic 5.5%, Asian 1.3%, Native American 0.9%, Other 2.8%

Famous Nebraskans: Fred Astaire, Marlon Brando, William Jennings Bryan, Buffalo Bill (William F. Cody), Warren Buffett, Johnny Carson, Willa Cather, Dick Cavett, Loren Eisley, Henry Fonda, Gerald Ford, Robert Henri, Malcolm X, Wright Morris, Nick Nolte, Mari Sandoz, Standing Bear

Significant Events Your Character Has Probably Thought About

- In 1854, the federal government passed the Kansas-Nebraska Act, and a large area of land labeled the Nebraska Territory became available for settlement.
- In 1855, Sally Bayne arrived in Omaha and was counted as the first free African-American person to settle in the Nebraska Territory.
- The Nebraska Territorial Legislature in 1855 demanded free public schooling across the state.
- The Kinkaid Act of 1904 allowed for 640-acre home-steads in designated areas, except for lands that were suitable for irrigation.
- The Enola Gay's bombing of Hiroshima in 1945—the legendary bomber was built in Omaha.
- The years the Nebraska Cornhuskers won national championships in football: 1971, 1972, 1994, 1995, 1997.
- When Omaha-born Gerald Ford took office in 1974, he became the only president not to have been elected to either the presidency or the vice presidency.
- The first time two women ran against each other in a gubernatorial race was in Nebraska in 1986, when Kay Orr defeated Helen Boosalis.
- In 2001, former longtime Nebraska football coach Tom Osborne became a U.S. Congressman.

Nebraska Facts and Peculiarities Your Character Might Know

- Nebraska football rules everything . . . conversations, talk radio, class lectures, sermons (you get the point).
- Nebraska nearly always votes Republican, though sometimes the lefties in Omaha opt for the donkey.
- There's an unwritten law that drivers merging onto a highway from an entrance ramp shouldn't expect those on the interstate to slow down, speed up, or switch to the left lane to let them on.
- Nebraska is the second leading cattle state in the nation, next to Texas.
- The concept of dialing "911" for an emergency originated in Lincoln.
- If lost in the country, all one must do is look around for grain mills—there's the nearest town.
- Nebraska weather changes drastically from one instant to the next.
- Omaha's Lied Jungle in the Henry Doorly Zoo is the world's largest indoor rain forest.
- The Mutual of Omaha corporate headquarters has seven floors underground (just in case a tornado strikes).
- Nebraska has more than its share of water: It holds the nation's largest underground reservoir (the Oga-

lala aquifer) and has more river miles than any other state.

- A high school's graduating class is typically rather small (about fifty) or extremely large (five hundred).
- Nebraskan's three favorite questions: "How's the crop?" "How's harvesting?" and "How about those Huskers?!"

Your Character's Food and Drink

If your character is from Nebraska, he loves the following: a Reuben sandwich, ribs, steak, hamburger, pizza, a Runza (a meal in a bun), corned beef, barbecue. He's also likely to buy Nebraska favorites Wimmer's Summer Sausage, Annie's Jellies & Jams, Mick-D-Angelos Pasta Sauce, The Heartland's Finest Bar-B-Que Sauce, Hollmon's Barbecue Sauces, Grandpa Jack's Hot Sauce, Dorothy Lynch salad dressing, and Poppycock popcorn. Valentino's Pizza is big in Lincoln. Nebraskans like to drink "pop" (not a "soda," "coke," or "soft drink"), milk, beer, Kool-Aid (it was created here), and wine.

Nebraska's famed Eagle Rock

Things Your Character Likes to Remember

- The best crop ever.
- The pioneer way of life.
- Nebraska men and women have a reputation as being hard workers with strong morals.
- The Cornhuskers.
- Small-town courtesies. People and businesses always greet others with a "Hi, how are ya?"
- Cruising the square, or the main drag, or the only street in town—just for the fun of it.
- The weather (when the farming's good).

Things Your Character Would Like to Forget

- The hailstorm that ruined the corn.
- The ice storm in October that killed half the trees.
- The year Halloween was cancelled because of a blizzard.
- Outsiders who think that Nebraskan girls are corn-fed hogs, that the boys are hicks, and that windmills were built to keep cows cool in the summer.
- People in Lincoln dislike Omaha. People in Omaha dislike Lincoln.
- The weather (when the farming's bad).

Myths or Misperceptions About Nebraska

- **The Nebraska Cornhuskers football team only cares about sports, not academics.** The Huskers have produced more Academic All-Americans than any other Division I school.
- **The state has no trees.** While Nebraska is a plains state, it was J. Sterling Morton (father of Morton Salt baron Joy Morton) of Nebraska City who came up with the idea of Arbor Day back in 1872. Also, the state's nickname was the "Tree Planter's State" until 1945, when it became the "Cornhusker State."
- **Nebraska is flat and boring.** Actually, Nebraska has more variety than one would think. There's a near five-thousand-foot elevation difference (the state's highest point is 5,426 feet above sea level, while its lowest is 840 feet above sea level), and the western part of the state contains sand hills, waterfalls, dinosaur fossil beds, and forests.

Interesting Places to Set a Scene

- **Boys Town USA.** The dream of Irish immigrant priest Father Edward Flanagan, this community has been a safe refuge since 1917 for delinquent, homeless,

For Further Research

Books

Faith in the Game: Lessons on Football, Work, and Life, by Tom Osborne

Fifty Years a Country Doctor, by Hull Cook

The Franklin Cover-Up: Child Abuse, Satanism, and Murder in Nebraska, by John W. DeCamp

Go Big Red: The Complete Fan's Guide to Nebraska Football, by Mike Babcock

Massacre Along the Medicine Road: A Social History of the Indian War of 1864 in Nebraska Territory, by Ronald Becher

The Nature of Nebraska: Ecology and Biodiversity, by Paul A. Johnsgard

Nebraska Hard-to-Believe (But True!) History, Mystery, Trivia, by Carole Marsh

A Salute to Nebraska's Tom Osborne: A 25-Year History, by Lincoln Journal Star

An Unspeakable Sadness: The Dispossession of the Nebraska Indians, by David J. Wishart

Web Sites

www.nebraskastudies.org/ (state history)

www.state.ne.us/ (official state site)

www.visitnebraska.org/ (tourism)

www.omaha.com/ (Omaha site)

http://lincoln.inetnebr.com/ (Lincoln site)

http://mockingbird.creighton.edu/NCW/ (state writer's site)

Still Curious? Why Not Check Out

Boys Don't Cry

The Dirty Shame Hotel, and Other Stories, by Ron Block

Goodnight, Nebraska: A Novel, by Tom McNeal

Heartland: A Novel, by David Wiltse

A Lantern in Her Hand, by Bess Streeter Aldrich

Muse, by Susan Aizenberg

Nebraska: Stories, by Ron Hansen

O Pioneers! or *My Antonia*, by Willa Cather

The Weight of Dreams, by Jonis Agee

---

abused, neglected and handicapped boys and girls. Nearly a thousand kids call it home today.

- **Lincoln.** The state capital is also a major midwestern railroad hub, busy with livestock companies, railroad cars (they're built and repaired here), grain elevators, and pharmaceutical and insurance companies. Of course, Lincoln is home to the University of Nebraska, so there are Cornhusker fans everywhere. It also has an art gallery, a natural history museum (called "Elephant Hall"), a planetarium, a sculpture garden, the state fairgrounds, several parks, and a state penitentiary.

- **Memorial Stadium during a Cornhusker game.** When the Huskers are playing at home, Memorial Stadium gets so full it becomes the third most populated area in the state. Not only does the place hold seventy-five thousand fans, it also holds the NCAA record for consecutive sellouts (the last game in Memorial Stadium *not* to sell out was held in 1962). Have your character "get red" amidst all the shouting of "Go Big Red!" "Go Huskers!" and "What's wrong with the Blackshirts?" (the name for the Huskers' defense).

- **Omaha.** This river city is Nebraska's major transportation, industry, and commerce center, with some of the biggest livestock markets and meat-processing centers in the world. Omaha also is home to many insurance companies and medical research facilities. It has a reputation as the friendliest city in Middle America, a great place for raising a family, thanks to the school systems, low crime rates, and cultural opportunities (an educational zoo, art museums, an aerospace museum, a Mormon cemetery, a forest, several parks, and an old fort).

- **Omaha's Old Market.** This twelve-block, walker-friendly market area by the Missouri River hosts over one hundred small shops and boutiques.

- **Pioneers State Park.** This vast preserve is a natural haven, with ponds, woodlands, wildflowers, prairies, wetlands, and a stream. There also are trails to areas with native Nebraskan animal exhibits, where your character can gaze upon bison, elk, white-tailed deer, raptors, vultures, and turkeys.

- **Red Cloud.** Named for the Oglala Sioux chief, this old railroad town is Willa Cather country, the setting for several of her novels and short stories. When the

Burlington and Missouri River Railway arrived here in 1879, it brought with it a wide variety of immigrants, making Red Cloud a midwestern melting pot. The architectural design of Webster Street is quite unique and well preserved, with intricate buildings of brick and stone that at one time were basic wood frame and log structures.

- **Valentine.** A gateway to many of Nebraska's natural wonders (the sand hills, Fort Niobrara National Wildlife Refuge, Fort Falls), Valentine is a town of shady streets and pleasant people in pickups. In February The Heart City's post office gets flooded with letters, which get postmarked "Valentine" and then are sent off to their real destinations: starry-eyed sweethearts.

Nevada

Nevada Basics That Shape Your Character

Motto: All for Our Country

Population: 1.9 million

Prevalent Religions: Christianity, with particularly large numbers of Roman Catholic and Baptist, and smaller numbers of Lutheran, Methodist, Presbyterian, also Jewish and Church of Jesus Christ of Latter-day Saints

Major Industries: Tourism, mining, machinery, printing and publishing, food processing, electric equipment, cattle, hay, dairy products, potatoes

Ethnic Makeup (in percent): Caucasian 75.2%, African-American 6.8%, Hispanic 19.7%, Asian 4.5%, Native American 1.3%, Other 8.0%

Famous Nevadans: Andre Agassi, Ben Alexander, Helen Delich Bentley, Hobart Cavanaugh, Abby Dalton, James A. Gibbons, Jack Kramer, Paul Laxalt, Pat Nixon, Jack Wilson Paiute, Edna Purviance, Harry M. Reid, David Derek Stacton, Sarah Hopkins Winnemucca

Significant Events Your Character Has Probably Thought About

- In 1899, Charles Fey invented a slot machine named the Liberty Bell. If he only knew what would follow . . .
- In March 1931, Governor Fred Balzar signed into law the bill legalizing gambling in the state. The Pair-O-Dice Club was the first casino to open on Highway 91, which later became the Las Vegas Strip.
- Hoover Dam began construction in 1933.
- In the 1950s, the Atomic Energy Commission began conducting nuclear tests at Frenchman Flat and Yucca Flat.
- The state's first community college didn't open until 1967 (Great Basin College).
- Thanks mostly to Las Vegas and retirees, Nevada's population increased by 650 percent between 1950 and 1990, making it the fastest-growing state in the country.
- In 1986 Highway 50 became "The Loneliest Highway in America" thanks to *Life* magazine; there are but a few road stops on the 287-mile stretch between Ely and Fernley.
- In 1987 the Department of Energy chose Yucca Mountain as the storage site for nuclear waste. The battle over the storage has been going since.

Nevada Facts and Peculiarities Your Character Might Know

- That Mississippi River man Mark Twain started his writing career as a reporter for the *Virginia City Territorial Enterprise*.
- Most of the state is desert, but the Sierra Nevada and Ruby Mountains are covered in snow for half the year.
- Nevada has been called "The Sagebrush State," "The Silver State," and "The Battle Born State."
- South Africa produces the most gold in the world; Nevada is second.
- Filmmaker John Huston gave the town of Misfits Flats its name when he used the area to film a wild horse roundup for *The Misfits*.
- Nevada has had a large population of Basques, especially in the northern part of the state, where they did a lot of sheepherding; about five thousand Basques

currently live here (but few are sheepherders these days).

- Nevada tribes that prevailed here in the nineteenth century included the Shoshone, the Washo, the Northern Paiute, and the Southern Paiute.
- Thanks to all its prostitutes, Las Vegas used to be called "Pay-for-Lay Central."
- The oldest church in Austin is St. Augustine; the church's bell ringer must pull a rope located in the men's restroom.
- The last film performance of the Duke (John Wayne) was in *The Shootist*, which was filmed in Carson City in 1974.
- Construction workers all over the world have the construction of the Hoover Dam to be grateful for—the hard hat was invented for its workers.

Your Character's Food and Drink

What your character eats depends upon where she is. In Las Vegas, of course, she'll be able to eat anything from around the world (Greek, French, Brazilian, Vietnamese, Mongolian, Indian, and so on) at the thousands of eateries, but in other parts of the state she'll have to settle for "eat here because it's the only diner within a one-hundred-mile radius" type places. Typical American fare (bacon, eggs, steak, hamburgers) is the choice in most small towns. Perhaps what the state of Nevada is most known for are its buffets, those cafeteria-like troths where your character can pick and choose her favorite mass-produced food for hours.

Basque food can be found in the north. At restaurants, Basque meals are served "family style," with everyone sitting side by side at long tables. The food is simple, the portions huge. Garlic is the primary seasoning. Typical Basque dishes included thick chateaubriand steaks (one big slab of meat between two thin ones; after being cooked, the two thin outer pieces are discarded and the mostly rare centerpiece is eaten), leg of lamb, spicy chorizo, paella, chicken, pig's feet, beef tongue, and various types of seafood.

Things Your Character Likes to Remember

- Fast marriages and lax divorce laws.
- The state marches to the beat of its own drummer.
- Smoking in public is not only accepted but encouraged.
- Hoover Dam.
- Lonely roads.
- Its Basque traditions and festivals.
- Cowboy poetry.
- Mining and prostitution (they've been profitable bedfellows throughout the state's history).
- The Depression. While the rest of the country suffered in the 1930s, Nevada thrived. In fact, the state actually found its calling then, thanks to legalized gambling, no-questions-asked marriage laws, automatic divorce laws, and the Hoover Dam.

Things Your Character Would Like to Forget

- People come here and lose a lot of money.
- The state enables and promotes gambling addicts.
- It's number one in the country for the most deaths from liver and lung cancer (all that drinking and smoking).
- Education. The state has one of the highest high school drop-out rates.
- That marriage is supposed to be a lifelong commitment (people get married and divorced faster than they change sheets).
- That outsiders perceive the state as full of little more than drunken gamblers and whoremongers.

Myths and Misperceptions About Nevada

- **It's just a flat desert.** Nevada has more mountain ranges than any other state.
- **Las Vegas is the capital.** Nope. It's Carson City.
- **Cowboys and Indians are still roaming in the state fighting.** While there are still cowboys and Native Americans in the state, they're not roaming or fighting each other.
- **Nobody lives anywhere in Nevada except in Las Vegas.**

Neon playing cards. Where else but in Nevada?

© PhotoDisc/Getty Images

For Further Research

Books

Basin and Range, by John McPhee

Desert Challenge: An Interpretation of Nevada, by Richard G. Lillard

The Girls of Nevada, by Gabriel R. Vogliotti

History of Nevada, by Russell R. Elliott

History of Nevada, 1540–1888, by Hubert Howe Bancroft and Frances Fuller Victor

In Nevada: The Land, the People, God, and Chance, by David Thomson

Madam: Chronicles of a Nevada Cathouse, by Lora Shaner

Nevada Place Names: A Geographical Dictionary, by Helen S. Carlson

Traditional Basque Cooking: History and Preparation, by Jose Maria Busca Isusi

Virginia City and the Silver Region of the Comstock Lode, by Douglas McDonald

Web Sites

www.westfolk.org/gathering.html (cowboy poetry site)

http://basque.unr.edu/Default.asp (Basque site)

http://silver.state.nv.us/ (official state site)

www.nevada-history.org/ (state history)

www.burningman.com/ (Burning Man site)

www.rgj.com/ (news)

Still Curious? Why Not Check Out

Bad Boys and Black Sheep: Fateful Tales From the West, by Robert F. Gish

Basque Family Trilogy, by Robert Laxalt

Breakdown

Contemporary Basque Fiction, by Jesus Maria Lasagabaster

Fools Rush In

The Greatest Story Ever Told

Independence Day

Lethal Weapon 4

Mark Twain's America

Misery

The Ox-Bow Incident

Rain Man

The River Underground: An Anthology of Nevada Fiction, by Shaun T. Griffin

Shoshone Mike: A Novel, by Frank Bergon

The Shootist

Total Recall

Universal Soldier

Vanishing Point

Vegas Vacation

Viva Las Vegas

Reno and Henderson are two of the fastest-growing cities in the country.

Interesting Places to Set a Scene

- **The Burning Man.** There's an overwhelming sense of community among the forty thousand or so participants of this uninhibited, expressive, participatory, creative gathering. Just before Labor Day, the barren four-hundred-square-mile Black Rock Desert becomes packed with RVs, "art cars" of all sorts, bizarre shelters, some drugs, strange displays and events, bodies covered in paint, flags, light sticks, sunscreen, or nothing (but dust). On Saturday night, the giant forty-foot wooden man is ignited, and everyone gathers in a circle to watch him burn. Every year has a theme. Some themes from years past: Fertility, Time, Hell, Outer Space, The Body, and The Floating World. Perhaps the closest thing to living on another planet with kindred spirits. . . .

- **Carson City.** The state capital only has fifty thousand residents, but its history and location make it important, for it is the gateway to Lake Tahoe and home to the U.S. Mint.

- **Elko's National Cowboy Poetry Gathering.** Every January this small town rains Stetsons, stirrups, and stanzas, as poetry lovers gather for "a jubilee of conversation, singing, dancing, great hats and boots, stories, laughing and crying, big steaks, incessant rhymes, and a galloping cadence that keeps time for a solid week." Have your character saddle up his sestina to partake in the rip-roarin' fun.

- **Hoover Dam.** It's only the most popular dam in the world and the largest single public works project in the history of the United States. This massive water-stopper is made of seven million tons of poured concrete, which people say is enough to pave a two-lane highway from coast to coast. Check out *Universal Soldier* for some exceptional shots of this concrete monster.

- **Lake Mead.** Thanks to Hoover Dam, this man-made lake was crated in the 1930s. It's the second largest man-made lake in the world, with over eight hundred miles of shoreline. Lake Mead supplies water for more than fourteen million people and is a big recreational area, offering everything from swimming and boating to diving. In the waters rest over twenty submerged "sites," from buried yachts to an old Mormon town and a graveyard.
- **Las Vegas.** (For more on Las Vegas, see page 202.)
- **Reno.** Billing itself as "the biggest little city in the world," Reno is in many ways a mini Vegas, with several resort facilities, entertainment spots, casinos, and quick chapel marriages. But Reno also has an international airport and is a distributing and warehouse center. It's also one of the fastest-growing cities in the country and a gateway to Tahoe.
- **Rhyolyte.** Remains of a depot, glass house, bank, and other buildings are still around in this ghost town that still echoes with the voices and visions of the early pioneers.
- **Virginia City.** This classic Victorian city of the western frontier was in its early days a city of miners, prostitutes, drinking, and general debauchery. Prostitution in the state started and thrived here, with up to three hundred "dens" or "cribs" of ill repute running at once. This also is where Mark Twain began his writing career as a reporter for the *Virginia City Territorial Enterprise*. The city remains one of the most authentic and colorful boomtowns in the West. Although the miners and brothels have mostly disappeared, the steam train still runs.

Las Vegas

Las Vegas Basics That Shape Your Character

Vegas at night—no other city quite like it

Population: 483,448 in the city; 1.4 million in the Greater Metro area

Prevalent Religions: Mostly Roman Catholicism, Protestantism, and some Church of Jesus Christ of Latter-day Saints and Judaism

Top Employers: Bellagio Hotel and Casino, MGM Grand Hotel/Casino, Bally's Hotel and Casino, Mirage Hotel and Casino, Caesars Palace, Mandalay Bay Resort and Casino, Paris Las Vegas, Venetian Casino Resorts, Clark County, State of Nevada

Per Capita Income: $29,605

Average Daily Temperature: January, 46° F; July, 91° F

Ethnic Makeup (in percent): Caucasian 72.2%, African-American 8.7%, Hispanic 12.3%, Asian 5.8%, Native American 1.0%, Other 8.6%

Newspapers and Magazines: *Las Vegas Review-Journal, Las Vegas Sun, Las Vegas Life, Vegas Golfer, In Business Las Vegas*

Free Weekly Alternative Papers: *Las Vegas Weekly, Showbiz Weekly*

Las Vegas Facts and Peculiarities Your Character Might Know

- The famous casino "The Flamingo" was named by owner Bugsy Siegel in honor of his showgirl sweet-heart, Virginia Hill, who had exceptionally long and thin legs.
- Not surprisingly, Las Vegas boasts of having more hotel rooms than does any other place in the world; it can also boast of having nineteen of the world's twenty largest hotels.
- Since 1959 the Follies Bergere at the Tropicana Hotel and Casino has been going on nightly, making it the longest-running show in Vegas.
- Producer, aviator, entrepreneur, crook, and eccentric billionaire Howard Hughes owned several Las Vegas hotels and casinos, including Castaways, Desert Inn, Frontier, Harold's Club, Landmark, Sands, and Silver Slipper. See Jonathan Demme's *Melvin and Howard*.
- Hollywood just loves Las Vegas. In the last twenty years, over eighty-five films have been shot in the city or in the desert just outside of the city.
- With the arrival of the $120 million MGM Grand in 1973, Las Vegas became an official mega-resort.
- When John F. Kennedy was assassinated in 1963, all casinos on the strip closed for three hours with the lights out.
- In 1984, a fire swept through the MGM Grand, killing eighty-four guests and injuring seven hundred.
- Steve Wynn's three-thousand-room Mirage put Las Vegas on the map as a spot for family vacations. Geared toward more wholesome fun, the Mirage houses a white tiger garden, a dolphin habitat, a huge aquarium with sharks, and a fifteen-acre rainforest.
- Thirty-two million people visit Las Vegas annually.
- Las Vegas typically issues over 100,000 marriage licenses per year—an average of one "I do" every five minutes.
- Miracles do happen in Sin City: In 1999, Suzanne Henley made a three-dollar slot machine bet and ended up winning a whopping $12,510,559 (yes, that's 12.5 million dollars).

If Your Character . . .

If Your Character Is Alternative and Grungy, he lives in North Las Vegas. This former poor part of town has recently gone through some redevelopment, but not enough to make it middle-class living. The area is still home to inexpensive housing, cheap hotels, and the area's lower-class population.

If Your Character Smells of Money, she lives in Lake Las Vegas. Out of town through a scenic road up in a mountain pass, you'll find this posh area with huge, custom homes on comparatively spacious lots. Spanish Trail and The Fountains are wealthy areas that are closer to town.

If Your Character Is a Family Man, he lives in Green Valley. These mostly two-story homes are stucco with red tile roofs and nice green yards. The yards are rather small, though, as the price of land is outrageous, and all have a cinder block wall in back (that's a Las Vegas thing).

If Your Character Is Trendy, she shops at The Venetian. This upscale, fancy resort has all the shopping anyone could want, with shops specializing in fashionable, cutting-edge clothes to expensive boot shops to regular mall fair like Gap and Structure.

Local Grub Your Character Might Love

There is really no specific food for which Las Vegas is famous, with the possible exception of the "$2 steak" or the "$5 prime rib." Your character can get any type of food here, as some of the nicer casino-hotels offer international meals. Some good places to eat in town include The Grand Lux Cafe inside the Venetian (there are almost too many good dishes to choose from, and it's not too expensive either). The Ming Terrace inside the Imperial Palace (best shrimp fried rice on the planet, some say). The buffet at Bally's is definitely the best in town (formerly a Chinese restaurant, the new owners kept the Chinese part and added a buffet around it—very good stuff). Rosati's pizza is in a class by itself. If your character likes to indulge in a little artery-clogging, The Fatburger has the best burgers in town.

Local Slang Your Character Might Hear or Utter at a Casino

Here's all the Las Vegas lingo directly from an expert casino dealer: "tokes" (tips); "george" (meaning generous, a good tipper); "king kong george" (a very, very good tipper); "stiff" (someone who never tips); "acorn"

(a novice-table game player with tipping potential); "back East" (pretty much means New York City or New Jersey); "comp" (complimentary food, room, airfare, etc. given to players based on how much money they have in action × how long they play); "86ed" or "black-booked" (someone permanently barred from a casino); "early out" (getting a break that ends at the same time as one's shift, allowing a person to leave a little earlier than usual); "the strip" (Las Vegas Boulevard, where most of the major casinos are located); someone "caught the ace-deuce" (died).

Interesting and Peculiar Places to Set a Scene
- **At the swim-up black jack table at the Hard Rock Hotel.** That's right—your character can lay down his chips with the big dogs while taking a dip in the hotel pool. Might not be a lot of places to store the winnings, but, hey, you can only do it Las Vegas . . .
- **At the top of the Stratosphere Tower.** Your character can cast her eyes upon the entire city atop this huge, three-legged monster that holds fifteen hundred rooms. The tower is at the northernmost part of he Strip.
- **Binions Horeshoe Coffeeshop.** This Las Vegas legend is the still-standing coffeeshop from Vegas's earlier days, when people sat at a counter drinking ten-cent cups of coffee. The place hasn't changed—it's still possible to get a hearty breakfast and a cup of coffee for five dollars, twenty-four hours a day. And your character can gamble, too!
- **Fremont Street.** Surrounded by Vegas's modest casinos and hotels, this main city vein is a five-block pedestrian promenade in the heart of town. "The Fremont Street Experience" (the area's official name) shines wildly every night as the overhead lights on the covered corridor are manipulated for an extravagant visual show.
- **Glitter Gulch.** When your character heads toward the intersection of Main and Fremont, he'll be greeted by those long-standing Vegas residents, cowgirl Sassy Sally and cowboy Vegas Vic (you know them, they're the two big neon figures on top of the casino signs). This is old-time Vegas, with casinos that have been around for years catering to the traditional Vegas gambler (the "I'm-here-to-gamble-not-to-play-with-the-kids" kind of guy).
- **Naked City.** That's not really the official name of this

For Further Research

Books

Casino, by Nicholas Pileggi

Las Vegas: As it Began, As It Grew, by Stanley W. Paner

Viva Las Vegas: After Hours Architecture, by Alan Hess

A Pictorial History of Las Vegas, by the Las Vegas Review Journal

The Everything Casino Gambling Book, by George Mandos

Las Vegas: Behind The Tables!, by Barney Vinson

Welcome to the Pleasuredome, by David Spanmier

Resort City in the Sunbelt, by Eugene Moehring

Web Sites

www.vegas.com/about/ (city info)

www.lvstriphistory.com/ (history of the strip)

www.nmhu.edu/region/lvhist.htm (city history)

www.quatloos.com/gamble/gamread.htm (guide to gambling)

http://members.aol.com/alicebeard/letters/vegas.html (writer's site)

Still Curious? Why Not Check Out

Bugsy

Casino

Con Air

Diamonds Are Forever

Fear and Loathing in Las Vegas, by Hunter S. Thompson

Honeymoon in Vegas

Indecent Proposal

The Desert Rose, by Larry McMurtry

Leaving Las Vegas

Literary Las Vegas, by Mike Tronnos

Ocean's Eleven

Rain Man

Rocky IV

Swingers

part of the Strip that goes into downtown; it's just what the locals call it. This is Sin City at its seediest: shabby buildings, skanky strip clubs, cheap motels, and in-and-out wedding chapels in a fifteen-block strip with a notorious reputation for its prostitution (hence the "Naked City" moniker).

- **Near or inside any of the really unique Casinos:** Luxor, Bellagio, The Venetian, Caesars Palace, New York New York, The Mirage, Bally's Paris—all themed, mega casinos that attempt to take you to another world (or at least another city). The Venetian, for instance, has its own canals, gondolas, and Venice architecture, while Bally's Paris has its own Eiffel Tower. You get the point.
- **North Vegas.** By far the most brutal area of the city, this is a place where your character would hate to get lost, especially on foot. Crime is much more prevalent here than in the more touristy areas of town.
- **The Strip.** Driving through this five-mile stretch of Las Vegas Boulevard is a slow jaunt through a jungle of massive casinos, small motels, expensive hotels, strip malls, and generic fast-food joints.
- **The Double Down Saloon.** This is the only true punk-rock bar in town, but it's not the punky kids, the psychedelic atmosphere, or the variety of live music that make this bar a gem. It's the lack of dignity. The midget porn flicks that would normally greet your character when he walks in have been banned, but he'll still be greeted by a bartender asking if he'd like to try the house drink—a spicy red concoction inventively called "Ass Juice." After experiencing that, your character will be surprised to learn the joint actually has a golden rule: "You puke, you clean." Who says Vegas has lost its edge. . . .
- **The VooDoo Lounge.** A glass elevator ride; a killer view of the strip; decor featuring snakes, crosses, hearts, and the colors purple, yellow, red, and black; and Haitian voodoo stuff—these are the makings of The VooDoo Lounge. Your character can drink a Witchy Woman, a Jamaican Hellfire, or a Sexual Trance, then she'll really be ready to party with the best of them at this ultra-hip rock 'n' roll club.

Exceptionally Grand Things Your Character Is Proud Of

- The many grand casinos.
- The surrounding desert and mountains.
- Nearby Hoover Dam and Lake Mead.
- There's no other place like it in the world.
- Crime is down, especially violent crime.

- The Las Vegas Motor Speedway.
- Las Vegas is the engine that drives the state of Nevada, providing about 70 percent of the state's taxable retail sales and about 80 percent of its taxable revenue.

Pathetically Sad Things Your Character Is Ashamed Of

- Compulsive gamblers.
- Drunk losers crying in their beer at every bar.
- Pickpockets and robbery crimes.
- Prostitution.

Your Character Loves

- The city lights.
- Vegas Vic and Sassy Sally.

- The fancy billion-dollar buildings.
- The twenty-four-hour excitement and nightlife.
- Seeing celebrities.
- The great food.
- Meeting people from every corner of the planet.
- Seeing gamblers beat the house.
- Bowling, golfing, rodeos, racing.
- He's only minutes away from a place that could make him a much richer man.
- Quick 'n' easy drive-through weddings.

Your Character Hates

- That outsiders think few decent people live in Las Vegas
- Losers complaining that the games are "rigged."

New Hampshire

New Hampshire Basics That Shape Your Character

Motto: Live Free or Die

Population: 1.24 million

Prevalent Religions: Christianity, particularly Roman Catholic, followed by Baptist, Methodist, and Episcopalian (smaller portions of Lutheran, Presbyterian, Pentecostal), also Judaism and Buddhism

Major Industries: Dairy products, electric equipment, rubber and plastic products, tourism nursery stock, cattle, apples, eggs, machinery

Ethnic Makeup (in percent): Caucasian 96%, African-American 0.7%, Hispanic 1.7%, Asian 1.3%, Native American 0.2%, Other 0.6%

Famous New Hampshirians: Bill Bryson, Salmon P. Chase, Robert Frost, Horace Greeley, Sarah Josepha Hale, John Irving, Franklin Pierce, Adam Sandler, Alan Shepard, John Stark, Steven Tyler (Aerosmith), Daniel Webster

Significant Events Your Character Has Probably Thought About

- The state's first settlement was Portsmouth, founded in 1630.
- Benning Wentworth was made the first official governor of New Hampshire in 1741.
- Anti-British sentiments were high here, and in 1774 a group of patriots took over British-controlled Fort William and Mary, which became Fort Constitution.
- In 1776, New Hampshire established its own government and became the first colony to declare independence from Britain.
- New Hampshire was the ninth and last "necessary" state to ratify the 1788 Constitution.
- Home-stater Franklin Pierce was elected president in 1853.
- New Hampshire was a strong supporter of—and contributed many troops to—Union forces during the Civil War.
- In the late nineteenth and early twentieth century, New Hampshire's economy started to boom as industries from textiles to lumber mills set up shop in the state.
- The state's one-industry towns were crushed in the 1930s, thanks to the Depression.
- In 1963, New Hampshire became the first state to establish a lottery to help pay for education.
- New Hampshire had one of the fastest-growing economies in the 1980s, as electronics and other high-tech industries came to the state.
- In 2001, two teenagers passing themselves off as Dartmouth students entered the home of Dartmouth professors Half and Susanne Zantop and killed them.

New Hampshire Facts and Peculiarities Your Character Might Know

- Locals have an interesting term for bad drivers from Massachusetts: "Massholes!"
- The state has no income tax and no sales tax (of course, that means high property taxes).
- The terrain in New Hampshire is incredibly diverse, from the massive Presidential Range to oceans, beaches, and lakes.

- Unlike its neighbors (Vermont and Maine, for instance), New Hampshire is quite a conservative state.
- It's like a grumpy old man, represented in the state symbol—and seemingly ubiquitous—Old Man in the Mountain (there really is a mountain formation that looks like an old man, and it really is the state symbol).
- Mount Washington has recorded the highest wind speed in the country (231 miles per hour!). It's also the highest point in the Northeast, and one of the region's most dangerous mountains.
- Novelist John Irving is from Exeter.
- New Hampshire seems to be closer in spirit and attitude to Montana and Idaho than to the rest of the Northeast (anti-government, individual rights, conservative, and so on).
- *Yankee Magazine*, the authority on life in New England, is published in Dublin.
- The state is popular with shoppers from other states—mostly Massachusetts—thanks to no sales tax.
- Although residents always have a gripe about Massachusetts, New Hampshire's economy benefits greatly from its neighbor.
- Not many people realize it, but New Hampshire does have a coastal shoreline—but it's only thirteen miles long.

Your Character's Food and Drink

While New Hampshire doesn't have the seafood reputation of Maine or Massachusetts, don't forget that the state does have ocean access and therefore shares in all the lobster, oysters, fried clams, and cod that the rest of New England feasts upon. Maple syrup and maple candy are big deals, too, of course, as is Stonyfield Yogurt. New Hampshire also has at least two reputable microbrews: Nutfield and Smuttynose. Other favorites include strong cider, wild blueberries, fresh produce, home-baked breads and muffins, lobster rolls, Necco wafers, and pies of all sorts. Some still drink Moxie cola.

Things Your Character Likes to Remember

- No taxes!
- New Hampshire holds the first primary in the nation.
- Their state motto ("Live Free or Die"). It's on all the license plates, and they take it seriously!
- The White Mountains—no other mountain range west of the Rockies can compare with their ruggedness and grandeur.
- Robert Frost had a farm outside of Franconia Notch.
- The mountain formation that makes up the Old Man of the Mountains, the state's symbol.
- Astronaut Alan Shepard was the first American to travel in space; he's from East Derry.
- Jenny Thompson won gold medals in swimming and is from Dover.
- Nashua was twice voted the number one city in the United States to live in by *Money* magazine.
- Roy Campanella and Don Newcombe both started their careers with the Nashua Dodgers (they were some of the first African-American players in professional baseball).
- Dartmouth is an Ivy League school.

Things Your Character Would Like to Forget

- Vermont and Massachusetts.
- Big government.
- Residents in the northern part of the state who stay up all night and compete to be the community with the first returns in the primaries.
- The lack of diversity—minorities make up only about 3 percent of the state's population.
- Pamela Smart. She's the teacher who had an affair with one of her students and had him kill her husband.

Myths and Misperceptions About New Hampshire

- **Robert Frost was born here.** He wasn't, instead the sage of New England was actually born in California.

One of New Hampshire's many tiny, steepled churches

© PhotoDisc/Getty Images

For Further Research

Books

Gathered Sketches From the Early History of New Hampshire and Vermont, edited by Francis Chase

The Indian Heritage of New Hampshire and Northern New England, edited by Thaddeus Piotrowski

Jacksonian Democracy in New Hampshire, 1800–1851, by Donald B. Cole

New Hampshire, by Kathleen Thompson

The New Hampshire Century: Concord Monitor Profiles of One Hundred People Who Shaped It, edited by Felice Belman and Mike Pride

New Hampshire in the Civil War, by Bruce D. Heald

Not Without Peril: One Hundred and Fifty Years of Misadventure on the Presidential Range of New Hampshire, by Nicholas Howe

Web Sites

www.nhhistory.org/ (state history)

www.nhwritersproject.org/ (writer's site)

www.nhhistory.org/museum.html (historical society)

www.theunionleader.com/ (state news)

www.visitnh.gov/ (visitor's info)

www.whitemtn.org (White Mountains)

www.dartreview.com (Dartmouth news)

Still Curious? Why Not Check Out

Affliction

Dispatches From the Cold: A Novel, by Leonard Chang

Lake News, by Barbara Delinsky

North of Boston and *New Hampshire*, by Robert Frost

A Prayer for Owen Meany, by John Irving

Random Hearts

Red River

Sea Glass: A Novel, by Anita Shreve

A Walk in the Woods, by Bill Bryson

He did, however, spend many years of his life here, composing such favorites as "Stopping by Woods on a Snowy Evening" and "The Road Not Taken" at his farm near Franconia Notch.

- **It's on the Atlantic Coast.** Only thirteen short miles....
- **It's the state that legalized same-sex marriage.** That would be Vermont, and the conservative residents of New Hampshire won't let you forget it.
- **It doesn't border Canada.** Guess again. It does (not much of it, though), but there's no major interstate to cross the border.

Interesting Places to Set a Scene

- **A hut in the White Mountains.** The Presidential Range is the East's undisputed champion of mountainous splendor. An outdoorsy character can't be in New Hampshire without being here, hiking, kayaking, rapelling, rock climbing, mountain biking, bird-watching, showering (under the one-hundred-plus waterfalls), or cross-country skiing. What's popular here is for hikers (and nonhikers) to rent a space in one of the many huts dotting the mountains. If your character doesn't care much for physical activity and just wants to get to the whispering-winded tops of Mount Washington, she can always take the cog railroad, which has been chugging up the mountain since 1869.

- **Concord.** The state's capital sits right on the Merrimack River and is known as the granite capital of the state (New Hampshire's nickname is "The Granite State"). The city has been an industrial center since the early nineteenth century.

- **Dixville Notch.** Okay, this is where people get crazy about presidential primaries. Every presidential election, residents of this tiny town rush to the ballot box minutes before midnight and cast their votes minutes afterward, being the first in the nation to do so. They just love all the media attention—and they should, for little else is going to happen here until the next election rolls around. But the scenery is beautiful.

- **Ensfield.** This small town used to be home to about three hundred or so Shakers in the nineteenth century. Several historic buildings rest on Lake Mascoma, which used to be called "The Chosen Vale," but now a series of condominiums have spoiled the area a bit. However, if your character has a thing for simple furniture and hearty architecture (especially the colossal Great Stone Dwelling), this is his place.

- **Hanover.** Home to the Ivy Leaguers of Dartmouth, this college town and river city has been trotted upon by everyone from Dr. Seuss (Theodor Geisel) and Robert Frost to Nelson Rockefeller and Daniel Webster. Have your character absorb the intellectual hunger in the air as she struts from class to class. Or, she can just nap on her backpack in the expansive village green that serves as a buffer between the city and the school.

- **The Kancamangus Highway.** It rips through the White Mountains and is arguably the most awesome mountainous drive east of the Rockies.
- **Manchester.** This is The Big City in New Hampshire, with several industries ranging from textile to clothing to electronics. Your character might be more impressed with Manchester's Currier Museum of Art, by far the best in the state, as it contains several European and American pieces. Also on the grounds is the fabulous Zimmerman House, designed by Frank Lloyd Wright himself. And who says there's no culture here. . . .

- **Motorcycle Week in Lake Winnipesaukee.** While the state's largest lake is a favorite relaxation getaway for city dwellers from New York and Boston, the Laconia and Weirs Beach stretch gets pretty loud in June. This is when thousands of motorcyclists come to town for Motorcycle Week, a Dionysian fest of roaring engines, halter tops, leather, whiskey, and cold beer. Hunter S. Thompson's *Hell's Angels* documents the 1965 riots that took place during this wild week.
- **Portsmouth.** This southwestern-corner ocean/river town is a rarity—an interesting combination of bridges and docks, tugboats and tour boats, small eateries and coffeeshops, tattoo parlors and old-time barber shops, fashionable boutiques and art galleries. Established in 1653, the historic Strawberry Banke neighborhood is a living history museum of its own. Your character can't ask for more New England splendor than this.

New Jersey

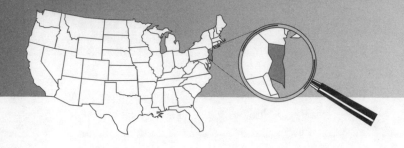

New Jersey Basics That Shape Your Character

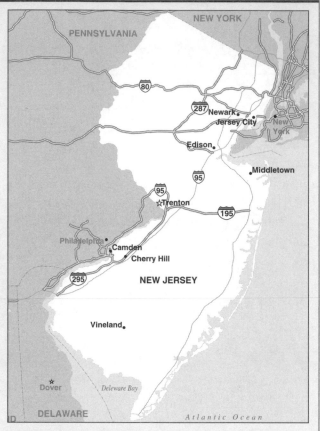

Motto: Liberty and Prosperity

Population: 8.4 million

Prevalent Religions: Christianity, particularly Roman Catholic (some Baptist, Methodist, Lutheran, Presbyterian, Episcopalian)

Major Industries: Chemical products, food processing, electric equipment, printing and publishing, tourism, nursery stock, horses, vegetables, fruits and nuts, seafood, dairy products

Ethnic Makeup (in percent): Caucasian 72.6%, African-American 13.6%, Hispanic 13.3%, Asian 5.7%, Native American 0.2%, Other 5.4%

Famous New Jerseyans: Alan Alda, Judy Blume, Jon Bon Jovi, Stephen Crane, Olympia Dukakis, Allen Ginsberg, Whitney Houston, Jerry Lewis, Norman Mailer, Joe Pesci, Susan Sarandon, General Norman Schwarzkopf, Bruce Springsteen, John Travolta, Dionne Warwick, Phyllis Whitney, William Carlos Williams

Significant Events Your Character Has Probably Thought About

- The first brewery in America opened in Hoboken in 1642.
- William Penn and fellow Quakers purchased East Jersey in 1681 with the hopes of creating a nonviolent society of peace and love. At least the intentions were good.
- In 1776, George Washington quietly crossed the Delaware to win the Battle of Trenton, which was quickly followed by a victory at the Battle of Princeton.
- Thomas Edison's invention years at Menlo Park included the first phonograph (1877), the first incandescent lamp (1879), and the first motion picture (1889), to name a few.
- The Frank Hague years. For thirty-five years (1913 to 1949) this Jersey City mayor almost single- if not under-handedly controlled Hudson County, the Democratic Party, and the entire state. He also jump-started major projects like the Holland Tunnel (1927) and the Pulaski Skyway (1932).
- During World War II, New Jersey shipyards cranked out aircraft carriers, battleships, heavy cruisers, and 25 percent of all destroyers built for the navy during the war. Paterson's Curtiss-Wright Company alone built 139,000 aircraft engines in five years.
- The Federal Housing Act of 1949 created public housing projects (essentially high-rise ghettoes for minorities).
- In 1976, the state voted to minimize the gap in school spending between wealthy suburbs and poor inner cities.
- The state also legalized gambling in 1976; the first casino opened in Atlantic City in 1978.
- In the 1980s, New Jersey started to run out of sites for disposing garbage and thus required each county to limit or recycle most of its waste.
- Christine Todd Whitman was elected the first female governor in 1994.
- Native Lauryn Hill gave hip-hop a name in 1999 by winning three Grammys, two Billboard Music Awards, and three NAACP Image Awards.

- In 2001 Governor Whitman resigned to lead the Environmental Protection Agency.

New Jersey Facts Your Character Might Know
- Camden can boast of having the world's first drive-in movie theater (1933).
- New Jersey has a reputation for being one of the best and most active research centers in the world.
- If your character is "heading into the city," he's actually leaving the state (and going to New York City).
- New Jersey has more diners than does any other state.
- Beat legend Allen Ginsberg was born in Newark in 1926.
- Nassau Hall at Princeton was the country's capital for a short time in 1783.
- New Jersey has 127 miles of pristine coastline and brags of possessing the most beautiful beaches on the East Coast.
- Campbell's soup company is in Camden.
- Orson Welles's "aliens" from his "War of the Worlds" radio broadcast supposedly landed in Grover's Mill, right outside of Princeton. The water tower still stands, replete with bullet holes from locals who shot at it thinking it was an alien spaceship. Who said people in Jersey do dumb things?
- Every year on Christmas Day, thousands of people from around the world come to watch the reenactment of Washington's crossing of the Delaware.
- Your character is likely to hear the following while hanging out in Jersey: "What exit?" (people are always lost), "Pockabook" (for pocketbook or purse), "I was standing on line . . . " (as opposed to "in" line), "Jevanotice?" (Did you ever notice?).

Your Character's Food and Drink
Your character can choose from the following: thin crust pizza, Italian ice, pork rolls, egg and cheese sandwiches (South Jersey), sausage and peppers, Stewart's root beer (served in a frosty mug and delivered to your car at Stewart's Drive-In), Kohr's frozen custard, gravy fries, and anything from a diner. Your character drinks soda, *not* pop!

Things Your Character Likes to Remember
- Woodrow Wilson's governorship. In the two years (1910 to 1912) before he became president (1913),

Wilson regulated big corporations, mitigated political scandals, provided compensation for injured workers, and restricted the illegal employment of women and children. He also was responsible for voting reform and the historic antitrust acts, called the Seven Sisters Acts.
- Albert Einstein, that great mind of the twentieth century, lived at 112 Mercer Street in Princeton.
- New Jersey can boast of having a plethora of U.S. "firsts," including: the first submarine, the first log cabin, the first Colt revolver, saltwater taffy, and Roselle was the first town in the country to be lighted by electricity (1890s). Also the first boardwalk in the world was built in Atlantic City, Eddie Cantor made his radio debut in Roselle Park over WDY, the first Miss America was crowned in Atlantic City, and the first intercollegiate football game, between Rutgers and Princeton, was held in New Brunswick (1869).
- Dining oceanside at Klee's Bar in Seaside Heights.
- Climbing up on top of Old Barney, the Barnegat Lighthouse, and watching the ships come in.
- Getting "comped" (receiving complimentary rooms, drinks, and so on from the casinos) in Atlantic City.
- Lucy, the hotel in Margate that's shaped like a big elephant.
- Frank Sinatra, Bruce Springsteen, Walt Whitman, Stephen Crane, Allen Ginsberg, Amiri Baraka.
- *The Sopranos.*
- Atlantic City (the casinos and the boardwalk).
- The beaches.
- Clubbing.
- Shopping (all those malls!).

Things Your Character Would Like to Forget
- The SS Castle. In 1934 it was grounded off Asbury Park and went up in flames, killing 122 people.
- The six-day Newark race riot in 1967.
- Taking the PATH Train from New Jersey to New York City, which is a dirty, often delayed, unpleasant commute.
- Camden.
- The Meadowlands.
- Bon Jovi.
- Skid Row (the band).
- Oyster Creek nuclear plant.
- The humidity.
- The cops.

- High car insurance rates.
- The commute into the city.
- Parkway and turnpike tolls.
- The corrupt politicians.
- The poorly run Department of Motor Vehicles.
- Taxes.

Myths and Misperceptions About New Jersey

- **That it's an industrial wasteland.** Actually, close to 20 percent of New Jersey is farmland.
- **That there are no "gardens" in the Garden State.** New Jersey does in fact rank high in the production of most garden vegetables, and it grows cranberries, blueberries, and peaches to boot.
- **That all New Jerseyans are crass and uneducated.** Just the poor and underprivileged, particularly in the projects and inner cities.
- **That all residents pronounce it "Joisey."** Guess again. This is a stereotype.
- **That all the women have big, teased hair and wear acid-washed jeans.** Mostly it's just the cheap prostitute wanna-bes in Atlantic City.
- **The Statue of Liberty and Ellis Island belong to New York.** Wrong. They are both in the state of New Jersey!

Interesting Places to Set a Scene

- **Asbury Park.** With its famous oceanside boardwalk, Convention Hall, and Paramount Theatre, this birthplace of saltwater taffy (the idea/recipe originated here) was also Stephen Crane's boyhood home (his house still stands as it did when he lived in it). What could really be fun, however, is to have your character catch a gig at The Stone Pony. This legendary Jersey nightclub is known for intimate concerts and surprise visits from nationally recognized musicians, including The Boss himself (Bruce Springsteen).
- **In a canoe on the Bass River in The Pine Barrens.** If your character needs a New Jersey water getaway that's not in the ocean, he can hop in a canoe on the Bass River and breeze though the whispering, wind-blown-but-sturdy pines in The Pine Barrens.
- **Wildwood.** The sometimes overdone and sometimes too simple 1950s-style hotels along the boardwalk make this southern-tip seaside destination an interesting place for your character to toss back a few drinks and lounge in a "postwar American getaway" setting. Historic little villages, casinos, and an amusement park are also nearby.
- **Cape May during the Bird Migration in April.** While swimming in Cape May in April isn't such a good idea, your bird-watching character will want to hit these beaches, back bays, marshes, creeks, and mudflats for some of the best bird-spotting in the country. Everything from waterfowl, herons, egrets, and ibis to red-throated loons and red-shouldered hawks can be seen here.
- **Clownfest on The Boardwalk at Seaside Heights.** Every year Seaside Heights hosts the country's largest clown parade. What began as the "Garden State Clown Convention" in 1981 on a boardwalk has mushroomed into the "National Clown Arts Project Inc." This is a family favorite and the highlight of the year at Seaside Heights.
- **Driving down Route 9 in South Jersey.** Your character should look for the big dinosaur at the carpet store in Bayville and the giant neon cowboy at the Cowboy Steakhouse and Saloon, where Willie Nelson and Johnny Cash stop by—really!
- **Paterson.** Called the "Silk City of the World," Paterson had its cotton-spinning mills running early, establishing the city as a harbinger for the textile and manufacturing industries. Now its home to aerospace, iron, electronics, paper products, metals, rubber, and plastics industries. African-Americans and Hispanics make up a good deal of this Jersey ethnic epicenter, as do weathered cobblestone streets, stone bridges, and old mills and factories. Samuel Colt manufactured the Colt revolver here, and William Carlos Williams made his home here.
- **Ocean Grove.** An oceanside village with beautifully re-

A boat on the beach near Atlantic City

For Further Research

Books

Down the Jersey Shore, by Russell Roberts and Rich Youmans

A Guide to New Jersey's Revolutionary War Trail for Families and History Buffs, by Mark Di Ionno

Looking for America on the New Jersey Turnpike, by Angus Kress Gillespie and Michael Aaron Rockland

The Meadowlands: Wilderness Adventures at the Edge of a City, by Robert Sullivan

New Jersey: An American Portrait, by April Bernard and Luc Sante

New Jersey: A History, by Thomas J. Fleming

New Jersey Women: A History of Their Status, Roles and Images, by Carmela Ascolese Karnoutsos

New Jersey, Yesterday and Today, by Elaine Fay and Charles A. Stansfield Jr.

The People of New Jersey, by Rudolph J. Vecoli

The Pine Barrens, by John McPhee

This Is New Jersey, by John T. Cunningham

When Dinosaurs Roamed New Jersey, by William B. Gallagher

Web Sites

www.state.nj.us/ (official state site)

www.ptnj.org/FramePps/FrameNJW.htm (New Jersey Writers Project)

www.nj.com/ (news)

www.state.nj.us/state/history/hisidx.html (historical society)

www.njhm.com/ (NJ histories and mysteries)

www.state.nj.us/travel/ (visitor information)

Still Curious? Why Not Check Out

The Barrens: A Novel of Suspense, by Joyce Carol Oates, writing as Rosamond Smith

Bluestones and Salt Hay: An Anthology of Contemporary New Jersey Poets, edited by Joel Lewis

Clockers, by Richard Price

The Collected Poems of William Carlos Williams, edited by A. Walton Litz

Fatal Vision, by Joe McGinnis

Garden State: A Novel, by Rick Moody

Gone for Good, by Harlan Coben

Independence Day and *The Sportswriter*, by Richard Ford

Leaves of Grass, by Walt Whitman

The Lost Legends of New Jersey, by Frederick Reiken

Mango Shoes and Other Stories, by Paul Drexel

The Stephanie Plum Series, by Janet Evanovich (All her books are set in Trenton.)

Sloppy Firsts: A Novel, by Megan McCafferty

The Sopranos

This Side of Paradise, by F. Scott Fitzgerald

---

stored Victorian homes, cottages, and gardens, this National Historical Landmark is said to feature the largest collection of Victorian architecture in the country. A great place for your character to pass away a spring day on a front-porch rocking chair, amidst the blossoming pear trees on Main Avenue.

- **The Cranberry Bogs in South Jersey.** The cranberry is actually one of only a few native North American fruits, and it grows in abundance in New Jersey's wetlands. These bogs are a lovely sight in spring (when the light pink blossoms begin to appear) and summer (when the flowers bloom and swarms and swarms of bees gather to pollinate). But nothing compares to harvesttime, when the bogs are afloat with bright, ripe cranberries. Drop your character in this setting, and she'll literally be swimming in a sea of red.

- **The Edison Tower in Menlo Park.** The site of what's

deemed the first modern research-and-development center in the world, this is where Thomas Edison came up with many of his over four hundred inventions, from the incandescent light bulb to the phonograph to the electric railroad to wireless transmissions. The museum contains some of Edison's inventions and lots of his memorabilia—an inventor-character's playground.

- **Hoboken.** With its port, shipyards, and warehouses, this small Hudson River city of thirty-five thousand across from Manhattan was an important industrial and commercial center in the 1800s. By the 1970s and 1980s, it was full of artists, writers, bohemians, students, and even professionals who came here for the reasonably priced housing and proximity to New York. Now Hoboken is its own cultural community, with art galleries, brew pubs, entertainment events, and a major riverfront face-lift. Frank Sinatra was born here and John Jacob Astor lived here, as did the likes of Washington Irving and William Cullen Bryant. Even *On the Waterfront* was filmed in Hoboken.

- **The Moon Motel on Route 9 in Lakewood.** This odd motel got its name because there allegedly used to be an amusement park nearby that had an astronomical theme. The neon sign on the outside of the place sports a cartoonish V-2 ("Hitler's Brainchild") style rocket. There's also a ringed planet and a giant crescent moon. There's got to be a way to have your character spend the night in this peculiar setting.

Significant Events Your Character Has Probably Thought About

- The 1680 Pueblo Indian Revolt forced Spanish survivors to flee to El Paso.
- In 1822, the Santa Fe Trail opened when William Becknell traveled from Independence, Missouri, to Santa Fe.
- Bishop Jean Baptiste Lamy came to New Mexico in 1851 and established schools, hospitals, and orphanages.
- New Mexico became a state in 1912.
- In 1924, oil was discovered on the Navajo Reservation.
- The testing of the first atomic bomb in 1945 took place at White Sands National Monument; it was built by the Manhattan Project at Los Alamos.
- Uranium was discovered here in 1950.
- Native Americans were finally willed the right to vote in state elections in 1948.
- In 1982, the space shuttle Columbia landed at White Sands, where the first atomic bomb was tested.
- The 1988 drought destroyed almost a million and a half acres.
- Voters opted for video gambling and a state lottery in 1995.
- The largest fire in the state's history was ignited in 2000, when a "controlled burn" got out of control, forcing the entire city of Los Alamos to evacuate.

New Mexico Facts and Peculiarities Your Character Might Know

- In 1947, a UFO allegedly crashed near Roswell.
- Most roads in New Mexico are unpaved because the climate is so dry (no worry of the rains washing away the gravel).
- The cliff-dwelling Anasazi Native Americans built stone homes and lived here about one thousand years ago.
- Many people have passive solar heating with their adobe-style houses.
- Founded in 1610, Santa Fe boasts of being the oldest capital city in the nation.
- The population (with its Native American pueblos and cliff dwellers) in the Los Alamos area was larger in A.D. 1300 than it is today.

New Mexico Basics That Shape Your Character

Motto: It Grows As It Goes

Population: 1.8 million

Prevalent Religions: Christianity, particularly Roman Catholicism, Baptist, Presbyterian, Lutheran, and Pentecostal

Major Industries: Scientific research, mining, electric equipment, petroleum and coal products, food processing, printing and publishing, stone, glass, clay, tourism, cattle, dairy products, hay, nursery stock, chiles

Ethnic Makeup (in percent): Caucasian 56%, African-American 1.9%, Hispanic 42.1%, Asian 1.1%, Native American 1.9%, Other 0.7%

Famous New Mexicans: Dennis Chavez, Robert Crichton, John Denver, Pete Domenici, Harvey Fergusson, Neil Patrick Harris, Conrad Hilton, Peter Hurd, Ralph Kiner, John Madden, Demi Moore, Kim Stanley Robinson, Harrison Schmitt, Slim Summerville, Al and Bobby Unser, Thomas Weaver, Linda Wertheimer

- New Mexican Native Americans use yucca leaves to make rope, baskets, and sandals.
- New Mexico can boast of having seven national for-

ests, including the whopping Gila National Forest (3.3 million acres).

- The idea of Smokey the Bear originated here when a cub was found trapped in a tree during a forest fire in the early 1950s.

Your Character's Food and Drink

New Mexicans love Southwestern and Mexican dishes. Here's what most folks eat regularly: *albondigas* (meatballs), *arroz a la española* (Spanish rice), *arroz con pollo* (chicken with rice), burritos, *caldillo* (stew), *carne adovada* (pork steak in chile sauce), *carne asada,* chalupas, *chauquehue, chicharrones,* green chiles stuffed with cheese or meat, enchiladas, *flautas,* gazpacho, guacamole, *huevos Rancheros,* paella, *posole* (hominy stew made with dried lime), quesadillas, *sopaipillas,* tacos, tamales, *taquitos,* and *tostados.* To drink, your character will have an *atole* (a blue cornmeal drink served with sugar, scalded milk, or both) or hot chocolate.

Things Your Character Likes to Remember

- The green chiles have more kick than the red chiles.
- Ski season begins in late November.
- The deep blue skies and rich sunsets are to die for.
- Cinco de Mayo. It's celebrated here as a huge festival with music, dancing, and good food.
- Hot air balloon festivals.
- New Mexico's white sands.
- The state's history—New Mexico has played a prominent role in the American Southwest.
- Camping in the mountains.
- Gathering with others at a powwow.
- Going to the Mountain Man Rendezvous in the fall.
- Traveling to the Mountain Film Festival in Taos.

Ruins from New Mexico's Pueblo Indians

Things Your Character Would Like to Forget

- New Mexico is one of the nation's poorest states.
- That many people think New Mexico is part of Mexico and not part of the United States.

Myths and Misperceptions About New Mexico

- **New Mexico is desert country.** While there are plenty of desert spots, the state does have many mountains for skiing and wet spots for waterskiing, sailing, and swimming (most lakes, however, are man-made).
- **It's part of Mexico.** Wrong. It's a U.S. state. The New Mexico Visitor's Bureau told us they get lots of calls daily from Americans asking, "Could you tell me about your country?"
- **Everyone speaks Spanish.** Not true. One local tourism clerk said, "People freaked when I went to Iowa and told them I was from New Mexico. They were shocked that I didn't have a Spanish accent!"
- **Natives like outsiders partaking in their powwows.** Not really. Many tribes aren't comfortable when non-natives are at the dances at powwows; they feel the ceremonies should be a spiritual moment between man and god, not man and god and onlooking tourist.

Interesting Places to Set a Scene

- **Albuquerque.** (See page 219 for more specifics on Albuquerque.)
- **Cimarron.** It has some of the largest cattle ranches in the United States, but the town itself is extremely small. The boast of the town is the Cimarron Inn— famous outlaws like Billy the Kid and Wyatt Earp stayed there, and their alleged bullet holes still remain in the walls and ceilings in the bar. It is said that several ghosts reside in the inn, too.
- **Española.** This mostly Hispanic town is rough and has a notorious reputation all over northern New Mexico as a place to avoid, unless your character is looking for trouble or drugs.
- **Las Cruces.** This is very much a college town, with lots of wild adolescents on skateboards and bikes, many of whom do a fine job toting around their books during the week and chugging their beer on the weekend. The big event here is October's Whole Enchilada Fiesta, in which they cook and eat the world's biggest enchilada.
- **Los Alamos.** What was founded in absolute secrecy in 1943 became known the world over when atomic bombs—the brain children of research scientists

For Further Research

Books

Anasazi Ruins of the Southwest in Color, by William M. Ferguson and Arthur H. Rohn

Bacon, Beans, and Galantines, by Joseph R. Conlin

Built to Last: An Architectural History of Silver City, New Mexico, by Susan Berry and Sharman Apt Russell

The Making of the Atomic Bomb, by Richard Rhodes

Mayordomo: Chronicle of an Acequia in Northern New Mexico, by Stanley Crawford

New Mexico: A History of Four Centuries, by Warren A. Beck

Philmont: A History of New Mexico's Cimarron County, by Lawrence R. Murphy

River of Traps: The Pueblo Revolt, by Robert Silverberg

Roadside History of New Mexico, by Francis L. and Roberta B. Fugate

They "Knew" Billy the Kid, edited by Robert F. Kadlec

A Village Life, by William DeBuys and Alex Harris

Web Sites

www.vivanewmexico.com/ (state information)

www.newmexico.org/index.html (official state site)

www.southernnewmexico.com/snm/history.html (state history and tales)

www.nmcn.org/ (state cultural site)

www.nmmagazine.com (*New Mexico Magazine*)

Still Curious? Why Not Check Out

Ben Hur

Black Mesa Poems, by Jimmy Santiago Baca

Bless Me, Ultima, by Rudolfo A. Anaya

Brothers in Blood, by Ken Englade

Canyon of Remembering, by Lesley Poling-Kempes

It Happened in New Mexico, by James A. Crutchfield

The Last Outlaw

Laughing Boy, by Oliver La Farge

The Milagro Beanfield War

The Milagro Beanfield War, by John Nichols

Santa Fe Silkwood

Any book by Tony Hillerman

White Sands

---

holed up here—were dropped on Japan in 1945. The town (called "The Hill"), with all its modern scientific buildings, sticks out like a sore thumb compared to the rest of the state. A lot of scientists live in Los Alamos, as it's still headquarters for much military and even environmental research.

- **Madrid.** A very artsy town, Madrid is becoming a popular destination for art collectors as well as artists. It used to be inexpensive to live here, but no longer.

- **Ojo Caliente.** In between Santa Fe and Taos, this city's claim to fame is mineral hot springs. Have your character soak away while she chats with one of the many local New Age "hippies."

- **Red River.** A ski town high in the mountains, Red River is most frequented by cowboys from the local ranch. There are two local bars that everyone hangs out in, shooting pool, dancing, or just drinking a cold one. Shotgun Willie's is the local eats, with the best breakfast in the area.

- **Rio Grande Gorge Bridge.** It is twelve hundred feet wide and six hundred feet deep. White-water rafting is the thing to do, especially if your character's an extremist.

Several people have died trying to run the rapids.

- **Roswell.** Aliens, anyone?

- **Santa Fe.** The state capital and one of the oldest cities in the United States (1607), Santa Fe is tucked in the foothills of the Sangre de Cristo Mountains and has an international reputation for its restaurants, art galleries, Native American jewelry shops, museums, and opera. The town is a haven for Southwestern artists and writers; Tony Hillerman put the place on the literary map. Santa Fe has almost six thousand hotel and motel rooms to handle the constant influx of tourists who join the city's sixty thousand residents. In addition, this is the place for specialized spas and wellness centers. Alternative healing practices—from hypnosis and massage to yoga and shamanism to astrology and Chinese medicine—can be experienced here. Georgia O'Keeffe's Ghost Ranch is not far from Santa Fe in desolate but starkly beautiful country.

- **Silver City.** This city is known for its historic lore in cowboys and Spanish conquistadors.

- **Taos Canyon.** Only one road leads through the pass. Your character can see lots of animals on that road, including coyotes, deer, bears, elk, bobcats, and mountain lions. It's extremely difficult to travel around Taos Canyon in the snow, but it's one of the state's most scenic areas.

- **Taos.** Taos is a mix of Hispanic, Native American, and Caucasian folks, with Caucasians in the minority. All cohabitate harmoniously, even though each is extremely proud of its own heritage. Taos used to be the sight of the Buffalo Commune in the sixties. There are still many "hippies" in Taos, but they have turned into New Agers who live a simple life, sometimes without electricity or running water. People in Taos walk everywhere, too. One more thing: The town is notorious for breaking up marriages. Rumor has it that if you go to Taos married, you'll leave single (or at least with your spouse *and* your new lover!).

Albuquerque Facts and Peculiarities Your Character Might Know

- It's New Mexico's largest city—about one-third of the state lives here—and its the commercial, industrial, and transportation center of the state.
- Its nickname is "Duke City."
- The city grew quickly after World War II, thanks to government interest in nuclear research.
- Albuquerque is a culturally rich city; it's a melting pot for Native American, Latino, and Anglo cultures.
- The city is divided into the old town (touristy and historic) and the new town (the downtown business center).
- Albuquerque underwent a major urban renewal in the 1970s.
- The Kirtland Air Force provides a lot of economic input to the local economy.
- The Sandia Mountains make a lovely backdrop for the city.
- It has one of the fastest-growing metropolitan areas in the country.
- Many high-tech industries call this their home, making Albuquerque a major site for electronic, industrial, and nuclear research.
- The daytime temperature is way hotter than you'd think, and the nighttime temperature is way cooler than you'd think.
- The state's largest university, the University of New Mexico, is here.
- Albuquerque located east of a bend on the Rio Grande.
- Painters, writers, poets, and photographers looking to the wide-open spaces for inspiration have made their home here over the years.
- The city's Central Avenue is legendary road old Route 66.
- You'll hear people speaking Spanish on the streets all the time.

If Your Character . . .

If Your Character Smells of Money, he lives in East Foothills. The Northeast and Southeast Heights are the gems of Albuquerque. Many homes are nestled in the

Albuquerque Basics That Shape Your Character

An aerial view of picturesque Albuquerque

Population: 448,607 in the city; 562,450 in the Greater Metro area

Prevalent Religions: Christianity, particularly Roman Catholicism, also Protestant, Episcopalian Judaism, New Age, Christian Science, and Church of Jesus Christ of Latter-day Saints

Top Employers: University of New Mexico, Sandia National Laboratories, Intel Corporation, City of Albuquerque, Philips Semiconductor, Albuquerque Public Schools, Bernalillo County, General Electric Aircraft Engines, Sumitomo Sitix Silicon Inc., Presbyterian Healthcare Services

Per Capita Income: $24,860

Average Daily Temperature: January, 34° F; July, 79° F

Ethnic Makeup (in percent): Caucasian 70.8%, African-American 3.0%, Hispanic 42.0%, Asian 1.8%, Native American 4.2%, Other 16.1%

Newspapers and Magazines: *The Albuquerque Tribune, Albuquerque Journal, New Mexico Business Weekly*

Free Weekly Alternative Paper: *Alibi*

foothills of the Sandia mountains, have awesome views of the city and the mountains, cost quite a bit of cash, and are owned by the doctors and lawyers in town.

If Your Character Is an Artist, she lives in Northwest Corrales. This rural community on the outskirts of town is home to gardens, horses, fruit trees, adobe houses, and artists who find this serene area and slow pace of life inspiring.

If Your Character Is a Family Man, he lives in Northeast Heights. This area is a rambling residential suburb dotted with strip malls. Rio Rancho in the northern part of the city is another option.

If Your Character Wears a Blue Collar at Work, he lives in South Valley. This is a mix of small rural mini farms and subdivisions, popular with those with a modest income and simple taste.

Local Grub Your Character Might Love

Hispanic food is popular here. For specific New Mexican foods and dishes, see the New Mexico chapter. Locals love to drink Cabernet Franc from the Casa Rondeña Winery. Favorite eateries include Gold Street Caffe, Frontier Restaurant, Flying Star Cafe, Murphy's Mule Barn, and Garcia's Kitchen (all great breakfast spots). Diners in town are the 66 Diner, Lindy's Diner, Vic's Daily Cafe, and La Familiar Restaurant. Albuquerque is also home to several world eateries, such as Kanome-Al Asian Diner, Japanese Kitchen Sushi Bar, Cajun Kitchen, Chow's Chinese Bistro, and India Kitchen Restaurant. Other favorites are La Crepe Michel, Restaurant Antiquity, Ranchers Club of New Mexico, and Capo's Villa.

Interesting and Peculiar Places to Set a Scene

- **Old Town.** This is the heart of the city's Hispanic heritage. An assortment of art galleries, boutiques, eateries, tourist shops, private patios, secluded gardens, serpentine pathways, and old Pueblo Revival-style structures make up the area, as do ancestors of the original early settlers, who still inhabit the Old Town.
- **Romero Street on a Sunday afternoon.** It might not be a gunfight at the OK Corral, but it is showdown time—staged gunfights take over the streets.
- **Old Town on Christmas Eve.** Half a million luminaries don the walkways, sidewalks, porches, and rooftops throughout the Old Town area, making this a romantic spectacle for your character to behold on a cold winter's night.
- **The Plaza.** Officially called "Old Town Plaza," locals just call it "the plaza." Surrounded by huge cotton-

wood trees, it is the people-watching center of the city. Everyone gathers to rest on the wrought-iron benches, to stroll the snaky walkways, or to just relax from all the shopping and sight-seeing.
- **KiMo Theatre.** The seemingly incompatible Art Deco and Southwestern styles meet in this landmark 1927 Pueblo Deco structure. Have your character catch a show in this unique picture palace.
- **The University of New Mexico.** Twenty thousand students spin around on bikes in the seven-hundred-acre campus noted for its Pueblo Deco architecture, stunning landscaping, pleasant plazas, and neat little pathways. Your character might partake in either the unparalleled anthropology or Southwestern studies programs, for which the campus is well known.
- **The Double Rainbow.** A popular hangout with the young bookstore crowd, this is the best place in town for your character to flip through her favorite magazine while drinking a splendid cup of coffee.
- **Central Avenue.** Route 66 cuts through this main vein of the city, which used to buzz with one-story motels and glowing neon lights but is now the site of big buildings, classy restaurants, flashy nightclubs, and painting, sculpture, and photography galleries.
- **In Crowd.** Albuquerque's funkiest outfitter draws the young, the free, and anyone who's looking to wrap themselves in a fashionable getup that's entirely different.
- **The Kodak Albuquerque International Balloon Fiesta.** It's a big party in the sky for the first two weekends in October, with over a million spectators and 850 balloon pilots from all over the world partaking in various ascending competitions and stunts. Particularly interesting is the "Night Magic Glow," in which the well-lighted balloons look like big lightbulbs in the dark New Mexican sky.
- **Fall Crawl.** This annual rock fest in October features more local bands than your character can listen to. The bands play on nineteen stages in the heart of downtown, and the beer is flowing.

Exceptionally Grand Things Your Character Is Proud Of

- Balloons.
- The University of New Mexico.
- The Indian Pueblo Cultural Center.
- The Rio Grande Zoological Park.

For Further Research

Books

Absolutely Albuquerque, by the Greater Albuquerque Chamber of Commerce

City-Smart: Albuquerque, by Brendan Doherty

Fodor's 1998 Santa Fe, Taos, Albuqerque, by Alison B. Stern

Frommer's Santa Fe, Taos, and Albuquerque, by Lesley S. King

Georgia O'Keeffe, in the West, edited by Doris Bry and Nicholas Callaway

Great River: The Rio Grande in North American History, by Paul Horgan

Old Town, Albuquerque, by Peter Hertzog and James C. Smith

Web Sites

www.abqtrib.com/ (*The Albuquerque Tribune*)
www.cabq.gov/ (official city site)
www.abqcvb.org/ (city visitors bureau)
www.aibf.org/ (balloon festival)
www.oldtownalbuquerque.com/ (guide to Old Town)

Still Curious? Why Not Check Out

Albuquerque and *Heart of Aztlan: A Novel*, by Rudolfo A. Anaya

Baby Face, by Steve Brewer

Dance Hall of the Dead, by Tony Hillerman

Dead Beat

North of the Border, by Judith Van Gieson

Pushing Tin

- The Sandia Mountain Aerial Tramway.
- Atomic Museum.
- Old Town.

Your Character Loves

- Tony Hillerman—he's put the area on the literary map.
- Ernie Pyle—the famous World War II correspondent even has his own museum and a school named after him.
- The Albuquerque Dukes.
- Balloon Fiesta Park.

- Its artists and writers.
- Tourists—without them the city could barely survive.
- El Pinto. To many, it's the most popular, most delicious, most beautiful, and most affordable restaurant in the city.

Your Character Hates

- The high altitude. Sometimes folks get a little lightheaded. . . .
- Rude tourists, of which there can be many during the scorching summer days.
- Visitors who don't realize that the temperature fluctuates greatly between day and night.

New York

Motto: Excelsior

Population: 18.9 million

Prevalent Religions: Roman Catholicism rules in New York State, followed by Judaism, with smaller numbers of Methodist, Lutheran, Presbyterian, Pentecostal, Baptist, and Episcopalian. Muslim, Buddhism, and all world religions are also present (especially in New York City).

Major Industries: Printing and publishing, scientific instruments, electric equipment, machinery, chemical products, tourism, dairy products, cattle and other livestock, vegetables, nursery stock, apples

Ethnic Makeup (in percent): Caucasian 67.9%, African-American 15.9%, Hispanic 15.1%, Asian 5.5%, Native American 0.4%, Other 7.1%

Famous New Yorkers: Lucille Ball, Humphrey Bogart, James Cagney, Aaron Copland, Tom Cruise, Sammy Davis Jr., Agnes de Mille, George Eastman, Millard Fillmore, Lou Gehrig, George Gershwin, Bret Harte, Edward Hopper, Washington Irving, Henry James, John Jay, Billy Joel, Jerome Kern, Vince Lombardi, Marx Brothers, Herman Melville, Ogden Nash, Rosie O'Donnell, Eugene O'Neill, George Pullman, Red Jacket, Christopher Reeve, John D. Rockefeller, Norman Rockwell, Mickey Rooney, Eleanor Roosevelt, Franklin D. Roosevelt, Teddy Roosevelt, Jonas Salk, Margaret Sanger, Barbara Stanwyck, Barbra Streisand, Louis Comfort Tiffany, Martin Van Buren, Mae West, George Westinghouse, Edith Wharton, Walt Whitman

Significant Events Your Character Has Probably Thought About

- In 1609 Samuel de Champlain hit Lake Champlain, and Henry Hudson sailed down the Hudson almost into what's now Albany.
- Revolutionary battles Fort Ticonderoga and Lake Champlain. About a third of the American Revolution took place in here.
- The legacy of Governor DeWitt Clinton.
- The building of the Erie Canal, completed in 1825.
- Alexander Hamilton, James Madison, John Jay, and the Federalist Papers—they tried to persuade New Yorkers to approve the Federalist Constitution, which emphasized that state sovereignty and an individual's freedom were most important.
- Robert Fulton showcased his steamboat on the Hudson.
- Thomas MacDonough's defeat of the British on Lake Champlain at Plattsburgh was a major naval victory during the War of 1812.
- New York led many nineteenth-century reform groups—many abolitionist groups made their headquarters here.
- In 1848 the first women's rights convention in the country was held in Seneca Falls.
- Thomas E. Dewey. This governor did an effective job handling everything from state activities to helping with national efforts in World War II to promoting social and antidiscrimination legislation.
- Under Nelson Rockefeller's governorship (1959 to 1973), the State University of New York grew, social-welfare programs were expanded, and Albany became a culturally and politically active city.
- Woodstock. This 1969 event is known the world over as the biggest party, love fest, and drug fest of the twentieth century.
- The election of Senator Hillary Rodham Clinton in 2000 certainly gave the state a lot to talk about.

New York Facts and Peculiarities Your Character Might Know

- Both the 1932 and the 1980 Winter Olympics were held in Lake Placid.

- New York City was briefly (1789 to 1790) the capital of the new nation and was also the state capital until 1797, when Albany succeeded it.
- The town of Oneontawas was once said to have more bars per capita than did any other place in the country.
- Muckrakers—a term coined by Teddy Roosevelt about writers who uncovered the corruption and dirt on large companies and powerful people—were writing about all sorts of issues all over the state in the late nineteenth and early twentieth centuries.
- Teddy Roosevelt was hiking in the Adirondacks when William McKinley was killed.
- Gilbertsville used to have international polo fields.
- Nobody knows how deep Seneca Lake is; it's never been completely sounded.
- Albany is allegedly the oldest continually settled place in the original thirteen colonies.
- Cooperstown is named after James Fenimore Cooper's father.
- The split of the Democrats over the slavery issue was a big deal—the two groups were the anti-slavery Barnburners and the pro-slavery Hunkers.
- Many upstaters went downstate to help after 9/11. That helpful, spirited move actually hurt the rest of the state's economy, especially in western and upstate New York.
- When people say "the city," they're referring to New York City.
- "Soda" is soda, except in western New York, where it's "pop." And people used to call those long sandwiches "hoagies," but now they're called "subs."

Your Character's Food and Drink

It's pretty typical American fare except in the larger cities, where ethnic restaurants of all sorts offer a variety of eats. In general, the smaller towns offer family restaurants, Italian restaurants, Chinese restaurants, and steak houses. Barbecue is big here as well.

Things Your Character Likes to Remember

- The 1980 U.S. hockey team gold medal.
- Cooperstown.
- The Underground Railroad, which went through New York.
- The Saranac Lake tuberculosis hospital.
- Mario Cuomo.

Myths and Misperceptions About New York

- **There's a monster in Lake Champlain.** Nope.
- **There is no New York except New York City and Buffalo.** Just read about the places on pages 226, 229.
- **The entire state of New York is paved.** Been to the Catskills or the Adirondacks?
- **There's a subway in everyone's backyard.** Upstate New York is beautiful, with lots of trees and rolling hills and mountains. Lots of dairy farms as well—and no subway lines!
- **Upstate towns are all the same.** Each town, of course, is different, but there are two distinct styles of town, depending on whether they were settled by the Dutch or by pioneering New Englanders.
- **Baseball was invented in Cooperstown in 1839.** Despite what Abner Doubleday and the Spalding Commission said, baseball is an outgrowth of cricket and other local games like town ball or one old cat. It's been around much longer than 170 years.
- **The Mohicans exist.** Sorry—James Fenimore Cooper made up the tribe.

Interesting and Peculiar Places to Set a Scene

- **The Adirondacks.** Fishing, swimming, kayaking, mountain biking, camping—you name it, as this is the

A taxi in Manhattan

place for your outdoorsy character to smell the fresh air and challenge nature on nature's terms. Or she could be a rich descendant of the Vanderbilts, Astors, Baches, or Durants, in which case she'll be spending time at one of the impressive "cottages" (to her, but mansions to us). Whatever the case, the Adirondacks encompass six million acres of land, has over forty mountain peaks, sports two thousand lakes, and makes up about one-sixth of the state.

- **Albany.** Poor Albany—many folks don't realize it's New York's capital city (they think New York City is). Albany today is undergoing quite a bit of restoration as it tries to preserve the architecture of the many nineteenth-century homes and buildings that grace the city. What your character might like is rubbing elbows with state legislatures or heading out along Wolf Road where all the discount outlet malls are— always jam-packed.

- **Bronxville.** Home to Sarah Lawrence College, this rather upper-crust community is perfect for a character with deep pockets who likes to pay top dollar for rent or home ownership.

- **Buffalo.** (See page 226 for information on Buffalo.)

- **Cooperstown.** The National Baseball Hall of Fame, the Farmer's Museum, the Fenimore House, the New York State Historical Association, the Glimmerglass Opera, a world-class teaching hospital . . . and it's quite quaint and pretty. There also are several breweries nearby. What else could your character want?

- **East Egg and West Egg.** Remember these two cities from *The Great Gatsby*? Well, they don't exist . . . but if they did, they'd be in Nassau County.

- **Hudson River Valley.** This river valley is dotted with many small towns with old canals that once relied on river traffic for their survival. Since those times are changing, however, this valley along the river has opted to produce gardens and nurseries, many of which grow plants and flowers that can't be matched in the state (so they sell them in the cities).

- **Lake Placid.** Site of the 1932 and the 1980 Winter Olympics, Lake Placid is just as its name insists: calm, cool, slow-paced, tranquil. Your character can either spend a few days on the impressive downhill slopes or enjoy a day or two of sight-seeing at the Olympic Park. If he's there in summer, he can always hike about the mountains and get a different, non-wintery view of the area.

- **New York City.** (See page 229 for information on New York City.)

- **Oneonta.** The population is young and the public library use is high. That's a big deal for a small town, and the reason is that the city benefits from having two liberal arts colleges and an involved little army of local arts organizations.

- **Rochester.** The city's nurseries gave the town the nickname "Flower City," but Rochester is mostly known for its interesting architecture, neighborhoods, and restaurants. Your character might be impressed with the one-hundred-foot waterfall, which does a good job powering the city. Of course, Rochester is best known as the headquarters of Eastman Kodak Company, Xerox Corporation, and Bausch and Lomb. The city has hosted its freethinkers and actors, too: Frederick Douglass published his paper, *The North Star*, here, and Susan B. Anthony was arrested in town for trying to vote. And this was a major stop on the Underground Railroad.

- **Saratoga.** This is the site of two major military engagements that many argue changed the course of the Revolutionary War by bringing France in to help the colonists. However, your character will be more interested in nearby Saratoga Springs, which boasts mineral baths, springs, geysers, spas, polo, and thoroughbred racing. Playing the ponies is a big deal here, but so is relaxing and being pampered (for those who have the money).

- **Seneca Falls.** A feminist character might love to step back in time here, as this is where Elizabeth Cady Stanton, Mary Ann McClintock, Jane Hunt, and others gathered in 1848 for the historic convention that called for "the social, civil, and religious condition and rights of women." It was a serious precursor for later generations of women wanting equal rights. The city is also known as the setting for *It's a Wonderful Life*. While the movie was filmed in Hollywood, many people are convinced Seneca Falls was the model for George Bailey's hometown, so locals hold an It's a Wonderful Life Celebration every year.

- **Syracuse.** This city in the Fingerlakes region used to be known as "Salt City" for all its salt mining, but most of its prosperity came from the Erie Canal. Today Syracuse is deemed a suburban sprawl area, but the university keeps the youngsters hopping.

- **The Hamptons.** Big money, lots of space, awesome

For Further Research

Books

The Adirondacks: A History of America's First Wilderness, by Paul Schneider

Colonial New York: A History, by Michael Kammen

The Encyclopedia of New York, by Thomas Gergel

The Geography of New York State, edited by John H. Thompson

The History of the Province of New-York, by William Smith Jr.

New York in the Age of the Constitution, 1775–1800, edited by Paul A. Gilje and William Pencak

New York: The Empire State, by Barry Kaplan

New York: A Physical History, by Norval White

William Cooper's Town, by Alan Taylor

Web Sites

www.state.ny.us/ (official state site)

www.nyhistory.com/ (state history)

www.nysl.nysed.gov/ (state library)

www.thruway.state.ny.us/ (travel)

http://nysparks.state.ny.us/ (state parks)

Still Curious? Why Not Check Out

The Bell Jar, by Sylvia Plath

Farmer Boy, by Laura Ingalls Wilder

How the Other Half Lives, by Jacob A. Riis

Any of James Fenimore Cooper's work

Last of the Mohicans

A League of Their Own

Rip Van Winkle and *The Legend of Sleepy Hollow*, by Washington Irving

The Secret of Mirror Bay, by Carolyn Keene (a Nancy Drew mystery)

The Sterile Cuckoo

Tootsie

The Way We Were

Wealth Against Commonwealth, by Henry Demarest Lloyd

---

views, cool breezes . . . you know what kind of character would live here.

- **West Point.** If you need to have your story set in the country's most honorable military academy, West Point is the perfect place. Why don't you have your character become one of the twelve hundred new cadets who enter West Point each year? Have him graduate and become a national war hero like other noteworthy alumni: Ulysses S. Grant, Robert E. Lee, Douglas MacArthur, Dwight D. Eisenhower, George S. Patton, and Norman Schwarzkopf. The foundation of the academy rests in its motto, "Duty, Honor, Country" and the Cadet Honor Code, which states "A cadet will not lie, cheat, steal, or tolerate those who do."

Then, of course, there's the unofficial motto: "Much of the history we teach was made by people we taught." Not too many places can brag like that.

- **Woodstock.** While your hippie, music-loving character might have to go about sixty miles southwest to Bethel to catch the vibes of the 1969 Woodstock event, this town of about 7,500 is a great little community. It began as an artist's colony (The Art Students League of New York had a summer school here), held the nation's first chamber music concert series in the country, and is still home to many artists, musicians, and those wanting small-town life but also the benefits of being within a manageable drive of the city.

Buffalo

Buffalo Basics That Shape Your Character

Buffalo's Historical Society building

Population: 300,717

Prevalent Religions: Christians, mostly Roman Catholic, and some Lutherans, Pentecostals, and Baptists

Top Employers: General Electric, IBM, Xerox Corporation, Samsung, Fisher-Price, EDS Enterprise Solutions, M&T Bank Corporation, Arthur Andersen LLP, University of Buffalo

Per Capita Income: $26,710

Average Daily Temperature: January, 24° F; July, 71° F

Ethnic Makeup (in percent): Caucasian 54.7%, African-American 37.2%, Hispanic 7.5%, Asian 1.4%, Native American 0.8%, Other 3.7%

Newspapers and Magazines: *The Buffalo News, Business First of Buffalo*

Free Weekly Alternative Paper: *Buffalo Beat, Art Voice*

Buffalo Facts and Peculiarities Your Character Might Know

- All the neighborhoods have their own ethnic makeup: Irish in south Buffalo, Polish in Cheektowaga, and so on (although it's becoming blurred these days).
- To always keep a shovel in his truck and know the proper technique for pushing a car out of the snow.
- Buffalo was the home of the Goo Goo Dolls and Ani DiFranco.
- President William McKinley was assassinated at the 1901 Pan-American Exposition in Buffalo.
- President Millard Fillmore is buried in Buffalo, where he had a law practice before entering politics.
- President Grover Cleveland was a prominent lawyer and the mayor of Buffalo before becoming governor of New York and eventually president.
- "Lake effect snow"—hear it all the time.

If Your Character . . .

If Your Character Is Trendy, she shops in Toronto. Although it's about two and one-half hours away, it is the getaway of choice for serious trendy shopping. Plus, the currency exchange rate is extremely favorable to Americans. Elmwood and Delaware Avenues, near Buffalo State University and the Albright-Knox Art Gallery, are the rather small epicenters of the coffeeshop and boutique scene in Buffalo.

If Your Character Is a Middle-Class Family Man, he lives just about anywhere outside the city limits. Most neighborhoods surrounding Buffalo are distinctly middle class. Hamburg, West Seneca, and Tonawanda are among the several nondescript, middle-class suburbs. Houses are inexpensive in most of Buffalo (but property taxes are high), so many city dwellers could make it to the inner suburbs without much of a cost-of-living increase if they had a mind to.

If Your Character Loves Nature, she's spending time in Ellicottville, south of the city, for skiing; Chestnut Ridge Park for sledding and hiking; and Lakes Erie and Ontario for water sports of all kinds. With the exception of Buffalo and the slightly smaller Rochester to the east, western New York is mostly rural and agricultural. As a result, camping, hunting, and fishing are all popular pursuits that can be found just about anywhere in all directions.

If Your Character Wears a Blue Collar at Work, he lives in one of the neighborhoods in the city, especially South Buffalo, Cheektowaga, Lackawanna, and Depew. At one time, many of these neighborhoods had distinct ethnic flavors: south Buffalo was Irish, for example, and Cheektowaga was Polish. Over time these ethnic influences decreased as populations shifted. Still, Buffalo is mostly a blue-collar, American car kind of town.

If Your Character Smells of Money, he resides in Amherst. With its tree-lined streets and grassy medians, Amherst is a fine example of a pre-sprawl suburb, although it is Buffalo's most populous suburb. It has loads of trees, lampposts, and big, older houses. It is frequently recognized as one of the safest cities in America. Williamsville, Orchard Park, and Clarence are typical strip mall, good school, and cul-de-sac outer suburbs, interchangeable with most of America.

Local Grub Your Character Might Love

Buffalo wings, invented at the Anchor Bar on Main Street in 1964, are Buffalo's main culinary contribution. Buffalonians never call them "Buffalo wings," though (just wings). Beef on Weck is Buffalo's second great food contribution: roast beef and horseradish on a salted kaiser roll (kummelweck). Your character also can get pizza and wings from just about anywhere—and blue cheese goes on both. Popular restaurants are Ted's Hot Dogs and Mighty Taco (cleans Taco Bell's clock any day). To drink, Buffalonians like "Genny" Genesee beer (actually from Rochester, but it's everywhere in Buffalo, too); for the upscale palate, Labatt's. They drink pop, not soda. Those with a sweet tooth take in orange chocolate and sponge candy.

Interesting and Peculiar Places to Set a Scene

- **Elmwood Avenue.** This is the city's trendy, college-type area, with adolescents bustling about with backpacks and flyers to post around the area for school events. Coffeeshops are big here, as the college kids need to stay juiced to make up for their lack of sleep.
- **Niagara Falls.** The Falls themselves are interesting, as are the seedy heart-shaped tubs in some of the hotels (catering to newlyweds honeymooning here). Have your character put on his slicker and board the "Maid of the Mist," which passes under the falls. Once he

dries off your character can head to one of the nearby wax museums. Hmmm . . .

- **Walden Galleria.** Also called "Galleria Mall," the area's largest shopping mall has lots of national stores like Gap, Eddie Bauer, and Abercrombie and Fitch. It's mostly filled with moms looking for school clothes for the kids or high school kids just hanging out.
- **Albright-Knox Art Gallery.** This fabulous museum houses one of the premier modern art collections in the country. Your character can take a first date to the Albright-Knox and impress her with all his knowledge of Louise Bourgeois, Gustave Courbet, Eugene Delacroix, Jackson Pollock, and Mark Rothko—all of whom are in the collection.
- **Across the border in Canada.** Your character can check out any of the strip clubs, Chinese food joints, or late-night doughnut shops. People of all sorts hang out here, looking for some sort of satisfaction.
- **Rich Stadium.** This is home of the Bills, and when the team's in town, the town's at the game. Many games are "snow bowls," as Buffalo gets all the snow from the Lakes. Have your character put on his earmuffs, Burlington coat, and winter gloves and head to the game for three hours of cold, beer-drinking fun. He might even enjoy watching the football game.
- **Old Fort Niagara.** This is a War of 1812-era fort and destination for every fifth-grade field trip in western New York. Kids go crazy standing behind the cannons or climbing up to the observation deck, all the while imagining they are the war heroes.
- **The Erie Canal.** This landmark canal dates back to the early nineteenth century. It runs from Buffalo heading east and goes all the way to New York City. Your character can still catch boats chugging along its waters.

Exceptionally Grand Things Your Character Is Proud Of

- Niagara Falls. The Niagara Falls power complex, Goat Island, and Rainbow Bridge are interesting as well.
- The Buffalo Bills.
- Chicken wings (what the rest of the country calls Buffalo wings).
- Snow—Buffalonians pride themselves on their ability to deal with, and thrive upon, large amounts of snow.
- The State University of New York at Buffalo—the school's Poetry/Rare Books Collection is the best in the country and is internationally held in high regard.

For Further Research

Books

Buffalo City Hall: Americanesque Masterpiece, by John H. Conlin

Buffalo: Lake City in Niagara Land, by Richard C. Brown and Bob Watson

Buffalo's Pan-American Exposition, by Thomas Leary and Elizabeth Sholes

City on the Lake: The Challenge of Change in Buffalo, New York, by Mark Goldman

Iron Riders: Story of the Buffalo Soldier Bicycle Corps, by George Niels Sorensen

Relentless: The Hard-Hitting History of Buffalo Bills Football, by Sal Maiorana,

Web Sites

www.buffalo.edu/ (university news)

www.ci.buffalo.ny.us/document_3.html (official city site)

http://bfn.org/preservationworks/hist/hist/hist.html (history)

www.buffalonian.com/history/ (histories of western New York)

www.buffalobills.com/ (official site of the Bills)

www.zuzu.com/worklink.htm (writer's resources)

www.buffalonews.com/ (news and current events)

Still Curious? Why Not Check Out

All-Bright Court, By Bonnie Porter

Buffalo Bill

Buffalo '66

City of Light, by Lauren Belfer

Commander Tom

Four and Twenty Bluebeards, by Loren Keller

Jesse

Killing Time in Buffalo, Diedre Laiken

Of Drag Queens and the Wheel of Fate, by Susan Smith

The Procedure, by Peter Clement

Stone Butch Blues, Leslie Feinberg

Pathetically Sad Things Your Character Is Ashamed Of

- "No Goal"—A controversial goal gave the 1999 Stanley Cup to the Dallas Stars over the Sabres. You can probably still see "No Goal" bumper stickers around town.
- "Wide right." The Bills' four consecutive Super Bowl losses in the early 1990s are a painful memory, especially Scott Norwood missing the game-winning field goal in Super Bowl XXV.
- O.J. Simpson. Buffalo doesn't talk much about the Juice anymore (once a hero, now a dolt).

Your Character Loves

- The snow. It does it all the time, and Buffalonians love the fluffy white stuff.
- Broadway market, especially at Easter [have to buy that butter lamb for Easter dinner (a butter stick molded in the shape of a lamb)].
- Snow (really, they do).
- Shakespeare in Delaware Park.
- The Buffalo Bills—Actually, this is an understatement. Buffalo is consumed by the Bills. The entire self-esteem of the Buffalo hinges upon the Bills' success on Sunday. In truth, it is Buffalo's one bright spot on the national level (unless you count "Buffalo" chicken wings), so the losses, especially the Super Bowl losses, go down hard.

Your Character Hates

- People who think Buffalo is right next to New York City.
- The Miami Dolphins.
- That Buffalo's tax money goes right to New York City.
- Canadian drivers and Canadian money (the loonies—one-dollar coins).

New York City

New York Facts and Peculiarities Your Character Might Know

- New York is made up of five boroughs: Brooklyn, the Bronx, Manhattan, Queens, and Staten Island.
- While Staten Island is deemed the safest and most sanitized area of New York, it's also home to the city's biggest pile of garbage. Residents in the city (Democrats) are tickled by that fact, and those on the island (Republicans) are ticked by it.
- As of late, the two big topics of conversation in the city are the quirks of billionaire mayor Michael Bloomberg and the events of 9/11.
- Times Square used to be called Longacre Square until 1904, when *The New York Times* moved from Park Row to between Seventh and Eighth Avenues on Forty-Third Street. So the new building spawned a new name for the square. Also, *The New York Times* publisher threw a New Year's Eve party that first year to celebrate the new building; the tradition has continued.
- New York City's subway opened in 1904 and now covers over seven hundred miles of track.
- Housing costs an unbelievable amount, and it's the first subject of conversation with a new acquaintance.
- About twenty acres of Central Park used to be home to sheep who roamed the areas between Sixty-Sixth and Sixty-Ninth Streets around the turn of the twentieth century, but then they were moved to Brooklyn's Prospect Park in 1934.
- SoHo stands for SOuth of HOuston Street.
- There's been a lot of debate over the years as to why New York is called "The Big Apple." While there's still some disagreement, according to the New York Public Library the term originated in Edward S. Martin's 1909 book *The Wayfarer in New York*; he referred to the national landscape as a big tree and New York as the big apple "that gets a disproportionate share of the national sap."
- The Macy's parade started in 1924.
- Gotham actually means "goat town," and the city was satirically nicknamed this by Washington Irving in his 1807 series *Salmagundi*. This is also how the Knicks got their name.

New York City Basics That Shape Your Character

Passengers awaiting a subway train

Population: 7.5 million in the city; 8.7 million in the Greater Metro area

Prevalent Religions: They're all here, but Protestant, Judaism, and Roman Catholicism are most prevalent.

Top Employers: Citigroup, AT&T, Verizon Communications, Philip Morris, American International Group, Morgan Stanley Dean Witter and Company, Merrill Lynch, AOL Time Warner, Goldman Sachs, MetLife, Pfizer Inc., Lehman Brothers Holdings, American Express, Viacom, Loews Corporation

Per Capita Income: $38,814

Average Daily Temperature: January, 60° F; July, 82° F

Ethnic Makeup (in percent): Caucasian 44.7%, African-American 26.6%, Hispanic 27.0%, Asian 9.8%, Native American 0.5%, Other 13.4%

Newspapers and Magazines: *The New York Times, The New York Daily News, New York Post, The Wall Street Journal, The New Yorker, New York Magazine, The New York Times Magazine, Literal Latte, Paper, SoHo Style, aRude, Interview, City Guide Magazine, Time Out New York, The Village Voice, New York Press, The New York Observer*

- Until the events of 9/11, the Fire of 1835 had caused the most property damage in the city's history.
- Madison Square Garden is actually the third Madison Square Garden. The first was built in 1879, the second

in 1925, and the one standing today was completed in 1968.

- In the late nineteenth and early twentieth centuries, the city experienced a huge influx of European and Asian immigrants, which increased the city's population.
- Tribeca stands for TRIangle BElow CAnal, which means Tribeca is a triangle-trapezoid neighborhood surrounded by Canal Street, Broadway, Barclay Street, and the Hudson River.
- After World War II, lots of African-Americans, Puerto Ricans, and Latin Americans came to the city looking for work, spiking the population numbers once again.
- The broad Brooklyn accent is a New York trademark and can still be heard here every day—and not just in Brooklyn.
- The city was the state capital until 1797, and then for a short time in 1789 to 1790, it temporarily became the U.S. capital.
- It's not uncommon to hear Jewish terms like *verklemmt* and *schmuck* (think of Mike Meyers on *Saturday Night Live*).
- The biggest noteworthy language shift of late is Spanglish—it's everywhere in the city these days. Since so many people speak both English and Spanish, it's typical to overhear conversations in which people switch effortlessly between the two (hence, they're speaking Spanglish).

If Your Character . . .

If Your Character Is Trendy, she shops in SoHo. This has become the hip place to shop for everything from the latest in fashion to the coolest new art to funky around-the-apartment kind of stuff.

If Your Character Is Wealthy and in need of Jewelry and Designer Clothes, she shops on Fifth or Madison Avenues. These are still the shopping and spending meccas for the Holly Golightlys of this world, although it's not uncommon to see a wealthy, tattooed rock star trying to impress his latest model girlfriend with something only he can afford.

If Your Character Wears a Blue Collar at Work, he lives on Long Island. He might also live in the farther reaches of some of the boroughs, like Brooklyn and Queens.

If Your Character Must See a Play, he's going to The Theater District. Over thirty theaters around Broadway dot the areas from Forty-First to Fifty-Third Streets and Sixth to Ninth Avenues. The most legendary block is Forty-Second Street.

If Your Character Is a Middle-Class Family Man, he lives on Staten Island. Although it's deemed "the forgotten borough," your Caucasian, middle-class, fairly conservative character will be right at home here. Those in Manhattan don't get a break from the filth and bustle—and they don't get to take a ferry to and from work when they feel like it.

If Your Character Must Rid Himself of the Body He Just Killed, he's taking the corpse to The East River. This is a classic spot for dumping bodies or having someone shot off a pier.

If Your Character Loves Nature, she's spending time in The New York Botanical Garden. One of the country's oldest, biggest botanical gardens (250 acres) also has about forty acres of uncut forest. The Bronx Zoo/International Wildlife Conservation Park and Brooklyn Botanic Garden are also good choices. Then there's always that little-known spec of green in Manhattan's concrete jungle: Central Park.

If Your Character Is in Dire Need of a Prostitute, he's scanning the Meatpacking District. This area is particularly famous for its transsexual prostitutes, but male and female prostitutes in vans looking for business can also be found here.

Local Grub Your Character Might Love

While San Franciscans and Parisians might disagree, many people think of New York as the restaurant capital of the world. With 12,000 or more restaurants to choose from, your character can get anything and everything here, from Harlem soul food to Brazilian, Chilean, Russian, French, Mongolian, African, Caribbean, and other dishes from around the world. Of course, there are the famous slices of New York pizza, the bagels, the knishes, the hot dogs and falafels from street vendors . . . it's endless. Some of the city's treasured eateries are (and the list is far from comprehensive) the following: 21 Club, Balthazar, Becco, Cafe Mozart, Jane, WD-50,

M, Kai, IL Vagabando, La Grenouille, Lot 61, Four Seasons, Patsy's, Djungo, Bouley Bakery, Letucé, Sugar Bar, Frankie's Restaurant, Dahiel, Lespihasse, Chanterelle, Le Cirque 2000, Le Bernardin, Jean Georges, and Alain Ducasse.

Interesting and Peculiar Places to Set a Scene

- **ABC Carpet and Home.** Yep, it sells carpet, but it's a whole lot more than a carpet store. It's more like a six-floor museum specializing in Americana kitsch, from country furniture and knickknacks to antiques. Probably the mostly colorful "carpet and home" spot in the world.

- **Artists Space.** This innovative Manhattan gallery was a pioneer in the alternative space movement in the early 1970s. It's been showcasing the visual arts since, including video, multimedia, performance, architecture, and design art.

- **Atop the Empire State Building.** Okay, tourists and lovers go here for the dramatic—some claim fifty-mile—view of the city and harbor. But what other building has an eighty-sixth floor observation deck, was the tallest building in the world for forty years, and is famed for having a big ape climbing on it? Only in New York City . . . .

- **Brooklyn Heights Promenade.** If your character needs to take a pleasant stroll along the East River and soak up a great view of lower Manhattan (it was better when the towers were there), this is her walking space.

- **Cathedral of St. John the Divine.** Manhattan's famous cathedral and longest work-in-progress also happens to be the world's second largest church. It's as unique as it is huge—home to one of the most powerful working pipe organs in the world, the famed poet's corner, interfaith chapels, lectures, and performance artists. And yes, it even holds mass, too.

- **Chinatown.** About 150,000 Chinese-speakers live here. It's the best area in the city for your character to eat on the cheap (Chinese, Thai, Vietnamese) and get stuffed at the same time, all the while feeling like he's in, well, Asia.

- **Coliseum Books.** This corner shop used to be a New York mega-store before big chains Barnes and Noble and Borders came to town. It's still a classic New York bookshop, with lots of history, academic books, and loads of paperbacks.

- **East Village.** Since the 1960s, this has been the gritty little brother of the more gentrified Greenwich Village. Things haven't changed much since, except there are more Puerto Rican and Eastern European immigrants these days, as well as young professionals. Your character will still have no problem befriending a grunger with a nose ring, tattoos, baggy pants, and anticonventional ideas.

- **Eighth Street in Chelsea.** Many gays moved here when Greenwich Village became dotted with more tourists than transvestites and the rent soared higher than Manhattan skyscrapers.

- **Fulton Fish Market.** This is the most legendary fish market in New York. Dating back to 1821, the market used to be the unloading spot for local fisherman who'd drag their catches here from their fishing boats. Now that the water's too polluted, most of the fish today comes from elsewhere. What's most interesting, however, is that the place is an absolute madhouse—even though it's only open between midnight and eight or so in the morning.

- **Gracie Mansion.** If your character wants to spot a mayor or is even a New York mayor himself, Gracie just might creep into the story—the Manhattan mansion literally houses the mayor.

- **Greenwich Village.** What was once the site of Stonewall and home to Bohemians and counterculturists has become somewhat gentrified. While coffeehouses still make a great place for a cup of java and good conversation, and the nightclubs on Bleecker Street are as prevalent as ever, the people here have changed—now your character is more apt to see tourists and privileged college kids than she is to run into the next Jack Kerouac or Jackson Pollock (she'll have to go to the East Village for that).

- **Greenwood Cemetery.** While it's no Central Park, this Brooklyn cemetery has a history that Central Park can't match. Not only is it home to more boxes of bones (lots of history there!), but the nearly five-hundred-acre architectural and horticultural marvel also possesses the famous Gothic gatehouse, built in 1861 and now a Brooklyn landmark and legend.

- **Hell's Kitchen.** Still deemed one of the roughest parts of town, with fenced-in playgrounds, drug dealers, gangs (the area got its name from the gang that ruled the area), and underground clubs. A perfect spot for setting a "life-is-tough-in-the-big-city" story.

- **The Lower East Side**. This was the sight where all the sweatshops were in the early days. They hired cheap immigrant labor (many of whom were displaced Jews). Today, however, the area is a mix of down-and-out immigrants (not Jewish anymore but Hispanic and Latin Americans), Bohemians, and expensive restaurants.

- **The Malcolm Shabazz Harlem Market**. When your character first walks into this Harlem bizarre, he'll pass the too-obviously phony minarets. Then, he'll be bombarded by vendors catering mostly to the African-American crowd, selling everything from West African clothes, Black Pride T-shirts, big gold jewelry, a myriad of hats, Ashanti dolls, and just about anything else the clientele will buy.

- **Mulberry Street in Little Italy**. This is the area's main drag and home to lots of delicious little trattorias, grocery stores, and Italian restaurants. The Casabella Restaurant is on Mulberry and has come to be the major spot for authentic Italian.

- **Rockefeller Center**. The nineteen-building complex has 388 elevators and includes Radio City Music Hall, NBC Studios, the G.E. Building, the Channel Gardens floral display, and the famous skating rink. Why not have your character have a drink in the Rainbow Room for yet another only-in-New York experience?

- **Socrates Sculpture Park**. Your sculpture-loving character will get an eyeful at this Queens exhibit space, as it's the major site for large sculpture exhibitions in the city. An extra bonus, however, is the breathtaking view of the Manhattan skyline.

- **SoHo**. This is where your hip artist character can be found living in a loft apartment in one of the cast-iron buildings, strutting the streets, hanging out at the bars and art galleries, drinking cappuccino, and mingling with rich and trendy friends who shop at the trendy stores.

- **Tribeca**. This is as hip as SoHo but a little less sanitized. The heart of Tribeca used to be the massive and long-standing Washington Market, which was the largest food market in the nation in the mid-1800s. Where the market once stood is now Washington Market Park.

- **Union Square Greenmarket**. Farmers everywhere from Pennsylvania to the Hudson Valley to Long Island and New Jersey set up shop for this legendary four-days-a-week market. Administered by the city, this is just one of the dozens of green-markets in New York. Have your character stop in for some produce, fish, breads, herbs, cheeses, cakes, meat, flowers—it's all for sale.

- **The Upper East Side**. A character with lots of cash would make her home in the Upper East Side, which is still the place for the city's wealthy, with its expensive penthouses, privacy, and lack of noise. It's no surprise that auction houses Sotheby's and Christie's International are here as well.

- **White Columns**. This gallery was a harbinger for cutting-edge artists with new ideas back in 1969, and it hasn't changed its mission since (although its location has; it was once on Christopher Street but is now on West Thirteenth near the Meatpacking District). It is New York's oldest alternative exhibition space, showcasing the works of hundreds of artists annually. Many artists from Gordon Matta-Clark to Alice Aycock to William Wegman got their first major exposure here.

Exceptionally Grand Things Your Character Is Proud Of

- New Yorkers' independence.
- The Yankees.
- Its theater.
- Its cultural and artistic life.
- Publishing—90 percent of all printed material comes from here.
- That it's the most happening city in the world.
- Its restaurants.
- Its snobbiness and sense of self-importance—that New York City is the center of the world, and everything else is the provinces.
- That not too many people get robbed, mugged, and shot anymore.
- How the city came together during and after the attacks on the Twin Towers.
- Former Mayor Rudy Giuliani—he cleaned up the city and was a great spokesman for its people after the attacks.

Your Character Loves

- Being a New Yorker.
- Central Park. All that green in the heart of Manhattan is truly amazing.

For Further Research

Books

AIA Guide to New York City, edited by Elliot Willensky and Norval White

American Metropolis: A History of New York City, by George J. Lankevich

Colonial New York: A History, by Michael G. Kammen

The Columbia Historical Portrait of New York, by John A. Kouwenhoven

The Encyclopedia of New York City, edited by Kenneth T. Jackson

Gotham: A History of New York City to 1898, by Edwin G. Burrows and Mike Wallace

In the Place to Be: Guy Trebay's New York, by Guy Trebay

Kafka Was The Rage: A Greenwich Village Memoir, by Anatole Broyard

Low Life: Lures and Snares of Old New York, by Luc Sante

New York Cookbook, by Molly O'Neill

New York: A Guide to the Metropolis, by Gerard R. Wolfe

New York Literary Lights, by William Corbett

New York Vertical, by Horst Hamann

Tales of Times Square, by Josh Alan Friedman

Up in the Old Hotel, and Other Stories, by Joseph Mitchell

World of Our Fathers, by Irving Howe

WPA Guide to New York City, by Works Projects Administration

Writing New York: A Literary Anthology, edited by Phillip Lopate

Web Sites

www.nytimes.com (*The New York Times*)
www.nycvisit.com/home/index.cfm (official city site)
www.gothamcenter.org/ (New York City history)
www.smartnewyorker.com/ (tourist stuff)
www.ny.com/ (visitor info)
www.newyorker.com/ (*The New Yorker*)
www.thenewyorker.com/ (site for locals, not the magazine)
www.stjohndivine.org/ (St. John the Divine site)

Still Curious? Why Not Check Out

42nd Street

Annie Hall

Bonfire of the Vanities, by Tom Wolfe

Breakfast at Tiffany's, by Truman Capote

Bright Lights, Big City: A Novel, by Jay McInerney

Call It Sleep, by Henry Roth

Catcher in the Rye, by J.D. Salinger

Complete Stories of Dorothy Parker, edited by Colleen Breese

Crazy Cock, by Henry Miller

The Daytrippers

Do the Right Thing

The Doorbell Rang, by Rex Stout

Eyes Wide Shut

Frankie and Johnny

The French Connection

The Godfather II

Going Down, by Jennifer Belle

Guys and Dolls

Here Is New York, by E.B. White

Kids

Manhattan

The Matthew Scudder novels, by Lawrence Block

Midnight Cowboy

Miracle on 34th Street

Money: A Suicide Note, by Martin Amis

The Movie Lover's Guide to New York, by Richard Alleman

New York Eats, by Ed Levine

The New York Trilogy, by Paul Auster

On the Waterfront

The Out-of-Towners

Ragtime, by E.L. Doctorow

Saturday Night Fever

Searching for Bobby Fischer

Smoke

Taxi Driver

Washington Square, by Henry James

When Harry Met Sally

- Walking Museum Mile and stopping to thoroughly check out an exhibit.
- Sidewalk shopping.
- Browsing—or maybe even shopping at—Prada, TSE Cashmere, Barneys New York, Tiffany, Bloomingdale's, Saks Fifth Avenue . . .

- Watching the chess players in Washington Square Park.
- Love Stores—the city's favorite pharmacy chain.
- Scouring the many green-markets for that special treat.
- Its sports team (Yankees, Knicks, Rangers, Jets, and Giants) and players (Roger Clemens, Mike Piazza).
- Woody Allen, Martin Scorsese, Spike Lee, Paul Simon, Joseph Mitchell, and others.
- Going to Roosevelt Island's Lighthouse Park for a great view of East River and the Manhattan skyline.
- Hanging out and wandering through the grand Frick Collection.
- Sauntering through the Village at night.
- Heading up to Times Square and getting last-minute half-price theater tickets.
- Spending hours leafing through books at the New York Is Book Country book fair.

Your Character Hates
- The traffic.
- The noise.
- The rude people.
- Ignorant tourists.
- The high cost of living—buying a house is nearly impossible.
- Former mayor David Dinkins.
- That all the sex shops on Times Square are disappearing (hey, this is New York).

North Carolina

Significant Events Your Character Has Probably Thought About

- The birth of Virginia Dare (in Roanoke) in 1587; she's said to be the first English child born in America. Many tourists go to Roanoke Island to see *The Lost Colony*, an outdoor drama about Virginia and her mother Eleanor.
- North Carolina seceded from the Union in 1861; it was readmitted in 1868.
- Hiram R. Revels became the first African-American member of the U. S. Senate in 1870.
- The 1901 election of Governor Charles B. Aycock, whose administration championed education and proved it by creating nearly 1,100 schools in four years.
- The first flight by the Wright Brothers in 1903 at Kill Devil Hills.
- North Carolina launched an innovative road-building campaign in the 1920s. The state has since become known as "The Good Roads State."
- The formation of the North Carolina Symphony in 1943, making it the first official state symphony. It still offers 175 performances a year.
- The establishment of Research Triangle Park in 1959. To kick-start North Carolina's economic growth, Duke University in Durham, North Carolina State University in Raleigh, and the University of North Carolina at Chapel Hill all became engaged in institutional, governmental, and industrial research.
- In 1992 Grandfather Mountain became the first private park in the world designated by the United Nations as an International Biosphere Reserve.
- The 2001–2002 "separation of church and state" controversy over whether the Ten Commandments should be posted in public schools.

North Carolina Facts and Peculiarities Your Character Might Know

- North Carolina is divided geographically into the High Country in the northwest, the Piedmont area in the east, and the sandy lowlands of the Outer Banks on the Atlantic shore.

North Carolina Basics That Shape Your Character

Motto: To Be Rather Than to Seem

Population: 8.1 million

Prevalent Religions: Christianity, particularly Lutheran, Pentecostal, Baptist, and Roman Catholic

Major Industries: Tobacco, textiles, chemical products, electric equipment, machinery, tourism, poultry and eggs, tobacco, hogs, milk, nursery stock, cattle, soybeans

Ethnic Makeup (in percent): Caucasian 72.1%, African-American 21.6%, Hispanic 4.7%, Asian 1.4%, Native American 1.2%, Other 4.7%

Famous North Carolinians: Doris Betts, David Brinkley, Howard Cosell, Roberta Flack, Eileen Fulton, Ava Gardner, Billy Graham, Paul Green, Andy Griffith, O. Henry (William Sidney Porter), Hatcher Hughes, Andrew Jackson, Andrew Johnson, Michael Jordan, Charles Kuralt, Sugar Ray Leonard, Ronnie Milsap, Edward R. Murrow, Guy Owen, James K. Polk, Reynolds Price, Sequoyah, Betty Smith, James Taylor, Doc Watson, Thomas Wolfe

- Barbecuing is so competitive in North Carolina that the state holds twenty-five annual cook-offs.
- Towering at 6,684 feet above sea level, Mount Mitchell is the highest peak in the East.
- Three North Carolina natives became U.S. president: Andrew Jackson, Andrew Johnson, and James Polk.
- Shore erosion prompted the Cape Hatteras Lighthouse to be relocated in 1999; it's the tallest lighthouse in the states and the tallest lighthouse in the world to be transported.
- "Cherry Point" in Havelock is the largest Marine Corps Air Base in the United States.
- North Carolina is the second highest producer of hogs in the country.

- At 480 feet high, Fontana Dam is the tallest dam in the East.
- North Carolina is the largest producer of sweet potatoes in the nation.
- Krispy Kreme sold its first doughnut—and thus had its first bakery—in Winston-Salem.

Your Character's Food and Drink

Barbecue has been as much a part of North Carolina as anything else in the state. It is served at almost any celebration, including political fund-raisers, church gatherings, and family picnics. Unlike in other parts of the country where "barbecue" means beef, in North Carolina "barbecue" is pork. The barbecuing in North Carolina is a slow-roasting process that lasts most of the day, with the carcass placed over an oak or hickory fire. North Carolina barbecue sauce is always vinegar-based and seasoned with various herbs and spices. There are also two different styles of North Carolina barbecue: western and eastern. The primary difference is that in the west (often called the "Lexington" style), they add a tomato base to the sauce and roast only the pork shoulders, whereas in the east they forgo the tomato base and cook the entire hog.

North Carolinians also like Southern fried chicken, chitlins, crackling bread, Brunswick stew, catfish, hush puppies, quail, all types of seafood (especially folks on the coast), tomato gravy, various salads (a big one is lettuce coated in a dressing of bacon fat and sugar), casseroles, pickles, preserves, coleslaw, boiled potatoes (with barbecue sauce added to the water), fried cornmeal, and corn bread. Breakfast favorites include homemade biscuits, bacon, country fried ham, redeye gravy, grits, sausage, and buckwheat pancakes. The state's drink is fresh-brewed, sweet iced tea.

Things Your Character Likes to Remember

- The birth of Virgnia Dare.
- Pepsi was invented in New Bern (1898).
- Sir Walter Raleigh founded the first English colony in America on Roanoke Island (1585).
- The University of North Carolina at Chapel Hill is the oldest state university in the United States (1795).
- The Outer Banks host some of the most beautiful beaches and coastal wildlife in the country.
- The Tarheels are always one of the best basketball teams in the nation.
- North Carolina barbecue. Even during the Jim Crow era and the Civil Rights movement, barbecue joints were places where African-Americans and Caucasians gathered together and ignored their racial differences.

Things Your Character Would Like to Forget

- Hurricanes.
- Dayton, Ohio. There's an ongoing feud over who owns bragging rights to the Wright Brothers, who grew up in Dayton. The Ohio town calls itself the birthplace of aviation, whereas Kill Devil Hills calls itself the home of the first flight.
- Kansas City and Louisiana barbecue.

Myths and Misperceptions About North Carolina

- **The only reason to visit is for the beaches.** The Smoky Mountains anyone?
- **Only country folk inhabit the state.** Lots still do, but Charlotte and Research Triangle Park have attracted many business people and tech professionals.
- **Basketball and barbecue are all residents care about.** Okay, maybe this is true.
- **There's really a town called Mayberry.** This town from *The Andy Griffith Show* never existed outside of your television set.

Interesting Places to Set a Scene

- **Asheville.** The Biltmore Estate, America's largest home and the once-private residence of the Vanderbilts, is here. With its 255-room chateau, award-winning winery and vineyard, and acres of beautiful gardens, it's a treasure. But Asheville also has a

© PhotoDisc/Getty Images

The Bodie Island Lighthouse

For Further Research

Books

Habits of Industry: White Culture and the Transformation of the Carolina Piedmont, by Allen Tullos

A Living Culture in Durham: A Collection of Writings by Durham Area Authors, edited by Judy Hogan

More Than a Game: Why North Carolina Basketball Means So Much to So Many, by Thad Williamson

North Carolina Barbecue: Flavored by Time, by Bob Garner

North Carolina Ghosts and Legends, by Nancy Roberts

The Scots-Irish in the Carolinas, by Billy Kennedy

Web Sites

www.ncgov.com/ (official state site)

www.ncdcr.gov/ (cultural resources)

www.visitnc.com/ (visitor's information)

www.ncwriters.org/ (writer's network site)

www.ibiblio.org/litfest/ (state literary festival)

http://ncmuseumofhistory.org/ (state history)

http://statelibrary.dcr.state.nc.us/nc/cover.htm (state encyclopedia)

www.news-observer.com/ (news and current events)

Still Curious? Why Not Check Out

Cold Mountain, by Charles Frazier

The Fiery Cross, by Diana Gabaldon

A Long and Happy Life, by Reynolds Price

Look Homeward, Angel, by Thomas Wolfe

The Notebook, by Nicholas Sparks

Out to Canaan, by Jan Karon

The Sharp Teeth of Love: A Novel, by Doris Betts

A Short History of a Small Place: A Novel, by T.R. Pearson

Walking Across Egypt, by Clyde Edgerton

---

flourishing and eclectic arts community, where mountain folk meet cultured urbanites. There's also lots of upscale shopping, art galleries, museums, restaurants, and nightlife. Literary lovers frequent Asheville because F. Scott and Zelda Fitzgerald lived here, and it's the setting for Thomas Wolfe's *Look Homeward, Angel*.

- **Barbecue Trail.** This twenty-five-mile stretch of U.S. 52 between Salisbury and Albemarle (including Lexington and Greensboro) was coined "Barbecue Trail" by barbecue guru Bob Garner, because the towns have become known for their tasty and numerous barbecue joints. Lexington, for example, has only about seventeen thousand residents but at least two dozen barbecue joints.

- **Blue Ridge Parkway.** The 250-mile stretch of the 469-mile parkway links Shenandoah National Park in Virginia to the Great Smoky Mountains in North Carolina. The numerous communities along this wildflower- and tree-filled road offer a variety of festivals, cultural events, and other activities that honor mountain living.

- **Charlotte.** Charlotte is the gem of the New South, sporting towering skyscrapers and successful banking, insurance, and transportation industries. The city is becoming culturally significant, too, as it showcases the splendid Mint Museum of Art, the interesting Discovery Place (science and technology), the Charlotte Symphony Orchestra, and the Charlotte Pops. The city still hasn't found its "cultural identity," though, as it has no great historical legacy and the new big boomtown is mostly filled with strip malls and suburban sprawl. One other disappointment is that while your Charlotte character might be proud of his city's business successes, he certainly won't be too happy with the state of Charlotte's once-beloved Hornets—the team split for New Orleans, leaving the state of North Carolina with no professional basketball team. Now that stings.

- **Grandfather Mountain.** Inhabited by bears, river otters, panthers, deer, eagles, and a nature museum, Grandfather Mountain is one of North Carolina's natural wonders. These days your character can drive to the mountaintop and enjoy the breathtaking vistas and curious rock formations. She'll even get a unique view of Charlotte's skyline, but she'll have to get out of her car to walk across the 228-foot Mile High Swinging Bridge.

- **The Outer Banks.** This chain of barrier islands can boast of having Cape Hatteras, wildlife refuges, maritime forests, the tallest sand dunes on the East Coast (Jockey's Ridge State Park), exceptional restaurants, and lots of vacationers having fun in the sun (without an overload of high-rise hotels, as in Myrtle Beach). It's also where Wilbur and Orville Wright made the first powered airplane flight in 1903 (in Kill Devil Hills). There's even a lovely herb, wildflower, and rose garden surrounded by an array of antique statuary. Deracoke Island is also a gem, as no cars are allowed on the island and wild ponies run free on a 160-acre expanse.

- **Triangle Park.** (See page 239 for details on Raleigh, Durham, and Chapel Hill.)
- **Wilmington.** The state's most frequented port, Wilmington is the economic, cultural, medical, and educational center of North Carolina's southeast coast. It's known for its weather-tracking, historic preservation (The World War II battleship *USS North Carolina* rests in Cape Fear River), Riverfest and Azalea Festivals, and Screen Gems Studios. Screen Gems Studios is home to more than three hundred film, television, and commercial productions, including *Dawson's Creek, Matlock, Lolita, Weekend at Bernie's, Blue Velvet, Crimes of the Heart, The Hudsucker Proxy,* and the heroic *Teenage Mutant Ninja Turtles.*
- **Winston-Salem.** With its restored colonial village that revisits the eighteenth-century Moravian way of life, Old Salem is a trip back in time. Your character can even feast on what the Moravians ate; beef ragout and chicken pot pie are two favorites. What makes Winston-Salem at large so distinct is that the community fosters its artists, writers, educational institutions, and museums—it proves why it calls itself the "City of Arts."

Raleigh-Durham-Chapel Hill Facts and Peculiarities Your Character Might Know

- The University of North Carolina at Chapel Hill, established in 1789, is the nation's oldest public university.
- Raleigh is The Tar Heel state's capital city.
- This area is not a city. The Raleigh-Durham-Chapel Hill Metro Statistical Area (MSA) is a five-county region.
- Raleigh can boast of four excellent museums, and all are free, which is why the city calls itself "the Smithsonian of the South."
- In 1924, Trinity College was renamed Duke University after the tobacco-farming-turned-tobacco-titan Duke family donated a forty-million-dollar endowment to the university.
- Research Triangle Park (RTP) was founded in 1959 and contains over 140 research-and-development organizations. The three anchoring corners of the triangle are North Carolina State University, Duke University, and the University of North Carolina at Chapel Hill. The park itself, though, is based in Durham County, so it's not right in the center of the three cities but is equidistant from the three universities in those cities.
- Chapel Hill has a reputation for being one of America's greatest book-loving cities.
- Durham gets a bad rap. Although it's accurate to say that RTP is in Durham midway between Chapel Hill and Raleigh, those who work in RTP prefer to say that they work in RTP—not that they work in Durham.
- This area consistently ranks among the nation's best places to live, visit, and do business.
- The Triangle Universities' Computation Center was established in 1966 and is one of the world's largest university computing centers.
- Booker T. Washington once referred to residents of Durham as the "sanest group of white people I have ever met."
- Chapel Hill has grown rapidly over the past thirty years, mostly because of the University of North Carolina at Chapel Hill, whose enrollment has tripled from 8,791 in 1960 to 24,872 in 2000.

Raleigh-Durham-Chapel Hill Basics That Shape Your Character

Typical Raleigh porches exhibit a "Southern feel"

Population: 1.3 million in the Greater Metro statistical area

Prevalent Religions: Baptist still rule the area, and there are smaller pockets of Roman Catholicism, Methodist, Presbyterian, Pentecostal, and Lutheran.

Top Employers: Research Triangle Institute, Nortel Networks Corporation, IBM, Northern Telecom Ltd., Cisco Systems, SAS Institute, GlaxoSmithKline, Blue Cross Blue Shield of North Carolina, U.S. Environmental Protection Agency, National Institute of Environmental Health Sciences

Per Capita Income: $30,680

Ethnic Makeup (in percent): Caucasian 69.3%, African-American 22.7%, Hispanic 3.1%, Asian 2.9%, Native American 0.4%, Other 1.6%

Average Daily Temperature: January, 39° F; July, 75° F

Newspapers and Magazines: *The Herald-Sun, The News & Observer, Triangle Business Journal*

Free Weekly Alternative Paper: *Independent Weekly*

- Famous politicians from the area include Elizabeth Dole, "Mutt" Evans, Maynard Jackson, William Mangum, Floyd B. McKissick Sr., Kenneth C. Royall Jr., Terry Sanford, Elna Spaulding, William B. Umstead, and Willis Whichard.
- The area has Southern tradition and hospitality, but it's a diverse and tolerant community that's home to a large population of gays and lesbians as well as immigrants from all over the world.

If Your Character . . .

If Your Character Is a Struggling Artist, she lives in Carborro. With a slogan like "Carborro, North Carolina . . . a little to the left," it's no surprise this is where an artist would live. Actually, the town was recently named by *USA Today* as one of the country's "ten great places with arts-filled spaces."

If Your Character Is All About the Business of Research, he works in Research Triangle Park. This massive research facility is like no other in the country.

If Your Characters Are Raising a Family, they live in Forest Hills. This 1920s-looking, middle-class neighborhood has many period revival-style houses and even looks a bit like some neighborhoods in Boston.

If Your Character Is Hip and Trendy, he lives in a condo in downtown Raleigh. Just make sure the condo is inside the belt line, because that's where the cool people live.

If Your Character Wears a Blue Collar at Work, she lives in Durham. This is known as a blue-collar town, more so than its counterparts Raleigh and Chapel Hill.

If Your Character Smells of Money, he lives in Hope Valley Country Club. Located in southwest Durham, this upper-class neighborhood is situated around a golf course and contains large homes on landscaped yards. This was the area's first country club suburb.

Local Grub Your Character Might Love

Of course, barbecue with fries and coleslaw and Southern dishes like chicken and mashed potatoes with gravy are still a favorite here, and many people stick with tried-and-true Southern recipes. However, what's great about this area of North Carolina is the variety. Some restaurants, for instance, might offer nonSouthern cuisine, like sushi, but then also offer something entirely Southern, like biscuits 'n' gravy as a side dish. RTP has brought lots of immigrants and with them a variety of international eateries. Long-standing local legends include Clyde Cooper's Barbecue, Raleigh's oldest barbecue shack (in an old red-brick building), and Big Ed's City Market Restaurant in Raleigh. Durham's Magnolia Grill is legendary for its wines and interesting, delicious entrées. The Southern Brewery's wood-grilled smoked meats—from blackened salmon to New York strip—are a hit. The Angus Barn is a pricey mainstay, as is the Old Bartlett Mangum House. Other favorites include the Hayesbarton Diner, the 42nd Street Oyster Bar, Chargrill, and many others.

Interesting and Peculiar Places to Set a Scene

- **Alive After Five at Fayetteville Street Mall.** Every spring this space in downtown Raleigh becomes the site of a huge party (which lasts from April until September), showcasing the best local music talent around. Locals leave work early, pack the cooler full of cold ones, and spend the evening hanging out with friends and jamming to the tunes. This event is a partying character's Southern paradise.
- **Capitol Corral.** If your character is up for a hopping dance floor with bright, flashing lights and big, mirrored walls, he needs to be at the Capitol Corral, the oldest club in the area.
- **Duke Homestead and Tobacco Museum.** This area will let your character get a taste of North Carolina tobacoo without taking a puff or a chew. He can see a tobacco curing barn, a tobacco packing house, one of old Ashington Duke's tobacco log factories, and the Duke Home. The tobacco museum offers all sorts of information, including living history demonstrations of what life was like on a typical yeoman farm in the 1800s.
- **Duke University.** Duke's west campus is one of the most beautiful campus areas in the world, thanks to the many Gothic buildings and the awesome landscaping. Of most distinction is the incredible Duke Chapel, one of the last great collegiate English Gothic structures. Amidst the rib-vaulted ceiling, flying buttresses, and pointed arches, the chapel boasts a 5,000-pipe organ, a 210-foot bell tower, a 50-bell clarion, and 77 stained glass windows with 800 figures. Even when

the Blue Devils don't make it to the Final Four, they still have the chapel. . . .

- **During Happy Hour at the Southend Brewery.** This is where your young professional will go when the working day is done. It's really a huge warehouse with exposed brick and art nouveau furnishings. One side of the building is a popular restaurant, while the other is a busy, here's-where-I-gotta-be-seen bar. It's a big hit with the RTP crowd.
- **During the Central Intercollegiate Athletic Association (CIAA) Men's and Women's Basketball Championships.** These folks don't perceive this as just another basketball tournament—it's a week of nonstop parties, concerts, step shows, contests, educational forums, fashion shows, and, oh yes, even exciting basketball games.
- **Foster's in Cameron Village.** If your character needs a good single's place, have him come here for lots of flirting, dancing, talking, drinking, and hooking up.
- **Museum of Life and Science.** This fifty-thousand-square-foot interactive science-technology center covers seventy-eight acres, is home to Apollo XVI (one of the nation's four unlaunched lunar landers), a restored Piedmont Airliner, and lots of other cool stuff. This would be a perfect place to set a family scene; the kids can go riding by on an amusement park railway en route to the dinosaur trail or the petting zoo.
- **North Carolina State University (NC State).** NC State is one of the nation's lead institutions for science, engineering, and technology, and it also has a strong humanities program, a vibrant theater, and one of the premier colleges of design. NC State's athletics program is outstanding.
- **Patterson's Mill Country Store.** This little turn-of-the-twentieth-century country store on Farrington Road is both a doctor's office and a pharmacy. It has on hand lots of Americana memorabilia, from pharmaceutical stuff to tobacco signs.
- **Research Triangle Park.** One of the largest research parks in the world, the park is eight miles long and two miles wide, with thirteen million square feet of building. The seven-thousand-acre site is dramatic, and buildings can cover only 30 percent of the land. The GlaxoSmithKline campus can be seen in 1981's *Brainstorm,* starring Natalie Wood.
- **Sarah P. Duke Gardens.** What was once a construction and a garbage dump is now one of the most peaceful settings in the area—and one of the most romantic.

Flowers, gazebos, little pathways . . . ah. The little white bridge just might be the perfect place for your head-over-heels character to propose to his lovely lady.

- **Shelley Lake Park.** Fishing, canoeing, sailing, rowboating, pedal boating, biking, hiking, and picnicking—that's what goes on here. Families love this place, as it has plenty of swings, a playground, and lots of hungry ducks ready to be fed by happy little kids.
- **Sunday Brunch Jazz at Weaver Street Market.** Have your character spend a Sunday picnicking on the grass as he smells the freshly baked bread and brewing coffee from across the green. Oh, there's also the live music, the market shoppers, the families and sweethearts on their blankets, and the aging hippies in their lawn chairs.
- **On The Manning House grounds.** This impressive Queen Anne in Old North Durham is an area gem, with ceiling medallions and ornate Victorian mantelpieces. Heck, if it was good enough for Kevin Costner and Susan Sarandon in 1987's *Bull Durham.* . . .
- **The University of North Carolina at Chapel Hill.** Touted as "The University of the People," this is to many the Southern side of heaven. It's the oldest state university in the country (1789), and it's situated on the top of a scenic hill. The campus is gorgeous, and the university has a solid reputation as one of the best schools in the country. Then there are the Tarheels. . . .

Exceptionally Grand Things Your Character Is Proud Of

- Research Triangle Park's reputation as a top research area.
- The cuisine.
- Local theater, deemed the best in the South.
- Duke's medical center—one of the most reputable in the world.
- The areas science museums.
- The Carolina Hurricanes, who in 2002 won their first Stanley Cup, which was held in Raleigh.
- Raleigh's downtown—places like Powerhouse Square, City Market, Cameron Village, and Glenwood Avenue are all hotbeds of activity.
- NC State graduates. They have a great reputation for creating start-up companies that do well. Also, in 2000 IBM announced that it had hired more graduates from NC State than from any other university in the country.
- Coach Kay Yow's U.S. women's basketball team,

For Further Research

Books

Celebrating a Triangle Millennium, by Charlie Gaddy

Chapel Hill: An Illustrated History, by James Vickers

Durham County: A History of Durham County, North Carolina, by Jean Bradley Anderson

A Generosity of Spirit: The Early History of the Research Triangle Park, by Albert N. Link

Homelands: Southern Jewish Identity in Durham and Chapel Hill, North Carolina, by Leonard Rogoff

Light on the Hill: A History of the University of North Carolina at Chapel Hill, by William D. Snider

A Living Culture in Durham, edited by Judy Hogan et al.

Raleigh: A Living History of North Carolina's Capital, edited by David Perkins

Taste of the Triangle: A Guide to the Finer Restaurants of Raleigh, Durham, Cary, and Chapel Hill With Recipes, by Juli Brown

Web Sites

www.rtp.org/ (Research Triangle Park info)

www.trianglecommunity.com/ (area community information)

www.durham-nc.com/ (Durham Convention and Visitors Bureau)

www.durhamchamber.org/ (Greater Durham Chamber of Commerce)

www.chapelhillnews.com/ (Chapel Hill news)

www.raleighcvb.org/ (Raleigh visitor information)

www.news-observer.com/ (Raleigh's *The News & Observer*)

http://triangle.citysearch.com/ (events and information)

www.ci.chapel-hill.nc.us/ (official Chapel Hill site)

Still Curious? Why Not Check Out

Bandwagon

Billie Bathgate

Black Business in the New South: A Social History of the North Carolina Mutual Life Insurance Company, by Walter B. Weare

Brainstorm

Bull Durham

The Handmaid's Tale

Immortal

Kate Vaiden, by Reynolds Price

Kiss the Girls

Oral History, by Lee Smith

Piedmont Plantation: The Bennehan-Cameron Family Lands in North Carolina, by Jean Bradley Anderson

The Portrait

The Program

Raleigh's Eden, by Inglis Fletcher

Raney, by Clyde Edgerton

Trespassing: My Sojourn in the Halls of Privilege, by Gwendolyn M. Parker

which won the gold medal in the 1988 Summer Olympics in Seoul.

Your Character Loves

- The area's world-class universities.
- Basketball, particularly Atlantic Coast Conference (ACC) and CIAA basketball.
- Exploris. Built in 1999, this is an interactive museum about cultures, economies, and natural environments around the world.
- Local authors, like Jean Bradley Anderson, James Applewhite, Clyde Edgerton, Eli Evans, John Hope Franklin, Pauli Murray, Gwendolyn Parker, Francis Gray Patton, Reynolds Price, Walter B. Weare.
- The Durham Bulls, the Carolina Storm, the Durham Braves, the Durham Striders.
- Southern hospitality and good manners.
- One of the following but not all three: The North Carolina Tarheels, The NC State Wolfpack, The Duke Blue Devils.

Your Character Hates

- Traffic problems in and out of RTP.
- Wild college kids partying on her property, often leaving empty beer bottles and bits of regurgitation on her lawn for her to clean up.
- Two of the following but not all three: The North Carolina Tarheels, The NC State Wolfpack, The Duke Blue Devils.

North Dakota

Significant Events Your Character Has Probably Thought About

- The Lewis and Clark Expedition wintered here from 1804 to 1805 with the Mandan Native Americans.
- In the early 1800s, Hudson Bay Company and The North West Company established trading posts here, spawning industry that dominated the region for more than half a century. However, conflict over the Red River settlement got intense between the companies and they merged in 1821.
- John Jacob Astor's American Fur Company controlled the region's trade during the middle of the 1800s.
- President Teddy Roosevelt visited the area in September 1883 to hunt bison, and he soon became interested in the cattle business, forming the Maltese Cross and the Elkhorn Ranches.
- Antoine de Vallombrosa, the Marquis de Mores, also came here in 1883 and made lots of money with his beef-packing plant, stagecoach line, freight company, refrigerated railway cars, and cattle and sheep ranches.
- Sitting Bull was killed during the Ghost Dance unrest of 1890.
- The Nonpartisan League was started in 1915.
- Governor William Langer was elected in 1932, convicted on a federal charge of misconduct in office in 1934, and was reelected in 1936.
- In 1981, gambling for "charitable purposes" became legalized.
- Ruth Meiers became the state's first woman lieutenant governor in 1984.
- In 1986, Democrats gained control of the North Dakota Senate—for first time in the state history.
- In 1988, the state saw its first major drought since the 1930s.
- In 1997, the state was rocked by a flooding Red River, which severely damaged areas including Fargo and Grand Forks.

North Dakota Facts and Peculiarities Your Character Might Know

- Rugby is supposed to be the geographical center of North America. It celebrates this with a fifteen-foot obelisk.

North Dakota Basics That Shape Your Character

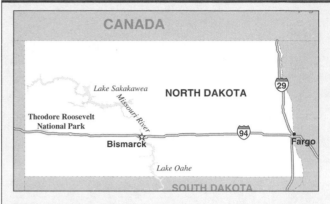

Motto: Liberty and Union, Now and Forever: One and Inseparable

Population: 642,200

Prevalent Religions: Christianity, mostly Lutheran, Roman Catholic, Methodist, and Baptist

Major Industries: Wheat, cattle, barley, sunflowers, milk, sugar beets, food processing, machinery, mining

Ethnic Makeup (in percent): Caucasian 92.4%, African-American 0.6%, Hispanic 0.6%, Asian 0.6%, Native American 4.9%, Other 0.4%

Famous North Dakotans: Angie Dickinson, Ivan Dmitre, Phyllis Frelich, William Gass, Phil D. Jackson, Louis L'Amour, Peggy Lee, Arthur Peterson, Eric Sevareid, Ann Sothern, Dorothy Stickney, Edward K. Thompson, Era Bell Thompson, Lawrence Welk, Larry Woiwode

- Dakota means "friends" or "allies"; it is a Sioux word.
- It's been called "The Sioux State," "Peace Garden State," "Flickertail State," and "Rough Rider State."
- The state is a land of prairies, ranches, rivers, small towns, and wheat farms.
- The International Peace Garden straddles the border between North Dakota and Manitoba.
- There's only one synthetic natural gas producer in the United States, and that's in North Dakota.
- The Dakota Dinosaur Museum in Dickinson is noted for its dozen or so full-scale dinosaurs, and its thousands of rock, mineral, and fossil specimens.
- North Dakota grows more sunflowers than does any other state in nation.

Your Character's Food and Drink

Milk is the official state beverage. Other than that, it's mostly meat and potatoes.

Things Your Character Likes to Remember

- Big burgers. The town of Rutland holds a spot in the *Guinness Book of World Records* for having cooked and eaten the world's largest hamburger. Almost ten thousand people showed up to munch on the 3,500-pound burger.
- Roger Maris—this baseball great came from Fargo.
- Hillsboro—it's supposed to have some of the most fertile farmland in the world.
- Buffalo. Frontier Village in Jamestown displays the world's largest buffalo monument.
- The Paul Broste Rock Museum in Parshall. The world-famous structure of natural granite was built entirely with volunteer labor.

Things Your Character Would Like to Forget

- The state's population keeps decreasing.
- The United Mine Workers strike in the late 1980s.
- The 1987 fire at the agricultural chemical warehouse in Minot, which caused ten thousand people to flee their homes because of the toxic fumes.

Myths and Misperceptions About North Dakota

- **Nobody lives here.** Actually, 642,200 people do.
- **It's all dry, rugged prairie land.** Check out Lake Sakakawea, which is almost two hundred miles long and allegedly covers about sixteen hundred miles.
- **North Dakotans wish they were somewhere else.** Actually, a lot of the residents love their quiet, big sky state. There's even a motto for the Minot Air Force Base: "Only the Best Come North."

Interesting Places to Set a Scene

- **A wagon train.** The Fort Seward Wagon Train is a weeklong ride in which old horse-drawn (and mule-drawn) wagons make a train and stop each night to camp as their forefathers did.
- **Bismarck.** Situated on a hill overlooking the Missouri River, this state capital was a campground for Lewis and Clark in 1804 and later benefited from both river traffic (thanks to a steamboat port called the "Crossing on the Missouri") and the building of the Northern Pacific Railroad. Today it's the state's major trade center for livestock, dairy, wheat, telecommunications, and oil (found in the reserves in nearby Williston Basin).
- **Fargo.** Named for William G. Fargo of Wells-Fargo Express Company fame, this is the state's largest city (seventy-five thousand) and the Red River Valley's retail and wholesale center, with many factories centering around the farm and cattle business. Now it's also the gaming center of the state, with about thirty casinos in the city.
- **Grand Forks.** This river town was once a French fur trading post and a popular railroad stop, but these days it's home to the University of North Dakota.
- **Kenmare.** If your character likes to hunt wild geese, send him here, as Kenmare is the "Goose Capital of the North," with an annual snow goose count of 400,000 birds.
- **Leipzig.** No, this isn't where Nietzsche broke down and hugged a whipped horse (that was in Germany),

The North Dakota horizon

For Further Research

Books

The Atlas of North Dakota, by L.R. Goodman and R.J. Eidem

Dakota: A Spiritual Geography, by Kathleen Norris

Ethnic Heritage in North Dakota, edited by Francie M. Berg

History of North Dakota, by Elwyn B. Robinson

Land in Her Own Name: Women as Homesteaders in North Dakota, by H. Elaine Lindgren

North Dakota Wildlife Viewing Guide, by Joseph Knue

Web Sites

http://discovernd.com/ (travel information)

www.ndtourism.com (tourism)

www.state.nd.us/hist// (state history)

www.minot.k12.nd.us/mps/cc/ndhistory.html (history)

www.sendit.nodak.edu/ndsl/cftb/ (writer's site)

www.bismarcktribune.com/ (news)

Still Curious? Why Not Check Out

Four Winds Returning: A Novel, by Richard Dreamwalker

Love Medicine, by Louise Erdrich

Old Indian Days, by Charles Alexander Eastman

Ranch Life and the Hunting Trail, by Theodore Roosevelt

Set the Ploughshare Deep: A Prairie Memoir, by Timothy Murphy

---

but this is a small, friendly German prairie town that's known for its annual Oktoberfest.

- **Medora.** Although the place has only about one hundred residents, in many ways it's one of the state's best towns, as it's maintained much of its historical glory. The flamboyant Marquis de Mores (Antoine de Vallombrosa) founded the town (and the historic Chateau de Mores house is still standing with its original furnishings). Teddy Roosevelt lived nearby in the 1880s.

- **New Rockford.** The annual Central North Dakota Steam Threshers Reunion (boasting a variety of antique farm machinery) is one of the state's main annual events, and it's held here during the third weekend of September.

- **Teddy Roosevelt National Park.** These seventy thousand acres of badlands and rugged landscape honor the conservationist president and contain deer, bison, and bighorn sheep.

- **United Tribes Powwow.** This is one of the biggest powwows in the country. Held in Bismarck in August, it's a festival of dancing, singing, food, games, and other Native American events.

Ohio

Ohio Basics That Shape Your Character

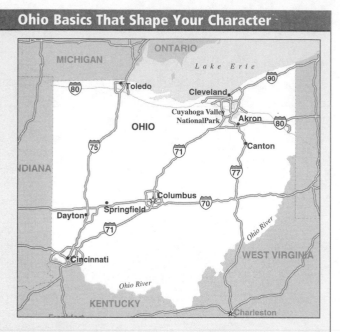

Motto: With God, All Things Are Possible

Population: 11.4 million

Prevalent Religions: Roman Catholicism, Protestantism (mainly Baptist and Methodist), and Judaism

Major Industries: Transportation equipment, fabricated metal products, machinery, food processing, electric equipment, soybeans, dairy products, corn, tomatoes, hogs, cattle, poultry, eggs

Ethnic Makeup (in percent): Caucasian 85%, African-American 11.5%, Hispanic 1.9%, Asian 1.2%, Native American 0.2%, Other 0.2%

Per Capita Income: $27,081

Famous Ohioans: Neil Armstrong, Halle Berry, Erma Bombeck, Dorothy Dandridge, Doris Day, Paul Laurence Dunbar, Thomas Alva Edison, John Glenn, Bob Hope, Dean Martin, Toni Morrison, Paul Newman, Annie Oakley, Jesse Owens, Norman Vincent Peale, Arthur M. Schlesinger Jr., Steven Spielberg, Gloria Steinem, Orville Wright

Significant Events Your Character Has Probably Thought About

- In 1763, France ceded the Ohio country to Great Britain at the end of the French and Indian War, and in 1783 Britain ceded the Ohio country to the new United States.

- The Ordinance of 1787 made the Ohio country part of the Northwest Territory.

- In 1794, General Anthony Wayne led American troops to victory over various tribes of Native Americans, headed by Miami Chief Little Turtle, at the Battle of Fallen Timbers (near what is now Toledo). A year later, the Native Americans formally surrendered by signing The Treaty of Greenville, which opened Ohio to white settlers.

- Ohio became a state in 1803.

- Americans defended Ohio land from British forces during the War of 1812, and in 1813 Ohio's northern border was secured by victories at the Battle of Lake Erie and the Battle of the Thames.

- Columbus succeeded Chillicothe as the state capital in 1816.

- In 1832, the 308-mile Ohio and Erie Canal opened in the eastern part of the state, and in 1845 the state's western canal, the 301-mile Miami and Erie Canal, was completed.

- The American Federation of Labor was founded in Columbus in 1886, marking a major development in the country's modern trade union movement.

- A statewide flood in 1913 left nearly five hundred dead and caused $100 million in damages in Dayton and the surrounding Miami Valley alone. This led to the founding of the Miami Conservancy District in 1914 to build a flood-control system.

- The 241-mile Ohio Turnpike was completed in 1955 and was traveled by forty-four thousand vehicles the first day it opened.

- Carl Stokes was elected mayor of Cleveland in 1967, making him the first African-American leader of a major American city.

- In 1970, four students were killed and nine were wounded when Ohio National Guard troops opened fire during an anti-Vietnam War demonstration at Kent State University.

Ohio Facts and Peculiarities Your Character Might Know

- Ohio is the birthplace of seven U.S. presidents: Ulysses S. Grant, Rutherford B. Hayes, James A. Garfield,

Benjamin Harrison, William McKinley, William H. Taft, and Warren G. Harding. Another president, William Henry Harrison, was an Ohio resident at the time he was elected.

- Oberlin College, founded in 1833, was the country's first interracial, coeducational college.
- Ohio is the thirty-fourth largest state in the United States, but the seventh most populated.

Things Your Character Likes to Remember

- Chief Wahoo, the culturally insensitive yet stubbornly adored mascot of the Cleveland Indians.
- Its two famous astronauts: John Glenn was the first American to orbit the earth (1962) and the oldest (age seventy-seven) to take part in a mission, and Neil Armstrong was the first person to step on the moon (1969).
- Its two famous Halls of Fame: Cleveland's Rock and Roll Hall of Fame and Museum, and Canton's Pro Football Hall of Fame.

Things Your Character Would Like to Forget

- The Kent State deaths.
- U.S. Representative James Traficant Jr., a nine-term Democrat congressman from Youngstown who was found guilty of bribery, racketeering, and tax evasion in a 2002 federal jury trial. That he chose to represent himself and made national news for his bizarre courtroom antics added to the embarrassment.

Myths and Misperceptions About Ohio

- **Ohio is just farmland.** Suburban sprawl continues to encroach upon Ohio's farms, and the percentage of the state's land devoted to agriculture decreased nearly 20 percent in the latter part of twentieth century.
- **All major cities rest on the banks of the Ohio River.** Only Cincinnati does. Cleveland is on the southern shore of Lake Erie, and Columbus is in the middle of the state where the Olentangy and Scioto Rivers cross.

Interesting Places to Set a Scene

- **Athens.** This is home of Ohio University, the state's first higher-education institution. The town's conservative residents are often at odds with the liberal campus, especially during the university's popular Hallow-

een celebrations and the traditional springtime change "riots," when students take to the streets to protest bars closing early.

- **Chillicothe.** What was the first capital of Ohio is now best known for its Mead paper mill and the outdoor drama, *Tecumseh!* Needless to say, in summer it's hopping with tourists, but in winter it's pretty dead.
- **The Circleville Pumpkin Show.** Touted by organizers as "The Greatest Free Show on Earth," the largest and oldest festival in Ohio features the Miss Pumpkin pageant, a hog-calling contest, and numerous parades. The highly anticipated opening event, the Pumpkin Weigh-In, has seen the likes of eight-hundred-pound pumpkins in recent years.
- **Cincinnati.** (See page 250 for more detailed information on Cincinnati.)
- **Cleveland.** (See page 254 for more detailed information on Cleveland.)
- **Columbus.** (See page 258 for more detailed information on Columbus.)
- **Dayton.** Home of the Wright brothers' bicycle shop, where they researched and built the world's first power-driven, heavier-than-air craft; site of tense 1995 negotiations involving presidents of Serbia, Croatia,

Amish road sign in Northeastern Ohio

© PhotoDisc/Getty Images

For Further Research

Books

The Great Road: The Building of the Baltimore and Ohio, the Nation's First Railroad, 1828–1853, by James D. Dilts

Elusive Empires: Constructing Colonialism in the Ohio Valley, 1673–1800, by Eric Hinderaker

Going to Cincinnati: A History of the Blues in the Queen City, by Steven C. Tracy

The Ohio Frontier: An Anthology of Early Writings, edited by Emily Foster

Ohio Oddities: A Guide to the Curious Attractions of the Buckeye State, by Neil Zurcher

Ohio Politics, edited by Alexander P. Lamis and Mary Anne Sharkey

Web Sites

www.ohiohistory.org (Ohio Historical Society)
www.state.oh.us (official state site)
www.oplin.lib.oh.us (Ohio Public Library Information Network)
http://www.onnnews.com/ (state news)

Still Curious? Why Not Check Out

Air Force One
The Budget (weekly Amish newspaper)
Go Tigers!
Ohio Magazine
Plain and Happy Living: Amish Recipes and Remedies, by Emma Byler
The Shawshank Redemption
Winesburg, Ohio, by Sherwood Anderson

---

and Bosnia that led to the signing of the Dayton Peace Accord; and location of Hangar 18, the Wright-Patterson Air Force Base storage facility that is rumored to contain alien spacecraft wreckage from the 1947 Roswell incident as well as living and dead alien specimens.

- **Holmes County.** The largest Amish settlement in the nation lives and works in this east-central Ohio county; nearly half of its 38,943 residents are of Amish descent. Your character is likely to get stuck driving behind a black buggy on the way to the county's most popular towns, Millersburg and Berlin, where stores offering handcrafted furniture and secret-recipe Swiss cheese abound. For a dose of everyday Amish life, your character should attend an auction and watch the locals bid on livestock, produce, and other essentials.

- **The Longaberger Home Office in Newark, Ohio.** The company headquarters of famously collected Longaberger baskets is a seven-story replica of one of their best-sellers. Built in 1997 of stucco-covered steel beams, the humongous basket welcomes collectors and other curious folk for thirty-minute tours.

- **Kelleys Island.** The largest American island in Lake Erie, Kelleys Island is a well-known vacation spot that caters equally to history buffs and outdoor enthusiasts. The former will flock to Glacial Grooves State Memorial to see the largest incidence of glacial scour-

ing in North America, as well as to Inscription Rock State Memorial to examine a limestone boulder covered with pictographs carved by the Lake Erie Native Americans hundreds of years ago. The latter will spend time bicycling and hiking the island's trails, boating and fishing, or scuba diving around the many shipwrecks. Your character can stay in one of the many bed-and-breakfast inns or pitch a tent at a prime campsite overlooking the North Bay shore at Kelleys Island State Park.

- **Mansfield.** The Ohio State Reformatory, built in 1896 and closed in 1990, is the city's claim to fame. A preservation society renamed the supposedly haunted penitentiary as Mansfield Reformatory and began offering guided tours of the facility in 1996. Movies such as *The Shawshank Redemption* and *Air Force One* have been shot here.

- **Marietta.** Ohio's first permanent Caucasian settlement is still a relatively small town (population 14,857) with intense pride in its history. Marietta maintains the most brick streets of any other Ohio city, and its downtown has been carefully preserved, with many of its buildings and homes more than one hundred years old.

- **Zanesville.** It has what's deemed "Zanesville Pottery"—maybe too much of it—and it's home to Zane Grey, the novelist for whom the city is named.

- **Yellow Springs.** Once a popular health resort for people seeking the Yellow Springs' supposedly curative waters, this small community is best described as "earthy," liberal, and welcoming. Antioch College students and the town's four thousand residents mingle harmoniously with a shared passion for social awareness and activism. Downtown offers an art-house movie theater, vegetarian-friendly restaurants, and independent shops selling books, Birkenstocks, hand-made jewelry, and more. The area is a nature-lover's kind of place, with miles of bike trails converted from railroads and hiking trails through Glen Helen Nature Preserve and John Bryan State Park. Young's Jersey Dairy, a working dairy farm, is a popular destination for families who want to pet goats, play putt-putt golf, and enjoy homemade ice cream.

Cincinnati

Cincinnati Basics That Shape Your Character

The Tyler Davidson Fountain in Cincinnati's Fountain Square

Population: 331,258 in the city limits; 1.98 million in the Greater Metro area

Prevalent Religions: Roman Catholic, Baptist, Pentecostal, Methodist, some Lutheran, Presbyterian, Episcopalian, Judaism, and Church of Jesus Christ of Latter-day Saints

Top Employers: University of Cincinnati, Procter & Gamble, Health Alliance of Greater Cincinnati, Kroger, Mercy Health Partners, Cincinnati Public Schools, TriHealth, Children's Hospital Medical Center, City of Cincinnati, Fifth Third Bank

Per Capita Income: $33,953

Average Daily Temperature: January, 31° F; July, 76° F

Ethnic Makeup (in percent): Caucasian 52.97%, African-American 42.92%, Hispanic 1.28%, Asian 1.55%, Native American 0.21%, Other 1.07%

Newspapers and Magazines: *The Cincinnati Enquirer, The Cincinnati Post, Cincinnati Herald, Business Courier, Cincinnati Magazine*

Free Weekly Alternative Papers: *CityBeat, Snitch*

Cincinnati Facts and Peculiarities Your Character Might Know

- The East Side vs. West Side thing. The East Side is considered more white collar, with more cultural events and many unique stores and restaurants. The West Side is thought to be more blue collar, with chain restaurants, bowling alleys, and stores that could be "Anytown USA." Many East-Siders rarely venture to the West Side.
- Cincinnati is known as "Porkopolis" due to its thriving pork industry in the early nineteenth century; "Queen City of the West" is the city's preferred nickname.
- History says that Cincinnati—like Rome—is built on seven hills; however, there are a total of twenty-four "hill" and "mount" communities in the area.
- The 1869 Red Stockings were deemed the first professional baseball club.
- In 1973, Theodore Berry became the first African-American mayor of Cincinnati. Three years later, Cincinnati elected its first female mayor, Bobbie Sterne.
- "Over-the-Rhine," the downtown area north of Central Parkway, received its name from German immigrants who settled there in the nineteenth century. At that time the Parkway was the Miami-Erie Canal, which the Germans affectionately referred to as the Rhine.
- The big sporting event in town is the Crosstown Shootout, a legendary basketball game between rivals Xavier Musketeers and Cincinnati Bearcats.
- Cincinnatians say "Please?" instead of "What did you say?"
- The city held its first "strong mayor" election in 2001, with Charlie Luken as its winner.

If Your Character . . .

If Your Character Is Alternative, he'll spend time in Clifton. University of Cincinnati's stomping grounds is, not surprisingly, packed with bars, coffeehouses, fast-food and ethnic restaurants, unique clothing and gift shops, and an art-house theater.

If Your Character Is Trendy, she shops in Rookwood Pavilion/Rookwood Commons. This two-part open-air shopping development offers its upscale shoppers many new-to-Cincinnati stores and restaurants. Even its organic grocery store is filled with Polo-wearing shoppers—few "earthy" people are in sight.

If Your Character Smells of Old Money, he lives in Indian Hill. No Wal-Marts, no apartment buildings, and practically no crime are what make people spend millions to live here. Homes are situated on no less than one-acre lots; 90 percent of the lots are between three and five acres.

If Your Character Smells of New Money, he lives in Mount Adams. This gentrified area, with its close proximity to downtown and amazing views of the skyline, commands Manhattan-like rents. Old row houses and contemporary condos are tucked between pubs, restaurants, art galleries, and boutiques.

If Your Character Is All About Business, she works in Downtown. Six Fortune 500 companies—American Financial Group, Cinergy, Federated Department Stores Inc., Fifth Third Bancorp, Kroger, and Procter & Gamble—call Cincinnati's downtown home.

If Your Characters Are Raising a Family, they live in Mariemont. Tree-lined streets and sidewalks, a beautiful square, and excellent schools make this suburban community attractive to families. Plus, mom and dad can hop on scenic, curvy Columbia Parkway and get to work downtown in about fifteen minutes.

If Your Character Wears a Blue Collar at Work, he lives in Norwood. This once-booming neighborhood was economically devastated when its General Motors Plant closed in the mid-1980s. Though the construction of several shopping centers has boosted the economy and drawn more white-collar folks to the area, Norwood proudly remains a blue-collar haven.

If Your Character is a Manual Laborer, he lives on the West Side. The western portion of the Greater Cincinnati area has traditionally been home to the city's manual laborers, the blue-collar folk who bowl on Friday nights and catch a Red's game on the weekend. Rows of residential homes with modest, but clean yards.

If Your Character Is a Yuppie, she lives in Hyde Park/Mount Lookout. These affluent, adjacent neighborhoods are teeming with young P&Gers and other professionals who take a daily run around its squares, party in the many upscale bars and restaurants, and live in apartments and houses with perfectly manicured lawns.

Local Grub Your Character Might Love

Cincinnatians love their Skyline Chili (a.k.a. "Cincinnati Chili") served on spaghetti. This un-spicy, secret-recipe chili is rumored to contain cinnamon, mustard, and chocolate. The service is always fast, and menus are only used by the uninitiated. Suit-wearing executives even frequent the chili shops, but they don bibs while eating lunch. An equally sloppy and beloved meal is ribs served at Montgomery Inn at the Boathouse. With fantastic views of the Ohio River, hungry Cincinnatians chow on ribs slathered in world-famous barbecue sauce that has won praise from celebrities like Bob Hope, Mark McGwire, and Britney Spears. Even during snowstorms, people often end their evenings standing in line at Graeter's for scoops of amaretto crunch, black raspberry chip, or eggnog ice cream. Favorite meals at baseball games, street fairs, and Catholic festivals include "brats and metts" (sausages of German heritage) and Hudepohl, a watery, locally brewed beer (also known as "Hudy Delight"). Goetta, a loaf of steel-cut pinhead oatmeal, pork, beef, and seasonings that is sliced and fried, is a popular breakfast item at local diners.

Interesting and Peculiar Places to Set a Scene

- **Union Terminal.** This Art Deco train station that resembles the Superheroes' Hall of Justice now houses three museums and an Omnimax Theater. Your character can explore an eight-thousand-square-foot limestone cave or walk through full-scale re-creations of nineteenth- and twentieth-century Cincinnati settings.
- **Mount Adams Holy Cross Immaculata Church.** Beginning at midnight every Good Friday, thousands of devout Catholics pray a bead of the rosary on each of the eighty-nine steps leading up to the church.
- **The Palm Court Bar at the Omni Netherland Plaza Hotel.** Locals rarely patronize this dimly lit Art Deco bar, making it a perfectly glamorous setting for a secret tryst.
- **Over-the-Rhine.** Its former grandness is still visible, though many of its buildings are run-down or completely abandoned. The poorest and most crime-rid-

den area of Cincinnati is where your character would run into trouble—or cause trouble.

- **A Catholic festival.** Every summer churches all over town set up beer gardens and gambling booths in their parking lots for three or four nights of debauchery that benefits their coffers. These are great places for your character to reminisce with high school friends and sweethearts.

- **The Maisonette.** Your character can celebrate a special occasion at the country's most noted five-star restaurant—it's received Mobil's top rating for thirty-eight consecutive years.

- **Bicentennial Commons.** Built in 1988 for Cincinnati's two-hundredth anniversary celebration, this mile-long park is where your character can really see pigs fly—two bronze, winged hogs flank the entrance. All summer long, visitors enjoy free concerts, after-work parties, festivals, fireworks, and recreational activities like sand volleyball, tennis, and skating.

- **Carew Tower.** For a few bucks, your character can get an unobliterated, fifty-story-high view of the city. Send him downstairs to Tower Place Mall for more grounded thrills.

- **An abandoned subway tunnel or station.** Construction of a subway system ended in 1925 when the six million dollars designated for the system ran out. Though most of the "remains" have been sealed or destroyed, there are still ways for vandals, graffiti artists, and others with nefarious intentions to get underground.

- **Spring Grove Cemetery.** A beautiful and peaceful place to stroll, this 733-acre cemetery includes twelve ponds, many massive stone mausoleums and statues, and the graves of Cincinnati's most notable historical figures.

- **The Roebling Suspension Bridge.** When Cincinnati's most beautiful bridge was finished in 1867, it was the longest in the country. Its designer, John A. Roebling, went on to create the similar-looking but much larger Brooklyn Bridge in 1883.

Exceptionally Grand Things Your Character Is Proud Of

- Her Cincinnati roots. Though Cincinnati's many international companies bring plenty of non-natives to the area, it seems that the majority of Cincinnatians were born and raised here.

- Rookwood Pottery—known all over the world for its tile and sculpture.

- Fountain Square. The heart of downtown, Fountain Square is the place to eat a brown-bag lunch, attend free concerts, or simply enjoy the sunshine. The square's focal point, the Tyler Davidson fountain, was erected in 1871 and painstakingly restored in 2000.

- The Public Library of Cincinnati and Hamilton County. With forty-one branches and nearly ten million volumes, it's one of the five largest libraries in the country.

- The Big Red Machine—one of the best teams in franchise history.

- Cincinnati Zoo and Botanical Gardens. From its "Zoo Babies" exhibit every summer to its "Festival of Lights" every winter, the second-oldest zoo in the United States is a favorite local attraction, especially for families.

Pathetically Sad Things Your Character Is Ashamed Of

- That many suburban Cincinnatians don't go downtown and aren't interested in issues impacting downtown.

- The Mapplethorpe Trial—the city became nationally known as censorship central, a close-minded conservative town that's anti-artistic expression.

- The radiation experiments. During the 1960s and early 1970s, about one hundred cancer patients (most of whom were African-American) became "guinea pigs" at General Hospital; they were exposed to excessive doses of radiation but not told of the dangers.

- Cincinnati has had seventeen riots in its history, more than half related to race issues. The latest riot occurred in April 2001 after a police officer shot a nineteen-year-old unarmed African-American man during a foot chase. The deadliest riot was in 1884; the city's courthouse was burned to the ground and fifty-six people were killed when ten thousand citizens protested the hanging of a half-black man for committing murder while his white accomplice only received twenty years in jail.

- Jerry Springer. Prior to his talk-show career, he was Cincinnati's mayor and a news anchor for the local NBC affiliate.

- Marge Schott. No one's complaining that the former Reds owner known for her racist and anti-Semitic slurs has dropped out of the spotlight.

For Further Research

Books

The Big Pig Gig: Celebrating Pigs in the City, edited by Rick Pender

Boss Cox's Cincinnati: Urban Politics in the Progressive Era, by Zane L. Miller

Changing Plans for America's Inner Cities: Cincinnati's Over-The-Rhine and Twentieth-Century Urbanism, by Zane L. Miller and Bruce Tucker

Cincinnati and the Big Red Machine, by Robert Harris Walker

Cincinnati Observed: Architecture and History, by John Clubbe

The Cincinnati Red Stalkings, by Troy Soos

Cincinnati Then and Now, by Iola Hessler Silberstein

I'll Cook When Pigs Fly . . . and They Do in Cincinnati: Bits and Bites of Queen City Cuisine, by the Junior League of Cincinnati

Practicing Community: Class Culture and Power in an Urban Neighborhood, by Rhoda H. Halperin

The Treatment: The Story of Those Who Died in the Cincinnati Radiation Tests, by Martha Stephens

Web Sites

www.cincinnati.com (daily news)

www.cincinnati.citysearch.com (local attractions and events)

www.rcc.org (city government)

www.cincinnatiusa.org (city information and statistics)

www.cincymuseum.org/ (museum and history site)

Still Curious? Why Not Check Out

Driving While Black: Coverup, by Kelvin R. Davis

Eyeshot, by Lynn S. Hightower

Grand Avenue, by Joy Fielding

The Jazz Bird, by Craig Holden

John Uri Lloyd: The Great American Eclectic, by Michael A. Flannery

Little Man Tate

The Music Lovers: A Harry Stoner Novel, by Jonathan Valin

My Life As a Gay Man in a Straight Woman's Body: An Autobiography, by Carol Sherman-Jones

The People Vs. Larry Flynt

Process: A Novel, by Kay Boyle

A Rage in Harlem

Rain Man

Traffic

Your Character Loves

- The Reds.
- Pete Rose—whether he's guilty or not.
- The Bengals when they win.
- The Blue Wisp jazz club.
- Local talk radio host Bill Cunningham.
- *WKRP in Cincinnati*—remember that sitcom?
- Oktoberfest-Zinzinnati. The city's celebrates its German heritage by gathering to drink lots of draft beer and gobble down foods like brats and sauerkraut.
- The Cincinnati Bearcats or the Xavier Musketeers—but not both.

Your Character Hates

- Change.
- Paul Brown stadium. This new Bengals home, built in 2000, went about $45 million over budget, had many overruns, and ended up costing a whopping $450 million.
- Cincinnati's conservative reputation.
- Larry Flynt. He loves the First Amendment, but local leaders hate him—he and his *Hustler* franchise have been a thorn in the city's side for years.
- The Cincinnati Bearcats or the Xavier Musketeers but not both.

Cleveland

Cleveland Basics That Shape Your Character

The bridges of "The Flats"

Population: 478,403

Prevalent Religions: Protestant, Roman Catholic, Judaism, Eastern Orthodox, Methodist, Lutheran, Baptist, Pentecostal, Amish, Mennonite, and Buddhist

Top Employers: Ford Motor Company, University Hospitals of Cleveland, Catholic Diocese of Cleveland, Cleveland Board of Education, The Cleveland Clinic Foundation, KeyCorp, FirstEnergy Corporation, The LTV Corporation, Alcan Inc., Tops Friendly Markets, Goodyear Tire and Rubber Company, Riser Foods Inc., Dillard Department Stores Inc.

Per Capita Income: $30,472

Average Daily Temperature: January, 25.5° F; July, 71.6° F

Ethnic Makeup (in percent): Caucasian 41.5%, African-American 51.0%, Hispanic 7.3%, Asian 1.3%, Native American 0.3%, Other 3.6%

Newspapers and Magazines: *The Plain Dealer, Crain's Cleveland Business*

Free Weekly Alternative Papers: *Cleveland Free Times, Cleveland Scene*

Cleveland Facts and Peculiarities Your Character Might Know

- Eliot Ness turned a sorry Cleveland police force into one of the best departments in the nation, decreasing crime in the Cleveland area by 38 percent.
- The suburb of Twinsburg holds an annual Twins Day Festival, the world's largest annual gathering of twins. It's taken place every August since 1976.
- Lots of companies mine salt under Lake Erie (on the Canadian side as well as the U.S. side). As a result, there are plenty of salt companies on the banks of Lake Erie in Cleveland.
- Bill Watterson, creator of *Calvin & Hobbes*, is from the eastern suburb of Chagrin Falls.
- The Cleveland Clinic is a world-renowned health-care facility, serving celebrities and dignitaries from around the world.
- Lakeview Cemetery is known for the famous people buried there, including President James Garfield, Eliot Ness, John D. Rockefeller, and former major-league baseball player Ray Chapman, the only player in the history of baseball to be killed by a pitch.
- The East Side of Cleveland starts the Snow Belt. It's not uncommon for eastern communities to get lots of snow, while western suburbs don't get any.
- Sam Sheppard (*The Fugitive*) was from West Side suburb of Bay Village.
- Former Cleveland disc jockey Alan Freed is credited with coining the phrase *rock 'n' roll* and emceeing the first rock concert in 1951.
- One of the writers for *Leave It to Beaver* was a graduate of Mayfield High School in Cleveland, which is why the school in the series was Mayfield.

If Your Character . . .

If Your Character Loves the Nightlife, he's hanging out in the Flats. This bar district near Lake Erie has been a local nightlife spot for years. Also, the Sixth Street Warehouse District has lots of upscale restaurants and bars.

If Your Character Is Hip and Trendy, she shops in Larchmere. With more than fifty unique specialty shops and the city's best and most unusual art galleries, this is where your character can find contemporary crafts, the latest in designer fashions, and one-of-a-kind shopping treats.

If Your Character Wears a Blue Collar at Work, he lives in Parma, Bedford, or Cleveland Heights. These neighborhoods are home to hardworking, middle-class Clevelanders.

If Your Character Smells of Money, she resides in Brantenahl. This small community on the East Side boasts huge lake-front homes. Gates Mills is another wealthy East Side community on the edge of Cuyahoga County. Shaker Heights and Westlake are also ritzy neighborhoods.

Local Grub Your Character Might Love

Pierogies are popular here, as are sandwiches from Panini's (especially at 2 A.M.). Stadium Mustard goes over well, as does anything from Little Italy. The Big Egg has egg-shaped menus and enough grease to run a battleship. Peanuts from the Peterson Company, located across from Jacobs Field, are a hit at and away from the ballpark. Rascal House Pizza near Cleveland State University is where the college students feast. And everyone loves beer from the Great Lakes Brewery. Favorite local restaurants are Moxie, Watermark, Sans Souci, Heck's, Luchita's, Lola's, The Palazzo, Tommy's, and Nate's.

Interesting and Peculiar Places to Set a Scene

- **Bookstore on West Twenty-Fifth.** This Ohio City institution used to be called "Six Steps Down." No matter the name change, it's still the best independent bookseller in town, with big shelves of old dust jackets (about 90 percent of the titles are used or rarities). Have your character pick up a copy of a Les Roberts novel, while Star, "the feline bibliophile," purrs and curls around her leg.
- **East Cleveland.** This rough neighborhood is frequently in the news for murders. It's also home to former pro baseball stadium League Park.
- **Li Wah at the Asian Market.** The Asian Market is Cleveland's own little Chinatown, and at Li Wah your character can get the most authentic dim sum in the region. This is probably the only area in Ohio (or even the Midwest/Great Lakes region) where Asians actually outnumber non-Asians.
- **Little Italy.** Once a community with a lot of Mob ties (the Mayfield Road Mob, for instance). This community has a great festival in August for the Feast of the Assumption, when the main thoroughfare, Mayfield Road, is shut down and taken over by booths with food, music, gambling, and plenty of drinking.
- **Lorain Antiques Row.** An industrial neighborhood at the foot of the Lorain Carnegie Bridge, this nationally known antiques district spans twenty-eight blocks and could have its own "Lorain Antiques Road Show" on PBS. Most of these shops are small, independently owned "grab it and keep it" flea-market stores that carry a hodgepodge of what to some are gold mines of collectibles and to others are mere piles of junk.
- **Major Hoople's Riverbed Café in the Flats.** At the corner of Riverbed and Columbus Roads, this is to some the last bar left in the Flats for your regular Joe. The food is cheap, the beer selection is wide (but highly domestic), and the regulars include everyone from factory hands and construction workers to bikers, college students, and medical professionals.
- **Ohio City.** This chic area of town sports an array of trendy little lunch spots, cozy diners, and corner pubs.
- **On a fishing boat.** Your character can take to the Rocky and Chagrin Rivers in the spring and fall to fish for steelhead trout. He can then follow the fish out to Lake Erie in the late spring/early summer, during which time he can also toss out a line in Lake Erie in the hopes of bagging some walleye.
- **On the Waterfront Line.** This light-rail rapid transit system links the Flats, Tower City, the Rock 'n' Roll Hall of Fame and the Great Lakes Science Center.
- **The Cleveland Museum of Art.** Located in University Circle and regarded as one of the finest museums in the nation, this gallery hosts more than thirty-four thousand works, including gems by masters Rembrandt, Monet, Van Gogh, and Picasso. Just as striking as what's inside is what's outside: The museum overlooks the Fine Arts Gardens of Wade Park. Breathtaking seasonal displays of flowers make this setting a popular place for wedding photos all year round.
- **Tremont.** This is the Greenwich Village of Cleveland, a historic melting pot where Greeks and Hispanics mix with African-Americans and Appalachians who also happen to rub shoulders with Eastern Europeans from Poland and the Ukraine. Young professionals and those interested in the arts are here as well, as evidenced by the small art galleries and studios, quaint cafes, and hip bars that dot the streets. Many

For Further Research

Books

Catalogue of Egyptian Art: The Cleveland Museum of Art, by Lawrence M. Berman

City Smart: Cleveland, by Nancy Peacock

Cleveland: A Concise History, 1796–1990, by Carol Poh Miller and Robert Wheeler

Cleveland Ethnic Eats: A Guide to the Authentic Ethnic Restaurants & Markets of Greater Cleveland, by Laura Taxel

Cleveland Fishing Guide, by John Barbo

The Cleveland Indians Encyclopedia, by Russell Schneider

In the Wake of the Butcher: Cleveland's Torso Murders, by James Jessen Badal

On Being Brown: What It Means to Be a Cleveland Browns Fan, by Scott Huler

Rock 'n' Roll and the Cleveland Connection, by Deanna R. Adams

Web Sites

http://www.lakeviewcemetery.com/famous_residents.html (Lakeview Cemetery)

http://www.twinsdays.org (Twins Days Festival)

http://cleveland.about.com/cs/360degreetours/ (tourist information)

http://www.plaindealer.com/ (*The Plain Dealer*)

http://www.rockhall.com/ (Rock 'n' Roll Hall of Fame)

http://www.digitalcity.com/cleveland/ (city guide)

http://www.travelcleveland.com/ (visitors information)

Still Curious? Why Not Check Out

Black Rain for Christmas, by Scott Malensek

A Christmas Story

Crooked River Burning, by Mark Winegardner

The Drew Carey Show

Finding Fish: A Memoir, by Antwone Quenton Fisher

The Lake Effect, by Les Roberts

Light of Day

---

of the Victorian homes hugging the winding drives have been restored and are now unique boutiques and upscale restaurants.

- **West Side Market.** This Ohio City old building is where your epicurean character can find local and international treats and dishes of all sorts and sizes. The atmosphere can be frenetic, with tourists, shoppers, and vendors scurrying about sampling, sipping, buying, and selling.

Exceptionally Grand Things Your Character Is Proud Of

- Former Mayor Carl Stokes was the first African-American mayor of a major U.S. city.
- The suburb of Brooklyn was the first community in the United States to ban handheld cell phone usage while driving (the law was enacted in 1999). Brooklyn also was the first Cleveland community to require the use of seat belts (1966).
- The Jake (Jacobs Field). The Tribe (Indians) holds the record for the most consecutive sellouts in major-league baseball history.
- The Dawg Pound. A rowdy section of fans near the end zone at Cleveland Browns' games.

- Cleveland Clinic Foundation, Cleveland Orchestra, Cleveland Museum of Art.
- Some famous Clevelanders: Halle Berry, Arsenio Hall, Drew Carey, Jesse Owens, Tracy Chapman, Robert Smith.
- The Rock 'n' Roll Hall of Fame.
- The first Monday Night Football game was played in Cleveland on September 21, 1970, with a record-setting attendance of 85,703 (Cleveland Browns vs. New York Jets).

Pathetically Sad Things Your Character Is Ashamed Of

- The infamous fire on the water (1969).
- 1974's Nickel Beer Night at Municipal Stadium. Fans got so rowdy that the game was stopped.
- The overall impression that Cleveland fans throw bottles and batteries.
- The giant "Free" stamp downtown. Some say it's art, most have no clue what it is.
- Cleveland Municipal Stadium—"The Mistake by the Lake," as they called it. Many fans hated it especially because its seventy-four thousand seats were never even close to full during baseball games.

Your Character Loves

- The Browns.
- Bernie Kosar.
- Jim Brown.
- The West Side Market.
- The Michael Stanley Band (Clevelanders thirty-five and over).

Your Character Hates

- Pittsburgh.
- Art Modell, owner of the NFL's Ravens who moved the Browns to Baltimore and left Cleveland without an NFL franchise for five years.
- People who think Browns fans are the rudest, most obnoxious fans in the NFL. Has anybody ever been to Oakland?
- The fact that the Rock 'n' Roll Hall of Fame induction ceremonies take place in New York. The museum is in Cleveland.

Columbus

⊙Columbus

Columbus Basics That Shape Your Character

The Book Loft in German Village

Population: 711,470 in the city; 1.5 million in the Greater Metro area

Prevalent Religion: Roman Catholics rule here

Top Employers: State of Ohio, The Ohio State University, Honda of America, Nationwide Mutual Insurance Company, AT&T, Anheuser-Busch, American Electric Power, Battelle Memorial Institute, CompuServe Interactive Services Inc., Limited Brands Inc., White Castle System Inc., Wendy's International Inc., Nationwide Auto Parts, Borders Group Inc., A&P Grocery, Kroger

Per Capita Income: $30,820

Average Daily Temperature: January, 26° F; July, 73° F

Ethnic Makeup (in percent): Caucasian 67.9%, African-American 24.5%, Hispanic 2.5%, Asian 3.4%, Native American 0.3%, Other 3.8%

Newspapers and Magazines: *The Columbus Dispatch, Ohio Magazine, Columbus Business First, The Daily Reporter, Columbus Parent*

Free Weekly Alternative Papers: *Columbus Alive, The Other Paper, Gay People's Chronicle*

Columbus Facts and Peculiarities Your Character Might Know

- Columbus is the state capital and Ohio's largest city.
- No other city produces stainless steel whistles—they're all made here.
- Columbus trains more seeing-eye dogs than does any other city.
- Columbus isn't known for its high life, but its unemployment rate is low.
- The Anthony-Thomas Candy Company is one of the largest family-owned candy-making facilities in the states.
- Eddie Rickenbacker, the famous World War I pilot and business executive, was born in Columbus (and its airport is named in his honor).
- The Ohio State University—with its thirty-five thousand students—is the largest educational institution in Ohio.
- Writer James Thurber is from Columbus.
- The oval on The Ohio State University campus is a local haven for sitting, lunch eating, and Frisbee tossing.
- Residents love their German heritage, as evident by German Village, a restored nineteenth-century community that boasts beautifully renovated homes, shops, and restaurants.

If Your Character . . .

If Your Character Smells of Money, she lives in New Albany. This wealthy suburb, northeast of Columbus, has beautiful Georgian-style houses and huge lots. Les Wexner (owner of The Limited Inc.) lives here.

If Your Character Can't Leave the House Without His Golf Clubs, he lives in Dublin. This wealthy, upper-middle-class suburb is home to Murfield Country Club, which hosts the Murfield Memorial Golf Tournament. Jack Nicklaus designed the course, and he apparently lived there for a time.

If Your Character Is a Family Man, he lives in Westerville. This upper-middle-class suburb is the home of Otterbein University. Similar suburbs include Hilliard, Reynoldsburg, or Pickerington.

Local Grub Your Character Might Love

Columbus isn't too well known for any only-in-Columbus signature dishes, but some local favorite eateries include Nancy's Home Cooking, Blue Danube, Garcias, Barleys, El Vaguera, the German Village Coffee Shop, Starliner Diner, Florentine, Thurman, Thirsty Ear, Old Mohawk, and Schmidts.

Interesting and Peculiar Places to Set a Scene

- **Mirror Lake.** This is a pond on The Ohio State University's campus. It's a great place to hang out on weekends and, for students, between classes.
- **Bicentenniel Park.** This is a downtown park on the Scioto River. Santa Maria (a working fifteenth-century sailing vessel modeled after the city's namesake ship) is there, as is COSI (Center of Science and Industry). The park is important because most summer festivals are held here, from the Columbus Arts Festival to the Rhythm and Food Festival to the Red, White, and Boom (Fourth of July party).
- **Comfest.** This annual community festival takes place the last full weekend in June in Goodale Park. No public or private sponsors, just several stages, each constantly filled with great local music. A barefoot area (no glass in the park). This is the place where you'll see anything and everything.
- **A Concert at The Newport.** This Music Hall on The Ohio State University's main drag brags of being the nation's longest continually running rock club, hosting jams since 1970. The institution is like a miniature run-down palace, complete with an oval balcony and lots and lots of smoke. It's very, very intimate. You name a rocker, and they've played The Newport, from B.B. King and Miles Davis to Todd Rundgren and The Grateful Dead to U2 and The Police to Pearl Jam.
- **Goodale Park.** This is a great park in the Short North area of town. Lots of people run, play tennis, roller blade, walk their dogs, or just hang out. This is by far the most popular public place to have sex in the city (is your character interested?). It also hosts the Summer Jazz Series on Sunday mornings.
- **OSU campus.** This is one of the country's largest college campuses.
- **Olde Claremont/Round.** The Claremont is a hotel and restaurant. The restaurant is not in the hotel; it's across the street. They recently renovated the hotel and hotel bar (The Round Bar), so they aren't so 1970s tacky as they used to be. The restaurant is still the same. Great food. Most of the people that go there have been going there for years and years.
- **The Book Loft of German Village.** This amazing bookstore in German Village is kind of an old house renovated into a bookstore. It's a maze of rooms, with each room housing different types of books: an entire room of art books. an entire room of cookbooks, and so on. It's easy for your character to get lost in here, physically and mentally.
- **An OSU tailgate party.** They say it gets crazy. For every OSU home game, fans bring campers and tents and cars and trucks—sometimes even old busses. Scarlet and gray are everywhere. People bring their televisions, satellite dishes, favorite foods, grills, and, of course, lots of beer. It's packed rain or shine or snow. The area bars/restaurants close off their parking lots and set up big-screen TVs for partygoers. Local bands play before and after the game at various locations. Your character could partake in some really good fun here.
- **Franklin Park Conservatory.** Botanical gardens and climate rooms. In the spring, they have a butterfly exhibit with thousands of butterflies in a big room. In the fall, they have a giant corn maze. They have a couple of plant sales every year, too.
- **Mozart's European Desserts.** These Austrian desserts are so good that while in Columbus promoting his national fitness show, Arnold Schwarzenegger stopped in to make sure he got a sampling—and apparently was delighted to find such authentic Austrian food in the Midwest.
- **The Fireside Book Company.** These guys sell books from a little frame house built in about 1850. The used and rare bookshop was started in 1993 by husband and wife and has been able to sustain itself in spite of the chains.

Exceptionally Grand Things Your Character Is Proud Of

- Its low unemployment rate.
- Berlinger Park.
- First Major League Soccer stadium (Columbus Crew).

For Further Research

Books

Columbus Celebrates the Millennium, by Mike Harden
Columbus: The Discovery City, by Harry B. Franken
Columbus, Ohio: A Personal History, by Henry L. Hunker
Dangerous Class: Crime and Poverty in Columbus Ohio 1860–1885, by Eric H. Monkkonen
Discover Columbus, by Mike Harden and Brooke Westrup
A Fragile Capital: Identity and the Early Years of Columbus, Ohio, by Charles Chester Cole
Ohio: An American Heartland, by Allen G. Noble and Albert J. Korsok
The Most Incredible Prison Escape of the Civil War, by W. Fred Conway

Web Sites

www.digitalcity.com/columbus/ (local news and events)
www.cityofcolumbus.org/ (official city site)
http://columbus.citysearch.com/ (news and entertainment)
www.outincolumbus.com/ (gay news)
www.cohums.ohio-state.edu/history/default.htm (The Ohio State University history)
www.dispatch.com/ (*The Columbus Dispatch*)
www.history.ohio-state.edu/old_columbus/default.htm (historic Columbus)

Still Curious? Why Not Check Out

Air Force One
Fast Women, by Jennifer Crusie
Goodbye, Columbus
The Right Man for the Job, by Mike Magnuson
Showcase and *Trunk Show*, by Alison Glen
Teachers
Traffic

- Tuskegee Airmen. The city has a new $1.8 million memorial devoted to the airmen.
- Its motorcycles. Columbus boasts America's oldest Harley-Davidson dealership, which started selling the two-wheeled demons in 1912.
- Script Ohio. Part of this marching band tradition is when a sousaphone player gets to go out and dot the *I* when the band spells "OHIO" on the field.
- Buckeyes basketball greats, like Bobby Knight, John Havlicek, Jerry Lucas, and Fred Taylor.

Pathetically Sad Things Your Character Is Ashamed Of

- Columbus is the fourth fattest city in the United States.
- The 1979 Buckeyes football team went 11-0 and then lost the national championship by one point.

Your Character Loves

- OSU football.
- Archie Griffin. This Buckeye is the only football player to win two Heisman trophies (1974 and 1975).
- Its summer movie series.
- Shakespeare in the Park.
- Woody Hayes—hey, he might have punched a few players, but by god his Buckeyes won!

Your Character Hates

- All those orange barrels from constant road construction.
- The University of Michigan.
- Cleveland and Cincinnati (they have major league sports teams).

Oklahoma

Significant Events Your Character Has Probably Thought About

- In 1541, Spanish explorer Francisco Vasquez de Coronado ventured through the area.
- Oklahoma land was part of the 1803 Louisiana Purchase.
- The Cherokee Trail of Tears, in which Five Civilized Tribes from the southeastern United States were forced off their lands by state and federal governments to go to "Indian Territory"—what is now Oklahoma.
- After the Civil War, Oklahoma became part of the booming cattle industry.
- In 1889, during the first homesteading or "land run" day, about fifty thousand people swarmed into the territory. Those who tried to beat the noon starting gun were called Sooners.
- There were six land runs between 1889 and 1895. Settlers came to stake their claims from as far away as Ireland, Germany, and Poland.
- In 1907, Oklahoma became the forty-sixth state, mostly because of the discovery of oil, which made Oklahoma the "place to go to strike it rich."
- In 1948, a tornado ripped through Tinker Air Force Base and caused a bit of damage but just a few injuries and no fatalities, thanks to Captain Robert C. Miller and Major Ernest J. Fawbush, who correctly predicted that atmospheric conditions were ripe for tornadoes. This was deemed the first tornado forecast.
- The bombing in Oklahoma City on April 19, 1995.
- On July 25, 2000, Governor Frank Keating announced plans to construct a dome on the Oklahoma State Capitol Building.

Oklahoma Facts and Peculiarities Your Character Might Know

- Astronaut Thomas P. Stafford is from here.
- Okmulgee has the biggest pecan festival anywhere, and holds world records for the largest pecan pie, pecan cookie, and pecan brownie.
- With over 250,000 Native Americans, Oklahoma has the largest Native American population of any state. It also is headquarters for thirty-nine tribes.

Oklahoma Basics That Shape Your Character

Motto: Labor Conquers All Things

Population: 3.45 million

Prevalent Religions: Baptists by far, also Methodist, Roman Catholic, Lutheran, Presbyterian, Pentecostal, and Episcopalian

Major Industries: Cattle, wheat, milk, poultry, cotton, transportation equipment, machinery, electric products, rubber and plastic products, food processing

Ethnic Makeup (in percent): Caucasian 76.2%, African-American 7.6%, Hispanic 5.2%, Asian 1.4%, Native American 7.9%, Other 2.4%

Famous Oklahomans: Johnny Bench, John Berryman, Garth Brooks, Ralph Ellison, James Garner, Vince Gill, Woody Guthrie, Paul Harvey, Tony Hillerman, Ron Howard, Mickey Mantle, Reba McEntire, Shannon Miller, Bill Moyers, Brad Pitt, Tony Randall, Oral Roberts, Will Rogers, Jim Thorpe, Jeanne Tripplehorn

- *On the Chisholm Trail*, a life-size statue of a cattle drive, in Duncan, serves as a monument to the American cowboy.
- African-American pioneers are little known these days but played a major role in the state, creating numerous all-black towns (twenty-seven of them!). African-Americans also were cowboys, settlers, gunfighters, and farmers, and they fought side by side with Caucasians during the Civil War, most notably the Battle of Honey Springs.
- In Oklahoma City, it's common to see coyotes on the airport grounds at night running across the entrance road.

- Oklahoma has more man-made lakes than any other state.
- If you make eye contact with an Oklahoman, he will always acknowledge you and say hello.
- It is extremely windy here. People often must lock their building doors on the windy side because the wind could catch the doors and damage them.

Your Character's Food and Drink

They love their steak and potatoes. Big, trough-ish, all-you-can-eat cafeterias are a big deal here as well. Pig roasts are always fun, as are the stews. Oklahoma chili (very spicy, like Mexican chili) has a long history here from when vendors used to sell it on the street. Oklahomans in general are notorious for not eating enough fruits and vegetables.

Things Your Character Likes to Remember

- Universities of Oklahoma and Oklahoma State University (OSU) football.
- Cowboys. The National Cowboy Hall of Fame is here, and most radio stations are country music stations.
- Their history of producing oil. Oil derricks can be seen almost everywhere, even on the capitol grounds in Oklahoma City.
- The cheapest gas in the country.
- How they've recovered from the bombing.
- Their big trucks and big rigs.
- Garth Brooks. He was born in Tulsa and grew up in Yukon.
- Oklahoma was the setting for the movie *Twister*.
- Bricktown (cobblestone streets, old buildings, lots of tourist dollars).

© PhotoDisc/Getty Images

Skyline of Oklahoma City

- Bob Dunn. A musician from Beggs, he apparently invented the first electric guitar in 1935.
- Governor Frank Keating. He really pulled the state together after the bombing.
- Will Rogers. First he was a Native American, then a cowboy, now a legend (there's the Will Rogers World Airport).
- The Amateur Softball Association of America. It was founded in 1933 and has evolved into the strongest softball organization in the country.
- The Oklahoma City National Memorial.

Things Your Character Would Like to Forget

- The "Trail of Tears."
- Timothy McVeigh.
- Breaking bridges. In 2002 a river barge crashed into a bridge near Tulsa, sending several vehicles into the Arkansas River.

Myths and Misperceptions About Oklahoma

- **It's flat.** Oklahoma has four mountain ranges (the Ouachitas, the Arbuckles, the Wichitas, and the Kiamichis).
- **It's not diverse.** It actually is, especially considering the unique role African-Americans have played in Oklahoma history.

Interesting Places to Set a Scene

- **Jenks.** Known as the "Antique Capital of Oklahoma," this home to the state's best variety of antique stores, gift shops, galleries, museums, crafters malls, and other collectible-filled.
- **Chickasaw National Recreation Area.** Springs, streams, and lakes are the attractions at, the first national park in the state of Oklahoma. Chickasaw lies in a transition zone where the Eastern deciduous forest and the Western prairies meet.
- **Anadarko.** This is home to the only authentic Native American city in the United States. It's located in the beautiful Washita River Valley in southwest Oklahoma.
- **Ardmore.** If there ever was an oil and cow town, this is it. However, Ardmore also prides itself on the Eliza Cruce Hall Doll Museum, which has a collection of hundreds of dolls of all sorts, shapes, sizes, materials, and ethnicities. If your character's got a thing for dolls, oil, and cattle.

For Further Research

Books

Cherokee Connections, by Myra Vanderpool Gormley

Historical Atlas of Oklahoma, by John W. Morris and Edwin C. McReynolds

Oklahoma: A History of Five Centuries, by Arrell Morgan Gibson

Oklahoma Place Names, by George H. Shirk

Progressive Oklahoma: The Making of a New Kind of State, by Danney Goble

The Real Wild West: The 101 Ranch and the Creation of the American West, by Michael Wallis

Web Sites

www.hm-usa.com/states/ok.html (travel and tourism)

www.state.ok.us/osfdocs/stinfo2.html (state history)

www.ou.edu/ (University of Oklahoma)

www.travelok.com/ (visitor's information)

www.okit.com/ (*Native American Times*)

www.okc-cityhall.org/ (Oklahoma City site)

Still Curious? Why Not Check Out

The Final Jihad: When the "Best of the Worst" Finally Come For Us, by Marin Keating

Harvesting Ballads, by Philip Kimball

Invisible Man, by Ralph Ellison

The Names of the Dead, by Stewart O'Nan

Paradise, by Toni Morrison

Remnants of Glory, by Teresa Miller

Twister

Way Down Yonder in the Indian Nation: Writings from America's Heartland, by Michael Wallis

---

- **Duncan.** While the city claims things like "The spirit that built the West and tamed the wide-open spaces lives on in Duncan" and "The spirit that turned cowboys into legends, cattlemen into men of fortune, and oilmen into giants lives on in Duncan," your character might think otherwise. Duncan is a touristy little town with more antiques than anyone could want, but it does have a colorful heritage, a historic downtown Main Street, and an interesting walking tour of its history.

- **Edmond.** Edmond likes to brag about its "firsts" in the history of the Oklahoma Territory: first public school house, first church, first library, first public institution of higher education . . . you get the point. But what this place is really proud of is that it's the home of Olympic gold-medal gymnast Shannon Miller.

- **Elk City.** With a perfect spot on Route 66, this town used to be a major stop for ranchers driving their cattle from Texas to Kansas on what was called "Dodge City Cattle Trail." Today, this town of eleven thousand is home to lots of natural gas and an Old Town Museum that contains many Native American and rodeo artifacts, as well as exhibits that hint at life here in the 1900s.

- **Norman.** This is Oklahoma City's little brother. What got its start from the 1889 land rush has grown into a university town (University of Oklahoma is here) and a city built on oil, education, industry, tourism, high-tech industries, research and development, and agriculture.

- **Oklahoma City.** The city got a fast start when someone struck oil, and it's been an oil-producing city since; underneath it is one of the nation's largest oil fields. No surprise that oil well equipment became one of the city's major industries (also big are stockyards, meat-packing plants, grain, iron and steel mills, tire manufacturing, and auto and aircraft assembly). To get a taste of the new Oklahoma City of today, have your character take a rubber-wheeled trolley (called The Oklahoma Spirit) to Bricktown, the city's hot new entertainment area. It was once an old warehouse district but is now filled with brick streets, quaint shops, and fashion stores. It's the place to be in Oklahoma City. Bricktown Brewey, the state's first microbrewery, is also here.

- **Stillwater.** With Oklahoma State University's nineteen thousand students making up more than half of the city's population, this is a college town. Your biology student might find herself here, as OSU is one of the top experimental farming and agriculture universities in the country, with its Noble Research Center for Agriculture and Renewable Natural Resources. The town also has its own little art community and a fine arts and jazz festival.

- **Spiro Mounds.** Oklahoma's only archaeological park is a 140-acre site encompassing twelve southern mounds that contain evidence of a Native American culture that occupied the site from A.D. 850 to A.D. 1450. The mounds are considered one of the four most important prehistoric Native American sites east of the Rocky Mountains.

Significant Events Your Character Has Probably Thought About

- The Lewis and Clark Expedition (1803–1806).
- The Oregon Trail (1848).
- The Construction of the Union Pacific Railroad (1888).
- Senate Bill 100, the breakthrough land-use law. The 1973 law created the Land Conservation and Development Commission and gave the state authority over growth. The law slowed urban sprawl and preserved farm and forest lands. It is still hailed as the nation's most progressive land-use law.
- The big, ongoing "event" of deforestation: In 1849 one could eye a virgin ponderosa pine forest in central Oregon that reached to California. Today less than 10 percent of Oregon's first-generation forests remain.
- The conservation leadership years under Governor Tom McCall. The broadcaster turned politician who once said "Industry must come here on our [Oregon's] terms" and "play the game by our environmental rules, and be members of the Oregon family." He also once quipped that he loved Oregon more than he loved his own life.
- The discovery of Senator Bob Packwood's diaries.

Oregon Facts and Peculiarities Your Character Might Know

- Eleven mountain ranges span the state.
- The Columbia Gorge hosts seventy-one waterfalls.
- The state's three million residents live mostly in urban areas; 66 percent reside in cities or towns.
- A state law prohibits self-service gasoline pumping; all stations are full service only.
- About 53 percent of Oregon is owned by the federal government, much of it on thirteen national forests spanning 15.5 million acres, an area the size of West Virginia.
- Oregon passed Washington as the nation's leading timber producer in 1938.
- After World War II, Oregon's national forests split the lumber that built the suburbs of California.
- The provisional Legislature of 18—it outlawed slavery, but the Oregon Constitution (1862) later banned African-Americans from the state.
- In 1973, Oregon was the first state in the United States to recycle bottles, offering five cents per returned bottle
- Oregon was the first state to grant physician-assisted suicide.

Your Character's Food and Drink

A lot of Oregonians eat good old-fashioned American cuisine (meat, potatoes, soup). There is, however, a

Oregon Basics That Shape Your Character

Motto: She Flies With Her Own Wings

Population: 3.47 Million

Prevalent Religion: Christianity, particularly Methodist, Lutheran, and Roman Catholic

Major Industries: Manufacturing, semiconductors, computers, services, trade, finance, insurance, real estate, government, construction, lumber and wood products, metals, transportation equipment, farming (hay, wheat, potatoes, berries, onions, Christmas trees), commercial fishing

Ethnic Makeup (in percent): Caucasian 86.6%, African-American 1.6%, Hispanic 8.0%, Asian 3.0%, Native American 1.4%, Other 4.2%

Famous Oregonians: Chief Joseph, Ken Kesey, Edwin Markham, Joaquin Miller, Linus Pauling, John Reed, Alberto Salazar, Mary Decker Slaney

Northwest cuisine with a strong local thrust, offering up dishes with fresh oysters, crabs, clams, Oregon spot prawns, tuna, and chinook salmon; local lamb and beef; mushrooms, apples, and pears; blackberries, cherries, raspberries, and cranberries; cheeses (such as Oregon blue); lots of nuts; and anything organic.

Lots of wine is homegrown. Chardonnay and zinfandel are popular, but pinot noir is the favorite. Microbreweries are in the cities. The orchards of the Columbia Gorge produce apples, pears, and peaches to create tasty brandies.

Things Your Character Likes to Remember

- Oregon Ungreeting Cards. They contain inscriptions like, "Best wishes on a safe trip to California, Nevada, or Washington—but don't even think about stepping foot in Oregon!"
- Governor Tom McCall. On an on-camera interview, he told the nation, "Come visit us again and again, but for heaven's sake, don't come here to live."
- Oregon's natural wonders (Crater Lake, Mount Hood, Columbia River Gorge, Oregon Dunes).
- The Oregon Trail.
- Oregon in the 1960s and 1970s.

Things Your Character Would Like to Forget

- The spotted owl controversy.
- The Packwood Diaries.
- World War II Japanese-American internment camps.
- The rest of the world.

Picturesque Crater Lake
© PhotoDisc/Getty Images

Myths and Misperceptions About Oregon

- **The people are isolationists and xenophobes.** They really aren't. They love to travel and love for strangers to visit.
- **The people are all tree huggers.** Many locals actually hug more coffee mugs than they do trees.
- **No traffic jams.** Try driving coastal 101 on a pretty summer's day.

Interesting Places to Set a Scene

- **Ashland.** One of the most pleasant and cultural towns in the state, this is home to the internationally renowned Oregon Shakespeare Festival.
- **Astoria.** Astoria is home to historic city housing with a 150-year-old maritime history, a reconstructed Fort Clatsop (where Lewis and Clark survived the winter of 1805 to 1806) and the world's longest truss bridge (4.1 miles).
- **Bandon.** This quaint, quiet coastal community is known for its berry picking, organic farms, cranberry festival, and old-town feel.
- **Bend.** Considered the hub of central Oregon, this famous logging town is known for its High Desert Museum.
- **Columbia River Gorge.** This is one of the Northwest's most popular, dramatic, and scenic destinations. Its yawning canyon cuts through the Cascade and Sierra Mountains and contains numerous waterfalls, ski resorts, fish hatcheries, lush green forests, and both historic and recent dams and bridges.
- **Crater Lake.** The deepest lake in the United States and Oregon's only national park are here. This also is home to hikers, boaters, and the rustic-but-rebuilt Crater Lake Lodge (there are still no phones or TVs in the rooms).
- **Eugene.** Considered the hippie town of the world by many, Eugene has lots of love, flowers, festivals, bikers, and runners. This is a great and interesting place to have a unique character bum around in.
- **Grants Pass.** There is lots of local color here, including a long-standing and still thriving farmer's market and The Cavemen, a civic organization whose members dress in Flintstone garb and claim the Oregon Caves as their ancestral home.
- **Hell's Canyon.** The Snake River runs through this deep gorge, and the area has lots of natural beauty and human history (such as The Hells Canyon Massa-

For Further Research

Books

The Best Towns in America: A Where-to-go Guide for a Better Life, by Hugh Bayless

Fodor's Gay Guide to the Pacific Northwest, by Andrew Collins

Hidden Oregon, by Maria Lenhart

On the Loose in the Pacific Northwest and Alaska, (The Berkeley Guide)

Oregon, by Judy Jewell

Oregon Handbook, Stuart Warren and Ted Long Ishikawa

Pacific Northwest: Oregon & Washington, (Lonely Planet Publications)

That Balance So Rare: The Story of Oregon, by Terence O'Donnell

Web Sites

www.oregon.gov/ (official state site)

http://traveloregon.com (travel and tourism)

http://Oregon.citysearch.com/ (travel and events)

www.travelportland.com (Portland, Oregon Visitors Association)

www.wunderground.com/US/OR/Oregon.html (Oregon weather)

Still Curious? Why Not Check Out

Clan of the Cave Bear, by Jean M. Auel

Dragonquest, by Anne McCaffrey

The Left Hand of Darkness, by Ursula K. Le Guin

The Man Who Fell in Love With the Moon: A Novel, by Tom Spanbauer

The River Why or *The Brothers K*, by David James Duncan

Sometimes a Great Notion: A Novel or *One Flew Over The Cuckoo's Nest*, by Ken Kesey

Undaunted Courage: Meriwether Lewis, Thomas Jefferson, and the Opening of the American West, by Stephen E. Ambrose

The Sky Fisherman, by Craig Lesley

---

cre in which Chinese miners were murdered by passing cowboys). Relics of mines can be found throughout the area.

- **Joseph.** Home to Chief Joseph Days, a four-day rodeo festival, this town has many original buildings from the 1880s and is now "The Place to Be" for artists, sculptures, and gallery owners.
- **Portland.** (See page 268 for an extensive look at Portland.)
- **Sisters.** Amidst three lovely peaks (called The Three Sisters), this is touted as a Western town, with cowboys, cattle ranchers, llama ranchers, and historic-but-phony-looking shop fronts.
- **Talent.** The city's motto alone is enough to make us want to mention this town: "Our name speaks for itself."
- **Umpqua River Valley.** This home of great fishing lodges, steep canyons with gushing waterfalls, and expansive vineyard valleys is called "Oregon's Mediterranean" by locals.

Portland

Portland Basics That Shape Your Character

A Portland street scape

Population: 509,610 in the city limits; 1.8 million in the Greater Metro area

Prevalent Religions: Various denominations of Christianity and Buddhism

Top Employers: Fred Meyer Stores, Intel Corporation, Oregon Health Sciences University, Providence Health System, Kaiser Foundation Health Plan Inc., Legacy Health System, Safeway Inc., Freightliner LLC, U.S. Bank, Louisiana-Pacific Corporation, Nike, Precision Castparts Corporation, Tektronix Inc., Willamette Industries

Average Daily Temperature: January, 33.5° F; July, 79.5° F

Per Capita Income: $29,430

Ethnic Makeup (in percent): Caucasian 82.2%, African-American 1.1%, Hispanic 11.2%, Asian 6.7%, Native American 0.7%, Other 5.9%

Newspaper: *The Oregonian* is the only daily

Free Weekly Alternative Papers: *Our Town, Willamette Week*

Portland Facts and Peculiarities Your Character Might Know

- Portland often ranks near the top of the list of most livable cities in the United States.
- It's often considered the "Bookstore Capital of the United States," thanks to Powell's City of Books and other local bookshops.
- It's deemed the most bicycle-friendly city in the states.

- It's only seventy-eight miles from the Pacific Ocean.
- It resides on the confluence of the Columbia and Willamette Rivers.
- It's relatively cold in the winter and relatively cool in the summer.
- OK, it's wet, with an average annual rainfall of thirty-seven inches (but it's not humid).
- No, it's *not* the wettest city in the states! Atlanta, Baltimore, Houston, and Seattle all get more rainfall.
- It's loaded with parks and greenery, containing thirty-seven thousand acres of parks in the metro area.
- It's one of the lowest cities (elevation-wise) to live in, only 173 feet above sea level.
- It's only sixty-five miles away from Mount Hood.
- Trade has kept the city going, not industry or natural resource exploitation.
- There's a cap on building height to keep the "city" part of the city in proportion to its natural surroundings.
- There's a mandatory 1 percent "tax for art" program, which is why Portland has so much art in so many public spaces.

If Your Character . . .

If Your Character Is Alternative and Grungy, he lives in The Hawthorne District. This is Portland's funkiest, most diverse neighborhood. All along Hawthorne Boulevard, bookstores, brew pubs, college students, hippies, gays, street dogs, street vendors, and pamphleteers vie for sidewalk space.

If Your Character Smells of Money, she lives in Northwest Portland. Filled with nineteenth-century homes, this neighborhood is as high end and trendy as it gets. There's lots of shopping, eating, drinking, and one-upsmanship.

If Your Character Is All About Business, he lives in Gresham. Minutes from downtown Portland, this area is a prime location for business, industry, and families just starting out.

If Your Character Is a Rich Computer Geek, she lives in Hillsboro. What started as a farm community is now the heart of Oregon's "Silicon Forest."

If Your Character Is a Family Man, he lives in Milwaukie. This area of town is often touted as one of the best places in the country to raise a family and is graced with the title "City of Dogwoods."

If Your Character Wears a Blue Collar at Work, she lives in Tualatin. Blue-collar families appreciate Tualatin's small-town feel and city facilities.

Local Grub Your Character Might Love

Your character will have ample opportunities to eat fresh seafood, fruit, veggies and cheeses, such as Oregon blue. Portlanders are also nuts about nuts. As for drinks, local wines are popular, especially pinot noir. Beer is the most popular alcoholic beverage, with brew pubs all over town (twenty-five microbreweries in all). And, of course, a coffeehouse can be found on almost any corner (there are eighty-two Starbucks alone in Portland). Some local favorites include Our Daily Bread, Delta Café, Cup & Saucer, Tube, Foothill Broiler, Mother's Bistro & Bar, Cafe del Toro, Leaf & Bean.

Interesting and Peculiar Places to Set a Scene

- **The Anne Hughes Coffee Shop.** In the corner of Powell's City of Books, this is where lonely hearts and active minds try to find kindred spirits.
- **Sellwood.** This old working-class part of town is now more like a forgotten ghetto, save the curio shops, small antique stores, and hip restaurants.
- **Pioneer Courthouse Square.** Deemed the center of downtown Portland, concerts, festivals, rallies, and exhibits occur here almost daily in the summer. A roaring fountain, a weather machine sculpture, and levels of open-air seating bring people to the square to lounge, play music, eat lunch, and gawk.
- **The Pearl District.** This old warehouse district is in an industrial part of town. Although still full of long blocks of warehouses, many parts of the area have turned into lofts, art galleries, boutiques, shops, restaurants, and nightclubs.
- **Portland Art Museum.** This museum is popular with tourists and known for hosting a permanent exhibit of Northwest Native American art.
- **Old Town.** This area used to be the center of late-nineteenth-century Portland but is now pretty rough and tattered. Several homeless shelters and missions share the area with art galleries and specialty shops.
- **The Portland Building.** Designed by architect Michael Graves, this blocky, pastel-colored edifice is decorated like a wedding cake and considered the world's first major structure in the postmodern style.
- **The Chinatown Gates.** At the entrance to Chinatown on NW Fourth Avenue and Burnside Street, these two gates have been around since the 1880s.
- **Skidmore Fountain.** A preserve of Victorian-era architecture, the district that surrounds the fountain bustles on weekends when the Saturday market sets up beneath the Burnside Bridge.
- **Japanese Gardens.** This tranquil and intimate garden encompasses five acres of tumbling water, pools of koi, flowers, a tea house, a sand garden, and views east on to Mount Hood.
- **Forest Park.** A seven-square-mile forest and the largest urban wilderness area in any U.S. city is a haven for bird-watchers, joggers, bikers, and secret lovers.
- **Pups and Cups.** This is a dog wash and coffeeshop all rolled into one innovative hangout. Where else but in Portland?
- **Montage.** This Creole nightspot with cheap meals, artsy and funky youngsters, and lots of jambalaya is one of the most popular night scenes in town.
- **The Gay Bar District.** A block of gay bars and an old downtown hotel (that still survives as a cheap, if dirty, place to rest one's head), this area is a ghost town during the day but loud and colorful at night.

Exceptionally Grand Things Your Character Is Proud Of

- *One Flew Over the Cuckoo's Nest* (the book's author, Ken Kesey, was from here).
- Naked bicyclers during the 120-mile race at Portland International Raceway (they're only bodies . . .).
- The cleanliness of the city.
- Concerned, active citizens.

Your Character Loves

- Progressive politics. Can't find more forward-thinking people north of Berkeley.
- Nature. It's all here: mountains, rivers, valleys, parks, gardens.
- Preservation. "Why throw it away?" is what most people think.

For Further Research

Books

The Insiders' Guide to Portland, by John Rumler

Portland Best Places, edited by Kim Carlson

The Portland Handbook: A Practical Guide for International Residents, by Margie Rikert and Carol Cowan

Portland: The Riches of a City, by Karen Christine Cowan

Wild in the City: A Guide to Portland's Natural Areas, by M.J. Cody and Michael C. Houck

Web Sites

www.oregoncitylink.com/portland/ (city info)

www.eastportlandchamber.org/ (East Portland Chamber of Commerce)

www.el.com/to/portland/ (official city site)

www.pdxchamber.org/ (Portland Metropolitan Chamber of Commerce)

www.digitalcity.com/portland/ (Portland entertainment guide)

Still Curious? Why Not Check Out

Blue Moon Over Thurman Street, by Ursula K. Le Guin

Body of Evidence

Drugstore Cowboy

The Island, by David Borofka

Merchants, Money, and Power: The Portland Establishment, 1843–1913, by E. Kimbark MacColl

My Own Private Idaho

One Flew Over the Cuckoo's Nest, by Ken Kesey

Round the Roses II: More Portland Past Perspectives, by Karl Klooster

Under Suspicion

Zero Effect

- Community involvement. Your community is your home, and Portlanders are proud to make their place its best.
- The Portland Trailblazers.
- Organic everything. Pesticides beware! You're not faring well in Portland.
- Polka parties. They love 'em here. Dancing anyone?
- Locally brewed beer. Portland ushered in the whole microbrew craze, and it's here to stay. You'll find few Bud drinkers in this town.

Your Character Hates

- Incomers. Portlanders like their special way of life and don't want others to screw it up.
- Pretense. Just be yourself in Portland, and you'll fit in well.
- Californians. Too much pretense.
- The Los Angeles Lakers. They've trounced on the Trailblazers too many times.
- Mass-produced fast food. Eat local, eat organic, eat well.

Pennsylvania

Significant Events Your Character Has Probably Thought About

- Philadelphia was the center of political opposition to the Stamp Act in 1765.
- Following the important Revolutionary War battles of Brandywine, Germantown, and Whitemarsh, General George Washington and his soldiers spent a hard winter at Valley Forge from 1777 to 1778.
- The Battle of Gettysburg was one of the bloodiest of the Civil War, and it proved to be a turning point: After three days of fighting, Confederate armies retreated to Virginia. Abraham Lincoln later read a brief address at a ceremony dedicating part of the battlefield as a graveyard to the soldiers who died there.
- The first steel mill in the country was built in Pittsburgh in 1873.
- On June 1, 1889, the South Fork Dam, which had been holding back the waters of Lake Conemaugh, broke. The mining city of Johnstown was flooded, killing 2,220 people and leaving many more homeless.
- Pennsylvania was a major supplier of the steel needed for weapons and transportation in World War I. Increased competition from other states and from abroad has led to a steady decline in the state's steel industry.
- The Pennsylvania Turnpike, begun in 1940 and completed in 1956, was the first multi-lane interstate highway. Originally, it was built to facilitate movement of military vehicles across the country.
- The first nuclear power plant in the United States opened in Shippingport in 1957.
- In 1979, an accident at the Three Mile Island nuclear power plant near Harrisburg caused panic as it threatened the release of deadly levels of radiation.
- In December of 2001, the state of Pennsylvania took over the Philadelphia school system, abolishing the school board and sparking a national debate about school privatization.

Pennsylvania Facts and Peculiarities Your Character Might Know

- During the Carboniferous Period, the great forests that once covered the state were transformed into de-

Pennsylvania Basics That Shape Your Character

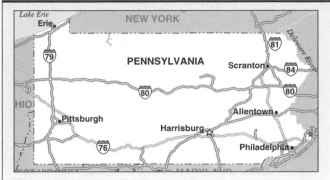

Motto: Virtue, Liberty, and Independence

Population: 12.3 million

Prevalent Religions: Pennsylvania was founded on the premise of religious tolerance, so for hundreds of years this has been home to Quakers, Lutherans, Mennonites, Amish, Baptist Brethren, Catholics, Presbyterians, Jews, Swedenborgians, Schwenkfelders, Moravians, and Methodists, among others.

Major Industries: Health care, banking, education, pharmaceuticals, manufacturing, food processing (ketchup, chocolate, ice cream, potato chips), agribusiness (dairy products, cattle, mushrooms, poultry, apples, sweet corn), coal, steel, hardwood forestry, tourism, shipping

Ethnic Makeup (in percent): Caucasian 85.4%, African-American 10.0%, Hispanic 3.2%, Asian 1.8%, Native American 0.1%, Other 1.5%

Famous Pennsylvanians: Marian Anderson, Samuel Barber, Pearl S. Buck, Alexander Calder, Rachel Carson, Bill Cosby, Stephen Foster, Martha Graham, Alexander Haig, Lee Iacocca, Reggie Jackson, General George Marshall, Margaret Mead, Man Ray, B.F. Skinner, Gertrude Stein, Jimmy Stewart, John Updike, August Wilson, Andrew Wyeth

posits of anthracite coal in the northeast and beds of bituminous coal in the west. These would form the basis of Pennsylvania's economic development from the late eighteeen century to the mid-twentieth century.

- King Charles II named Pennsylvania ("Penn's Forest") in honor of Sir Admiral William Penn, the father of the Quaker William Penn, whom the king owed £16,000.

- By the time of the American Revolution, a third of Pennsylvania's population was composed of German immigrants. German heritage remains strong in the center of the state ("Pennsylvania Dutch" is a corruption of "Pennsylvania Deutsch [German]").
- The Pennsylvania Gradual Abolition Act of 1780 was the first emancipation statute in the United States.
- The Conestoga wagon, developed in Pennsylvania, was the prototype for the primary vehicle of westward migration. It was capable of carrying as much as four tons.
- The University of Pennsylvania in Philadelphia, the only nondenominational college of the colonial period, remains a strong Ivy League school today.
- KDKA in Pittsburgh was the first commercial radio station in the world. It began broadcasting on November 2, 1920.
- One-third of Pennsylvanians live in rural areas, the largest proportion of any state in the country. Pennsylvania also has the second oldest state population (16 percent are over the age of sixty-five).
- Many people in the western part of the state, when directly addressing or speaking of more than one person, use the pronoun "yunz" or "yinz"; in Philadelphia, it's often "youse."
- Pennsylvania has 220 colleges and universities, the third most of any state.
- In February each year, national attention is focused on Punxsutawney, where a groundhog emerges from its burrow to determine how many weeks of winter remain.
- Pennsylvania has the most registered hunters of any state. Your character better wear that orange cap when he goes out hiking in the woods.

Your Character's Food and Drink

Pennsylvania Dutch country provides all kinds of homey dishes, from chicken stews and cured hams to fruit pies and caramel candies. Dried sweet corn is popular around Thanksgiving time. Syrups and preserves go with pancakes for breakfast. Teaberry is a mintlike plant used to flavor ice cream and candies in central Pennsylvania. One curious Pennsylvania food is scrapple, a meat product made of pork parts and cornmeal that's usually eaten for breakfast. In the western part of the state, Eastern European influences can be tasted in *halupki*, *halushki*, and *kielbosa*. In addition, "hoagie" is part of common parlance throughout Pennsylvania.

Things Your Character Likes to Remember

- Among all U.S. states, people born in Pennsylvania are the most likely to stay in their home state throughout their lives. Why leave, anyway?
- Pennsylvania steel has strengthened the infrastructure of the country, including the I-beams of the first skyscrapers, the Brooklyn and Golden Gate Bridges, the steam shovels that excavated the Panama Canal, and over half the rail lines in the United States.
- The Gettysburg Address is one of the most quoted historical documents, along with the Declaration of Independence and the Constitution, which also were penned in Pennsylvania.
- After years of research, Dr. Jonas Salk developed the polio vaccine at the University of Pittsburgh in 1952.
- Governor Tom Ridge was asked to serve as the director of Homeland Security after the 9/11 attacks.

Myths and Misperceptions About Pennsylvania

- **Between Philadelphia and Pittsburgh lies Alabama.** This disparaging remark, which manages to insult

© PhotoDisc/Getty Images

Canons at Gettysburg Battlefield

For Further Research

Books

African-Americans in Pennsylvania: Shifting Historical Perspectives, edited by Joe W. Trotter and Eric Ledell Smith

Better in the Poconos: The Story of Pennsylvania's Vacation Land, by Lawrence Louis Squeri

Big Steel: The First Century of the United States Steel Corporation, by Kenneth Warren

Discovering American Folk Life: Essays on Folk Culture and the Pennsylvania Dutch, by Don Yoder and Henry Glassie

Guide to African-American Resources in the Pennsylvania State Archives, by Ruth E. Hodge

The Johnstown Flood, by David G. McCollough

Land of Giants: Where No Good Deed Goes Unpunished, by Steve Lopez

Pennsylvania Firsts: The Famous, Infamous, and Quirky of the Keystone State, by Patrick M. Reynolds

The Riddle of Amish Culture, by Donald B. Kraybill

Susquehanna Heartland, by Ruth Hoover Seitz and Blair Seitz

And the Wolf Finally Came: The Decline of the American Steel Industry, by John P. Hoerr

Web Sites

www.state.pa.us (official state site)

www.phmc.state.pa.us (history and museums)

www.pennlive.com/patriotnews (central Pennsylvania news)

www.legis.state.pa.us (political goings-on)

www.800padutch.com/amish.shtml [Amish site (and that's not an oxymoron)]

www.upenn.edu (University of Pennsylvania)

www.psu.edu (Penn State University)

Still Curious? Why Not Check Out

Gettysburg: A Novel, by James Reasoner

Grievance, by K.C. Constantine

Guilty of Innocence: A Novel, by William C. Costopoulos

In the Gloaming: Stories, by Alice Elliott Dark

The Killer Angels: A Novel, by Michael Shaara

The Quilter's Apprentice: A Novel, by Jennifer Chiaverini

Rabbit, Run, by John Updike

Tales of the Mine Country, by Eric McKeever

---

two states at once, is often made about the population of the vast rural portion of Pennsylvania. Although most of the radio stations there are devoted to country music, and there are in fact two counties with no traffic lights, central Pennsylvania is not a province of hayseeds. In fact, much of the region is given over to state and national forests, so there's nobody living there anyway!

- **The Amish are backward, isolationist hypocrites.** The Amish don't claim to be perfect, and while some of their practices may seem contradictory (for example, accepting rides in cars but refusing to own cars themselves), their practices are rooted in their religious beliefs. For example, car ownership would create obvious distinctions between the wealthy and the poor. Education is provided only through the eight grade, but children are not forbidden from continuing their education elsewhere if they wish; in fact, at age sixteen, they are encouraged to go out and experience the wider world, returning to Amish life only if they wish. The Amish don't view the outside world as evil in itself; they just want to maintain their way of life and their families as they are.

Interesting Places to Set a Scene

- **Hershey.** There's your character now, at the corner of Cocoa Street and Chocolate Avenue. . . . Hershey is a city devoted to chocolate, with a huge factory that you can tour and even a theme park with roller coasters. The factory, however, has occasional labor-management problems, which lead to not-so-sweet "kiss-off" strikes.
- **New Hope.** This old Delaware River village has a history as being a haven for artists. The surrounding Bucks County has been a writer's retreat for such notables as George S. Kaufman, Moss Hart, John Steinbeck, and James A. Michener.
- **State college.** Right in the middle of the state, far from any other cities, is the home of Penn State. (Pennsylvania State *University*, that is, not penitentiary, although sometimes the students do feel a little hemmed in. . . .)

- **Scranton or Wilkes-Barre.** These cities developed through mining of the anthracite coal in the surrounding region, but their fortunes and populations have been declining since the 1970s. A Pennsylvanian will know that it's pronounced "Wilks-Berry."

- **Lancaster County.** Although there are large towns here, Lancaster County is also the home of many Old Order Amish, a religious group that is best known for rejecting modern devices such as electricity and automobiles that they feel will not contribute to living a simple life and to keeping families together. They have a rich religious history, profess belief in nonviolence and hard work, and would mostly just like to be left to themselves. (Be sure to pronounce it "AH-mish," not "AY-mish.")

- **Holmes County.** There are actually more Amish here than in the better-known Lancaster County.

- **The Pocono Mountains.** For decades these mountains have served as a vacation retreat for people from Pennsylvania as well as from other Middle Atlantic states. In the first half of the twentieth century, the Poconos were known for their resorts that catered to Jewish vacationers who wanted a good laugh.

- **Harrisburg.** This is the state capital and home to hundreds of legislators, lawyers, and lobbyists. With the declining importance of heavy industry and of labor unions, the capital is influenced more and more by the professional lobbying efforts of special interest groups.

- **Erie.** Pennsylvania does in fact have beaches, and they're all on Lake Erie. Presque Isle State Park, a green peninsula off the downtown area, is a popular site for family picnics, swimming, fishing, even sunbathing. In winter popular activities include snowmobiling and staying warm.

Philadelphia Facts and Peculiarities Your Character Might Know

- William Penn, hoping to establish a place of religious tolerance, began planning "The City of Brotherly Love" in 1682. The streets were laid out in a grid pattern, which was novel at the time, in order to prevent a disaster along the lines of London's Great Fire of 1666, still fresh in Penn's mind.
- Philadelphia boasts a long list of "firsts" in North America: the first public park, brick house, paper mill, public school, hospital, library, botanical garden, volunteer fire department, city water system, medical society, U.S. flag, corporate bank, stock exchange, daily newspaper, steam vessel, law school, federal mint, and zoo.
- Philadelphia was the capital of the United States from 1790 to 1800.
- Fairmount Park is the largest city park in the country.
- Leopold Stokowski and the Philadelphia Orchestra collaborated with Walt Disney for the score of *Fantasia*.
- Going "Donna Shore" ("down the shore," that is, to the beach) is a popular summer pastime.
- Philadelphia is ranked as the fourth safest large city in the United States.
- Philadelphia cream cheese is made all over the world now.
- Some famous Philadelphians include Benjamin Franklin, Richard Gere, Will Smith, Patti LaBelle, Marian Anderson, Kevin Bacon, Boyz II Men, Mary Cassatt, Wilt Chamberlin, Bill Cosby, Frankie Avalon, W.C. Fields, Stan Getz, Grace Kelly, W.E.B. DuBois, Margaret Mead, Man Ray, Betsy Ross, Anna Quindlen, Mario Lanza, Todd Rundgren, and Chubby Checker.

If Your Character . . .

If Your Character Is a Young Artist, she lives in Old City. Large, sparse loft spaces and a profusion of art galleries make this area north of Market Street on the east side of town attractive to aspiring Warhols.

If Your Character Is an African-American Family Man, he lives in Germantown. This was the site of the first anti-

Philadelphia Basics That Shape Your Character

John Barry Monument & Independence Hall

Population: 1,517,550 in the city; 5.1 million in the Greater Metro area

Prevalent Religions: Founded by Quakers, Philadelphia remains predominantly Christian, with sizable groups of Jews, Muslims, and Buddhists.

Top Employers: Bell Atlantic Corporation, CIGNA Corporation, Conrail Inc., Crown Cork & Seal Company Inc., Unisys Corp, Campbell Soup Company, Alco Standard Corporation, Provident Mutual Life Insurance Company, The Vanguard Group Inc., Subaru of America, DuPont, SmithKline Beecham Company, QVC Network Inc., Strawbridge & Clothier, Comcast Corporation, Philadelphia Electric Company, Arco Chemical Corporation, CoreStates Financial Corporation, United Parcel Service of America Inc., University of Pennsylvania

Per Capita Income: $25,055

Average Daily Temperature: January, 33°F; July, 75°F

Ethnic Makeup (in percent): Caucasian 45.0%, African-American 43.2%, Hispanic 8.5%, Asian 4.5%, Native American 0.3%, Other 4.8%

Newspapers and Magazines: *The Philadelphia Inquirer, Philadelphia Daily News, Philadelphia Magazine, Philadelphia Business Journal, SBN Magazine*

Free Weekly Alternative Papers: *Philadelphia Weekly, City Paper, Philadelphia Gay News*

slavery protest in North America (in 1689), and it still has many historic homes. It is now predominantly African-American and somewhat run-down in spots.

If Your Character Is a Caucasian Family Man, he lives in The Northeast. This blue-collar section of Philadelphia is larger than most cities. Row after row of single-family homes fronted with tiny patches of green line the straight streets.

If Your Character Is a Wealthy Socialite, she lives in Rittenhouse Square or Washington Square. Uniformed doormen ward off the riffraff from the pricey high-rise condos surrounding these two city parks.

If Your Character Is a Heroin Dealer, he lives in North Philadelphia, a.k.a. "The Badlands." North Philly is the America that America has given up on. Abandoned apartment buildings and crumbling factories slowly sink to the ground next to the tired tenements where people eke out meager livings.

If Your Character Is Steeped in Old Money, he lives in Society Hill. Colonial and Federal-style brick row houses, courtyards, cobblestone streets, and hundreds of historically significant townhouses make up this area. You can buy your way into Society Hill, but it's better to have been born into it.

If Your Character Is an Asian Immigrant, she lives in Chinatown. It's no stereotype, because this area just north of Market Street isn't some tacky tourist spot: It's home to many Asian immigrants and businesspeople.

If Your Character Commutes to the Office on Her Bike, she lives in the Art Museum District. Newly fashionable and increasingly unaffordable, an address in the Art Museum District has just the right amount of cachet and humility.

If your Character Is the Fresh Prince, he lives in West Philadelphia, born and raised, on the playground is where he spends most of his days. This also is the home of the University of Pennsylvania, but West Philly is marked by decay and blight as much as by its prestigious educational institution.

Local Grub Your Character Might Love

The cheese steak, that friend of every dieter, was first popularized here and remains a local favorite. Other foods associated with Philly include soft pretzels (easy on the salt), water ice (a cool summer treat of flavored crushed ice in the Italian tradition; say "wudder ice" if you want to be understood), and Tastycakes (locally baked snack foods now sold in many supermarkets in other regions). However, Philadelphia is hardly the home of only junk food: Several world-class restaurants are here, including the five-star Le-Bec Fin and The Fountain. The Striped Bass was recently named Restaurant of the Year by *Esquire*. Chinatown boasts a number of fantastic restaurants, including a few that specialize in kosher vegetarian cuisine. And the Italian restaurants and bistros in South Philly, such as Ralph's Italian Restaurant, are the best this side of the Tiber. Other favorite local establishments are Fuji Mountain, Morning Glory, Maggiano's, Butcher's Café, Porcini, Morimoto, Manny Brown's, Charles Plaza, Cedars, Aden, Bitar's Pita Hut, Essence Café Citrus, Kingdom of Vegetarians.

Interesting and Peculiar Places to Set a Scene
- **Reading Terminal Market.** Once a train station, it's now an enormous indoor market in the center of downtown. Amish bakers work alongside Vietnamese fry cooks in pleasant chaos. Reading Terminal is a popular lunchtime hangout and meeting place for all who work downtown.
- **Fairmount Park.** This huge city park is characterized by winding wooded trails, stone bridges spanning meandering creeks, roller-bladers, rowing teams, horticultural gardens, nineteenth-century mansions, and a Japanese house and garden ("Shofuuso"). The neighborhoods surrounding the park can be a bit sketchy.
- **Rittenhouse Square.** Surrounded by cafes, bookstores, and high-rise condos, this quintessential city park is populated by every type of person, from lunching businesspeople to pigeon aficionados to dog-walking professors.
- **The Rodin Museum.** This charming building surrounded by tall trees and shaded benches houses the largest collection of the sculptor's works outside Paris. Everyone's here, from *The Thinker* to *Victor Hugo* to *The Burghers of Calais*. Your character can even contemplate *The Gates of Hell*.
- **Broad Street.** Because of its preponderance of cultural

For Further Research

Books

Acres of Skin, by Allen M. Hornblum

First City: Philadelphia and the Forging of Historical Memory, by Gary B. Nash

From Paesani to White Ethnics: The Italian Experience in Philadelphia, by Stefano Luconi

Miracle at Philadelphia: The Story of the Constitutional Convention, by Catherine Drinker Bowen

Philadelphia: A 300-Year History, edited by Russell F. Weigley

Philly Firsts: The Famous, Infamous, and Quirky of the City of Brotherly Love, by Janice L. Booker

A Prayer for the City, by Buzz Bissinger

W.E.B. Dubois, Race, and the City: The Philadelphia Negro and Its Legacy, edited by Michael B. Katz and Thomas J. Sugrue

Web Sites

http://www.gophila.com (general information)

http://www.libertynet.com (regional information)

http://www.pcvb.org (Philadelphia Convention and Visitors bureau)

http://www.phillymag.com (city magazine)

http://www.philly.com (general info, linked to local papers)

http://www.phila.gov (official government information)

Still Curious? Why Not Check Out

The Ambidextrist, by Peter Rock

Blow Out

The Bluest Blood, by Gillian Roberts

Good in Bed: A Novel, by Jennifer Weiner

The Magnificent Ambersons

Philadelphia Fire: A Novel, by John Edgar Wideman

The Philadelphia Story

Pipe Dream: A Novel, by Solomon Jones

Rocky (just the first one)

The Sixth Sense

There Is Confusion, by Jessie Redmon Fauset

Trading Places

Witness

---

organizations, the stretch of Broad Street north and south of City Hall is called "The Avenue of the Arts." Here you have architectural backdrops that include the brand-new Kimmel Center for the Performing Arts, the neon-bedizened Wilma Theater, the Doric-columned University of the Arts, and the stately Academy of Music (home to the Philadelphia Orchestra, the Opera, and the Pennsylvania Ballet). And towering above it all is City Hall, an architectural masterpiece in itself, topped by an enormous statue of William Penn.

- **The Mutter Museum.** The strong-of-stomach often visit the medical collections here, which include thousands of fluid-preserved anatomical and pathological specimens. Yecch.

- **Eastern State Penitentiary.** From the outside it looks like a castle; on the inside, this abandoned prison's rows of individual cells once put it at the forefront of nineteenth-century prison reform. Nevertheless, it seems that Al Capone didn't enjoy his stay here, nor did Brad Pitt in *12 Monkeys*.

- **International House.** This huge dorm and cultural center is for students and professors from all over the world. Concerts and film showings bring in people from all over the city.

- **South Street.** This eclectic, youthful area is reminiscent of Greenwich Village. "Vintage" clothing stores, bins of used CDs, used bookstores, and head shops abound. An absence of body piercings may make you stand out.

- **Chinatown.** An authentic Chinese gate straddles Arch Street just north of Market, and the street signs here are in English and Chinese. Restaurants, video stores, and martial arts studios line the streets, and the smells of fried pork and won ton soup hover in the air.

- **The Zoo.** Hey, why not? Rocky and Adrian were standing in front of the tiger cage when he popped the question.

- **The Steps of the Museum of Art.** Rocky again, this time running up the steps in anticipation of pugilistic triumph.

- **Manayunk.** Revitalized haven for those seeking food-oriented nightlife, Manayunk ("Manny-unk") is loaded with hot restaurants and outdoor cafes. This neighborhood is so crowded on Friday and Saturday nights that valet parking is needed just to park on the street.

- **The Book and the Cook Festival.** Held annually in March, cookbook authors and restaurant chefs from all over the country come to Philadelphia to serve up their finest culinary treats.
- **The Italian Market.** The social center of South Philly, this open-air market is the site of numerous transactions punctuated with that fundamental Philly monosyllable, "Yo!"

Exceptionally Grand Things Your Character Is Proud Of

- The Declaration of Independence, the Continental Congress, and the Constitution.
- Benjamin Franklin.
- The Liberty Bell.
- The Orchestra.
- The Philly Sound.
- The two thousand murals painted on buildings throughout the city.

Pathetically Sad Things Your Character Is Ashamed Of

- In 1985 former mayor W. Wilson Goode ordered the police to drop firebombs on the housing units of MOVE, an African-American back-to-nature group. Eleven people were killed.
- Philadelphia sports fans don't hesitate to boo their own teams.
- Parts of Veteran's Stadium occasionally collapse, taking people down with them.

Your Character Loves

- A good hoagie (and don't call it a grinder, a sub, or anything else stupid).
- Telling it like it is.
- Making fun of New Jersey.
- The Sixers.
- The Flyers.
- The Phillies.
- The Eagles (say "Iggles").

Your Character Hates

- Pretense.
- The Yankees, the Mets, the Giants, and the Jets.
- The city wage tax.
- L&I (The Licensing and Inspection Department).
- The Vet (Veteran's Stadium).

Pittsburgh Facts and Peculiarities Your Character Might Know

- Pittsburgh's KDKA was the first radio station in the United States; it has an annual Christmas drive for Children's Hospital.
- Much of the city lies in the fork of the Ohio, Allegheny, and Monongahela Rivers, known as "The Golden Triangle."
- Prior to 1980, Pittsburgh was nicknamed "Iron City," "Steel City," and "City of Bridges," but today it relies on health care and retail trade as its major sources of income and jobs.
- Although it was no Kansas City, Pittsburgh had an active jazz district in the heyday of jazz.
- Heinz (ketchup and mustard king) started here.
- Some Pittsburghisms: *warsh* ("wash"); *pop* ("soda"); *yuenz* ("you guys"); *dahntahn* ("downtown"); *jumbo* ("bologna"); *the Mon* ("the Monongahela River").
- One of the city's great landmarks is the sixty-four-story U.S. Steel Tower. When completed in 1970, it was the world's highest tower outside of New York City and Chicago. It was called the U.S. Steel Building for years, then it was changed to USX Tower, but in 2002, it was officially renamed the U.S. Steel Tower.
- Pittsburgh is home to many colleges and universities—Carnegie Mellon University, Chatham College, University of Pittsburgh, and Duquesne University are all close to each other.
- Carnegie Mellon University (CMU) students go to "PHI" (Panther Hollow Inn) and get drunk on "purple hooters" (a mixed shooter's cocktail with vodka, Chambord, bar mix, and 7Up).
- At Pittsburgh football games people yell, "Here we go, Stillers here we go!" (Steelers) and wave gold and black "terrible towels."
- Everyone goes around singing, "It's a beautiful day in the neighborhood. . . ." Okay, they don't, but Mr. Rogers (Fred Rogers) does live here!

If Your Character . . .

If Your Character Is All About Money and Culture, she's spending time in Mount Washington. This is a ritzy neighborhood on top of the mountain overlooking the city

Pittsburgh Basics That Shape Your Character

Iron City's Duquesne Incline

Population: 375,000 in the city; 2.4 million in the Greater Metro area

Prevalent Religions: Christianity (predominantly Roman Catholic, Lutheran, Methodist, Presbyterian, and Episcopalian), also Judaism, Muslim, and Church of Jesus Christ of Latter-day Saints

Top Employers: University of Pittsburgh Medical Center, US Airways, Mellon Financial Corporation, University of Pittsburgh, Allegheny University Hospitals, Giant Eagle Inc., PNC Bank Corporation, Kaufmann's, Allegheny County, Marathon Oil Corporation, JC Penney/Eckerd Corporation, Allegheny Teledyne, Carnegie Mellon University

Per Capita Income: $28,381

Ethnic Makeup (in percent): Caucasian 84.3%, African-American 12.4%, Hispanic 1.7%, Asian 1.7%, Native American 0.1%, Other 0.3%

Newspapers and Magazines: *Pittsburgh Post-Gazette, Pittsburgh Tribune-Review, Pittsburgh Magazine, Dynamic Business, Pittsburgh Business Times, Pittsburgh TEQ*

Free Weekly Alternative Paper: *Pittsburgh City Paper*

(hence the "Mount" part) with expensive property, plenty of nice restaurants, and spectacular skyline views.

If Your Character Is a Devoted Family Man, he lives in Swissvale. An ethnically diverse, mostly working-class community, this area is home to many families who've been here for several generations. Edgewood is another good choice.

If Your Character Loves Nature, she's spending time in Shenley Park. This place is a local favorite natural getaway, as its home to Phipps Conservatory and Botanical Gardens. People also love North Park and McConnell's Mill State Park.

If Your Character Is a Carnegie Mellon College Student, she's hanging out in Shadyside. This is where many Carnegie Mellon students make their homes. It's a shopping and residential district with stores like Banana Republic and the Gap, as well as smaller eclectic boutiques, flower shops, and bars.

Local Grub Your Character Might Love

Your Pittsburgh character will love pierogies and kielbasa, as well as the soft-on-the-inside-but-crispy-on-the-outside "O" fries, a local favorite served in huge portions at The Original Hot Dog Shop frequented by Pitt students. Another local favorite is to get a big sandwich from Primanti Brothers—the reason the sandwiches are so big is that they put fries and coleslaw on them. This is still a sports and steel town, so wings, ribs, sandwiches, and beer are king. And on the last issue, Iron City Beer is not surprisingly a hit in Iron City. Glen's Frozen Custard is a big deal. Favorite local establishments include Stone Mansion Restaurant, Monterey Bay Fish Grotto, Le Mont, Hyeholde Restaurant, Top of the Triangle, Ritter's Diner Restaurant, Grand Concourse, and Abruzzi.

Interesting and Peculiar Places to Set a Scene

- **Carnegie Science Center.** Billed as "An amusement park for the mind," this interactive museum offers your character the opportunity "to feel an earthquake, eat a science experiment, pitch a fastball, play in a sea of clouds," as well as "experience 250 hands-on exhibits, a world-class, interactive planetarium, and an authentic World War II vintage submarine."
- **Duquesne Incline.** This four-hundred-foot cable car incline goes from the South Side (on the bottom) up to Mount Washington. Have your character soak up the view as he ascends the hills of Iron City.

- **East Carson.** Called "Great American Main Street," this nineteen-block corridor of coffeeshops, bars, colorful storefronts, cozy eateries, and funky music stores is where your alternative and grungy character would hang out.
- **Gateway Clipper Fleet.** Have your character hop on one of these riverboats for dinner, dancing, or just a river cruise.
- **Kennywood Amusement Park.** Kennywood celebrated its hundredth anniversary a few years ago. It's a neat mix of new and old, including some great old, wooden coasters like the Jackrabbit. Many think Kennywood has seen its heyday, but it's still a local favorite; lots of companies and schools hold "Kennywood Days." Kenny Kangaroo is the mascot.
- **Point State Park.** This is the park where three rivers meet. The remnants of Fort Pitt are also here, along with the Fort Pitt Museum. Lots of events—like the annual Pittsburgh Arts Festival—are held here. There's a fountain at "the Point," where people go just to teem in the misty air—a pair of young lovers might come here to steal a kiss.
- **The Hill District.** This is a high-crime area where your character would hate to run out of gas or run into a stranger. Littered streets, drug dealers, and homeless folk make this place home. *Hill Street Blues* was based on "The Hill District" (Steven Bochco and lots of actors went to Carnegie Mellon University).
- **The Strip District.** An open-air market reminiscent of New York City's SoHo, the Strip District is on the Allegheny shoreline not far from downtown. Here your character will find open-air markets with fresh produce and seafood, flower stands, mom-and-pop shops, specialty shops, and great eats, from Italian to Cajun. The place smells great, too—coffee beans, bakeries, and so on. There's a lot of night life—an entire strip of dance clubs with valet parking.
- **Cathedral of Learning at University of Pittsburgh.** Your student character can step inside Beijing, Damascus, Athens, and more at this forty-two-story Gothic building, the city's Cathedral of Learning (at the University of Pittsburgh). Classes are held here in "Nationality Rooms"—twenty-six classrooms with ethnic themes. Gifts to the university from the city's ethnic communities, these unique classrooms take you on a voyage of world cultures and global traditions, from Byzantine and Classical to Renaissance and Romanesque.

For Further Research

Books

Hometown Heroes: Profiles in Sports and Spirit, by Jim O'Brien

Pittsburgh Sports: Stories From the Steel City, edited by Randy Roberts

Pittsburgh, Then and Now, by Arthur G. Smith

Pittsburgh: An Urban Portrait, by Franklin Toker

Seeing Pittsburgh, by Barringer Fifield

Steel Shadows, by Douglas Cooper

Triumphant Capitalism, by Kenneth Warren

Witness to the Fifties, by Constance B. Schulz and Steven W. Plattner

Web Sites

www.city.pittsburgh.pa.us/ (city site)

www.phlf.org/ (Pittsburgh History and Landmarks Foundation)

http://pittsburgh.citysearch.com/ (local events and news)

www.post-gazette.com/ (*Pittsburgh Post-Gazette*)

www.nauticom.net/www/maduro/ethnic.htm (Pittsburgh ethnic history)

www.carnegielibrary.org/subject/pgh/famous/writers.shtml (local writers)

Still Curious? Why Not Check Out

An American Childhood, by Annie Dillard

Andrew Carnegie, by Joseph Frazier Wall

Bone Wars, by Tom Rea

Creepshow

Doing It Right, by Jim O'Brien

The Fall-Down Artist, by Thomas Lipinski

Flashdance

The Guardian

Hill Street Blues

Inspector Gadget

Monkeybone

The Mysteries of Pittsburgh, by Michael Chabon

Wonder Boys

Exceptionally Grand Things Your Character Is Proud Of

- The Steelers and Penguins—sports fans are amazing and loyal.
- New stadiums: Heinz Field (Steelers), PNC Park (Pirates).
- The city has really cleaned up a lot of old steel town pollution.
- Bob Prince, who broadcasted Pittsburgh Pirates' games for nearly three decades.
- Myron Cope, the Steelers broadcaster whose name is on some terrible towels.
- Its culture: Pittsburgh Symphony Orchestra, Benedum Center for the Performing Arts, and the Carnegie Library.
- Heinz Hall, Benedum Center, Phipps Conservatory, Andy Warhol Museum.

A Pathetically Sad Thing Your Character Is Ashamed Of

- Reputation of "The Burgh" as a dirty steel town. It used to be, but it's not anymore.

Your Character Loves

- Steelers!
- Pittsburgh's nightlife.

- Mount Washington. The awesome and unobstructed view of downtown Pittsburgh and the city's three rivers—the Monongahela, the Allegheny, and the Ohio—can't be matched.
- PNC Park, Heinz Field, Mellon Arena.
- The bridges at night.
- Carnegie Museums.
- Biking/walking/skating the trails converted via the "Rails to Trails" program.
- Frick Art and Historical Center.
- Ohiopyle State Park.
- Roberto Clemente, Willie Stargell, Terry Bradshaw, Mario Lemieux, Lynn Swann, John Stallworth, Mean Joe Green, Franco Harris, Dan Marino, Tony Dorsett, Bill Cowher, Honus Wagner . . . the list of worshipped sports figures goes on.
- Station Square with its shops and restaurants along the river, historic train station and steel memorabilia, outdoor concert venue, night clubs, restaurants, Sheraton hotel and Gateway Clipper Fleet, plus two inclines up the mountain.

Your Character Hates

- The Cleveland Browns.
- Road construction.
- Going through "the tunnels" at rush hour—they're always backed up.

Rhode Island

Rhode Island Basics That Shape Your Character

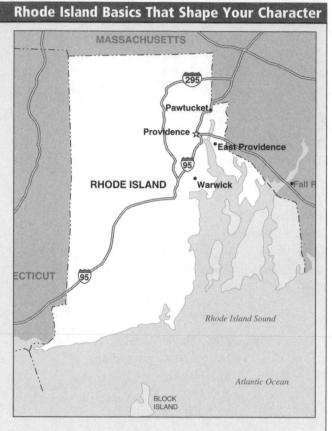

Motto: Hope

Population: 1.04 million.

Prevalent Religions: Largely Roman Catholic, and small pockets of Baptist, Episcopalian, Methodist, and Buddhist

Major Industries: Nursery stock, vegetables, dairy products, eggs, jewelry, fabricated metal products, electric equipment, machinery, shipbuilding and boat building, tourism

Ethnic Makeup (in percent): Caucasian 85.0%, African-American 4.5%, Hispanic 8.7%, Asian 2.3%, Native American 0.5%, Other 5.0%.

Famous Rhode Islanders: Harry Anderson, George M. Cohan, Eddie Dowling, Peter Farrelly, Spalding Gray, David Hartman, Ruth Hussey, Thomas H. Ince, Van Johnson, Galway Kinnell, H.P. Lovecraft, Dana C. Munro, Gilbert Stuart

Significant Events Your Character Has Probably Thought About

- In 1635, Roger Williams was barred from the Massachusetts Bay colony and established a settlement near Providence in 1636.
- Rhode Islanders burned and sank the British cutter *Gaspee* in 1772.
- In 1776, Rhode Island became the first colony to declare its independence from Great Britain.
- Those involved in Dorr's Rebellion of 1842 tried to establish an illegal state government. Although the new government failed, the rebellion forced the state to adopt a new constitution.
- Rhode Island was a major supporter of the Union during the Civil War.
- In the nineteenth century, immigrants (English, Irish, Scottish, French Canadian, Poles, Italians, and Portuguese) flooded into the state to work in the textile mills. By 1900, nearly 70 percent of the state was foreign-born or had foreign-born parents.
- Throughout the nineteenth and early twentieth centuries, mill owners such as Nelson W. Aldrich ruled much of the state.
- Rhode Island suffered after World War I from a major Blackstone Valley textile strike and from the migration of mills to the South where labor was cheap.
- For the first time since 1854, Democrats controlled both houses of the state legislature in 1935. They got rid of all existing Supreme Court justices and reorganized the state's executive branch; this was called the Bloodless Revolution.
- John F. Kennedy and Jacqueline Bouvier tied the knot in 1953 at Rhode Island's St. Mary's Catholic Church.
- Rhode Island's textile industry severely declined from the 1950s through the 1970s, as the number of textile workers dropped from over sixty thousand in 1950 to less than fifteen thousand by the 1970s.
- High-tech businesses and service industries gave the state a boost in the 1980s. By 1986, the state's unemployment rate was at its lowest in years, and real estate values were at their highest.
- In 1989, the state underwent a wave of economic woes

as property values dropped, unemployment rose, and the state's credit union system failed.

- In 1993, downtown Providence had a construction boom with the development of a new urban mall and Waterplace Park.

Rhode Island Facts and Peculiarities Your Character Might Know

- Rhode Island is the smallest state in the nation in terms of area.
- Newport can brag that it held the country's first circus in 1774.
- Jews and Quakers came here in large numbers and settled in Newport around the mid-1600s. Also, The Touro Synagogue, built in 1763, is the oldest synagogue—and possesses the oldest Torah—in North America.
- The state has no county government but instead is divided into thirty-nine municipalities, each with its own local government.
- Rhode Island used to have many covered bridges, but today only one survives: the Swamp Meadow Covered Bridge in Foster.
- Some of the world's fine silverware and jewelry is manufactured in Rhode Island, which has been producing these items for well over a century.
- The Battle of Rhode Island featured the first Afro-American regiment to fight for America.
- Tennis is a big deal here, with Rhode Island housing the Tennis Hall of Fame.
- Although it seems the United States is overloaded with monuments these days, there wasn't a single one when the Nine Men's Misery monument was erected in memory of the colonists killed during King Philip's War in 1676; it's the oldest known monument to veterans in the country.
- When they were outlining the Constitution, Thomas Jefferson and John Adams sang the praises of Roger Williams for originating the principles of freedom of religion, freedom of speech, and freedom of public assembly, all of which are tenets of the First Amendment.

Things Your Character Likes to Remember

- Roger Williams.
- Religious freedom. Rhode Island was never admitted

to the New England Confederation because of its position on religious tolerance and freedom.

- The Industrial Revolution. It started in Rhode Island back in 1790 with Samuel Slater's water-powered cotton mill.
- Nathaniel Greene. Although Greene was second in command to George Washington, many historians deem him the most significant general of the Revolutionary War.
- George M. Cohan. Yes, the man who wrote such national favorites as "Yankee Doodle Dandy" and "You're a Grand Old Flag" is from here.
- Julia Ward Howe. Another patriotic songwriter, she composed the "Battle Hymn of the Republic."
- The White Horse Tavern. Built in 1673, this is the oldest operating tavern in the nation.
- Independence Day. Bristol has the longest unbroken series of Fourth of July observances in the country, dating back to 1785.
- Quonset's Electric Boat facility. It created many new jobs that were lost when the navy station left the state.
- Education. Not only does the state possess the oldest schoolhouse and oldest library in the country, it also houses the well-respected Brown University, an Ivy League institution. Providence alone has twelve colleges and universities.

Things Your Character Would Like to Forget

- The U.S. Navy. It dealt a crushing economic blow to Rhode Island in 1973 when, as the state's largest employer, it closed its Newport Naval Base and Quonset Point Naval Air Station.
- Doris Duke. She allegedly killed her chauffeur lover

Sailboats and a bridge at sunset in Newport

© PhotoDisc/Getty Images

For Further Research

Books

An Album of Rhode Island History, 1636–1986, by Patrick T. Conley

Providence: A Pictorial History, by Patrick T. Conley and P.R. Campbell

The Rhode Island Atlas, by Marian I. Wright and Robert J. Sullivan

Rhode Island and the Formation of the Union, by Frank Greene Bates

Rhode Island: A History, by William Gerald McLoughlin

Rhode Island: Off the Beaten Path, by Robert Patrick Curley

The Transformation of Rhode Island, 1790–1860, by Peter J. Coleman

Vital Record of Providence, Rhode Island, by James N. Arnold

Web Sites

www.providenceri.com/ (official Providence city site)
www.newportri.com (Newport happenings)
www.projo.com (Providence news)
www.visitri.com (tourism)
www.rilin.state.ri.us/studteaguide/RhodeIslandHistory/ rodehist.html (state history)
www.rootsweb.com/~rigenweb/ (genealogy and history)

Still Curious? Why Not Check Out

Blue Moon, by Luanne Rice
Fade to Black, by Wendy Corsi Staub
I, Roger Williams: A Fragment of Autobiography, by Mary Lee Settle
Me, Myself, and Irene
Moonlight Becomes You: A Novel, by Mary Higgins Clark
Mr. North
Newport Houses, by Jane Mulvagh, Mark A. Weber, and Roberto Schezen
One Kid at a Time: Big Lessons From a Small School, by Eliot Levine
Outside Providence
The Survivor's Club, by Lisa Gardner

but was never convicted because of her wealth and donations to the city of Newport.

- Operation Plunder Dome. This FBI operation in 2000 sent several Providence officials to the slammer for bribery, tax favors, and general corruption.

Myths or Misperceptions About Rhode Island

- **Rhode Island is the state's official name.** Guess again. The official state name is "Rhode Island and Providence Plantations."
- **Only the rich and famous live here, in all those big seaside mansions.** While Newport's southeastern shore was the summer home of choice for several wealthy aristocrats, the state at large is home to many middle-of-the-road, common folk.

Interesting Places to Set a Scene

- **Block Island.** Have your character set off on a ferry from Point Judith to Block Island, the state's favorite summer resort that everyone teases is air-conditioned because it's ten to fifteen degrees cooler on the island than on the mainland. The island is a nature lover's dream and quite popular with bird-watchers.

- **Little Compton.** Home to the gravesite of the first girl born to colonists in New England (the daughter of pilgrims John and Priscilla Alden), this sleepy little town is quiet and quaint, especially Gray's store, which was built in 1788. It was the area's first office back then, and today it still sports wheeled cheese, an antique soda fountain, and lots of other old-time stuff.
- **Newport.** Called the "City by the Sea," this is the place that epitomizes "The Gilded Age" in Rhode Island, when Newport was a summer resort for the rich and famous. At the time, the likes of the Astors, the Vanderbilts, and the Belmonts lived here; huge, ocean-view mansions still dot the eastern shore. Few places, in fact, can match Newport's history. The area was home to several different groups of immigrants, from Quakers to Jews, and the *Rhode Island Gazette*, the state's first newspaper. Newport also played a major role in the American Revolution. These days the area is well known for its wharves, boating, and yachting. *Amistad* was filmed here.
- **Providence.** Called "Renaissance City" these days, the state capital has a great deal to offer—museums, the-

aters, a new convention center, historic sites, colleges and universities, an award-winning zoo, and world-class dining. Well, if it's good enough to have a TV show named after it, it's probably good enough to be the setting for your novel.

- **College Hill.** Home to Brown University and the highly reputable Rhode Island School of Design (which has several cool buildings that encapsulate the Brown campus), The Hill is filled with college students, dreamy professors, artsy folks, and many colonial and Victorian homes. Just near the campus is the legendary Thayer Street, a happening, funky shopping strip that bustles with students and counterculture types.

- **Sakonnet Point.** This isolated southeastern tip of the state is where your character would go—or live—to be away from it all. She's likely to run into roadside produce stands, mom-and-pop stores, a few antiques shops, and locals who don't particularly want her there. The point itself is a mix of marshy lands, a tiny harbor, and stone-filled beaches.

- **The Sakonnet Vineyards.** Near Tiverton, this winery produces the most wine in New England. The vineyards can make for a great-tasting getaway.

- **Warwick.** The state's second largest city enjoys the state's largest commercial airport, the T.F. Green Airport; nearly forty miles of coastline along the Narragansett Bay; about fifteen or so marinas; and a reputation as Rhode Island's retail and industrial capital. This is definitely the place where your character could shop 'til she drops, especially at the Warwick Mall and the Cadillac Shopping Outlet. New England's oldest village, Pawtuxet (settled in 1642), is also in Warwick.

- **WaterFire.** This fire sculpture is composed of a series of one hundred bonfires that blaze on the surface of the three rivers that pass through the middle of downtown Providence. The fires illuminate urban public spaces and parks. Your character can come and watch the many residents and visitors who gather to stroll along the river.

South Carolina

South Carolina Basics That Shape Your Character

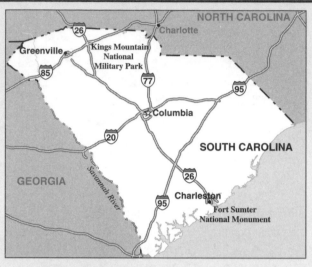

Mottoes: Prepared in Mind and Resources *and* While I Breathe, I Hope

Population: 4 million.

Prevalent Religions: Christianity, particularly Protestant (Lutheran, Methodist, Presbyterian, Episcopalian, and Southern Baptist), and a small percentage of Roman Catholics

Major Industries: Tobacco, poultry, cattle, dairy products, soybeans, hogs, textile goods, chemical products, paper products, machinery, tourism

Ethnic Makeup (in percent): Caucasian 67.2%, African-American 29.5%, Hispanic 2.4%, Asian 0.9%, Native American 0.3%, Other 1.0%.

Famous South Carolinians: Whispering Bill Anderson, James Brown, John C. Calhoun, Dizzy Gillespie, Andrew Jackson, Jesse Jackson, Andie MacDowell, Ronald McNair, Micky Spillane, Strom Thurmond, General William Westmoreland, Vanna White, Woodrow Wilson

Significant Events Your Character Has Probably Thought About

- In 1670, a permanent English settlement was established on the coast near Charleston.
- The slave trade. In the late 1600s and early 1700s, African slaves were shipped here in such large num-

bers that by 1720 they formed the majority of the state's population.
- South Carolina was the first state to secede from the Union (1860); it was readmitted in 1868.
- The first shots of the Civil War were fired at Fort Sumter in April 1861.
- Near the war's end, General William Tecumseh Sherman marched his troops through South Carolina, burning plantations and most of the city of Columbia.
- In 1877, the last federal troops overseeing Reconstruction left South Carolina.
- Sumter adopted a city-manager type of government in 1912, being the first city in the nation to do so.
- Strom Thurmond was elected to his first of eight terms as a U.S. senator in 1954.
- In September 1989, Hurricane Hugo devastated the South Carolina coast, claiming thirteen lives and causing $3.7 billion in damage.

South Carolina Facts and Peculiarities Your Character Might Know

- It's divided into six basic regions: the Sea Islands off the coast (estuaries, salt marshes), the coastal Lowcountry plantation/Charleston area, the Myrtle Beach/Grand Strand area, the Coastal Plains (swamps, pastures, farmland), the Piedmont (manufacturing), and the Blue Ridge Mountains in the northwest (waterfalls, lakes, streams, forests, gorges).
- American Classic Tea farm is the nation's singular commercial tea farm.
- Brookgreen Gardens possesses the world's largest collection of outdoor sculptures.
- Francis Beidler Forest Sanctuary contains the largest remaining virgin stand of bald cypress and tupelo trees in the world.
- Fort Jackson in Columbia is the country's largest military training base.
- The North Carolina-South Carolina border is home to Whitewater Falls, the highest waterfall in eastern North America.
- An abandoned African-American church-turned-nightclub in Columbia was the birthplace of that 1930's dance craze called "The Big Apple."

- South Carolina is home to more than three hundred golf courses.

Your Character's Food and Drink

South Carolinians like traditional Southern dishes, such as fried chicken, ham, steak, prime rib, catfish, chitlins, crackling bread, stew, catfish, hush puppies, all types of seafood, salads, casseroles, pickles, preserves, coleslaw, corn bread, black-eyed peas, turnip greens, peach cobbler, fried okra, sweet potato pie, and boiled peanuts. They prefer whiskey and sweet iced tea to drink. Breakfast favorites include homemade biscuits, bacon, fried ham, gravy, grits, sausage and pancakes.

Things Your Character Likes to Remember

- Strom Thurmond. Not only was he the first U.S. official elected as a write-in, he has also served more years than anyone in the U.S. Senate. South Carolinians love him. (They've even named a huge lake and a high school after him.)
- South Carolina's prominence in U.S. history, especially its political, cultural, and economic importance from colonial times to the Civil War.
- Clemson University's 1981 national championship in football.
- Its gorgeous coast and historic towns.
- It's the place to go for great golfing.

Things Your Character Would Like to Forget

- Hurricane Hugo.
- General Sherman's March to the Sea.
- Negative press associated with the Confederate flag flying above the Statehouse in the late 1990s.

Myths and Misperceptions About South Carolina

- **There is an island in South Carolina named Gullah Island.** Gullah is not an island but a distinctive African-American culture in the Lowcountry and along the coast. It even has its own language, a combination of King's English, American English, and an African dialect.
- **Cotton created all the wealth in the coastal areas of colonial South Carolina.** Guess again—it was rice. African slaves brought it with them and knew how to plant it well, so that's what they did (but rice barons, not slaves, made all the money). Cotton didn't become

profitable until after the Revolutionary War, when Eli Whitney invented the cotton gin (1793).
- **South Carolina isn't a leading peach producer.** Guess again. Both South Carolina and California grow more peaches than "The Peach State," Georgia.

Interesting Places to Set a Scene

- **Abbeville.** With its red-brick streets, historic homes, and old courthouse, Abbeville is the gem of the Piedmont area. It's also deemed "the birthplace and death-bed of the Confederacy," because the first secession meeting was held here, as was the last cabinet meeting of the Confederate government.
- **Aiken.** This is horse country at its finest. Wealthy aristocrats (Vanderbilts, Whitneys, Mellons, Astors, Roosevelts) started coming here years ago, and today it boasts mansions, horse tracks, unpaved streets, Kentucky Derby and Preakness winners, and the Thoroughbred Hall of Fame.
- **Beaufort.** Spanish explorers first came here in 1514 and others have followed, from French Huguenots and English privateers to the notorious pirates of the 1800s. Beaufort is a popular Lowcountry tourist destination these days, with its waterfront vistas, old "town" homes, history, and wonderful architecture. Beaufort has recently been popular with Hollywood as well, with movies such as *The Prince of Tides*, *The General's Daughter*, and *Daughters of the Dust* having been filmed here.
- **Charleston.** (See page 289 for specifics on Charleston.)
- **Columbia.** Although it's the state capital and boyhood home of Woodrow Wilson, Columbia is best remembered because Sherman torched the city, sparing only

Spanish Moss draping over a coastal South Carolina garden

© Michael Peeden

For Further Research

Books

The American South and Southern History, by David R. Goldfield

Red Hills and Cotton: An Upcountry Memory, by Ben Robertson

Still Fighting the Civil War: Reminiscenses of Sea Island Heritage, by Ronald Daise

South Carolina: A History, by Walter B. Edgar

South Carolina: The WPA Guide to the Palmetto State, edited by Walter B. Edgar

Web Sites

www.discoversouthcarolina.com/asi.asp (tourism)

www.sciway.net/hist/ (state history)

www.schumanities.org/ (state humanities council)

www.schistory.org/ (South Carolina Historical Society)

www.state.sc.us/arts/index.html (state arts commission)

Still Curious? Why Not Check Out

Bastard Out of Carolina, by Dorothy Allison

Beach Music, by Pat Conroy

Clover: A Novel, by Dori Sanders

The Hard to Catch Mercy: A Novel, by William Baldwin

Scarlet Sister Mary, by Julia Mood Peterkin

---

a few structures. One still standing is the granite statehouse. These days Columbia typifies sprawl, a mix of modern office buildings, and suburbia.

- **Edgefield.** With its rich deposits of clay, Edgefield is a potter's town and has been since 1800 (actually archeologists have found pottery here dating back to 2,500 B.C.). The entire city is listed on the National Register of Historic Places, thanks to the courthouse square and numerous structures from the nineteenth century. There's also a clay pottery museum.

- **Georgetown.** Founded in 1729, this historic waterfront town was the heart of the colonial rice-baron era (yes, there's a rice museum). Not surprisingly, Georgetown offers a peak into the past, with its many historic homes and well-preserved churches.

- **Hilton Head.** A resort destination for the wealthy and middle class, this barrier island was settled by cotton planters in the 1700s. Of course, it has its share of beachfront hotels, resorts, and plantations, but what make the island special are the nature preserves.

Most impressive is the Sea Pines Forest Preserve, which boasts a 3,400-year-old Native American shell ring, a 605-mile wilderness area, several lagoons, and woods full of majestic oaks and pines.

- **Myrtle Beach.** This is lower-to-middle-class American summer playground and sunny getaway is loaded with beachfront hotels, wax museums, nightclubs, shops, water parks, and more minigolf courses than any putter could wish for.

- **The Piedmont.** In between the mountains and the lowlands, this area has a history of farming hard and living simply—quite unlike the more leisurely folks on the coast. These days Piedmonters are still hard at work but doing less farming and more manufacturing.

- **St. Helena.** This and surrounding islands are where the Gullah culture began. A museum documents the history and lifestyle of the African-American sea island communities. It's also home to Penn Center, the first school established for freed slaves after the Civil War.

Charleston

Charleston Facts and Peculiarities Your Character Might Know

- Charleston lies on a low, narrow peninsula between the Ashley and Cooper Rivers.
- Named after King Charles II, it was established in 1670 and then called Charles Town.
- It's known as the "Holy City" for its numerous churches.
- Founded in 1770, the College of Charleston is one of America's oldest educational institutions.
- The world's first successful submarine attack took place in Charleston Harbor in 1864 when the Confederate *The HL Hunley* rammed the Union *Housatonic*.
- Charleston has no skyline. Thanks to an ordinance dating back to the late 1700s, no building can be higher than the highest church steeple in Charleston proper.
- Charleston is deemed one of America's friendliest cities.
- It's the oldest city in South Carolina and was the colonial center for culture and trade.
- The first shots of the Civil War were fired on Fort Sumter in April 1861.
- Charleston is one of the chief ports of entry in the Southeast; only New Orleans gets more traffic.
- Harleston Greens (built in 1786) was the first golf course in the United States.
- Charleston was frequented by pirates Blackbeard, Stede Bonnet, and Calico Jack (among others) during the early 1800s.
- *Porgy and Bess*, George Gershwin's famous musical, is set in Charleston and based on the novel *Porgy* by DuBose Heyward.
- The Cooper River Bridge will be the largest single-span suspension bridge in North America when completed in 2006.

If Your Character . . .

If Your Character Is a Generation X-er, she lives or hangs out in Folly Beach. Also known as "The Edge of America," this area is Charleston's minimecca for hippies, grungers, skateboarders, and surfers.

Charleston Basics That Shape Your Character

The glorious Boone Hall Plantation

Population: 312,007 in city; 549,033 in the Greater Metro area

Prevalent Religions: Mainly Protestant, especially Episcopalian, Presbyterian, Lutheran, and Methodist. Large numbers of Southern Baptists and, to lesser extents, Roman Catholics. Nondenominational parishes are popular among the younger crowd.

Top Employers: South Carolina Port Authority, MeadWestvaco Paper Mill, U.S. Navy, U.S. Air Force, Blackbaud Corporation, Bayer Corporation, Robert Bosch Corporation, Nucor Corporation, BP Amoco, Medical University of South Carolina

Per Capita Income: $41,799

Ethnic Makeup (in percent): Caucasian 61.9%, African-American 39.5%, Other 1.0%, Hispanic 2.4%, Asian 1.1%, Native American 0.3%.

Average Daily Temperature: January, 48° F; July, 82° F

Newspapers and Magazines: *The Post and Courier*

Free Weekly Alternative Paper: *The Charleston City Paper*

If Your Character Is All About Business, he works in the Downtown Business District. Broad, King, and Queen Streets are dotted with accounting, law, and banking companies and several restaurants and bars. Charleston's business district is unlike others because it has no high-rise office buildings.

If Your Character Is a Tourist, he's on a horse-drawn carriage touring downtown's historic district and visiting

For Further Research

Books

The Buildings of Charleston: A Guide to the City's Architecture, by Jonathan H. Poston

The CSS Hunley: The Greatest Undersea Adventure of the Civil War, by Richard Bak

Mary's World: Love, War, and Family Ties in Nineteenth-Century Charleston, by Richard N. Côté

Mrs. Whaley and Her Charleston Garden, by Emily Whaley and William Baldwin

A Short History of Charleston, by Robert N. Rosen

The Siege of Charleston 1861–1865, by E. Milby Burton

Silver Spoon Restaurants: A Culinary Tour of Charleston's Finest, by Jamie Minster

The Sweet Hell Inside: A Family History, by Edward Ball

Web Sites

www.charleston.net/ (The Post and Courier Web site)

www.charlestoncvb.com/ (Charleston Area Convention and Visitors Bureau)

www.sciway.net/ (news, history, events)

www.jewishcharleston.org/ (Charleston Jewish Federation)

www.discovercharleston.com (travel, tourism, and history)

Still Curious? Why Not Check Out

Drums of Autumn, by Diana Gabaldon

The Legend of Bagger Vance

North and South, Books I and II

On Leaving Charleston, by Alexandra Ripley

The Patriot

Plantation or *Sullivan's Island*, by Dorothea Benton Frank

Porgy, by DuBose Heyward

Porgy and Bess, by George Gershwin

Scarlet Sister Mary, by Julia Peterkin

---

places such as The Market, Fort Sumter, Patriots Point, Rainbow Row, The Battery, the shops of King Street, and the several plantations.

If Your Characters Are Raising a Family, they live in Mount Pleasant. Charleston's high-middle-class suburb, this quaint, historic (founded in 1680) coastal town boasts some of the prettiest streets and homes in the state, including the majestic avenue of moss-draped live oaks leading to the Boone Plantation.

If Your Character Smells of Money, he lives on Charleston Peninsula. The area south of Broad Street is loaded with extravagantly huge homes on big lots and is rumored to contain some of the most expensive real estate in the country.

If Your Character Wears a Blue Collar at Work, she lives in James Island or West Ashley. These are residential areas with small brick or wooden houses and rows of neighborhood blocks. James Island is becoming more popular with the young professional crowd.

Local Grub Your Character Might Love

Charleston is home to many Southern coastal and uniquely Charleston dishes. Favorites include shrimp 'n' grits (Charleston signature dish), steamed oysters, low-country crab cakes, Beaufort stew (a mixture of seafood, sausage, and corn), collard greens, bread pudding, crème brûlée, barbecue, and fried chicken. Notable upscale restaurants abound, such as Carolina's, Slightly North of Broad (SNOB), Magnolia's, High Cotton, Cypress, The Peninsula Grill, 82 Queen, Elliot's, and Garibaldi's.

Interesting and Peculiar Places to Set a Scene

- **The Market.** What was once an old slave-trading center is now an open-air market for arts and crafts. Restaurants, cafes, boutiques, and clubs line each side of the market, which is situated between North and South Market Streets.
- **Rainbow Row and The Battery.** Large colonial homes dominate this area that hugs the Charleston Harbor shoreline.
- **Plantation Homes.** Charleston is home to several colonial plantation homes, including Drayton Hall, Magnolia Plantation, and Boone Hall. Nearly all are in splendid condition.
- **Sullivan's Island.** This quiet barrier island community has quaint homes and uncrowded beaches. It's home to the Sullivan Island Lighthouse and Fort Moultrie (Revolutionary War).

- **The Citadel.** One of the nation's oldest military colleges, this once all-male academy gained worldwide recognition in 1995 when Shannon Faulkner challenged tradition to become the first woman accepted to the school (although she left shortly thereafter).
- **The Dock Street Theatre.** The oldest production theater in the United States, established in 1736, is a gem. Modern playhouses might have many modern amenities, but this is old-time theater is at its finest.
- **The Spoleto Festival.** Charleston hosts this nationally renowned festival each May/June. It is recognized as one of the world's most comprehensive arts festivals, focusing on theater, dance, and music.

Exceptionally Grand Things Your Character Is Proud Of

- Charleston's place in U.S. history.
- Its historic sites.
- Its plantations.
- Southern hospitality.
- Fine Southern dining.
- The Citadel.

- Sweet-grass basket making. At over three hundred years old, this is one of the oldest art forms of African origin in the United States, and Mount Pleasant is the only place where this particular type of basketry is still practiced.

Your Character Loves

- Seafood.
- Historic homes.
- Good Southern cooking.
- The Confederate flag.
- Either Clemson or the University of South Carolina, but definitely not both.
- The beach.
- Southern hospitality.
- Good manners.

Your Character Hates

- Bad food.
- Either Clemson University or the University of South Carolina, but definitely not both.
- Bad manners.

South Dakota

South Dakota Basics That Shape Your Character

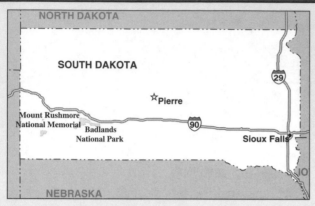

Motto: Under God the People Rule

Population: 755,000

Prevalent Religions: Lutheran, Roman Catholic, and Methodist

Major Industries: Tourism, manufacturing (predominately food processing), agriculture (wheat, corn, oats, soybeans, sunflowers), mining, banking (credit card processing)

Ethnic Makeup (in percent): Caucasian 88.7%, African-American 0.6%, Hispanic 1.4%, Asian 0.6%, Native American 8.3%, Other 0.5%.

Famous South Dakotans: Sparky Anderson, Tom Brokaw, Crazy Horse, Mary Hart, Cheryl Ladd, Russell Means, George McGovern, Dorothy Provine, Red Cloud, Joe Foss, Tom Daschle

Significant Events Your Character Has Probably Thought About

- Before white settlement, the area was dominated by the Sioux nation, a nomadic people who hunted bison on the Great Northern Plains.
- In 1804, the Lewis and Clark Expedition traveled through South Dakota along the Missouri River, charting the territory as part of the Louisiana Purchase.
- In the 1820s, 1830s, and 1840s, fur companies built forts and trading centers in the area, mostly along the Missouri River. The most powerful figure of the time was Pierre Chouteau of the American Fur Company.

The capital city of Pierre (pronounced "peer") is named for him.

- Gold was discovered in the Black Hills in 1874. Colonel George A. Custer was sent to confirm the discovery. At first his assignment was to keep prospectors off the Native American land, but this soon changed to protecting the flood of miners from the Sioux tribes who had been given the land in the 1868 treaty.
- The Dakota Territory continued to boom in the 1870s as railroads eased access to the state. Immigrants, mostly Scandinavian, poured in to farm the rich land east of the Missouri. When political battles heated up in 1883 between the northern and southern regions of the territory, both pushed for statehood.
- Droughts, grasshoppers, and dust storms destroyed thousands of acres of farmland in South Dakota during the 1930s, and many farm families left the state.
- On February 27, 1973, members of the American Indian Movement began a seventy-one-day occupation of the town of Wounded Knee to protest government treatment of Native Americans. The Sioux nation later won a lawsuit for the illegal appropriation of the Black Hills and was awarded $105 million in compensation.

South Dakota Facts and Peculiarities Your Character Might Know

- The state is divided roughly in half by the Missouri River. The east side of the river is flat and is covered with grassy plains. The west side is mountainous and includes the Black Hills and the Badlands.
- Harney Peak in Custer State Park rises to 7,242 feet. It is the highest point in the United States east of the Rocky Mountains.
- The largest U.S. gold mine for many years was located in Lead, but closed in 2001.
- Sculptor Gutzon Borglum took fourteen years (from 1927 to 1941) to complete the Mount Rushmore monument featuring busts of Presidents George Washington, Abraham Lincoln, Thomas Jefferson, and Theodore Roosevelt. The monument is South Dakota's leading tourist attraction.
- The Crazy Horse monument on Thunder Mountain in the Black Hills will take significantly longer than

Rushmore to complete. Sculptor Korczak Ziolkowski began work in 1947. When he died in 1982, the face was not yet finished. The completed face was unveiled in 1998, and work continues on the body and the horse.

- Jack McCall, famous for the murder of Wild Bill Hickock, at the No. 10 Saloon in Deadwood, was convicted and hanged after a short trial in Yankton. His grave is unmarked.
- Several cities have been the capital of the Dakota Territory. When the land was divided into North and South Dakota, cities competed fiercely to be the capitals. Citizens of Pierre spent a lot of money to win the honor and then spent the next thirty years paying off the debt.
- A distinct divide exists within the state. Most of the state's residents live east of the Missouri River in cities and towns and on farms. "West River" residents are more likely to be ranchers.
- The state legalized low-limit gaming in the 1980s, providing a new revenue stream but adding new social problems such as addiction that needed to be addressed.
- Citicorp moved a large portion of its credit card processing operations to Sioux Falls in the 1980s, creating thousands of white-collar jobs and slowing the exodus of the state's young people.

Your Character's Food and Drink

If your South Dakota character likes exotic food, he needs to move. The fare here is meat-and-potatoes American. Sioux Falls offers the widest variety. The open, grassy spaces in the state are perfect for pheasant. Because hunting is a popular sport in the state, elk, deer, quail, and other game are frequently served for dinner.

Things Your Character Likes to Remember

- The state's cowboy heritage.
- South Dakota is clean: clean air, clean water, clean towns and cities.
- The crime rate is low, even in the most populated areas. During the coldest months, it's not unusual for people to leave their cars running while shopping for groceries.
- People here are friendly. As you would expect in such a sparsely populated area, they're self-reliant and a bit

guarded, but on a day-to-day level, they are open and genial. They pride themselves on being this way.
- The movie "Dances With Wolves," much of which was filmed here.

Things Your Character Would Like to Forget

- Poverty is too prevalent on the Native American reservations in various parts of the state.
- Long, cold winters.
- It takes a long time—by car or plane—to get anywhere else.

Myths and Misperceptions About South Dakota

- **It's dullsville.** True, there's not a lot of excitement, but it has many beautiful places and is a paradise for people who like the outdoors. The scenery, particularly in the southwest corner and along the Missouri River, is breathtaking.
- **It's cold.** Winters are long, no question. But the heat of summer is hot—sometimes in the 100s. Visitors expecting a cool July won't find it here.
- **It's conservative.** While the legislature and most state offices are controlled by Republicans, this is also the home of U.S. Senate Majority Leader Tom Daschle and is the state that sent George McGovern, the Democrats' 1972 presidential nominee, to Washington.

Interesting Places to Set a Scene

- **Aberdeen.** People socialize at Wylie Park, an entertainment center offering water slides, a man-made lake, go-carts, and picnic areas. *Wizard of Oz* author L. Frank Baum lived here for a time, so enterprising townsfolk created the Land of Oz theme park, which attracts locals as well as families from nearby areas.

Mount Rushmore

© PhotoDisc/Getty Images

For Further Research

Books

Great Plains and *On the Rez*, by Ian Frazier
Looking for History on Highway 14, by John E. Miller
South Dakota: A Bicentennial History, by John R. Milton
South Dakota: The Face of the Future, by William J. Reynolds
South Dakota: The South Dakota Experience, by Carole Marsh and Kathy Zimmer

Web Sites

www.pierrechamber.com/ (Pierre Chamber of Commerce)
www.state.sd.us/ (state government site)
www.travelsd.com/ (state tourism site)
http://blackhills-info.com/sdhistory/ (South Dakota history)

www.crazyhorse.org/ (site focused on the Crazy Horse monument)
www.dwu.edu/sdlitmap/onmap.html (South Dakota writers)

Still Curious? Why Not Check Out

Black Elk Speaks, by John G. Neihardt
Dakota: A Spiritual Geography, by Kathleen Norris
Dances With Wolves
Deadwood, by Pete Dexter
Feels Like Far: A Rancher's Life on the Great Plains and *Windbreak*, by Linda M. Hasselstrom
Works by Hamlin Garland
Lakota Woman, by Mary Crow Dog and Richard Erdoes
Works by Laura Ingalls Wilder

- **Badlands National Park.** Visitors feel like they're on the surface of another planet when they look at the strange, erosion-scarred buttes and spires of this park.
- **Black Hills.** Covered with pine trees, which the Native Americans thought made the hills look black from a distance, this landmark contains over a million acres and attracts great numbers of tourists and locals.
- **Custer State Park.** Located in the Black Hills, this park is best known for its herds of bison. More than fifteen hundred of them graze the park, sometimes stopping traffic as they amble across park roads. The state's highest peak, Harney Peak, is located here, too.
- **Deadwood.** A wild town during the gold-rush years, Deadwood remains a center for gambling, skiing, and the high life. Wild Bill Hickock, who was killed here, and Calamity Jane (Martha Canary) are fixtures in the local culture. Movie star Kevin Costner owns a popular restaurant in town called Jake's.
- **Mount Rushmore.** Alfred Hitchcock used the monument in the famous scene in *North by Northwest*, but the four faces carved into the Black Hills could work as a great scene in a novel, too. The monument is located twenty-five miles from Rapid City, near the town of Keystone.
- **Pierre.** This small town on the Missouri River is the state capital. The name is pronounced "Peer." There's a mix of East River and West River life here. People like to spend time outdoors at Farm Island or on the Missouri River near the Oahe Dam.
- **Rapid City.** Located in the western part of the state, Rapid City is a straight shot across I-90 from Sioux Falls. It's the seat of Pennington County, which contains many tourist spots. It was the site of a horrific flood in 1972 that left 238 people dead and 3,057 injured.
- **Sioux Falls.** Most of the city's businesses and social life are found on the south and east sides. Citicorp is among the major employers. Sioux Falls is also home to the state's primary prison. Falls Park features a picturesque waterfall.
- **Sturgis.** Tens of thousands of people—from biker gangs on Harleys to weekend wannabes—flood this tiny town every year for the Black Hills Classic Motorcycle Rally. Nearby, 1,400-foot Bear Butte rises alone out of the flat surrounding prairie. It was called "Sacred Mountain" by the Plains Native Americans and was the source of many legends.
- **Yankton.** This original capital of the Dakota Territory lost the honor in 1883. Hometown to NBC news anchor Tom Brokaw, Yankton is proud of its river heritage; Gavins Point Dam is the hot spot for recreation.

Significant Events Your Character Has Probably Thought About

- The New Madrid Earthquake. During the winter of 1811 to 1812, the largest earthquake in American history rattled Tennessee; it created Reelfoot Lake and Lake Counties.
- The bottling of Coca-Cola in 1899. Two Chattanooga attorneys purchased the bottling rights to the drink for one dollar, and America has been adequately caffeinated since.
- Andrew Johnson becoming president. The Tennessean was inaugurated as the seventeenth U.S. president in April of 1865, after Lincoln's assassination.
- The 1868 impeachment of Andrew Johnson. The Tennessean became the first U.S. president to be impeached, thanks to his lenient Reconstruction policies and his vetoes of the Freedmen's Bureau Act and the Civil Rights Act.
- The Cumberland-Georgia Tech football game in October of 1916. Cumberland lost by the ungodly score of 222 to 0. The Georgia Tech coach became quite a success; he was John Heisman, after whom the Heisman Trophy was named.
- The 1925 opening of Nashville's Grand Ole Opry. This legendary radio show has become the longest continuously running live radio program in the world and is still broadcast live every Friday and Saturday.
- The 1925 Scopes Monkey Trial in Dayton, in which high school teacher John Scopes served as the test case in a fight over the state's law requiring that creationism, not evolution, be taught. Creationism forces won.
- Elvis Presley recording his first tracks in the summer of 1953. Just out of high school, The King began the first of many recording sessions at The Memphis Recording Service (Sun Studios).
- Martin Luther King Jr.'s assassination on April 4, 1969. The civil rights leader was gunned down outside the Lorraine Motel in Memphis.
- The establishment of The Farm in 1971. This hippie community started near Summertown and became a harbinger of self-sufficient communal living for the rest of the country.

Tennessee Basics That Shape Your Character

Motto: Agriculture and Commerce

Population: 5.7 million

Prevalent Religions: Christianity, particularly Pentecostals, Southern Baptists, and a few Roman Catholics

Major Industries: Soybeans, cotton, tobacco, livestock and livestock products, dairy products, cattle, hogs, chemicals, transportation equipment, rubber, plastics

Ethnic Makeup (in percent): Caucasian 80.2%, African-American 16.4%, Hispanic 2.2%, Asian 1.0%, Native American 0.3%, Other 1.0%

Famous Tennesseans: James Agee, Chet Atkins, Davy Crockett, Morgan Freeman, Tennessee Ernie Ford, Aretha Franklin, Nikki Giovanni, Al Gore, Isaac Hayes, Benjamin L. Hooks, Dolly Parton, Minnie Pearl, Wilma Rudolph, Cybill Shepherd, Dinah Shore, Tina Turner

- The 1996 Summer Olympics. The Ocoee River became the site for the Atlanta-based Olympics' whitewater canoe/kayak competition.
- The 2000 presidential election. Vice President Al Gore failed to win his home state's eleven electoral votes in his run against George W. Bush, who won the national election by only four electoral votes.

Tennessee Facts and Peculiarities Your Character Might Know

- The state is divided into three geological areas: Mountains comprise the eastern region; the highlands make up middle; and the lowlands are in the west.
- Tennessee has more than 3,800 caves.
- Tennessee was the last state to secede from the Union

during the Civil War, and the first state to be readmitted.

- Oak Ridge, known as the "Energy Capital of the World," played a major role in developing the atomic bomb.
- Tennessee's favorite daughter, Dolly Parton, is from Sevierville.
- Knoxville hosted the 1982 World's Fair.
- Known as "The Volunteer State," Tennessee got its moniker in 1812 because so many citizens volunteered to fight in the War of 1812.
- Living up to its nickname, Tennessee had the most soldiers per capita in the Civil War and the most National Guard soldiers per capita in the Gulf War.
- Alex Haley's childhood home in Henning was the first Tennessee historic site devoted to African-Americans.
- There is no state or local personal income tax in Tennessee.
- Lost Sea in Sweetwater is said to be the largest underground lake in the United States.

Your Character's Food and Drink

"Meat 'n' three" restaurants are popular here. Most "meat 'n' threes" are walk-up-and-pick-it-yourself cafeterias. Your character picks one meat entree (beef pot roast, meat loaf, fried chicken, fried catfish, salmon croquets, chicken n' dumplings) and then chooses three vegetables from a long list (macaroni and cheese is considered a vegetable). Sides include baked apples and cottage cheese. Homemade biscuits or corn bread are also part of the meal. All this typically gets ingested with a big glass of sweetened iced tea, followed up by a cup of coffee and a slice of pie.

© PhotoDisc/Getty Images

The Pioneer Farmstead in the Great Smoky Mountains

Things Your Character Likes to Remember

- Sequoyah. A Cherokee from Tennessee, he was the only man in the history of the world known to have developed single-handedly an alphabet.
- Jack Daniels.
- The Grand Ole Opry.

Myths and Misperceptions About Tennessee

- **They have poor aesthetic judgment.** Take a look at the magnificent BellSouth (Batman) Tower in Nashville; it's one of the coolest buildings in the world.
- **Everyone in Nashville loves country music.** No, they don't; many folks can't stand the pluck of a string and dread the thought of having to learn the boot scoot.
- **Nashville musicians only make country records.** Actually, more commercial jingles for television and radio are recorded in Nashville than anywhere else in the states.

Interesting Places to Set a Scene

- **Bristol.** This is a curious area, because Bristol, Tennessee, and Bristol, Virginia, meet right at the state line, which runs directly down the middle of the main street. Bristol is about steel, paper, furniture, leather goods, and mining cars, and it's home to country music, which allegedly started here in 1924 by superstar Jimmy Rodgers. NASCAR races at Bristol International Speedway are all the rage these days, with partying before and after, including women pulling up their tops to get everybody in the mood for raw entertainment.
- **Chattanooga.** Ahead of the curve environmentally and technologically, Chattanooga has developed an extensive greenway system. The city also supports a downtown shuttle fleet of zero-emission electric buses—manufactured in Chattanooga—for commuters and visitors wishing to park and ride. The city has won repeated awards for outstanding "livability" and excellence in housing and consolidated planning. Moon pies came from here, too.
- **Clarksville.** This city features full-service restaurants and delis, stylish boutiques and antique shops, a museum and live performance venues, plus fascinating historic architecture in both commercial and residential applications. Historic Franklin Street features tree-lined brick sidewalks, period lighting, benches, nice trash receptacles, and planters.

For Further Research

Books

Faithful Volunteers: The History of Religion in Tennessee, by Stephen Mansfield and George Grant

Homewords: A Book of Tennessee Writers, edited by Douglas Paschall

My Own Country: A Doctor's Story, by Abraham Verghese

Myra Inman: A Diary of the Civil War in East Tennessee, edited by William R. Snell

Tennessee: A Political History, by Phillip Langsdon

Trials of the Monkey: An Accidental Memoir, by Matthew Chapman

Web Sites

www.tennesseeanytime.org/ (official state site)

www.utk.edu/ (University of Tennessee)

www.legislature.state.tn.us/ (Tennessee General Assembly)

www.tnstate.edu/ (Tennessee State University)

www.tennessee.worldweb.com/ (travel and visitor guide)

www.east-tennessee-history.org/ (East Tennessee Historical Society)

Still Curious? Why Not Check Out

An Affair of Honor: A Novel, by Richard Marius

Child of God: A Novel, by Lolita Files

Christy, by Catherine Marshall

The Family Holvak

Inherit the Wind

A Letter From Death Row

Night Whispers: A Story of Evil, by Emmett Clifford

Walking Tall

Where the Heart Is, by Billie Letts

White Trash in a Trailer Park, by Randal Patrick

- **Dayton.** This city made itself famous as the setting for the Scopes Monkey Trial, and you, too, can have your courtroom drama in the very same chambers that William Jennings Bryan and Clarence Darrow exchanged wits. Create your own H.L. Mencken to report it all.

- **Great Smoky Mountains.** Although this is beautiful country with misty mountains, all is not placid in the Great Smokies. Backpackers disappear. Poisonous snakes bite at least a few hikers a year. Human–bear encounters are a regularity. In other words, this is a good place for an adventure story.

- **Greenville.** Greenville has the only monument in the United States honoring both the Union and Confederate Armies. It is located on the lawn of the Green County Courthouse.

- **Jonesborough.** Set in the picturesque hill country of eastern Tennessee, the state's oldest town is a time capsule of early America. From the top of Main Street, you can behold dozens of restored, early-nineteenth-century brick buildings, punctuated by the white spires of churches. Storefronts and sidewalks wear seasonal decorations, while locals and tourists alike rest on benches outside the courthouse. Jonesborough combines country style with polish, and its pulse is easy to take. This is small-town Appalachia at its finest.

- **Knoxville.** The University of Tennessee calls Knoxville home, making an array of educational and cultural opportunities available to area residents. Affordable housing, health-care costs below the national average, a low crime rate, and a pleasant climate with lakes and mountains nearby are factors that make Knoxville an attractive place to settle.

- **Lynchburg.** This home to Jack Daniels is an economically sound town that has retained its small-town charm.

- **Memphis.** (See page 298 for more information on Memphis.)

- **Murfreesboro.** A mixture of commercial and residential architecture, both historic and modern, gives downtown Murfreesboro its unique appearance and identity.

- **Nashville.** (See page 301 for more information on Nashville.)

- **Pigeon Forge.** While your character will likely find a lot of campgrounds in southeastern Tennessee near Pigeon Forge (like the Smoky Mountains), once in Pigeon Forge, all he'll get is camp—at its finest. Boardwalks and sidewalks are swarming with tourists, knickknack shops, fast-food joints, and, of course, believe-it-or-not-types of attractions.

- **Rogersville.** This is home to the oldest courthouse and oldest inn in the state. In fact, the whole city is on the National Registry of Historic Places.

Memphis

Memphis Basics That Shape Your Character

Michael Peeden

The King's "Home Sweet Home" (Graceland)

Population: 650,100 in the city limits; 1.92 million in the Greater Metro area

Prevalent Religions: Church of God in Christ (largest African-American denomination in the world), Roman Catholicism is popular, but Pentecostals abound

Top Employers: FedEx Corporation, Memphis City Schools, Shelby County Government, Memphis City Government, Baptist Memorial Health Care Corporation, General Medical and Surgical Hospitals, AutoZone Inc., Kroger, Methodist Healthcare System, Naval Support Activity, University of Tennessee, M.S. Carriers

Per Capita Income: $28,828

Average Daily Temperature: January, 39.6° F; July, 82.1° F

Ethnic Makeup (in percent): Caucasian 47.3%, African-American 48.6%, Hispanic 2.6%, Asian 1.6%, Native American 0.2%, Other 1.5.

Newspapers and Magazines: *The Commercial Appeal, Memphis Magazine, Memphis Business Journal*

Free Weekly Alternative Papers: *Memphis Flyer, Tri-State Defender*

Memphis Facts and Peculiarities Your Character Might Know

- Flat and full of cotton fields, the Memphis area is more akin geographically and culturally to Arkansas and Mississippi than it is to other places in its home state.
- Cotton is still important to the city, as almost a third of the United States's annual cotton crop passes through the Memphis Cotton Exchange.
- Memphis is a mixed bag of laid-back locals with conservative political ideologies and liberal creative types working the streets and club scenes on and around Beale Street.
- An 1878 epidemic of yellow fever sent more than half of the city's population out of town and killed a quarter of those left in town, decreasing the population to fifteen thousand and causing the city to declare bankruptcy.
- In 1909, W.C. Handy wrote "The Memphis Blues," which is deemed the first blues song ever composed on paper.
- Over 43 percent of Tennessee's African-American residents live in Memphis.
- Graceland is the second most visited house in the country (that insignificant alabaster house at 1600 Pennsylvania Avenue ranks first).
- The Lorraine Motel (site of Martin Luther King Jr.'s assassination) is now the National Civil Rights Museum.
- Memphis has been called "Bluff City," "America's Distribution Center," "Home of the Blues," and "The Birthplace of Rock 'n' Roll."
- In 1991, Dr. W.W. Herenton was elected the first African-American mayor of Memphis.
- Visitors from all over the world make Memphis their destination, thanks to its music history.

If Your Character . . .

If Your Character Is All About the Blues, he's hanging out on Beale Street. This is the heart, rock, and soul of Memphis. Now revitalized and hopping, this is where your character will be if he's a tourist (probably B.B. King's Blues Club) or a local looking for some of the best blues in the world.

If Your Character Is All About the Blues and Needs a Big Party as Well, she's at the Beale Street New Year's Bash. Probably the biggest blues party in the world and also known as "Bury Your Blues Blowout on Beale," this is where crazed blues fans go crazy on the crowded streets and inside smoky clubs.

If Your Character Smells of Money, he lives in The Village in East Memphis. An affluent suburban neighborhood with galleries and the Memphis Botanic Garden, Dixon Gallery and Gardens, Lichterman Nature Preserve, and several shopping centers.

If Your Character Needs His Football Fix, he's at The Liberty Bowl. This is the top event in Memphis, held every December for two of the nation's best college teams.

Local Grub Your Character Might Love

Bluff City's pork barbecue is legendary—there are more than two thousand "swine-dining" establishments in Memphis. Payne's Barbecue, Tom's BBQ and Deli, Gus's World Famous Hot and Spicy Chicken, and Earl's Hot Biscuits are some local favorites. Many say the best ribs in the city (served dry) come from The Rendezvous. There are also a number of upscale restaurants that require jackets, but not one demands that your character wear a tie. Arcade Restaurant has 1950s decor and boomerang-patterned countertops; the ambiance has barely changed since the doors opened in 1954. Elvis was a big fan of the Arcade (he loved those creamsicle shakes).

Interesting and Peculiar Places to Set a Scene

- **The Peabody Hotel.** Your character can either dance on top of the building and see views of the city or stay down in the lobby and watch the world-renowned Peabody Duck March, held daily at 11 A.M. and 5 P.M. This is Memphis's most expensive hotel, which not surprisingly also happens to be a good place for spotting celebrities, who are often asked to emcee the duck-marching ceremonies.
- **The Gazebo Outside the National Ornamental Metal Museum.** Have your character sit on the side of the gazebo and grasp the beautiful views of the Mississippi River Valley just below. A most romantic place, especially looking west over the water at sunset.
- **South Main Historic District.** The area between Central Station and the National Civil Rights Museum has been slated for redevelopment, but at press time the effort was only in its infancy. The area remains dominated by boarded-up warehouses.

- **Ernestine & Hazel's.** This used to be a brothel on the inside and a storefront on the outside. This place is the hellhole that everybody wants to go to but not everybody can get in, especially when it's packed and crazy from midnight until three in the morning. Although it looks like it's ready for the wrecking ball, it's actually a top nightspot in Memphis.
- **Overton Square.** This entertainment area at the corner of Cooper and Madison is where "Memphians love to meet, eat, shop, and play!" Overton hosts several festivals and events each year and also houses movie theaters, live theatre, several restaurants and bars.
- **Orpheum Theatre.** Gold stars that is, with the names of performers who have graced the Orpheum's stage over the past one hundred years. The "Sidewalk of Stars" includes such great names as Yul Brynner, Cary Grant, Helen Keller, Louis Armstrong, Gregory Peck, Carol Channing, and Mae West. There are sixty-two brass stars in all, including hometown favorites like B.B. King and Cybill Shepherd.
- **Graceland During Elvis Tribute Week.** Every August thousands of Elvis fans head to Graceland and surrounding areas for the biggest Elvis extravaganza in the world. Have your character dress up, play trivia games, dance, or head to the Heartbreak Hotel for some serious Memphis fun.
- **Cooper Young Historic District.** Guaranteed to send your character back in time, this quaint area of town sports buggies, horse-drawn carriages, big shady trees, and glorious, stately homes.
- **Schwab's Dry Goods Store.** The only original shop from Beale Street's 1940s glory days, this is the place your character needs to go for voodoo powders, wild hats, handcuffs, cheap neckties and other odd "accessories."
- **At The Cotton Makers Jubilee.** This ten-day carnival— filled with rides, games, concessions, and cotton— takes place each May and has the nation's largest African-American parade, with more than 100,000 residents partaking in the festivities.

Exceptionally Grand Things Your Character Is Proud Of

- The revitalization of downtown's urban decay. The total downtown population grew 18 percent from 1990 to 2000, making it one of the fastest-growing downtowns of any city.
- The *Memphis Belle.* Flown by Robert K. Morgan, this

For Further Research

Books

Deep Blues, by Robert Palmer

Good Rockin' Tonight: Sun Records and the Birth of Rock 'n' Roll, by Colin Escott and Martin Hawkins

It Came From Memphis, by Robert Gordon

Last Train to Memphis: The Rise of Elvis Presley and *Careless Love: The Unmaking of Elvis Presley*, by Peter Guralinck

The Man Who Flew The Memphis Belle: Memoir of a WWII Bomber Pilot, by Robert Morgan and Ron Powers

Mine Eyes Have Seen: Dr. Martin Luther King Jr.'s Final Journey, by D'Army Bailey

Wheelin' on Beale, by Louis Cantor

Web Sites

www.ci.memphis.tn.us/ (official city site)

www.commercialappeal.com/ (daily newspaper)

www.gomemphis.com/ (news)

www.digitalcity.com/memphis (news and tourist information)

www.memphismagazine.com/ (city monthly magazine)

www.memphisguide.com/ (overall guide to Memphis)

www.memphisflyer.com/ (alternative newspaper)

Still Curious? Why Not Check Out

The Firm, *The Client*, or *The Rainmaker*, by John Grisham; movie versions of the Grisham's novels

A Family Thing

Great Balls of Fire!

Memphis

Memphis Afternoons: A Memoir, by James Conaway

Mystery Train

Paradise Lost: The West Memphis Childhood Murders

The People Vs. Larry Flint

September, September, by Shelby Foote

was the first B-17 bomber to complete twenty-five missions over Europe and return to the United States safely on its own.

- In addition to being the "Birthplace of Rock 'n' Roll," Memphis also gave birth to several businesses: FedEx Corporation, Holiday Inn, AutoZone Inc., Piggly Wiggly Company, Greyhound Lines Inc., and Continental Trailways.
- The Church Health Center. This nonprofit hospital offers the working poor quality health care that they couldn't otherwise afford.

Your Character Loves
- The Blues.
- Elvis, B.B King, and Rufus Thomas.

- WDIA radio.
- The Gibson Guitar Factory and Museum is the most popular museum of its kind in the world.
- Hollywood—Several films have been shot in town in recent years, adding a boost to the economy.
- Memphis City Schools. They've improved greatly over the years, making many residents proud of their public school systems.

Your Character Hates
- Hard rock.
- Nashville.
- Tourists.
- Arkansas.

⊙ Nashville

Nashville Facts and Peculiarities Your Character Might Know

- Nicknames include "Music City USA" and "Athens of the South." Recently, it's been known as "The Third Coast," next to entertainment megacities Los Angeles and New York City.
- Nashville first became known for its music back in 1870, when the Jubilee Singers of Fisk University opened the world's ears to the African-American spiritual.
- Forty-five thousand registered songwriters call Nashville home.
- Citizens Savings Bank and Trust Company is the United States's oldest African-American financial institution, and McKissack and McKissack is the nation's oldest African-American architectural firm.
- Both country music and Christian music are headquartered in Nashville—more of these types of labels call Nashville home than they do in any other city.
- The decade between 1956 and 1966 is deemed "Nashville's Golden Age," because 188 songs written or recorded in Nashville made the Billboard Top 10, with 27 hitting number one.
- A replica of the Parthenon in Athens, Greece, stands in Nashville's Centennial Park: It's an art gallery containing a forty-one—foot-high statue of Athena.
- The Grand Ole Opry was first broadcast live from Nashville's Ryman Auditorium in 1925 (but then moved to its Opryland complex in 1974).
- Nashville was the first Southern state capital to fall under Union control (1862).
- With the founding of Fisk University and Meharry Medical College in the 1870s, Nashville became known as "The Black Athens of the South."
- If you're from Nashville, you're always "fixin' " to do something (grab a bite to eat, go to the store, take a shower, and so on).

If Your Character . . .

If Your Character Likes to Shop and Spend Money, he's walking the streets in Green Hills. Dotted with upscale restaurants and high-priced boutiques, this is the Rodeo

Nashville Basics That Shape Your Character

The highway to Nashville

Population: 569,891 in the city; 1.2 million in the Greater Metro area

Prevalent Religions: Christianity, Protestants, particularly Southern Baptist, rule. Catholics and others are here as well but in much smaller numbers.

Top Employers: Saturn Corporation, Gaylord Entertainment Center, Dell Computer Corporation, Hospital Corporation of America, CNA Financial Corporation, Shoney's Inc., Aladdin Industries, Cracker Barrel Old Country Store Inc., Caterpillar Financial, BT Services, Primus Automotive Financial Services, Dollar General Corporation, Nissan, Genesco Inc., Vanderbilt University, University of Tennessee, O'Charley's Inc.

Per Capita Income: $30,510

Average Daily Temperature: January, 36° F; July, 79° F

Ethnic Makeup (in percent): Caucasian 67%, African-American 25.9%, Hispanic 4.6%, Asian 2.3%, Native American 0.3%, Other 2.4%

Newspapers and Magazines: *The Tennessean, Tennessee Tribune, Nashville Magazine, Nashville Business Journal, Nashville Post*

Free Weekly Alternative Papers: *Nashville Digest, Nashville Scene*

Drive of Nashville. West End Avenue and Hillsboro Village also offer upscale restaurants and shops.

If Your Character Is an Average Joe, he lives in Antioch. This lower- to -middle-income residential area is where your blue-collar character lives, in a small, modest home.

If Your Character Is Steeped in Old Money, she lives in Belle Meade. With its large, stately, historic mansions and famous cafes and shopping spots, this area is for the socially elite. Period. Brentwood and Franklin also are high-income areas, but they're more new money than old.

If Your Character is a Twenty-First-Century Henry David Thoreau, he hangs out in Radnor Lake State Natural Area. Locals go to this green place to get away from the noise on Music Row; appropriately, they call it "Nashville's Walden Pond."

If Your Character's Got a Song in Her Heart, she lives in Lieper's Fork or Southwest Williamson County. Lots of the city's successful songwriters, performers, session players, and label executives live in this middle- to upper-class suburb.

If Your Character Is a Family Man, he lives in Berry Hill, Hermitage, Donelson, South Nashville, Belleview, or Franklin. With modest but well-kept lawns and homes, these residential neighborhoods are cookie-cutter bedroom communities like those you'd find in any city.

If Your Character Likes to Brush Shoulders With Authors, she goes to The Southern Festival of Books. Held annually in October, this is the big literary event in Nashville, with local and blockbuster scribes partaking in lectures, workshops, and signings.

Local Grub Your Character Might Love

The deal when it comes to eating in Nashville is going to a "meat 'n' three." Favorite Nashville "meat 'n' threes" are Arnold's Country Kitchen, Norman Couser's Country Cooking, Belle Meade Cafeteria, The Pie Wagon, Swett's (in a bad part of town, but the food is awesome), and Sylvan Park Restaurant. Other favorite local restaurants include Corky's, the Elliston Street Soda Shop (an old-fashioned soda shop near Vanderbilt), Barbecutie, Herbert's, and Catfish House. Gerst

beer comes from the original Gerst House Restaurant and Brewery.

Interesting and Peculiar Places to Set a Scene

- **The Palm at 140 Fifth Avenue.** This could be the place for your character to go for an upscale, impressive dinner.
- **Music Row.** With 29 major record labels, 150 recording studios, and thousands of registered songwriters, the row is brimming with creative musical types, from country to Christian to gospel. Have your character get in on some of the yahooing and hallelujahing.
- **The District.** The area surrounding Second Avenue and Broadway is the liveliest entertainment area in the city, with chic boutiques, microbreweries, ethnic restaurants, and hipatoriums of all sorts.
- **The Ernest Tubb Record Shop.** This old store opened its doors in 1947 and draws quite a mixed crowd, from tattooed, pierced grunge rockers to cowboy hat-wearing, country-western enthusiasts. All have one thing in common: They know Tubb's is the place to find rarity and bootleg vinyl albums.
- **Tootsie's Orchid Lounge.** The wallpaper in this old, honky-tonk Nashville institution contains, among other things, Willie Nelson smoke stains and thousands of autographed photos. Throughout the years, its owners have played surrogate parents to some of country music's biggest stars.
- **Robert's Western World.** This western-wear store turned bar is the place that launched the career of country stars BR5-49. It's a hot spot in town and a great place to see the next star band.
- **Bluebird Café.** With its excellent acoustics and two shows a night, The Bluebird is Nashville's most famous venue for country songwriters. Only the best make it here, and many of the people who play here get discovered by a major record label.
- **Dangerous Threads.** Call it a cutting-edge trend shop tailored toward musicians and others wanting to call attention to themselves. This is the place your character will go for leather, rhinestones, fringe, studs, and anything else fashionably weird. As the store motto goes, "Everyone needs to look a little dangerous."
- **Wildhorse Saloon.** Nowhere else in the world will your character sit down for a drink only to encounter ten life-size horses galloping across the ceiling and bellying up to the bar next to him. The large dance floor

For Further Research

Books

Classical Nashville, Athens of the South, by Christine Kreyling

Dreaming Out Loud: Garth Brooks, Wynonna Judd, Wade Hayes, and the Changing Face of Nashville, by Bruce S. Feiler

Embrace an Angry Wind: The Confederacy's Last Hurrah, by Widley Sword

Music City Babylon: Inside the World of Country Music, by Scott Faragher.

Shrouds of Glory: From Atlanta to Nashville, by Winston Groom

Stories Behind the Street Names of Nashville and Memphis, by Denis Strub

Web Sites

www.nashville.gov/flashpgs/flashhome.htm (official city site)

www.nashvillecvb.com/ (Nashville Convention and Visitors Bureau)

http://nashville.bizjournals.com/nashville/ (Nashville business journal)

www.nashscene.com/ (alternative weekly)

www.walkbikenashville.org/ (walking and biking in Nashville)

www.nashvillesports.com/ (Nashville sports council)

www.nashvillemusicguide.com/home.htm (music industry guide)

Still Curious? Why Not Check Out

Dead Folks' Blues, by Steve Womack

I Still Miss My Man But My Aim Is Getting Better, by Sarah Shankman

Nashville

Nashville 1864: The Dying of the Light, by Madison Jones

Nashville Girl

Nashville Rebel

Nashville Tales, by Louise Littleton Davis

The Road to Nashville

---

gets jammed. Free lessons for those who can't tell the "Cotton-Eyed Joe" from the "Wildhorse Stampede."

- **Dad's Old Bookstore.** This place is so small you could wrap a dust jacket around it and call it a book. The smell of the old books alone sends you back in time. Have your character stop here for a first edition, an out-of-print title, or maybe even one of the many autographed press photos and posters.
- **Atop the BellSouth "Batman" Building.** With its needlelike twin towers pointing skyward and resembling the Cape Crusader's hood, this 632-foot-high building is the tallest in the state. It makes for great views of the city, of course, but why not have your jaded and malicious music man toss one of his label executives from the top of it?

Exceptionally Grand Things Your Character Is Proud Of

- Presidents Andrew Jackson (The Hermitage) and James Polk.
- Centennial Park and the Parthenon.

- Its City Parks Program.
- The Grand Ole Opry.
- The Tennessee Titans (and Adelphia stadium).
- The Predators.
- The Opryland Hotel.
- Al Gore.

Your Character Loves

- Nashville's famous Goo Goo candies.
- Teddy Roosevelt. While sipping coffee at the old Maxwell House Hotel, he was so impressed with its flavor that he said it was "good to the last drop." Maxwell House went on to adopt the phrase as its official slogan.
- Oprah Winfrey. Her father owned a barbershop here, and she went to Tennessee State University.
- Music and book publishing.
- RC Cola.
- Moon pies.
- Hosepipe—that's what locals (and other Southerners) call a regular, tubed rubber hose.

Texas

Motto: Friendship

Population: 20.8 million

Prevalent Religions: Baptist, Roman Catholic, Pentecostal, Methodist, and Lutheran

Major Industries: Energy, oil production and refining, natural gas, chemical and petrochemical products, computer and high-tech-related industry, agriculture (primarily cattle, sheep, and cotton), machinery, tourism

Ethnic Makeup (in percent): Caucasian 71%, African-American 11.5%, Hispanic 32.0%, Asian 2.7%, Native American 0.6%, Other 11.7%

Famous Texans: Gene Autry, Clyde Barrow, Carol Burnett, George W. Bush, Joan Crawford, Dwight D. Eisenhower, A.J. Foyt, Larry Hagman, Ben Hogan, Buddy Holly, Howard Hughes, Jack Johnson, Lyndon Johnson, George Jones, Tommy Lee Jones, Janis Joplin, Mary Martin, Roger Miller, Willie Nelson, Roy Orbison, Bonnie Parker, Ross Perot, Katherine Ann Porter, Wiley Post, Dan Rather, Gene Roddenberry, Stevie Ray Vaughn, Mildred "Babe" Didrikson Zaharias

Significant Events Your Character Has Probably Thought About

- A number of Native American societies lived in the Texas area before the Europeans arrived. In the east, the Caddo people occupied the land, while in the west, the Hasinai were the dominant tribe. The Wichita and Tonkawa lived in central Texas, and the Karankawa lived in the south, along the Gulf of Mexico.

- European entry to the area began in the far west, as Spanish explorers settled near El Paso in 1682. The Spanish neglected their mission settlements in the Southwest until the early 1700s, when the French began exploring and settling the eastern part of the state.

- In the 1700s, two strong Native American tribes moved into the state: the Apache and the Comanche. Throughout the 1800s, these tribes would clash with Caucasian residents. The Texas Rangers were formed, in part, to fight these tribes.

- In 1821, Americans moving west began to build settlements along the Brazos River on land ruled by Mexico. Led by Stephen F. Austin, these settlers began to expand their presence, leading to the war for independence in 1835.

- The war lasted from October 1835 until the next April. Its most famous battle took place in San Antonio at the Alamo mission, where 189 volunteers held on through a thirteen-day siege before being massacred by the Mexican army led by General Antonio Lopez de Santa Anna.

- The Texans defeated Santa Anna on April 21 at the Battle of San Jacinto and were granted independence. The Republic of Texas lasted for ten years, despite problems with the Mexican government, with native tribes, and with financial debts. On December 29, 1845, the republic signed a treaty to enter the United States.

- Governor Sam Houston, hero of the war for independence, was removed from office in 1861 for his opposition to joining the Confederacy.

- Unlike many Southern states, Texas thrived during the postwar decades, becoming a center for cattle ranching and, in the western area, for cotton.

- In 1901, the first large oil deposit gushed forth at Spindletop, near Beaumont. The East Texas region grew rapidly in exploiting the oil reserves, and the city of Houston became a center for oil money. Oil fields later were discovered throughout the state.
- In 1963, after the assassination of President John F. Kennedy in Dallas, Texas native Lyndon Johnson became president. The following year he was elected to the post.
- The healthy and diversified economy received a new boost in the late 1960s when the state became a leader in high-tech industries. Austin and Dallas became two of the fastest-growing areas in the country because of the boom in these industries.

Texas Facts and Peculiarities Your Character Might Know

- The name is derived from the Hasinai Native American word *tejas*, meaning "friends" or "allies." When the Spanish arrived in the area, the Native Americans greeted them with the word, which the Spanish used to name the area.
- Texas is known as the "Lone Star State" because of the single star on its flag, which asserted its independence from the stars on the U.S. flag. Though most people think of the song "Deep in the Heart of Texas" when they hear of the state, the official song is "Texas, Our Texas."
- Texas is the only state in the United States that was not annexed. It entered the Union by territorial treaty.
- Texas is number two in both size (Alaska is first) and population (California is first).
- Texas contains more farmland than does any other state. Much of the land is used for growing cotton. An even larger percentage is used as rangeland for cattle and sheep.
- Texas is home to the Bush family, which produced the country's forty-first and forty-third presidents, only the second father-and-son team in U.S. history.

Your Character's Food and Drink

Tex-Mex is number one—and Texans like it spicy hot. The Fiery Foods Festival, held annually in Austin, allows Texas chefs to compete with their spicy sauces. Texas chili is a state tradition. Again, the hotter the better. To wash the fire off their tongues, Texans love Lone Star Beer. Beef barbecue is another tradition. It's particularly popular at backyard picnics and grill-outs, which are much a part of Texas eating traditions. Steak, too, is a state specialty. Southwestern cooking is popular and pervasive, especially in the western part of the state. In the major cities of Texas, any type of ethnic food is available. Authentic Mexican is, of course, a favorite and a specialty of the state.

Things Your Character Likes to Remember

- Their rich history and culture. Texans tend to be experts on Texas. They know the state's history, its facts and traditions, as well as anything it's first, best, or biggest in.
- The Republic of Texas. The only state that formerly was an independent country, Texans pride themselves on their independent past and attitudes. They "Remember the Alamo."
- The Cowboys. Pro football's Dallas Cowboys call themselves "America's Team," and they certainly are the state's team.

Myths and Misperceptions About Texas

- **Big money, big hats, big mouths.** When people think of Texas, they think of rich oil and cattlemen with lots of money and little sophistication. The stereotype of Texas women is a thick accent and big hair. Though these stereotypes are not totally mythic, they're certainly not the whole story. Texas has many sophisticated cities and a well-educated population. It's also home to many world-renowned medical centers and universities.
- **Everything's bigger in Texas.** In some ways, that's true. Visitors often are overwhelmed by the size of the state, and Texans do sometimes crow about their size.

An oil pump in Texas

For Further Research

Books

(A large number of books have written about the state, too many to include here. The following list includes some of the best and most recent.)

Calling Texas Home: A Lively Look At What It Means to Be a Texan, by Wells Teague

Folklore and Culture on the Texas-Mexican Border, by Americo Paredes

Isaac's Storm: A Man, A Time, and the Deadliest Hurricane in History, by Eric Larsen

Lone Star: A History of Texas and the Texans, by T.R. Fehrenbach

Lone Star Justice: The First Century of the Texas Rangers, by Robert Marshall Utley

Oil in Texas: The Gusher Age, 1895–1945, by Roger M. Olien and Diana Davids Olien

Texas Almanac (published annually)

Texas: A Photographic Tour, by Carol M. Highsmith

Web Sites

www.thc.state.tx.us/heritagetourism/httravel.html (Texas Historical Commission)

www.traveltex.com/ (travel information)

www.texashighways.com/currentissue/index.php (*Texas Highways* magazine)

www.tacvb.org/ (Texas Association of Convention and Visitor Bureaus)

http://tourtexas.com/ (state information and tourism with extensive links)

www.texasescapes.com/ (tourism and visitor site with links)

www.texasfun.com/ (state entertainment)

www.noplacebuttexas.com/ (state links and information)

www.texasmart.com/ (links directory for Texas sites)

www.texas.gov/ (state government)

Nearly every city and town in Texas has a Web site, and many are helpful. There are far too many to list here.

Still Curious? Why Not Check Out

A large number of films and novels have been set in Texas, far too many to list here. The following list includes some of the best known.

All the Pretty Horses, by Cormac McCarthy

Barbarosa

The Best Little Whorehouse in Texas, by Larry L. King

Dazed and Confused

Giant

Happy, Texas

Hud

Lonesome Dove and *The Last Picture Show* (novel and film), by Larry McMurtry

Molly Ivins Can't Say That, Can She? by Molly Ivins

Paris, Texas

Tender Mercies

Texas, by James A. Michener

But for every South Fork Ranch, there's a suburb of working folks doing their best to get by.

Interesting Places to Set a Scene

- **Abilene.** Connected by four interstate highways to the major cities in the state, Abilene retains more Western heritage than do the thriving financial centers of east Texas. Developed as a "cow town" in the 1860s, Abilene treasures its past. Skilled makers of saddles and boots still ply their crafts in this city.

- **Amarillo.** The commercial and cultural center of the Texas Panhandle, Amarillo is far less glamorous than many of its fellow cities in Texas. It's a hub for meat-packing and petrochemical industries, especially rubber, as well as for processing grain. The beautiful Palo Duro Canyon is just a short drive away.

- **Beaumont-Port Arthur.** A heavily industrialized, oil-refinery area on the Gulf, Beaumont and Port Arthur team with the town of Orange to create the Golden Triangle. Much money comes from the industries here, but it goes to Houston and Dallas. The area itself is somewhat bleak and dirty. At nearby Spindletop, a marker commemorates the spot where oil was first discovered in the state.

- **Brownsville.** The southernmost city in the state, Brownsville has a strong Mexican atmosphere and culture. It's located on the Rio Grande River and is close to the Gulf of Mexico. It's a port city known for shipping and fishing.

- **Corpus Christi.** Though it's an industrialized port city, Corpus Christi is more beautiful and more of a tourist mecca than are most cities in East Texas. The pride of the city is its beaches along Corpus Christi Bay. Nearby Padre Island is the country's longest barrier island and is a popular spring break destination for college students. Municipal Marina is the vortex of the city's entertainment life, while nearby King Ranch is one of the largest working ranches in the world.

- **El Paso.** Located on the western tip of the state, El Paso was for many years far from its fellow Texas cities in miles as well as economy opportunity. In recent years, however, information technology and health-care industries have made it one of the fastest-growing and economically sound areas in the region. Through architecture and local festivals, it retains its cultural connections to Mexico and the Old West.

- **Laredo.** A fast-growing border city on the Rio Grande River, Laredo is the largest inland port in the country. Home to Texas A&M University, it's a center for trade with Mexico and Latin America. For many years, it relied mainly on shipping, farming, and ranching, but in recent years it has become a wholesale/retail center.

- **Lubbock.** The hub of the state's southwestern plains area, Lubbock is a midsized commercial and industrial center. Its best-known native is rock 'n' roll legend Buddy Holly, who is honored with a large bronze statue, a museum center, and a walk of fame.

- **Midland/Odessa.** A West Texas oil city now known mostly as the home of the Bush family (who don't spend much time here), Midland lies midway between Fort Worth and El Paso. Its metro area has combined with Odessa to form a single metro area of 250,00 people. The city economies rely mostly on the oil-producing Permian Basin, which contains over 20 percent of the country's oil and gas reserves.

- **Waco.** Home to the Texas Sports Hall of Fame and the Texas Rangers Hall of Fame, Waco is located on the Brazos River in the central part of the state. It's also the birthplace of Dr Pepper, and at the Dr Pepper Museum, an animatronic Charles Alderton explains how he invented the drink in 1885. The city's Cameron Park is one of the largest city parks in the state.

Austin

Austin Basics That Shape Your Character

A view of South Congress

Population: 650,000 in the city; 1.25 million in the Greater Metro area

Prevalent Religions: Baptist, Roman Catholic, Pentecostal, Methodist, and Lutheran

Top Employers: Dell Computer Corporation, University of Texas, State of Texas, Motorola Inc., Texas Instruments Inc., Vignette Corporation, Samsung, Tivoli Systems Inc.

Per Capita Income: $31,794

Average Daily Temperature: January, 49° F; July, 85° F

Ethnic Makeup (in percent): Caucasian 65.4%, African-American 10.0%, Hispanic 30.5%, Asian 4.7%, Native American 0.6%, Other 16.2%

Newspapers: *Austin American-Statesman, Austin Business Journal*

Free Weekly Alternative Paper: *The Austin Chronicle*

Austin Facts and Peculiarities Your Character Might Know

- The Tonkawa Native Americans lived throughout central Texas for hundreds of years before the Europeans arrived. Spanish missionaries founded several settlements along the Colorado River in the early 1700s. Around the same time, nomadic Native American tribes, the Apaches and the Comanches, moved into the area.
- In the 1830s, pioneers from the United States established the first permanent white settlement, naming it Waterloo. In 1839, the name was changed to honor Stephen F. Austin, a leader of the rebellion against Mexico.
- Austin was one of several cities vying for selection as the state capital. In 1850, it won the honor in a state-wide election. Other cities, especially Houston, continued to fight for the title until a second election in 1872 settled the dispute.
- For much of its history, Austin's economy has depended mostly on state government activities and the University of Texas, established in 1883. It also was a commercial center for ranching and farming in central Texas.
- The city became known nationally in the 1960s for its thriving music culture and now calls itself "The Live Music Capital of the World." From country to blues, Southern rock to rockabilly, folk to honky-tonk, your characters will find it here in more than a hundred venues for live performances.
- In the late 1960s, Austin began to build a reputation as a home for high-tech industries, beginning with IBM and Texas Instruments. As a result, it has been one of the fastest-growing areas in the country in the past twenty years and calls itself "the Silicon Hills."
- The Colorado River divides the city. North Austin, home to downtown and the university, was long considered more sophisticated. Northerners called people living south of the river "Bubbas"; Bubbas called the northerners "liver lilies." With the expansion and gentrification of the town during recent decades, these distinctions have disappeared.

If Your Character . . .

If Your Character Is Alternative and Artsy, she lives on South Congress Avenue. This is one of the funky spots in town, a street full of restaurants, shops, nightclubs, antique shops, and plenty of street life. The University of Texas students and struggling artists live north of downtown around the campus. Guadalupe Street, known as "The Drag," is the main center for the neighborhood. Your artsy character also might live in South Austin.

If Your Character Smells of Old Money, he lives in Tarrytown in west or west-central Austin. The mansions here are full of character.

If Your Character Has New Money, she lives in the northwest or the southwest neighborhoods farther from the center of town, where big new homes are being built. Mount Bonnell and Cat Mountain are also possibilities. She may live in the Hill Country or in the Arboretum area or along Highway 360. In the west, she might live in West Lake.

If Your Character Is All About Business, he works downtown. All the government and high-tech businesses are downtown; Dell Computer Corporation, however, is in a newer area north of downtown.

If Your Character Is a Rising Professional, she lives in the new high-rise condos downtown. The move is on to revitalize the downtown area as a living area for Austinites. Stores and trendy stops are helping attract the well-heeled professionals from the suburbs.

If Your Characters Are Raising a Family, they live in the southwest, which is growing rapidly. The Circle C is a popular area. The western suburbs are growing, too.

If Your Character Wears a Blue Collar at Work, he lives in the south and north-central area, in the older suburbs.

Local Grub Your Character Might Love

Tex-Mex is the most popular cuisine, as would be expected. Z Tejas is a popular spot, but there are too many favorites to pick just a few. Southwestern cooking styles appear in many restaurants in the city. Authentic Mexican is less pervasive, but there are good places, such as Curra's, that are frequented by locals. Tacos are great for breakfast, lunch, or dinner; Taco Xpress can serve your character all three. The façade of the restaurant features a giant sculpture of a Mexican woman, the owner. The high-tech industries attract employees from all over the world, and Austin is becoming a more international town. Ethnic foods of every type can be found without much trouble. Barbecue, a Texas tradition, is popular here. The County Line, Artz Rib House, and the Salt Lick are local favorites. Lamme's candy also is a favorite. There's a factory in north Austin, but there are Lamme's candy stores throughout the city. Famous for their chocolate-covered strawberries, Lamme's is a local tradition.

Interesting and Peculiar Places to Set a Scene

- **Auditorium Shores.** Auditorium Shores, on the south side of the river across from downtown, is a popular spot for concerts. A well-known statue to guitarist Stevie Ray Vaughn is located on the Shores.
- **Deep Eddy.** A popular spring-fed pool with a long history in the city. Be sure your character dips a toe in first, because the water is cold.
- **Mount Bonnell.** Right in the heart of northwest Austin, it provides the best view of the city, Lake Austin, and the Hill Country. At the top of the cliff, there are observation areas. If your character needs a fresh perspective on life in the city, send him up here.
- **Sixth Street.** The young crowd comes here for music and partying on East Sixth. Bars with live music line the street. The Driskill Hotel, a taste of old Austin, has been restored and gives a note of elegance to the street. West Sixth is an entertainment center, too, but is for more sedate Austinites.
- **The Broken Spoke.** This golden-oldie club in south Austin preserves the city's roots in country-and-western music. Plenty of cowboys and cowgirls are here.
- **The Capitol Building.** An impressive building even by Texas standards, the pink granite Capitol Building is the largest domed statehouse in the country. In true Texas style, locals are quick to note that it's fifteen feet taller than the nation's capitol in Washington, DC.
- **The Hill Country.** A short drive west from downtown Austin, the Hill Country is a favorite area for locals, especially in the spring when bluebonnets blanket the hillsides. Going to see the flowers in bloom is an annual ritual.
- **The University of Texas.** Home of the cherished Longhorns as well as a first-rate educational institution, the University of Texas is a source of pride and interest for Austinites. The campus, located just north of downtown, also is home to a number of the art and culture facilities, such as the Blanton Museum of Art and the Lyndon B. Johnson Library and Museum.
- **The Congress Avenue Bridge.** It spans the lake, and in the spring and summer, a million bats live beneath it. It's a local tradition to go to the bridge and the lake at dusk and watch the bats fly out from below.
- **Town Lake.** Located in the center of the city, Town Lake is a focal point of entertainment and relaxation, a setting for picnics and leisure. Ten miles of walking

For Further Research

Books

Austin: A History of the Capital City, by David C. Humphrey

The Capitol of Texas: A Legend Is Reborn, by Mike Ward

Overcoming: A History of Black Integration at the University of Texas at Austin, by Almetris Marsh Duren

The Sniper in the Tower: The Charles Whitman Murders, by Gary M. Lavergne

UT History 101, by Margaret Catherine Berry

Web Sites

http://www.ci.austin.tx.us/ (Austin city government site)

http://www.austinchronicle.com/ (site for weekly entertainment guide)

http://www.austintexas.org/media_austinmed.php (visitor's bureau site)

http://www.utexas.edu (University of Texas site)

http://www.austin360.com/ (sister site of *Austin American-Statesman*)

http://www.austinwebpage.com/ (city information and links)

Still Curious? Why Not Check Out

Deep in the Heart, by Sharon Oard Warner

Devil Went Down to Austin, by Rick Riordan

Michael

My Austin: Remembering the Teens and Twenties, by Emmett Shelton

Résumé With Monsters, by William Browning Spencer

Slacker

Still Breathing

The Underneath

---

trails attract joggers as well as strollers. This is where Austin gathers for festivals and city events.

- **Warehouse District.** If your characters can't find enough music on Sixth Street, they can head to the Warehouse District on the west side of Congress Avenue. It's the other center for bars and music venues, and it will put your characters in the middle of the city's buzzing nightlife. The crowd here is a bit older than on Sixth but just as rowdy.
- **Zilker Park.** This is Austin's favorite park, a 350-acre spread located in the middle of the city. Its most popular feature is the Barton Springs pool, a three-acre, spring-fed pool with a constant temperature of sixty-eight degrees (a bit chilly in the cool months but bliss in the summer). The pool attracts locals of every age and background.

Exceptionally Grand Things Your Character Is Proud Of

- Austin itself. Though it's a city full of high-tech industry and opportunity, the charm of its days as a music and art center remains.
- Music. It's still a primary element in the day-to-day life of the city. *Austin City Limits*, a long-running show on PBS, is a particular source of pride.

- The film industry. Austin is home to a thriving independent movie scene. Well-known actors and directors such as Owen Wilson, Richard Linklater, and Joe Johnston started here.
- The weather—for most of the year. During the long summer, however, even natives shrink under the heat.

A Pathetically Sad Thing Your Character Is Ashamed Of

- The University of Texas Tower lights up in orange when the Longhorns sports teams win. But on August 1, 1966, Charles Whitman made the tower part of American crime history when he killed fourteen people and wounded dozens others with several sniper rifles. He also had killed his mother the previous night and his wife earlier that day. After four suicide leaps from the tower in the next few years, it was closed in 1974 and was not reopened until 1999.

Your Character Loves

- Barton Springs and Zilker Park.
- The South by Southwest Music Festival.
- The bats. They're a city tradition.
- It's a very open atmosphere—hip and laid-back. Newcomers bring a certain gentrified air to the city, but they quickly adapt.

Dallas-Fort Worth

Dallas-Fort Worth Facts and Peculiarities Your Character Might Know

- The Dallas-Fort Worth metro area—the ninth largest in the country—includes Dallas, Fort Worth, and a number of other growing cities. It's one of the fastest-growing metro areas in the country (and *the* fastest growing of the top ten metro areas) with a population exceeding 5.3 million.
- Dallas is the glitz-and-glamour city and is considered more sophisticated and Eastern. Fort Worth, which was built by its meatpacking and stockyard industry, is considered more Western and earthy; it calls itself "Where the West Begins."
- Fort Worth was established as a military outpost to protect Caucasian settlers from Native American attacks. It's named for William Worth, commander of the Texas army during its war for independence from Mexico. Dallas was established as a trading center and is thought to be named for the vice president at the time, George Mifflin Dallas.
- Though Fort Worth thrived through its location along the Chisholm Trail and is known for its stockyards, its economy is diverse and includes oil, banking, and finance. Dallas's early economy focused mostly on cotton and transportation of Texas goods to the North and East. It became an oil boomtown in the 1930s. It's now home to many corporate headquarters and is a leader in high-tech industries.
- A number of famous folks are from the Dallas-Fort Worth area, including Kate Capshaw, Ornette Coleman, Patricia Highsmith, Fess Parker, Rex Reed, and Liz Smith (from Fort Worth) and Tex Avery, Ernie Banks, Morgan Fairchild, Aaron Spelling, Stephen Stills, and Lee Trevino (from Dallas).
- The integrated-circuit computer chip was discovered in Dallas, sparking a rapid development of high-tech industries in the area, which is known as "Silicon Prairie."
- Market Center in Dallas is the world's largest wholesale merchandise mart, a fitting locale for a city that loves to shop. The Neiman Marcus chain started here, and NorthPark Center claims to be the first covered shopping mall in the country (though several other malls make this claim). Dallas has more shop-

Dallas-Fort Worth Basics That Shape Your Character

The Dallas skyline

Population: 1,188,000 in Dallas; 534,000 in Fort Worth

Prevalent Religions: Baptist, Catholic, Methodist

Top Employers: Texas Instruments Inc., Electronic Data Systems (EDS), JC Penney, Exxon Mobile, Nortel Networks, Nokia, Mary Kay Cosmetics Inc., American Airlines Inc., Frito Lay, Pizza Hut Inc., 7-Eleven Inc., LockheedMartin, Bell Helicopter Textron

Per Capita Income: $34,690 in Dallas; $28,035 in Fort Worth

Average Daily Temperature: January, 45° F; July, 86° F.

Ethnic Makeup (in percent): Dallas: Caucasian 50.8%, African-American 25.9%, Hispanic 35.6%, Asian 2.7%, Native American 0.5%, Other 17.2% **Fort Worth:** Caucasian 59.7%, African-American 20.3%, Hispanic 29.8%, Asian 2.6%, Native American 0.6%, Other 14.0%

Newspapers: *The Dallas Morning News, Fort Worth Star-Telegram*

Free Weekly Alternative Paper: *Dallas Observer*

ping centers per capita than any other U.S. city.
- The world's largest bronze statue (featuring cowboys on horseback herding longhorn steers) is located at the entrance to the Dallas Convention Center.

If Your Character . . .

If Your Character Is Alternative and Bohemian, he lives in Deep Ellum or the McKinney Avenue/Oaklawn Avenue area. These are the centers of the artsy and grunge scenes.

If Your Character Smells of Old Money, he lives in University Park, Highland Park, or the Turtle Creek area. During the white flight of the 1970s, much of the old money moved out of the city into the northern suburbs.

If Your Character Is All About Business, she works in Downtown Dallas, where the well-established financial institutions and corporate headquarters have been for many years, or in Downtown Fort Worth, especially in oil and related industries. North Dallas also has a growing number of business areas.

If Your Character Is New Money, he lives in Willowbend or one of the many high-priced new suburbs in the northern area. Well-heeled young professionals also might live in the lofts downtown or uptown.

If Your Characters Are Raising a Family, they live in a variety of the commuter suburbs. Larger pockets of young families can be found in Coppell, Grapevine, Plano, Frisco, Richardson, Allen, and Southlake.

If Your Character Wears a Blue Collar at Work, she lives in the Euless/Bedford area or in Hurst, Garland, North Richland Hills, Grand Prairie, Duncanville, or DeSoto. The areas south of Dallas and those in between Dallas and Fort Worth tend to be blue collar. South Dallas is known as the more economically challenged section.

Local Grub Your Character Might Love

Tex-Mex is the metro favorite. The chicken fajita, for example, was invented in Dallas, as was the frozen margarita. The Blue Mesa restaurants and a number of other spots in the metro area are known for their margaritas. Barbecue, steak, and Southwestern cuisine are done in great style here. Lone Star Beer is still big, though not in the wealthy northern suburbs. Texas chili is another classic dish. As this is a cosmopolitan metro area, locals can find every type of ethnic food here.

Interesting and Peculiar Places to Set a Scene

• **Arlington.** Located south of Dallas and Fort Worth, Arlington has bloomed as an entertainment center convenient to both cities. The main attraction is the new Ball-

park in Arlington, home to baseball's Texas Rangers. Its other big draw is Six Flags Over Texas amusement park, which features more than a hundred rides as well as a three-hundred-foot observation tower that affords a view of the Dallas and Fort Worth skylines.

• **Bass Performance Hall.** Fort Worth's crown jewel, this world-class opera house is a magnificent, state-of-the-art concert space and is home to the Fort Worth Symphony, opera, and the Fort Worth Dallas Ballet.

• **Fair Park.** Located two miles east of downtown Dallas, Fair Park is a 277-acre area that contains nine museums and six performance facilities, including the Cotton Bowl, the Dallas Aquarium, the science and natural history museums, and the Discovery Gardens. Its buildings comprise the largest collection of Art Deco architecture in the world. Your characters could find more than a dozen great settings in one place.

• **Fort Worth Stockyards Historic District.** This national historic district evokes the city's beginnings as a key point along the Chisholm Trail. It's now mostly an entertainment area and a tourist mecca.

• **Garland.** The growth in North Dallas has brought the city of Garland into the sprawl. Located fifteen miles northeast of downtown Dallas, Garland is a commuter city of 200,000, where shopping malls and suburbs spread far and wide.

• **John F. Kennedy Memorial Plaza.** Located in the West End Historic District close to where the president was shot, the thirty-foot monument commemorates a historic moment in U.S. history. At nearby Dealey Plaza, the Sixth Floor Museum presents a collection of photographs and artifacts at the spot where Lee Harvey Oswald fired the shots.

• **Mesquite.** More than 250,000 people flood this city every year for the Mesquite Championship Rodeo. Located due west of downtown Dallas and well within the sprawling metropolis, Mesquite is the official "Rodeo Capital of Texas," though mostly it's a large bedroom community.

• **Plano.** For many years a small farming community a half hour due north of Dallas, Plano joined the sprawl in the 1980s and is now a commuter city of wealthy suburbs and more than 200,000 residents. A few historic buildings commemorate the area's farm heritage, but mostly Plano is about big suburban homes and escape from the city.

• **Sundance Square.** A masterpiece of urban redevelop-

6

For Further Research

Books

As Old as Dallas Itself and *Big D: Triumphs and Troubles of an American Supercity in the 20th Century*, by Darwin Payne

Dallas: The Making of a Modern City, by Patricia Evridge Hill

Dallas Then and Now, by Ken Fitzgerald

Dallas Uncovered, by Larenda Lyles Roberts and Kay Threadgill

Decker, by Jim Gatewood

Fort Worth Then and Now, by Carol E. Roark

Gamblers and Gangsters: Fort Worth's Jacksboro Highway in the 1940s and 1950s, by Ann Arnold

Reminiscences of the Early Days of Fort Worth, by J.C. Terrell

Web Sites

www.dallascityhall.com/ (Dallas city government)

www.dallascvb.com/ (Dallas Convention and Visitors Bureau)

www.dallasnews.com/ (*The Dallas Morning News*)

www.dallas.thelinks.com/ (links directory for Dallas and Fort Worth)

www.dallasobserver.com/ (*Dallas Observer*)

www.fortworth.com/ (Fort Worth Convention and Visitors Bureau)

http://ci.fort-worth.tx.us/ (Fort Worth city government)

www.dfwi.org/ (downtown Fort Worth business and entertainment)

www.fortworthcoc.org/ (Fort Worth Chamber of Commerce)

www.ci.arlington.tx.us/ (Arlington city government)

www.arlington.org (Arlington entertainment and culture)

www.ci.garland.tx.us/ (Garland city government)

www.planotx.org/ (Plano city government)

Still Curious? Why Not Check Out

Big Town, by Doug J. Swanson

Dallas

The Day That Dusty Died, by Lee Martin

Doin' Dirty and *Jitter Joint*, by Howard Swindle

The Loop, by Joe Coomer

North Dallas Forty

Queen: The Making of an American Beauty

Texas Justice Bought and Paid For, by Mona D. Sizer

The Thin Blue Line

Walker, Texas Ranger

---

ment, this twenty-block area is networked by red-brick streets and lined with stores, restaurants, nightclubs, theaters, and galleries set in historic buildings. The TV show *Walker, Texas Ranger* was set in this area.

- **West End Historic District.** A renovated area on the west side of downtown Dallas, this district is known for great restaurants, shops, and nightclubs. The restored buildings and trendy interiors and people give the area a mix of history and excitement. Great people-watching here, too.

Exceptionally Grand Things Your Character Is Proud Of

- Fort Worth is proud of its ability to reinvent underused areas, such as the Stockyards Historic District and the Sundance Square area. Bass Performance Hall is a source of pride as well.
- The Cowboys. Win or lose. And they've won a lot. They've appeared in eight Super Bowls, more than any other team.

- The Texas State Fair, held in Fair Park in Dallas. It draws more than three million people every year and is the largest fair in North America. Big Tex, a fifty-two-foot statue of a smiling cowboy, greets visitors at the fair entrance and is a well-known landmark. The "Texas Star" Ferris wheel is another beloved tradition of the fair.
- Being a Texan. In Texas, residents take more-than-usual pride in the state itself—they also are proud of its history and culture.
- Dallas prides itself on its urbane sophistication, especially its artistic attractions—museums, orchestra, opera, and theater. Fort Worth cherishes its Western roots and its mix of big business and Texas authenticity.

Pathetically Sad Things Your Character Is Ashamed Of

- The assassination of John F. Kennedy in Dallas.
- The antics and arrests of various Cowboys players.

When the Cowboys are behaving badly—or playing badly—locals call them "the Cryboys."

- In the wealthy Plano area, teens have had more than their share of drug problems and suicides.

Your Character Loves

- The Cowboys and the Longhorns are nearest and dearest to their hearts, but the cities have embraced the Rangers and Mavericks in recent years. Sports are big in Texas. High school sports are followed more closely here than they are in most states. Pitcher Nolan Ryan, who played for the Rangers and is a native Texan, is beloved as is former Cowboys coach Tom Landry.
- They're also proud of their sports facilities, such as the Ballpark in Arlington, Texas Stadium (in Irving), and even the aging Cotton Bowl.
- The death penalty and the right to bear arms.
- The bluebonnets. When these flowers bloom, it's almost mandatory to see them.
- Eating out. There are four times more restaurants per capita in Dallas than there are in New York City.
- Fort Worth loves Billy Bob's Texas, a seven-acre entertainment complex featuring a restaurant, general store, twenty-five bars, and an indoor rodeo. It's known as the "World's Largest Honky-Tonk."
- Reruns of *Dallas*. In the 1980s, it was one of the most popular shows on television. The Southfork ranch remains a tourist site and an events center.

Your Character Hates

- Each other . . . well, not really. The spread of the metro area has united Dallas and Fort Worth, and the rivalry has been softened considerably by the influx of residents from throughout the country. There's still a bit of rivalry between the cities but far less than in decades past.
- Archrival University of Oklahoma. The big football game, held every September in the Cotton Bowl, is very important. Any team who plays the Cowboys is suspect, but the Washington Redskins and the Philadelphia Eagles are particularly despised.

Houston

Houston Facts and Peculiarities Your Character Might Know

- Houston was the first capital of the Republic of Texas, which was formed after the rebellion against Mexico. The city was named for Sam Houston, the leader of the rebellion and the first president of the republic.
- Houston goes by the nicknames "The Bayou City," which it pretty much has outgrown, and "Space City," a nod to the role of the aerospace industry in the city. Houston has the huge Space Center Houston museum, as well as NASA's Johnson Space Center.
- Epidemics of yellow fever were common in Houston until the turn of the twentieth century, when concerted efforts were made to combat the mosquitoes that carried the disease.
- Like many large commercial centers in the South, Houston depended on cotton as its economic base, even after oil production had become big business.
- Oil was discovered in nearby Spindletop in 1901, ushering in the industry that would become synonymous with the city.
- In 1914, the Houston Ship Channel opened, making Houston an inland ocean port. The port of Houston handles more international tonnage than does any other in the city and is second in total tonnage.
- The port also brought oil companies to the city who were seeking easy access to the Gulf of Mexico but inland safety from storms and hurricanes, like the one that decimated Galveston in 1900. By 1930, Houston was a key center for oil production.
- The Texas Medical Center, located in Houston, is the largest medical facility in the world. It employs more than fifty-two thousand people.
- A number of famous folks come from Houston, including Allen Drury, Shelly Duvall, Howard Hughes, Barbara Mandrell, Dennis and Randy Quaid, Kenny Rogers, and Patrick Swayze.
- Houston is the fourth largest city in the country. Over 4.6 million people live in the metro area. With 8,778 square miles, Greater Houston is the largest metro area in the country. The city itself is spread over 617 square miles.

Houston Basics That Shape Your Character

Johnson Space Center

Population: 1.95 million

Prevalent Religions: Baptist and Roman Catholic

Top Employers: Texas Medical Center, Compaq Computer Corporation, NASA Johnson Space Center, Reliant Energy Inc., Continental Airlines, Conoco Inc., Shell Oil/Chemical Corporation, Dynergy Inc., Lyondell Chemical Company

Per Capita Income: $32,386

Average Daily Temperature: January, 52° F; July, 84° F

Ethnic Makeup (in percent): Caucasian 49.3%, African-American 25.3%, Hispanic 37.4%, Asian 5.3%, Native American 0.4%, Other 16.5%

Newspaper: *Houston Chronicle*

Free Weekly Alternative Paper: *Houston Press*

If Your Character . . .

If Your Character Is Alternative and Grungy, she lives in the Museum District, around Rice University. The Montrose area nearby is a bit more upscale but is sophisticated and artistic, a haven for individualists.

If Your Character Smells of Old or Big Money, she lives in River Oaks or the Heights (for old, old money). The houses here are grand and classic.

If Your Character Is All About Business, he works in Downtown or, perhaps, along the I-10 "Energy Corridor." The Uptown/Galleria area is another business center and includes the sixty-five-floor Williams Tower, the world's tallest building not located in a central business area. Or, try Greenway Plaza or the Houston Port area.

If Your Character Is a Rich Computer or Energy Geek, he lives in Katy, Clear Lake, or the Galleria area. Sugar Land is a bit of a drive, out on the western fringe, but more folks are building out there and commuting to the city.

If Your Characters Are Raising a Family, they live outside the 610 loop, in places such as Sharpstown, First Colony, and other suburbs in the southwest. Next to Sharpstown, the town/suburb called Bellaire is a strongly Asian community.

If Your Character Wears a Blue Collar at Work, she lives in Pasadena and other southeastern towns and suburbs on the way to Galveston. This is *Urban Cowboy* country.

Local Grub Your Character Might Love

As it is throughout the state, Tex-Mex is king here. Downtown's Caba's Mix-Mex Grille is a three-story restaurant that's well known for its Tex-Mex cuisine. A close second to Tex-Mex is Cajun cuisine. Your characters will find dozens of places that specialize in Cajun dishes, and many of the locals have a Cajun specialty or two that they like to cook for guests. The Magnolia Bar and Grill on Richmond is the most popular of the city's Cajun restaurants. The city also boasts thousands of restaurants of every ethnic variety. It's tough to name a type of cuisine that you *can't* find in Houston. The proximity of the Gulf makes seafood plentiful—either at fine restaurants or off the back of a fisherman's truck. Barbecue is another specialty of the city—and in Houston, barbecue means beef.

Interesting and Peculiar Places to Set a Scene

- **Astros Field.** One of the new classic-style ballparks, Astros field is a great place to see a game. It replaced the cavernous Astrodome, which was a state-of-the-art facility when it opened in the 1960s. Astros Field originally was called Enron Park, but after the scandal involving Enron in 2002, the name was changed.
- **Galveston.** An hour's drive from Houston, Galveston is an old port city located on the Gulf of Mexico. In recent years it has undergone extensive renewal, especially the waterfront area, which attracts Houstonians on the weekend. For many of the locals, going "to the beach" means going to Galveston.
- **Hermann Park.** A key entertainment center for the city, this area includes the Houston Zoo and the Museum District. In the Museum District, your characters will find the Museum of Fine Arts, the sixth largest museum in the country, as well as ten other museums. There's also a lot of green space here for walking and enjoying nature within the big city.
- **The ferry to Bolivar Island.** If your characters are looking for a cheap date, send them on the ferry from Galveston to Bolivar Island, where many people—especially the young and single—go to camp and "party."
- **Memorial Park.** Located near the upscale Galleria area, this lovely park is full of joggers with cell phones. It's a green space in the middle of town, surrounded by the buzz of the city.
- **Rice University campus.** Spanish oaks and moss grace the campus, which is old and elegant in a place that prides itself on newness. There's a rich history—beginning with the murder of the founder by his butler—and a who's who list of alumni.
- **The San Jacinto Monument.** Located a short drive east of the city, the monument marks the San Jacinto battlefield where Texans defeated Mexico to win their independence. The monument itself is a tall, white column similar to the famous Washington Monument, though Houstonians are quick to point out that their monument is fifteen feet taller.
- **Theater District.** A source of pride for Houstonians, the Theater District, a seventeen-block area in downtown Houston, is home to the city's ballet, opera, and symphony. Locals frequently compare the district to New York City. From the Alley Theater—Houston's center for dramatic arts—to lighter dramatic fare at Theater Under the Stars, the performing arts are located here. After the show, chic nightclubs and restaurants in the district attract crowds.
- **The Tunnels.** A system of pedestrian walkways built beneath downtown Houston, the Tunnels connect major office buildings, parking garages, and entertainment centers, restaurants, and shopping areas. A cool respite from the heat of Houston summer, the Tunnels are clean and safe, if a bit sterile.

For Further Research

Books

Houston 2000: People, Opportunity, Success, by Ray Viator

Houston: Deep in the Heart, by Ted Landphair and Carol M. Highsmith

Invisible Houston: The Black Experience in Boom and Bust, by Robert D. Bullard

The Man With the Candy: The Story of the Houston Mass Murders, by Jack Olsen

No Color Is My Kind, by Thomas R. Cole

Web Sites

www.cityofhouston.gov/ (city government)

www.houston-guide.com/ (Greater Houston Convention and Visitor's Bureau)

www.houstonmetropolis.com/ (guide to city buildings, especially skyscrapers)

www.houston-texas-online.com/ (city links directory)

www.houstonhistory.com/ (detailed city information, including history and links)

www.houston.org/ (city economic and chamber of commerce site)

www.chron.com/ (*Houston Chronicle*)

www.houston-press.com/ (*Houston Press*)

Still Curious? Why Not Check Out

The Eagle and the Raven, by James A. Michener

Farewell to the Mockingbirds, by James McEachin

Gone Fishin', by Walter Mosley

Houston, by Doug Bowman

The Lord's Motel and *God's Country Club: A Novel*, by Gail Donohue Storey

Urban Cowboy

Exceptionally Grand Things Your Character Is Proud Of

- The sports teams. Pro basketball's Rockets in the early 1990s won championships, which have been rare for Houston. The Oilers had to move out, though they've been replaced by the Texans, and the Astros have had good years. The most successful franchise has been the Women's National Basketball Association's Comets.
- The size. Texans like things big, and Houston is the biggest in all kinds of ways—and it's continuing to grow. In a survey of the ten largest cities in the country, Houston ranked second in job growth.
- The arts and culture. Houston has a world-class ballet, opera, and orchestra. "It's just like New York," Houstonians like to say.
- It's an international city full of cultural diversity.

Pathetically Sad Things Your Character Is Ashamed Of

- The Enron scandal. Houston's largest employer and most powerful company attracted national attention in 2002 when many top executives divested their holdings before the stock price plummeted, virtually destroying the retirement savings of thousands of employees.
- Andrea Yates. A resident of suburban Clear Lake, Yates drowned her five children in the bathtub. Her trial in 2002 caught national outrage as many people, particularly in Houston, hoped she'd receive the death sentence. She didn't.
- Competition with Dallas. Houston has a wide-open, brawling history, while Dallas is more chic and sophisticated. Some Houstonians compare themselves constantly with their more beguiling neighbor to the north.

San Antonio

San Antonio Basics That Shape Your Character

The Alamo

Population: 1.1 million

Prevalent Religions: Roman Catholic, Baptist, Pentecostal, and Methodist

Top Employers: USAA Real Estate Company, SBC Communications Inc., Frost National Bank, Ultramar Diamond Shamrock Corporation, Valero Energy Corporation

Per Capita Income: $24,716

Average Daily Temperature: January, 49° F; July, 86° F

Ethnic Makeup (in percent): Caucasian 67.7%, African-American 6.8%, Hispanic 58.7%, Asian 1.6%, Native American 0.8%, Other 19.3%

Newspaper: *San Antonio Express-News*

Free Weekly Alternative Paper: *San Antonio Current*

San Antonio Facts and Peculiarities Your Character Might Know

- Coahuiltecan Native Americans lived in a settlement near the current city. Spanish priests and explorers discovered the San Antonio River in 1691 on the feast day of Saint Anthony of Padua and named it in honor of the saint. The city later took its name from the river.

- The Spanish began building a permanent settlement in 1718, including a *presidio* and a mission, the latter called San Antonio de Valero, better known today as the Alamo.

- In December of 1835, during the rebellion from Mexican rule, a small group of Texians captured the Alamo. By February of 1836, 189 volunteers occupied the mission. From February 24 until March 6, a large Mexican army made many efforts to take the mission and finally succeeded, killing the entire group. "Remember the Alamo" became a rallying cry for the Texian army, which defeated Mexico six weeks later to win independence.

- The Alamo, located in the heart of downtown, is the city's leading tourist attraction. San Antonio is called "The Alamo City."

- The Alamo is part of a cluster of Spanish missions built in the area near the San Antonio River during the eighteenth century. Others include Concepción, Espada, San Juan, and San Jose. Each has its own charms and history and makes a great setting for a San Antonio scene, evoking the Spanish heritage and culture of the place.

- Throughout much of its history, San Antonio has been a center for the transportation of cattle. Cattle herders made it an unruly "cow town" throughout the nineteenth century.

- The Mexican revolution in the 1910s brought an influx of Mexicans to the city. The growing Mexican population diversified the city but, at times, polarized it. Racial tensions between Caucasians and Mexicans were part of the city's life for decades afterward.

- Water is always an issue, especially now that the city is growing so rapidly. The Edwards Aquifer is the sole source of water, and new housing, especially in the quickly expanding north, causes no end of concern for people who worry the aquifer will soon run dry.

- San Antonio is the ninth largest city in the country.
- The city is a center for military bases. Fort Sam Houston, the birthplace of military aviation and now a leading army medical center, is the best known. Three large air force bases also make their homes here: Brooks, Lackland, and Randolph.

If Your Character . . .

If Your Character Is Alternative and Grungy, he lives in downtown, especially in the Lavillita area, or the near North Side.

If Your Character Smells of Old Money, she lives in Alamo Heights or in Terrell Hills slightly north of downtown.

If Your Character Is All About Business, he works in Downtown, especially if he works in banking, law, insurance, government, or a paper profession. The business area is expanding in the north or along the I-410 loop.

If Your Character Is a Rich Computer Geek, she lives in the northwest portion of town near the medical district beyond the loop, such as Converse, Thelma, and Universal City. Due west lies The Dominion, which is on the high end of the new money.

If Your Characters Are Raising a Family, they live in Converse and the expanding suburbs in the north and northwest.

If Your Character Wears a Blue Collar at Work, he lives in the aging suburbs of the near north side.

Local Grub Your Character Might Love

Mexican here runs the gamut from horrible to outstanding. La Fogata is a local favorite. Most ethnic cuisines are available, particularly downtown along River Walk. Tex-Mex is available throughout the city, as is Southwestern cuisine. Tamales are a specialty of the area; any group gathering will include them. The stockyards are closed, but the city's love of steak lives on.

Interesting and Peculiar Places to Set a Scene

- **Brackenridge Park.** Your characters will find a mix of tourists and locals in this huge park that contains the zoo, the botanical gardens, and the Japanese Tea Gardens, as well as jogging trails, picnic areas, and a golf course. Above it all, Swiss cable cars slide along cables strung high in the air.
- **La Villita.** A neighborhood located in the heart of downtown on the east side of the San Antonio River, La Villita is a one-block cluster of art galleries and unique shops. The focus here is on art and artists. Your characters will mix with local bohemians and well-heeled tourists.
- **Market Square.** It's the largest Mexican marketplace outside of Mexico. Known by locals as "the Mexican Market," it's a Spanish-style plaza with restaurants, art galleries, and shops. On weekends, dances and festivals are held here. For colorful details and a diversity of people, this area makes a great setting.
- **Paseo del Rio.** Next to the Alamo, the River Walk is the best-known landmark in the city. Located on both sides of the San Antonio River in the heart of the city, the River Walk is a cobblestone path stretching for more than two miles. The path runs through commercial and entertainment areas as well as through green, parklike settings. Cobblestone bridges span the narrow river in a number of spots, making it easy to move from one side to the other. Tour boats packed with tourists make their way up and down the river.
- **Tower of the Americas.** Take a scene to new heights by setting it in the observation areas atop this 750-foot tower that overlooks the city. Built in 1968 as part of the Hemisfair celebration, it features glass-enclosed elevators to give your characters a scenic ride and a touch of vertigo.
- **The Alamo.** The Alamo got its name from Spanish soldiers garrisoned there in the early 1800s; they named it after their hometown of Alamo de Parras. Tours are conducted here throughout the day. Locals have taken the tour, but your characters will find most people in line are visitors to the city.
- **The Missions.** Visitors to the Alamo can head south along a nine-mile trail along the San Antonio River where they'll see four other Spanish missions, all of which are well-maintained and great places to set a scene. Though the Alamo is the best known because of the famous stand against the Mexican army, the Mission San Jose is considered "Queen of the Missions" for its beauty and size. The others (see "San Antonio Facts and Peculiarities Your Character Might

For Further Research

Books

Many books have been written about the Alamo and the famous battle, viewing it from every possible perspective. There are too many to list here.

Crown Jewel of Texas: The Story of San Antonio's River, by Lewis F. Fisher

Place Names of San Antonio, by David P. Green

San Antonio de Bexar: A Community on New Spain's Northern Frontier, by Jesus F. de la Teja

San Antonio: Outpost of Empires, by Lewis F. Fisher

San Antonio: The Soul of Texas, by Gerald Lair and Susanna Nawrocki

San Antonio Uncovered, by Mark Louis Rybczyk

Web Sites

www.sanantoniovisit.com (San Antonio Convention and Visitors Bureau)

www.mysanantonio.com/ (*San Antonio Express-News*)

www.thealamo.org/ (tourism)

www.ci.sat.tx.us/ (city information and links)

www.alamocity.com/ (city links directory)

Still Curious? Why Not Check Out

The Alamo

The Ballad of Gregorio Cortez

The Battle of the Alamo

Cloak and Dagger

Last Night at the Alamo

Not Between Brothers: An Epic Novel of Texas, by D. Marion Wilkinson

Pee-Wee's Big Adventure

Places Left Unfinished at the Time of Creation, by John Phillip Santos

San Antonio

Something Borrowed, Something Black, by Loren D. Estleman

Still Breathing

Know") offer their own unique architecture and details.

Exceptionally Grand Things Your Character Is Proud Of

- Friendliness. The city prides itself on its geniality.
- The Alamo and the other missions. Yes, they boost the economy, but locals see their beautiful Spanish missions as much more than just tourist traps.
- The River Walk. It's a unique attraction of the city, and no visitor passes through without spending some time here.

A Pathetically Sad Thing Your Character Is Ashamed Of

- The Mexican Mafia. A network of drug dealers that extends deep into Mexico, they frequently make the local news for arrests and murders.

Your Character Loves

- The Spurs. The city's only major-league sports team, pro basketball's Spurs inspire fanatical devotion.
- Fiesta. This ten-day, citywide event held annually in April features parades, concerts, food, and much good cheer to celebrate the city's Mexican heritage.
- The Spanish heritage and culture, in all its forms—from food to festivals, architecture to accents.

Your Character Hates

- Drought. The water issue haunts the city. During dry months, locals get nervous.
- The heat. It's the hottest large city in the state, and moisture from the Gulf adds humidity. But fall and winter are mild, and locals prefer the heat to the cold and snow of the North.

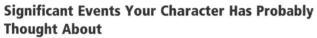

Utah

Significant Events Your Character Has Probably Thought About

- Brigham Young becoming first governor of the Utah Territory (1851).
- The 1857 removal of Young as governor by James Buchanan. Rumors spread that Mormons were rebelling against federal authorities, so Buchanan ousted Young by sending 2,500 troops to accompany newly appointed governor Alfred Cumming. This started the Utah War.
- Utah officially becoming the forty-fifth state in 1896. Heber Wells was inaugurated as governor.
- In 1943, the federal government's largest wartime construction project, the Geneva steel plant, started operation in Utah County.
- The 1964 completion of the Flaming Gorge Dam on the Green River.
- Lake Powell became the nation's second largest artificial lake, thanks to Arizona's Glen Canyon Dam.
- Moderate Democrat Calvin Rampton was first elected governor in 1965 and became the state's only three-term governor, holding office until 1977.
- In 1997, a wagon train traveled the old pioneer wagon trail from Winter Quarters to the Salt Lake Valley to celebrate the 150th anniversary of the Mormon's arrival in the area.
- A tornado ripped through the state in 1999, causing more than $100 million in damage.
- The Winter Olympics in 2002 galvanized the state, boosting tourism and economy and putting Utah on the international map.

Utah Facts and Peculiarities Your Character Might Know

- The Golden Spike National Historic Site at Promontory is where the Central Pacific and Union Pacific Railroads met on 1869 to complete the world's first transcontinental railroad.
- Utah is a natural wonder. It has five national parks (Arches, Canyonlands, Zion, Bryce, Capitol Reef), seven national monuments (Cedar Breaks, Natural Bridges, Dinosaur, Rainbow Bridge, Grand Staircase-Escalante, Timpanogos Cave, Hovenweep), two national recreation areas (Flaming Gorge, Glen Canyon),

Utah Basics That Shape Your Character

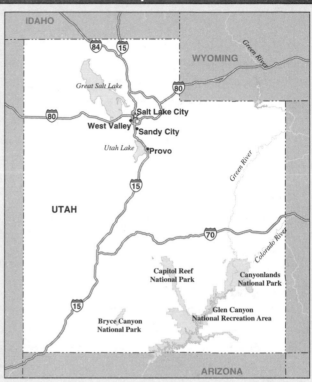

Motto: Industry

Population: 2.3 million

Prevalent Religions: Church of Jesus Christ of Latter-day Saints, Roman Catholic, Methodist, Lutheran, Presbyterian, Muslim, and Episcopalian

Major Industries: Cattle, dairy products, hay, turkeys, machinery, aerospace, mining, food processing, electric equipment, tourism

Ethnic Makeup (in percent): Caucasian 89.2%, African-American 0.8%, Hispanic 9.0%, Asian 1.7%, Native American 1.3%, Other 4.2%

Famous Utahans: Frank Borzage, Butch Cassidy, Laraine Day, Bernard De Voto, Philo Farnsworth, John Gilbert, J. Willard Marriott, Merlin Olsen, The Osmonds, Reed Smoot, Mack Swain, Everett Thorpe, Robert Walker, James Woods, Loretta Young

six national forests (Ashley, Dixie, Fishlake, Manti-LaSal, Uinta, Wasatch-Cache), over 11,000 miles of streams and rivers, and 147,000 acres of lakes and reservoirs.

- The section of I-70 from the Colorado border to Cove Fort is one of the most deserted stretches of interstate in the country.
- Thanks to its steep slopes, Alta ski center was a key training camp for paratroopers during World War II.
- Utah ranks as one of the top ten locations in the United States for film production
- Utah has quite an array of climates, from the arid Great Salt Lake Desert, which receives less than five inches of rain annually, to the northern mountain ranges, which get more than sixty inches (and average five hundred inches of snow each winter).
- Beaver is the birthplace of outlaw Butch Cassidy and television inventor Philo T. Farnsworth.
- Heber Valley Railroad can boast that its steam engine and old-time railroad cars have appeared in more than thirty movies.

Your Character's Food and Drink

Some folks still eat lots of meat, including big game like deer, elk, bison, and antelope. Some chefs in the state are now taking a healthy, natural approach to cooking, using locally grown herbs, grains, and vegetables as well as fish (bass, trout, salmon) from Utah's mountain streams.

Things Your Character Likes to Remember

- Its professional sports teams: Utah Jazz (basketball), the Salt Lake Buzz (baseball), the Utah Grizzlies (hockey), and the Utah Starz (women's basketball).
- Their spaceman senator. In 1985, Senator Jake Garn

orbited the earth 108 times and traveled 2.5 million miles as a payload specialist on the STS-51D *Discovery* mission.

- Utah has the highest literacy rate in the nation.
- The Treasure Mountains Resort (now Park City). It created the world's first underground ski lift in 1965 using an electric mine train. The skiers traveled three miles into the mine and then up an 1,800-foot elevator shaft to the slopes. The lift stopped, however, in 1969, because passengers got tired of the long, slow underground ride.
- Rainbow Bridge. At 278 feet wide and 309 feet high, it's the world's largest natural-rock span.
- Printing and publishing. They started here in 1850 and have been mainstay industries since.

Things Your Utah Character Would Like to Forget

- Its chemical weapons facilities. The mishandling of chemical weapons—and taking shortcuts in destroying some of them—caused major environmental concerns recently.
- All the chaos and scandal before and during the 2002 Winter Olympics.

Myths and Misperceptions About Utah

- **Utah is one big desert.** While parts of it are, the state is filled with thirteen-thousand-foot mountains and lush, green river valleys as well.
- **Mormons are polygamists.** Not true today—that practice was outlawed years and years ago (1890).
- **Salt Lake City is right on the Great Salt Lake.** It's actually fifteen miles east of the lake.

Interesting Places to Set a Scene

- **Arches National Park.** This place contains the world's largest concentration of natural stone arches—nearly two thousand of them. With inspiring areas possessing names like Devil's Garden and Fiery Furnace, you should have no problem finding ways to set a unique scene here.
- **Bryce Canyon.** Oops, wrong planet! That's what your character will think once he steps foot in Bryce, an otherworldly, Mars-ish wonder of this world. It's a massive series of horseshoe-shaped amphitheaters carved by wind and rain into thousands of sparkling spires, fins, pinnacles, and mazes (collectively called "hoodoos"). The colors of these strange-looking formations range

© PhotoDisc/Getty Images

Arches National Park

For Further Research

Books

The Great Railroad Race: The Diary of Libby West, Utah Territory, 1868, by Kristiana Gregory
A History of Utah's American Indians, by Forrest S. Cuch
Nothing Like it in the World: The Men Who Built the Transcontinental Railroad, by Stephen E. Ambrose
The Peoples of Utah, edited by Helen Z. Papanikolas
The Poet and the Murderer: A True Story of Literary Crime and the Art of Forgery, by Simon Worrall
Utah History Encyclopedia, edited by Allan Kent Powell
Utah: The Right Place: The Official Centennial History, by Thomas G. Alexander

Web Sites

http://history.utah.org/index.html (state historical society)
www.utahhistorytogo.org/amnindtime.html (history)
www.utah.gov/index.html (official state site)
www.utahwriters.org/friends.htm (writer's site)
www.mormon.org/ (Church of Jesus Christ of Latter-day Saints)

http://utah.citysearch.com/section/attractions/ (visitor information)
www.thespectrum.com/ (state news)
http://parks.state.ut.us/ (state park site)

Still Curious? Why Not Check Out

2001: A Space Odyssey
Butch Cassidy and the Sundance Kid
City Slickers II: The Legend of Curly's Gold
Desert Sojourn: A Woman's Forty Days and Nights Alone, by Debi Holmes-Binney
Downwinders: An Atomic Tale, by Curtis Oberhansly and Dianne Nelson Oberhansly
The Executioner's Song, by Norman Mailer
Footloose
The Greatest Story Ever Told
Independence Day
Mission Impossible II
Red Water, by Judith Freeman
Thelma and Louise

from pastel orange to sore-throat red to crispy golden brown. This is a science fiction writer's paradise.

- **Fandango! Writer's Retreat.** This gathering of writers and storytellers in six languages takes place in Bluff, an area that has roller-coastered its way through the rise and fall of mining, cattle ranching, and farming. Today, this San Juan River town is an art-and-craft haven, with painters, sculptures, photographers, and fabric and bead makers all about.
- **Kanab.** This southern town near the Arizona state line is known as "Utah's Little Hollywood," for the many motion pictures filmed in the area. It's also deemed "Park Central" because it's so close to so many national parks, monuments, sand dunes, and so on.
- **Moab.** "The Heart of the Canyonlands," Moab is the only city in the state located on the Colorado River. The setting is awesome, with the city is nestled between colorful red rocks and the lofty peaks of the La Sal Mountains. Mountain bikers think of this as heaven on Earth, and Hollywood and advertisers consider it a great spot to film.
- **Monument Valley.** Massive rock formations jut hundreds of feet into the air in this mile-high, monument-studded paradise on the Navajo Reservation. Amidst the rock and dirt roads is Scenic Byway U.S.-163 at the Utah/Arizona line, which is both desolate and world-famous at once—nobody inhabits the place and few have visited it, but millions have seen it repeatedly thanks to scores of movies and commercials.

- **The Festival of the American West.** The northern town of Wellsville becomes a busy west-fest each summer as it glorifies nineteenth-century Utah. Your character can no doubt find something interesting to do at one of the Western art shows, cowboy poetry readings, horse parades, Dutch oven cook-offs, quilt shows, pioneer settlements, or military encampments.
- **The Sundance Film Festival in Park City.** This winter wonderland packs in more than twenty thousand filmmakers, dealmakers, skiers, stars, sycophants, and cell phones—all ostensibly celebrating independent filmmaking (but secretly celebrating themselves for being at the coolest festival this side of Cannes). Even when Sundance isn't in town, Park City is a yuppie's shopping and recreational hotspot, filled with quaint shops, outdoor concerts, theater and dance performances, art festivals, a symphony, and several art galleries.

Salt Lake City

Salt Lake City Basics That Shape Your Character

Salt Lake City's skyline

Population: 181,743 in the city; 1.3 million in the Greater Metro area

Prevalent Religions: Church of Jesus Christ of Latter-day Saints, some Roman Catholic, Baptist, and Episcopalian

Top Employers: U.S. Federal Government, Utah State Government, Church of Jesus Christ of Latter-day Saints, University of Utah, Kennecott Corporation, Delta Airlines

Per Capita Income: $21,271

Average Daily Temperature: January, 28° F; July, 78° F

Ethnic Makeup (in percent): Caucasian 79.2%, African-American 1.9%, Hispanic 18.8%, Asian 3.6%, Native American 1.3%, Other 12.1%

Newspapers and Magazines: *The Salt Lake Tribune, Deseret News, Utah Business*

Free Weekly Alternative Paper: *Salt Lake City Weekly*

Salt Lake City Facts and Peculiarities Your Character Might Know

- The area used to be home to the Shoshone, Ute, and Paiute Native Americans.
- Brigham Young and the Mormons came here in 1847; that first Mormon wagon train included three women and three African-Americans.
- Salt Lake City was actually named Great Salt Lake City, but officials decided to drop the "Great" in 1868.
- The surrounding mountains get five hundred inches of snowfall each winter.
- Salt Lake City is the industrial, financial, religious, and commercial center of Utah, as well as the state capital and the largest city in Utah.
- The city has a low housing vacancy rate due to the rapid job growth, and housing costs have been rising.
- The Mormon Temple took a glacial forty years to complete—but it was worth it!
- Salt Lake City hosted the 2002 Winter Olympics.
- TRAX, a twenty-four-kilometer light-rail system running from downtown to the Salt Lake Valley, was completed in 1999.
- Young Mormon men serve a "mission" around ages eighteen to twenty.
- Mormons tend to prefer to be called "Latter-day Saints," as the official name of the church is the Church of Jesus Christ of Latter-day Saints.
- Contrary to popular opinion, you *can* get an alcoholic beverage in Salt Lake City.

If Your Character . . .

If Your Character Is a Devout Mormon, he's hanging out in—Mormons don't "hang out." Everything has a purpose. They might socialize at home, at their ward, or their stake center (similar to a Catholic priest). Or they might go to dinner or a cultural event. But they don't "hang out."

If Your Character Is Trendy, she's shopping in Gateway. This outdoor shopping mall will satisfy the shopping urges of any character. The Crossroads Mall, with typical mall fare, is another popular place.

If Your Character Loves to Ski, he's heading to the slopes at Brighton or Park City. Although in the past these have been primarily skiing hills, snowboarding is becoming popular. In fact, many prefer it over skiing, especially the young crowd.

If Your Characters Are Raising a Family, they live in Sandy. This is the place for family in Salt Lake City, with a variety of recreational and cultural options, a low

For Further Research

Books

Approaching Zion, by Hugh Nibley

The Doctrine and Covenants of the Church of Jesus Christ of Latter-day Saints, by Joseph Smith

Encyclopedia of Mormonism, edited by Daniel H. Ludlow

A Gathering of Saints: A True Story of Money, Murder, and Deceit, by Robert Lindsey

The Mountain Meadows Massacre, by Fuanita Brooks

Salamander: The Story of the Mormon Forgery Murders, by Linda Sillitoe and Allen D. Roberts

Secret Ceremonies: A Mormon Woman's Intimate Diary of Marriage and Beyond, by Deborah Laake

Web Sites

www.slweekly.com/ (arts and entertainment)

www.digitalcity.com/saltlakecity/ (current events)

http://deseretnews.com (news)

www.sltrib.com/ (news)

www.lds.org/ (official church site)

Still Curious? Why Not Check Out

Fault Line, by Sarah Andrews

Footloose

The Killing of America

Recapitulation, by Wallace Earle Stegner

SLC Punk

Touched by an Angel

---

unemployment rate, a growing economy, and a strong family atmosphere. Nice, respectable homes make up this pleasant area.

If Your Character Wears a Blue Collar at Work, she lives in Rose Park. This community was quickly erected after World War II and contains lots of similar-looking, row-by-row homes and lawns.

Local Grub Your Character Might Love

The standard Mormon meal is baked ham, funeral potatoes, and lime Jell-O with carrots. Funeral potatoes got its name because women would make this casserole dish and freeze it, so it would be ready to go if there was a funeral. Locals tend to love Chuck-O-Rama and other places that serve family-style cooking, but the city boasts lots of international and nontraditional restaurants as well.

Interesting and Peculiar Places to Set a Scene

- **Pioneer Park.** Dirty benches, old newspapers, litter, old shopping carts, overgrown weeds, and people down on their luck set the scene here. Recently many of the park's trees, which were planted by the first settlers, have been cut down. This is definitely the place in town to hide a body or to commit a murder.
- **Memory Grove.** With its war monuments, pond, canyon, and babbling creek, this place is a pleasant pause from the business of the city. It's an especially great place if your character is a dog lover, as it offers one of few places in town where Rusty can roam free in the designated "off-the-leash-is-okay" area.
- **A Liberty Park Festival.** One of the city's favorite fair and festival locations, your character can easily come across everything from someone selling snow cones and hemp jewelry to belly dancers and drumming musicians looking to bag a few bucks.
- **Antelope Island.** This is the largest island in the Great Salt Lake, popular for recreational activities like swimming, boating, picnicking, sunbathing, hiking, mountain biking, horseback riding, and camping. Your character can even observe the large herd of wild bison inhabiting the island.
- **Temple Square.** Enclosed within fifteen-foot-high walls, this ten-acre block in the middle of downtown bustles with tourists from all over the globe, which is no surprise since it contains the Mormon Tabernacle, Assembly Hall, a huge multilingual Jesus statue (speaks over twenty languages!), and numerous other monuments.
- **Olympic Park.** There's no other place like this in the state ... and few in the world. The Winter Sports Park boasts the bobsled, luge, ski jump and other Olympic-event venue sites.
- **Trolley Square.** Utah's historic festival marketplace is one of the state's most popular tourist attractions. It offers shopping, dining, and entertainment in a charming, turn-of-the-century setting.

- **Gilgal Gardens.** This is a sanctuary of Mormon art and sculpture, the most unforgettable of which is the sphinx sculpture with the face of Joseph Smith on top of it (it's made out of twenty-five tons of rock and occupied a large spot in Smith's backyard).
- **Lagoon.** This country-western theme park has a shaky, aged roller-coaster, a Pioneer Village, a rifle-shooting gallery, a log ride, an ice-cream parlor, a beach, and kitschy shops that are supposed to evoke memories of the Wild West.

Exceptionally Grand Things Your Character Is Proud Of

- Temple Square and the Mormon Tabernacle Choir.
- The mountains, canyons, and all their outdoor opportunities.
- Downtown—it's clean and safe.

- Mary Jane Dilworth. In 1847 this seventeen-year-old opened the area's first school in her tent.

Your Character Loves

- Lime green Jell-O with carrots.
- The television series *Touched by an Angel*—it's filmed here.
- Joseph Smith.
- Donny and Marie Osmond.
- History.
- Documentation—this plane is known the world over for millions of stats on millions of people.
- Giving and receiving a friendly smile.
- Hard work and discipline.

Your Character Hates

- Californians.
- Rude skiers from out of state.
- Agnostics and atheists.

Significant Events Your Character Has Probably Thought About

- Ethan Allen and company captured Fort Ticonderoga in 1775.
- In 1791, Vermont became fourteenth state in the Union.
- Montpelier became the state capital in 1805.
- In 1826, Martin Henry Freeman became the first African-American college president in the country.
- Vermonters didn't elect their first Republican governor until 1855—but then Republicans controlled that office for more than one hundred years, until 1962.
- Vermonter Calvin Coolidge became president in 1923.
- Consuelo Northrup Bailey was elected as the first woman lieutenant governor in the states in 1954.
- Billboards were officially banned from dotting the Vermont landscape in 1968.
- Vermont's economy has grown well since the 1960s, thanks to the tourist industry and the high-tech firms (mostly in and around Burlington).
- In 2000, the state's legislature granted gays and lesbians the right to apply for a certificate for what's called a "civil union"—but it's not deemed a "marriage."
- Republican Senator James Jeffords shocked constituents and the country in 2001 when he left the party to become an independent.
- Vermont's Senate Health and Welfare Committee unanimously approved a medical marijuana bill in 2002.

Vermont Facts and Peculiarities Your Character Might Know

- When Calvin Coolidge was vice president, he was vacationing in Vermont when he received an urgent call on August 3, 1923, informing him of the death of President Warren Harding. It was 2:47 A.M., but Coolidge was immediately sworn in as the thirtieth president of the United States—by his father, who was a notary public.
- With a population of less than nine thousand, Montpelier is the smallest state capital in the nation.
- Bill Clinton couldn't have survived as governor of Vermont, as Montpelier doesn't have a single McDonald's (it's the only state capital without one).

Vermont Basics That Shape Your Character

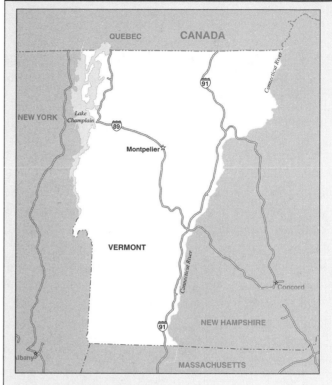

Motto: Freedom and Unity

Population: 608,000

Prevalent Religions: Christianity, particularly Roman Catholic, Methodist, Lutheran, Presbyterian, Pentecostal, Baptist, and Episcopalian

Major Industries: Dairy products, cattle, hay, apples, maple products, electronic equipment, fabricated metal products, printing and publishing, paper products, tourism

Ethnic Makeup (in percent): Caucasian 96.8%, African-American 0.5%, Hispanic 0.9%, Asian 0.9%, Native American 0.4%, Other 0.2%

Famous Vermonters: Chester A. Arthur, Orson Bean, Calvin Coolidge, John Deere, John Dewey, Stephen A. Douglas, Richard Morris Hunt, William Morris Hunt, Moses Pendleton, Joseph Smith, Ernest Thompson, Rudy Vallee, Brigham Young

- Montpelier is the largest producer of maple syrup in the country.
- Vermonters used to have to drive to the state capital

just to get a drivers license with their photo on it.

- Ben & Jerry's doesn't believe in throwing away good stuff—the company gives all its ice-cream waste to local hog farmers to feed to their oinking friends. The pigs love it, except for the oreo mint flavor, which they just won't eat.
- Motorists still have to stop on some country roads to let herds of cattle cross.
- After they escaped from Austria, the Von Trapp family of *The Sound of Music* fame made their new home in Stowe. The area is now a thriving ski resort.

Your Character's Food and Drink

Yankee cooking is what's going in your character's mouth here, including foods like pot roast and pudding, sticky buns and homemade corn relish. New England foods like fiddlehead ferns, maple syrup, cheese, fruits and berries, venison, quail pheasant, and other game go over well here, too. Vermonters also like lots of variety, as it's home to those with a wide variety of tastes—especially near Burlington—so it's not too surprising to see ethnic dishes being whipped up around the state.

Things Your Character Likes to Remember

- Longtime governor George Aiken.
- Milk. It produces most of the New England region's dairy products.
- Writers. The Bread Loaf Writers' Conference in Middlebury is one of the most noteworthy summer writing workshops in the world.
- Skiing. Killington is the king of skiing east of the Rockies.
- Weaving and sheep sheering. Sheep farming was reintroduced to the state in the last twenty-five years.

A wood shed in Vermont

- Made in Vermont. If it says it, locals buy it, whether it's maple syrup, sharp cheddar cheese, Vermont gin, Vermont apple wines, Vermont chocolate, or Ben & Jerry's ice cream.
- The Marlboro Music Festival. Every summer this small town becomes quite sonorous as musicians from around the world come to play their classical and chamber music.
- The Green Mountains.

Myths and Misperceptions About Vermont

- There are more cows than there are people. While this used to be true, it is no longer. However, Vermont does still have the highest ratio of cows to people in the country.
- Ben & Jerry's is Vermont's largest employer. Nope—it's IBM.
- They're all a bunch of socialists. Not true—it's just the only state in the nation to be represented by an independent socialist congressman.

Interesting Places to Set a Scene

- **Bennington.** This college town has history (the Battle of Bennington and Ethan Allen's Green Mountain Boys), and it can boast of having one of the most expensive and progressive liberal arts schools in the country. Vermont's favorite poet, Robert Frost, is buried here; his tombstone reads, "I had a lover's quarrel with the world." Who hasn't . . .
- **Brattleboro.** Once an industrial town filled with blue-collar workers, Brattleboro is now home to many bohemians, progressives, counterculturists, and activists. However, it also is the heart of commerce for southeastern Vermont. Vegetarian eateries and shops abound. If your character's into tofu, pine nuts, and left-wing politics, this is her place.
- **Burlington.** The state's biggest city (only about forty thousand) is mostly a college town filled with people who want an alternative to big-city life. The city's three claims to fame are Ben & Jerry's, the rock band Phish, and former socialist mayor Bernie Sanders, whose now the state's only representative in Congress. Church Street's pedestrian mall is good old-time shopping at its best, with people walking about from store to store in support of small business owners. This is also where Ethan Allen made his home for many years.

For Further Research

Books

The Beauty of Vermont, by Tom Slayton

Granite and Cedar: The People and the Land of Vermont's Northeast Kingdom, by Howard Frank Mosher and John M. Miller

Off the Leash: Subversive Journeys Around Vermont, by Helen Husher

Roadside Geology of Vermont and New Hampshire, by Bradford B. Van Diver

Robert Frost's New England, by Betsy Melvin and Tom Melvin

The Soul of Vermont, by Richard W. Brown

Vermont: A History, by Charles T. Morrissey

Vermont: A Bibliography of Its History, by Thomas D. Seymour Bassett

Vermont: A Guide to the Green Mountain State, by Federal Writers' Project

Vermont: An Explorer's Guide, by Christina Tree and Peter S. Jennison

Vermont's Land and Resources, by Harold A. Meeks

Web Sites

www.state.vt.us (official state site)

www.uvm.edu/ (University of Vermont)

http://vermont.indymedia.org/ (news)

www.vpr.net/vt_news/ (Vermont Public Radio news)

www.vermonthistory.org (state history)

www.middlebury.edu/%7Eblwc/ (Bread Loaf Writers' Conference)

Still Curious? Why Not Check Out

Crossing to Safety, by Wallace Earle Stegner

Disappearances, by Howard Frank Mosher

The Freshman

The Gore: A Novel, by Joseph A. Citro

The Inn at Lake Devine: A Novel, by Elinor Lipman

Midwives: A Novel, by Christopher A. Bohjalian

The Price of Land in Shelby: A Novel, by Laurie Alberts

Shelburne, Vermont: A Novel, by Richard S. Conde

Tales From the Edge of the Woods, by Willem Lange

Three Wishes, by Barbara Delinsky

A Stranger in the Kingdom

Sweet Hearts Dance

White Christmas

Where the Rivers Flow North

- **Chester.** Its picture-book Victorian homes and quaint Main Street are lovely, but what makes Chester special is its stone village, two rows of stone houses constructed during the Civil War, many of which were apparently stops and safe havens on the Underground Railroad.

- **Manchester.** Manchester proper was once a rather quiet and subdued town, but nearby Manchester Center is now "The Place to Shop" in Vermont, as seen by the shoppers cramming the discount malls. The old town itself still has quaint marble sidewalks, shady streets, and stately homes. It also was home to Robert Todd Lincoln, Abe's son, and his four-hundred-acre estate and mansion.

- **Middlebury.** Middlebury sits in the rolling hills of Vermont and has a creek running through its downtown. It also has white steepled churches, small chapels, and over three hundred historic buildings. Your character can partake in the Bread Loaf Writers' Conference, where he can be tutored by America's best authors and get drunk with a bunch of fellow aspiring writers. If he spends the summer here, he's sure to overhear many conversations in different foreign languages, as Middlebury also is home to summer language programs where students must make a pledge not to speak English in or out of the classroom.

- **Montpelier.** What other state capital can claim to have less than nine thousand residents and a beautiful dome amidst a backdrop of green mountains?

- **Waterbury.** Can you say ice cream? The Ben & Jerry's factory is here, and so are lots of tourists who come for a tour and the inside scoop on one of America's great success stories.

- **Woodstock.** This quintessential New England village has twelve hundred residents, historic inns, and country stores. Its quaint downtown has shops and neat little galleries, which can be found in alleys and alongside hidden side streets.

Virginia

Virginia Basics That Shape Your Character

Motto: Thus Always to Tyrants

Population: 7.1 million

Prevalent Religions: Mostly Baptist and Roman Catholic, with varieties of international religions in the Washington, DC area

Major Industries: Tobacco, cattle, poultry, dairy products, textiles, food processing, printing, electric equipment, chemicals, hogs, soybeans, transportation equipment

Ethnic Makeup (in percent): Caucasian 72.3%, African-American 19.6%, Hispanic 4.7%, Asian 3.7%, Native American 0.3%, Other 2.0%

Famous Virginians: Arthur Ashe, Pearl Bailey, Warren Beatty, Willa Cather, William Clark, Joseph Cotton, Ella Fitzgerald, William H. Harrison, Patrick Henry, Sam Houston, Thomas Jefferson, Robert E. Lee, Meriwether Lewis, John Marshall, James Madison, Shirley MacLaine, Opechancanough, Bill Bojangles Robinson, George C. Scott, Jeb Stuart, Thomas Sumter, Zachary Taylor, Nat Turner, John Tyler, Booker T. Washington, George Washington, Woodrow Wilson, Tom Wolfe, James Monroe

Significant Events Your Character Has Probably Thought About

- The founding of Jamestown in 1607.
- The American Revolution.
- Virginia was admitted to the Union on June 25, 1788.
- Nat Turner's Rebellion in 1831. Turner led slaves into the Travis house in Southampton County where they killed five family members; this ignited about sixty more slaves to go kill fifty-eight whites in the next thirty-six hours. See William Styron's *The Confessions of Nat Turner*.

- Virginia seceded from the Union in 1861; it was readmitted in 1870.
- In 1862, the U.S.S. *Monitor* and the C.S.S. *Virginia* clashed in one of the nation's most famous naval battles at Hampton Roads.
- Stonewall Jackson was killed at Chancellorsville in 1863.
- In 1865, Lee surrendered at Appomattox Court House.
- Henry O. Flipper became the first African-American to graduate from West Point, in 1877.
- In 1954 the Supreme Court ruled for school integration, but many schools throughout the state closed to avoid compliance with the law.
- L. Douglas Wilder in 1989 became the state—and the nation's—first African-American governor.
- In 1994, Democrat Charles Robb was reelected in a close Senate race against Iran-Contra man Oliver North.

Virginia Facts and Peculiarities Your Character Might Know

- More than half the battles fought in the Civil War were fought in Virginia.
- About one-fourth of Virginia's worker are employed by the U. S. government.
- It's the home base for the U.S. Navy's Atlantic Fleet.
- Eight presidents were born here: George Washington, Thomas Jefferson, James Madison, James Monroe, William Harrison, John Tyler, Zachary Taylor, and Woodrow Wilson.
- Founded in 1693, The College of William and Mary is the second oldest college in the country.
- Virginia was named in honor of Elizabeth I, England's "Virgin Queen."
- Tobacco is still the state's major cash crop, and the livelihood of many Virginians is tied to the tobacco industry.
- Edgar Allan Poe spent his boyhood in Richmond; the house is now a museum.
- Many folks don't realize it, but Virginia is the second largest seafood processor in the nation.
- Those Virginia hams are a big hit in the state, and

Smithfield is deemed the ham capital of the world.

- Colonial Williamsburg is one of the top ten tourist destinations in the United States.
- Although Virginia has become home to many non-natives who don't speak Virginia lingo, natives still toss around phrases like "y'all," "might could/should," "say what?," "do what?," and "thank ya, dear."

Your Character's Food and Drink

Some favorite foods include barbecue crab-cake sandwiches, Virginia hams, "hog and hominy" mixtures (pork and corn prepared in a variety of ways), oysters, and ham pie. Veggies include okra, collard greens, black-eyed peas, green beans, and corn on the cob. Breakfast favorites tend to be bacon, sausage, ham, hash browns, flaky biscuits, biscuits 'n' gravy, and grits. Side and dessert dishes are corn bread, pecan pie, pudding, and peach cobbler. Burgers, hot dogs, and beer are picnic foods.

Things Your Character Likes to Remember

- The First Battle of Manassas on July 1, 1861. This major Confederate victory is where General Thomas Jackson got his nickname "Stonewall."
- The Chesapeake Bay Bridge Tunnel.
- Monticello and Mount Vernon.
- Its shipbuilding and military presence.
- Pleasant summers and mild winters.
- The Blue Ridge Mountains.
- The seashore.
- Its proximity to Washington, DC.
- Common local phrases are "down yonder" and "y'all come back now, hear." However, the Southern flavor is slowly diminishing as more northerners live here than natives.
- Tides games (Norfolk's baseball team—the Mets' farm league).
- Norfolk Admirals hockey.

Myths and Misperceptions About Virginia

- **Virginia has never had a professional sports franchise.** While it's true no Virginia *city* has ever had its own pro sports organization, in the early 1970s The Virginia Squires contested (if you want to call it that) in the American Basketball Association (ABA). Although the team reeked, it will always be remembered for unearthing future NBA Hall of Fame players Julius

"Dr. J" Erving and George "The Iceman" Gervin.

- **All Virginians are Southern Confederate sympathizers.** Nope. Most aren't today, especially since a large portion of the state consists of newcomers from the north. Plus, we are in the twenty-first century . . . .

Interesting Places to Set a Scene

- **A winery.** Charlottesville has become home to many fine wineries, including the Barboursville Vineyard, Oakencroft and Whitehall Wineries, and Prince Michel Vineyards, to name but a few. All are open for tours and tastings.
- **Alexandria.** When George Washington and company laid out the street plans here, they had no idea this would be such a major capital suburb. Government buildings (Crystal City and Pentagon), research firms, and vast office developments have significantly changed Alexandria, making it one of the area's leading suburbs.
- **Charlottesville.** This town has a right to be proud of its heritage, as it's the birthplace of three U.S. presidents (Thomas Jefferson, James Monroe, James Madison) and the University of Virginia (UVA), founded and designed by Jefferson himself. While Jeffersonian ideals and influence still play a large part in the life of the school and the community, both are also big tourist draws. In addition, the spirit of former UVA student Edgar Allan Poe still lingers there. His room on the historic Lawn remains intact and is a tourist attraction, as is the famous Rotunda.
- **Fredericksburg.** This historic river town in the Virginia hills is made up of red-brick and clapboard homes, arts and crafts boutiques, antique shops, people dressed in colonial garb, and, of course, plenty of his-

George Washington's Mount Vernon

© PhotoDisc/Getty Images

For Further Research

Books

Black Confederates and Afro-Yankees in Civil War Virginia, by Ervin L. Jordan

Lee's Miserables: Life in the Army of Northern Virginia From the Wilderness to Appomattox, by J. Tracy Power

Life in Black and White: Family and Community in the Slave South, by Brenda E. Stevenson

Notes on the State of Virginia, by Thomas Jefferson

Richmond: A Renaissance City, by L. White-Raible

Touring Virginia's and West Virginia's Civil War Sites, by Clint Johnson

Uncommon Wealth: Essays on Virginia's Wild Places, edited by Robert M. Riordan

Virginia Landscapes: A Cultural History, by James C. Kelly and William M.S. Rasmussen

Virginia's Past Today, by Chiles T.A. Larson

Web Sites

www.myvirginia.org/ (official state site)

www.virginia.org/home.asp (tourism)

www.arts.state.va.us/wivintro.htm (state writers)

www.vahistorical.org/ (state historical society)

www.virginia.edu/vfh/ (state humanities)

www.vamuseums.org/museum_dir.asp (state museum site)

www.pilotonline.com/ (news)

Still Curious? Why Not Check Out

The Blue and the Gray

Circle of Three: A Novel, by Patricia Gaffney

The Civil War

The Confessions of Nat Turner, by William Styron

Isle of Dogs or nearly any book by Patricia Cornwell

Marching Through Culpeper: A Novel of Culpeper, Virginia, Crossroads of the Civil War, by Virginia Beard Morton

Ollie's Army

The Red Badge of Courage, by Stephen Crane

Remember the Titans

Shenandoah

They Stooped to Folly. A Comedy of Morals, by Ellen Anderson Gohlson Glasgow

Thomas Jefferson

---

tory. Battles were fought here, Washington's sister Betty lived here, and James Monroe practiced law here. While your character can step into the past, he'll have to remember that although this is a town, it's also a city of museums. Rising Sun Tavern probably has more drunken stories about our founding fathers than any other establishment in the area.

- **Hampton Roads.** Comprising Newport News, Chesapeake Bay, and Virginia Beach, this southeastern peninsula of Virginia—called "the Tidewater"—is a mix of natural, bone-white sand beaches and man-made steel shipyards. The cities, the navy, the marshes, the wetlands, and the sea all go hand in hand in this coastal area, but the cities have become sprawling metropolises these days, with lots of cookie-cutter homes and fast-food joints. There still, however, are crucial aspects of American history here, from the battle between the U.S.S. *Monitor* and the C.S.S. *Virginia* to stations on the Underground Railroad to the several historic homes.

- **Lynchburg.** This community is noted for its friendly residential neighborhoods and outstanding public ed-

ucation. Lynchburg can regularly boast of having one of the top school systems in the state (thanks to its Partners in Education program).

- **Richmond.** Fine arts, theater, cool architecture, culture, fancy high-rises—Richmond has it all, with history at its core. St. John's Church is where Patrick Henry made his "Give me liberty, or give me death" speech. Thomas Jefferson designed the state capitol building. The capital of the Confederacy (the White House of the Confederacy) was here. Much of the town was burned when the Confederates evacuated the area. Have your character take a trip to the National Battlefield or, better yet, send him to General Robert E. Lee's House, with all its statues of Confederate leaders. The city is home to several universities.

- **Roanoke.** What used to be an industrial railroading center is now one of the country's primary electron manufacturing centers. However, Roanoke also has become culturally sophisticated, as it is home to a thriving arts and theater community, several museums, and exceptional educational institutions, making it an all-American town that's called both "Star

City of the South" and "Capital of the Blue Ridge."

- **The Shenandoah Valley.** This is nestled between the Allegheny Mountains and the Blue Ridge Mountains. Although it is a valley, it's an expansive one that played a major role in both the Revolutionary War and the Civil War (called the "Breadbasket of the Confederacy"). Even today the landscape is a fine blend of neatly kept farms, rolling green pastures, preserved historic communities, and isolated hillside homes built in the 1700s and kept intact.
- **Virginia Beach.** Not only is this the largest city in the state, it's also one of the largest on the East Coast, with a population of 400,000. This resort area is a vacationer's town, with twenty-eight miles of beaches, a three-mile boardwalk, a wax museum, and plenty of recreation and dining. Camp Pendleton is also here, as is the Association for Research and Enlightenment, which is the research headquarters for ESPer Edgar Cayce.
- **Williamsburg.** If your setting requires you to jump back in time to colonial America, historic Williamsburg is your place. This eighteenth-century village, known by tourists the world over, has a plethora of restored or reconstructed colonial homes, a local tavern and jail, horse-drawn carriages on sandy gravel streets, and plenty of workers dressed in their colonial bests.

Washington

Washington Basics That Shape Your Character

Motto: By and By

Population: 5.9 million

Prevalent Religions: Christianity, particularly Roman Catholic, Methodist, Lutheran, Presbyterian, Pentecostal, Baptist, and Episcopalian

Major Industries: Software development, aerospace, food processing, paper and lumber products, chemical products, tourism, seafood, dairy products, apples, cattle, wheat, potatoes, nursery stock

Ethnic Makeup (in percent): Caucasian 81.8%, African-American 3.2%, Hispanic 7.5%, Asian 5.5%, Native American 1.6%, Pacific Islanders 0.4%, Other 7.5%

Famous Washingtonians: Bob Barker, Dyan Cannon, Bob Crosby, Howard Duff, John Walker Kendall, John Knowles, Kenny Loggins, Phil Mahre, John McIntire, Patrice Munsel, Jimmie Rogers, Francis Scobee, Adam West

Significant Events Your Character Has Probably Thought About

- The Lewis and Clark Expedition in Washington (1805 to 1806).
- The Grand Coulee Dam across the Columbia was completed in 1942; at the time, it was the largest dam ever built.
- During World War II, more than fifteen thousand Japanese Americans were forced from their homes and placed in internment camps in eastern Washington.
- In 1974, the state ruled that the Puyallup people of the Puyallup River were guaranteed at least half of the fish caught off reservations.
- Dixy Lee Ray became Washington's first female governor in 1976.
- The 1980 eruption of Mount Saint Helens killed fifty-seven people and caused billions of dollars in damage.
- The timber industry peaked in the 1980s, thanks to exceptional harvests.
- Gary Locke became the nation's first Chinese-American governor in 1997.
- In 1988, Congress granted twenty thousand dollars to each Japanese American sent to an internment camp during World War II.
- Many timber mills had to close in the 1990s because of the enforcement of strict environmental restrictions.
- Initiative 200 in 1998 banned most government-sponsored affirmative action programs.

Washington Facts and Peculiarities Your Character Might Know

- Washington is the only state to be named after a president.
- It has more glaciers than do all the other contiguous states combined.
- Washington's capitol building was the last state capitol constructed with a rotunda.
- Mark Fuhrman of O.J. fame is an icon in Spokane; his radio show is extremely popular (so is his book about a local murder).
- Spokane was the smallest city to host a World's Fair (1974).
- The Columbia River and its tributaries have the best hydroelectric power sites in the country and quite possibly in the world.
- Washington has more than one thousand dams and just as many lakes.
- More than half the state's population is concentrated in the Puget Sound region.
- Washington is surpassed only by Oregon in lumber production.
- Woody Guthrie wrote his famous "Roll on, Columbia" when he was sent to Washington by the federal gov-

ernment to write songs about the construction of the Grand Coulee Dam.

Your Character's Food and Drink

Seafood is big here, especially oysters, crab, shrimp, shellfish, halibut, flounder, tuna, cod, rockfish, pollock, and sablefish. The salmon, of course, can't be beat. Washington also happens to be a leading producer of apples, lentils, dry edible peas, hops, pears, red raspberries, spearmint oil, onions, potatoes, and sweet cherries—all of which the locals devour. Most of the state's fruit and vegetable products are grown in the Yakima Valley. Kennewick has an important grape-processing plant and has been the site of a growing wine-making industry. Cold microbrews and leaded coffee are right up there with the wine. There's also Mount Rainer canned beer.

Things Your Character Likes to Remember

- Spokane's 1974 World's Fair. Called "Progress Without Pollution," the fair resulted in an urban renewal project that put a lovely park in the center of downtown.
- During World War II, Washington had the second highest number of defense contracts in the nation.
- Auntie's Bookstore in Spokane. One of the best new and used bookstores in the country, Auntie's allegedly started the whole "sit and read on one of our big, comfy couches" craze.
- Bill Gates—he gives lots of cash throughout the state.

Things Your Character Would Like to Forget

- Centralia on Armistice Day in 1919 when an American Legion parade ended with several men killed, one lynched, and almost one thousand sent to jail.
- The 1990 northern spotted owl controversy.
- Hanford. This was a helpful plutonium production site during World War II, but radioactive waste has since leaked from the tanks, possibly contaminating the Columbia River.
- Japanese-American internment camps.
- Serial killer Robert Yates. He lived in a quiet, upscale neighborhood until he confessed to killing thirteen people in two decades.

Myths and Misperceptions About Washington

- **That everyone is an environmentalist.** They're not. Many residents are even "anti-environment" because the logging and fishing industries have suffered so much due to environmental restrictions.
- **That it rains in Eastern Washington like it does in Seattle.** It doesn't. In fact, it barely rains at all compared to the downpours they get over Puget Sound.
- **All Washingtonians are addicted to coffee.** While Seattle is probably the most caffeinated place in the world, the rest of Washington is not (probably because it's not gray and rainy all the time).

Interesting Places to Set a Scene

- **Bellingham.** A partially industrial area just twenty miles from the Canadian border, this is a spirited, hippie-ish college town (Western Washington University), especially Fairhaven, with its Victorian architecture, casual cafes, and artsy bars. Nearby Mount Baker is deemed the state's best ski area. Have your character take the Alaska Marine Highway for a three-day cruise from Bellingham to Alaska.
- **Bloomsday run.** Former Olympian runner Don Kardong started this marathon of a race in 1976. A quarter of Spokane's 200,000 residents partake in the fun, as the run is open to parents with strollers, seniors

A Sasquatch Crossing road sign

For Further Research

Books

Between the Mountains: A Portrait of Eastern Washington, by John A. Alwin

Exploring Washington's Past: A Road Guide to History, by Ruth Kirk and Carmela Alexander

From Wilderness to Enabling Act: The Evolution of a State of Washington, by Paul L. Beckett

Murder in Spokane: Catching a Serial Killer, by Mark Fuhrman

The Pacific Northwest: An Interpretive History, by Carlos A. Schwantes

River-horse: The Logbook of a Boat Across America, by William Least Heat Moon

Undaunted Courage: Meriwether Lewis, Thomas Jefferson, and the Opening of the American West, by Stephen E. Ambrose

Valley Walking: Notes on the Land, by Robert Schnelle

Washington: A History of the Evergreen State, by Mary Williamson Avery

Washington Times and Trails, by Joan Olson and Gene Olson

Web Sites

http://access.wa.gov/ (state information)

www.parks.wa.gov/ (parks and recreation site)

www.tourism.wa.gov/ (tourism)

www.wshs.org/ (state history)

www.spokanecity.org/ (Spokane information)

www.bellinghamherald.com/ (Bellingham news)

Still Curious? Why Not Check Out

Angus

Benny and Joon

Dante's Peak

The Lone Ranger and Tonto Fistfight in Heaven, by Sherman Alexie

An Officer and a Gentleman

One Stick Song, by Sherman Alexie

Snow Falling on Cedars, by David Gutterson

This Boy's Life: A Memoir, by Tobias Wolff

Twin Peaks: Fire Walk With Me

The Vanishing

Vision Quest

Vision Quest: A Novel, by Terry Davis

Whale Talk, by Chris Crutcher

---

with canes, wheelchair-bound participants, and dedicated walkers and runners of all ages. The race has even been featured on ESPN.

- **Gingko Petrified Forest.** What at first might seem like just a windblown area of barren hillsides and dried-up lava flows was once a subtropical swamp and is now one of the largest fossil forests in the world. It has more than two hundred different types of fossilized trees that simultaneously turned to stone about fifteen million years ago. There's a *Jurassic Park*-type story in here somewhere.

- **The Great Bavarian Ice Fest in Leavenworth.** This makes for an only-in-the-Pacific-Northwest scene: a snow-in-your-boots tug-of-war, an ice cube hunt, snowshoe races, snow-sculpture contests (they don't melt in forty-eight hours), dogsled races, and the ever-popular "Great Leavenworth Smooshing Contest."

- **Hoopfest.** Spokane's Hoopfest is the biggest and best three-on-three basketball competition in the world. It

actually consumes the city, which pretty much shuts down, as the streets are roped off for the 5,600 teams and 22,000 competitors. Hundreds of teams, who come from all over the region, have to be turned away annually because there's just not enough court space.

- **The International Snowshoe Softball Tournament in Winthrop.** Yes, it's softball on snowshoes! While the rules of the game are pretty much the same, the action is not (the footwear becomes an issue).

- **Manito Park.** A rose garden, greenhouses, a duck pond . . . it's a nature lover's dream.

- **Riverfront Park.** Frederick Law Olmsted (New York City's Central Park) designed this wonderful city park. This is the place in Spokane to catch happy parents playing with the kids, young lovers kissing under a bridge, and old cable cars crossing a rushing river.

- **Rocky Reach.** Here your character can sit on the riverbank and watch the salmon as they swim upstream to spawn.

- **The San Juan Islands.** Noted for their spa resorts, rustic waterfront cabins, and small scenic villages, these great spaces of greenery put the rest of the Puget Sound to natural shame. Have your character take a break here on one of the many bluffs or bays, as she watches bald eagles fly overhead and "killer" orca whales glide in the waters just off the shore.
- **Seattle.** (See page 338 for an extensive look at Seattle.)
- **Spokane.** Spokanites consider their friendly town a well-kept secret. Popular with Canadians (the Canadian flag even flies here), there's a huge subculture of hippies and gypsies that mostly hang around the South Hill area. The city is also a big test market area for services such as the drive-through pharmacy and "make your own pizza" joints. Residents here take to Seattle ("the coast") for a long vacation or head to a nearby lake ("the beach") for a short one. Although Spokane is a relatively small town, it has its own symphony, opera house, and several city parks, and it's home to Craig T. Nelson, Bing Crosby, and Rob Thomas, among others.

Seattle

Seattle Basics That Shape Your Character

A ferry set against Seattle's skyline

Population: 542,000 within the city; 1.74 million in the Greater Metro area

Top Employers: Microsoft Corporation; Starbucks Corporation; Seattle Metro; Seattle City Light, Nordstrom Inc.; University of Washington; Preston, Gates & Ellis LLP; U.S. Federal Government; APCO Associates; Seattle School District; Boeing; Argosy Cruises; AT&T; Imagio/ JWT; Immunex Corporation; Cell Therapeutics Inc.; Fred Hutchinson Cancer Research Center

Per Capita Income: $32,784

Average Daily Temperature: January, 42° F; July, 67° F

Ethnic Makeup (in percent): Caucasian 70.1%, African-American 8.4%, Hispanic 8.4%, Asian 13.1%, Native American 1.0%, Other 2.4%

Newspapers and Magazines: *The Seattle Times, Seattle Post-Intelligencer*

Free Weekly Alternative Papers: *Seattle Weekly, The Stranger, The Seattle Press, The Rocket, Earshot Jazz*

Seattle Facts and Peculiarities Your Character Might Know

- More than half of the residents of metropolitan Seattle were born outside the state of Washington.
- Seattle hosted the 1962 World's Fair, which gave the city international attention and the Space Needle.
- In the early 1930s, many shantytowns went up, as many of Seattle's homeless had nowhere to go. The shacks were called "Hoovervilles," and authorities kept burning them down.
- If someone says, "The Mountain is out," they mean that Mount Rainer is in view.
- It's nicknamed "The Gateway to Alaska," "City of Eternal Views," "The Cannery City," "Gateway to the Orient," "The Northwest Gateway," and "The Emerald City."
- City mayoral firsts: Bertha Landes became the city's first female mayor in 1926, and Norm Rice became the city's first African-American mayor in 1989.
- If someone says, "Meet me at the Pig," they mean at the statue in Pike Place market.
- The term *Skid Row* came from Yesler Avenue when Seattle was first settled. They used to "skid" the logs down to the mill and barges.
- Several times Seattle has been rated by various publications and organizations as the best place to live in the country.
- In 1989, residents got fed up with the all the high-rise buildings and voted for a cap on the size (both height and width) of buildings.
- The Smith Tower was the largest building outside of Manhattan when it was built in 1914.
- Boeing's final assembly plant in Everett is the world's largest building.
- People in Seattle say things like "Ya, sure, you betcha" (there's a large Scandinavian populace in Ballard); "Sodo Mojo" (Seattle Mariners); "How 'bout those M's" (also the Mariners); "Bad traffic in the 'S' curves" (famous traffic jam on I-405).
- 'The box the Space Needle came in" refers to the Sea-first bank building, which is a mighty fifty stories high.
- When someone says, "go the Puyallup," they're saying, "Go to the Evergreen state fair."

If Your Character . . .

If Your Character Likes Alternative Housing, he lives in his boat. Many of Seattle's non-urban dwellers like to make their homes on Lake Union or the Shilshole Bay Marina.

If Your Character Is a Rich Computer Geek, he lives in Magnolia. This is one of the many pockets of wealthy neighborhoods throughout the city that are often within blocks of extreme poverty. A few other neighborhoods known for Microsoft types are Broadmoor, Blue Ridge, Capitol Hill, Medina, Bellevue, New Castle, Woodinville, and, of course, Redmond.

If Your Character Is the Richest Man in the World, he lives in Medina. Yep, it's home to Microsoft's Bill Gates.

If Your Character Is All About Business, he works in Downtown Proper. Parts of Seattle's business district look surprisingly familiar, especially the Times Square area, which resembles New York City's famed intersection.

If Your Characters Are Raising a Family, they live in Ballard. This area houses a large Lutheran population and is typical middle-class Seattle, with decent-sized homes, pleasant yards and shady streets, and plenty of walkers and bicyclers. Wallingford, Bothell, Edmonds, and West Seattle are other similar areas.

If Your Character Wears a Blue Collar at Work, she lives in Everett. This home to Boeing workers is Seattle's most well-known blue-collar area. It was also the site of The Everett Massacre of 1916, in which several were killed and wounded in labor conflicts. Other blue-collar neighborhoods are Kent, Lynnwood, Renton, and Georgetown.

Local Grub Your Character Might Love

Those in Seattle love oysters and salmon. Four varieties of oysters are found in the area: the European flat oyster, Olympia oyster, Kumamoto oyster, and Pacific oyster. Five varieties of salmon come from the area: spring salmon (also called chinook or king), silver salmon, chum salmon, steelhead, and stockeye salmon. Mussels, pink swimming scallops, clam chowder, octopus, and Dungeness crab also are big local favorites.

On an establishments-only-level: Dicks has the best burgers in town; Taco Del Mar has noted burritos; Ivars is the place for fresh fish and chips; Ray's Boathouse and Elliott's Oyster House & Seafood Restaurant serve great fish at large. Locals also like Washington Merlots and, no surprise here, Starbucks, the biggest coffee chain in the world (which was founded in Seattle).

Interesting and Peculiar Places to Set a Scene

Pike Place Market. This nearly one-hundred-year-old farmers and butchers market offers as much to the eye as it does to the mouth. And we're not just talking about the bright yellow bananas and crimson red peppers—more than six hundred different vendors from all ages, shapes, and colors come with their own specialties to make this place a spectacle. Your character can stroll this market and purchase anything from bacon and crabmeat to squid, sushi, and strawberries. Not only is this a great place to fill up the grocery sacks, it also offers several in-the-market restaurants, such as Lowells, The Athenian, and Place Pigalle.

U.S. Bank Centre at Fifth Avenue and Pike Street. This is the city's big living room. Well, it's really a big second-floor lobby, but your character will love meeting a friend or lover and relaxing on the cushy leather chairs and couches.

The Chittenden Locks. Next to those on the Panama Canal, these locks are the biggest in the Western world.

Sit & Spin. Your character could have a blast at this combination bar/restaurant/Laundromat/theater. Not only can he wash his clothes, he can also drink his favorite microbrew, eat a sandwich, play board games under a lava lamp, watch a movie, or groove to the tunes of the jukebox.

Ruby Montana's Pinto Pony. If your character is into pink flamingos, ant farms, cowboys, or Elvis, she'll love this joint. Amidst the cowgirl Christmas lights and lava lamps, this place will sell your character kitsch of every ilk from just about any era.

Alki Point. The bright warning beacon at Alki Point Light Station in Elliott Bay has been steering sailors clear of disaster since the 1870s. Have your character go up on the lighting deck on a dark, misty night. It could be very romantic—or very scary, if your character plans to kill someone and toss him off the lighthouse into the bay.

Chateau Ste. Michelle Winery. This is the state's oldest and most prestigious winery, regularly concocting some of the top wines in the world. Have your character go to the chateau and historic grounds for a wine tasting, a dinner, or even to take classes or to see how they grow their grapes.

For Further Research

Books

Bertha Knight Landes of Seattle: Big City Mayor, by Sandra Haarsagen

Digressions of a Native Son, by Emmett Watson

The Good Rain: Across Time and Terrain in the Pacific Northwest, by Timothy Egan

Hunting Mister Heartbreak: A Discovery of America, by Jonathan Raban

Meet Me at the Center, by Don Duncan

Prisoners Without Trial: Japanese Americans in World War II, by Roger Daniels

Seattle in the Twentieth Century, by Richard C. Berner

Skid Road: An Informal Portrait of Seattle, by Murray Cromwell Morgan

Websites

www.ci.seattle.wa.us (city information)

www.seattlechamber.com (chamber of commerce site)

http://seattletimes.nwsource.com/html/home/ (news)

www.seattle.com/history/ (historical site)

http://members.tripod.com/seattlewriters_assoc/ (writer's site)

Still Curious? Why Not Check Out

Disclosure

Fish Story, by Richard Hoyt

Frasier

Half Asleep in Frog Pajamas, by Tom Robbins

Hype!

It Happened at the World's Fair

Picture Postcard, by Fredrick D. Huebner

Say Anything

Singles

Sleepless in Seattle

Snow Falling on Cedars, by David Guterson

Twin Peaks

Without Due Process, by Judith A. Jance

Around a Totem Pole. The giant pillars have been around for centuries, and they're in high numbers in Seattle, telling symbolized myths or just showing mythical figures. Most popular is the fifty—foot-tall pole in Pioneer Place Park. Others are on Washington Street and Alaskan Way, at Victor Steinbrueck Park, and at Montlake Bridge on East Shelby Street.

Bud's Jazz Records. Your character might think he's descending into hell when he opens the big metal gates and enters this cluttered dungeon of a place that's filled with what could be the most jazz records in the West. Remember the pop music junkies in *High Fidelity*? Folks are kind of like that here, except the topic is jazz.

Pioneer Square on the first Thursday of every month. Most of the city's local art galleries and specialty shops stay open late (with craftspeople and artists on hand), drawing lots of art enthusiasts of every age and ethnicity. Although the complimentary wine is no longer flowing, the crowds and art buyers are still out in full force, if only to stroll around on the cobblestoned triangle. Panhandlers and pigeons seem to like the area as well.

Exceptionally Grand Things Your Character Is Proud Of

- Their Northwest hospitality.
- The magnificent views—of Mount Rainer, the Lakes, and Elliot Bay.
- Floating bridges. Okay, so the Lacey V. Morrow sank in 1990, but it was reconstructed!
- Great restaurants.
- Active theater and outdoor music venues abound.
- Mount Rainier. It's the highest point in Washington, it can be seen from Seattle, and it's only a car drive away when it's time to get away from it all.
- Ferries. Seattle ferries serve Puget Sound, Alaska, and Canada.
- Starbucks, Microsoft, Nordstrom, and Amazon.com (they've provided lots of jobs).

Pathetically Sad Things Your Character Is Ashamed Of

- Loss of Boeing corporate headquarters.
- The Washington Public Power Supply System, which defaulted on a seven-billion-dollar debt in the early 1980s. People nicknamed it "Whoops!"

- The World Trade Organization riots in 1999. Thousands of protesters marched in the streets, busted storefront windows, stole goods, and generally vandalized the city in what came to be known as the "Battle in Seattle." However, many protesters were peaceful as well.

Your Character Loves.

- Sunshine! (even though she rarely gets it).
- Gardening. Citizens are known the world over for their green thumbs, and the Northwest Flower and Garden Show is legendary.
- The Mariners, SuperSonics, and Seahawks.
- Microbeers/Northwest wines.
- Northwest seafood.
- Grunge music. Seattle was a cradle for the movement in the early 1990s.
- Outdoor activities (skiing, hiking, waterskiing, golfing, and so on).
- Theater and the arts.
- Cultural casualness that allows one to go anywhere dressed in jeans and raincoats.
- Concerts at the Pier (on the downtown waterfront).
- Great dining.
- Espresso/coffee.
- Jimi Hendrix, Kurt Cobain, and Bing Crosby.

Your Character Hates

- All the rain. The city gets 154 rainy days annually.
- Californians. There was a big influx of them in the 1980s, and they've raised the cost of housing.
- Portland. There is great rivalry between Seattle and Portland for the trade of eastern Washington.
- Trying to plan outdoor activities—the rain keeps getting in the way!

Washington, DC

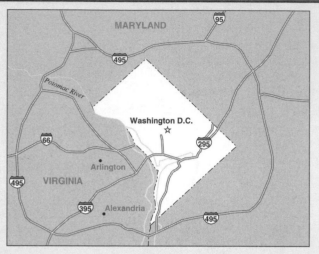

Washington, DC Basics That Shape Your Character

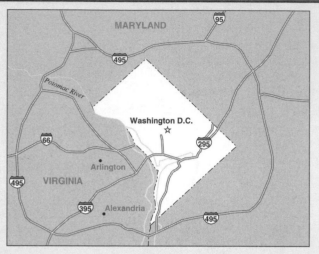

Population: 573,000 in the city; 5.5 million in the Greater Metro area

Prevalent Religions: Roman Catholicism, Baptist, Judaism, Muslim, Buddhist, and small pockets of about any other type of worship—this is a melting pot of a town.

Top Employers: Lockheed Martin Corporation, General Dynamics Corporation, Marriott International Inc., US Airways Group Inc., Gannett Company Inc., America Online, Sodexho, Crestline Capital Corporation, Nextel Communications, AES Corporation, *The Washington Post*

Per Capita Income: $38,403

Average Daily Temperature: January, 35° F; July, 78° F

Ethnic Makeup (in percent): Caucasian 30.8%, African-American 60.0%, Hispanic 7.9%, Asian 2.7%, Native American 0.3%, Other 3.8%

Newspapers and Magazines: *The Washington Post, The Washington Times, The Washingtonian, Capital Style*

Free Weekly Alternative Paper: *Washington City Paper*

Famous DCers: Edward Albee, Billie Burke, Ina Claire, John Foster Dulles, Duke Ellington, Jane Greer, Goldie Hawn, Helen Hayes, J. Edgar Hoover, William Hurt, Roger Mudd, John Philip Sousa, Frances Sternhagen

Washington, DC Facts and Peculiarities Your Character Might Know

- Beltway traffic congestion is second only to Los Angeles, but the Metro subway system is excellent.
- Citizens used to be ineligible to vote in federal elections. They resented this and even displayed their displeasure with license plates bearing the motto, "No taxation without representation." The good news is that they are now able to vote for president.
- Many residents are attached to foreign embassies and therefore immune from prosecution in the United States, whether they run a red light or kill someone.
- The area seems to be populated with a high percentage of former high school valedictorians—definitely a high achiever town.
- Washington has the highest average income for African-Americans in the nation.
- Where the Capitol stands was once a swamp off the Potomac River.
- "Inside the Beltway" means closer to the heart of the political action.
- "The Hill" means Capitol Hill.
- "Bureaucrat-speech" is flat, emotionless, rational prose—a bit like reciting government regulations. It's not slang, but everywhere in Washington, your character is constantly exposed to a multitude of foreign languages from almost every part of the world; a lot of the spoken English is so heavily accented that it sounds like a foreign language.
- Federal law requires that no building be taller than the Capitol.

If Your Character . . .

If Your Character Has Lots of Money and Loves to Shop, she's going to Tysons Corner. This is a place where the Beltway and other highways meet. There are at least two big indoor malls and lots of other big department stores nearby. The shopping in Tysons Corner is upscale, with fancy, full-price places like Nordstrom.

If Your Character Has Little Money but Still Loves to Shop, she's going to Potomac Mills. This massive indoor mall, about thirty minutes south of Washington, is allegedly the biggest discount mall in the East; there are also countless stores springing up nearby.

If Your Character Likes Cool Art and Hates Shopping in Malls, he's going to Old Town Alexandria. This quaint riverside area is populated with unique shops, including the Torpedo Factory, a former World War II torpedo factory that now houses art studios, small galleries, and co-ops—as well as a torpedo on display.

If Your Character Is Hip, Alternative, and Grungy, he lives in Adams Morgan. This is definitely "The Place to Be" in Washington. Your character will find a mix of big Catholic churches, lots of Latinos, and edgy, hip, young single folks who really want to live in the city. There are lots of ethnic restaurants—Brazilian, Spanish, Ethiopian, Thai, and so on. It's impossible to find a parking spot but a piece of cake to find a bar, as nightclubs and pubs are everywhere.

If Your Character Smells of Money, he lives in Chevy Chase. This old-money area is packed with large mansions and mature trees. West of the city in North Virginia there's Great Falls, with its huge, very private mansions. The wealthy also call Spring Valley home.

If Your Character Is a Former Vice President, he lives in Arlington Ridge. If you think Al and Tipper rushed back to Tennessee after the 2000 election, guess again. They sought their pleasant Tudor home here, in the same area where Tipper was raised and the Gores raised their own kids during Al's years as a congressman. On a ridge overlooking the city, this quiet, tree-lined neighborhood is also home to many big-timers in the military, as it's only minutes from the Pentagon.

If Your Character Loves Nature, she's spending time in Rock Creek Park. This eighteen-hundred-acre park was set aside as a nature preserve in 1890 by Benjamin Harrison. Once home to bear, elk, and bison, the area is still fairly rough and wild, although your character is more likely to see a deer, horses, ducks, bird-watchers, and picnickers these days (unless of course he goes to the zoo, which also is located in the park). The Rock Creek runs through the guts of the area before emptying into the Potomac.

If Your Character Is a Middle-Class Family Man, he lives in Silver Spring. This Maryland neighborhood is the affordable little sister of the more expensive Takoma Park. Its modest, mostly brick homes and cul-de-sac streets are perfect living quarters for those with enough money to afford a home who don't care to overdo it. Prince George's County, east of the city, is a similar middle-class area.

Local Grub Your Character Might Love

There are few unique Washington foods, but blue crab (especially "whole soft-shell") and crab cakes are popular. Fish also is popular, especially rockfish, and so are barbecued ribs and "half-smokes" from roadside vendors in trailers. A huge variety of ethnic restaurants are here, from Asian (Thai, Vietnamese, Chinese, Indian) to Latin American (Salvadoran, Guatemalan, Mexican) to African (Ethiopian) and European (French, Italian, Spanish). Politicians still go to "shad fries" in the spring when these fish are running in the streams to spawn.

Interesting and Peculiar Places to Set a Scene

- **Annual Smithsonian Folklife Festival on the Capitol Mall.** For two weekends in the summer, the Mall becomes swamped with musicians, artists, craftspeople, cooks, and interesting people from all over the globe. Different regions, countries, and cultures are featured every year with crafts, dances, food, and songs from each. It's deemed the best festival in town.
- **In one of the massive, cavernous federal buildings.** High ceilings, lots of marble, plenty of big columns, and slightly dated office furniture will give your scene that congressional office feel.
- **Tow Path along the C&O Canal.** This is a popular hiking, biking, and birding area running alongside the Potomac River. It had old locks, planned by George Washington himself, but they were soon replaced by railroads. The path starts in Georgetown just behind the ritzy shops and restaurants.

The National Capitol Columns

- **Dupont Circle on the first Friday of the month.** On the first Friday of each month, art galleries host what's called "First Friday." With works by local and national artists, the galleries set up booths and line the streets of Dupont Circle (mostly on R street). The circle and nearby streets get crowded with art collectors, artists, and those who just want to hang out with a cool crowd.

- **Georgetown.** Home to Georgetown University, this neighborhood is actually forty years older than Washington. Right on the Potomac, it's one of hippest, trendiest, wealthiest, and most historic neighborhoods in town, with many eighteenth- and nineteenth- century homes (and a neo-Victorian shopping center) on shady, tree-lined streets. Bars and eateries line the main veins and are packed with college students (cheap eats) and older professionals (fine dining). Perhaps no area of town has had more writers, either, as the likes of Louisa May Alcott, Sinclair Lewis, Katherine Anne Porter, Archibald MacLeish, and even Francis Scott Key have all made Georgetown their home.

- **At a rally on the Capitol Hill Lawn.** Your character can join with a million moms rallying against violence or she can protest drilling in the Arctic Wildlife Refuge. While the powers that be might be more than a stone's throw away, there's no other place like this in the nation for political visibility.

- **Southeast DC.** This is the area's least affluent section and somewhere in which your character would hate to have car trouble. There are also parts of Washington north of the Convention Center that haven't been restored since the riots in the 1960s—they're quite dilapidated and even abandoned.

- **Rafting or canoeing down the Potomac.** Have your character don a life jacket and set off to glide down America's historic river. She'll be happy to pass historic Mount Vernon and will love waving to fellow water-lovers and the crowds at Washington Harbour, which overlooks the Potomac.

- **In front of the Vietnam Memorial.** Only the most powerful and sobering stretches of granite in the world. Rarely will your character see laughter here; it's a place that elicits reflection and, for many, tears.

- **Takoma Park.** This area is unusual because Takoma Park's framed houses with wooden porches—like the old kit house Sears and Roebuck used to sell—stand out in a region dominated by brick houses. People who live here call it "Berkeley East," but you would have to be a lawyer or a doctor to afford a house in this neighborhood. These large houses were frequently shared by groups of young hippies until the zoning police started cracking down, so lately it's become occupied by baby-boomer families. No other neighborhood has such a fierce sense of community, though, from the organic local farmer's market to the everyone's-involved parades.

- **At one of the many different monuments on the Mall.** Grand edifices honoring Washington, Lincoln, Jefferson, Roosevelt, war veterans . . . add lots of picture-snapping tourists, and you have an only-in-Washington experience.

- **Bonsai Gardens at the National Arboretum.** This Japanese compound of buildings houses an extensive collection of miniature plants, many of which are hundreds of years old. Some structures are open-air, and others have glass roofs. It's only open in the middle of the day while a curator—usually pruning or watering the plants—is around to keep an eye on things.

- **Union Station.** It's more than just a place to hop off a train; it's one to meet friends for lunch, shopping, catching a movie, people-watching, or gazing at the breathtaking entrance hall, with its decorated vaulted ceiling and statues of Roman warriors. Some people come here just to exit the station because they know they'll be amazed at the spectacular view of the Capitol when leaving the front doors.

- **Maryland Sheep and Wool festival.** Held at Howard County Fairgrounds the first full weekend in May, this is the biggest fiber festival in the country. The whole fairgrounds are filled with fiber-producing animals (sheep, goats, alpaca, rabbits). People bring sheep from as far away as New England and the Midwest for the competitive shows. Fiber fanatics from all over the East come to stock up for the year on fleeces and yarns and to check out all the spinners, knitters, weavers, exhibits, seminars, and sheepdog demonstrations.

- **Eastern Market.** This long-standing Washington market (dating to 1873) is legendary, as old market butchers, grocers, cheese-makers, bakers, and seafood vendors offer what's deemed the freshest food in town. On the outside is a farmer's market, in which green thumbs from neighboring states sell everything from produce to plants. Frenetic Capitol Hillers bustle

For Further Research

Books

Eyewitness Travel Guide to Washington, DC, by Alice L. Powers, Susan Burke

The Inside-Outside Book of Washington, DC, by Roxie Munro

Lost in the City: Stories, by Edward P. Jones

Mastering DC: A Newcomer's Guide to Living in the Washington, DC Area, by Kay Killingstad

Reveille in Washington: 1860–1865, by Margaret Leech

Strange and Fascinating Facts About Washington, DC, by Fred L. Worth

Washington, by Meg Greenfield

Washington: A History of the Capital, 1800–1950, by Constance McLaughlin Green

Washington Itself: An Informal Guide to the Capital of the United States, by E.J. Applewhite

Web Sites

www.washingtonpost.com/ (news)

www.si.edu/ (Smithsonian site)

http://hswdc.org/index.asp (historical society)

www.dcnet.com/ (area neighborhood site)

www.washington.org/ (visitor site)

Still Curious? Why Not Check Out

Cupid and Diana, by Christina Bartolomeo

Democracy: An American Novel, by Henry Adams

The District

The Man Who Loved Children, by Christina Stead

The Patron Saint of Unmarried Women, by Karl Ackerman

Primary Colors: A Novel of Politics, by Anonymous

Twilight at Mac's Place, by Ross Thomas

Waking the Dead, by Scott Spencer

Washington, DC, by Gore Vidal

Washington Week in Review

The West Wing

about shopping and eating on Saturday mornings (your character can easily say he spotted a congressperson or a media person here), and arts and craftspeople sell their creations on the plaza. A flea market takes over the food booths on Sundays.

• **The Sixteenth Street Corridor.** Your character won't find a better architectural wonderland than here, as it contains everything from Queen Annes to Romanesques to Italianate and Beaux-Arts-inspired structures. This historic stretch of grand mansions, quaint row houses, churches, and buildings is also home to the exceptional Meridian Hill/Malcolm X Park (cascading staircase waterfall, terraced landscape, statues).

Exceptionally Grand Things Your Character Is Proud Of

• Living and working in the supreme capital of the known universe.

• Maybe getting to go to the Kennedy Center with the "A" list when the president honors famous artists with lifetime achievement awards.

• Showing out-of-town relatives and friends the many monuments and the various Smithsonian Museums, most of which are free.

• The miles of bike trails in the area.

• Marion Barry Jr. The four-term mayor and civil rights activist was a soldier for Washington's African-American communities and an indefatigable champion of district rights. Heck, he even took a bullet in the chest while defending the District Building from Black Muslim terrorists.

Pathetically Sad Things Your Character Is Ashamed Of

• Most people come to the Washington area from other places, but they usually love to deride it and prefer to live outside of it.

• The high crime rate. Murders are commonplace and the murder rate per capita is usually near the top of U.S. cities.

• The district government bureaucracy is incredibly bad, including schools, hospitals, government agencies, police, road crews, and so on.

• Nobody in the Washington area seems to know how to drive in the snow, and the road crews don't seem very interested in removing it. It's actually commonplace for people to just leave their cars in the snow.

• Marion Barry Jr. The same four-term mayor is a convicted drug offender—he was videotaped smoking crack and then was busted for cocaine possession (1990); he spent six months in the slammer.

Your Character Loves

- Neighborhood ethnic restaurants.
- Spring and fall.
- Dozens of free music events offered each week.
- Reading *The Washington Post* as the hometown morning paper.
- The abundance of art/theater/music events—enough to warrant *Around Town,* a weekly PBS program devoted to these events.

Your Character Hates

- Exploding manhole covers. Ridiculous but true— many underground electrical cables become frayed (due to age, corrosion, heat overload, even gnawing rats), then they spark, mix with underground gasses, and ignite, causing some serious combustive pressure. Over fifty manhole covers take to the air annually in Washington, mostly in Georgetown (the oldest cables in town). One even exploded on the grounds of the White House in 2000.
- Bureaucracy—especially if he works in one. It seems to stifle individual initiative and often feels like a giant amorphous conspiracy to prevent anything from actually being accomplished. The stereotype is true: It takes forever to get the smallest thing done.
- That the local government has no voice—it isn't independent and always has to be negotiated with Congress, who can give or withhold power. In recent years, a government-appointed control board managed the purse strings more than the mayor or the Washington Council.
- The heat and humidity in August.

West Virginia

Significant Events Your Character Has Probably Thought About

- John Brown's raid. In 1859 Brown raided the federal arsenal at Harper's Ferry to obtain arms for a slave insurrection. He was caught and hanged for treason.
- Stonewall Jackson captured twelve thousand Union troops at Harpers Ferry in 1862, the largest surrender of Union troops during the Civil War.
- The Matewan Massacre in 1920. In this fierce coalfield struggle, the mayor, two miners, and seven armed coal company men were killed in a shootout.
- The Battle of Blair Mountain in the 1921. Three thousand angry, striking miners attacked owners, killing several of them, including three deputy sheriffs. President Warren Harding had to send in federal troops.
- The Hawk's Nest Tunnel Disaster of 1931. Deemed the worst occupational health disaster in American history: 476 men died and over a thousand fell ill from silicosis while building the Union Carbide tunnel.
- On November 20, 1968, an explosion at a Consolidation Coal Company mine along Buffalo Creek at Farmington killed seventy-eight people.
- In 1972, the Buffalo Creek dam burst, spilling 132 million gallons of black coal wastewater, killing 125 people, injuring 1,100, and demolishing 943 houses and mobile homes.

West Virginia Facts and Peculiarities Your Character Might Know

- Many streams and creeks in West Virginia are a rusty orange thanks to coal mining.
- During the Depression, the state had more miles of railroads (used for coal mining) than roads (for people).
- West Virginia has a median age of forty, the oldest of any state.
- Forests make up nearly 75 percent of West Virginia, and the entire state is mountainous.
- Many deem West Virginia the southernmost northern state and the northernmost southern state.
- The first federal prison for women opened here in 1926.

West Virginia Basics That Shape Your Character

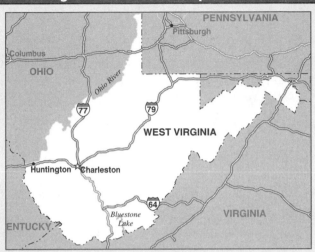

Motto: Mountaineers Are Always Free

Population: 1.8 million

Prevalent Religions: Mostly Southern Baptist, also some Methodist, Roman Catholic, Presbyterian, Pentecostal, and Lutheran

Major Industries: Chemical products, mining, primary metals, stone, clay, and glass products, cattle, dairy products, poultry, apples

Ethnic Makeup (in percent): Caucasian 95.0%, African-American 3.2%, Hispanic 0.7%, Asian 0.5%, Native American 0.2%, Other 0.2%

Famous West Virginians: Pearl S. Buck, Jennifer Garner, John Henry, Homer Hickam, Don Knotts, Matt Lauer, Kathy Mattea, Randy Moss, John Nash, Mary Lou Retton, Sam Sneed, Jerry West, Jason Williams, Chuck Yeager

- West Virginia was the first state to implement a sales tax (1921).
- The Golden Delicious apple comes from West Virginia.
- "Ya" is you; "slicky slide" is a child's playground slide; "buggy" is a shopping cart; "sweeper" is a vacuum cleaner; "awallagoa" is "a while a go"; "up yonder" means "in the general direction of"; "naw" is no; "mommaw" is grandmother, and "poppaw" is grandfather.

Your Character's Food and Drink

This is a real meat-and-potatoes state where lots of Southern dishes are popular as well. A "ramp" (related to the onion and garlic families and sometimes called a "wild leek") is a common, spring wild vegetable that is picked and cooked, and to some smells nothing less than awful—but they eat it. Many West Virginians love slaw on their hot dogs. In Charleston Skeenies has a reputation for the best slaw hot dogs. After going out in Charleston, the locals go to Southern Kitchen late at night to get a greasy meal. It stays open all night and is closed only one day a year (Christmas). Fazio's Italian Restaurant and Laury's Restaurant are also Charleston favorites. Bob Evans, Big Boy, Cracker Barrel, and Dinner Bell are popular chains throughout the state.

Things Your Character Likes to Remember
- The New River.
- West Virginia regularly has the lowest crime rates in the country.
- Outdoor advertising. It allegedly started in Wheeling around 1908 when the Block Brothers Tobacco Company painted bridges and barns with the wording: "Treat Yourself to the Best, Chew Mail Pouch."
- Gov. Cecil H. Underwood. When he was first elected governor in 1956, he was the youngest person to hold the state's highest office. Then, after he was reelected forty years later (he took a long hiatus), he became the oldest governor in the history of the state.

Things Your Character Would Like to Forget
- All the mining strikes and disasters.
- It's one of the poorest states in the country.
- The 1974 Kanawha County textbook controversy. Critics called school textbooks anti-American and

A West Virginia mill

anti-religious and threatened to pull them. Then twelve hundred students at George Washington High School walked out in protest. The community was violently divided; one man was even shot.

Myths and Misperceptions About West Virginia
- **West Virginia is just the western part of the state of Virginia.** Locals hear this all the time and hate it. West Virginia is its own state, with senators and all.
- **West Virginians are all hillbillies.** They do have running water, and they do wear shoes.
- **The Blue Ridge Mountains and Shenandoah Valley are in West Virginia.** Nope. They're in Virginia. (John Denver did a little geographical misrepresentation in "Take Me Home, Country Roads.")
- **John Denver is from West Virginia.** Sorry. He's from New Mexico and never lived a day here (although the aforementioned song has become a staple at weddings and funerals).

Interesting Places to Set a Scene
- **Berkeley Springs.** George Washington called this the "Town of Bath" because of its healing natural hot springs. Although an April 2002 report showed the springs were flowing at an all-time record low, the hot water still boils well enough for the eccentric massage therapists, artists, writers, and homeopathic healers who make up this quaint community. If your character's in need of a heated Roman bath and a relaxing massage . . .
- **Charleston.** The heart of the highly industrialized Kanawha Valley, Charleston is a big producer of coal, salt, metal, gas, clay, sand, timber, and glass, and is an important transportation and trading center. However, it's been a major polluter as well. On the bright side, it boasts of having the first brick street in the world (1870) and one of America's most beautiful capitol buildings. The Gilt dome shines three hundred feet above the street (higher than the nation's Capitol dome) and is quite a sight, especially at night.
- **Morgantown.** This being the state's college town, it's often a big party, especially during the Florence Merow Mason-Dixon Festival, in which there's a circus calliope, arts, crafts, concerts, pageants, a talent show, bicycle and tricycle races, foot races, street and river parades, and more.
- **New River Gorge Bridge on Bridge Day.** Not only is

For Further Research

Books

Culture Change and the New Technology: An Archaeology of the Early American Industrial Era, by Paul A. Shackel

Far Appalachia: Following the New River North, by Noah Adams

A History of Appalachia, by Richard B. Drake

The Life and Death of a Rural American High School: Farewell, Little Kanawha, by Alan J. DeYoung

This Holler Is My Home, by Alyce Faye Bragg

Thunder in the Mountains: The West Virginia Mine War, 1920–21, by Lon Savage

Transforming the Appalachian Countryside: Railroads, Deforestation, and Social Change in West Virginia, 1880–1920, by Ronald L. Lewis

Web Sites

www.wvgazette.com/ (*Charleston Gazette*)
http://wvde.state.wv.us/ (education)

www.mountainlit.com/centuryauthos.htm (writer's site)
www.wvculture.org/ (culture and history)
www.mgtn.com/pages/activities.html (Morgantown Convention and Visitors Bureau)

Still Curious? Why Not Check Out

At Home in the Heart of Appalachia, by John O'Brien

The Coalwood Way, by Homer Hickam

The Good Earth, by Pearl S. Buck

Hawk's Nest, by Hubert Skidmore

Life in the Iron Mills, by Rebecca Harding Davis

Matewan

The Mothman Prophecies

October Sky

The Purchase of Order: Stories, by Gail Galloway Adams

The Sowing of Alderson Cree, by Margaret Prescott Montague

The Unquiet Earth: A Novel, by Denise Giardina

the New River Gorge Bridge the second highest steel arch bridge in the United States, it is also the longest steel arch bridge (seventeen hundred feet) in the world—and it's a good place for a big party. Every October on Bridge Day, the states closes the bridge to traffic, so individuals can parachute and bungee jump off it. Bridge Day is the state's largest event, attracting about 100,000 people annually.

- **Shepherdstown.** On a bluff overlooking the Potomac River, this is one of the state's oldest towns. Although Shepherd College (known as "Georgetown West") sustains most of the community's economy, outsiders from Washington, DC and Maryland do visit often for the brick streets, small shops, restaurants, inns, and history—the Battle of Antietam turned every building in the community into a makeshift hospital, as wounded Confederates flooded the city (many died here; the local cemetery is their resting place).
- **Snowshoe and Canaan Valley.** These are the state's two major mountain resorts, and they offer some of the best skiing mountains in the east in the winter and mountain biking and golfing in the summer.
- **The Greenbrier.** One of the finest getaways in the

country, this White Sulphur Springs resort has been a haven of fun and relaxation for the rich and famous, from presidents and royalty to Hollywood stars and World War II diplomats (the hotel was turned into a hospital during the war). Its golf courses are legendary, as are the architecture and the grounds. During the Cold War, a secret bunker was built at the resort to house members of Congress in case of a nuclear attack.

- **Wheeling.** Once the gateway to the West, this old river town tucked in coal country is quite depressing today but can make a great place for a down-and-out story. Its Oglebay Park and Lake, high above the city, are uplifting getaways from those down on their luck below.
- **A white-water raft on the New River.** When most people plan to go to West Virginia in the spring and fall, they've got white-water rafting on the New River in mind. Not only is it the oldest river in North America and one of only two rivers that runs north, it has many massive boulders and drops and swells, making it the best place in the East to go for a splashing, wild river ride.

Wisconsin

Wisconsin Basics That Shape Your Character

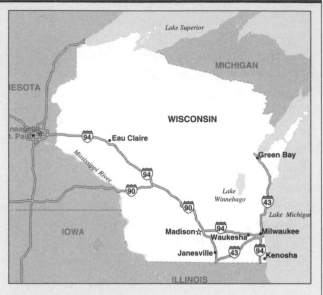

Motto: Forward

Population: 5.4 million

Prevalent Religions: Roman Catholic, Lutheran

Major Industries: Agriculture and dairy farming; production of dairy products; manufacture of paper products, beer, and processed foods

Ethnic Makeup (in percent): Caucasian 88.9%, African-American 5.7%, Hispanic 3.6%, Asian 1.7%, Native American 0.9%, Other 2.8%

Famous Wisconsinites: Walter H. Annenberg, Willem Dafoe, Jeffrey Dahmer, Zona Gale, Eric Heiden, Woody Herman, Harry Houdini, Liberace, Georgia O'Keeffe, Charles and John Ringling, Spencer Tracy, Orson Welles, Thornton Wilder, Frank Lloyd Wright

Significant Events Your Character Has Probably Thought About

- The first Frenchman to explore the state was Jean Nicolet, who arrived in Green Bay in 1634.
- Jesuit priests led early exploration and settlement of the area, building several missions. The most famous explorers of the area were Louis Joliet and Jacques Marquette, who crossed the state to reach the Mississippi River in 1673.
- The Treaty of Paris ended the French and Indian War in 1763, and the Wisconsin lands were surrendered to the British. Twenty years later, they were made part of the Northwest Territory, which was surrendered to the United States following the Revolutionary War.
- Fearing too much government control and higher taxes, the people of the Wisconsin Territory refused statehood four times in the 1830s and 1840s.
- On May 29, 1848, Wisconsin achieved statehood.
- An influx of German immigrants in the middle of the century enlarged the population. German culture shaped the state's identity. Later in the century, many Polish immigrants arrived.
- The first hydroelectric plant in the nation opened in 1882 on the Fox River.
- Early in the twentieth century, Governor Robert La Follette enacted a number of laws to reform taxes, railroad rates, and to empower the average citizen. His program became known as the "Wisconsin Idea." La Follette won a seat in the Senate in 1906 and served until 1925, continuing to promote his reform ideas and progressive politics. He ran for president in 1924.
- The progressive political ideas born in Wisconsin—such as its 1931 unemployment compensation law—were used as templates for federal laws adopted during the New Deal.

Wisconsin Facts and Peculiarities Your Character Might Know

- The name *Wisconsin* comes from the Ojibwa word for "grassy place."
- Wisconsinites lead the country in milk and cheese production. They also invented the ice-cream sundae. In addition, they claim to be the world capital of the bratwurst, ginseng, jump rope, the loon, the snowmobile, and toilet paper.
- The first Ringling Brothers circus was held in Baraboo, where the circus makes its winter home.
- Though Minnesota is known as "Land of 10,000 Lakes," Wisconsin has approximately 8,500, the largest being Lake Winnebago. Tourists come for great fishing and boating.
- The Hamburger Hall of Fame is located in Seymour;

the Mustard Museum is located in Mount Horeb. The state is a world leader in the production of cheese. Tourists, therefore, can build an entire sandwich from the attractions they find here.

- Wisconsin hosts the largest cross-country skiing race in North America, the American Birkebeiner. The race from Cable to Hayward is fifty-two kilometers long.
- Wisconsin has called itself "The Badger State" for many years but didn't officially recognize the badger as the state animal until 1957.
- Spring Green is home to Taliesin, which was home to (and designed by) Frank Lloyd Wright.

Your Character's Food and Drink

If you think Wisconsinites eat a lot of sausage and cheese, you're right. Colby cheese was created in Colby, Wisconsin, and Swiss cheese is a state favorite. Cheese curds also are popular; they look like deformed cheese balls and are served at restaurants (often deep-fried) and can be bought at grocery stores. Outside grilling is a popular way to prepare food, even in the depths of winter. Tailgating parties are an event in themselves before Brewers and Packers games. The cannibal sandwich has been a popular food at Packers games for years; it's made of raw ground chuck and covered with onions. Though it's no longer a national leader in brewing, Wisconsin still is proud of its brewing tradition. The industry still has a presence here, and microbreweries have sprung up in great number. Towns and cities throughout the state hold ethnic festivals, especially the Germans and the Poles.

In Door County, the peninsula that juts into Lake Michigan and the bay of Green Bay, red cherries are grown in great number, making cherry pies and jellies a common part of the state's diet. Cherry wine also is popular. Door County also hosts frequent "fish boils." Freshly caught fish is thrown into big vats of boiling water. Various spices and potatoes are added to the mix, and guests line up with plates to be served cafeteria style. Many towns and organizations throughout the state host weekly fish frys, especially during Lent. Wisconsin also is a leading producer of cranberries.

Things Your Character Likes to Remember

- The Green Bay Packers and Vince Lombardi.
- Progressive politics. Though he died more than sev-

enty-five years ago, Robert La Follette remains a great source of pride for the state.

- Education is highly valued here. The state prides itself on its schools. The first U.S. kindergarten was founded in Watertown in 1856.

Things Your Character Would Like to Forget

- Wisconsin Senator Joseph McCarthy led the Communist "witch-hunts" of the early 1950s. McCarthyism destroyed many lives and led to a repressive reign of fear and conformity that resonated throughout the decade.
- Ed Gein, the "Mad Butcher of Plainfield," killed at least twelve people in the early 1950s, carving their corpses and using their flesh for clothes and to repair furniture. He was the inspiration for Norman Bates in *Psycho* and Buffalo Bill in *The Silence of the Lambs*.
- For many years, Chicago gangsters vacationed in Wisconsin. The Hideout in Couderay was a favorite of Al Capone, and John Dillinger's gang was involved in a shoot-out at the Little Bohemia Lodge in Manitowish Waters.

Myths and Misperceptions About Wisconsin

- **It's a wilderness area full of wolves and bears.** The state is pretty tame. Areas in the north still are wild in spots, but your characters will find more cows than wolves.
- **They're a bunch of cheeseheads.** For the most part, this is true (see "Your Character's Food and Drink.") But it's a progressive, well-educated state with a strong sense of equality and community.

Farm setting in Wisconsin

For Further Research

Books

Indian Nations of Wisconsin: Histories of Endurance and Renewal, by Patty Loew

Oddball Wisconsin: A Guide to Some Really Strange Places, by Jerome Pohlen

Wisconsin Death Trip, by Michael Lesy

Wisconsin Jeopardy: Answers and Questions About Our State, by Carole Marsh

Wisconsin's Best Breweries and Brewpubs: Searching for the Perfect Pint, by Robin Shepard

Web Sites

www.escapetowisconsin.com/ (state travel and tourism information)

www.wisconsinhistory.org/ (state historical society)

www.wisconsinstories.org/ (state historical society and public television Web site)

www.wisconsin.gov/state/home (state government and general information)

www.weird-wi.com/index.htm (information on state occult and criminal events)

Still Curious? Why Not Check Out

A number of the works of Hamlin Garland, including *The Son of the Middle Border* and *A Daughter of the Middle Border* (also associated with Iowa, Minnesota, and South Dakota)

The works of Laura Ingalls Wilder (also associated with Minnesota and South Dakota)

Off Keck Road, by Mona Simpson

A Peculiar Treasure, by Edna Ferber

The Story of My Boyhood and Youth, by John Muir

The Straight Story

Wisconsin Death Trip

Wisconsin Quilts: Stories in the Stitches, by Ellen Kort

The Wolfing: A Documentary Novel of the Eighteen-seventies, by Sterling North

Interesting Places to Set a Scene

- **Appleton.** A medium-sized city located in the Fox River Valley, Appleton is the birthplace of Harry Houdini and Edna Ferber, whose novel *A Peculiar Treasure* is a fictional account of her youth. The city's history and atmosphere have been shaped by the paper industry.

- **Door County.** The Door County peninsula is seventy-five miles long and ten miles wide, jutting northeast into Lake Michigan. It's primarily a tourist area with a number of quaint towns, notably Ephraim (pronounced "e-from"). Your characters will find cherry and apple orchards and a beautiful, well-maintained shoreline.

- **Green Bay.** Known for the Packers, Green Bay actually enjoys more moderate weather than the northern parts of the state. It's a blue-collar town known for its ports, shipbuilding, and meatpacking industry. It calls itself "Titletown U.S.A."

- **Lake Geneva.** A playground for the wealthy of Chicago and Milwaukee for more than a hundred years, this resort is full of history and old money. Victorian mansions—summer homes for rich families escaping the heat of the city—line the streets and the lakeshore.

- **Madison.** The capital city, Madison was built on an isthmus between Lakes Monona and Mendota. Beautiful parks ring the lakeshore, and the city has many great walking areas. It's home to the University of Wisconsin-Madison and is known for its liberal politics.

- **Racine.** Located on Lake Michigan, this city features the 125-year-old Wind Point Lighthouse, the oldest and tallest lighthouse still operating on the lake. Though not a major port city, its atmosphere and culture are strongly tied to its location on the lake.

- **Stevens Point.** It's a college town, where students at the University of Wisconsin-Stevens Point have a strong presence. The town natives are largely blue-collar workers of Polish descent. Not far from town, cranberry bogs are plentiful and give the town a rural atmosphere.

- **Wisconsin Dells.** The Wisconsin River flows in a seven-mile stretch through glacially sculpted cliffs that captivate visitors. The Dells have attracted even more tourist dollars recently by building water parks, golf courses, and casinos.

Milwaukee

Milwaukee Facts and Peculiarities Your Character Might Know

- Begun as a center of the French fur trade, Milwaukee shifted its focus to shipping in the 1830s. It was incorporated as a city in 1846, two years before Wisconsin became a state.
- German settlers streamed into the area in the 1840s and 1850s and made it a city of German culture. They called it *Deutsch Athen*, meaning "German Athens."
- Several theories exist for the origin of the name. The one most commonly cited is that it's derived from the Algonquian word *Milliocki*, which means "gathering place by the waters."
- Harley-Davidson motorcycles are made in Milwaukee. During anniversaries or other company celebrations, the town fills with bikers.
- The ten-day Milwaukee Summerfest, held in late June and early July, is the largest music festival in the country. Featuring dozens of entertainers, it draws more than a million visitors.
- Milwaukee has produced its share of famous folks, including James Arness, Peter Graves, Woody Herman, Al Jarreau, Douglas MacArthur, and Gene Wilder.
- Milwaukee is the nineteenth largest city in the United States. Nearly half its citizens (roughly 48 percent) have German heritage. Fifteen percent have Polish heritage.
- The city is divided by two major rivers—the Menomonee and the Milwaukee. Numerous bridges unite the sections of the city, but the natural barriers have allowed neighborhoods to retain their ethnic flavors.
- Chicago is less than a two-hour jaunt down I-94 and remains a great rival in sports and commerce.
- While Marquette is the city's best-known university, its largest is the University of Wisconsin-Milwaukee, which has more than twice as many students as Marquette, a private Catholic school.

If Your Character . . .

If Your Character Is Alternative and Grungy, he lives on the east side, around the university and the lakefront. Bradford Beach is another area with an artsy atmosphere.

Milwaukee Basics That Shape Your Character

Aerial view of Milwaukee

Population: 1.7 million

Prevalent Religions: Catholic, Lutheran, Methodist

Top Employers: Allen-Bradley Inc., Johnson Controls Inc., Harley-Davidson Inc., Briggs and Stratton Corporation, Miller Brewing Company, Northwestern Mutual Life Insurance Company, Patrick Cudahy, A.O. Smith Company

Per Capita Income: $31,805

Average Daily Temperature: January, 19° F; July, 71° F

Ethnic Makeup (in percent): Caucasian 50%, African-American 37.3%, Hispanic 12%, Asian 2.9%, Native American 0.9%, Other 6.1%

Newspapers: *Milwaukee Journal Sentinel*

Free Weekly Alternative Paper: *Shepherd Express*

If Your Character Smells of Money, she lives in Fox Point or Whitefish Bay.

If Your Character Is All About Business, he works in downtown. He also might work in Waukesha County, west of Milwaukee, where a number of the downtown companies have moved.

If Your Character Is a Yuppie, she lives on the east side or in Wauwatosa on the west side. She also might live in Elm Grove.

If Your Characters Are Raising a Family, they live in Brookfield, or New Berlin. You might also put them in one of the other western suburbs, which provide an easy commute to downtown.

If Your Character Wears a Blue Collar at Work, he lives in South Side, mostly southwest. The neighborhoods Southeast is the Latino area and the industrial valley.

Local Grub Your Character Might Love

Beer and brats are always favorites. Tailgating parties with various types of picnic foods are popular before Brewers and Packers games. See "Wisconsin" on page 350 for more on food and drink.

Interesting and Peculiar Places to Set a Scene

- **The area around Marquette University.** The mansions on Wisconsin Avenue provide a look back to old Milwaukee. On the campus, your characters could meet at the St. Joan of Arc Chapel, a fifteenth-century French chapel that was shipped to the United States and reconstructed. It's claimed that St. Joan prayed in this chapel before her execution.
- **Maier Festival Park.** From May through October, there's an ethnic festival held every weekend at Maier Festival Park on Lake Michigan. The water provides a great background while you have your choice of ethnic themes to explore in the details of the festival.
- **Allen-Bradley Building.** If your scene needs a ticking clock to add tension, put your characters near the Allen-Bradley building. Its tower features the largest four-faced clock in the world. The clock won't chime, however. Good sports that they are, Milwaukeeans didn't install chimes so that London's Big Ben could remain the largest four-faced *chiming* clock in the world.
- **Grand Avenue Mall.** This mall is a popular downtown gathering place with plenty of places to shop and eat. If your characters want a slightly surreal experience, take them to the Mall's International Clown Hall of

Fame. If they aren't afraid of clowns, they will be.
- **Historic Third Ward District.** This old Irish and Italian neighborhood that has been renovated and revitalized is a great place for walking and window-shopping. It has many specialty shops, art galleries, and interesting little restaurants. It's the place where locals mix with tourists, and the people-watching is terrific.
- **Westown.** If your character is in town for a convention, she's probably staying in Westown, which is part of the city business district. Large conventions usually are held at the cavernous Midwest Express Center on Wisconsin Avenue.
- **Potawatomi Bingo Casino.** Your characters have never played bingo like they'll play at the Potawatomi Bingo Casino. Imagine Las Vegas-style glitz while bingo balls percolate and rows of players vie for big bucks. The casino is located just outside the downtown area and attracts locals on the weekends and tourists almost every night. There are slot machines and black jack tables here, too. The clientele is, well, anxious to win.

Exceptionally Grand Things Your Character Is Proud Of

- The brewing tradition. Miller is headquartered here (though it's now part of a larger conglomerate), and the city produces 11 percent of the country's malted beverages. The smell of roasting hops and barley still is familiar to locals driving past the big breweries.
- Lake Michigan. The city identifies heavily with the lake.
- The Milwaukee Ballet, one of the best in the country.

Pathetically Sad Things Your Character Is Ashamed Of

- Jeffrey Dahmer. The serial killer is not one of the city's favorite sons.
- Milwaukee has lost its crown as the king of beer towns. The closing of all of its major national breweries except Miller led not only to unemployment but also to the loss of a source of great pride.

Your Character Loves

- The Packers and Vince Lombardi. The Brewers (baseball) and the Bucks (basketball) are popular, too, but not as beloved as the Packers.

For Further Research

Books

Magnificent Milwaukee: Architectural Treasures, 1850–1920, by H. Russell Zimmermann

The Making of Milwaukee, by John Gurda

The Milwaukee Road: Its First Hundred Years, by August William Derleth

Milwaukee, Wisconsin, by Richard Klatte Prestor

Web Sites

www.ci.mil.wi.us/ (city government)

www.onmilwaukee.com/ (news and local topics)

www.creamcitysuds.com/ (local brewing information)

www.historicmilwaukee.org/ (city historical society)

www.milwaukee.org/ (news and travel info)

Still Curious? Why Not Check Out

Caesar's Park

Drowning Ruth, by Christina Schwarz

A Father's Story, by Lionel Dahmer

Lady in the Box

Throwing Roses, by Elizabeth Ridley

- Miller Park. The state-of-the-art home of the Brewers opened at the start of the 2001 season and is a great place to see a ball game.
- Beer, cheese, sausage, and just about any other food high in fat content.

Your Character Hates

- People from Illinois.
- Low-fat food.
- Atlanta, for stealing the Braves. For that matter, they hate the Braves for leaving.

Wyoming

Wyoming Basics That Shape Your Character

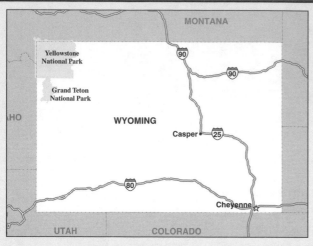

Motto: Equal Rights

Population: 500,000

Prevalent Religions: Protestant and Roman Catholic

Major Industries: Mining (especially coal and natural gas), tourism, agriculture (especially sheep and cattle)

Ethnic Makeup (in percent): Caucasian 92.1%, African-American 0.8%, Hispanic 6.4%, Asian 0.6%, Native American 2.3%, Other 4.2%

Famous Wyomingites: Jim Bridger, Tom Browning, Dick Cheney, Curt Gowdy, Tom Horn, Jackson Pollock, James Watt

Significant Events Your Character Has Probably Thought About

- Mountain men in search of beaver pelts were the first Caucasians to explore the state, in the early nineteenth century. Men such as Jim Bridger, Kit Carson, and Jedediah Smith roamed the area.
- The Oregon Trail cut through the state, giving many Americans their first look at its incredible beauty. Fort Laramie, established in 1834, was an important stop along the trail, as was Independence Rock, located near Casper. Many people on the Oregon Trail stopped to carve their names into the rock, which is now a tourist attraction.
- Yet another attraction associated with the trail, The Ruts, located near Guernsey, marks the passage of thousands of wagons headed westward. The wheel tracks of the wagons are still deeply carved into the earth.
- Yellowstone was designated the first national park in 1872.
- The Wyoming Territory was admitted as a state in 1890.
- President Teddy Roosevelt proclaimed Devils Tower the country's first national monument in 1906. Wyoming also is home to the country's first national forest—Shoshone.
- In 1924, Wyoming elected the first female state governor, Nellie Tayloe Ross. In 1933, Ross was selected as the first female director of the U.S. Mint, a position she held until 1954.
- Forest fires ravaged Yellowstone Park in 1988, destroying over a million acres.

Wyoming Facts and Peculiarities Your Character Might Know

- Wyoming has the lowest population of all the states but is ninth largest in square miles. Only Alaska has a lower population density. Wyomingites like the open space.
- Sheep and cattle outnumber people in the state by more than a five to one ratio.
- The Black Thunder coal mine in Wright is the largest in the country.
- The Grand Teton Mountains were named by John Colter, who thought they resembled breasts.
- The state's unofficial symbol, and one that has appeared on its license plates since 1936, is a man riding a bucking bronco. The horse's name is "Old Steamboat." The symbol also appears on road signs throughout the state as well as on official letterhead stationery.
- Wyoming has the second highest mean elevation of the states. No. 1 Colorado is first with fifty-four peaks above fourteen thousand, while Wyoming has none. Its highest point in the state is Gannett Peak at 13,804.
- James Cash Penney opened his first store in the mining town Kemmerer in 1902. It was part of a small chain called the Golden Rule stores, for which he

worked as a manager. He eventually bought out his partners in the chain, and in 1913, with thirty-four stores scattered throughout the West, he changed the name to JC Penney stores.

- Wyoming was the first state to have a county public library.
- White Hall, a twelve-story dormitory on the University of Wyoming campus, is the tallest building in the state.

Your Character's Food and Drink

Wyomingites eat beef and lots of it. There are a number of traditional Mexican restaurants scattered throughout the state, usually small, mom-and-pop places. Wyoming-ites pride themselves on cooking it the real way. Many towns have an old-fashioned diner or two, where you'll find strictly American cuisine, and plenty of it. Wyoming-ites love the outdoors, so barbecues and picnics are common. Hunting and fishing are huge; almost everybody does it. And they eat a lot of what they kill, such as wild game, elk, and brown and rainbow trout. Wyomingites also love their beer. Moose Drool is a particular favorite.

Things Your Character Likes to Remember

- Richard Dreyfuss made a model of Devils Tower with his mashed potatoes in the film *Close Encounters of the Third Kind*. Later in the movie, aliens landed next to the tower.
- The state motto "Equal Rights" is not just empty talk. Wyoming was the first area in the country to give women the right to vote, serve on juries, and hold public office. It elected the first female justice of the peace and the first female governor.
- Winning seasons for the 'Pokes. The lack of professional teams or any other four-year colleges makes everyone in Wyoming a 'Pokes fan.
- Low state taxes. They do without some services but prefer it that way.
- A strong sense of community—from town to town and even within the state as a whole. As former governor Michael Sullivan put it, "Wyoming is a medium-sized city with very long streets."

Things Your Character Would Like to Forget

- The state has only one four-year university, the University of Wyoming. It prides itself on its primary and secondary school systems, but students often leave the state to attend college. After graduating, many seek jobs

elsewhere, such as the front-range cities of Colorado.
- The Teapot Dome Scandal. In 1924 Secretary of the Interior Albert Fall secretly leased the naval oil reserve near Casper to the Mammoth Oil Company.
- Anything involving the sports teams of Colorado State or Brigham Young, the hated rivals of the beloved 'Pokes. Stealing Colorado State University's mascot (a sheep) before the annual football game is an old tradition.

Myths and Misperceptions About Wyoming

- **Wyoming is one big dude ranch.** The dude ranch got its start here; even the name *dude ranch* got its start here. And you'll find plenty of these "guest ranches" spread across the state, giving city slickers a week or two of the Western experience. But Wyoming is not faux West. The rugged terrain and sparse population create a tough, self-reliant people.
- **Wyoming is one big national park.** Tourism is a major industry in the state, but mining actually brings in more dollars. Wyoming is the leading coal-producing state in the country.

Interesting Places to Set a Scene

- **Yellowstone Park.** Old Faithful is the best-known geyser in the world, and the park's 2.2 million acres abound with waterfalls, rivers, mountains, and a variety of wildlife, including elk, bison and pronghorn antelope.
- **Jackson Hole.** The state's famous ski resort is still a favorite with trendy skiers looking for great slopes and beautiful people. A fifty-mile-long valley south of the Grand Tetons, Jackson Hole, and the town of Jackson, also draws tourists through Old West museums, hiking, and fishing. The valley inspired the famous

Buffalo at Yellowstone National Park

For Further Research

Books

Legacy of the Tetons: Homesteading in Jackson Hole, by Candy Vyvey Moulton

The Medicine Bows: Wyoming's Mountain Country, by Scott Thybony et al.

The Natural World of Jackson Hole: An Ecological Primer, by Tim W. Clark

Teewinot: A Year in the Teton Range, by Jack Turner

Wyoming: A Sourcebook, by Roy Jordan and S. Brett DeBoer

Yellowstone, by Norbert Rosing

Yellowstone, by Erwin A. Bauer and Peggy Bauer

Web Sites

www.state.wy.us/ (state government site)

http://wyodex.com (Wyoming links directory)

www.wyolinks.com/ (Wyoming links directory)

www.wyomingcompanion.com (Wyoming's leading magazine, with many links)

www.wyomingtourism.org/ (Wyoming visitor site)

Still Curious? Why Not Check Out

Angel Fire: A Novel, by Ron Franscell

Close Range: Wyoming Stories, by Annie Proulx

Leaving Normal

The Mountain Men

Shane

The Solace of Open Spaces, by Gretel Ehrlich

The Virginian, by Owen Wister

Western Swing, by Tim Sandlin

Wyoming, by Barry Gifford

Western novel *The Virginian* (which was a popular Western TV drama in the 1950s and 1960s).

- **Cheyenne.** This is the state capital and largest city, though the metro area holds only a little more than seventy thousand residents. The only time to find much of a crowd is the last week of July during the annual Frontier Days celebration, known locally as "the Daddy of 'em all." It's the largest outdoor rodeo in the world. The rest of the year, things are peaceful, full of Western tradition and atmosphere.

- **Laramie.** A short drive west on I-80 from Cheyenne, this town, like the capital, continues Old West traditions—cowboy hats and boots, blue jeans, denim shirts. Though it hardly seems like a college town, it is home to the University of Wyoming. There are lots of tourist centers here, mostly related to the town's roots along the Oregon Trail.

- **Sheridan.** The fourth largest town in the state, Sheridan is a cozy mix of Old West and new money. Old-time cowboys mix (but not often) with polo-playing corporate executives, and the main shopping district is restored to its turn-of-the-century glory. The Wyoming Theater boasts a surprising number of top-name performers. It's also one of the country's great centers of hang gliding.

- **Devils Tower.** Steven Spielberg beat you to this setting, using it in his famous climactic scene in *Close Encounters of the Third Kind*. However, it's such an unusual place, it could probably work for you, too. The gray monolith rises 1,267 feet above the Belle Fourche River and is a sacred site for many Native Americans. Devils Tower is near Moorcroft in eastern Wyoming.

CANADA

Provinces and Cities

Alberta

Alberta Basics That Shape Your Character

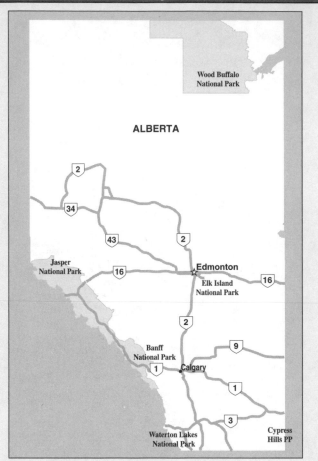

Population: 2.8 million

Capital: Edmonton

Largest City: Calgary (765,000)

Prevalent Religions: Roman Catholic, United Church of Canada, and Anglican

Major Industries: Oil mining and refining, natural gas mining, petrochemical industries, coal mining, agriculture (primarily wheat, barley, and cattle), tourism

Alberta Facts and Peculiarities Your Character Might Know

- Before Europeans arrived, the province was occupied by a variety of Native American tribes, primarily the Assiniboine, Blackfoot, and Cree.
- Fur traders from the Hudson's Bay Company ex-

plored the area in the 1750s. By the end of the eighteenth century, French and American traders had moved into the area to share the bounty of furs.

- By the middle of the nineteenth century, much of Canada had been settled under British rule, though the middle provinces, including Alberta, remained mostly wild and lawless until forts were built in the 1870s for the Northwest Mounted Police.
- In 1905, Alberta became a province. It prospered as a center for wheat farming and cattle ranching.
- After World War II, oil fields were discovered near Edmonton. A few years later, fields of natural gas were discovered. Edmonton boomed, becoming the industrial center of the province.
- Alberta ranks fourth among the provinces in population. More than half of Albertans live in the Edmonton and Calgary metro areas.
- The eastern part of the province lies in the Great Plains and is known for its sprawling wheat farms and cattle ranches. The western part rises into the Rocky Mountains and boasts several of the country's most famous and beautiful parks.
- The West Edmonton Mall is known locally as "the largest shopping center in the world." Several other malls in the world make this claim.
- Calgary has two major sports teams, the National Hockey League's Flames and Canadian Football League's Stampeders. Edmonton boasts the National Hockey League's Oilers and the Canadian Football League's Eskimos.
- Calgary is the fastest-growing major city in the country.

Interesting Places to Set a Scene

- **Banff National Park.** The oldest and one of the most famous national parks in the country, Banff also is one of the most photographed. Its striking views of the Rocky Mountains and its spring wildflowers make it a favorite for Canadians across the country. The town of Banff's a popular starting point for exploration of the park and is famous for its mineral springs.
- **Calgary.** The cultural and financial center of the province, Calgary is a thriving city and a leader in high-tech industries. It was the host of the 1988 Winter

For Further Research

Books

Alberta, by Susan LeVert

Alberta, by Tanya Lloyd

Box Socials: A Novel and *The Fencepost Chronicles*, by W.P. Kinsella

From Summit to Sea, by George Buck

Roses Are Difficult Here: A Novel, by W.O. Mitchell

Trails of a Wilderness Wanderer, by Andy Russell

The Trojan Horse: Alberta and the Future of Canada, by Gordon Laxer and Trevor Harrison

Web Sites

www.alberta.com/ (site for Alberta, with many links)

www.findalberta.com/ (province visitor site)

www.worldweb.com/ParksCanada-Banff/ (Banff park site)

www.discovertherockies.com/index.html (Alberta's Rocky Mountain site)

www.calgary.net/ (Calgary visitor and entertainment site)

www.calgaryalberta.net/ (Calgary/Alberta visitor site)

www.visitor.calgary.ab.ca/ (Calgary visitor site)

www.gov.edmonton.ab.ca/ (Edmonton city government site)

www.discoveredmonton.com/ (Edmonton tourist site)

www.edmontonview.com/ (Edmonton visitor information)

www.medicinehatchamber.com/ (Medicine Hat Chamber of Commerce)

www.city.medicine-hat.ab.ca/ (Medicine Hat city government)

Olympics, a great source of pride for the city. It is located at the confluence of the Bow and Elbow Rivers. The University of Calgary is one of the most respected schools in the country, and its campus offers a variety of possibilities for settings.

- **Calgary Exhibition and Stampede.** This annual event, which draws more than a million people, is the most popular event in the province. Begun in 1912, the festival features a rodeo and other cowboy events and celebrates the province's still-thriving cattle-ranching industry. It's billed as "The Greatest Outdoor Show on Earth."

- **Edmonton.** The provincial capital and the primary industrial area in the province, Edmonton also is one of the cultural centers. Like Calgary, it's one of the fastest-growing cities in the country, primarily because of its thriving oil and gas industries. Though a cultural center and the home of the University of Alberta, people from Edmonton take their greatest pride in the Oilers hockey team, which Wayne Gretzky led to five National Hockey League championships.

- **Head-Smashed-in-Buffalo-Jump.** If you set a scene here, the name alone will get your reader's attention. This popular historic center commemorates the place where plains Native Americans drove herds of buffalo over a cliff and to their deaths. Guided tours are conducted by Blackfoot Native Americans.

- **Klondike Days.** Held annually in July in Edmonton, this festival celebrates—and reenacts—the gold rush of 1898. Though Edmonton's booming metro area seems far removed from its humble origins, the festival is a local favorite.

- **Jasper National Park.** The largest park in the Rockies, Jasper is located north of Banff along the western border of the province. Like Banff, it attracts tourists from throughout North America for its spectacular mountains and lakes.

- **Lethbridge.** Though it's the third largest city in the province, Lethbridge is considerably smaller than Calgary and Edmonton and is far less of a cultural center. It's primarily a commercial center for the farming and ranching communities in the region.

- **Medicine Hat.** A small city located in the southeast corner of the province, Medicine Hat is known as "The Gas City" for its involvement in Alberta's natural gas industry. It's perhaps most famous for the world's largest teepee, a twenty-story-high steel structure called the Saamis Teepee.

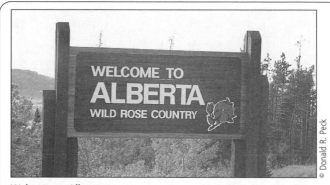

© Donald R. Peck

Welcome to Alberta

British Columbia

British Columbia Basics That Shape Your Character

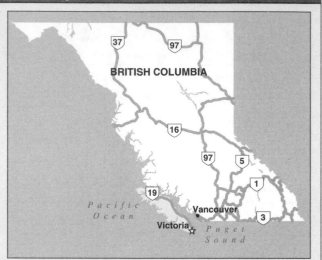

Population: 4 million

Capital: Victoria

Largest City: Vancouver (515,000)

Prevalent Religions: United Church of Canada, Roman Catholic, and Anglican

Major Industries: Lumbering, wood processing and paper products, food processing, tourism, fishing (especially salmon), farming (primarily fruit, dairy, and livestock)

British Columbia Facts and Peculiarities Your Character Might Know

- A number of Native American societies lived in the area before Europeans arrived. These societies settled mostly in the south and southwest and relied heavily on fishing. These tribes are known as the First Nations.
- Captain James Cook arrived in Nootka in 1778 and established a British presence in the area, but Spain also laid claim to it. The two countries fought, with Spain seizing British ships in 1789. The dispute was settled in 1794.
- The Oregon Treaty settled the border dispute with the United States and established British Columbia's southern boundary at the forty-ninth parallel in 1846.
- In 1858 gold was discovered on the Fraser River in the Cariboo Mountains, sparking a rush to the area

that lasted nearly ten years. When it was over, many miners moved on, though a number of those who stayed were Asian; this marked the beginning of British Columbia's continuing relationship with Asia.

- In 1871, British Columbia became a province of Canada, mostly to ensure rail connection to the East. Work on the railroads attracted more Asian settlement. By the turn of the century, the area suffered race riots and anti-Asian demonstrations.
- Chinese is the second most spoken language in the province, and trade with Asia is a key part of the British Columbian economy.
- British Columbia is an almost wholly mountainous area, which has made farming difficult and limited. The steady depletion of its timber has forced it to rely heavily on tourism.
- The province has four national parks—Glacier, Kootenay, Mount Revelstoke, and Yoho.
- Three-fourths of the province's population lives in the southwestern tip in the Vancouver/Strait of George area. The north is largely unsettled.
- West Vancouver Island receives more rain than does any other place in North America.
- After Los Angeles and New York City, British Columbia is the third largest film production center in the world, and it's Canada's leading film and television center.

Interesting Places to Set a Scene

- **Kamloops.** One of the few cities of any size outside the Strait of George area, Kamloops boomed during the 1860 gold rush. It's now the hub of the south-central region and the Big City for the surrounding farm and lumber communities.
- **Prince George.** The province's largest northern outpost, Prince George services the lumber industry of the north. It's an industrial city filled with sawmills, pulp mills, chemical plants, and an oil refinery. Located on the Fraser River, Prince George is not scenic, but the wilderness of the north is not far away.
- **Queen Charlotte Islands.** These 150 small islands located off the coast of central British Columbia are sometimes called the "Misty Islands" because they're often shrouded in mist and fog. The population here

For Further Research

Books

British Columbia Ferries and the Canadian West Coast, by David Spalding

British Columbia: A Natural History, *Geology of British Columbia: A Journey Through Time*, *Life in the Pacific Ocean*, and *Mountains and Northern Forests*, by Sydney and Richard Cannings

British Columbia Railway, by John Garden

The Curve of Time, by M. Wylie Blanchet

Helicopters: The British Columbia Story, by Peter Corley-Smith and David N. Parker

I Heard the Owl Call My Name, by Margaret Craven

The Intemperate Rainforest, by Bruce Braun

Journeys Through the Inside Passage, by Joe Upton

Maps and Dreams: Indians of the British Columbia Frontier, by Hugh Brody

Mythic Beings: Spirit Art of the Northwest Coast, by Gary Wyatt

Shoot! by George Bowering

Smith and Other Events, by Paul St. Pierre

Strangers and Sojourners: A Novel, by Michael D. O'Brien

Web Sites

www.gov.bc.ca/ (British Columbia government site)

www.britishcolumbia.com/ (British Columbia information site and links)

www.bcinformation.com/ (British Columbia information and links)

www.discoverbc.com/ (British Columbia travel and tourism site)

www.bctravel.com/ (British Columbia travel and tourism site)

http://parkscanada.pch.gc.ca/parks/Bc_np_e.htm (British Columbia National Parks information)

www.bc-rockies.com/ (British Columbia Rocky Mountain information)

www.city.victoria.bc.ca/ (Victoria city government site)

http://victoriabc.com/ (Victoria area travel guide)

is sparse, which adds to the aura of mystery pervading the islands. Queen Charlotte City on Graham Island is the center of civilization with a population of less than a thousand.

- **The Gold Rush Region.** The towns in this region of central British Columbia have names like Horse Fly and Likely, which suggest a colorful past. Some towns, such as Barkerville, have historic sites to mark the gold rush period in this rugged country dominated by the Cariboo Mountains and many large lakes.

- **The National Parks Region.** The four national parks in British Columbia are located in the southeastern section of the state in the Columbia Mountains region, which some Canadians believe is the most beautiful area in the country. Dramatic mountains and hidden streams bring visitors in droves for fishing, hiking, and camping in the summer and skiing in the winter. However, the area is so vast your characters won't feel crowded.

- **Vancouver Island.** At 280 miles long and 80 miles wide, Vancouver Island is the largest island on the North American Pacific Coast. It's also a populated area with more than a half million residents, most of whom work in the fishing or timber industry. Its cragged coast, foggy inlets, and endless rains make it a tough but dramatic place to live.

- **Victoria.** The provincial capital of British Columbia, Victoria is a small city of less than 100,000. It's located at the southern tip of Vancouver Island and separated by the Strait of George from the large mainland it governs. It's primarily a port town, and its fishing and shipping industries dominate the atmosphere much more than government does. When they're not on the water, locals gather for recreation at Beacon Hill Park.

A cabin at Kootenay Pass Summit

© Trevor Knowlton (www.phototour.ca)

Vancouver

Vancouver Basics That Shape Your Character

Vancouver skyline

Population: 571,708 in the city; 1,986,965 in the Greater Metro area

Prevalent Religions: Protestant, Roman Catholic, Sikh, Buddhist, Muslim, Jewish, and Hindu

Top Employers: The Jim Pattison Group, Canadian Airlines International, Westcoast Energy, West Fraser Timber Company Ltd., Teck Cominco Ltd., Simons International Corporation, Spectra Group Ltd. Inc., St. Paul's Hospital, CIBC, WIC (Western International Communications), MacMillan Bloedel, Weyerhaeuser Canada, Vancouver City Savings Credit Union

Per Capita Income: $29,664 (Canadian dollars)

Average Daily Temperature: January, 35° F; July, 62° F

Ethnic Makeup (in percent): Caucasian 68.1%, African-American 0.9%, Hispanic 0.3%, Asian 29.4%, Native American 1.8%, Other 4.5%

Newspapers and Magazines: *The Vancouver Sun, The Province, The Vancouver Courier, Vancouver: The Magazine*

Free Weekly Alternative Paper: *The Georgia Straight*

Vancouver Facts and Peculiarities Your Character Might Know

- Greater Vancouver is usually referred to as the Lower Mainland, and it includes the surrounding cities of Richmond, Surrey, and Burnaby. Downtown Vancouver is a peninsula that juts out into the Burrard Inlet; much of this peninsula is a preserved wooded area called Stanley Park.
- The Lions Gate Bridge links downtown Vancouver, via Stanley Park, with the North Shore on the other side of the Burrard Inlet. With only three lanes, this bridge gets slow at rush hour, but few in this nature-loving city want to cut any additional roadways through Stanley Park.
- The North Shore is divided into North Vancouver ("North Van") and West Vancouver ("West Van"). Don't confuse West Van with the West Side (the area south of downtown across False Creek) or the West End (downtown between the City Center and Stanley Park).
- Much of Vancouver's history is tied up with timber, trade, and transportation, all three of which converged around the Canadian Pacific Railway (CPR).
- Thanks to its felicitous geographic location, Vancouver has the mildest climate of any city in Canada.
- The mild climate, a diversity of locations, and favorable tax breaks for moviemaking have made Vancouver attractive to the film industry. About twenty feature-length films and twice as many TV movies are shot in the Lower Mainland annually.
- Thirty-five percent of Vancouver's population is foreign born, one of the highest figures for any city in the world. It has the highest proportion of Asians in any North American city.
- Fierce local opposition has kept Vancouver's downtown free of freeways. The city has good public transportation, with extensive bus lines, an elevated commuter train (the Sky Train), and a commuter ferry line (the Sea Bus), but the transportation system is occasionally hobbled by strikes.
- Vancouver is the economic engine of British Columbia, and it's difficult to talk about one without mentioning the other.
- Some famous Vancouverites: Michael J. Fox, Pamela Anderson, James "Scotty" Doohan, Jason Priestley, Bryan Adams, Rae Dawn Chong, Margot Kidder, Douglas Coupland, and the band Loverboy.

If Your Character . . .

If Your Character Is a Chinese Family Man, he lives in Strathcona. Over 60 percent of the residents of this neighborhood east of downtown, which includes Chinatown, speak Chinese as their native language. Because of the decay and drug culture of East Hastings Street to the north, however, newer Chinese immigrants are settling in Richmond, south of the North Arm of Fraser River.

If Your Character Is an Ordinary Joe, he lives in Mount Pleasant. This area west of Cambie Street is Vancouver's original "uptown," but for the past century or so it's been characterized by lot after lot of small, single-family houses. People who live here come from a great variety of ethnic backgrounds, including Greek, Punjabi, and Italian.

If Your Character Is a Heroin Addict, she lives in Downtown Eastside. The area around Hastings and Main is populated by all sorts of down-and-out types, including many drug addicts whose problems are compounded by HIV infection. This is said to be the poorest neighborhood in all of Canada.

If Your Character Owns a Small Business Downtown, she lives Downtown. No need to commute from the suburbs. Many of those tall buildings in the West End are actually high-rise apartments, not office buildings, so getting to work on a bike is no problem.

If Your Character Is Old Money, she lives in Shaughnessy. Between Sixteenth and Forty-First Streets, from West Boulevard to Oak Street, Shaughnessy has always been Vancouver's most exclusive neighborhood, where the house prices have been kept out of the reach of all but the wealthiest residents. Interspersed among the large homes with lush lawns on tree-lined streets is the occasional stunning baronial mansion.

If Your Character Wears a Blue Collar to Work, he lives in The East End in such neighborhoods as Hastings-Sunrise or Grandview-Woodland. This area has been home to immigrant communities, particularly Italian and Chinese, for over a century.

If Your Character Is a Gay Professional With No Money, he lives in Yaletown. This section of downtown south of City Center is zoned for commerce, but the lofts and warehouses are becoming popular as trendy and (relatively) low-rent living spaces near the hottest nightspots.

If Your Character Is a Gay Professional With Money, he lives in Kitsilano. This former hippie enclave is now out of the price range of the students who used to inhabit it. Kits Beach is *the* hip beach for the young and lovely, as well as for the formerly young and lovely who can now afford large, expensive homes.

Local Grub Your Character Might Love

Salmon in all its forms is king of the plate in Vancouver. Steamed rock cod and halibut are also popular. Fruits of the sea include the geoduck (pronounced "GOO-ee-duck") clam and the mild-tasting West Coast oyster. Perhaps the strongest influence on local cuisine has come from Asia. Chinese food in Vancouver is probably the highest-quality Asian cuisine available in North America, rivaling even that of Hong Kong, and Vancouverites eat out often at these Asian restaurants. In a Japanese vein, Vancouver rolls are sushi *norimaki* with barbecued salmon and vegetables. The increasingly popular "bubble pearl tea," which is sweetened iced tea, frothed with milk, flavored with lychees or similarly exotic tastes, and containing small, gelatinous "pearls" of potato starch that are sipped up through an extra-wide straw. Vancouverites' love of the grape is on display every year at The Vancouver Playhouse International Wine Festival. For dessert, Nanaimo bars are the local standout: These are exquisite, no-bake, chocolate-covered three-layer dessert bars made with graham cracker crumbs, chocolate, caramel, and lots of fat.

Interesting and Peculiar Places to Set a Scene

- **The Night Market in Chinatown.** The Saturday night market is common in Asia, and the phenomenon has spilled over into Vancouver's Chinatown during the summer months. Produce stores stay open until 11:00 P.M., along with blocks and blocks of stalls featuring cheap electronics, baby clothes, cell phone covers, tiny plastic toys, watches, Chinese books, sunglasses, sandals, incense—anything you could need, really. It's noisy, busy, smoky, smelly, and fun.
- **Queen Elizabeth Park.** This park right in the middle of the Lower Mainland is 153 meters above sea level and affords great views of the city, sea, and mountains. In addition to the botanical gardens, it has sports fields (baseball, tennis, lawn bowling, Frisbee, golf) and the Bloedel Conservatory, a Plexiglas-covered home for tropical birds and plants. You're almost certain to en-

For Further Research

Books

The Chinese in Vancouver 1945–80: the Pursuit of Identity and Power, by Wing Chung Ng

Down From the Shimmering Sky: Masks of the Northwest Coast, by Peter Macnair et al.

The Greater Vancouver Book: An Urban Encyclopedia, edited by Chuck Davis

Legends of Vancouver, by Emily Pauline Johnson

Making Vancouver: Class, Status, and Social Boundaries, 1863–1913, by Robert A.J. McDonald

Pacific Press: The Unauthorized Story of Vancouver's Newspaper Monopoly, by Marc Edge

Vancouver, From Milltown to Metropolis, by Alan Morley

Vancouver and Its Writers, by Alan Twigg

Web Sites

www.canada.com/vancouver (the newspapers)

www.city.vancouver.bc.ca (general and government information)

www.canada.com/vancouver (regional information and news)

www.straight.com (*The Georgia Straight*)

Still Curious? Why Not Check Out

Carnal Knowledge

The Cherry Tree on Cherry Street and Other Poems, by George Woodcock

Cougar Annie's Garden, by Margaret Horsfield

Disappearing Moon Cafe, by Sky Lee

Itsuka, by Joy Kogawa

McCabe and Mrs. Miller

Paper Boy, by Stuart Keate

The X-Files

---

counter a wedding party being photographed here.

- **Pacific Spirit Regional Park.** This huge forest of cedars and firs stretches from the Burrard Inlet to the North Arm of the Fraser River. There's a large bog with a boardwalk in the middle. This forest is what most of Vancouver looked like for millions of years.

- **Wreck Beach.** Down a steep path to the shore west of the University of British Columbia, you'll find the city's only nude beach.

- **Library Square.** The new public library resembles a beige Colosseum, with seven stories in the library itself and twenty-one in the connected office building. The cafes and restaurants on the ground floor and around the complex are popular with bookish types and thrifty students.

- **The Granville Street Bridge.** This bridge has pedestrians on the right, bicyclists on the left, and oblivious drivers speeding by in the middle. There are sidewalks on each side, from which you can look down to see a jumble of colorful buildings and dingy gray factories.

- **Gerard.** Because it's a center of the film industry, Vancouver is a haven for movie stars seeking a night out after a hard day's shoot. This low-key, wood-paneled bar in the Sutton Place Hotel on Burrard is a place you're likely to spot a celebrity out on the town.

- **A tubing or tobogganing snowfield.** Sliding down a hill covered with compacted snow and ice is a quintessential Canadian pastime, so why not have your character spend a day at Seymour Hill or Manning Park? Playdium in Burnaby even has a "virtual" toboggan ride that offers the thrills without the chills, eh?

Exceptionally Grand Things Your Character Is Proud Of

- The city's natural beauty: parks, beaches, nature trails, mountains, rivers, the ocean, forests. . . .
- You can go skiing in the morning, sailing in the afternoon, and then spend the night out in the city.
- The United Nations rates Vancouver as one of the best places in the world to live.

Your Character Loves

- The beach, the mountains, the woods, the ocean.
- Riding a bike around the Stanley Park Seawall.
- The Canucks (National Hockey League team).
- Skiing, on both water and snow.
- Shakespeare Under the Stars on Granville Island in August.
- Coffee at the Bean Around the World Café.
- Those little doughnuts at the Pacific National Exhibition (PNE).

Manitoba

Manitoba Facts and Peculiarities Your Character Might Know

- Cree, Assiniboine, and other plains Native Americans ruled the area before European settlement. British explorers seeking the Northwest Passage began to arrive in the early 1600s, the first of whom was Captain Thomas Button in 1612.
- The Hudson's Bay Company explored and mapped the area in the late 1600s to expand their fur-trading dynasty. They built their first post, known as Rupert's Land, on the Nelson River in 1670.
- In the early eighteenth century, French explorers moved into the area and built posts, including one next to Lake Winnipeg. France and England battled for the area until the French surrendered their claims in 1763, following defeat in the French and Indian War.
- French-Canadians in Montreal continued to explore and settle in the area, which caused fighting between the factions until the merger of the Hudson's Bay and North West fur companies in 1821.
- The province of Manitoba was created in 1870, following the Red River Rebellion of the Metis people, a mixed race of French and Native Americans. The leader of the rebellion, Louis Riel, was captured and hung.
- In the late nineteenth century, the spacious prairies drew many immigrants, who grew wheat and other grains. By early in the twentieth century, the province enjoyed a thriving economy, and Winnipeg was a leading center for storing and processing wheat and other grains.
- The influx of immigrants reduced the political and economic power of French-speaking residents. Struggles between French and English speakers have continued ever since.
- In the 1950s, manufacturing industries began to replace agriculture in importance, a trend that shifted the provincial identity—and interests—from farming to industry.
- More than half the population of Manitoba lives in Winnipeg's metro area.
- During World War I, a Canadian captain from Winnipeg took a black bear cub named for the man's hometown to England as a regimental mascot. He donated

Manitoba Basics That Shape Your Character

Population: 1.1 million

Capital: Winnipeg

Largest City: Winnipeg (620,000)

Prevalent Religions: Roman Catholic, United Church of Canada, Anglican, and Lutheran

Major Industries: Manufacturing (primarily transportation and farm equipment and products), farming (primarily wheat and barley), fishing and fish processing, paper products and printing

the bear to the London Zoo, where it was a favorite of author A.A. Milne and his son; the bear was the inspiration for Winnie the Pooh. A statue of Winnie stands at the Assiniboine Park Zoo.

- Winnipeg has a thriving artistic scene. It's home to the country's oldest ballet and is hometown to a number of famous pop stars, including Randy Bachman, Burton Cummings, Neil Young, and the Crash Test Dummies.

For Further Research

Books

All We Know of Heaven, by Rémy Rougeau

Dictionary of Manitoba Biography, by Jim Bumstead

Faces of the Flood: Manitoba's Courageous Battle Against the Red River, by Jake MacDonald and Shirley Sandrel

Kiss of the Fur Queen, by Tomson Highway

Manitoba, by Harry Beckett

Manitoba: The Province and Its People, by Ken Coates and Fred McGuinness

The Northern Lights, by Howard Norman

Oh Susannah, by Selena Mindus

The Ojibwa of Behrens River, Manitoba, by A. Irving Hallowell

The Plains Cree, by John S. Milloy

Purple Springs, by Nellie L. McClung

River Road: Essays on Manitoba and Prairie History, by Gerald Friesen

The Stone Diaries and *Larry's Party*, by Carol Shields

Winnipeg: A Prairie Portrait, by Martin Cash

Web Sites

www.travelmanitoba.com/ (travel and tourism information)

www.gov.mb.ca/index.shtml (provincial government site)

www.manitobavirtualtours.com/ (virtual tours of the province)

www.fyiwinnipeg.com/ (Winnipeg news and entertainment information)

www.tourism.winnipeg.mb.ca/ (Winnipeg and tourism and information)

www.discoverwinnipeg.ca/ (Winnipeg information)

Interesting Places to Set a Scene

- **Brandon.** Located in the southwestern part of the province, Brandon is the financial center of its wheat-growing area. Visitors flock to the city—which has less than forty thousand residents—for the annual Manitoba Winter Fair.

- **Churchill.** A tiny town in the north, Churchill is an important provincial port on Hudson Bay. It's also the only settlement in North America where polar bears can be seen in the wild, and it's a great place to view the aurora borealis.

- **Folklorama.** The world's largest multicultural festival draws visitors from throughout North America to Winnipeg. It's a colorful festival that is especially good for seeing northern Native American, Inuit, and French cultural dress and ceremony.

- **International Peace Garden.** This landscaped park straddles the border of Manitoba and North Dakota and is located at the approximate center of the shared east-west border of the United States and Canada. Its Peace Tower—twin hundred-foot columns—is a well-known landmark in the region. The park also includes an auditorium, the Peace Chapel, and sunken pools that reflect the tower and the landscaped gardens.

- **The Forks.** Located near downtown Winnipeg, this fifty-six-acre recreation area is the meeting and entertainment center of the metro area. Shops, galleries, restaurants, and the scenic river walk attract thousands of visitors every day.

- **Selkirk.** Located on the Red River to the northwest

© Trevor Knowlton (www.phototour.ca)

Wheat in a Manitoba field

of the Winnipeg metro area, Selkirk was settled by Scottish and Irish immigrants. Nearby Lake Winnipeg makes Selkirk, so locals claim it the "Catfish Capital of the World." A ten-foot statue of Chuck the Channel Cat boosts the claim. The Scottish heritage of the city is obvious in the themes of its parks, restaurants, and festivals.

- **Universities of Manitoba and Winnipeg.** Both schools are located in Winnipeg and draw students from throughout the province as well as the country. The University of Manitoba is the bigger of the two and is known as a research center. Its spacious campus offers a variety of settings.

- **Winnipeg.** The only city of significant size in the province, Winnipeg is the cultural, educational, economic, and social center of Manitoba. It features a number of urban parks, the best known being Assiniboine Park, which contains the zoo and the conservatory. In winter the park is a favorite place for locals to sled, toboggan, and cross-country ski. Another great setting is the St. Boniface Cathedral in the heart of the city's French Quarter.

Ontario

Ontario Basics That Shape Your Character

Population: 11.7 million

Capital City: Toronto (Ottawa, the nation's capital, is located in this province)

Largest City: Toronto (700,000)

Prevalent Religions: United Church of Canada, Anglican, and Roman Catholicism

Major Industries: Manufacturing (machine tools, automotive parts, electrical machinery, metal products, computers), finance and banking, information and telecommunication services, food processing, tourism, farming (primarily dairy, corn, soybeans, and fruit)

Ontario Facts and Peculiarities That Your Character Might Know

- The Algonquin, Cree, and Ojibwa Native Americans lived in the area before the arrival of the British in 1611 and the French in 1615. The two countries battled for control of the region until the French surrendered their interests in the Treaty of Paris in 1763.
- Ontario became Upper Canada and Quebec Lower Canada in the eighteenth century, the former having closer cultural ties to England, the latter to France. Since then, these provinces have been unable to re-solve their cultural and political differences. Quebec's efforts to secede drove away a number of its leading industries, which resettled in Ontario. By the 1960s, Ontario was clearly established as the country's economic as well as political leader.
- The provincial name is derived from the Iroquoian word for "big lake," which was the name of Lake Ontario.
- More than a third of Canada's population lives in Ontario, and 80 percent of Ontarians live in urban centers. Toronto is the country's largest city, while Ottawa is fourth largest.
- The Toronto and Ottawa metro areas are the country's centers for manufacturing and high-tech industries. More than half the country's manufacturing takes place in Ontario.
- The cities of Kitchener, Cambridge, and Guelph form Canada's "Technology Triangle."
- Ottawa's famous Canadian Tulip Festival in May began in 1945 when Holland sent 100,000 bulbs to the city in gratitude to the Canadian army that liberated the European country during World War II. The festival is one of the best known in the country.
- Manitoulin Island in Lake Huron is the largest freshwater island in the world.

Interesting Places to Set a Scene

- **Hamilton.** Canada's equivalent to Pittsburgh, Hamilton is "Steel City." Connected to nearby Toronto by the massive Skyway Bridge, Hamilton is a blue-collar town known for its heavy industry, football (the beloved Tiger-Cats), and beer. Of course, it's much more diversified than that and has its share of parks and museums, but it takes special pride in being home to the Canadian Football League's Grey Cup and the Canadian Football Hall of Fame.
- **Hull.** Ottawa's neighbor across the Ottawa River, Hull is a French-speaking city closer in atmosphere and attitude to Montreal or Quebec City than to Ottawa. However, Ottawa-Hull is a single metro area and one of the fastest-growing areas in the country.
- **Kitchener.** Known as Berlin until it changed its name in 1916, Kitchener retains its Germanic heritage in

For Further Research

Books

Beautiful Ontario Towns, by Fred Dahms

Great Lakes Suite, by David W. McFadden

In a Glass House, by Nino Ricci

In the Mad Water: Two Centuries of Madness and Lunacy at Niagara Falls, by T.W. Kriner

Killarney, by Kevin Callan

Ontario, by David Peterson

Ontario, by Suzanne LeVert

Ontario's Wildlife, by Dave Taylor

Steel City: Hamilton and Its Region, by M.J. Dear

The Witching of Ben Wagner, by Mary Jane Auch

Web Sites

www.ontariotravel.net/ (Ontario travel)

www.gov.on.ca/ (Ontario government)

http://onwebguide.ca/ (directory of Ontario links)

www.thehilltimes.ca/ (national political and business information)

www.canada.com/ (Canada's main site)

http://canada.gc.ca/ (Canada's government)

www.thecanadadomain.com/ (Canadian links directory)

www.canadatravel.ca/ (Canada travel)

www.canada.com/ottawa/ (Ottawa information section of Canada's main site)

www.tourottawa.org/ (Ottawa tourism)

---

its architecture, culture, and its annual Octoberfest. Though Mennonite horse and buggies still can be seen around here, Kitchener is a thriving high-tech city. Its metro area has joined with neighboring Waterloo, and the area is now usually called Kitchener-Waterloo.

- **London.** This city takes its name seriously. It's located on the Thames River, and it's street names are taken from those in the other London. It also has the Covent Gardens market and red, double-decker buses. London calls itself the "Forest City" and prides itself on its trees and parks.

- **Mississauga.** The sixth largest city in the country, Mississauga is becoming part of the Toronto metro sprawl. It's home to L.B. Pearson International Airport, Canada's busiest, and miles of suburbs and golf courses. Lake Aquitane Park is where the city goes to play.

- **Niagara Falls.** Canadians are quick to note that their Horseshoe Falls are bigger than the American Falls. More than twelve million people visit the site every year, making it one of North America's most popular destinations. Your characters can see the falls by boat, car, or helicopter or from two observation towers.

- **Ottawa.** Ottawa has some interesting setting possibilities. Embassy buildings located throughout the city add an international air, and the National Gallery is a strikingly designed building of steel and glass. Every day at noon (except Sunday) in Major's Hill Park, the city fires a small (but loud) cannon. In May the annual tulip festival brings color and visitors.

- **Parliament Hill.** The home of Canada's government, "the Hill" features the stately Parliament Buildings, with their Gothic architecture and green copper roofs. The buildings sit high above the Ottawa River. Every day at ten in the morning, visitors and locals gather to watch the Changing of the Guard, which is full of pomp and bagpipes.

- **Rideau Canal.** Threading through the heart of Ottawa, the Rideau Canal is one of the city's best-known landmarks. It's a tourist stop for summer visitors, and locals use it in winter as the world's longest skating rink. Some even use it for a skating commute to work.

- **Sudbury.** A northern city that made its nickel by mining nickel, Sudbury has been in slow decline since its

The rushing Niagra Falls

mining industry began to suffer in the 1970s. It's still home to the world's biggest nickel (photo op here) and is reinventing itself as a science center. Lake Ramsey in the middle of the city provides graceful scenery for a midday walk.

- **Thunder Bay.** Once a busy center of storage and transportation for the Wheat Belt, Thunder Bay's port business has declined in recent years. It now sells itself as a hip, cosmopolitan arts center. It's best known for a huge land formation at the mouth of the bay that looks like, and is called, "The Sleeping Giant." Tourists come to see Old Fort William, a large reconstruction of a fur trading post, where actors in period costume evoke the past.

- **Windsor.** Located on the southwestern tip of the province and right across the river from Detroit, Windsor is a center for the auto industry and is the leading port of entry between the United States and Canada. Its casinos used to lure Americans by the thousands until Detroit built its own casinos. Though not exactly Las Vegas, there's a wide-open atmosphere of fun in Windsor that much of the province lacks. Windsor has an international flavor. Nearly 7 percent of its 200,000 residents were born in Asia (your character will find many great ethnic restaurants) and about 16 percent of residents were born in Europe.

Toronto

Toronto Facts and Peculiarities Your Character Might Know

- Hockey's Toronto Maple Leafs are commonly referred to as "The Buds."
- Someone talking about the "ROM" is referring to the Royal Ontario Museum; someone talking about the "AGO" is referring to the Art Gallery of Ontario.
- The "CNE" is the Canadian National Exhibition, a midway-style amusement park open for a few weeks each September.
- Toronto is often ranked as the safest large metropolitan area in North America.
- "Wonderland" is Paramount Canada's Wonderland, Canada's premier theme park.
- "Queen's Quay" (pronounced "key," which even locals often mispronounce as "kway") runs east-west along the harbor-front.
- People will get all dressed up to go see *The Lion King* or *Mamma Mia!* downtown and then race back home to catch the end of the Leaf game.
- Toronto is sometimes referred to as "Hogtown," but nobody seems to know why.
- The "TTC" is the Toronto Transit Commission, the city's extensive subway, bus, and streetcar network; commuters coming from the suburbs or outlying communities use GO Trains (their actual name), which are faster and more comfortable than the city trains.
- There's a joke among Torontonians that goes a little something like this: "Vancouver hates us because we're too stuffy. The Prairies hate us because we have no soul. The Maritimes hate us because we're money-driven. And Montreal hates us because we've taken over as the economic center of Canada and stolen most of their eighteen to thirty-five generation."

If Your Character . . .

If Your Character Is Trendy, he shops in The Eaton Centre. This immense downtown shopping mecca is architecturally impressive and sports beautiful artwork of a flock of Canadian geese flying overhead.

If Your Character Is a Bohemian, she's hanging out at The Beaches. The name is a slight misnomer, because

Toronto Basics That Shape Your Character

A snapshot of Toronto

Population: 700,000 in the city; 5.2 million in the Greater Toronto area (called CMA for Census Metropolitan Area)

Prevalent Religions: Protestant, Roman Catholic, Sikh, Buddhist, Muslim, Jewish, and Hindu

Top Employers: The Bank of Nova Scotia, Canada Post Corporation, Canadian Imperial Bank of Commerce, City of Toronto, General Motors of Canada Ltd., The Great Atlantic and Pacific Company of Canada Ltd., Hudson's Bay Company, Loblaw Companies East, Magna International Inc., Peel District School Board, Royal Bank of Canada, TD Bank Financial Group, TD Canada Trust, Toronto District School Board, Toronto Transit Commission, University of Toronto

Per Capita Income: $23,900 (Canadian dollars)

Average Daily Temperature: January, 24° F; July, 69° F

Ethnic Makeup (in percent): Caucasian 79.5%, African-American 6.0%, Hispanic 6.1%, Asian 2.1%, Other 6.3%

Newspapers and Magazines: *The Globe and Mail, National Post, The Toronto Star, The Toronto Sun, WHERE Toronto*

Free Weekly Alternative Papers: *Now, Eye, Xtra!*

Used with the permission of *Navigator*

you don't actually swim here. The Beaches is Toronto's bohemian community on the eastern section of the lakefront, where cyclists, roller-bladers, joggers, dog-walkers, beach-volleyball players, and sun-worshippers abound during summer.

If Your Character Loves Castles, she's roaming around in Casa Loma. This is a big castle in the middle of the city. Businessman Sir Henry Pellatt spent $3.5 million to build the medieval style castle, which was completed in 1914. Since 1937, Casa Loma has been in the hands of the Kiwanis Club of Casa Loma.

If Your Character Is All About Business, he's spending time in Bay Street. The heart of Toronto's thriving Financial District, this is Canada's answer to Wall Street. Towering glass skyscrapers house the big banks, insurance companies, and law firms whose suited, cellphone-toting yuppies pack the sidewalks during the summer months for a quick bite from a hot-dog vendor and a power bottle of water.

If Your Character Is Asian and Smells of Money, he resides in Richmond Hill. There has been a large influx of wealthy Asians (largely from Hong Kong) into Toronto over the past decade; the wealthiest (or at least those with the biggest homes) are concentrated here.

Local Grub Your Character Might Love

One of Toronto's strongest drawing points is its incredible variety of restaurants. What many folks do to take advantage of the variety is to patronize a few favorite spots in one evening. On a given night, you might go to The Danforth for *souvlaki*, Little Italy for penne, Chinatown for dim sum, or enjoy one of the French, Hungarian, Vietnamese, or Thai restaurants in town. Sushi is big here—there are a number of good Japanese restaurants around—as is the occasional steak. The most popular restaurants in town include Scaramouche, North 44, Centro, Canoe (on the fifty-fifth floor of the Toronto-Dominion Tower), and 360 (a revolving restaurant near the top of the Canadian National (CN) Tower).

Interesting and Peculiar Places to Set a Scene

- **Harbourfront.** This popular promenading area hugs Toronto's harbor. It's a great place to have an ice cream, watch the sailboats, or take in a reading at the International Festival of Authors, the largest event of its kind worldwide.
- **The CN Tower.** Built in the 1970s and shooting skyward past the roofs of downtown's tallest skyscrapers, this needle-shaped building is the world's tallest freestanding structure. Out-of-towners tend to freak out

in the glass-windowed, high-speed elevators as they hurtle upward 113 stories (or, if they go to Sky Pod, another thirty-three stories up). This is said to be the world's highest public observation deck.

- **Ontario Place.** This is an extensive amusement complex built on Lake Ontario (the giant golf ball on the water is actually a 360-degree IMAX theater).
- **In a theater.** Toronto's theater and performing arts community is the third largest in the world after New York City and London. Your character will be sure to find something to fit his taste here, whether it's watching a Broadway-style production at the Princess of Wales or Royal Alexandra Theatres, listening to one of the international musical acts at Roy Thompson Hall, laughing at Yuk Yuk's or The Second City, or jamming to the beat of the city's annual jazz festival.
- **Yorkville.** This former 1960s hippie hangout is now a popular upscale shopping area abutting downtown to the north, with art galleries, cafes, chic shops, and outside eateries.
- **Kensington Market.** While it might seem like a disorganized mess of apparel and salespeople, this is actually Toronto's best spot for buying vintage clothes and curious toys. How can your character resist shops with names like Asylum; Dancing Days; and Courage, My Love?
- **University Avenue.** Your character has seen this stretch before, as the area has stood in for Chicago, New York City, and numerous other cities in many Hollywood productions.
- **Greektown.** Toronto is a city with lots of Greeks, which means lots of late-night bars, lots of Øuzo (an anise-flavored liqueur), lots of singing and dancing, and lots and lots of food.
- **On a subway train.** For some, this is a favorite part of the day (for winding down, mostly). In any given car your character is likely to find at least a few—but often several—of the following mix of people: a European, an Asian, an Indian, a Portuguese, an African, a Ukranian/Russian, a Hispanic, a Greek, or a Filipino. Most Torontonians wouldn't know racism if it struck them in the face.

Exceptionally Grand Things Your Character Is Proud Of

- Its multiculturalism and multiethnicity. Toronto is heralded as one of the most multicultural cities in the

For Further Research

Books

Accidental City: The Transformation of Toronto, by Robert Fulford

Blues and True Concussions: Six New Toronto Poets, by Michael Redhill

Doing Good: The Life of Toronto's General Hospital, by J. T. H. Connor

The Estates of Old Toronto, by Liz Lundell

Get Stuffed Toronto, by Julie Crysler

The Rough Guide to Toronto, by Rough Guides

Secret Toronto: The Unique Guidebook to Toronto's Hidden Sites, Sounds, and Tastes, by Scott Mitchell

Toronto: Considering Self-Government, by Jane Jacobs et al.

Toronto's Many Faces, by Tony Ruprecht et al.

The Waning of the Green: Catholics, the Irish, and Identity in Toronto, 1887–1922, by Mark G. McGowan

Web Sites

www.thestar.com (*The Toronto Star*)

www.city.toronto.on.ca (city site)

www.gaytoronto.com (gay guide to the city)

www.fyitoronto.com (*The Toronto Sun*)

Still Curious? Why Not Check Out

Algonquin, by Roderick MacKay

Alias Grace, by Margaret Atwood

Brown Girl in the Ring, by Nalo Hopkinson

Fifth Business, by Robertson Davies

I'm Supposed to Be Crazy and Other Stories, by John Grube

In the Skin of a Lion: A Novel, by Michael Ondaatje

Poor Tom Is Cold, by Maureen Jennings

The Stone Carvers, by Jane Urquhart

Summer Gone: A Novel, by David Macfarlane

Swimming Lessons and Other Stories From Firozsha Baag, by Rohinton Mistry

---

world, and rightly so. The running joke is that the only way Canadians can define themselves is that they're not American. There's a reason: This is a place where anyone is welcome, so it's harder to describe the typical Torontonian than it is to describe, say, the typical American businessman.

- The city's comedians: Mike Myers, Jim Carrey, John Candy, Martin Short, Eugene Levy.
- Its authors: Michael Ondaatje, Rohinton Mistry, Margaret Atwood, Robertson Davies.
- Singers and musicians: Shania Twain, Alanis Morrisette, Celine Dion.
- SkyDome. This is major-league baseball's first stadium with a retractable roof.
- Toronto Maple Leaf fans—they're ever loyal and proud despite the performance of their team.
- The Hockey Hall of Fame—it's here and people frequent it often.
- That no one ever thinks about visiting Toronto, but once they do, they always love it.
- The Ontario Science Centre and The Toronto Zoo (the city's two most popular school field-trip destinations).

Pathetically Sad Things Your Character Is Ashamed Of

- That the Maple Leafs haven't won a Stanley Cup since 1967.
- That the Blue Jays play on turf instead of grass.

Your Character Loves

- Canadian politeness. Though you wouldn't know it from the breakneck speed of downtown, they're fiercely proud of their innate laid-back, obliging nature. They enjoy the hustle and bustle of New York City without the aggressive energy.
- The city's cleanliness—something Torontonians take for granted until they go to a city in another country.
- Their safety. Residents know they can walk virtually anywhere in the city at virtually any hour without being harmed.
- The sports community. Most Canadian kids play hockey in winter and baseball or soccer in summer, though the city is becoming increasingly basketball-mad these days. Skiing and snowboarding also have plenty of devotees.
- Hockey. On any given day from May to October you'll

see frequent road-hockey games (now played mostly in roller-blades instead of sneakers) along residential streets.

Your Character Hates

- American ignorance toward Canada (but they don't hate Americans!). When Americans ask how cold it gets, or if there's still snow in June, or whether Toronto actually experiences summer, Torontonians are ready to throttle them.
- The "Eh?" joke, which does apply to most Canadians (since Canada is made up mostly of rural towns and people) but not really to Torontonians.
- That people assume pleasant and clean means boring and dull.

Quebec Facts and Peculiarities Your Character Might Know

- Quebec is Canada's largest province, covering 595,000 square miles.
- Much of the exploration of Canada began in Quebec. In 1608 Samuel de Champlain built a trading post on the site of present-day Quebec City, and most explorations of Canada initiated from there.
- The region was known as New France throughout much of the seventeenth and eighteenth centuries, until French General Louis Montcalm was defeated by British General James Wolfe on the Plains of Abraham near Quebec City in 1759.
- Though the region fell under British rule in 1763 after the French and Indian War, the new government allowed much of the French customs and legal traditions to continue. However, disagreements between the British and the French residents continued and sparked a rebellion in 1837.
- Quebec was known for a time as Lower Canada, while Ontario was called Upper Canada. Later they were called East and West Canada. In 1867, when the confederation of Canada was officially formed, they became the provinces as we now know them, though Quebec maintains its French character and tensions about this continue.
- Quebec has made a number of attempts to secede from Canada. Provincial votes have been taken, and one in 1995 nearly approved separation. In 1998, the Canadian Supreme Court ruled it illegal for Quebec to secede.
- Quebec City is built in tiers. Lower Town lies on the shores of the St. Lawrence River, and Upper Town sits at the top of the hill. The tiers are divided by a steep rock escarpment.

Interesting Places to Set a Scene

- **Basilique Notre-Dame-de-Quebec.** The oldest Catholic parish in North America is centered in this grand old basilica full of ornate architecture and details. It's just one of the many grand historic buildings in Quebec City's Upper Town, which is known for its splendid churches, museums, hotels, and government buildings.
- **Charlevoix.** A large pastoral region stretching east

Quebec Basics that Shape Your Character

Population: 6.8 million

Capital: Quebec City

Largest City: Montreal (1 million)

Prevalent Religions: Roman Catholicism and United Church of Canada

Major Industries: Finance, insurance, banking, tourism, communication services, manufacturing (primarily paper products), lumber and wood products

from Quebec City to the Saguenay River and north to Saguenay-Lac-Saint-Jean in the north, Charlevoix is where the Quebecois go to play outdoors. The region offers a mix of rolling hills and valleys, rivers and streams to more dramatic scenery, including waterfalls and glacial mountains. It's a popular area for campers and hikers as well as for less adventuresome visitors seeking respite from the city.

- **Chateau Frontenac.** Built in 1624, this turreted building in Quebec City's Upper Town is the city's most famous landmark. Now a hotel, it once housed the colonial governors. Its green roof and turrets and its commanding position above the city and the river make it a symbol of the city's strength.
- **Gaspe Peninsula.** If your characters want to escape the buzz of Quebec's big cities, take them to Gaspe Peninsula, where moose, caribou, and bears still roam the

For Further Research

Books

Behind the Embassy Door: Canada, Clinton, and Quebec, by James J. Blanchard

The Black Hunter, by James Oliver Curwood

The Bridge at Quebec, by William D. Middleton

French Fun: The Real Spoken Language of Quebec, by Steve Timmins

La Rage and *Cowboy*, by Louis Hamelin

Pluralism and Inequality in Quebec, by Leslie Laczko

Quebec, by Harry Beckett

Quebec City: 1765–1832, by D.T. Ruddell

Surfacing, by Margaret Atwood

Town House, Country House, by Hazel Boswell

Whistling Past the Graveyard, by David M. Thomas

Web Sites

www.tourisme.gouv.qc.ca/ (Quebec travel and information)

www2.marianopolis.edu/quebechistory/ (Quebec history)

www.quebecweb.com/tourisme/quebec/introang.html (Quebec City and region information)

www.quebecregion.com/ (Quebec City and Area Tourism and Convention Bureau)

www.ville.quebec.qc.ca/ (Quebec City information)

www.quebecplus.ca/ (Quebec City and area)

www.telegraphe.com/ (Quebec City *Telegraph*)

www.tourisme-charlevoix.com/ (information about Charlevoix)

dense forests of the Chic-Choc Mountains. The rough shoreline is bounded by steep cliffs. Tiny, rugged villages still focus on fishing, though some cater to hardy tourists.

Trevor Knowlton (www.phototour.ca)
Quebec City

- **Grosse Isle.** Canada's Ellis Island, this island is located in the St. Lawrence River and was the entry point for immigrants arriving from Europe in the nineteenth century. Some of the old processing and quarantine buildings are still open to tourists. A huge Celtic cross stands on its shore in memory of Irish immigrants lost at sea.

- **Montreal.** (For specifics on Montreal, see page 379.)

- **Quebec City.** It's the oldest city in the province and retains its French heritage in its architecture and magnificent old buildings. It looks like a European city, and, to some extent, it is one. French-speaking residents make up more than 90 percent of the population, and there's a strong emphasis on tradition here. The part of the city built on the waterfront is called Lower Town; Upper Town rises about 300 feet above the St. Lawrence River on Cape Diamond Bluff.

- **Sherbrooke.** The economic and cultural center of the southeastern corner of the province, Sherbrooke is far less glamorous than Montreal and Quebec City. Its proximity to the U.S. border makes it a transportation center, but it's best known for its "sugar shacks" where maple syrup is made.

- **Vieux-Quebec.** This historic district in Quebec City's Lower Town is lined with narrow, crooked cobblestone streets. The area was restored in the 1970s and is now densely packed with trendy shops, galleries, and restaurants. It's a great walking area and a major tourist attraction.

● Montreal

Montreal Facts and Peculiarities Your Character Might Know

- Explorer Jacques Cartier was the first European to see the area, which he claimed for France in 1535. A large village of Hochelaga Native Americans stood on the spot. The Native Americans took him to a hill overlooking the area, which he named *un mont real,* or "royal mountain."
- Montreal grew up as a fur trading center in the seventeenth and eighteenth centuries. It was home to the North West trading company, which merged with the Hudson's Bay Company in 1821.
- After the American Revolution, Montreal became the leading trade center for the British in North America. When the fur trade died in the 1830s, the economic focus shifted to lumber and other industries. Tens of thousands of immigrants, many of them Irish, poured into the city to find jobs in the shipyards and flour mills.
- Throughout the nineteenth century and well into the twentieth, Montreal was Canada's most important city. Since World War II, it has gradually lost a number of its industries to Toronto, mostly as a result of the secessionist issues.
- In 1967, Montreal hosted Expo '67, a World's Fair that brought international attention to the city and established a thriving new identity for it. Two years later, it became the first Canadian city to have a Major League Baseball team, which was named, fittingly, the Montreal Expos.
- In 1976, Montreal hosted the Summer Olympic games. Olympic Park, which includes the dynamically designed Olympic Stadium, is a great place to set a scene.
- Montreal is an island city in the St. Lawrence River. The corporation limits of the city did not extend to the entire island until January 1, 2002, when the island became a single municipality.
- Montreal is the second largest French-speaking city in the world. Paris is the largest.
- Quebec laws prohibit signs posted in any language other than French, so if your characters don't speak French, they'll need to learn to read it. In the city,

Montreal Basics That Shape Your Character

Trevor Knowlton (www.phototour.ca)

The facade of Notre Dame

Population: 1 million

Prevalent Religions: Roman Catholicism, Protestantism, and Judaism

Top Employers: Bombadier, BCE, Quebecor, Bell Canada, Alcan, Power Corp., Power Financial, Canadian National Railway

Newspapers: *The Gazette* (English daily), *Journal de Montréal* (French daily)

Free Weekly Alternative Papers: *Mirror* (English), *Voir* (French)

most people can speak English, so there's little problem. Rural towns in the area tend to speak only French.
- The neighborhood of Old Montreal has the largest concentration of nineteenth-century buildings in North America.
- *Le Gros Bourbon,* a bell in the Perseverance Tower of the Notre Dame Basilica, weighs more than twelve tons and is one of the largest bells in North America.
- At the turn of the twentieth century, residents of the "Golden Square Mile" in downtown Montreal owned 70 percent of Canada's wealth. Though high-rise apartments and office buildings now dominate the area, a number of the majestic homes are still there.

If Your Character . . .

If Your Character Is Alternative and Grungy, he lives in the Quartier Latin, which includes the red-light district (still seamy but less dangerous than in its heyday), and the the gay village. Also consider the Carre St. Louis, or, especially if your character is artsy, the Plateau Mont Royal (known locally as "the Plateau.") The Boulevard Ste. Laurent is full of bohemian cafes and trendy shops.

If Your Character Smells of Old Money, she lives in Westmount if she's not French, or Outremont if she is French. Or, your character might live in one of the Golden Square Mile mansions, especially on Rue Sherbrooke, Montreal's most elegant old street.

If Your Character Is All About Business, he works Downtown. Some of the growing cities in the metro area, such as Laval, have their own business districts.

If Your Character Is a Rich Young Professional, she lives in Outremont (if French), the mile-high district of the Plateau, or in Mont Royal. Commuting to work downtown by bicycle is common for this character.

If Your Character Is a Family Man, he lives in one of the suburban cities or neighborhoods in the Montreal metro area, off the island.

If Your Character Wears a Blue Collar at Work, he lives in Cote-des-Neiges or Notre-Dame-de-Grace. He could also live in the residential neighborhoods in the southwest.

Local Grub Your Character Might Love

Trempette—bread, cream, and maple syrup—is a local favorite. (Maple syrup is a Quebec specialty in itself.) French pastries, baguettes, croissants, cakes, and chocolates are sold in boutiques throughout the city. Truffles are another local favorite. Montreal is also known for smoked meats, especially spiced beef and pork. Schwartz's is viewed by many as the best place for smoked meat. Smoked meat sandwiches can be found all over town. *Tourtiere* (a meat pie spiced with cloves and onions) is popular, both homemade from Grandma's recipe or takeout on the fly. Coffee is big here. Debates rage about where to find the best café au lait.

Interesting Places to Set a Scene

- **Mount Royal.** Visitors as well as locals love to hike to the seven-hundred-foot crest of Mount Royal, located in Mount Royal Park, for a panoramic view of the city.

At the top, your characters can look down at the city and see the river beyond it and the Monteregian Hills beyond the river. Locals call it simply "the mountain."

- **Notre Dame Basilica.** One of the city's best-known landmarks and a popular tourist attraction, the basilica is immediately recognizable by its twin bell towers, Temperance and Perseverance. It was built in 1829 and features neo-Gothic architecture and beautiful stained glass windows. The interior is dazzlingly ornate, with paintings and statues as well as a blue vaulted ceiling speckled with hundreds of twenty-four-karat-gold stars.
- **Old Montreal.** The Vieux Montreal is the main tourist area, with plenty of landmarks and attractions along its cobbled streets. It's primarily a walking area and is crowded during summer tourist season. (Locals tend to avoid it at that time of year.)
- **Ste. Catherine Street.** This is the main commercial shopping district in the city. It's a buzzing mix of locals and tourists ambling through stores and restaurants, all of them speaking a variety of languages. It's a great place for people-watching, too.
- **The Underground City.** An eighteen-mile network of tunnels beneath the city, "the Underground" is more than a pedestrian walkway. While it does connect above-ground buildings, it has many stores and restaurants of its own. In the cold of winter, your characters can window-shop in comfort.
- **The universities.** Campuses, and their usually funky-trendy environs, can provide good settings. Montreal has several, including the University of Montreal, the University of Quebec at Montreal, and, perhaps best known and most prestigious, McGill University. Try any of them, though McGill and the neighborhoods surrounding it are the hippest grunge spots in the city for young people.
- **Vieux-Port.** The shipping port area on the St. Lawrence River is in transition. It used to be a shabby area but is becoming an entertainment center. There's an IMAX theater and other attractions, while remnants of the old port area remain intact—for better and worse.

Exceptionally Grand Things Your Character Is Proud Of

- The Olympic Games. The timing of the games, when Montreal was losing industry to Toronto and

For Further Research

Books

Bedlam on the Streets, by Caroline Knowles

City Unique: Montreal Days and Nights in the 1940s and '50s, by William Weintraub

A City With a Difference: The Rise and Fall of the Montreal Citizen's Movement, by Timothy Lloyd Thomas

The Living Past of Montreal, by Eric McLean

Montreal: A Guide to Recent Architecture, by Steven Ware

Opening the Gates of Eighteenth-Century Montreal, edited by Phyllis Lambert and Alan Stewart

Storied Streets: Montreal in the Literary Imagination, by Bryan Demchinsky and Elaine Kalman Naves

Web Sites

www.canada.com/montreal/ (Montreal page of Canada's main site)

www.montreal.com/ (main city page)

www2.ville.montreal.qc.ca/ (Montreal city site)

www.toutmontreal.com/ (Montreal city information)

www.canada.com/montreal/montrealgazette/ (*The Gazette*)

www.lookmontreal.com/ (Montreal links)

www.montrealfood.com/ (Montreal food, restaurants, and general information)

www.tourism-montreal.org/ (Montreal travel and tourism)

Still Curious? Why Not Check Out

The Apprenticeship of Duddy Kravitz and *Joshua Then and Now: A Novel*, by Mordecai Richler

City of Ice: A Novel, by John Farrow

Cracks, by Anne Dandurand

Fat Woman Next Door Is Pregnant: A Novel, by Michel Trembley

Lies My Father Told Me

The Tin Flute, by Gabrielle Roy

---

the Quebecois debate raged, gave the city a lift that has lasted.

- The Canadiens. The city loves hockey, and the Canadiens have been one of the National Hockey League's most successful franchises.

Your Character Loves

- French culture and tradition. Even the locals who don't have French lineage enjoy the tradition and heritage.
- Winter sports. They like to get out of the city on the weekends to head north for cross-country and downhill skiing, sledding, ice skating, and tobogganing.
- Café au lait.

Your Character Hates

- Ontario, particularly Toronto. *Hate* might be too strong a word, but Montrealans tend to resent losing

a number of industries—and therefore economic opportunities and therefore its young people—to the now more robust financial centers, particularly Toronto.

- Quebec City. There's always been a (sort of) friendly rivalry between the two cities, Montreal being considered the more energetic and cosmopolitan, Quebec City the more sophisticated and traditional. As Montrealans resent Toronto's providence and vitality, they resent the stubbornness of their fellow Quebecois.
- Visitors who assume no one speaks English here. It's an international city with a great many English-speaking residents.

Saskatchewan

Saskatchewan Basics That Shape Your Character

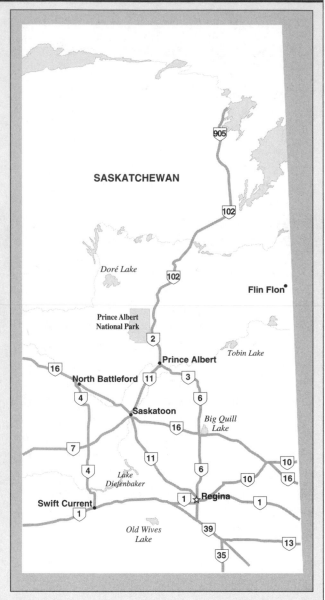

Population: 1 million

Capital: Regina

Largest City: Saskatoon (230,000)

Prevalent Religions: United Church of Canada, Roman Catholicism, Anglican, and Lutheran

Major Industries: Farming (primarily wheat and barley) and mining (primarily uranium, potash, oil, and natural gas)

Saskatchewan Facts and Peculiarities Your Character Might Know

- The name of the province is taken from the Saskatchewan River and is derived from the Cree word *kisiskatchewan* for "river that flows swiftly."
- As part of the Great Plains, Saskatchewan was home to plains Native American tribes, such as the Cree, Blackfoot, and Sioux. The Gros Ventres and Assiniboine tribes also occupied the area.
- The Hudson's Bay Company explored and trapped here in the mid-eighteenth century. French traders from Montreal soon entered the area, which was rich in fur. The first settlement was a post built in 1774 by Samuel Hearne of the Hudson's Bay Company.
- One of the most famous events in the province's history occurred in 1885 when Louis Riel led the mixed-race Metis against the Canadian government in the Northwest Rebellion. The Metis, part French and part Native American, objected to white settlement of the area and the vanishing buffalo herds on the plains. The Metis were quickly defeated and Riel was captured and hanged.
- Immigrant settlers poured into the area in the late nineteenth century to farm the rich and wide lands. Saskatchewan's identity as an important wheat producer and agriculture center had begun.
- In 1905, Saskatchewan was made a province. It continued to be a major farming region throughout the twentieth century. Its economy has benefited from oil and gas fields, but not nearly as much as Alberta, its neighbor to the west.
- Saskatchewan is the world's largest producer of uranium.
- The province's low population and large land area give it a low population density, especially in the sparsely settled north. More than one half of the province is covered by forest.
- Last Mountain Lake is home to the oldest bird sanctuary in North America.
- As opportunities in farming have decreased over the years, young people of the province have moved out.

Interesting Places to Set a Scene

- **Moose Jaw.** Located due west of nearby Regina, Moose Jaw has a colorful name and a colorful past.

For Further Research

Books

As for Me and My House, by Sinclair Ross
Canadian Sioux, by James H. Howard
Cornerstones: An Artist's History of the City of Regina, by William Argan with Pam Cowan
The Englishman's Boy, by Guy Vanderhaeghe
The Lonely Land, by Sigurd F. Olsen
Lost Geography: A Novel, by Charlotte Bacon
People Place: A Dictionary of Saskatchewan Place Names, by Bill Barry
Saskatchewan: A History, by John H. Archer
Saskatchewan Politics: Into the Twenty-First Century, edited by Howard A. Leeson

Saskatchewan Saga series, by Ruth Glover
A Student of Weather, by Elizabeth Hay

Web Sites

http://saskatchewan.worldweb.com/ (tourism, travel, and general information)
www.sasktourism.com/ (visitor information)
www.sasksearch.com/ (general information and links)
www.cityregina.com/ (Regina city government and information)
www.rreda.com/ (Regina regional development)
www.tourismsaskatoon.com/ (Saskatoon tourism)
www.moosejaw.ws/ (Moose Jaw visitor and entertainment)

Set a scene in the "Tunnels of Little Chicago," underground passages used for smuggling Canadian liquor during the American prohibition era. The city also attracts visitors to its well-known mineral springs and calls itself "The Friendly City."

- **Prince Albert.** The province's northernmost city of any size, Prince Albert is a commercial and processing center for the northern industries, such as lumbering and uranium mining. It also is a popular entry point for Prince Albert National Park.

- **Prince Albert National Park.** Though it lacks the dramatic peaks of the national parks to the west, Prince Albert attracts visitors from throughout the country, especially those seeking a greater sense of wilderness. It's best known for muskeg, a thick mat of swamplike vegetation.

- **Regina.** A pretty city and very clean for its size, Regina is the provincial capital as well as the artistic and cultural center. It also claims to be sunniest capital in the country. Wascana Centre is one of the largest urban parks in North America and features respected science and art museums as well as manicured green space. During the long winters, locals love to skate on Wascana Lake. The city is home to the University of Regina and the training academy for the Royal Canadian Mounted Police.

- **Saskatoon.** Though it's the largest city in the province, Saskatoon has only 200,000 residents and is by no means a big city in any regard. However, it does have a relaxed yet sophisticated atmosphere, especially in the university area and the Broadway shopping district. Saskatoon berry pie is a local favorite and a tradition.

Canola Fields

Trevor Knowlton (www.phototour.ca)

The Atlantic Provinces

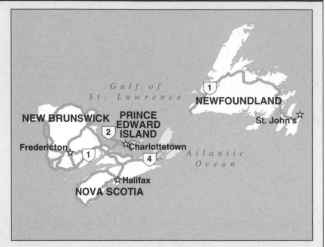

Provincial Facts and Peculiarities Your Character Might Know

- New Brunswick, Nova Scotia, and Prince Edward Island are called the Maritime Provinces. The province of Newfoundland is officially called Newfoundland and Labrador. The combined population of the Atlantic Provinces makes up less than a tenth of the country's population.
- Life in the Atlantic Provinces is heavily influenced by water. If your characters are in the Maritimes or Newfoundland, they're less than a hundred miles from the ocean. The seas control the economy as well as the weather—which is often damp and breezy and sometimes foggy. People here have a special kinship to the sea and have braved its worst for generations.
- The Maritimes built their economy on shipbuilding

and fishing in the eighteenth and nineteenth centuries. The shift from wooden to steel ships and the slow depletion of nearby fisheries has damaged the economy, which now relies heavily on tourism.

- The Inuit Native Amerians lived in the Atlantic Provinces before and during the arrival of Europeans, as did Algonquian-speaking tribes such as the Micmacs and the Malecites. Viking explorers are believed to have reached the area in A.D. 1000.
- In 1497, explorer John Cabot reached the area and named it "New Founde Lande" and claimed it for England. Further exploration was done by the British, the French, and the Basques, all of whom were drawn by cod fishing on the Grand Banks.
- In 1610, French settlers established an area they called Acadia, near Port Royal in Nova Scotia. The culture thrived until the 1750s when the British began deporting all Acadians who refused to sign a loyalty oath. Nearly three-fourths of the Acadians were deported, eventually finding homes in Europe, the American colonies, and the Caribbean Islands.
- In 1864, delegates from New Brunswick, Nova Scotia, Prince Edward Island, Ontario, and Quebec met at Province House in Charlottetown on Prince Edward Island to discuss forming a union. The British government approved the confederation of provinces in 1867.
- Newfoundland was the last to join, becoming a province in 1949. It is made up, confusingly, of the island of Newfoundland (known as "the Rock") and the mainland region of Labrador. Its people tend to identify far less with Canada than do those in other provinces, and they refer to themselves as "Newfies" far more than they do "Canadians."
- Prince Edward Island is the country's smallest province but also the most densely populated, with fifty people per square mile. It produces more than half of Canada's potato crop, earning it the nickname "Spud Island."
- Before the detonation of the atomic bomb, the largest man-made explosion in history occurred in Halifax in 1917. A French munitions ship loaded with TNT collided with another ship. Several thousand people

For Further Research

Books

Anne of Green Gables series, by Lucy Maud Montgomery

Anne's World, Maud's World, by Nancy Rootland

The Colony of Unrequited Dreams and *Baltimore's Mansion: A Memoir*, by Wayne Johnston

Hunting Down Home, by Jean McNeil

Kit's Law, by Donna Morrissey

Labrador Village, by John C. Kennedy

Losing Eddie, by Deborah Joy Corey

Moncton Mantra, by Gerald LeBlanc

Newfoundland, by Harry Beckett

No Great Mischief, by Alistair MacLeod

Nova Scotia, by Suzanne LeVert

Prince Edward Island Sayings, edited by T.K. Pratt and Scott Burke

Random Passage, by Bernice Morgan

The Shipping News, by Annie Proulx

Web Sites

www.new-brunswick.com/ (New Brunswick information)

http://new-brunswick.net/ (New Brunswick information and travel)

www.gov.nf.ca/ (Newfoundland/Labrador government)

www.gov.nf.ca/tourism/ Newfoundland/Labrador tourism)

www.gov.ns.ca/ (Nova Scotia government)

www.gov.ns.ca/tourism.htm (Nova Scotia tourism)

http://gonovascotia.com/ (Nova Scotia travel)

www.gov.pe.ca/ (Prince Edward Island government)

www.peionline.com/ (Prince Edward Island travel)

---

were killed, hundreds were blinded, and the northern part of the city was wiped out.

- New Brunswick is the largest and most populous of the Maritime Islands.

Interesting Places to Set a Scene

- **Cape Breton Island.** One of the most beautiful areas in the country, Cape Breton Island is a mecca for tourists. For setting a scene, consider the 175-mile Cabot Trail, a road that cuts through gorgeous hills and valleys and hugs the coast of the island.
- **Halifax.** A main gateway for visitors to the craggy coasts of the Maritimes, Halifax is perhaps the busiest and most economically robust city in the region. Its port has provided an important connecting point with England for several hundred years. Its best-known landmark is the Citadel, a star-shaped fort built on a hill above the city.
- **New Brunswick.** The pleasant capital city of Fredericton is a bit dull, and the largest city, St. John, isn't much better. However, the St. John Valley offers great scenery, and your characters can stop in Grand Falls, where seventy-foot waterfalls add a note of drama. The Passamaquoddy Bay area is interesting, too, with the charming town of St. Andrews drawing locals and tourists.
- **Newfoundland.** Far less scenic and far less populated than its sister provinces, Newfoundland has a rugged, textured quality that at times is even harsh. All of this, of course, can make for great settings, as Annie Proulx proved in her novel *The Shipping News*. The people here, too, are less open and accommodating. Gros Morne National Park offers spectacular view of mountainous fjords and inlets.
- **Nova Scotia.** Its name is Latin for "New Scotland," but this province is only partly rooted in British traditions. The eastern part is much more French. For settings, try Peggy's Cove, an idyllic fishing village with weathered clapboard houses and a pristine lighthouse. It's how the Maritimes imagine themselves to be at their best. Or try Louisburg for a French influence, or Lunenberg, a German-Swiss fishing and shipping town.

The Anne of Green Gables house

- **Prince Edward Island.** Prince Edward Island is a beautiful if economically struggling island. It's best known as the home of Lucy Maud Montgomery's Anne of Green Gables. The town of Cavendish offers several Green Gables tourist sites, and throughout the island Anne's sweet visage is unavoidable. The island also offers miles of beautiful red-sand coastline and more lobsters and oysters than your characters can eat.

- **The Bay of Fundy.** For sheer power, you can't beat the tides of this rollicking water. For using the setting at a safer distance from your characters, there's a national park and a number of islands, the most famous of which is Campobello, where the Roosevelt family summered for years before FDR was stricken with polio. The family mansion is now a museum.

Canadian Territories

Territorial Facts and Pecularities Your Character Might Know

- All told, Northwest Territories, Nunavut, and Yukon Territory account for nearly 40 percent of Canada's land mass. Yet, combined the territories account for only about 0.25 percent of the country's population. Consider these places for a character who wants—or needs—to get away from it all.

- Although the Northwest Territories encompass 1,171,918 square kilometers, the area is sparsely populated, with only 42,083 residents. There is only one official city (Yellowknife) in the Northwest Territories, and only four towns, three settlements, and one village.

- Nearly half the population of the Northwest Territories is aboriginal, divided into two basic groups, the Dene and the Inuit, neither of which likes being called Indian or Eskimo. Dene and Inuit, by the way, both translate as "The People."

- The Northwest Territories has no political parties. It does have a Legislative Assembly, but the governmental system is called a "consensus government," is formed of nineteen members, representing the nineteen constituencies in the Northwest Territories. Once these nineteen members are elected, they vote amongst themselves for the Premier; they also elect a Speaker and a seven-member cabinet, the "Executive Council."

- The world's oldest "discovered" rocks—called tonalite gneiss and dated at about four billion years—were found in the Northwest Territories and have become a popular collector's item. Your character can find "authentic" rocks at almost any souvenir shop.

- The Northwest Territories is quite a geographical potpourri, as it's made up of numerous mountains, forests, rivers, and lakes.

- Tourism is vital to the economy, with some estimates showing that its revenue is greater than that of all other renewable resource industries combined.

- The Northwest Territories has many official native languages. The Dene has five: (Chipewyan, Dogrib, Gwich'in, North Slavey, and South Slavey) and the Inuit has one (Inuvialuktun). Then, of course, English

and French are the two Canadian national languages.

- Your character can find abundant and unique wildlife in this region, such as moose, caribou, bison, white wolves, and white whales.

- This is where the northern lights light up the winter sky the Midnight Sun never sets in the summer.

- Nunavut became a territory in 1999, splitting from the Northwest Territories after decades of debate. A mere 13 percent of Canadians even knew the area existed when it was slated to become its own territory.

- The Nunavut government is public, granting equal representation to all residents.

- Nunavut, which means "our land" in the Inuit language, encompasses most of Canada's Artic islands and is spread out over roughly 772,260 square miles.

- The majority of Canada's Inuit live in Nunavut. Hunting, fishing and trapping are still vital means of survival for many Inuits in Nunavut.

- Nunavut's three regions are the Qikiqtaaluk (or Baffin) Region, the Kivalliq (or Keewatin) Region, and the Kitikmeot Region.

- Nunavut is huge, covering many regional variations of arctic climate, landforms and ecosystems. It has flat barren lands, lakes, fiords, mountain ranges, and icebergs.

- As with the Northwest Territories, Nunavut's legislatures do not represent political parties. Decisions are made by consensus, though a simple majority is required to pass legislation.

- Inuktitut, English, and French are the three official

languages of Nunavut. Inuktitut, the language of the Inuit, is alive and growing.

- The best-known event in the history of the territories was the Klondike Gold Rush of 1897 and 1898, when thousands of miners poured into the boomtown of Dawson after gold was discovered in Bonanza Creek, a tributary of the Klondike River. By 1904, the rush was over and many of the miners left to follow new strikes in Alaska.
- Among the fortune hunters who came to the Klondike were Wyatt Earp, Jack London, and Canadian poet Robert Service, who captured the life of the gold rush in classic poems like "The Shooting of Dan McGrew." Earp ran a bar and gambling house, London mined for gold and left penniless, though he used the experience to write his famous novels of the northern wilderness. Service gained a reputation as a wild, rugged poet of the frontier, but he actually worked in a bank.
- Mount Logan, located in the Yukon Territory, is Canada's highest peak, rising to 19,551 feet (5,959 meters).
- The Royal Canadian Mounted Police are the law enforcement agency for all of the territories.
- In 1972, Kluane National Park opened, becoming the first national park in the Yukon Territory. The countries highest peaks are located within the park, and it also contains the world's largest non-polar icefield.
- The Alaska Highway, which runs from Dawson Creek, British Columbia, to Delta Junction, Alaska runs for more than 600 miles through the Yukon Territory, is the principal road linking Alaska to the continental states. It was built during World War II as a defensive measure, allowing military vehicles to more easily reach the northern regions of North American.

Interesting Places to Set a Scene

- **Yellowknife.** Resting near the North Arm of Great Slave Lake (ninth largest lake in the world), Yellowknife is quite a hike from the nearest big Canadian city, as its 981 driving miles and 600 air from Edmonton. Many locals call it the biggest small town in Canada. In fact, it wasn't until the 1960s that a road was established to connect Yellowknife with southern Canada. The big event of the year was the arrival of the first supply barge in June. While many natives live in the surrounding areas, over 80 per cent of Yellowknife's population is non-native.
- **Hay River.** Deemed "The Hub of the North" for its role as a major link between northern and southern Canada, Hay River is also the southern terminus for all water-based shipping that comes and goes along the Mackenzie River and the Arctic Islands. Lots of big boats, weathered sailors, and lonely travelers can be found here.
- **The Mackenzie Delta.** Situated in the Gwich'in the Arctic Circle, The Delta is a natural wonder, dotted by about 25,000 lakes, tundra shrubs and piney forests, and one of the most flourishing raptor population in the world (during summer months Bald eagles, golden eagles, peregrine falcons, tundra swans, snow geese, scoters, and belted kingfisher make their home here). And five communities of Gwich'in (two) and Inuvialuit (three) natives are in the area.
- **Winter Road.** The winter road between Fort Smith and Fort Chipewyan has a reputation for being dangerous. Stretching a lonely 228 km, the road is not only long but also hazardous, as much of it is narrow, rough and bumpy with many sharp curves. Oh, and you can only travel the road in winter because several ice bridge crossings are required. That's how it is with all Winter Access Roads in the Northwest Territories—they're open only from January to March, are mostly privately owned and maintained, and therefore offer no emergency road services.
- **Lac de Gras.** This is where gem-quality diamonds were discovered in 1991, making headlines around the world. Actually, the diamonds were found in the nearby Barren Lands, where more than 12 million hectares (30 million acres) have been staked for diamond mining. Prospecting crews, carried by helicopter and charter "bush" planes, buzz about the area looking to spot more gems. This is Canada's first diamond mine, one that provides hundreds of jobs for the people of the Northwest Territories and millions of dollars to the region's economy.
- **Iqaluit.** At 4,200 residents, this is no sprawling metropolis. But it is the capital city of Nunavut. The main portion of Iqaluit (pronounced "ee-ka-loo-eet") rests on Koojesse Inlet, which boasts some of the longest stretches of exposed beach area at low tide. These beaches used to be dotted with small communities of Inuit huts until modern houses and buildings came along. It's still a quaint village compared to some of the big cities down south. A few Arctic movies have been shot here, too, so locals get a little curious when

For Further Research

Books

Arctic Smoke and Mirrors, by Gerard Kenney

Nahecho Keh Our Elders, by Margaret Thom and Ethel Blondin

Here I Sit, by Rene Fumoleau

People and Caribou in the Northwest Territories, edited by Ed Hall

Yellowknife: How a City Grew, by Erik W

Arctic Revolution: Social Change in the Northwest Territories 1935–1994, by John David Hamilton

The River Guide, by Peter Jowett

Denison's Ice Road Nahanni, by Edith Iglauer

North of Reliance, by Dave Olesen

Aurora: The Mysterious Northern Lights, by Candace Savage

Arctic Dreams, by Barry Lopez

Shield Country, by Jamie Bastedo

Nunavat: Canada in the 21st Century, by Norma Jean Lutz, and George Sheppard

The Road to Nunavut: The Progress of the Eastern Arctic Inuit Since the Second World War, by R. Quinn Duffy

Nunavut (Hello Canada Series), by Lyn Hancock

Nunavut Handbook: Traveling in Canada's Arctic, by Marion Soubliee

Into the Great Solitude: An Arctic Journey, by Robert F. Perkins

Faith of Fools, A Journal of the Klondike Gold Rush, by William Shape

Journey, James A. Michener

Klondike, by Jack London

Part of the Land, Part of the Water: A History of the Yukon Indians, Catherine McClellan

The Yukon Fact Book: Everything You Ever Wanted to Know About the Yukon, by Mark Zuehlke

True North: The Yukon and Northwest Territories, by William R. Morrison

Walking the Yukon: A Solo Trek Through the Land of Beyond, by Chris Townsend

Yukon Poems of Robert Service. (Service's poems and stories of the Yukon are collected in various volumes under different titles)

Yukon Territory, by Penny Rennick

Web Sites

www.bmmda.nt.ca/default.htm / (McKenzie Delta)

www.hayriver.com/main2.htm / (Hay River)

http://city.yellowknife.nt.ca// (Yellowknife)

www.gov.nt.ca// (government site of the Northwestern Territories)

www.nunavut.com/home.html (information gateway to Nunavat)

www.tunngavik.com/site-eng/nlca/articl3.htm (Nunavut Settlement Area information)

www.gov.nu.ca/Nunavut/ (official government site)

www.arctictravel.com/maps/rankinmap.html (Travel and tourism in Nunavut)

www.gov.yk.ca (Yukon territorial government site)

www.touryukon.com (Tourism and travel in Yukon)

www.yukonweb.com (Many links to Yukon-related sites)

www.yukoninfo.com (New and tourist info for the territories)

Hollywood types come to town with their big money, big production crews, and big stars. Iqaluit's population is a mix of cultures (less than two-thirds of residents here are Inuit, compared to other communities that are more than 90 percent Inuit) and a mix of languages (the town even has a French-language radio station).

- **Rankin Inlet.** This small town challenged Iqaluit in the run for capital city back in 1991. It lost, but that doesn't mean the town is dying. Rankin Inlet is in fact bustling, as it's the hub of Nunavut and is the capital of the Kivalliq. It is where the Kivalliq Inuit Association is headquartered. Rankin Inlet is also located between Whale Cove (south), Chesterfield (north) and Baker Lake (west), so for the past thirty years the town has been the regional center for the government of the Northwest Territories and now the Government of Nunavut. The community was formed with the discovery of nickel in the 1950s, which prompted many Inuits in the region to flocks to the area to fill the jobs. Although the mine has been shut down since the 1960s, the community and its people has remained.

- **Whitehorse.** Despite its tiny size, Whitehorse is the

leading population, trade, and government center in the Yukon Territory. Located on the Yukon River as well as on the Alaska Highway, tourists and business folk traveling to or living in the Yukon are likely to pass through Whitehorse. It boasts the territory's only international airport.

- **Dawson.** A boomtown created during the glory days of the Klondike gold rush, Dawson now has little more than a thousand residents. Also known as Dawson City, the town survives mostly as a trade center for the Klondike mining region and as a tourist attraction, offering historical attractions from the gold rush days. A turn-of-the century mansion called the Commissioner's Residence is a popular tourist spot as are a handful of saloons, stores and other buildings of the period.

- **The Southern Wilderness.** The southern section of the territories is heavily forested and is home to a variety of wildlife not found in abundance elsewhere in North America. In an attempt to get away from it all, your character could come here and find grizzly bears, black and brown bears, timber wolves, wolverines and other friendly creatures. Moose, caribou, and deer also live here in great number.

- **The Chilkoot Trail.** A 31-mile (53 k) trail extending from Dyea, Alaska, to central Yukon Territory, the trail was a primary artery for fortune hunters during the Klondike Gold Rush. Wagon wheels, boots, and mining equipment from the time still litters the trail, and it's against the law to take anything away. A rugged climb even in good weather, the trail is a challenge to modern hikers and was a treacherous trip for miners at the end of the nineteenth century.

Get More Of The Best Writing Instruction From Writer's Digest Books!

Snoopy's Guide to the Writing Life—*Snoopy's Guide to the Writing Life* presents more than 180 heartwarming and hilarious Snoopy "at the typewriter" comic strips by Charles M. Schulz, paired with 32 delightful essays from a who's who of famous writers, including Sue Grafton, Fannie Flagg, Elmore Leonard and more. These pieces examine the joys and realities of the writing life, from finding ideas to creating characters.
ISBN 1-58297-194-3 ✳ hardcover ✳ 192 pages ✳ #10856-K

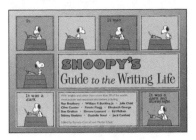

The Pocket Muse—Here's the key to finding inspiration when and where you want it. With hundreds of thought-provoking prompts, exercises and illustrations, it immediately helps you to get started writing, overcome writer's block, develop a writing habit, think more creatively, master style, revision and other elements of the craft.
ISBN 1-58297-142-0 ✳ hardcover ✳ 256 pages ✳ #10806-K

The Writer's Idea Book—This is the guide writers reach for time after time to jump start their creativity and develop ideas. Four distinctive sections, each geared toward a different stage of writing, offer dozens of unique approaches to "freeing the muse." In all, you'll find more than 400 idea-generating prompts guaranteed to get your writing started on the right foot, or back on track!
ISBN 1-58297-179-X ✳ paperback ✳ 272 pages ✳ #10841-K

Lessons from a Lifetime of Writing—Best-selling author David Morrell distills more than 30 years of writing and publishing experience into this single masterwork of advice and instruction. A rare and intriguing mix of memoir and writer's workshop, *Lessons* pulls no punches. Morrell examines everything from motivation and focus to the building blocks of good fiction: plot, character, dialogue, description and more.
ISBN 1-58297-143-9 ✳ hardcover ✳ 256 pages ✳ #10808-K

45 Master Characters—Make your characters and their stories more compelling, complex and original than ever before. This book explores the most common male and female archetypes—the mythic, cross-cultural models from which all characters originate—and shows you how to use them as foundations for your own unique characters.
ISBN 1-58297-069-6 ✳ hardcover ✳ 256 pages ✳ #10752-K

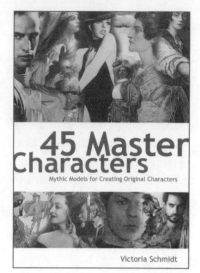

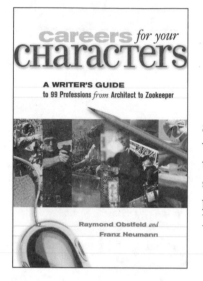

Careers for Your Characters—To create realistic, well-developed characters, you have to write with authority, describing their professional lives with the accuracy and detail of an insider. Here Raymond Obstfeld shares the hard-to-find specifics for 50 intriguing occupations, including professional jargon and buzzwords, education requirements, salaries, benefits, perks, expenses and more!
ISBN 1-58297-083-1 ✳ paperback ✳ 352 pages ✳ #10765-K

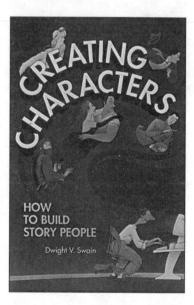

Creating Characters: How to Build Story People—Grab the empathy of your reader with characters so real, they'll jump off the page. You'll discover how to make characters come alive with vibrant emotion, quirky personality traits, inspiring heroism and other uniquely human qualities.
ISBN 0-89879-662-8 ✳ paperback ✳ 192 pages ✳ #10417-K

Picture Writing—This unique book applies the principles of whole-brain creativity to writing for young readers, allowing you to tap your imagination more deeply and powerfully than you ever thought possible. Whether you write fiction, nonfiction, or poetry, for reading levels ranging from picture books to young adult, this method will work for you.
ISBN 1-58297-072-6 ✳ paperback ✳ 224 pages ✳ #10755-K